Institute of Czech Literature of the CAS
Karolinum Press
2024

FROM LAUGHTER TO FORGETTING

A Sourcebook of Czech Avant-Garde Discourses

Zuzana Říhová (ed.)

With an introductory essay
by **Peter Zusi**

Institute of Czech Literature of the CAS
Karolinum Press
2024

INSTITUTE OF CZECH LITERATURE is part of the Czech Academy of Sciences
Na Florenci 1420/3, 110 00 Prague 1, Czech Republic
www.ucl.cas.cz

KAROLINUM PRESS is a publishing department of Charles University
Ovocný trh 560/5, 116 36 Prague 1, Czech Republic
www.karolinum.cz

This publication was created with the support of Research Development Program RVO 68378068.
This book was published with support from the Czech Academy of Sciences.
During the work on this text book, use was made of Czech Literary Bibliography resources/services (ORJ identifier: 90243).

Cover and graphic design Stará škola
Translation support Barbora Bartůňková (pp. 40–73, 78–145, 159–201)
Copyediting Nikola Dlabajová, Matthew Sweney
Set and printed in the Czech Republic by Karolinum Press
First English edition

Reviewed by Jindřich Toman (University of Michigan, Ann Arbor)
and Wolfgang Müller-Funk (Universität Wien)

Cataloguing-in-Publication Data is available from the National Library of the Czech Republic

ISBN 978-80-7658-090-9 (Institute of Czech Literature of the CAS)
ISBN 978-80-246-5308-2 (Karolinum)
ISBN 978-80-246-5309-9 (pdf, Karolinum)
ISBN 978-80-246-5310-5 (epub, Karolinum)

Contents

III. Coming of Age: Crises and New Perspectives / 273

IV. Complicating the Real: Czech Surrealism / 335

Introduction

In his memoirs the Czech poet Jaroslav Seifert recalled his final meeting with Roman Jakobson, the Russian linguist, literary theorist, poet, and central figure of 20th-century Structuralism. They met by chance on the platform of a train station as Jakobson, who was Jewish, was preparing to leave Czechoslovakia "at the critical hour" in March 1939, following the arrival of Nazi German occupying forces in Prague and a few months before the outbreak of World War Two. Jakobson had lived in Prague for nearly two decades and during that time had been a central figure in the internationally influential Prague Linguistic Circle, as well as friend of and collaborator with many of the leading figures of the vibrant avant-garde cultural scenes in interwar Prague, Brno and Bratislava. But all that was now ending. Seifert's account of their hurried, happenstance meeting on that train platform under gathering clouds of war conveys a decidedly elegiac tone. "'I was glad to be in this country, and I was happy here'," Seifert reports Jakobson as having said. "'And if it is any consolation, let me say that I feel myself to be Czech, and I am sad'." Seifert concludes his sketch by observing: "At that moment [Jakobson] had two small, broken tears in his eyes. He looked right at my face, and it seemed to me as if he were looking past me and talking with someone else. But aside from me there was no one else there."[1]

This anecdote says much about the fate of the interwar avant-garde in Czechoslovakia. A sense of ending and loss hangs over this scene; indeed the final sentences almost give the impression that Seifert himself is disappearing, being left behind, replaced, forgotten. Jakobson, to be sure, continued to recall and refer to his Prague years throughout his later, eminent career in the United States (and his apparently

1 Jaroslav Seifert, *Všecky krásy světa*, 3rd, rev. ed. (Praha: Československý spisovatel, 1992), 365.

distant gaze was in fact due to nothing more than a slight eye defect). But for a long time thereafter the wider world *did* largely forget this place, this period. Lost was the milieu symbolised by friendship between a Czech poet who at the height of the Cold War in the 1980s would be awarded the Nobel Prize for literature, and an émigré Russian linguist and theorist who in the 1950s would revolutionize French and American academia through the Structuralist principles he brought to them from Prague. Also lost was the memory of just how cosmopolitan, international, and convivial the intellectual life in this young Czechoslovak democracy could be.

Established in October 1918, upon the collapse of the Habsburg Empire at the end of World War One, and dismembered in stages between 1938 and 1939 around the time of Seifert and Jakobson's final, transitory encounter, the first Republic of Czechoslovakia had nourished a remarkable period of cultural achievement. Over the twenty years of its existence, central figures in the cultural life of the republic cultivated ties, cooperation, and influences among leading modernist groups across Europe and the world, and Czechoslovakia also provided a home to a range of European artists, writers and thinkers displaced from their native lands in the turbulent interwar years. During this period Czechoslovak modernism and its avant-garde generated vibrant art and literature, for example producing some of the most significant examples of modernist architecture (in the early 1930s Le Corbusier praised how "the Czechs have shone so brightly in the emerging sky of the new times"[2]), providing fundamental impetus to the development of semiotics and structuralist thought, and even giving world culture a new word: "robot," from Karel Čapek's 1920 play *R.U.R.* about man-made humanoids who are first exploited as cheap labor but then, having developed consciousness, revolt against and defeat humanity.

Seifert's anecdote thus relates a double loss. The outbreak of war, and later the imposition of Soviet influence, brought *de facto* an end to an all too brief florescence under what is now called the "First Republic," when Czechoslovak culture was internationally engaged and at the forefront of some of the most advanced European modernist trends. But further, in the decades following the war the avant-garde traditions and accomplishments of this "far-away land of which we know nothing" faded from wider consciousness and were effectively written out of mainstream accounts of the European avant-garde.[3] In many ways Czechoslovakia was not unique in undergoing this erasure, but rather stands as a particularly striking example of the fate that befell other avant-garde and modernist traditions in Central and East-

---

2 Le Corbusier, "In Defense of Architecture," trans. by Nancy Bray, André Lessard, Alan Levitt and George Baird, *Oppositions* 4 (1974): 93–106 (p. 94).

3 The quotation glosses the notorious phrase that British Prime Minister Neville Chamberlain used when defending his attempt to appease Hitler in the September 1938 Munich negotiations, which ceded large parts of Czechoslovak territory to the German Reich. On historical forgetting of the Czech avant-garde (and for useful bibliographic references), see Derek Sayer, "How We Remember and What We Forget: Art History and the Czech Avant-garde," in Dariusz Gafijczuk and Derek Sayer (eds.), *The Inhabited Ruins of Central Europe: Re-Imagining Space, History, and Memory* (Houndmills and Basingstoke: Palgrave Macmillan, 2013), 148–177.

ern Europe as well, in particular those that found themselves on the "wrong" side of the Iron Curtain during the Cold War period. How did this process of forgetting play out? And what conditions emerged later that have allowed the recovery of some sense of the vibrancy and diversity of the avant-garde not only in Czechoslovakia, but in interwar Central and Eastern Europe as a whole?

One evident key is to be found in the intellectual mapping that accompanied the Cold War itself. After a constitutional coup in 1948, which allowed the Communist Party of Czechoslovakia to seize control of the entire government, Czechoslovakia found itself solidly within the Soviet Bloc and underwent a swift and thorough process of Stalinization that saw mass nationalization of industries, curtailment of individual liberties, show trials of political opponents, and even a cult of personality (modeled in many respects upon the bombastic cult around Stalin) centered on the figure of the "worker President," Klement Gottwald. These radical changes affected not only social, economic and political life, but culture as well. During the 1950s, officially sanctioned culture in Czechoslovakia, as throughout the Soviet Bloc, was dominated by the doctrine of Socialist Realism, a deeply ideological aesthetic platform adopted in the Soviet Union in the early 1930s, which demanded that art and literature be "comprehensible," address questions of class struggle, and reflect the ideals and principles of the Communist Party. In particular the criterion of comprehensibility set Socialist Realism in direct conflict with the radical aesthetic experimentation, and consequent "difficulty," of much art and literature of the interwar period. Stalinist cultural orthodoxy of the 1950s thus vehemently rejected the avant-garde traditions of the First Republic as representing "bourgeois decadence" and unhealthy "formalism" (a term of condemnation that acquired particular truculence). After 1948 many major figures of the interwar avant-garde either emigrated to the West or were effectively forced into internal exile, as they were prevented from publishing and banned from public cultural life. Some succumbed physically to the pressure campaigns directed against them; others committed suicide or even were exccuted during the political show trials.[4] Yet others made their peace with the new regime, though this required "self-criticism" and renunciation of their earlier avant-gardist work.[5] This internal purgation of avant-garde traditions within the Soviet Bloc made it all too easy for commentators on the other side of the Iron Curtain to forget those traditions as well. The cultural map on which the Cold War played out thus set up an Iron Curtain of its own by equating the experimental free-

4 The poet František Halas (1901–1949) and the theorist and artist Karel Teige (1900–1951), both targeted by Communist authorities in official smear campaigns, died of heart attacks. The poet Konstantin Biebl (1898–1951) committed suicide. The historian, philosopher and sympathizer with Surrealism Záviš Kalandra (1902–1950) was one of four people judicially murdered following the infamous show trial centered on the politician Milada Horáková (1901–1950).

5 The poet Vítězslav Nezval (1900–1958) turned towards Socialist Realism and published poems praising Stalin in the late 1940s. The literary theorist Jan Mukařovský (1891–1975) was made rector of Charles University in Prague in 1948 after having denounced the methods of Czech Structuralism, which he had played such a central role in developing during the 1930s and 40s.

doms of modernism and the avant-garde with "the West," in stark contrast to the ideological oppressiveness of Socialist Realism in the Soviet Bloc.[6]

A related, though less obvious key to this process of forgetting requires understanding an odd paradox in that postwar Western critical reception of the literary and artistic avant-gardes. Most European avant-garde groups and movements had been consciously cosmopolitan, intentionally international. This was true even in the case of groups that, like the Italian Futurists, allied themselves with nationalist or indeed fascist politics: F. T. Marinetti's 1909 "Futurist Manifesto" was published in Paris, in French, within weeks of its original publication in Italy, and perhaps no single document of the interwar avant-garde had such wide international resonance in the interwar period. This internationalism was not coincidental but inhered in the underlying dynamic of the avant-garde, in the claim to represent not a specific national "spirit" or "identity" but the cutting edge of art itself (even while that cutting edge was often turned against the very notion of "art").[7] Yet despite such internationalism, Western critical reception (and, consequently, public awareness) of these avant-garde movements long displayed a stubborn tendency to attach a national modifier to each movement. Futurism thus becomes "Italian" and then "Russian"; Expressionism becomes "German"; Surrealism becomes "French." Even Dada—that most rambunctious and rebellious assault on national traditions—appeared to have had necessary geographical groundings in its Zurich, Paris, Berlin or New York variants, each of which has been presumed to reflect something of the wider national culture surrounding it. So the paradox is how much Western critical reflection in the postwar period has felt oddly comfortable in placing these internationalist European avant-garde movements within traditional, national literary and cultural histories. And, perhaps not surprisingly, those national traditions that lay on the "near side" of the Iron Curtain received the most attention. The cutting edge of art in early twentieth-century Europe was thus divided up among the major Western European national traditions.[8]

---

6 This ideological mapping also guided Western impressions of postwar "dissident" culture within the Soviet Bloc. The notion of heroic resistance against an oppressive official culture was often taken as creating a spiritual kinship between postwar dissident practice and the interwar avant-garde, even though in practice much dissident culture made no use of avant-gardist techniques.

7 The understanding of the interwar avant-garde as a practice of "anti-art" has its classic formulation in Peter Bürger's widely influential thesis of an avant-gardist "liquidation of the institution of art"; see Peter Bürger, *Theory of the Avant-Garde*, trans. by Michael Shaw (Minneapolis: University of Minnesota Press, 1984 [1974]).

8 Russia and the Soviet Union are the exception in this list of otherwise Western European national appropriations. The significance and influence of these Russian and Soviet impulses were impossible to ignore but western accounts often treated them hesitantly or associated them largely with émigré groups in the West (Wassily Kandinsky in Munich in the 1900s and later at the Bauhaus, for example, or the Russian Constructivist circles in Berlin in the 1920s). Further, the Soviet suppression of avant-garde cultural trends during the 1930s meant that the influence of the Soviet avant-garde could be presented as intense but short-lived, thus

The last thirty years or so have brought developments allowing a correction—slow, piecemeal, unfinished, but a correction nonetheless—of that process of forgetting that had obscured the significant role Central and Eastern European traditions played in the interwar avant-garde. Most obvious are the seismic political shifts in 1989–1991, when the collapse of the Soviet Bloc, followed by the disintegration of the Soviet Union itself, led to the scrapping of first the political and then the mental maps that had governed during the Cold War. The establishment of new or renewed democracies in states such as Poland, Hungary, Romania, Czechoslovakia (divided into the Czech and Slovak republics after the so-called "Velvet Divorce" in 1993) and elsewhere energized and expanded interest in the cultural history of those states as well. In particular their vibrant modernist and avant-garde traditions, so long smothered by official hostility from within and ignorant indifference from without, emerged as obvious objects of investigation.

This resurgence had its own complexities. The convoluted legacies of the interwar avant-garde in Czechoslovakia, for example, harbored currents that could appear quite ambivalent for audiences in the post-1989 period. Following the deepest Stalinist phase in the 1950s, bold scholars and intellectuals in Czechoslovakia had engaged from the late 1950s through the 1960s in efforts to rehabilitate central figures of the interwar avant-garde, in an implicit (or often explicit) rejection of the earlier cultural orthodoxies. Scholarly studies and critical editions of important avant-garde works and figures appeared, and the distortions in the accepted official accounts of such works, and often the injustice of what had befallen many of those artists and authors at the hands of the postwar Socialist regime, were discussed with increasing frankness. Much of this work of reappropriation attempted to reclaim these avant-gardists as key figures in a Marxist cultural tradition that, it was argued, a socialist state should embrace rather than suppress. This groundbreaking 1960s revisionist scholarship on the interwar avant-garde should thus be understood as a significant cultural component in the build-up to that striking period of social and political reform culminating in the 1968 Prague Spring, with its vision of a "socialism with a human face." (The same is true of scholarly efforts

---

keeping in place the "cultural Iron Curtain" discussed above. Contrast, for example, the fame of the Bauhaus (familiar enough to have provided the name for a popular English gothic rock band in the 1980s) with the obscurity of the Soviet VKhUTEMAS (an acronym for the Higher Art and Technical Workshop), an institute of comparable importance for the development of modern architecture and design, which interacted extensively with the members of the Bauhaus; see Anna Bokov's recent monograph *Avant-Garde as Method: Vkhutemas and the Pedagogy of Space, 1920–1930* (Zurich: Park Books, 2020). Both the Bauhaus and VKhUTEMAS were state-sponsored institutions, and both eventually closed (in 1933 and 1930 respectively) under the pressure of rising totalitarianism. Yet VKhUTEMAS has remained little known, while the Bauhaus has always played a central role in accounts of interwar modernism, largely due to its role in the 1920s avant-garde in the Weimar Republic and then to its later transplantation to and domestication within the United States when László Moholy-Nagy founded the "New Bauhaus" in Chicago in 1937.

beginning in the early 1960s to reclaim the work of Franz Kafka—another towering feature of interwar Czechoslovak and late Habsburg culture that the Stalinist orthodoxy of the 1950s had condemned and repressed.) The violent suppression of the Prague Spring through the Soviet-led invasion in August 1968, and the ensuing, nearly 20-year occupation of Czechoslovakia and imposition of renewed political and cultural orthodoxy, meant that in the 1970s and 1980s the interwar avant-garde was once again subject to censure and censorship.[9] Yet here lies the root of a serious complication in the rediscovery of these avant-garde traditions after 1989. Marxism had been extremely influential within much of the interwar avant-garde, and many of the major figures in that period had been confirmed supporters of communist ideals and of the Soviet Union. So despite their bitter fate later at the hands of the postwar Czechoslovak Socialist regime, these figures were often regarded with some suspicion or distaste in the 1990s, when the trend was to emphatically discard anything smacking of Marxism or Soviet influence. To some degree this paradox—on the one hand the celebration of the interwar avant-garde for its aesthetic independence and its "martyrdom" under the postwar Czechoslovak regime, and on the other the suspicion of the Marxism and pro-Soviet convictions of so many of its central figures—remains within public reflection on this topic to the present day.

Study of the European avant-garde has also pushed back in recent decades against that other feature that contributed to the forgetting of the Central and Eastern European avant-gardes: the Western European national appropriations that had long remained unquestioned. Not only were the inaccuracies in such national accounts too glaring, but it became increasingly difficult to ignore that the countries to which most such accounts gave a controlling interest—France, Germany, Italy, Britain and, with caveats (see note 8), Russia and the Soviet Union—were also the major colonialist powers of that period, contributing to a sense that academic study was, wittingly or not, reflecting geopolitical bias and cultural hegemony. The push-back has taken several forms. First, scholars pointed out how the national labels obscured the varied origins of many of the most significant figures. For example, the "French" avant-garde was shaped in fundamental fashion by many Romanians (e.g., Tristan Tzara, Constantin Brâncuşi), the "German" avant-garde by many

9 This see-saw dynamic is well illustrated by the fate of one of the most important of those 1960s revisionist publishing projects. Karel Teige, a key figure in the Devětsil and Czechoslovak Surrealist groups and a name that features prominently in this anthology, had been denounced during the Stalinist 1950s and his work had been suppressed as a prime example of "decadent formalism." In the early 1960s, however, editors Vratislav Effenberger, Jiří Brabec, Robert Kalivoda, and Květoslav Chvatík began work on a three-volume critical edition of Teige's selected works (*Výbor z díla*). The first volume appeared in 1966. The second volume, due for publication in 1969, was completed and printed, but before it could be published nearly the entire print-run was destroyed following the August 1968 invasion and the ensuing political changes (the few surviving copies became a valuable rarity). Volume three did not appear until 1994.

Hungarians (e.g., László Moholy-Nagy, Marcel Breuer); the "Russian" avant-garde by many Ukrainians (e.g., Kazimir Malevich, Vladimir Tatlin); and so on. Second, increasing attention has been paid to the fact that the most prominent nations by no means had a monopoly on many of the familiar movements: Expressionism and Futurism flourished in Poland, for example, as did Cubism and Surrealism in Czechoslovakia. Third, international scholarship (especially that written in English, French or German) has begun to explore more deeply the unique, original movements and styles that arose in what had previously too often been ignored as "peripheral" regions of Europe: Zenithism in Yugoslavia, for example, or Poetism in Czechoslovakia. The rediscovery of such movements, and the presentation of them often as "alternative avant-gardes," has rejuvenated the study of the interwar avant-garde by opening up what many had begun to perceive as an ossified canon of works, figures and movements. Taken together, these trends have done much to raise awareness of the geographical diversity in the early twentieth-century European avant-garde, and in particular of the contributions of Central and Eastern European avant-gardes that accounts centered on the "major," primarily Western European national traditions long obscured.[10]

This push for greater inclusiveness has in many ways learned from and echoed academic critiques first developed within postcolonial studies. The process of national appropriation described above is easily framed as a sort of "colonialization" within the postwar critical discourse on the European avant-garde. The ways in which postcolonial studies have worked to upend set hierarchies of cultural power, to decolonialize cultural canons, to reframe notions of non-European Otherness and the abject, and to recuperate what had for so long been excluded from Eurocentric master narratives, offer clear models for efforts to push back against both "Iron Curtain" and "west-centric" accounts of the European avant-garde. Further, such efforts dismantle from within the notion of an undifferentiated European master narrative, replacing it with a more complex, variegated, and hybridized image of the European avant-garde. Critical literatures on different Central and Eastern European modernist traditions have responded with varying degrees of enthusiasm to the postcolonial parallel. Scholars of Ukrainian modernism, for example, have often embraced the model, as it dovetails neatly with accounts not only of Stalinist suppression of the avant-garde but also of a longer history of Russian appropriation or oppression of specifically Ukrainian cultural phenomena, a history that can make the all too common glossing of the Soviet avant-garde as "Russian" particularly vexing. Scholars of other areas, however, such as Czechoslovakia, have been more skeptical about the usefulness of the postcolonial paradigm, focusing instead

---

10 English-language readers seeking insight into this broadened European avant-garde corpus should consult Timothy O. Benson and Éva Forgács (eds.), *Between Worlds: A Sourcebook of Central European Avant-Gardes, 1910–1930* (Cambridge, MA: MIT Press, 2002); and the essays in the companion volume, Timothy O. Benson (ed.), *Central European Avant-Gardes: Exchange and Transformation, 1910–1930* (Cambridge, MA: MIT Press, 2002).

on the various forms of interconnection across the European avant-gardes and thus pursuing a model of inclusion within, rather than oppression by, the main European accounts.

There is in any event no question that the process of opening up the catalogue of European avant-gardes to include Central and Eastern Europe has faced several of the same obstacles that postcolonial studies faced in its early phases in the 1970s and 80s as it argued for the decolonization of literary studies and the importance of wider attention to non-European cultural traditions. The first of these could be labelled "ghettoization." This occurs when the significance of the previously overlooked traditions comes to be acknowledged more widely yet is not granted any particular impact on the accepted narrative. "New" movements are admitted into the house, as it were, but are left standing alone in the corner. In such a situation Czech Poetism, for example, may become a more familiar term to a larger number of scholars of the European avant-garde and its originality may be acknowledged, but as a movement that never spread internationally it will be understood as only really having significance for specialists on Czech culture. Capsule descriptions or general summaries of the new movements are then deemed sufficient, as the notion that a deeper understanding of Poetism could reveal anything substantial to a scholar of Breton's Surrealism, for example, will appear eccentric. So when previously overlooked traditions are ghettoized in this manner, the catalogue of avant-garde movements may be broadened but the central canon remains intact.

A second obstacle is when the previously overlooked traditions are understood as "belated" versions of what is already familiar, as merely echoes or copies (which may be adjudged more or less successful, more or less interesting) of phenomena that originated elsewhere. Under this model, for example, Czech Surrealism may be acknowleged to have produced striking works of art and literature, yet is understood simply as evidence of the growing influence, the "exportation" of (or colonization by) Breton's conception of Surrealism. The "belatedness" model takes much of its persuasiveness from its apparent foundation on indisputable chronological facts (the Prague Surrealist group was indeed founded a decade later than Breton's Parisian group, for example). So here too the original canon is left untouched by an expanded catalogue of movements—indeed the original canon may even be reinforced by the apparently irrefutable evidence of its spreading influence.

If the recuperation of Central and Eastern European avant-gardes from the forgetting in which they had lingered so long is to reveal deeper significance, it is necessary to move beyond the twin pitfalls of ghettoization and belatedness. We must seek to understand how these newly appreciated traditions interconnect with—and even potentially alter—our understanding of the "major" movements around which accounts of the European avant-garde have so long been constructed.

How this might work can be illustrated through a specific example. The major theoretician of two important Czech avant-garde groups that feature prominently in this anthology, Devětsil in the 1920s and the Czechoslovak Surrealist Group in the 1930s, was Karel Teige (see notes 4 and 9). From the early 1920s onwards Teige constructed a wide international network of contacts and cooperation with other avant-gardist figures who nowadays are far more famous. And many of those figures came to appreciate Teige's important role within what could be called the "international republic of the avant-garde." The words of Le Corbusier quoted at the beginning of this introduction were in fact addressed directly to Teige, and can here be cited more extensively: "If since 1921, the Czechs have shone so brightly in the emerging sky of the new times, it is largely because of you people, your magazines, your manifestos, your poems, people such as Teige, Nezval, Krejcar, etc." Similarly, evidence of the international reputation enjoyed by Teige and other Czech Surrealists (such as the poet Vítězslav Nezval) is provided by André Breton's praise during his 1935 visit to Prague: "[For] many long years I have enjoyed perfect intellectual fellowship with men such as Vítězslav Nezval and Karel Teige, whose trust and friendship is a source of pride to me. [....] Constantly interpreted by Teige in the most lively way, made to undergo an all-powerful lyric thrust by Nezval, Surrealism can flatter itself that it has blossomed in Prague as it has in Paris."[11] Such quotations demonstrate that a figure who may now be unfamiliar to many people interested in the avant-garde was once far better known. For a scholar of the Czechoslovak avant-garde hoping to persuade others to take an interest in a figure like Teige, the temptation is strong (and I confess to having done this myself at times) to cite such strong praise from these major authorities, and trust that those who are interested in Le Corbusier or Breton will feel inspired to investigate further. This may or may not lead to a successful outcome, but in any event one must recognize that such marshalling of borrowed authority is not only patronizing but remains beholden to the twin traps of ghettoization and belatedness. Le Corbusier's praise may inspire some more or less decorative mentions of Teige's name, thus including him in the main narrative about the international architectural avant-garde, yet Teige is likely to be left standing, "ghettoized," in the background, for nothing about such praise indicates how Teige's work could convey something of deeper significance to those interested in Le Corbusier. Similarly, Breton's praise may well come off as little more than diplomatic protocol, since Breton was, after all, visiting Prague to cement relations with a Czechoslovak Surrealist group that can easily appear to be simply a satellite of the Paris movement, a "belated" effort to catch up with *le dernier cri*.

Yet if one knows more about the context of Teige's interactions with these more famous figures, things appear differently. Let us start with Le Corbusier. His praise of Teige and the Czechoslovak modernist architecture movement was not offered randomly but rather in response to a sharp critique that Teige, who had been a strong supporter of Le Corbusier for years, had made of what he deemed the "monumentalizing" and "historicizing" tendencies in one of Le Corbusier's

11 André Breton, "Surrealist Situation of the Object," in André Breton, *Manifestoes of Surrealism*, trans. by Richard Seaver and Helen R. Lane (Ann Arbor: University of Michigan Press, 1972), 255–278 (p. 256).

major projects. Given Le Corbusier's acknowledged status as a towering master of modern architecture at that time, this critique came as a surprise. That Le Corbusier responded at all was unusual (he generally left such criticism unanswered), let alone that he responded in such a mollifying tone, and indicates that Teige's critique struck a nerve. Historians of modern architecture have taken note of this exchange and have generally framed it as illustrating the moment when the modernist movement in architecture split between a radically "utilitarian" faction (supposedly represented by Teige) and a "humanistic" practice (represented by Le Corbusier). That framework does go some way towards identifying a deeper significance in this exchange, yet it remains ignorant of Teige's broader aesthetic positions, in which his alleged utilitarianism was inseparable from the whimsical, playful, and deeply anti-instrumental impulses that came bundled under the label of Poetism. Only a fuller understanding of the surprising range and complexity of Teige's positions releases him from the "ghetto" and allows the fuller resonance of his exchange with Le Corbusier, and its potential consequences for thinking about avant-garde aesthetics more generally, to emerge. And now Breton: the "lively" interpretation of Surrealism that Breton attributes to Teige in fact refers to Teige's roughly 15 years of rigorous *critique* of Breton and his group. Teige had only come to embrace Surrealism fully a few months before Breton's Prague visit, and not because he wished to join in with a more famous movement but because he felt that Breton's Surrealists had finally matured their positions sufficiently to dispel the whiff of idealism and mysticism Teige had always found suspicious about their activities. In Teige's understanding, Czech Poetism during the 1920s had represented a far more defensible position than had Breton's Surrealism in that period; in the early 1930s, he argued, both movements had evolved to the point where they could merge into a shared enterprise, represented by the foundation of the Czechoslovak Surrealist Group in 1934—but it was the Parisians, not the Praguers, who had had the rockiest path to that point. So the apparent "belatedness" that mere chronology would seem to demonstrate conclusively—the decade or so separating the foundations of the French and Czechoslovak Surrealist groups—in fact obscures a far more nuanced (and more interesting) picture.[12]

The point of course is not necessarily to claim that Teige's critiques get the better of these famous figures, but rather to acknowledge that only deeper awareness of the particularities of the Czechoslovak context allows one to perceive how these exchanges might potentially speak to new insights about those famous figures—and thus of the interwar avant-garde more generally. The initial dynamic, in which the borrowed authority of those commendatory quotations from Le Corbusier and Breton might perhaps serve to bring Teige's name more fully into the avant-garde catalogue yet leaves the canonical figures untouched, gives way to a more nuanced exchange, speaking to our understanding of *all* the figures involved. This deeper

12 I discuss both of these interactions in more detail in Peter Zusi, *The Integrity of the Avant-Garde: Karel Teige and the Biography of an Ambition* (Cambridge, England: Legenda, 2023).

sense of nuance, however, is impossible without a more granular understanding of those Central and Eastern European contexts that remained so long obscured.

Which brings us to the crucial role played by an anthology such as the present volume. Few people have the linguistic competence to read widely across the different avant-garde traditions at stake here, so translation is an essential task. Anthologies offering a broad sweep across the region (see note 10) are essential in allowing larger comparative perspectives to emerge, but they necessarily can only provide some of the "greatest hits" within each tradition. The requisite level of granular detail, however, can only be achieved through a more generous selection, rendering the major positions, practices and polemics that determined a particular historical time and place. Every such effort inevitably makes certain compromises, of course, yet the present anthology, containing a wide range of primary texts set into their historical context through Zuzana Říhová's historical introductions to each section, provides the most thorough resource currently available to an English-language reader interested in the Czechoslovak interwar avant-garde. What emerges is by no means a neat or coherent picture; indeed, in many ways granular detail always makes the picture messier, more ambiguous, open to different interpretations. Thus, for example, the usual emphasis in accounts of the Czech avant-garde (in secondary literature in both Czech and in English) on the narrative arc leading from Devětsil in its early "proletarian art" phase through its subsequent Constructivist and Poetist period, then to the foundation of the Levá fronta (Left Front) in the early 30s, and finally to the establishment of the Czechoslovak Surrealist Group in 1934, is here complemented by a selection of texts from less familiar groups: the Brno-based Literární skupina (Literary Group), for example, or the Slovak DAVists, or the group around Vít Obrtel and the journal *Kvart* (Quarto). The sense of a single narrative arc thus gives way to a wider field of avant-garde positions and activities. Similarly, should one feel inclined to understand the position of the Czechoslovak avant-garde within the wider European narrative through a decolonizing framework emphasizing rectification of its marginalization and distortion (indeed much in the present Introduction shows such an inflection) then one may be surprised by, for example, the degree to which the Czech avant-garde often echoes tropes that exoticize and orientalize Eastern European or non-European "Others" in troubling ways. Firmer inclusion of the Czechoslovak tradition within the larger European narrative account of the avant-garde may also mean inclusion within some of those broader prejudices and blind spots as well.

For most readers making a first acquaintance with the interwar avant-garde in Czechoslovakia, one of the most striking discoveries is the programme and practice of Poetism, which has already been referred to several times. The most original credo of the Czech interwar avant-garde, Poetism is also one of the most appealing, most endearing movements of the European avant-garde as a whole, marked by both humility and an enthusiastic focus on discovering the beauty of the modern world and the happiness that is to be found there. Teige's famous 1924 "Poetismus" (Poetism) manifesto refuses to *define* what Poetism is and rather merely *suggests* the atmosphere it supports: "The art that is brought by Poetism is nonchalant, frolicsome, fantastical, playful, unheroic, and amorous. [...] It was born in an atmosphere of exuberant sociability, ***in a world that laughs***; no matter that tears are running from its eyes."[13] Much about the interwar Czechoslovak avant-garde inevitably appears in the melancholic light with which this introduction began, with its opening anecdote of Seifert and Jakobson parting on a bleak train platform. It is impossible for us now to ignore the end of this story; the horrors of World War Two and the Shoah cast a pall over the entire period. Yet those years of the avant-garde were primarily years of creativity and exuberance. The present anthology will have served its purpose if it succeeds in reviving interest in and refreshing the memory of that laughter that long ago fell into forgetfulness.

Peter Zusi

13 See below, p. 153.

Chapter 1

The Birth of the Czech Avant-Garde: Between Avant-Garde, Expressionism, and Proletarian Art

Stand still and look! says the narrator in the preface to the prose piece *Měsíc* (The Moon, 1920) by Jiří Mahen, poet and prose writer whose work the young Czech avant-gardists took as their model after World War One. However, in the first years after the war, the young avant-gardists most definitely did not want to stand still — the slogan of the time was *forward*. They threw themselves enthusiastically into a radical transformation of society and the building of a new art. Things happened quickly, animatedly, and frantically. The period, felt as broken, needed to be mended by a new order, which was defined in connection with the doctrines of communism, proletarianism, or socialism. The proposed theoretical programs were clearly staked out within the framework of the newly founded artistic groups. In the initial years after the war there was no room for the fantasy, imagination, and "divine image-creation," for which Jiří Mahen appealed. However, the time for these would soon arrive. Austria-Hungary had fallen apart; and the foundation of the independent state of Czechoslovakia on 28 October 1918 was accompanied by an atmosphere full of euphoria, but also misgivings and concerns, as Richard Weiner noted in *Třásničky dějinných dnů* (On the Fringes of Historic Days, 1919). In 1919 the period of building occurred, a stylization of programs capable of replacing a cultural paradigm.

Although the Czech avant-garde presented itself as an artistic movement that arose from a "point zero," it developed some postulates and principles of pre-war modernism and drew on pre-war associations, in particular ones in the fine arts, among them Skupina Osma (Group Eight, 1907: Emil Filla, Bohumil Kubišta, and others) and Skupina výtvarných umělců (Group of Visual Artists), 1911: Emil Filla, Vincenc Beneš, and others). In 1918, two former members of the latter, Josef Čapek and Jan Zrzavý, formed the core of the Tvrdošíjní (Obstinate) group (Václav Špála, Rudolf Kremlička, and others), within the framework of which, and under the influence of Cubism, they tried to continue in the activities of the pre-war avant-garde.[1] However, the exhibition of the Obstinate, held under the name A přece! (And After All!) in March and April 1918 was one of the last attempts to maintain the activity of the post-war avant-garde in the context of the Czech fine-arts avant-garde of the 1910s. The incoming generation of artists was markedly critical towards a range of attributes of the pre-war artistic scene. Its gesture was no longer that of individual creative activity, but was unequivocally group-based and collective.[2] In the first post-war years, modernity was associated with communism. In his preface to Seifert's poetry collection *Město v slzách* (City in Tears, 1921) prose writer Vladislav Vančura wrote: "New, new, new is the star of communism. [...] apart from it [collective work] there is no modernity."[3] The reconstruction of society was to be implemented on the basis of Marxist theses.

---

1 On Czech visual arts groups, cf., for instance, Marie Rakušanová et al., *Degrees of separation: Bohumil Kubišta and the European avant-garde* (Praha: Karolinum Press, 2021); Jiří Padrta, *Osma a Skupina výtvarných umělců 1907–1917 : teorie, kritika, polemika* (Praha: Odeon, 1992); Miroslav Lamač, *Osma a Skupina výtvarných umělců 1907–1917* (Praha: Odeon, 1988).

2 Even though the Czech avant-garde was already forming before the war, especially as concerns the fine arts groups the Group Eight and the Group of Visual Artists, the *consciousness of being avant-garde* was not yet characteristic for it in this period: it did not promote itself with group manifestos and collective programmatic declarations. This characteristic appeared only in the post-war period, at a time when the actors themselves perceived and experienced (meta)literary communication as a form of breakthrough or as breaking point. In his article "Kulturní smysl doby" (Cultural Sense of the Period), Josef Hora exclaims: "The slogan of the period is: Quickly. The sense of the period is: Transformation." Josef Hora, "Kulturní smysl doby," in Štěpán Vlašín (ed.)., *Avantgarda známá a neznámá* 1 (Praha: Svoboda, 1971), 56–60 (p. 56). Similarly, the program of the Devětsil Artistic Group opens with a declaration of a period at breaking point; cf. "U. S. Devětsil," in Štěpán Vlašín (ed.), *Avantgarda známá a neznámá* 1 (Praha: Svoboda, 1971), 81–83 (p. 81). In his programmatic essay "Novým směrem" (In a New Direction), Karel Teige also writes about a disruptive, style-less period; Karel Teige, "Novým směrem," in Štěpán Vlašín (ed.), *Avantgarda známá a neznámá* (Praha: Svoboda, 1971), 90–96 (p. 91). In the introduction to his collection *Nesrozumitelný svatý* (Incomprehensible Saint, 1922), A. M. Píša describes his poems as a product of the stormy period of the years 1919 and 1920, in which a revolutionary transformation of the world, life, and the human being occurred, and describes the post-war period as *liquid*, in which currents of red-hot lava over the stale dry earth create a new reality and fore-images of the tomorrows of humankind; cf. A. M. Píša, *Nesrozumitelný svatý: cyklus básní z roku 1920* (Praha: František Svoboda, 1922), 8. This transformation of the world and the destruction of the current orders was also identified by F. X. Šalda: "We are living in the eve of a great world transformation. Orders on which the world has stood for thousands of years are loosening, collapsing, being replaced by others. Private property is disappearing; it is receding in favor of collectivist forms of ownership." František Xaver Šalda, *Kritické projevy 11. 1919–1921. Soubor díla F. X. Šaldy 20*, Zina Trochová (ed.) (Praha: Československý spisovatel, 1959), 159.

3 The preface is signed by the Devětsil Artistic Group; the author is Vladislav Vančura, cf. Jaroslav Seifert, *Město v slzách* (Praha: Komunistické knihkupectví a nakladatelství R. Rejman, 1921), unpaginated.

In the early 1920s the young Czech avant-garde was represented by two groups: Devětsil in Prague and the Literární skupina (Literary Group) in Brno.[4] The artistic association Devětsil was founded on 5 October 1920 and its first public appearance took place in Prague's Mozarteum on 15 December. Among its founding members were Karel Teige, Jaroslav Seifert, Adolf Hoffmeister, and Vladislav Vančura in the role of chairman. The group published the journals *Disk* (1923–1925), *Pásmo* (1924–1926), and *ReD* (1927–1931). In 1922 the group published the *Revoluční sborník Devětsil* (Devětsil Revolutionary Collection), containing key studies on the relationship between proletarianism and art. In the collection, the authors also expressed themselves on current visual arts, cinematography, functionalism in architecture, and similar matters. In the same year, the *Život* (Life) collection, subtitled *Sborník nové krásy* (A Collection of New Beauty), was also issued, with a striking typographical layout. This collection already reveals the shift away from proletarianism towards avant-garde inter-disciplinarity and inter-mediality. The theoretical articles and studies were accompanied by illustrations or photographs of automobiles, airplanes, transatlantic liners, and skyscrapers. Along with these, the work of the foremost representatives of the French avant-garde (A. Ozenfant, Man Ray, Le Corbusier) also appeared here. In an atmosphere of proclaimed proletarian literature, the *Život* (Life) compendium represented the first step in the postulates of Czech Poetism, which was fully developed in 1924 and became the only original Czech direction of the inter-war avant-garde.

---

4 For more on the history of the Devětsil group, compare, for instance, Jitka Ciampi Matulová et al., *Devětsil 1920–1931*, trans. by Gwendolyn Albert, Vladimíra Šefranka Žáková (Praha: Prague City Gallery, 2011). In 1923 a branch of Devětsil was founded in Brno. For more, compare: Petr Ingerle, Lucie Česálková, *Brno Devětsil and multimedia overlaps of the artistic avant-garde*, trans. by Miloš Bartoň, Alan Windsor (Brno: Moravian Gallery, 2014).
The following provide some starting points of the literature on Czech avant-garde written in English. See for example: Petr A. Bílek, Josef Vojvodík and Jan Wiendl (eds.), *A Glossary of Catchwords of the Czech Avant-Garde*, trans. by David Short (Praha: Faculty of Arts, Charles University; Togga, 2011); Karla Huebner, *Magnetic Woman: Toyen and the Surrealist Erotic* (Pittsburgh: University of Pittsburgh Press, 2020). Photography and picture poems: Matthew S. Witkovsky (ed.), *Foto: Modernity in Central Europe, 1918–1945* (New York: Thames & Hudson, 2007); Vladimír Birgus (ed.), *Czech Photographic Avant-Garde, 1918–1948* (Cambridge, MA: MIT Press, 2002); and Jaroslav Anděl and Anne Wilkes Tucker (eds.), *Czech Modernism, 1900–1945* (Houston: Museum of Fine Arts, 1989). Theatre: Andrea Jochmanová, "Liberating the Theatre," in Petr A. Bílek, Josef Vojvodík and Jan Wiendl (eds.), *A Glossary...*, 251–262; and Veronika Ambros, "Prague: Magnetic Fields or the Staging of the Avant-Garde," in Marcel Cornis-Pope and John Neubauer (eds.), *History of the Literary Cultures of East-Central Europe: Junctures and Disjunctures in the 19th and 20th Centuries, Vol. 2* (Amsterdam: John Benjamins, 2004), 176–182. Architecture: Rostislav Švácha, *The Architecture of New Prague 1895–45*, trans. by Alexandra Büchler (Cambridge, MA: MIT Press, 1995), chapters three and four. Journals: Nicholas Sawicki, "The View from Prague," in Peter Brooks, Sascha Bru, Andrew Thacker, and Christian Weikop (eds.), *The Oxford Critical and Cultural History of Modernist Magazines, Vol. 3: Europe 1880–1940, Part I* (Oxford: Oxford University Press, 2013), 1074–1098; Peter Zusi, *The Integrity of the Avant-Garde: Karel Teige and the Biography of an Ambition* (Cambridge: Legenda, 2023).

Karel Teige, the theoretical spokesman of Devětsil, in his articles "Novým směrem" (In a New Direction) and "Obrazy a předobrazy" (Images and Fore-Images, both 1921) presents the intellectual foundation of the emerging Czech avant-garde. For the first time concepts appear here which, albeit in a different way, will stand at the center of the Czech inter-war avant-garde for a further two decades: a new art, a new person, a new modern order and reality. In the early 1920s Teige promotes an art that is absolutely engaged — in Teige's deliberations, the individual artist becomes an "agitator for socialism" who is invigorated by the needs of the masses. In the context of the tension between individualism and collectivism, the first paradoxes of the Czech inter-war avant-garde already appear here.[5] Teige formulates in a very radical way that the only possible subject (not object!) of a work of art is a human being (not, however, as an isolated individual) with their psychological depths and giddiness of internal dramas, and with their unutterable need for harmony and happiness. In the case of Teige, these opinions are strongly influenced by a leftist-oriented proletarianism. Emotionality expressed through a human being anticipates a Utopian fore-image of art as a kind of the purest form of humanity — that is, traditional folk art and primitive art, which have always been closest to human beings and literally arise from them. The turn towards folk creation was supposed to prevent a return to negative individualism, because according to Teige's notions, folk art captured pure, true reality. The art of the emerging young generation was, therefore, supposed to create only a functioning fore-image for the new art, which would free human beings from narrow individuality and would incorporate them into society.

The art of this generation set as its aim only the creation of functioning "fore-images" (Teige's term) for a new art. Teige proposes replacing the currently functioning and conventional literary-critical terms with new terms that were anchored in traditional aesthetics: he proposes replacing the concept "intuition" with the concept "idea," and the concept "creation" with the concept "human work." In a comment on Teige's essay "Images and Fore-Images", Karel Čapek warned that it presented a retreat from the Utopian plans of the younger generation. A few years later, Čapek expressed himself on the matter of the relationship of proletarianism and literature even more explicitly. In an article with the portentous name "Proč nejsem komunistou" (Why I Am Not a Communist), he makes use of wordplay to connect the efforts of the young generation to achieve a new order of the world not with an order, but with a bad order (in Czech, respectively řád, zlořád). Čapek

5 The opposition of individualism and collectivism is a key concept of my monograph *Vprostřed davu* (In the Midst of the Crowd), which deals with the formation of the Czech avant-garde in the 1920s. Even though the avant-garde presented itself as a movement almost without artistic roots, as emerging from itself, it reacted to transformations of the modern world and the standing of the human being in it. It reacted to what was perceived and identified as modern. Cf. Zuzana Říhová, *Vprostřed davu: česká avantgarda mezi individualismem a kolektivismem* (Praha: Academia, 2016).

unmasked the almost aggressive post-war desire for the collective as an attempt to drown the "unease of the heart" in a review of Neumann's deliberations about new art *Ať žije život!* (Long Live Art!, written 1913–4, published in book form only in 1920 with illustrations by Josef Čapek): "*Yes, mainly unease*. When I read many books of modern poetry today, energetic, making a noisy racket, full of revolutionary optimism and celebration, I cannot rid myself of the impression that we are deluding ourselves about this surfeit of life just as though deluding ourselves that our pockets are full of banknotes."[6]

In the role of translator, Karel Čapek discovered French avant-garde poetry for Czech poets (*Francouzská poezie nové doby*, Contemporary French Poetry, 1920), in particular the personality of G. Apollinaire and his long poem *Zone* (in Czech, *Pásmo*). The influence of Apollinaire's *Zone* was unprecedented — it became a *de facto* original element in the development of Czech poetry, a new poetic model of the relationship between poetry and reality. In his studies from the early 1920s, Karel Teige describes *Zone* as an initiatory poem of our era, as a hymn from which the era of new poetry begins. The formal (interchangeability of first and second persons, free verse) and graphic (suppression of punctuation) aspects of the poem, together with its futuristic orientation, suited the Czech avant-garde oriented exclusively towards the future. *Zone* poetry became a genre in Czech literature and *Zone*-style compositions (among others, Jiří Wolker, Vítězslav Nezval, Vilém Závada, and Konstantin Biebl) represent a specific form of Czech avant-garde epic. [7]

---

6 The intoxication with the unification of humankind among the Czech avant-garde was also relatively precisely limited in time. After Devětsil found a "way out of the disharmony of world opinions" — Poetism — S. K. Neumann and A. M. Píša went their own ways, and the collectivism of the first post-war years became rather an unfortunate recollection. For this post-war generation, Čapek's words written in a private letter to Olga Scheinpflugová while working on the collectivist drama *R.U.R.* would become ever more clear: "While writing, a terrible fear descended on me. I wanted to warn in some way against production of the mass and depersonalized slogans, and all of a sudden I was gripped by anxiety that this would one day come to pass, maybe soon, that I will no longer save anything with this warning; that just as I the author led the forces of these blunt mechanisms wherever I wanted, one day someone will lead the stupid mass-man against the world and God." Karel Čapek *R. U. R. Rossum's Universal Robots: kolektivní drama o vstupní komedii a třech dějstvích* (Praha: Československý spisovatel, 1966), 106.

7 In spite of the lack of understanding that accompanied the first reading of *Zone*, this poem became a conscious genre choice — a number of Czech poets expressed their desire to "write like Apollinaire." Among the most significant *Zone*-style compositions we can enumerate *Svatý kopeček* (1921) by Jiří Wolker, *Podivuhodný kouzelník* (Strange Magician, 1922) by Vítězslav Nezval, Závada's *Panychida* (Memorial Ceremony, 1927), and Biebl's *Nový Ikaros* (New Icarus, 1929). Nezval included his further *Zone* compositions in his collection *Básně noci* (Poems of the Night, 1930), which can be read as a farewell to Poetism. Czech *Zone*-style poems as representatives of the Czech epic have been examined most recently by Říhová (Zuzana Říhová, "A Farewell to the Whole Epoch: the Zone as the Beginning and End of the Czech Avant-Garde," in *Journal of Modern Literature*, 2020, 43 (4): 45–61.

Leftist-engaged proletarianism appealed in particular to the young artists of Devětsil. In his manifesto "Proletářské umění" (Proletarian Art, 1922), a text written together with Karel Teige, Jiří Wolker defined the fundamental features of the new art: its revolutionary nature, collectivism, tendentiousness, optimism. He added a clear concluding slogan: "The proletariat are the workers of the new world. Artists want to be the workers of the new beauty in it." Similarly, for Teige in his text "Nové umění proletářské" (New Proletarian Art, 1922), the working class and communism represent the connection of modern art with revolution in reaction to the exhaustion of pre-war modernism and the necessity of building the world and a new art from their foundations in a different way. In the proletarian poetry of this period, the frequency of the image of the heart increases, which is associated with the formation of an idyllic post-war world, albeit in many cases connected paradoxically with a revolutionary perspective. In his collection *Host do domu* (Guest in the House, 1921), Jiří Wolker offers a paradise of poetry of the heart, a world like a miracle, enhanced by a harmonious connection between people and the unsubstantial world.

In 1921 an avant-garde association was founded in Brno with the name Literary Group, which acted as a group without a precisely formulated program, with no clear ideological and political direction. The absence of a program, considered by some members at the beginning as a positive aspect of the group, nevertheless showed itself to be unsustainable in an intensifying conflict with Devětsil. Therefore, František Götz, the group's spokesman, formulated a political and "intellectual" program for the group, *"polyphonic" socialism.*

The Literary Group's manifesto, "Naše naděje, víra a práce" (Our Hope, Faith, and Work) was not written by Götz until 1922. Even though phrases such as the following here also occur — "grand cosmic brotherhood of humankind" and immersing one's heart "in the mass consciousness of the crowds of workers" — and at the center of interest is the human being seen "through the fates of the masses, of classes, of entire worlds" and great emphasis is placed on the moral transformation of humankind and its "achievement of brotherhood," it was read by members of Devětsil as a reactionary, non-modern program. In particular, one concept, used by Götz seemingly without any great emphasis, became the impulse for an extensive polemic. František Götz never adopted a Marxist conception of culture and art, but nevertheless in accord with Teige's group he sought in socialism a path to the liberation of human beings and the proletariat. The artistic activities of the Literary Group were influenced by Expressionism, a concept that was significantly connected with the activities of the German avant-garde around the year 1910. However, for the Marxist theoreticians of Devětsil, Expressionism was like an imaginary red cap to a bull. In reaction to the accusation of Devětsil member Artuš Černík that Expressionism was a part of the individualist-anarchist tradition of German poetry, in his article "O Hosta a o ty, co za ním stojí" (On the Magazine Host and Those Who Stand Behind It) František Götz described the Unanimist creative work of Georges Duhamel, Charles Vildrac, and René Arcos as "French Expressionism" and determined it as the basis of the Expressionism of the Literary Group. It might seem that aligning the Literary Group to an artistic model that the early post-war avant-garde admired primarily for its depiction of the collective soul of the crowd would be a sufficient reason for ending the exchange of opinions between the two theoreticians. However, František Götz only achieved the result that Karel Teige, hitherto an enthusiastic adherent of Unanimism, and primarily of the work of Charles-Louis Philippe, whom contemporary critics connected with Unanimism, immediately turned his back on this movement and condemned it as one of the directions of spurned bourgeois art. Götz's declaration of the commitment of the Literary Group to Expressionism — that is, a direction that was pre-war, superceded, bourgeois, and individualistic — led Teige to make the following declaration in his article "O expresionismu" (On Expressionism, 1922): "Contributors to *Host*, who did not want to participate in creating proletarian art, are not revolutionary artists — they are *passéiste*." By connecting the program of the Literary Group with the repudiated individualism, bourgeoisie, and passiveness (in a period of the apotheosis of collectivism and revolutionary activism), Karel Teige in essence disarmed František Götz. Even though in reaction to Teige's invective František Götz in his article "Trochu polemiky, trochu vyznání" (A Little Bit of a Polemic, a Little Bit of a Confession, 1922), after providing an explanation of all the things that the concept Expressionism meant for him, tried to bring the polemic to an end with the appeal: "we are just as artistically contemporary as Devětsil." In doing so, he transforms this postulate into an empty formulation which lacks the necessary resonance for the opposing side. Teige's rejection of Unanimism is thus in the final instance a symptom of the turning away from France towards the Soviet Union by part of the Czech avant-garde (Devětsil), the process of which is captured in a condensed form by the title of Neumann's article "Paříž? — Moskva!" (Paris? — Moscow!, 1923). Within the abating polemic, Teige also mentions painter Zdenek Rykr — in his opinion, an avant-garde chameleon — who was constantly in dispute with Teige, as evidence of the treacherousness of the Literary Group, because personalities like Rykr contributed to *Host* — the journal platform of the Literary Group.

"We are going to compete together. We are perhaps even going to quarrel. But nevertheless, I think, we are going to be friends."[8] Such was the declaration of František Götz shortly after the foundation of the Literary Group about its relationship to Devětsil. Only the first two sentences of this declaration showed themselves to be prophetic. Practically from his first studies, Karel Teige claimed the quality of being avant-garde exclusively for the Devětsil group. Already in 1921 in his article "S novou generací" (With the New Generation), among the first things that Teige notes is that he does not speak for the entire generation, but only for its *avant-garde* (visual arts, less so literary). In Teige's early articles we can observe a strategic securing of first place in newness — modernism — which is the very essence of the avant-garde.

8 František Götz, "Devětsil v Brně", in Štěpán Vlašín (ed.), *Avantgarda známá a neznámá* 1. *Od proletářského umění k poetismu. 1919–1924* (Praha: Svoboda, 1971), 130–133.

František Götz comes forward with the "theoretical basis" of the Literary Group only later, after Teige already has his program formulated and is looking around for a partner for polemics in which he will reinforce the avant-garde claims of Devětsil, as well as his own claims as its spokesman. For Teige, Götz's Expressionism became an ideal concept that enabled him to maneuver Götz and his group outside of the avant-garde. Teige made similar use of concepts such as collectivism, revolution, and proletarianism (as well as optimism and tendentiousness), which (together with Jiří Wolker) he determined as the foundational concepts of the emerging avant-garde, without paying any attention to Götz's systematic efforts to promote collectivism as the main idea of a new, post-war art.

In a certain sense, the creative output of the Literary Group proved Teige right. Short stories with an emphasis on an examination of the psychological states of the poet (Čestmír Jeřábek, Miloslav Nohejl) did not leave any significant trace in the history of Czech literature. In his article "Likvidace konkurzní podstaty expresionismu" (Bankruptcy Proceedings of Expressionism, 1924), Bedřich Václavek compared the members of the Literary Group, just like the entire Expressionist movement, to a corpse on account of its conception of literature as an instrument for penetrating into a person's soul.[9] However, in 1924 the entire Czech proletarian avant-garde could be regarded as a corpse. The speed of the period and the tempo of change are also apparent in how quickly members of Devětsil and Literary Group rejected the infant period of proletarian art. For the participants in the generational discussion that took place on the pages of the journals, this phase was considered as closed once-and-for-all and was attributed the character of a youthful, laughable mistake. The Czech post-war avant-garde wanted to be adult. However, it was only in its next step, in Poetism, that it first entered the phase of youthful play and a light-headed intoxication with the beauties of the world. Shortly after the publication of the *Revoluční sborník Devětsil* (Devětsil Revolutionary Collection, 1922), Jiří Wolker writes in a letter to A. M. Píša: "The Devětsil collection showed that the slogan "proletarian art," to which we both once upon a time declared our allegiance, is becom-

9 Bedřich Václavek, "Likvidace konkursní podstaty expresionismu," in Štěpán Vlašín (ed.), *Avantgarda známá a neznámá* 1. *Od proletářského umění k poetismu. 1919–1924* (Praha: Svoboda, 1971), 520–525. According to Václavek, in Expressionism the powerless soul becomes absorbed in itself; instead of synthesis, only the powerlessness of subjectivity appears. Václavek criticizes the Literary Group primarily from the position of a radical pioneer of collectivism in art. He regards as desirable only such a generation as fills its works exclusively with the desires of the collective, and he perceives Devětsil's movement towards Poetism as a supplementing of the purposefulness of art with an intense poeticness, which in his opinion constantly ensures the place of the masses: "In their [the young generation] case the conflict between individualistic, subjectivist, bourgeois culture and the new, collectivist culture of tomorrow occurs clearly for the first time. They have given up footling subjectivism; they are going in the direction of the objectivity of the poetic method and of a level above individual persons." Bedřich Václavek, "Naše generace," in Štěpán Vlašín (ed.), *Avantgarda známá a neznámá* 1. *Od proletářského umění k poetismu. 1919–1924* (Praha: Svoboda, 1971), 656–659 (p. 657).

ing so to speak a laughing stock."[10] Wolker was not mistaken. In Karel Schulz's essay "Poetika" (Poetics, 1923), tendentious (politically-engaged) poetry, which one year earlier was still a serious aim of members of Devětsil, is subjected to caustic irony. From 1924 onward, the number one theme for the Czech avant-gardists is life, and very soon regardless of whether that life is class-based.

---

10 Jiří Wolker, *Dopisy. Korespondence Jiřího Wolkera*, Zina Trochová (ed.) (Praha: Československý spisovatel, 1984), 510. The early Czech avant-garde rejected its own postulates with admirable speed. Similar emotions to those expressed by Jiří Wolker in the context of proletarian art (a laughable mistake) are expressed by the narrator of Karel Schulz's novel *Dáma u vodotrysku* (Lady at the Fountain, 1926) within the framework of condemning the "grotesque promises and stone jugs full of decoctions of the poison of equality and brotherhood"; cf. Karel Schulz, *Dáma u vodotrysku* (Praha: Ladislav Kuncíř, Rozmach, 1926), 13. Also some literary critics who one year earlier had still praised the inclination of the young for the crowd and the masses, now followed their abandonment of this orientation with enthusiasm: in 1923 S. K. Neumann welcomes the fact that the young artists from Devětsil have done something sensible and left behind declamations and deluded theories about proletarian art and have (correctly) started to give precedence to the commotion of the circus and a colorful bustle over educating the proletariat for revolution. Cf. Květoslav Chvatík and Zdeněk Pešat (eds.), *Poetismus: antologie* (Praha: Odeon 1967), 116. *Revoluční sborník Devětsil* was reissued in 2010 by Akropolis publishing house.

Richard Weiner: The Curtain Rises; At the Castle

The Curtain Rises

October 28th, afternoon. On a visit in Dejvice. The periphery of Prague. A friend. He talks about all kinds of things. And because there has been no shortage of sensations this last week, we did not even get excited when my friend mentioned in passing that someone on the tram said that Austria-Hungary had capitulated. "Hang on a minute! That is pretty strong stuff." But the thought would not let us go and by midday our curiosity got the better of us. "Let's go into town." — All quiet on the streets of Dejvice. — "See, just idle gossip! A historic day does not look like this. People are walking too slowly." — At Klárov. Nothing. — Kaprova Street, and hey! Something is happening. How do we recognize this? God knows, but something is certainly happening. — Old Town Square. A special edition of *Národní Listy*. "Citizens, what is going on?" — "Citizens!" Where did that word "citizen" come from? — Austria-Hungary has accepted all of Wilson's conditions; in particular, it recognizes the claims of the Czechoslovaks and the Yugoslavs. At double trot! — Železná Street, the old German theater, Havířská Street. Příkopy. The "Bohemie" bank building. A huge American flag on it. We open our eyes wide, two friends looking at each other. Out of breath. Then, hands in the air, all together: Praise be to Wilson! — A huddle of young German students smile uneasily — A few flags on Příkopy boulevard. Large banks are hesitating. People running around confusedly. Over there, an acquaintance. He raises his hands. "What is going on?" "Don't know!" — "The end." — "Abtreten!" — "We have reached the goal!" — In front of the *Národní Politika* building. Special edition. — We know already. — On all sides: "Oh!" — "Ah!" "Lord Jesus!" "Done and dusted!" — A police officer is shuffling around at his post. "Extraausgabe Bohemia." — "Not in German," says the officer. "Today it does not matter, citizen officer! And don't provoke!" — The officer smiles. — Flags are showing up. On the flagpole of the Museum they are in the process of raising a second red-and-white canvas powerfully inflated by the wind. Around the statue of St. Wenceslas it is dark. A poster on the pedestal: Long live the Czech republic! — A people's orator is speaking from the balcony of the "Parlament" coffee house. We hear: "Wretched Austria-Hungary! — The final hiccup! — Rotting... — Tyrants and murderers." Today, these are not *loci comuni*. — On the way down from Můstek the supernumeraries of great days are streaming along: clusters, conglomerations. — Caps and hats are flying in the air. — On Ferdinand Boulevard! In Spálená Street we meet councilor Mattuš. He tells us: "Now the National Council has taken over. The test of statesmanship is beginning." — Who would have guessed that this civilian would present himself to us on this evening as the station commander of Prague? — It is half past one. Our stomachs remind us that we have not eaten. But when we think about indulging them, they inform that they do not actually feel like eating.

To the cemetery. To notify a new, expensive grave. The only way to get there by tramway is by a roundabout route. In the main streets whole rosaries of vehicles are lined up. They cannot move at all. At Olšany the conductors are saying that the trams are going back to depot. — At the Strašnice Cemetery a funeral. — I am carrying a wild mignonette flower. "A peace mignonette!" says an old beggar-woman. Now even the dead know that That Day has arrived. — The only way to get back is on foot. From Strašnice, from Vinohrady, whole families, whole processions are streaming into the city center. — Along field paths singing people are making their way in procession. They can be heard as far as the cemetery. Their cries are exuberant, but they do not disturb the peace of the dead. Even they are listening. On the horizon massive snow clouds. A freezing wind is blowing. However, when — dusk already falling — we come down from Vinohrady a mild early evening sets in that quite invites to strolling around. — In the meantime the flags have proliferated into white-red-blue waves, endless, beating high. Where were you sleeping, you treasonous *tricoleurs*, where have you come from, you countless three-colored cockades, lion cubs, banners, and pennant garlands? We go down a triumphant street. All the arched lamps are burning, music is playing, and from the ramps of the Museum something can be seen that no one remembers, not even if he or she remembers the greatest Prague days. An enormous boulevard literally crammed full with a mass of people that cannot move. Not even a quarter of a centimeter has been left unfilled by this human sea. And how they clamor! How they roar! And it can be observed that there is a complete absence of any kind of hateful sound. This moment is reserved only for a great thanksgiving. — A German lady, pointing at her husband, says to her companion: "Why is he so nervous? After all, it is astounding, amazing, fairy-tale beautiful — and it is a fairy tale in which there is no man-eater. Why, then, is he nervous? I am enthusiastic, even though it pained me." They lived our joy, which they purchased by risking everything they had, unable however to join their voice with ours in one cry welcoming the victor. Ah, this day that we are experiencing — who is to say whether for them a drop of regret, which they cannot resist, will not be mixed in its joyousness?

Only two days — and the delightful chaos of today will be sorted in the order of enthusiasm. I recall for the third time how we, we journalists, who just like the others are confronted by a miracle, well knowing, just like all of you, that there is no picture nor word adequate for it, equally excited by a feeling of happiness that is so great that it is similar to terror... and yet: We alone submit ourselves to a senseless task of work, and our resisting pens — more sensible than us — overcome by the brute force of journalistic duty will write words, words about something that can be expressed precisely as little as the Word itself.

At the Castle

One thing, it seems, was well and truly removed from the republic in the first days: that is what we have called the Prague fairy tale. The Prague fairy tale was palaces, and what was fairy-tale like about them was their dereliction, melancholy, and the blindness of their windows. The Prague fairy tale has for ever been a cheerless one.

Well, it is all over for the gloomy charm of Prague palaces. Even the most cursed of them, such as the Clam-Gallas Palace on Hus Street, the Fürstenberg Palace on Valdštýnská Street, and the Maltézský Palace on Velkopřevorské Square, have opened their doors, lighted their windows, and the once silent halls and corridors are now noisy with the comings and goings of people, the ringing of telephones, and the clacking of typewriters. The gloomy fairy tale is gone, but the reality, simple, transparent, and civic, is no less a charm, albeit clearer. We are adapting to an amiable fairy tale.

Prague Castle, however, has "become magical!" so suddenly and so thoroughly that certainly some time a fairy tale will be written about this. The end of the castle's enchantment took place with such vehemence that there is no other option than to believe in magic. For many long years the enormous castle resided on its hill like a famous corpse, exhibited in its sarcophagus with great, magnificent pomp: thus so during the day. In the night, however, it appeared as an exalted and somber giant, whom they had defeated and who rested without movement and without breath, inspiring plaintive respect by its lack of life. From one side, that from which it can be seen across the Rudolf Bridge, it looked down almost gloomily into the ravine of Letenská Street, and if from its motionlessness here and there a light could be spotted in some window in an institution of minor nobility or from someone's service accommodation, this was like the unclosed eye of a dead person, which terrifies. — One evening, however, a late-night walker noticed a big change. There were lights shining in the castle's windows. However, this was not ceremonial lighting for some fairy-tale play. It was a case of several discontinuous windows on two or three floors, behind which common yellow lights were shining such as light up human dwellings, offices, and shops, lights somehow concentrated and unexalted, lights of work and life. It is as though the gloomy majesty of inaccessibility and introversion has been wiped away. But look behind this, a kind of intimate trust spoke through these endless walls and these windows in a language comprehensible and serious, talk that repudiates fearful respect for the feudal past, extolling instead respect for the authority of civic institutions, in which you and I have the same share as creators and at the same time as those who obey them. The imagination of the late-night walker went to work: It depicted how, behind those windows, there are people performing night service for the republic, which is deep in a night-time sleep. No gentlemen with rapiers and ruffled sleeves; no gentlemen in tailcoats with bored faces, expounding in a nasal voice their noble family trees; none of those who moved around on the Earth like invisible spirits, embodying their physical state only on the occasion of state ceremonies, when their amazed subjects observed them as though they had descended from the clouds, behind the impenetrable veil of which they spent the remainder of their lives. Not at all! The late-night walker realized that present there in the service of the republic were citizen A., with whom he talked this evening in a coffee house, citizen B., with whom he was going to go out reveling tomorrow, citizen C., who had told him this afternoon about his problems in moving house, citizen D., with whom he walked around Ferdinand Boulevard at five o'clock today and who had an unfortunate accident when his braces snapped. He knows that these citizens there, with cigarettes in their mouths, work quite honestly, taking care not to overload themselves, that they accept dispatches, send other dispatches, answer the telephone, chatter, write, propose, argue with one another and then again agree — and they do all this, quite simply human in their tasks, full of good will, susceptible to lapses, mistakes, and errors, but also marked by honesty, endeavor, astuteness, and success. In other words, taken all together this or that ministry, which is also attested to here and there by a provisional nameplate on the doors with the names of citizens employed in this or that department. The late-night walker climbed up to his room with the consciousness that he lives in a republic in which everyone should obey (or he ***will*** have to obey) for the simple reason that no one and nothing prevents him in advance (or no one and nothing ***will*** prevent him in advance) from also participating and deciding; in a republic administered by people with whom he must speak frankly and directly, in a republic with a machinery that is complicated, but not however mysterious, in a republic in which state affairs do not appear as a monstrance for silent admiration and to be bowed down to, but rather in which everyone can put in some hard work and see for themselves what is involved in these state affairs. In a republic in whose engine it still rattles a bit here and there, but in which people are working thoroughly and meticulously to ensure that it rattles a bit less as every day goes by. In a republic which said to the old, morose castle: "Rise Up!" and helped him on to his feet.

And in the morning, in order to persuade himself whether his night-time vision of the lighted castle windows had not been merely a deception of the senses, he went to have a look. And he found what he had guessed he would find. He found, in sum, nobility, but of a purely humanized kind. The long facades of the castle courtyards, cathedral, fountains, the canonical quarters, and also that strangely reserved "Vikárka" (although even before this was only a pub), it is as though all this was to wipe its freshly open eyes and say: "Was all this just a dream for us?" Already at the Powder Bridge (Prašný most), that once-upon-a-time so gloomy castle entrance, it seemed to him that he was entering the castle in a different way than previously: not as a guest who could be thrown out already by the first soldier on guard, but rather like someone who has an ownership share here.

How everything was different from before! This change can be seen already in the guards, around whom one previously walked like around a fierce dog, but who now seem to welcome being addressed: Our people are keeping watch, for us. Castle attendants and clerks, once upon a time stiff faces lined with imperial side whiskers, which used to serve stupid swellheads as a substitute for dignity, have recognized necessity and have humanized their appearance. In reply to the question: "Where is Mr. Čapek?" they are no longer permitted to reply with a haughty shrug of the shoulders. Now, the usage pleasantly expected is "here and there" or "I don't know" or "I don't know him." And politely spoken.

From the fountain in the second courtyard that hideous metal eagle, which seemed to be deliberately provocative in that place, a disfigurement of the fountain's architecture, has disappeared. A little further on, the 1st Czechoslovak field artillery battalion is cooking in a mobile kitchen and nearby a number of vehicles decorated with pine branches are prepared for the journey to Ústí nad Labem. — Bustle and hum. Above a narrow door, a band with the sign: "Czechoslovak Ministry of National Defense — Presidium." Soldiers are taking some kind of furniture out of the building and a pretty girl is walking across the courtyard with some documents. — I enter through another narrow gate with the sign above it: "Castle Administration." — Inside the castle for the first time. So far it does not exactly look entirely royal: narrow meandering corridors with standard office paint, doors and more doors, winding staircases, alcoves, and bends. In the office two balding attendants, old regime types, who are making an effort to adapt to the new state of affairs and forcing themselves to a politeness that once upon a time was not a custom for visitors such as me. "Mr. Čapek? He's not here. He is moving office somewhere in the castle." — Into the third courtyard. Everywhere bricklayers, painters, locksmiths, carpenters; mechanics are laying electric cables. Ten new lines. Under a large balcony in the third courtyard — and up to the ministerial presidium. On the right, an improvised waiting room: plush red seats, and sitting on them male and female citizens of all types. On the left, a long corridor that goes on and on forever, stepladders, painters, electric wiring, dishwashers, cleaners, attendants, people hanging around. There follows a number of rooms with polished floors; with light furniture and also heavy furniture in all possible kinds of styles — Louis XVI, Rococo, Baroque, and Empire; old paintings — court scenes, landscapes, battle scenes and feudal portraits; splendid upholstery of red and heavenly blue; golden moulding; marble hearths, in which fires are burning. In order to melt away the musty courtly atmosphere. In spite of all this splendor — and splendor there is! — the permeating warmth from the hearths makes the chambers of the prime minister and the president of the republic habitable and cozy. And how appropriate all this is considering the fact that it will be from here that we are going to be ruled by our own people! A thought that constantly accompanies you and warms you until your heart melts. — We have known nothing other than foreign rule. Now for the first time it is possible to feel how much depression and bondage these two words meant.

And we enter a long corridor — a gallery, once again doors and more doors, a stairway — it is incredible all the things that are hidden in this giant building! Finally, we find sculptor Čapek, who together with architect Hilbert is "commander" of the castle. Right now, he is commanding a group of soldiers carrying a heavy cupboard. "We are quickly furnishing Beneš's apartment for the president. We are expecting him any moment now. He will stay for six weeks for the meanwhile." — He leads us to the German and Spanish halls. Of the "unhistorical" parts of the castle only these two were accessible: the smaller German one, where a representative national gallery will be established; and the larger Spanish one, assigned for major state events and ceremonies. "For instance, Wilson is coming, the English king is coming, Poincaré is coming..." At Prague Castle people now talk even in this way — and no one bats an eyelid. Yes, Wilson is coming, Poincaré is coming — what could be more natural?!

"This cupboard to the president's dining room!" — "And for a mirror go to the apartment of our dear Charles IV: that is, to the apartment of former Emperor Charles!"

Here is a part of the behind-the-scenes of the new state, the hall of requisites. This was what most enticed and impressed citizens, because it was carefully concealed so as not to disturb the illusion of the distinctiveness of the ruling luster. Kings ate, slept, and also had other needs, but it was to supposed to appear as though angels served them, as though there was no kitchen, bed or — toilet. By the way, there are really very few of them at the castle. In contrast, everywhere along the corridors, here, that portable chamber pot, a fatal reminder of the natural human needs of monarchs appointed by God's mercy. — In front of the press office, a group of our Russian soldiers. They have come from the Ukraine to look at the liberated homeland. We take them along with us. Once again, presidential suites and rooms of the Ministry of Foreign Affairs, shining with gold: No, the highest state offices are not going to be Cinderellas. And in this magnificence, once upon a time cold and self-enclosed, but now in some way simple-minded and affable, our people are going about their business. Our people, more meritorious and less meritorious, the talented and the less talented (time will sift them), are moving about; they perform their offices and believe in their tasks; all of them — how can it be doubted! — filled for the meanwhile with the best will, or even with idealistic intentions.

We are once again in the courtyard. It is midday. The troops with their vehicles are leaving for Ústí nad Labem, beaming faces, things are going well. There is hustle and bustle throughout all the courtyards, and "Vikárka," the good old Vikárka of Svatopluk Čech, is packed, and even though there is no talk there either of a trip to the moon or back to the 15th century, yesterday's pedestrian nevertheless feels like Mr. Brouček, finding himself suddenly in a wonderful world, but he no longer fears that he may perhaps wake up in a barrel on a rubbish heap.

U. S. Devětsil: The Age Has Broken in Two...

The age has broken in two. The past has been left behind, condemned to the dust of bookshelves; a new day glitters before us. All must have a voice, but all must also begin building towards a new life. Today young artists, writers, architects and actors are stepping forward as a family, to stand together on the front lines with those in blue collars, with those heading into battle for a new life that the bourgeoisie will not fight for.

Artuš Černík, Josef Frič, Josef Havlíček, Adolf Hoffmeister, Karel Prox, Jaroslav Seifert, Ivan Suk, Ladislav Süss, Vladimír Štulc, Karel Teige, Vladislav Vančura, Karel Vaněk, Karel Veselík and Alois Wachsmann have founded the Devětsil Art Group [U. S. Devětsil]. You're asking why, perchance? Because they are well aware that the individual alone cannot achieve anything significant on either an organizational or artistic level. A group of people sharing a new idea is needed to achieve this. No matter how young and humble, they must realize this. For the literature of the past, no matter how it is called, was always elitist and always served the needs of the rich. Yet these artists are young, they are revolutionary, and can therefore only accompany those who are revolutionary — the proletariat.

The fact that "the little crier calling himself in turn Expressionism, Cubism, Futurism and Orphism, born in the year 1909 of Our Lord, died in 1919..." was grasped by young Russian artists, and they are right. If today's young generation has turned away from this art, if it has turned away from Léger and Delaunay, if it has turned away from Marinetti and Apollinaire, it only does so because it was a fatal error to believe that this art of the machines was at least the art of the worker, imprisoned amongst the monsters of machines and stultified by them; to believe that the worker can be enthused by an art extolling automobiles, in which he will never ride, and glorifying airplanes, which will never carry him in his lifetime, but in which he will see wallowing those who lord over him and leech from him. This was much more the art of the capitalist than of the proletarian. It was an art that did not see things much closer, things with which it was in the closest contact, in everyday contact, things closest to the heart. It was incapable of noticing the table that we sit at, the lamps that provide us with light, the small vases with posies shrouding the face of our room with a smile or the girls we walk with every day. These young artists know how to draw inspiration from the simplest things surrounding any of us. In this, they have even turned away from Stanislav K. Neumann, until now the head and teacher of the youngest generation.

Not all the young, whether writers or artists, have embraced Devětsil. A right-wing group of young writers, organized in the Šak Art Club [Šakův umělecký klub], differs from Devětsil in that they are influenced by the impressionist style of Fráňa Šrámek. This group doesn't even have a set program. "We're young," they tell themselves, "and we want to be young." That's the whole premise on which the group is based. They are mainly formalists, similar to the young rightist artists Vlastimil Rada and Alois Moravec.

Devětsil has set forth a clear program that it intends to follow: the events that it plans on organizing are for the broadest public, accessible to all. Its program includes lectures on art for the public, recital evenings, theatre performances and the publication of anthologies and art catalogues. Yet its events are limited by its meagre financial means and it would be quite helpful if our revolutionary proletariat supported the group's activities by joining Devětsil as dues-paying members. Annual dues amount to twenty crowns; every member receives a discount on all events and every year gets a bonus gift in the form of an artwork that will in itself exceed in value the dues payment.

Having just been established, Devětsil will hold its first public literary evening at the Mozarteum on 15 December at 8 pm. Among those invited to its following event, namely the Proletarian Culture lecture series, is Stanislav K. Neumann.

Josef Hora: On New Art

Art is creation. Knowledge does not equal skill. Knowledge alone is insufficient for creation. Imagine the wisest polymath, who knows the history of humanity, the development of religions, who understands the workings of machines and horticulture, who is able to speak coherently about schools of painting and poetry. Enter a poor embroiderer from Slovakia who spreads before us beautifully and delicately embroidered fabric, a shawl, a blanket, a festive gown, and suddenly the barren scholar, who has absorbed all the wisdom of the world but has never put his knowledge to use, is put to shame. Science in and of itself solely impacts reason; only when it is connected with the imaginative mind, a spirit of enquiry and creativity does it touch your soul and make it fertile. What good is a lifeless map of the starry skies to you? Only when you look up to the star-speckled heavens on a freezing night informed by the map is your heart stirred, sparking inquiry and igniting a desire to take part in the active creation of the world. Only when you join knowledge and the art of observation will your relationship to the things you know become fruitful and deeply affect your everyday life. I myself know people who have studied socialist literature, yet have never seen a living socialist, people living in an ivory tower, entirely incapable of bringing together theory and practice.

The modern world, unfortunately, has reared more and more people here who, due to the ballast of knowledge, do not have the time to be in touch with natural, creative life. These people understand the task of civilization to be the reworking of the whole person to serve a predefined role, to embody a specialization. The word engineer today no longer means technician in the broad sense of the word, not entirely. The mechanical engineer does not and cannot understand civil engineering, nor can the civil engineer grasp electrification. That itself is not the problem. Highly skilled work demands expertise. But the tendency of our age is to turn material expertise into intellectual expertise. We are so preoccupied with gaining this expertise that we walk around with blinders on. The rest of life—the majority of life—slips away from us. And this can be avoided only when society learns again to value something higher than mere expertise, when it makes space for all that makes us human, when it does not discourage wonder of nature, when it stops depriving us of participating in all manifestations of the human spirit. This can only be achieved if it is instilled in people that what makes us human is not merely fulfilling a role, but experiencing our full range of feeling and using our full range of expression.

Take how far specialization has gone in modern art. There are painters who paint only the noonday sun, others only portraits of women; some work with oil, others only with a chisel. But the diagnosis, the narrowing of the field of vision, applies to far more than art technique. True, art is a calling like any other, but beauty is infinite and in the end creation is not only in the hands of the artist by trade, but the whole aggregate of humanity. The only differentiating factor here is intentionality. It seems to me that the more intention, the less beauty. This applies, above all, to technical intent, which keeps pure fantasy from spreading its wings and reduces art to its technical qualities. Where society limits itself to something fully formed, rigidly formal and run by tradition, where new creative elements are no longer brought in to supplement the old, technique wins over inner malleability. And with that art becomes artistically accessible only to the technical experts and those with a capacity for beautiful discernment are excluded; if only because professional and crafts-based works of art permeate the society and thus make the society's own artistic creation redundant.

Just consider the waning capacity in our people for musical creation and decorative arts, how factory production everywhere is winning over tailor-made products, how our sense for harmonious home furnishings and garment details is disappearing. Socialism is often accused of pedantry, but it is actually the capitalist, income-driven mode of mass production that distorts and makes uniform people's taste in everything from children's toys, furniture and pictures on the wall, to gramophones, which drive musical instruments out of homes, etc. This is however the iron tendency of the income-driven age. People, who are bound to exhausting, dismal, and monotonous work, earning minimum wage, do not have time to develop their internal ability to create their own quality of life. They do not yet have the means that would afford for a complete education and that would replace their primitive domestic culture, liberating them from their simple, laughable thinking on the basis of which they create and decorate their surroundings. The iron law of work has alienated people from a loving relationship to nature, which used to nourish their emotional faculties and lend them the gift of melody and an eye for decoration, and has instead provided mediocre compensation in the form of cheap industrial goods that lack taste and inspire no emotional reaction.

It is necessary to make peace with this state of things. The new way of life—in which its new forms, politics, social struggle, highly specialized work, and loss of fundamental and regional distinction play a role—nearly prevents creation dependent on life forms, which are slowly dying out. Only far from urban and industrial centers does the tradition of collective artistic creation survive. But it is necessary to compensate people for that of which they have been deprived. It is necessary to take care that they are given only the best, that immaculate taste is instilled in them instead of trash, run-of-the-mill products from urban rubbish heaps. They murdered the national song with Kmoch and Hašler, they eliminated mythology with the gory novel and traditional village houses with the barrack walls of estates. Instead of providing the city with fresh air and green space and more room, they are rebuilding villages into human chicken coops where there is electricity but where trees are cut down and gardens destroyed with land speculation. The capitalist economy closes people off into dark, tight living quarters, and deprives them of nature, but does not endeavor to build a new, modern law of beauty and taste to fit our new living conditions.

Comfort, health, and beauty are things you can only secure through an ascendance into the class of the moneyed bourgeoisie, who are drowning in luxury in their spacious villas, where nearby in the cellars the poor curse their life, lost love, and sociability—and if they are liberated from personal destitution by forming an anti-capitalist resistance, they are called Bolsheviks just as quickly as they may have previously been called socialists. One of the most beautiful socialist poems, written by the German poet Richard Dehmel, says:

> We have our love and child, our dowry,
>   my wife.
> And we have work, which brings us together,
> and we have the sun and the wind and the rain.
> So little is missing, so that we again
> were like birds and freer still:
>   Only time.

And here we arrive at the fundamental problem of our age. The slow rhythm of the world emanating from old tales of slowly moving village life is history by now. The world, work, pleasure, pain, history, and people—are all mostly motivated by hustle and bustle. Quick! Don't let anyone surpass you! What was the old generation's source of harmony? What was the great classic artists' source of creative strength? What was the source of family bliss in the past? It was the free, regular pulse of their life. Is it our life purpose to work, to hustle? Yes, or so says the industrial age, the age of making money. But isn't the purpose of work to *simply* allow us to live, to teach us not to be lazy but to enjoy rest, to concentrate our mind, to develop our dreams and fantasies, if you like, but mainly to support liberal, creative work on one's own soul, on one's health, on building one's existence into a beautiful, perfect example of humanity?

Even today the bourgeoisie laugh at attempts by the proletariat to shorten the workday. This is entirely reasonable from their point of view because they couldn't possibly allow workers to use their free time to potentially match the intellectual level of the bourgeoisie, who have access to public education. And that is despite modern technology's tendency—and that is its most positive side—to generate the most intensive performance possible, the greatest amount of production in the shortest time. But the application of this tendency is not possible where production is regulated by profit margins instead of need. Superfluous goods are made in excess and production of necessary goods is limited to make the process as expensive as possible.

The bourgeoise simply cannot wish that the creative strength of the people be totally and freely expressed. They permit it only where they can use it to their benefit in their capitalist endeavors, simultaneously detracting from their inner value as well as their moral and pure aesthetic appeal because focus on the financial value strips products of other values. This is the shortcoming of the modern art industry. The art workers creating it are, however, alongside the majority of tinkerers, compelled to subordinate the artistic value of goods to their market value, and thus the spectacularly low level of our mediocre art. The average artist understands before long that they can utilize their talents more advantageously if they discard their artistic consciousness and substitute it with appealing qualities and the run-of-the-mill tastes of the old, dominant, monied crowd. Their production not only kills off the last bits of fantasy, the creative abilities of a human collective, but it also precludes uncompromising artists access to the folk soul, poisoned by conventional banality.

Thus, the majority of today's art is a dangerous weapon in the hands of the bourgeoisie pointed at the proletariat. What does it matter if the lives of thousands and millions are based on socialism *politically* when they are obliged morally and aesthetically to share the tastes and pastimes of the old bourgeoisie, whose market power does not permit the consumption and the art of beautiful things, created, according to them, in an irritating spirit, against their life forms? A bourgeoisie, rigid approach to history, morality, religion, and sense for life in all its breadth has been stifling the proletariat, which is hopefully still politically and economically conscious. Just how easily opportunistic socialist leaders succumb to the bourgeoisie way of life, how easily they adopt its nature, privileges, and comforts, that I presume is quite clear. Individualism, and by that I mean old, wasted, philistine individualism, is proletarians' most dangerous tempter. Neither hatred of the bourgeoisie and all the violence of its weaponry, nor the split opinions among socialists, or the poverty of the masses are as detrimental to the people, their drive for revival and ambiguous desires as the unrelenting comingling of the middle proletariat with the middle bourgeoisie, adopting the bourgeoisie's domestic and artistic customs and opinions, etc.

How can we restore humanity's purity and emotional authenticity, how can we ignite a collective endeavor to elevate its inner spirituality with joyful, autotelic collaboration on the revival of a sense of beauty stemming directly from the soul, independent of art, theater, literature, music, and optics in the awful, profit-hungry basements of cinemas? How can we make art the norm and not the fashionable exception? How can the masses be inspired to crave original creation again?

To this day, history of literature only tells us about poetic geniuses, hundreds of names and schools and forms, but rarely takes notice of how people have reacted to these values, related to ballast, or what reception this or that work, this or that movement, has received. It seems that 19th-century art was created only for a specific social caste, that it was associated solely with personages and created artificially, without the collaboration of the audience. That is why its forms of expression changed so frequently and why the individual generations of art aged so quickly that few works lived to see any appreciation from younger generations. Art was created by individuals for individuals of a similar temperament, it was created selfishly by selfish individualistic souls who created only from within themselves for themselves and whose artistic struggles and triumphs stemmed from their own problems, sorrows and hopes, psychology and skepticism.

Even in art, socialism is oriented towards collaboration, towards the individual's devotion to the collective, towards the belief that only a wave of like-minded people justifies and immortalizes in beauty the flourishing of the individual's soul. Socialism does not forbid variety in temperament and inclination of the individual to impart the work with its own taste and color per se, but it will pursue systematically and without exception all art (which at any rate is not art by our standards) that displays a desire to make itself interesting and distinctly charming by treating the masses and the age with arrogance, by closing itself off, unaffected by a tempestuous exterior. If the artist creates for their own personal delight, well then, let them contain their pride and their soul's greed for fame in their work—for us it will be but a monument that will be of interest only to their children and grandchildren. And only when they make their mortal soul immortal and add the symbolic force of race, age, and generational waves, when they put aside their family name and elevate the soul of the world to a greatness of forms and dramatic pressure will they be read, seen, and listened to by thousands.

I have always dreamed that art in its current form will perish as soon as humanity wins its fight for the primitive needs of the body and rises together to conquer matters of the spirit. Why is there a need today for artistic individuals who can be heard from miles away? Are they not merely destiny's substitute for our inability to create our own artistic life in this money-driven age, just like the simple breed of anonymous singers and artists did before? And will these individuals not be tossed aside like useless tools once Dehmel's lamentation "only time" is redeemed and the harmonious collective, freed of class subjugation and the frenzied haste after material, starts thinking about the higher meaning of life and finds a renewed delight for individual creation? Once this delight tempers the collective's hunger for foreign creation, which it has been forced to live off but which, however refined, has never been capable of offering it what it holds most dear and what it would create itself?

Artists will have no need for fame or giving off the impression of greatness. They will be co-workers and co-creators, creating not for their own ascendance above the anonymous masses, but for the sociable beautification of the world. They will not leave behind the work of an individual, but the work of a generation.

Jiří Mahen: The Moon

Stand still and look! Today he again gleamed with the purest shine. Sometime in the early ages, innumerable ages ago, giants found him deep, deep below us in mountain ranges of infinity, where they searched for traces of gods. A golden helmet was left behind, belonging to the one whose name has been lost in the abyss of the stars. And it was a god: his body was of the whitest ivory, eyes black like precious stones, legs like fiery columns, brain like a diamond, the most revered of all materials. The giants took the golden helmet and threw it into space—it flew for three thousand days and three thousand nights, it danced its dance above all of creation, and finally it paused above the earth, along which humans tread. And now it suspends above us ... it shines ... it remembers ... it observes ...

They say that he is dead. That is a lie. He is not dead. Yesterday he felt like dancing for a while once again; he started to sway, wanting to break out running to great heights, heights only the most daring of thoughts ever reach. And ten thousand lovers prayed to him and a murmur of vows sounded all around. It was as though all the dormant volcanoes wanted to awaken — their craters trembled and wailed and a crackle and roar rang all the way to the seventieth constellation above us, like on that day when Australia was born at the Pacific Ocean's edge, and when an enormous wheel of ur-material flew towards the golden helmet ...

Stand still and look!

Run and don't look back!! God is coming down slowly, but with a horrifying certainty comes closer and closer. In an instant, he will smash with annihilating horror all windows and all walls of our being and my soul. Madness follows it—

— What are you doing here?

— I want to speak with you!

— Then speak!

Stanislav K. Neumann: Devětsil

At the matinee on Sunday, the 6th of February at the "Revolutionary Stage," the first recitation event of the artists' collective "Devětsil" took place. The very aggressive but somewhat unclear and jumbled introductory remarks were delivered by Karel Teige and then more or less dilettantish verse and prose were recited by the presenters A. Černík, J. Suk, Vl. Vančura, Jar. Seifert, A. Hoffmeister and Karel Vaněk, of whom Seifert had the greatest success, followed by, to a lesser extent, Hoffmeister. In the days preceding the event, paintings and drawings by members of this collective—A. Hoffmeister, K. Vaněk, and K. Teige—were on display at the bookstore "U zlatého klasu" (At the Golden Cob) on Spálená Street. The works exhibited an ardent passion, a youthful yearning and happiness (especially those by Hoffmeister and Vaněk), somewhat leaning (at least for the time being) on the work of Jan Zrzavý, but omitting his occasionally slightly morbid tendencies.

These are expressions of self-help, certainly justified and reasonable, the youth fighting for themselves, and rightfully so. Naturally, the main question now is: *what do they want and what can they do already?*

It will in no way surprise us that this youth is already inclined to deny all that has come before; that is only a good sign, and they would certainly be a bad youth group if they worshiped craftsmen like the young epigones at "Zvon" (The Bell) and similar superfluous magazines. Instead, we might wonder why the coalition of "Devětsil" is not more strict and more complete — why, if Jirko is not in attendance, Černík and Suk are present, and why Hoffmeister turns up if Kalista and Wolker do not, or why wherever there is Teige, you never see Havlíček, Rykr, Süss, and Wachsmann, not to speak of František Němec, who, due to his notorious naughtiness, unfortunately does not fit in well with serious company. But ask them why Petr doesn't get on well with Pavel or Adolf with Zdeněk—that is their business, something that has always been and always will be among people, including the youth, something we have to come to terms with.

We can then for our own needs somewhat violate these young men and compose a picture of today's literary and artistic youth under the catchword of "Devětsil," from which we have the full right to expect something, and whose activities so far have shown that they are working on a specific program. To this end we list these twelve names:

J. Havlíček (sculptor), A. Hoffmeister, Zd. Kalista, A. M. Píša, Zd. Rykr, Jar. Seifert, L. Süss, K. Teige (as a critic above all), Vl. Vančura, Karel Vaněk, A. Wachsmann, Jiří Wolker.

Visual artists excluded, these names are usually best known to readers of "Kmen" and comprise the young core of the periodical's textual-artistic content. It would as such be pointless to talk about them individually; what is important is what they have in common, the new things they bring to the table as a group.

We do not think many words are needed to characterize it. These young artists along with František Němec, that rascal, continue the literary and artistic revolution which we started in the last few pre-war years, and they do so by *deepening* the revolution's spiritual aspect. That is not a mistake, but on the contrary a gain, and this gain will endure and keep growing as long as they persist and *continue deepening* in the spirit of the age, as long as the developing artistic revolution aligns with the post-war social and moral revolution more and more consciously and has in mind ever more clearly the *person*, the new person.

And this youth understands so correctly that today the most important thing is the person as a collective and not as an individual—that is if they do not want to create solely for the bourgeoisie. We hope the youth does not come to understand collective art as intellectually and coldly as Karel Čapek in R.U.R., but that they also do not, god willing, end up seeking a path to the "soul" like M. Rutte has proposed to them.

It is interesting to observe which bourgeois writers, who stood at the beginning of our artistic revolution, now step away or cultivate playful virtuosity. Individuality and the interests of individuals surpass artistic and human interests. It is becoming apparent that there is no understanding for the person as a figure of the collective where there is heartlessness, where the bourgeois mentality surpasses feelings of the heart.

If we want to speak of the soul again today, it might be better, for the sake of those well-oriented, to instead speak of the heart, for which the bourgeois order never had any understanding because its personal interests always had the upper hand over emotional ones, whereas the soul as a word and concept has been compromised by bourgeois art and science: the soul has always been a refuge to the bourgeois individual when they did not know which way to turn.

We naturally have the closest relationship to the literary and artistic youth named above, which is the only group of people that, of all the things that pop up here and there, produce anything worth our attention, since they have faith, ability, and are a bearer of progress. Their art also echoes with the clamor of modern life and the beautiful melody of sensual nature. What we have managed to achieve for modern art has not been lost; it is looking to be transferred to a lower tone so that the young, faithful heart of the comrade can clearly pronounce itself. It is a beautiful endeavor, which we want to support and protect against the cold hands of dexterous intellectuals and the onslaught of the selfish soul of the bourgeoisie.

Karel Teige: Images and Fore-Images

"It'll be necessary to make everything over again. Very well, we'll do it. The house? Gone. The garden? Nowhere. All right, we'll rebuild the house, we'll remake the garden. The less there is the more we'll make over again. After all, it's life, and we're made to remake, eh? *And we'll remake our life together, and happiness. We'll make the days again; we'll remake the nights.*"[1]—says Barbusse's Poterloo in *Under Fire.* So stands the whole of a person's creative work today before the enormous task of building the world anew, or better said: of building a new world. There are no more proposals for modern art being brought forward, now it is all plans for a new life, a new organization of the world and its consecration. The work of the designer and the poet is connected with the work of the farmer and laborer, the thinker and the scientist stand beside the soldier of the revolution: their task is one and the same. They do not just implement theory but rather create a new world. The only path is that which leads to tomorrow.

That the outburst of a war would bury the world which produced it in rubble, or at the very least tear apart its foundations, was clear far before we knew who would come out victorious. The world of industrialism and technology, civilization, factories, transatlantic steamers, and airplanes once astonished and exalted us, but now we have experienced it in the fiery days of Europe's bloodshed, bringing it close to failure and collapse, creating a destructive civilization of suffocating gases, submarines, and land mine launchers; the technology of war. In the deep unhappiness of the material struggle of the world, the fore-image of a new life grew from human anxiety and human hope like a comforting and touching illusion and is truly the germ of all present creative endeavors and developments, which constitute it

1 Henri Barbusse, Under Fire: The Story of a Squad, trans. Fitzwater Wray (London, 1917; Project Gutenberg, January 20, 2002), https://www.gutenberg.org/files/4380/4380-h/4380-h.htm.

a body. George Duhamel's books arose out of this anxiety and firm faith in future happiness. The most needed of his works in this time—*Possession du Monde* (Possession of the World)—proclaims new, good tidings over the ruin of the world, over the grave of yesterday's society, culture and civilization; it preaches the glorious gospel of a great love of life, a burning, beatific dream of the kingdom of the heart. Today the human soul burns with desire for what is next; it no longer believes blindly in the disruptive force of life in the form of an aggressive machinic and technological civilization; it would no longer believe in an art that did not know but to sing of material conquest and the progress of yesterday's world and to which war (which they did not hesitate to openly confess!) was the sole way to cleanse the world. That is the Futurists, who chase after war and praise it, some of whom resemble the clergy, blessing cannons and bayonets!

How aesthetic was this art really in its view of life when it could be furiously spit onto the Altar of art! And how formalist and hollow! It was characterized by a remarkable ignorance of causes, it did not penetrate into, as they say, the soul of everything, possibly because while it viewed objects from many angles, it clung only onto their material existence; meanwhile any sense, purpose, and connection to the person was often evaded. It wanted only to be optimistic, in praise of life, an excited Whitmanesque "Salut au Monde!" and a rash sycophant to the given state of things, not realizing that sometimes that same art actually celebrates desecrators and exploiters of life and gives into the plundering of human happiness. When its poems celebrated the stock market for instance, it got seduced by appearance, the rush and bustle, and this perception of nervous movement was more essential than moral content, which it did not touch upon at all. Was there not something impressionistic about it, when the swarming of colorful stains, the rush and bustle of the stock market could, despite everything, trick the eye and nerves?

The art of yesterday—no matter if you call it Cubism, Futurism, Orphism, or perhaps Expressionism—found everything "in and of itself" beautiful and that sufficed. It did not evaluate things consciously with regards to content; I would say: according to their purpose and moral sense, in connection with human work and the happiness of living. Without this evaluation of the spiritual integrity of life, all that could remain was formalism and aestheticism. Teacher Ferd. Krch writes in *Náš směr* (Our Direction) about someone who is more a person and less an aesthete—the child, for whom visual perception or stimulation of the nerves do not suffice as a means to capture things and who instead needs complete and thorough knowledge of a thing. While working on a little drawing... the child asks: "How many eyes does a hare have?" "Two, of course!" ... The question is asked for a reason. The child has seen pictures of little hares many times, drawn on the page and in motion, with only one eye showing—the child accepts this in a picture and has nothing against it, but when the child is drawing a little hare itself, it cannot maim it by drawing it only with one eye. Therefore, the child confirms that hares have two eyes, not one.—And what vast wealth manifests in the content of the child's drawing, what fantasy and action!——Besides this little anecdote, allow me to remind you of a statement made by Fernand Léger, who, enchanted by the truly wondrous and extraordinary forms presented to us by contemporary industry and mechanics, by the curves of steel cylinders, levers and nuts reflecting light a thousand-times over, has found things like the mitrailleuse or the lock of a 75-mm artillery gun the most suitable subjects for painting. Because it only stimulates the senses, this art is hollow, as the only content of a work of art (not the subject!) can be the person (but not as an isolated individual) and must include the person's emotional depths and exorbitant inner dramas as well as the unspoken need for harmony and happiness.—

In today's transforming world, such art, which is only an inventive game and an indulgence of superficial beauty, cannot any longer provide the person with profound safety, which is very much needed in this time of crisis, facing the final battle. This art experiences agony together with the society from which and for which it arose. Just like the civilization whose downfall we are witnessing, this art has developed ad absurdum: are vague, ordinary Expressionism and impetuous Dadaism not the final consequences of past art and the reason for its bankruptcy? Artistic Civilism flowed out to emptiness, into nothingness, becoming a desert, boredom. Before long it was possible to glimpse its end: we are talking about the case of Kandinsky and the like.—We turn to other sources today.

Although this art was tightly restricted to its class, addressing only an exclusive, clearly defined group of individuals, as Paul Cézanne has himself said, although it was as individualistic as bourgeois philosophy, which grew into destructive hermitage and infertile solitariness, and although it masked all manner of egotism, the bad lever of the world, today this art, which is necessarily aristocratic (we speak of the aristocratism of the aristocratized bourgeoisie), threatens all nations with its poor imitations and enters even into the domestic space of the worker: just look at today's signs, leaflets, advertisements, illustrated magazines, and book covers as well as the manifold trinkets of the art industry! From all sides, you are accosted by depraved Cubism and exhausted, mottled Expressionism, just as banal as the hollow Art Nouveau of the past. The decline of the past. Stagnation. An external, but unequivocal sign that the real progress in art is elsewhere, further along.

* * *

We are again living through an extensive artistic transformation as well as a sharp social turn. We are simply living through a transformation of the world, or better put: through the birth of a new world. We are living through the birth of a new reality, we project a dream long in the making onto today, or the day just after that. It is impossible to imagine richer and more sacred times.

If you have not yet glimpsed art that is truly new in public competitions held by state governments, if you have not found it in galleries claiming a spot besides recognized, salon "beauty"—there is absolutely nothing official or conventional about it—if you have not heard its voice on the streets, it is because this art has very little time to concern itself with such things, as it is entirely engrossed in its creative work. *It creates the fore-image of a new life*. Comrade H. says that the fore-image is an abbreviation, simply all-encompassing, a simplification of complication, a thing or person existing in thought and dream. In this sense, the task of the whole of spiritual creation is the fore-image of a new world. New pictures painted today are a painter's shorthand for an all-encompassing tomorrow, they are tomorrow itself, which exists through the faith in our souls. They are the poems of our life, our communal life, which we dream up and build, having faith in the consummation of our work. In the pre-dawn darkness, we believe in a red daybreak, just as beautiful as it is undeniable, a beginning of an infinitely clear, sweet, brotherly life. It is above all about the person, one's happiness and a new, vital milieu, and that is why there is an emphasis on the criterion of content and psychological narrative in a picture, which we place above the precondition of form.

The coming art, as we have already said, is too preoccupied, its sights set fervently on a resolution of the future... If it only had time, it would address the past—(do not forget that every rise of a young art is necessarily a contrarian reaction to that preceding it, that there is a preoccupation with disapproval to the point of unfairness—)perhaps with these determined and clear words:

"We no longer like either your pictures, so inorganic and violent as the concrete jungle of the big cities, or your poetry, rumbling with express trains, with the honking of car horns, with boat sirens, with the cries of the boulevards and the drone of airplane propellors, because they look too much like your cities, which we are no longer fond of, either. Because they are nothing but chaotic and unscrupulous, aimless conglomerations of energy units, these cities of yours, unorganized and undirected, a magnet of the collective will and discipline to create a higher measure of sociability and transpersonal validity; they are about quantity, not richness. In short, we do not like your world; the pain and suffering of many is Atlas, who holds it up. No signs of life remain within him, and we believe the prince of this world is long condemned. Therefore, our kingdom of the heart is not a part of this present world, but a part of the future one."

* * *

On yesterday's horizon a brilliant constellation shines: Cézanne, Matisse, Picasso, Braque, Delaunay, Metzinger, Gleizes—Whitman, Verhaeren, Marinetti, Apollinaire, Max Jacob, the great creators and masters of new form. Today's harvest ripens below other well-known figures: Van Gogh, Seurat, Derain, Henri Rousseau, Chagall—Dostoevsky, Charles-Louis Philippe, Vildrac, Duhamel, Arcos, Romains, *artists of a wholeness of life*. The new world is being built from pure and precious materials: from dream, faith, love and hatred of the past, and from beautiful virtues.

We see new portraits of faces desirous and sad, having a happy or trusting look, or big, loyal eyes! New landscapes with tall, stately trees and palms, miraculous vegetation, geysers and waterfalls and intoxicating views! Scenes from cities, saturated by their own plaintive and unfathomable atmospheres. New still lifes, whose tranquility and festivity flows from a harmony among all things, a table, a chair, a book, a pipe, a musical instrument or a picture on the wall, among the lovely details of your domestic life. New genres, tableaus of our dreams and fantasy, stories of the heart, warm with love and empathy.

—So painters paint the fore-images of tomorrow, imbuing reality with enchanting and poignant landscapes: the avenues down which we stroll on quiet early evenings after work, gazing at the setting sun, which resembles a smiling and gracious human face or a magnificent magical flower; or the gorgeous solid trunks of trees that provide shade for us to lie down on supple grass when we are wearied by the journey or by our thoughts; and the homes, cottages, villages, small towns, cities, farmsteads and rooms in which we reside. Oh, what a homeland we want, a realm of the youthful soul and peace! The painter and the poet, the builder of a new world, the apostle of a new paradise and the coming of the kingdom of the heart is also an agitator of socialism.

Our spiritual construction is, as we have said, built upon dream and desire, love and hatred of evil, not gold and precious metals or sudden conquests of markets and colonies, which defined the old world, shot up by the drum fire of war. The next life will not see us buying things with money, stealing or killing for these things out of malice. When did the nations ever go to war for human happiness, for some beautiful dream, for the charm of a blooming flower?

It is not sentimentality but a little bit of the safe and untreacherous generosity of intimacy that is needed for the moments between the past and coming struggle, which is still not over, for the brief intervals of respite from the hard-hitting whirlwind of time.

A nook of nature in the spring, the commencement of thousands of lives in the dreamlike beauty and enchantment of blossoming flowers and butterflies dancing in the sun, could likely be the fore-image of new art as well as new life.

* * *

These pages are nothing other than a first look at the state of art and spirit as it is taking shape at present. The first look tends to present a bold vision, but at the cost of distortion and inaccuracy. Further progress will presumably correct many of the opinions expressed here, but still: the certainty of some of these assertions does not come from the strength of personal conviction, but from a fanaticism for a certain sociability, a certain community, and cannot be a delusion.

The path of young art cannot be a wandering one. It is defined by an unmistaken faith in the person, by love of life, by desire to lift up the human soul from orphancy and isolation, to lift it up from the jail of a narrow, individual life to an incarnate interrelation with society and all of creation. It draws its support on its path from primal sources of creative strengths: if you observe its proximity to folk art, children's drawings, and artistic manifestations of natural tribes, it can be proof that new construction is not just old fittings redone, but that it is a real province of youth.

The force of revolution is not only a struggle for justice and economic democracy, but also for a new human, moral, and spiritual order, for a precondition of style and culture, and it is mostly a force created by budding youth.

If you look around the whole world, you will already see new artists in the process of this work. In Italy as well as France, in Czechoslovakia as well as Germany and Russia. Real artists have long abandoned the severity and impertinence of Futurism, late Cubism and Expressionism, leaving it to the epigones. Today they build on the ruins of yesterday's order and the old world: they make the poetry of new days and new nights, more sacred, peaceful and lovely. For you and for us all.

Karel Čapek: A Note

A note: what you have just read was a declaration of faith and a view towards the future, both of which are indeed hard to dispute. But the text also presented a picture of the present, and to that I note: not only does today's transformation of the world and society not appear to me all that divine, uplifting, and so wholly internal, but I also do not see the state of art today as so unambiguously defined as the author of the "fore-images." Yes, it is possible to simplify the rather complicated picture of today's art by simply dividing it in two directions, "yesterday" and "tomorrow"; but that division is artificial and arbitrary. In art, yesterday and tomorrow are connected too deeply and in a veiled way for a circumstantial division to be anything more than a superficial classification.—We are speaking of art, not about the order of the world—the order of the world does not help us with anything here; let us rather speak about the order of painting. And in that respect, I think not enough has been "overcome" in the order which we take up from today's state of art. The demand for formal purity, compactness, and spatial harmony remains henceforth the task of the good art worker, who is at the same time a good worker for progress. And in these values of painterly work thus remains the great and exemplary *moral* value of modern painting.

Devětsil:
A Poem Is Not an Apparition...

A poem is not an apparition, but difficult and modest work, like that of a laborer. Revolution pervades the world; the order of new creation is germinating. This age rumbles with the explosion of wars, class struggles, the fall of civilization, and a communist country is being born from chaos like at the beginning of the world. The silly and sophomoric fabrications of the literati count for nothing. Yes and no, your consent, comrade, and your resistance are voiced in this book of poems, and all parts of your conquered world are rendered here. Because you are poor and not liberated, and because you live only halfway, a no is proffered to you more often than a yes. Your poet cannot do otherwise. You will not read about the glory of a city, but about its sorrow. For yours is a valley of tears. The revolutionary song will exhort you because struggle is your instrument. This book is about class and its content is you. New York, roaring before you with its greatness, its economic enterprise, is monstrous and hostile. Well then, may it no longer exist! New, new, new is the star of communism. Its communal work builds a new style and outside of it there is no modernity.

Vladislav Vančura: The Form of Things

Reality in pictures is an imaginary world, it persists and is rendered only through form. More than description, more than a definition of space it is a method, which makes something out of nothing and a lot from a little, which turns flowing might into a site of action, a life force into effect.

An emerging picture first moves along a curve, which first ascends and then suddenly drops for a want of visionary momentum, a pulse of tenderness and lyrical weightiness.

The glass you are looking at is defined by its perfectly curved surface. The inside is an upside-down cone, observe its surface, the concentricity of ever smaller circles, their boundedness.

When you use this glass and when you happen to think of it, give its perfections as they move twofold towards infinity a mission and you will grant the glass a purpose like a word that serves as a sign and promotes understanding. For then the thing will be more drinking vessel, less cut glass; more a work of art, less worked-over material.

If you were a painter, you would create another glass on the axis of poetry, purely and specifically for your thirst.

But no one is ever alone, nothing is ever by itself and each display of originality by miraculous children reeks with a forgotten ordinariness. Why should I think up new things when I can do less than I have to?

Order, the truth of the time, great like the migration of peoples and like a genesis, is the wind that sways with all of contemporary life, ever darkened by the shadow of civilization. From its ferment legitimate forms come together, like crystal from a solution. This or that, but the border of definability cannot be crossed without damage. A substance and its effect are defined one by the other. In this sense, form is certainly not a mere set of surfaces and lines going in a certain direction, but a whole area, structure, proportionality, and a sum total of their attributes.

František Götz: On the Magazine Host, and Those Who Stand Behind It

Artuš Černík, a member of the Prague Devětsil group, has come out with notes on every issue of Host published so far. His comments have been heavily disapproving in general and far from respectful—which would be no crime if his critiques were not also exaggerated, if Černík had any semblance of tact that would hold him back from resorting to grousing and slander. We have stressed several times that we do not strive for recognition in the field of polemics. And what is more: we hate all the pointless and personal literary scuffles devised for the sole reason of devaluing people and getting a dubitable reaction from the so-called literary cafés. We did not respond to Černík's commentary the first time, nor the second, simply because what he wrote in those days was nothing but a representation of his simple personal opinion, unsubstantiated by any defined aesthetic or other judgments; two or three non-committal ideas and diatribes just hanging in the air, completely unground-ed. His little article on the third issue of Host does pass more universal judgments, which, however incomplete, fragmentary, and unclearly pronounced, open up the possibility to strike up a matter-of-fact debate pertaining only to principles, ideas, and values instead of personal matters.

One thing to get straight: I speak to Černík as one intellectual to another. For the time being, I want to move away completely from his overall dismissal of all the poetic production of the artists behind the Host magazine and pay no heed to his personal invectives, since I truly do not know who his personal interventions and inept attacks are aimed at and who Černík meant by "literary miser." For now, I believe that we can come to a mutual understanding through a matter-of-fact discussion since I believe that Černík doesn't speak from a place of malice, but that he is simply going through a phase of excitement over having come out swinging with his daring opinions, triple-stepping over everything everywhere.

Upon reading the first two issues of Host, he harangued about our symbolicalness or decadence or some such thing. After the third issue, it suddenly hit him: we are actually Expressionists. He presently worked out a theory about our position. If I understand his statements correctly, he wants to associate us with the individualist-anarchist tradition of German poetry at any cost, to make it seem as though we as a whole are trailing after the opinionated ego-centrism of German Expressionism, as though our lyrical solipsism makes us prioritize perception instead of reality.—However, the only thing he holds against us is the very thing I set as the guideline for our progress: taking joy in reality, trying to use to the fullest the essence of things and the tangible world in general, the positive nature of poetry. References to Duhamel, Vildrac, and Romains certainly show that he places our supposedly Germanistic-individualistic standpoint against the Franco-Latin tradition, the tradition of the beliefs of Classicism and Rationalism, as is it reflected in the works of the named artists, and that he wants—if I can surmise from his insinuations thus—to perhaps position Literary Group, which is caught up in German individualism and expressionist, lyrical solipsism, against Devětsil, which professes the ideal of Latin Classicism as far as both form and ideology. I always carefully think everything through— and I think that Černík's curt notes cannot have any other meaning. And since I do not want to polemicize for the sake of polemicizing, but so that we can come to an understanding and clearly express what binds us together and what sets us apart, I want to give this polemic a definite, clear-cut base, drawing conclusions from what Černík has hinted at.

It is not true that we draw from German Expressionism. And in general: Expressionism is not a uniquely German phenomenon. I will have the opportunity to speak more on that a few paragraphs on. What I do want to emphasize right away is that Expressionism was something like a lifestyle to the whole preceding age, as was erstwhile Romanticism, that it is the heat, blood, and air of the age just passed, which you must have taken note of unless you have such a thick skin that nothing reaches you. For instance, the fact that Bolshevism, which made such a mark on the world, is nothing other than political Expressionism, can be demonstrated in every respect: just take its lack of esteem for current objects and orders, its blind obedience to a new idea, its dictatorship of thought, passivity with respect to civil life and activity with respect to the spiritual, an orientation towards the spontaneity of creation of all constituent parts of the national organism, which leads to the embodiment of that creative uncertainty in the council system, etc.

And thus: the phenomenon that we call Expressionism is not a phenomenon uniquely German, but rather a method of perceiving the whole cultural world prevalent right before the war, during the war, and right after it.

It is clear that in Germany Expressionism acquired the most revolutionary character, since the conditions there were favorable to pushing the movement to the farthest bounds. The volcanic tremor that upset this country, that destroyed the proud structure of this state, but also its culture, built on the principle of power, was so powerful here that it might seem like the German nation was truly incapable of tending to its culture in the period just after the war. Is it by chance that the revolution in Germany was carried out by Jews, that the majority, around 90 percent, of all expressionist writers are of Jewish origin? It is as though in the period that meant the collapse of all culture, a helpless nation gave the cultural reigns over to those whose morals were not nearly as shaken up by the collapse—the Jewish people. What else could rise up from that collapse but the art of resistance, decay of the phenomenal world, revolt of the spirit against nature, humanity, and society, art of a wide-spanning abyss, being ripped out from all order, and an overall passionate surge of a flame that has torn itself away from its eternal oil source and quickly burns in torments and curses or in anxious prayer.

We grew from different soil. Here, we saw no violent tremor, no miserable chaos, no fallen idols or piled ruins, no crisis of the spirit like in Germany. On the contrary: we saw the fulfillment of a long-time desire, the creation of a new state. In this way the atmosphere here was closer to that of post-war France. But we can say with certainty that anyone with any shred of attentiveness and sensitivity could feel that the soil across all of Europe was volcanic, that there were explosive materials piling up everywhere, that dark, cloudy, chaotic, nameless currents had burst forth onto the world and shook up all certainty, brought about a transformation of the world, its orders, humankind, and society and gave all of life a single law: change. In the East, from which these currents flowed to us, fore-images of a new world shone in bright red. The West defended itself against new forms of life. This can explain our clear turning away from the cultural France. Out of this atmosphere, we created. The works of Duhamel, Vildrac, Arcos, etc. can indeed be called French Expressionism, and again it is possible to confirm this with comprehensive analysis: the one thing I will point out is that both contemporary French and German poetry mostly concerns itself with humankind in all its ugliness and beauty. The Germans write books such as for instance, *Der Mensch in der Mitte* [The Person in the Middle] (L. Rubiner), and it is a declaration of love and a celebration of humankind and human sociability. When reading Duhamel's cry about the joining of pure hearts for the salvation of an unhappy world, you will be reminded of Rubiner, whose celebration of humankind definitely had the same impact in Germany as Duhamel's plea in France. One thing is impossible not to notice: Rubiner moves from humankind to the social collective, to brotherhood. Duhamel is French—he was born in a collectively creative country. His starting point is the social collective itself.

So, there is German Expressionism and there is French Expressionism, even if it is not regularly spoken of in those terms. Both grow from the volcanic soil of today. Both arrive at some certainties—by different methods. The French are not mired in despair and unrest. They cannot withstand those conditions for too long. They have to get away. They quickly introduce order, lawfulness, intention into the chaos of the present; they push disorder aside and move towards harmony and the cosmic equalization of contradictions, eurythmy, and the enchantment of all phenomena towards the certainty of reality. They quickly attain peace and quiet, rhythm and the organization of new world affairs.

Černík wants to use French Expressionism, which has achieved the reconciliation of the soul and the universe, to defeat German Expressionism, where an abyss yawns wide between the two—and, according to his own words, do the same with Czech Expressionism, which he apparently considers markedly German in character. I am afraid I must contradict him: our Expressionism is neither French nor German, but Czech. It rises up from our specific conditions and grows into an original form. Here, it is not marked by absolute psychism, but we have great love for the reality, which resounds so strongly in Wolker and Píša, Blatný, Kalista, Chaloupek and Jeřábek, etc. Here, it is not marked by aversion to order, which Germans consider a tyranny, nor is it marked by opinionated and emotional nihilism or absolute ambivalence. The attentive reader who wants to see will understand that Slavic strings resound here: the strange tenderness of the soul which connects dream and fact, the soul and the world, god and material in one reality. A reality that concerns flowers, the moon, or a dog, that forms a real phenomenon—a Sunday—a funeral—and yet a reality that is permeated by the rhythm of the soul. What it offers is a spiritual reality vibrating with all the anxiety, pain, destruction, and unrest of the time without ever actually speaking of current events.

If we have not yet achieved a firm, balanced precision and rendering of form, even as we are moving in that direction, just as we are moving in the direction of Classicism and towards a Latin creative stance, if we have not yet achieved a harmony of all the elements of our world, a harmony of form, it is simply because our soil is still so powerfully volcanically disturbed that we have been unable to build solid constructions on top of it. We do not want to fake brightness, balance, faith, or hope when we do not possess them, we do not want to lean on foreign crutches to be able to boast of a firmness of attitude, whether the crutches be the work of Duhamel or Vildrac. We, too, are moving towards an anchoring in the certainty of being. But that anchoring will be our work, our belligerence, and as such our inalienable property. Today and tomorrow, our gradual redemption from the fog and chaos will be owed to our own efforts. We feel that it would be dishonest to attempt to copy the young French. We create in other conditions. The soil is more turbulent here. The certainties that are a birth right to the French must still be fought for here. We are closer to the East. We do not want to deprive ourselves of the most beautiful parts of development. We want to experience for ourselves the whole essence of the time and overcome in ourselves the unrest, pain, destruction, and use the experience to create a new form of life and art. Duhamel and Vildrac, translated among others by Černík, as he bombastically advertises (if I were him, I would keep quiet about his sloppy translations, which are generally not to his credit), can perhaps advise us but cannot help in our development. There is no helping art. The soul alone determines its fate—even when that fate is art itself.

If the revolutionary spirit is not reflected in our words, it is reflected in our heart. We know that words are the roots of the soul and that they must stay buried deeply in the soil so as not to wilt.

And one more thing: our hands are clean. We do not fight for recognition. We go quietly along our own path. We exalt every artistic victory, no matter who it belongs to. We are hurt by every artistic defeat—even on the part of our enemies, insomuch as we have any. Our youth (a word Černík also wants to deny us) is a youth of pure enthusiasm, love and goodness. One thing all of us hate: hatred. And malice.

Karel Teige: On Expressionism

In the Socialist Future (January 6, 1922), Fr. Götz published an extensive feuilleton, partly polemicizing with regards to essays printed in this paper about Host by comrade Černík, and partly pointing out the contrasts and differences that, according to his interpretation, exist between the Literary Group and Devětsil. As far as concerns Host itself, it is certainly one of the best amongst among Czech magazines, but it is far from being the revue that the truly young and modern generation needs and is capable of creating. It seems that contributors to Host do not fully realize that we are living through a historic moment: this pertains not only to modern Czech art, but also new proletarian and revolutionary art—and its problems have nothing to do with provincial art issues, but rather with problems that are cosmopolitical and international alone. For this reason, it cannot be classified as something as simple as a Czech variety of Expressionism. It is not about how the strings of our work are Slavic, or Czech or Moravian, it is about them being revolutionary or proletarian. The Literary Group is not revolutionary: it is not even tempestuously bourgeois, nor properly *young* and *combative*. If it were, it could not hate hatred, as F. Götz writes, because love and hate are two sides of the same coin, fundamentally inseparable; after all, where there is potent love, there must be a hatred still more potent. Contributors to Host, who did not want to participate in creating proletarian art, are not revolutionary artists—they are *passéiste.* By the way: Zdenek Rykr could hardly contribute to a modern paper, that weak, naturalist-impressionist painter, and an even more decrepit and backwards art critic.

Mr. F. Götz indicates further alleged programmatic differences between the Literary Group and DEVĚTSIL. While there are differences between the two, they are by no means programmatic for the simple reason that while Devětsil is an association bound together by a common program, the Literary Group is not. The group's only programmatic announcement appeared on the cover of Host, saying that the magazine would completely shut out old forms of poetry, but what it really appears to be shutting out are new poetic forms, with the vaguely post-impressionistic and pre-expressionistic poetry of Chalupa, Chaloupka, Stejskal, Jeřábek, Vlček, Knap, Jirko, and Ráž making up the overwhelming majority of its poetic content. The Literary Group is an interest association, not a unilaterally programmatic one. It is the work of compromise, bringing bourgeois and passéist artists together with more or less revolutionary ones: “It is entirely impotent programmatically and opinion-wise it is in pieces,” a leading member of the Literary Group wrote to us in a letter, emphasizing that individual contributors at Host differ in opinion. The very praiseworthy efforts of Mr. Götz to consolidate the heterogenous group around a definite, firm, artistic, and philosophical opinion seem futile to us, since the Literary Group is not uniform. And there is another question here, of whether Expressionism could be the catchword for a truly young and modern generation, or even Czech Expressionism. We seriously doubt it.

Mr. Fr. Götz states that Expressionism is not a specifically German phenomenon: that depends on what is meant by that. In the study The Meaning and Illusion of Expressionism, prepared in manuscript form for some time now and to be published whenever possible, I attempted to formulate the mission of Expressionism and delineate the true boundaries of the artistic phenomenon using an applied arts perspective. Here I can say only this: the Post-Impressionist crisis, which arose in France many years ago, has spread everywhere. If you want to call it Expressionism, then it was definitively resolved and “overcome” around the year 1906 with the work of Picasso. Czech art has taken inspiration from French development up until now. If we can even speak of Czech Expressionism, we can only speak of Osma (The Eight), which could be called expressionistic. The Group of Fine Artists, established in 1912, now subscribes to Cubism, brought to us by Bohumil Kubišta. Literary Expressionism is, I believe, difficult to find here. Expressionism in the broadest sense of the word—reaction against Impressionism—is mostly mirrored in the Classicism of the stories of the Čapek brothers, the academicism of *Bohyně, světice, ženy* (Goddesses, Female Saints, Women), and in the historicizing Primitivism of Langer’s play *Saint Wenceslas.* The creative method of New Songs is Cubist and fundamentally influenced by Marinetti’s Futurism. Crossroads, in its cinematic technique, strict form, and austere materiality is a characteristically Cubist work. Similarly, Modern French poetry is far from Expressionist, especially the poetry listed by Götz.

If the so-called Unanimists come from the school of Philippe, they have namely inherited his creative method, which I attempted to characterize as Cubist some time ago in the magazine Kmen. For that matter, their Anthropocentricism came earlier than the Anthropocentricism of German Expressionism. Duhamel published his *Person in the Lead* and *The New Book of Martyrs* earlier than Rubiner published *The Person in the Middle* and than L. Frank’s *The Person Is Good.* The second wing of French poets is expressly bourgeois and nationalist (the spirit of Unanimists is the spirit of Clarté and some of them are even Communists), including the great deceased artist Apollinaire and the vast legion of his followers, such as Cendrars, P. Albert-Birot, L. Aragon, Ivan Goll (!), N. Beauduin—and all the Dadaists, Dermée, Cocteau, the painter Picabia, Ribemont-Dessaignes, etcetera, who irresponsibly take Apollinaire's lead *ad absurdum*. Apollinaire, who also made a big impression on Czechs like Hoffmeister and through him on Kalista, Píša, Wolker, Hůlka, and other contributors to the magazine *Červen*—(before the war, he had influenced a portion of the remaining work of Erwin Taussig)—could perhaps be considered an Expressionist, as he is also the *magnus parens* of the German poets of Der Sturm; but he, too, mostly holds the views of a Cubist and radiates the vibrant, innovative energy of a Futurist, not the mysticality and solipsism of German Expressionism. Ivan Goll, cited by the French and Götz, states that Expressionism is a *typical German* phenomenon, and truly, only in Germany did it develop to such a remarkable depth and cultural importance. The ideology of German Expressionism, as long as it is not Rubiner describing it, is Hiller's Activism. The difference between Activism and Marxism is, *mutatis mutandis*, the difference between Expressionism and the new art. It is reasonable to regret that Götz studies modern art so one-sidedly; he knows the German Expressionist literature perfectly and yet the current quest of non-French artists living in France escapes him.

Let us concede that the orientation of Devětsil is French, though that is not entirely the case. Mr. Götz is very mistaken if he thinks that it is about French Classism for us. We have said numerous times that our banner reads, above all, the beloved names Henri Rousseau, painter, maestro amongst folk picture-makers, and Ch.-L. Philippe, exceptional poet of the class of the offended and humiliated; that we consider the following painters our foreign co-conspirators—the Scandinavian Per Krogh and the Russians Zadkine, Chagall, Vasiliev; analogous literary and cosmopolitan confraternity is as yet not known to us, but we are of the conviction that it latently exists, that likeminded artists everywhere take the same paths toward the same goals. It was over two years ago, before Germany ever woke up from its Expressionist chaos, that we said it was necessary to developmentally account for Cubism, which was soon to reach its peak and subsequent end, stripped of its ground by the World War and even more so the world revolution, just like Italian Futurism. Classicism has always been, even in Cubism, a latent tradition of French art, and with it, Western culture comes full circle today. In the initial period of our shift away from Cubism, which occurred as a developmental necessity, without contact with contemporary efforts abroad, it became a transitional stage for a few individuals. Yet the connection between the East and the living relationship of new creation to all of the expressions of primary and primitive creation, to folk, Eastern, and exotic art, to children's drawings, etc., emphasized already in that initial period, excludes the possibility of any form of Classicism. Just as the art of the French civil revolution was related to antiquity, which became stronger as it grew into the Empire style, so is the art of the current proletarian revolution related to Primitivism. There is no other way out of today's crisis: revival comes through Primitivism. Perhaps more than these lines set down here, the pictures of F. Muzika or the literary works of V. Vančura, J. Hořejší, A. Černík, and J. Seifert will enlighten Mr. Götz about that.

I did not understand and I do not understand Mr. Broj's words at the recitation evening "Some," where he said that young textual creation overcomes Impressionism and that it stands at the threshold of Expressionism. He has thoroughly confused the concepts if he concludes that after Futurism comes Expressionism. Similarly, I did not understand it when comrade Píša asserted against Mr. Rutte that new literary work is Expressionist. Impressionism had been overcome around the globe by the time today's youth was even born, and Expressionism—or rather non-German Post-Impressionism—was channeled into Cubism more than fifteen years ago by Picasso. The issues of Expressionism, which is a reaction to Impressionism, cannot possibly be considered acute anymore, including by our truly modern artists. After all, compared to the rest of Europe—we're all caught up!

Regrettably I cannot exhaust the subject of a polemic here that demands more expertise than can be quickly written up in a journalistic repartee; in that regards I ask Mr. Götz that he kindly read my above-mentioned article once it is published. It seems to me however that any artist that still looks to Expressionism, which is being abandoned even in Germany, is lagging behind the times. Perhaps what lies between him and new art is "the most beautiful parts of development," of which he does not want to be deprived, as Mr. Götz writes: nevertheless, that does not change anything about him lagging behind.—It is not so much Ivan Goll but Hausenstein that is the bearer of post-Expressionist tendencies in Germany. Because Ivan Goll, by the nature of his work, remains a mystical Symbolist, or: a German Expressionist. Comrade Černík had every right to use these terms interchangeably. Even Apollinaire is a descendent of Symbolism, and German Expressionism, fathered by Scandinavian artist Munch, has within itself too much of a decadently mystic and spiritual atmosphere. Mr. Götz will concede that Werfel and Hasenclever are Neo-Symbolists and that even Píša's book *The Incomprehensible Saint* clung somewhat to a Symbolist accent and atmosphere. Similarly, the "Expressionist" Matisse and the Futurist Severini are the successors of Impressionism.

If German Expressionism influences some of our young artists today, it is presumably caused by the economic situation and foreign exchange, by the fact that cheap German books are more easily accessible here than French ones. It is then only owed to an outside influence and misplaced fashion, in which we cannot possibly be interested.

Every young artists' group must face the fire of polemics, one that serves to steel it, and it is not wise to give up fighting in advance. Any opinion developed with certain implications, that is, what is disdainfully called a theory in our circle, must inspire dissent in old-timer and bourgeois critics and disoriented individuals if it is truly revolutionary. And it must be fought for.

Mr. Götz correctly relates German Expressionism to the history of his country; it is however not correct that Communism, in its strict regularization of life, is a phenomenon parallel and coincidental to it, because it does not know the mysteries and the abysmal spiritual collapse, the issues and exaltedness, romanticism and religiosity of it.

Here in Bohemia, German and Jewish Expressionism were ignored and trivialized for chauvinist reasons, and so it is necessary to appraise them fairly today. However, today's artistic tendencies do not overlap with their tendencies, just as they depart from the tendencies of post-war France; they are very foreign even to the postulates of the "Unanimists." An entirely new art is emerging, worthy of glorious times—as was the Migration Period—starting at the beginning and growing out of the proletariat: Primitivism.

František Götz: A Little Bit of a Polemic, a Little Bit of a Confession

My polemical article about Host and those who stand behind it, which was printed not long ago in this paper, touched upon some general problems of new art and the relationship between the *Literary Group* and *Devětsil*. Perhaps because of that, the leading critical spokesperson for Devětsil, Mr. K. Teige, responded to it in the paper Rovnost (Equality). I welcome his objective article as a significant step towards understanding, which is what I desired in the first article.

Mr. Teige discerned well that the dividing line for both of the young Czech literary associations is their relationship to Expressionism, which he wrote in the article "On Expressionism." I would like to reiterate right at the outset of my response: I strongly sense that I do not stand on firm ground. Mr. Teige knows what I call Expressionism. He has read my article in Host and its supplement in Socialistická budoucnost (The Socialist Future). After a detailed study of the greatest phenomena of German and French Expressionism, I outlined in both writings a picture of that current, I observed its contemporary foundation, its philosophy and aesthetics, in short, its *concrete contents*. Mr. Teige however does not indicate in his article at all what is meant by Expressionism, and he defines it *merely as a reaction against Impressionism*, which is in no way sufficient because the construction of a relationship is justifiable only if we know what objects are being brought into relationship. I eagerly await Mr. Teige's promised article, "The Meaning and Illusion of Expressionism," in which I am sure he will clearly define the spiritual essence of the phenomenon, delimit it and stabilize its value. I simply refuse to believe that Mr. T. thinks the purpose of Expressionism is simply to be a *reaction*, that he does not see truly new and original content in it. In his previous article, Mr. T. only speaks about who is not an Expressionist and corrects my supposedly incorrect categorization of several phenomena, but at the same time he himself does not explain the problem using a single coherent observation or judgement. Hence my feeling of ambivalence at the base of the discussion. It would perhaps be better if I deferred to comment until Mr. T's promised study is published. Some things however cannot be deferred. It is necessary to respond immediately.

Mr. Teige certainly has great artistic erudition, but more with regards to the fine arts than to literature. I know that Cubist visual art is very closely connected to Cubist literature (similarly to Expressionism, etc.), but I also know that the laws of Cubist visual art are impossible to apply perfectly to Cubist literature. To a great extent, both artistic fields are autonomous, they have their own laws, their distinct spiritual foundations. Mr. Teige perpetrates an error in relating the criteria of the visual arts to the sphere of textual development because it makes him look at the development of literature and art in general very schematically and I would almost say in a formalist mode, as if these histories were only a quick game of alternating forms without deeper content. When talking about literary Cubism, for example, he delimits it as follows: cinematographic technique, strict formalism and curt matter-of-factness. I know that the focus of the literary critic and historian is on *developments* and the mainstream, and that definite, possibly violent constructions are necessary to orient oneself in that current. It is however also necessary to remain conscious of the fact that these constructions do not fully epitomize the essence of the phenomenon, that they are only a rather formal fiction, that we cannot look upon them as if they were complete, that we must always penetrate into the elementary reality of their essence—into the developments, the current, so that we understand the basic context. Specifically: Czech literary Cubism, for instance, as embodied in the stories of Richard Weiner, K. Čapek, Josef Čapek, and, to an extent, by Miroslav Rutte (*Prisoner*), stems from a painful awareness of the aimlessness of life and the world, from nihilism, which considers life to be a nonsensical whirlwind of coincidences layered into vicious circles that lead nowhere. And it strives, through a concrete analysis of a certain life act, an event in and of itself, to capture the event's order, logic, and a summary of the conscious and irrational powers within it so that it acquires, after this imperfect induction, the right to even remotely believe in a meaning, purpose, and goal of life in general. From there, it is possible to infer all the formal attributes of literary Cubism. If Mr. T. had penetrated into this spiritual foundation, from which both Czech and French literary Cubism stem (which I believe includes Al. Mercereau, whose *Contes des ténèbres* [Tales of Darkness] influenced K. Čapek very strongly, and, of course, G. Apollinaire, Max Jacob, Blaise Cendrars, P. Reverdy, P. Albert-Birot, etc. whose works don the banner of literary Cubism), he could perhaps have understood early on that there is not an enormous chasm separating literary Cubism and Expressionism, that they are spectacularly, fundamentally related, that they share the same core, the same situation-based, European emotions and beliefs—and that the only difference between the two is that Expressionism echoes cries and the occasional roar of the heart, cast out onto an aimless world whose horizons are flooded with darkness, whereas Cubism reflects the glistening, widened pupils of intellect, which struggles with the darkness, looking for a single reliable piece of knowledge. He would have understood that these are two branches which point in different directions but grow from the same trunk. In turn, he would have understood why he himself could consider the most distinctive French lyricists Cubist, lyricists who—headed by Apollinaire—presented themselves as a singular school in the reviews *Elan*, *Nord-Sud*, etc. and offered a theory parallel to painterly Cubism (resistance to imitation, emphasizing the autonomy of works of art, their surrealism and hypernaturalism, etc.). Confusion here is very likely. These are two wholly parallel currents, mostly flowing together. Further, I would like to point out that literary Cubism in France and Expressionism in Germany developed fully *in the same period*—during the World War. That Rubiner's *Der Mensch in der Mitte* (The Person in the Middle) was created contemporaneously with Duhamel's books. Here it is necessary to closely consider the development of literature, not the visual arts.

I agree with Mr. T. to the last letter if what he is asserting is that Unanimism has a Cubist tradition, speaking not only of the orthodox Unanimism of Romains—who does not allow for a realization of individuality, for whom it is always about the group consciousness, about the construction and destruction of that consciousness, which is built on the permeation of real and abstract thoughts and which excludes most individual components—but also the emotional "Unanimism" of Duhamel and Vildrac, for whom the core of creativity lies in the intense experience of one's own existence and its expansion through love into new individualities and objects. I agree so animatedly because here I feel an immense affinity with a pure Expressionism, though not with the corrupt and distorted forms of the most ragged German Expressionists. This also upholds my assertion that Expressionism is not a solely German phenomenon, that all of Europe shares a single great soul and wave, one with a single core but many crests with different names. It is necessary to take into consideration the essence and not to impoverish the richness of artistic progress with stark formulas, which make the current into differentiated things that mechanically remain alongside one another.

It still remains to discuss Bolshevism. I said in my article that *Bolshevism* is *political and social Expressionism*. Mr. Teige rejects this and declares: "It is however not correct that Communism, in its strict regularization of life, is a phenomenon parallel and coincidental to it, because it does not know the mysteries and the abysmal spiritual collapse, the issues and exaltedness, romanticism and religiosity of it." In the last months, I have read much literature on Bolshevist Russia, a number of concrete news reports from travelers and the writings of philosophers. And it is with this gained insight—which I have worked on deepening because I felt that is where the main problem of all of the new Europe lies, that it is the key to a new life—that it is possible for me to emphatically disagree here. I spoke of *Bolshevism*—that is, about Russia. And to me, Russian Bolshevism is infinitely more encompassing than the term Communism, Marxism. It seems incorrect to me to believe Russian Bolshevism is a mere consequence of German Communism. Bolshevism is an enormous historical movement, in which new races acquire a voice—Slavs and Mongols—and create something like a revolutionary pandemonium of all human spiritual forces, suppressed by Western European civilization, a new nebulous, intuitive human type and a new world in general which differs from the world of the Western European bourgeoisie so greatly that we must first educate the soul to be able to understand it. In this critical period of time, which is not dissimilar to the beginning of Christianity or the Reformation (or a migration period here and there), we see a burst of the whole ensemble of religious, moral, social, economic, scientific, and philosophical forces—and one of them is revolutionary Marxism.

Bolshevism is a new organism, which has devoured many conceptions of all kinds including Marxism. *But it is not its product.* Bolshevism has its mysticism, romanticism, and religiosity. Travelers in today's Russia have a lot of interesting things to say about it (Holitscher or Matthias, for example). I insist on the assertion that Bolshevism runs parallel to *Expressionism*: they both represent a revolution for the people, they both harbor a desire to overcome the Nihilism of Western Europe, they both emphasize an active mind, spontaneity of creation, transition and improvement of the world and its people.

That is how we arrive at the valuable insight of the unity of the spiritual wave in all of Europe, of the cohesive rhythm of the whole age, of the new sociability of all the purest people today. It is somewhat similar to Romanticism. The "Realism" of Balzac has been spoken of as something standing in opposition to it and the "Naturalism" of Flaubert has been spoken of as something overcoming Romanticism, Symbolism and Decadence, and they were put down as new phenomena—and lo, a deeper look uncovered that the majority of these phenomena have roots in Romanticism. If we look upon today from some distance, we will see a similar phenomenon.

Mr. Teige criticizes us for being behind the times by identifying with Expressionism. But it is easy to demonstrate that he has a very narrow and formal idea of Expressionism. He says: "The issues of Expressionism, which is a reaction to Impressionism, cannot possibly be considered acute anymore, including by our truly modern artists." I have shown in my earlier writings that Expressionism is not mere reaction—on the contrary, that it has positive contents, which make it part of the revolutionary wave of life and art which moves the world today; that it contains the same utopia of love, goodness, inner purity, peace, bright vital order, brought about by the dictatorship of a new idea, as is the case in socialism, which also wants to dictate new laws of love and good to the world. What survives today are perhaps only select compulsive offshoots of German Expressionism, which have become bogged down in the abstraction of a shadow empire of chimeras, succeeding entirely from reality. The true content of Expressionism is a component of the revolutionary pandemonium flowing through the world—and it is a living component of today.

In our group, there are poets who matured into Expressionism on their own without having known about its theory or the models of its art beforehand, such as Blatný, Jeřábek, Chaloupka, and Chalupa. We are moving towards a new, original, Czech form of Expressionism: the poems of Wolker, Píša, and Kalista elbow their way towards a very solid form.

Because we are *Expressionists*, we are *Socialists*. For us, these two concepts are simply inseparable. They are so closely connected that one without the other is almost unimaginable. We must emphasize that the orders of the world in which we live are not the embodiment of our imagination, that between today's topia (as Landauer says) and our utopia stretches the unbridgeable chasm that leads towards revolution. And that revolution is taking place in the world today: the spirit of change flows through every corner, always rocking the relative certainty of the bourgeois world. We rejoice in this change (see Chaloupka's Reorganized City, Chalupa's Revolution, Blatný's Cock-a-doodle-doo, the poems of Píša, Wolker, Kalista, etc.) and actively participate in it. We feel that the first condition of this revolution is: *the transformation of the person*, the removal of bourgeois, intellectual mercenariness, which constitutes the worst deformation of the human soul there is, which arose from excessive intellectualization: the bourgeois with the soul of a mercenary is able to internally adapt to every situation, betrays oneself ten times a day, surrenders loyalty to material possessions in an instant, adopts false religious mysticism with any change of fashion, regards hatred and malice as the most beautiful power in a time of war yet sings the praises of love in a time of peace. Their reason can justify anything—excuse anything—it is a device of irresponsibility and malice.

Against this the *mercenariness* of the soul we build our *humanism*. We profess unambiguously that we love humankind as it will come out of the revolution, as it will have grown from within the deepest layers of the human soul. We love humankind and that love makes us aware of our *responsibility* for it. We want to sow love around the world. Once it grows, a great community of *souls* and *hearts* will be established.

Even we are *anti-civilization* in the sense that we do not recognize civilization as a sufficient link between the world and its peoples, that we do not see steam and electricity as powers that bring together and unite people and nations, and the same goes for socialist organizations if they are not founded in *love*, which is the first and foremost element of human nature. We proclaim *human sociability* as the renewal of humanity. We are decidedly anti-subjectivist. We believe that the human being is not a lonely crystal in a vacuum. If it possesses a darkly unique core, then there is also a sphere consisting of people, the world, society—where we are all interconnected. Our poetry wants to be the creation of this new human sociability, it wants to build a firmer bridge between people, just as bridges are built between close islands. Ours is a *poetry of love*, as is the poetry of the greatest creators in France and Germany today. There is no need to emphasize that this poetry has a deep relationship to the worker. We love people and we want each person to achieve their human purpose. We stand, without a doubt, with those who were not proffered the fate to fulfill their own purpose: with *proletarians*. We thus do not pay attention to the narrowly personal, but to the *superpersonal, general, social aspects* of the individual's soul. Our religious sentiment is so strong because we feel a member of a whole, of a network of brothers. Ours is a religion of human sociability. We know well that today it is not about cultivating a play of forms, creative virtuosity, or art for art's sake in today's art. We know that today it is about creating art that contributes to the renewal of the world, the people, and life. We broke free from drunkenness caused by our own soul and the world, we wedged ourselves into the soaring wheel of sociable life and brotherly heart, and we want to use our art to participate in the building of the new person and a better life for them.

Today, we call this art *Expressionism*, but it is not German Expressionism. It is broader. German Expressionism knows only one reality: the soul. Ours however goes after a praiseworthy correspondence of the soul and matter, God and the earth. And we call this correspondence *Classicism*.

If Mr. Teige places Primitivism in opposition to us, let us shake his hand. Primitivism does not exclude Expressionism. On the contrary: they mutually complement each other. E. von Sydow concludes in his book *Deutsche expressionistische Kultur und Malerei* (German Expressionist Culture and Painting, 1920) that Primitivism is one of the fundamental components of Expressionism.

That is all I have to say on behalf of myself and my circle. The polemic gave the impression of a declaration. And not only on my behalf. On all of ours. Mr. Teige will soon understand that he relegates us to the literature of yesterday in error. We are the art of today, just like Devětsil.

Jiří Wolker: Proletarian Art

This article should not be taken as the writer's personal opinion. It is rather the basis of a programme upon which some other artist-friends and I have agreed. Even though our personal opinions on some particulars were different, we do not want to resolve these differences in opposition to each other but rather among ourselves. On the fundamental basis we are united. I will here declare the opinions of the group of communist artists called "Devětsil'.

We perceive the unsustainability and injustice of the current order, and we believe in a better reconstruction of society. Finding a firm and concrete plan for this reconstruction in the theses of Marxism, we view the world through the lens of historical materialism. Therefore, for us the new art is a class-based, proletarian, and communist art. We do not intend to debate the possibility of such an art. For us, this kind of art is a belief and a reality. We are concerned here about its characteristics and growth.

What is the fundamental feature of this new art? The collapse of the bourgeois order is accompanied by the fall of its ideology and thereby its bourgeois art. Viewing the world as Marxists, we do not use the term "bourgeois' in a derogatory way. When we use the term "bourgeois', we have in mind real art arising from the conditions of the capitalist order in the 19th century and the early 20th century. We are talking here about good art, because bad art is not art. In the category of bourgeois art we also include the art of progressive or social feeling, which in its formal and artistic means remains an authentic expression of the bourgeois era. Naturally, we also include here the cluelessness of all the numerous -isms, all those experiments produced by the path of cold speculation which succeeded one another like images on a film screen and in the end finished up in absolute nihilism.

Young artists do not merely want to criticize reality; neither do they want to depict a fairy-tale future. They want to fight for the future, and struggle is their main connection between today and tomorrow; struggle is what combines the present and the future in their hearts. This is why the fundamental characteristic of the new art is its revolutionary nature.

What does revolution in art mean? First and foremost, revolution in art means liberating oneself from the pertinacity of the old art and striving to produce a new proletarian art. The artist casts aside the cult of personality. He joins together in the throng of those struggling for the same goal. He gets organized in a collective united by an idea. It is here that he wants to be heard. His creative approach is not outside of this throng, but inside it, fully inside it. This is why the main features of proletarian art are in direct contradiction to the features of bourgeois art. Individualism is replaced by collectivism; *l'art pour l'art* is replaced by partisanship.

What is collectivism? Collectivism is a conception of life not as the actions of certain individuals, but rather as the actions of entities combined by an idea. It does not emphasize how one person differs from another, but rather how they are mutually similar. And this is also the basis on which it is built. Already the final era of bourgeois art attempted a depersonalization of works of art. The group of Unanimists, formed in France, set this aim out in its programme. To a certain degree, the proletarian artist takes over this group's collectivist opinions. However, for him, these opinions are not the sense of art, but rather one of its tasks. The proletarian artist does not stand above the movement of the masses, but within this movement; for him collective feeling is not merely an artistic experiment, but a living reality. He does not merely want to express artistically this movement of the masses, but also the sense and reasons of this movement. In practice, collectivism means the consciousness of class solidarity.

What do we understand by partisanship in art? Every art conscious of its task has been partisan. Proletarian art is more partisan than any other art, because it is more aware of its task than any other art and it concretely expresses this task. It does not want to be stuck together with some kind of ingenious wisdom; it does not want to play on both sides, in the end saying nothing — like most of the final works of bourgeois art. Its speech should be: yea, yea — nay, nay; and whatsoever is more than these is of the evil one. Therefore, we should not understand partisanship as putting a few political theses into verse; for us partisanship is not an external coating, but rather an opinion and an internal conception. In the cases of Smetana, Aleš, and Neruda, a nationalist partisanship is the angle of view of their artistic vision. Such will be the internationalist partisanship of proletarian art. This will not be achieved though partisan objects. We are not going to seek new objects to view, but rather new ways of viewing.

As I am talking about partisanship in art, I cannot resist citing several sentences by Havlíček from the preface to his review of Tyl's "*The Last Bohemian*': "It is usually said that art is complete in and of itself, that its only aim is that of creating, that it does not need to have any partisan tendency, and so on. However, this — it seems — is merely empty talk, perhaps in the same way that states are autonomous and independent of one another, but only for as long as one of them does not overpower the other. The same thing applies to partisanship in poetry. Perhaps there could be poetic beauty even if there were no people in the world, but such beauty is of no consequence to people — and cannot even be so. The following principle seems to be much more practical: that poetry is in the world so that people can enjoy it. And this is also precisely the best reply to everything that has been, and can be, said about partisan poetry. Some things in human nature are repeated eternally, while some other things change; some things therefore are always appealing, while some things are only so for a time. However, in every case partisan poetry is better than non-partisan poetry because it is more: that is, it is first and foremost poetry, but also something more. However, it is understood that partisan poetry must primarily be truly poetry, because bad poetry, even with the best partisanship, can never be partisan poetry."

Optimism. One more characteristic of the new art flows from its fundamental assumptions. This characteristic is not so much a specific feature of the new art, but rather it takes on a different function for the new art as a result of the characteristic's arising from different conditions. This is the new art's optimism. Romanticism divided life into reality and dream. Placing the highest ideal of happiness outside of the possibilities of this world, it become anchored in pessimism. For something to be beautiful, it had to be unattainable. It did not want happiness; it wanted to suffer in search of happiness. It wanted to be God or the devil, but never a human being. Therefore, for Romanticism the typical sentiment in which life was lived was one of futility, and Romantic art was a reflection of this. Proletarian wisdom knows only this world as a basis of life. It does not long for celestial joy; it wants only human happiness within the scope of its possibilities. I have written earlier in this publication that it is coming down from irresponsible celestiality to responsible humanity, and that it wants a concrete change of the concrete. This is possible, and it can be achieved through struggle and human courage.

Proletarian art, not being internally cloven, is optimistic. But beware! The final sprouts of bourgeois philosophy were also optimistic. What is the difference between these two characteristics called by one and same name? The difference between them, as I have already commented, lies in their different tasks. One was wings, the other is a weapon. The first was indulgence, the second is fervency. The first kind of optimism elevates a human being above the world; with the second kind of optimism a human being fights for the world. The new optimism does not consist in a faith in the perfection of the existing world, but rather in a faith in the possibility of its improvement. Therefore, it does not lead a human being to resignation about the world, seeing in it only the best. The new optimism is a faith in himself, a guarantee of victory, and thereby also a call to arms.

Optimistic periods are periods of faith; pessimistic periods are ones of little faith — sometimes even nihilistic. The object of our faith is not God and gods, but mankind and the world. The mediaeval age believed ardently in the abstract. We believe ardently in the concrete. Therefore, the new art will be realistic. Not the realism of F. X. Svoboda, but that of Ch. L. Philippe; not the formation of one's own impressions and sensations, but the experiential perception of things and people outside of us. It will not be illusory, but rather objective. It is not going to depict and describe, but to provide facts that will constitute a reality. As real things are mutually dissimilar, incomparable, and immeasurable, a work of art — especially a work of visual art — will be a kind of new thing, a new artefact that is non-synonymous and immeasurable with other things. Previously — in naturalism and realism in the usual sense of the world (which was actually naturalist) — a work of art was an imitation and a transcription of these real things.

And now a few words about the development of proletarian art. Its current state (when we are only just on its threshold) and a static conception of literary history could lead someone to contend that proletarian art will only be possible in a proletarian state.

On this matter we judge as follows: proletarian culture — that is, an art developed in its full stylistic breadth — will only be possible in a proletarian state; proletarian art, however, is also possible today. Revolution is its counterpoint. And revolution's mental sphere does not comprise merely the accomplishment of revolution, but also the preparation for it — that is, this mental sphere belongs not only in the future proletarian state, but also in today's world, which is preparing for the struggle to achieve this state.

Finding ourselves in a time of the extinction of one style and the birth of another style, we do not wish to disregard the fact that the new art, albeit mostly through negation, is nevertheless linked to the old art in accordance with all the laws of the sequence of development. Even though the new art is the opposite of the old art, it nevertheless grows from it. However, this is a case here of more than the difference between two generations. Just as bourgeois art is the final period of the great epoch of an individualistic lifestyle, so proletarian art is merely a precursor of a great epoch of a lifestyle of communal social responsibility.

Viewing proletarian art also in Marxist terms, we can ascertain that it is a transitional art. When the period of the dictatorship of the proletariat comes to an end, social classes will thereby cease to exist. The extinction of classes will also lead to the fall of class-based proletarian art. Or rather than a fall — this art will blossom out in all directions from the narrow confines of class and will grow into new cathedrals of socialist culture.

The proletariat are the workers of the new world. Artists want to be workers of a new beauty in this world.

Karel Teige: New Proletarian Art: An Introduction

The Russian Revolution strives not only towards the realization of economic equality and fairness, but also towards the liberation of human work, both material and spiritual, in order to render a higher, truly productive kind of work—creation. Liberating the proletariat from the subjugation of the inhuman order of the old world, it also liberates culture from its dependence on the bourgeoisie and focuses its public enlightenment exclusively on the proletariat. It liberates art. In this its efforts appear paradoxical. The absolute freedom of art was, for so many, its most precious privilege. It remained outside of the world and its early order, according to the opinion of artists and aestheticians, unrestrained by political and moral laws; in a vacuum of unrestrained movement, it could not become firmly anchored in concrete life. The artist wanted to separate oneself from the class structure, unlimited by it as a free **entrepreneur** on whom society has no claim or influence. **Art for art's sake distanced itself from its broad and abundant audience and refused to be associated with it.** Despising its own class—while for a number of good and historically justified reasons—it called itself aristocratic, and going as far as denying its human origin at times, it embarked on a mystic-religious platform.—It is only natural that the class then became alienated from its own art and did not provide it with material and cultural support through which it could have grown in stylistic breadth and magnitude. To liberate art, which is in its essence very constricted and which, not wanting to be sterile, must make good in its tasks and fulfill its mission, would mean rescinding the artistic work's social obligations, it would be its obviation and annihilation. The Russian Revolution's public enlightenment comes from a recognition of **the reciprocal connection and boundedness of art with life**, liberating the work of the artist by rebinding it to its social mission. Operating with Marxist concepts, it sees art as one of the greatest components of the **ideological social superstructure** and as such recognizes its class basis determined by the economic-political state of the period from which the ruling class draws its ideology. The thesis that art was, is, and will be a class-based art for the foreseeable future naturally generated a stir and tenacious dissent from defenders of a free and independent art. It is generally acknowledged, though sometimes unwillingly, that the problem of proletarian art and proletarian culture, as formulated in the writings of Lunacharsky's "The Cultural Tasks of the Working Class," is the **central and most current point** for the development and advancement of current artistic production. Both left-wing and right-wing papers fill their columns with reflections and articles that either oppose or promote the idea of a proletarian culture, but we must admit that it would be far easier to empty an ocean using nothing but a seashell than to ascertain a clear opinion and firm, concrete direction in these reservoirs of printer's ink.

If an institution as ancient and stiff as Charles University in Prague was able to provide a place for a debate on this topic by an organization just as stiff, it is apparent that the question of proletarian culture unsettles even the most intolerable circles. The approach was, however, thoroughly philosophical; it was necessary that the ever so clear and rational question first be obscured and complicated in order to make it worthy of a learned debate. It is conceded without objections that past arts were the arts of gods, kings, aristocrats, the Pope, the hierarchy; it is even conceded that the Florentine school was a civil (i.e., bourgeois) one; but most evade admitting that the art of the 19th and early 20th century is bourgeois, even though all it takes is a simple look at our history to be convinced of it. Those who do not admit this art to be bourgeois clearly cannot recognize the existence of proletarian art, either; after all, their philosophical lenses of delusion make them unable to see things as enormous as the current radical changes transforming the world.

It is irrelevant that the debate ended with a conditional and somewhat involuntary acknowledgement of the *possibility* of proletarian art. Even if it had ended with a denial, it would not have changed the fact of its existence, just as all of today's philosophizing has yet to result in a finding that would shatter the earth or even come near it. After all, idealistic philosophy never leads to the clarification and resolution of problems and reality, but to their obscurement. Those of healthy beliefs never doubt reality, they want to stand firmly on solid ground, use it for support and as an instrument. We learn about the irrefutable existence of reality early in life. When we sit at a table, that which we sit upon is a chair; a thing, tangible matter, something real. Post-Kantian philosophy does not know of the real, solid chair; it tells you to take a seat on your sensory input condensed into a cerebral, empirical experience. There is no question which of these is the safer, more solid, more practical option.

This little diatribe against idealistic philosophy, which denies even the fundamental basis of human life—the **simple existence of concrete reality**—was only a brief detour, although related to the rest of my observations. Now I return to my main point.

First, some **assumptions and *assertions.*** I consider Marxism not only the only possible and useful worldview, but also one capable of influencing all theoretical subjects. Hence the necessity in replacing today's idealistic, Bergsonian-Crocean art history with a different, new art history, aesthetics, and criticism, which will draw from the principal points of Marxism. For the same reason, if we rely on Marx's historical view, the notion of proletarian art is not a problem, but a fact, even if this art were only going to be realized in the subsequent decades. Its potential and historical legitimacy have been, as I have already touched upon, demonstrated by Lunacharsky as well as countless other Russian authors, albeit regretfully not always the most competent. I want pick up with my reflections where Lunacharsky left off. Lunacharsky resolved the existential problem of proletarian art; today we engage with his aesthetic questions and questions of genesis. Since it was said that a proletarian art will emerge in the nearest future, I want to approach it as a concrete task and attempt to describe **what this proletarian art will be like**. Using the terminology of bourgeois, proletarian, and socialist art, Lunacharsky's study offers three firm points. But not even the most revolutionary antitheticalism can realize itself or crystallize at once; when speaking of sharp opposition, we must also be conscious of **interrelatedness**, which persists, even if only in the form of tension between polarities. When predictions are made about the aspects in which new art will differentiate itself from bourgeois art, it is also tacitly asserted that **it is firmly bound up with what came before**. Take so-called Expressionism: when understood in its actual and narrow bounds, it is nothing but a programmatic anti-thesis to Impressionism, yet in a certain way, it emphasizes some of its predecessor's achievements, namely those of a technical nature. The anti-Impressionist Matisse,—this can be proved very easily—is, in several regards, a late Impressionist. That means that progress is spurred on just as much by **the reactive revolutionary rise of the new times**, which form more or less direct opposition to the preceding times, and that there is an **almost inviolable progressive continuity**, a natural progressive line, something that we call tradition. Sometimes, artistic renewal and reactivity do not balance out the legacy of tradition; other times, the revolutionary character of new generations is so pronounced that it seems as though its only aim is to disrupt the current line of progress and to then continue it using the interrelatedness of the dialectical tension between two opposites. The first is a traditionalist period, the second bitterly anti-traditional. But not even an epoch of the most revolutionary anti-traditionalism and mania for innovations sees its art and culture just drop from the sky. It must necessarily draw on preceding forms, even if it would rather fully abandon them and pursue completely opposite ones. Even in their case, the immediately preceding period must be a precursor for their path.

Yet if we were to speak about degrees of artistic progress instead of time periods, it would mean that we understand art as a movement of the times, oriented towards a certain higher goal. But the logic of historical progress does not play out so clearly and directly; it lets off steam in tumultuous contradictions and radical changes. And so, the period of proletarian art is actually **not degrees above the art of the bourgeois epoch; it is on the same level, just at the opposite pole.**

Marxist art history is and will possibly remain for some time a thing of the future; naturally, mere outlines and preliminary works of art can arise at this point; because proletarian culture and especially proletarian art history have not yet found its Marx. But from Marxist beliefs **flow some unconditional consequences for aesthetics** that can be used as a guide to build a new, Marxist art history. From Marxist beliefs flows, above all, the absolute necessity to **depsychologize**, which means to despiritualize and demystify aesthetics. It is not necessary that artistic intellect and sensibility be interpreted spiritually or cabalistically, it is not necessary that the artist be offensively declassified as a visionary cretin, a mere interpreter of the transcendental world as seen by their ecstatically widened eyes. **There is no intuition nor inspiration.** If you come across these somewhat aristocratic and melodious words in modern studies, translate them into a more prosaic expression: **an idea**. From this point on, the word **creation** shall not equate to the mysterious inception of something *ex nihilo*; it shall be a **more poetic, more aristocratic synonym for harmonious human work**. The conception of artistic work is truly as physical and human as the conception of a person; it is born of the fertilized brain **with conscious and subconscious recognition of reality**. If "genius" is an empty word and talent is mere ability and aptitude, it would be best if the modern critic used neither word, because to speak about how an artist has no talent is nonsense, and to say that one has talent **goes without saying**. And the Muses of poetry are no godlier than the Muses of engineering or history, or even the Muses of carpentry. Perhaps the only thing one could say is that they are more human. And if art is truly the **humanization of science**, as Gino Severini says (in the book *From Humanism to Classicism*)—and an actively scientific mission is certainly more dignified when it comes to art than the passive and problematic religious tradition—there is definitely just as much metaphysics in the work of the artist as in the work of the scientist or the laborer, which however does not mean the work of the artist does not involve more of the **heart and human warmth**. The new aesthetics will be more a sociology than a psychology of art; because the psychology of art has been only a mere, general psychology so far. Psychological-aesthetic interpretations of impressions, as for instance evoked by a landscape, have been identical in all professorial reflections, whether interpreting a landscape in a painting or on planet Earth. If the new aesthetics are **sociological**, it means, figuratively speaking, that it will be **historical**: which assumes the creation of a general history of art from a Marxist historical viewpoint. The need for a history of art is urgent, but it is clear that it will take more than a day or two to get there. We have, however, seen attempts at a sociology of art and social aesthetics here and there.

But this does not include the work of Lalo, Taine, Riegl, Guyau, Worringer, Verworn, and naturally also Ruskin, Morris—or it does so **indirectly** at best. What is more important is sociological sketches of the progress of art as found in Hausenstein's writings: *Der nackte Mensch in der bildenden Kunst aller Zeiten und Völker*, *Kunst und Gesellschaft*, *Bild und Gemeinschaft* (The Nude in Art Across All Times and Nations, Art and Society, The Picture and Community) and to some extent also *Kunst in diesem Augenblicke* (Art in These Times). It is likely that further work in this direction will correct and fill in some of the findings of Hausenstein, handled in places in too unscientific a manner, but it is clear that these writings are of considerable significance to laying the groundwork for a proletarian Marxist art history. Beside the writings of Hausenstein, I present another attempt of smaller scope and lesser importance: Lu Märten's *Historischmaterialistisches über Wesen und Veränderung der Künste* (Historical Materialist Being and the Transformation of Art) and Herzfeld's book: *Künstler, Gesellschaft und Kommunismus* (The Artist, Society, and Communism). In Czechoslovakia, only one notable brochure was published by Josef Hora: *Culture and Class Consciousness*.

The task of this article is neither to show the potential of proletarian art, which has already been done, nor to outline its philosophy, which is yet to come; I wish by discussing it not just as a social fact **but mainly as art**, as a field of human work, to establish and precisely state the tasks and responsibilities it places on contemporary, revolutionary artists. However, it is difficult to speak about contemporary art and the postulates of this age in the first place; it is difficult to exhaust so comprehensive a topic and to survey an expanse as wide and unbridled as our whirling and multi-faceted present. It is difficult to speak about phenomena and realities as complex as those we are faced with today and nearly impossible to trace and elucidate the threads of their mutual relationships. Because: where does the present start and end? And where does its art start and end? Delimitating it chronologically would mean engaging in academic pigeonholing, whose **static understanding** of progressive action would not clarify things but confuse them further rather than simplify and classify them. For a static understanding breaks the evolutionary curve into several precisely delimited parts that elude historical connectivity and logic when in isolation from each other. Progressive continuity, I repeat, is not mechanical continuation; progress is realized in oppositions, and over the polarizing tension of thesis and antithesis, it constructs a great synthesis, **which becomes the thesis for the subsequent period, once again forming an antithesis to the preceding one.** And for a second time: as I begin to reflect on the current state of artistic production and its resulting postulates, I hesitate as to where to begin. If I begin at the beginning, if I proceed from the cradle of so-called modern art, then I introduce it with a historical retrospective. Where is the beginning and birth of new art situated? Does it date from Impressionism as it is generally believed? Because Impressionism first introduced abstract elements, which characterize a major portion of new art, if not the whole of it. Impressionism came before Expressionism, which is in no way its integral antithesis, and it came before Futurism, which is its paroxysm. But: before Futurism and before Impressionism, William Turner stood on the doorstep of the 19th century.—Some, looking upon the modern with reserve, date it from the Renaissance, taking into account the individualism and physiocratic positivism that characterized the 19th and beginning of the 20th century, and if they have in mind that Renaissance art came about in an age of a developed monetary economy and the victoriously advancing market enterprise of the bourgeois Italian republics, they correctly note the connection between the art of the 19th century and that of the Italian Cinquecento. Because the aesthetic norm and ideal was the ideal of the Renaissance and Classicism, while the Gothic had no recognition.—Eventually others, namely with respect to the area of French creation, which was a decisive center of gravity in the preceding period, would say that this art began with the arrival of Leonardo on French soil. From then on, an uninterrupted line of tradition developed: from the tradition of French Rationalism and positivist Classicism, which advanced via Fouquet, Clouet, the Le Nain brothers, Poussin, and Claude Lorrain, to the period of the Revolution, to Chardin, Greuze, Vigée Le Brun, and from there to David, Ingres, Corot, Courbet, Manet, Degas, Renoir, Cézanne, to Picasso, Derain, and the contemporary school of Neoclassicism (Lhote, Galanis, Bissière), which **definitively closed** this large and interdependent historical circle.—For my considerations, however, the most well-suited and precise dividing line between the 18th and 19th centuries seems to be the fateful moment when the flame of the French Revolution was ignited, with its fundamental social reconstruction mirrored in art, which saw a parallel phenomenon of stylistic transformation. Since we can trace a direct line from today to post-revolutionary empirical Classicism, dating the beginning of this art back to this point might be the most precise option as it would clearly delimit not only the aesthetics but also the sociology of art.

"In rivers, the water that you touch is the last of what has passed and the first of that which comes; it is so with present time," says the wise Leonardo. Indeed. Every present moment means the death of the past and the birth of the future. In the present, the past and the future meet, and thus it has two faces, appearing just like a Janus face. These two faces appear in art. A typical example is Paul Cézanne, who not only represents the peak of Impressionism, but also surpasses it. He is an Impressionist and at the same time its antipode: a Classicist. If he gleaned his Impressionism from Pissarro, he based his Classicism on Poussin. His interest in both naturalist Impressionism and Classicism is expressed by a single statement: it is necessary to rework Poussin according to nature; that is all. Impressionism and Classicism are indeed in a certain respect the two faces of contemporary art; a contradiction in the fading epoch itself.

If I am to start from Adam, or better yet, if this is concerning modern art and life since David, Percier, Fontaine, Robespierre, Danton, and also perhaps the pre-revolutionary realists Greuze, Chardin, Goya, or from the encyclopedists, this is a comprehensive summary. And so that I may be extremely brief, I will frequently lean on Hausenstein's concise and apposite characterization of the period.

—The eighteenth century is particularly interesting. It is the simple development of the Baroque. Watteau, and more so Boucher, are the direct descendants of Rubens. And the gallant Rococo art attaches itself to the last scions of the Renaissance. The continuing blossoming of affluence and education amongst the bourgeoisie, however, hindered art from staying as festive and arabesque as in the style of Louis XVI. And this is where, before the Revolution and new Empire-style art, an anti-Rococo reaction laid down its roots, starting with the style of Louis XVI, an intermediary period that most evidently displays progressive continuity and discontinuity. If it is certain that there is a deep chasm within the mature revolutionary Empire style, it is also true that the short interim period of contact between the two centuries, defined by a rather hasty and radical change in style, does not interfere with continuity in development. The style of Louis XVI, which was already in full force 40 years before the Revolution, is an indicator of that continuity. It is also a connecting link, in a sense, just as is proclaimed by a Classicist anti-Rococo reaction striving for simplification and streamlining, which, despite it being a courtly style, is not without relation to the crystallization of the third democratic state in the bosom of the aristocratic and feudal order. Naturally, the style of Louis XVI, with its refined Primitivism, does not mean more change of the basic tendencies of Rococo and its whole concept; it is simply the beginning of a reaction, an opposition to an excessive opulence and flimsiness of form. If a reaction against the Rococo appears in the increasingly abundant use of Classical motifs, in ornament still firmly and geometrically unorganized, the whole concept as well as other socially characteristic details (such as, for example, an inclination for Chinese decorative arts) repeatedly show a continuation of a taste and fondness for the Rococo.

The consequent and complete reaction against Rococo (against Rococo as the last consequence and scion of the Renaissance) **is Empire**, which adopted a Classical style, the style of fifth-century cosmopolitan Greece, and reflections of that style in as much as Etruscan, Roman, Crusader, and Renaissance art administers them. It would, however, be a mistake to assume that its essence lies in a fuller reliance on Classical antiquity. From the age of the Renaissance, the Classical serves as a living model and it is interesting to observe how it is always reconfigured, its essence transformed in line with the tendencies of the time. The Empire Style also looks upon Greek and Egyptian Classicism "unobjectively," even though contemporary science ushers in new findings with the discovery of Herculanea and Pompei, with the archeological excavations at Palmyra and Baalbek, and with archeological research in Egypt. Despite the fact that during the reign of Napoleon the First, art attempted to precisely resemble the Classical, seen by contemporaries as art of literal copies, today we can clearly see the distinct features of the art they created, how it differs from the Classical. No style adopts foreign elements without assimilating, adapting, revising some of them in itself. As the Italian Renaissance is not a rebirth of Roman antiquity, neither is the Empire Style a renewal of the Hellenistic period. As the Renaissance indeed adopted motifs from Roman art, since they corresponded to the majestic splendor that it wanted to express, so did the Empire Style draw from Hellenic art, as it brought calm and harmony of form, which an age oversaturated by the Rococo longed for. Both styles, Renaissance and Empire, recreated preexisting models both consciously and unconsciously according to their needs and conditions. Sometimes the unconscious, unwitting differences between the model and the new style are the most significant characteristics of the new style's essence and character. It would be too superficial to assert that the discoveries at Pompei and Herculanea produced Empire Style. They only had a decisive, formal influence on its development, just like Napoleon's expedition to Egypt. If Empire style was only a copy of the Classical, it would have been possible for it to emerge any time before the discovery of Pompei in Italy, because artists in Italy always had the beautiful temples at Paestum and Agrigento right before their eyes. And yet it emerged in France, not out of the excavations at Pompei **but from the style of Louis XVI**, getting its name not from the Classical but from the **Napoleonic Empire** due to historically sociological necessity. Similarly, proletarian art is not born of Primitivisms and the fruits of primary creativity, which (such as Negro sculpture and the whole of exotic art, the art of the people, of children, and the paintings of the people's child H. Rousseau) are related to one another in a similar way the Classical and Empire are; that is, through their model, pillars, foundations, source of knowledge and renewal. Proletarian art will not be born from them; it will grow from bourgeois art, from Cubism and Futurism, its last chapter and subsequent antithesis. Its Primitivism will not be archaic, but contemporary; it will not be an insipid recollection of bygone beauty but will create the beauty of today. It will be born from the bourgeois order, through **negation**, just as the proletariat, the representative of the new society, was born from the bourgeoisie.

As far as it stems from the Classical, Empire art adopts the style of the previous bourgeois epochs (the Classical and Renaissance) by selecting certain relations to its whole. David, the citizen David, is as monistic, as rational (as Hausenstein says) as the most bourgeois of the Periclesean Classicists; he is as bourgeois as the Florentine generation of Donatello; like the Classical and Renaissance, David's forms are entirely without imagination; something finite, rational, irreligious. The pathos of the motifs and the tendencies are not translated into poetic form, just as religious theme does not render Raphael's art religious.

The economic conditions of the 19th century steered the community mentality towards individualism, to the criminal ideological and social anarchy that has eliminated style, corroded the primal collective pathos of the age of Empire, and, with a stylized degeneration, spread the cruel plague of historicizing eclecticism in architecture, turning the streets and cities into a museum of frightful examples. As far as the art of the 19th and 20th centuries, it is a direct and positive product of collective culture, it is a product of a culture that is highly problematic. That is because the bourgeois community, which is essentially non-aesthetic, did not provide art with positive impulses; hence historicism and a romantic turn towards the past—in certain decades, an escape from the everyday, current reality was an ostensible way of preventing art from a general banalization. Delacroix (writes Hausenstein), rejected by the majority of his contemporaries, appears to have painted for the civic public of Titian and Veronese and not for the descendants of the revolutionary generation in France. The artist, due to the influence of historical, economic, and political shifts and conditions, lived apart from the bulk of society. In such an extreme circumstance, one cannot live in a vacuum and therefore makes up another society, past or future; like a historian, or like a rebel, one addresses their works to imagined societies and communities. Art of the bourgeois epoch indicates a positive relationship to the current society and reality only in two cases: the first is the wisdom of Goethe and the civic, disciplinary classical school of David, while the second is the divisive, blinded craziness and technical megalomania of the enraptured Civilist and Futurist art. Other than that, it has always lived with the spirit of negation, directed at the past and the future. The artist's protesting stance has become historic necessity. Not recognized by the bourgeoisie, the art aims to frighten it; and yet it remains bourgeois. It belongs to its class, though rejected by it. The works of Baudelaire, Hugo, Verlain, Delacroix, Daumier, and Manet are all examples of bourgeois art, though repudiated by their class, while the art of Dumas, Sardou, Jirásek, Sv. Čech, Makart, Delaroche, Gallait, Brožík, Piloty, or the pseudo-realists in the Kondelik language of Thoma, Defregger, Rossegger, etc. is not—for the simple reason that it is not art at all. Even the work of Courbet and Van Gogh is bourgeois art because a change in style does not occur if the artist, a sharp emotional revolutionary, subscribes to socialism subjectively: **essential**, not **thematic**, changes would be necessary as only those would demonstrate collective sentiment and views, not an isolated belief or mood; the social side of art lies in essence and character, not in a program and theme. An artistic transformation requires **an achieved reality of a newly organized society** or at least a graspable hint of a new reality. New proletarian art does not grow from personal socialist viewpoints (which would make it bourgeois art with socialist tendencies) but from the reality of the existence of a new society. Courbet's "The Stonebreakers," Van Gogh's "Prisoners' Round," and tendencies in the draughtsmanship of the 19th century are authentic works of bourgeois art.

*

A single look at the present condition of textual and visual creation reveals a deep crisis — the artistic process, which seemed to reach a boiling point before the war but was then brought down to nothing, has parallels in all human work under the conditions of the capitalist order. Due to historical circumstances, the life of the society does not directly result in art. All efforts to interconnect art and life, such as in Ruskin's case, later manifest as leprous moralism, for his dream of purification's empty assumption and fundamental condition was a new organization of life, a new social order; it could become reality only in a young community born from the revolution—or cocooned in the ideal of l'art pour l'art as in the case of Cubofuturist Civilism. Art closes itself off, or gets closed off, in salons and ateliers as though a peculiarity, and its only relationship to contemporary life is evident in its share in the process of individualization and the distribution of work. Art, whose tense formalistic esotericism becomes a mannerism, loses its former seriousness as a public affair. Literature succumbs to the infection of salon snobbism and painting becomes a private affair, the purchase and order of a job from a haphazard amateur, of the art stock market and exchange, and critique a thing of rational intellect—valued the more today the more the individual separates oneself from the integral parts of the whole using this very intellect, aiding to further the ongoing general decline.

Creative problems become the final aims and self-purpose of artistic work, which is, with time, degraded to an internal affair of the atelier; issues of abstraction and deformation are meditated upon; creation does not turn outward, towards life and reality, but is held captive, becoming stuck in a vicious circle, it intensifies its formal means, not having an ascertainable aim. It turns only to a narrowly delimited number of individuals, as Paul Cézanne has already said, and it is a historically indispensable fact that today artists do not work for society, or even for the whole of the firmly crystallized currently reigning class, but rather for a narrow aesthetic sect. Art has forgotten that it is in the world **for the viewer, for the world, for the person**: divorced from life, separated from the surrounding world, it believed itself to be above life and above the world: it demanded that the world, the person, the viewer lived for art. Art only knew experts, who were just as clueless about the world and life, only knowing art. And so this art, which bragged about standing on the firm ground of current life, like Futurism for example, ultimately became a greenhouse flower.

A serious issue which should de facto not be an issue but a categorical necessity is the issue of the positive **relationship of art to society, which is reemerging** as a topic of discussion. And it is the revolutionary undercurrent of today that makes this issue into a dilemma: **art for art's sake on one side, and so-called tendentious art on the other**. If Ruskin and Morris wanted life and craft to ennoble art, today the focus is on innervating art with the specifics of current life. This shows that all is not well with art as a living organism. Artists can feel the burning tragedy of the constellation that has separated art from the world and real life: never had so much alarm been expressed in manifestations and proclamations, emphasizing that art and life are tightly connected, never had such learned tracts been written asking for two plus two to equal four. 2 + 2 = 4 is a fact just as much as the logical boundedness and connection of art with the life of society. Always and everywhere, in all circumstances. If there are immutable and material principles of art, then one of them is that principle. If it is demanded today that this principle, as certain as two and two is four but even clearer and more comprehensible, is to be realized—despite the fact that it is already a reality—it is because it appears not to be the case. And that again is because it has taken up a highly unprecedented and paradoxical form. The confusion of form and the helplessness of today's art originated in this paradoxical situation, one so truly strange, extremely disturbing, and unfavorable to creation that it would hardly be possible to find a parallel in history (unless the end of ancient history and the antiquity were considered one), a situation with deep sociological roots.

—Today, the conclusion of the present is coming; a point at which the age divides in two and its present becomes the past. A direct, transverse incision is wielded between the two faces of the Janus head, not a reckoning, but a sword's cut. The revolution is splitting the world, time, culture with this incision; it divides our thinking in two. It is an intermezzo and interregnum, it is not a pause. It is not a pause as it is intensified development, an accelerated progress of the age. Thus we stand at the threshold of the future. Though I would like to speak about tomorrow, I do not want to make baseless predictions. **It is possible to speak about tomorrow only in so far as it grows out of today**, which really means as far as it grows out of yesterday.

How does tomorrow's art grow out of the art of today and yesterday? I said that its relationship to the immediately preceding period will be antithetical. If you compare works which announce a new style of art and life, at least in hints, with art of the immediately preceding period, you will see at first glance a decided, radical and **unconcealed contradiction**. For example, the contradiction between the poetry of the youngest generation with that of the generation best described as belonging to Cubofuturist Civilism. It was poetry that wanted to redeem itself from decadent Subjectivism and Romanticism by lending its stanzas the life of the machine, the motor, by busying itself with the apotheosis of Euro-American civilization instead of subjective feelings.

After the animal era comes the era of the machine, which is now beginning, as the Futurists have announced. Their wireless imagination, liberated words, essential and synthetic lyricism, and civilized sensibility created a truly singular current of the time, which breathed with the greedy passion of modernity. Then war arrived, which felled the movement and disrupted it; it ruined people's faith in it. What lives of it today are grieving survivors, not the avant-garde of the modern, but weak animals and devastated castaways. The Futurist manifesto proclaimed: we can work for ten more years! Marinetti, and with him a number of young, active artists, are attempting to prolong the life of the movement, which has become a chronic humbug and has regrettably existed more than fifteen years already. Its newness grew old terribly fast; it became stiff and the artist Marinetti, became a kitsch writer with "The Pope's Monoplane," an author of surprising, synthetic theater.

The artistic bankruptcy of the movement is most clearly visible in the second generation of Italian Futurism (Carrà and Soffici abandoned Futurism and pursued, slong with Cirici, their own metaphysical variety of Neoclassicism in the magazine *Valori Plastici*), in so-called German Expressionism, and in the daring pieces of Russian extremists. It was not even necessary for Dadaism to reveal the full extent of its absurdity.

Today's poetry creates an opposition to Cubofuturist poetry with these characteristics: **tendentiousness and collectivity**, and also with the fact that the relationship to the civilized world is not optimistic, **but pessimistic**. And still, it is clear that the past movement did not fall from the sky or grow from the will and initiative of one individual. It was the cultural atmosphere in the few years preceding the war characterized by an extreme exertion of American economic civilization and struggle in the colonies that gave birth to an oppressive atmosphere which had to be cleared up by the storm of war. And just as a war caused by a criminal societal order and the politics of capitalist expansion was able to deliver the death blow to a culminating and advanced capitalism, it was able to uproot its cultural reflection: Cubistfuturist Civilism, which was the natural fruit, the climax, a proud outcome that pronounced its own fall, a culmination and the sunset of bourgeois culture.

I do not aim to perform its aesthetic analysis or evaluate it, I aim to discover its sociological diagnosis. It is not about the criticism of distinguished phenomena, but about the explanation of phenomena and events characteristic of the movement and the era. That is because the subject of my considerations on this topic will be books, portraits of people who would be found too superficial on the scales of artistic values. For such a problematic cultural atmosphere, truly second-rate art is a better pressure gauge. It was not Březina, but Ignát Herrmann, not Picasso, but far more so Léger, Delaunay, and Tatlin who testify, who **convict**. The era of Cubist-futurist Civilism yielded these names on the crest of its temporal wave: Marinetti, Apollinaire, Cendrars, Neumann, and the complete later literature of Birot, Epstein, Goll, Dermée, Salmon, perhaps most characteristically manifested in Apollinaire's famous "Zone" with its later reverberations in Goll's poem: "Paris is Burning." The poetry of Apollinaire and Goll are the benchmarks of the temporal and qualitative range of the whole movement. With Apollinaire's work a new poetry developed in a frenetic animacy.

The clarions of this movement were, above all, the Futurist manifestos. An art made up with an unconditional admiration for the external form of the world, pictures provided by the commercial and mechanical civilization of global Americanism, it sang the praises of the present: that is, it consciously or involuntarily sang the praises of maturing capitalism and colonialism, of mounting war. Poetry about machines and pictures of machines is art for the American engineer and factory owner; even if it is scoffed at by them, their renaissance villas decorated with sentimental kitsch, and bookcases in the study filled with salon literature.

It is possible to substantiate this: the art of mature, individualist capitalism was necessarily individualistic. It was formalist (which was an aesthetic necessity) and **art for art's sake** (which was a necessity of the age). Matisse conceived of the role of art in life thus: that which concerns me is an art of balance, calm and peace, without moving and compelling topics for reflection, an art that could provide pleasure and a respite to a person working with their mind—a statesman, engineer, writer. I want an art of equilibrium and purity which is not disquieting nor confusing, so that the tired, overburdened and exhausted person might enjoy calm and rest in front of my painting—it is a concept of art as a comfortable armchair in which it is possible to take a breather, as was the concept of the futurist Soffici, who asserts that art is not a serious thing, but a trifling, social game, a diversion. This concept, which constitutes the whole support structure of Dadaism, is typically **bourgeois**. The civilized city slicker considers art an inconsequential diversion suitable for the amusement of women and girls and takes artists as miserable fools whom it is necessary to pity and support. This is a conception of badly conveyed bourgeois snobbism. The artist, as Gleizes says, is now a product so deformed, so subjugated by the formula of specialization, that they have become the best advocate of their adversaries and themselves support the thesis of art for art's sake, which reduces their role to that of an entertaining jester and frees them of their own role as broadcaster.

I will not speak about the emotional causes for the contemporary revolution in art because I have already said enough times what the war taught us; we shivered in horror and condemned the order whose civilization devoured ten million human souls within four years of war. The artists, who were not only acrobats and pure formalists but also men with their hearts in the right place, soon spoke a resolute "no" against the bourgeois order and bourgeois civilization.

It was their hearts that regulated this negation; it is their understanding which seeks new, positive paths. Irritably condemning the past, mathematically researching the function of the future. Their thinking was entirely of **revolt, opposition, reaction**; born of absolute resistance to the given state. To prevent the revolt from remaining sterile, to prevent it from dissolving into foam, it was necessary that it become a goal-oriented revolution, it was necessary to precisely determine the causes of the fall of the old order and the path to a new world. The study of the fall and rebirth of the world is today **Marxism.**—I also cannot agree with the literary exuberance of revolutionary artists and critics. Drowning up to the ears and gulping the dirty water of the bourgeois ideology, they confusedly throw about catchwords of salvation and renewal, making the ideological water, which is already cloudy, cloudier still. The lifeboat of their theories is too tiny for the shipwreck of the world. Millions of the proletariat are living and dying with the desire for a new and just order; they cannot be rescued with the tinkerer of political Expressionism. So: emotion commanded us to deny the old world. On the path to the new, we can lean only on rational belief. In art it is precisely so. And as far as we know that art is a function of life, it is essential that artistic opinion as a fragment fit into the whole of the world's belief system. Marxist belief led to definite consequences for the aesthetic. **The antithetical nature of the historical** sequence above all. And here: I have concluded indifference towards a social mission to be a feature of the bourgeois individualism of Cubofuturism. New proletarian art will see this feature transform into collectivism and sociability.

First, let me speak of the **tendency of new art**, which is an easily perceptible trait, albeit less essential than its collectivism.

All epochs of mature and proud cultures used their art to proclaim and pronounce to the world the purpose, aim, and ideals of their day. It was a profession of faith through tendency, it was a collective pathos. How small and individualistically impotent nineteenth- and twentieth-century culture appears, unfriendly towards its own apostles. It was forbidden to proclaim tendency as soon as it was clear that the tendency must be anti-bourgeois. As long as the bourgeoisie as a whole lived by its collective beliefs, such as nationalism, it also owned up to their manifestations; the development of Capitalism put the interests of the individual entrepreneur above the interests of the whole = of the nation. And nationalism, no longer a faith or an ideal, became a matter of market speculation. Both ideology and life arrived at individualism. It was no longer possible to control the spiritual world, which was in collective hands. Every tendency born from collective faith would have to deny this state of things. It was thus advisable to avoid it.

The collective proletarian movement is again capable of rendering tendentious art just as it was before the thousand-year movement of Christianity. The collective movement of the proletariat, in the midst of its fight today but victorious tomorrow, needs such art as that which Kurt Hiller calls **political**: that is art fertilized by the age, born from the great collective political group, living in its faith and sentiment. Kurt Hiller rightly states: "In revolution we reject greenhouse literature, we want one that entirely bristles with the tendency to cease to exist as literature." A certain camp pathos, echoing with the polyphonic cries of demonstration, a pungency of expression bordering on proclamation, catch words, and poetry approaching the tone of a Communist journal, is the native form of so many poems. Because, in the words of Hiller, the writer cannot be a bit player, but must be the hero. There is no need to search for words to describe events but to use words to influence them; not reportage but prophecy; not proclamations, but demands!

Nevertheless, a number of allegedly Communist stories and poems exist. We have also seen pictures in which there is regrettably no Communism apart from the political formula. They cannot speak to the proletariat through their form; they are useless for agitational camp speech, nasty and undignified for art. They are didactic in the worst sense of the word, textbook Communist rhymes, whose formal impotence and naivety call to mind similar tendentious and dilettantish patriotic tales, which originated in the Czech National Revival era.

It is truly not inappropriate to draw a parallel between the current conditions in Czechoslovakia and that era. And I pronounce my judgement on day-to-day, ordinary tendentious pseudo-poetry with one sentence. Not "The Last Czech," "The Rose of One-Hundred Leaves," or "Three Eras in the Czech Lands"; we need a "**Grandmother**" for the proletariat. If you substitute the proletarian tendency for the patriotic one of Tyl, Jablonský, Kollár, Čelakovský, and Tomíček, there will be no gain, because only the socialists Němcová, Neruda, and Bezruč are needed. And we need a socialist critic, capable of discerning true value from false values, one as prescient today as Havlíček was some years ago. We need to resolutely do away with supposedly proletarian poetry the same way the supposedly national literature of the antediluvian "Last Czech" was buried. **It is necessary to advocate for tendency in art, which is why it is important to prevent the misuse of tendency in art**. Fully aware of the dust of the years that have settled over his articles, I will explain my view by citing Havlíček:

"It is typically said that art is completed in and of itself, that creation is its only purpose, that it does not have to have a tendency, etc. These are however, as it seems, only empty statements. The same thing goes for tendency in poetry. Perhaps there can be poetic beauty even if there are no people in the world; such beauty does not have anything to do with people nor should it. What appears to be far more practical is the sentence: poetry is in the world for people to enjoy. And that is also the best answer to all that has ever been said and can be said of tendentious poetry. Some things in human nature constantly repeat and always stay the same while some things change; some things are always enjoyed, while others only sometimes.

But in every way, tendentious poetry is better than non-tendentious poetry because it is, above all, poetry and something more. Granted, it must qualify as ***poetry*** **in the first place because not even the best tendencies could make bad writing into tendentious poetry.**"

It is certain that tendentiously belligerent, provocative, aggressive poetry, just like revolutionary drawing and caricature, somewhat pamphlet-like, is but one branch in the wide treetop of proletarian art. It is its **own style of revolution**, the song at the barricades, the chronical of civil war, the heroic epoch of radical change. It was precisely the same way with the French Revolution. Pamphlet caricatures, tendentious drawings, bloody satire that still breathes the bitter mood of the times into your face a century later. Ephemerally and sharp as an arrow, these revolutionary songs and drawings, born out of the need to preserve, can evoke the heat of the revolutionary season centuries later. But that belligerent tendency cannot be merely based on tone, it cannot be superficial; it must be intertwined with the organism of the work.

I compare here the age of today's radical change to the period of the French Revolution; that is why I discussed this period in more detail at the outset. What the so-called Directoire style as well as the aforementioned revolutionary caricature and satire was to revolutionary French art is today analogous to the propagandistic art demanded and cultivated by Proletkult. I have said that both are styles of the revolution, so if you find there is a qualitative decline, remember that sometimes during an uproar of arms, the Muses fall silent. This production is almost of an official partisan nature, inspired from above and ultimately considered, rightly or wrongly, as propaganda. It is a production that is disseminated by propagandistic, literary, and instructional trains in Russia.

That is enough about tendency in the narrow sense of the word, as it is commonly understood. I have said that this tendency **is not an essential characteristic of the whole of proletarian art**, but only a **distinguished trait of one of its branches**.

The essential characteristic of proletarian art is **collective feeling and sentiment**. Expressing this characteristic cannot be non-tendentious, but here I talk about tendentiousness in the broad sense of the word; not only a revolutionary slogan, but a proletarian **interpretation and viewpoint**. In truth, it is likely that other development, which will broaden the riverbed to proletarian creation, will forsake the narrow limits of political-revolutionary tendency so as to connect art with feelings and class-related, **purely collective**, thinking.

Whereas Cubofuturist art was derived from the machine of a defective civilization, we want to derive proletarian art from the person, seek it out amongst people and the crowd, the place where Charles Louis Philippe found its first hints. Among people and the crowd is where the group of so-called Unanimists sought the instrument of creation, or actually just the creator of Unanimist methods, Jules Romains. Romains's Unanimism was labeled some kind of sociological descriptive geometry, a way of thinking grounded in the fact that we are conscious of the autonomous life of the group both within the self and outside the self. Romains's view perceives the development of the individual from the prehistoric being all the way up to the author of the theory of relativity as complete and thus already inconsequential. The development of the human species, which has already begot the perfect individual, is entering into a great new era. Only at its end does Humanity come into existence. The beginning of new development is dependent on the creation of the group. Groups melt down and ravage the individual, and collective sociability and solidarity grows. Romains's poetry lives by the life of the group, it sings about how the individual is absorbed into it and about how it is the glorification of strength and feelings, which are born from human coexistence once people forsake their own seclusion.

Unanimist belief, which Jules Romains laid out in the conclusion to "The Power of Paris" ("Puissances de Paris") has its roots mainly in the sociology of Durkheim, Le Bon, and Tarde and the psychology of the crowd. It is a conscious denial of the individual and a stepping onto the path towards collectivism. Whereas Cubofuturist Civilism arouses consistent reaction in today's movement, the work of Jules Romains is a point of contact between the young movement and the past, it is a point that mediates the continuity of the line of development, that which we call tradition. The new movement, denying Cubofuturist Civilism with its art-for-art's sake and individualism, develops from Unanimism with the greatest evolutionary consistency into a stable and articulated final form: **collectivism**. Romains's Unanimism is nothing more than the first indication of this approach. He succeeded in overcoming the subjective arbitrariness of the preceding age with austere objectivism, though he did not develop it into a codified collectivist conception. Because the unity, already occurring in the whole of Romains, was accidental and occasional. It arose and vanished with the convergence and dispersal of groups. It was not an ideological oneness, a community spirit of thought. A crowd waiting on a steamer, as soon as it disperses, loses its single-minded wholeness: the isolated individual is what remains. The soul of revolutionary collectivism—pardon me for using Romains's phrasing—does not manifest in immediate and fleeting flashes—but is unceasing. The members of the revolutionary collective, which is the class, the proletariat, are not alone even where they are by themselves. Not only at a demonstration, but also at home in their attics and basements, they are a part of the crowd. But just like the work of his peers such as Chennevière, Vildrac, and Arcos, Romains's oeuvre is significant for emerging art in another sense—because through it, we are led towards the central point of the next artistic development: Charles Louis Philippe. Romains could do without an individual hero because he did not write psychological novelistic studies. His books are—**I emphasize strongly—pictures from life**, in which resides the essence of Philippe's legacy.

It is not necessary to illustrate Philippe's significance for proletarian literature here. That would require a detailed analysis of its formal structure, an aesthetic evaluation of his work. Perhaps it suffices if I say **that he is to the art of today and tomorrow *mutatis mutandis* as Verhaeren and Whitman were to the literature of yesterday**.

What is the shared characteristic of the literary branch that we call a picture taken from life and the scope of which ranges from the calendar story and the play of Matěj Kopecký, through the trashy, nickel-and-dime novel, to Philippe's "Father Perdrix," which constitutes its classical form, but which nevertheless fits here? It is a **folksiness**. A folksiness which demands the work to be comprehensible and entertaining.

If proletarian art is to conserve its positive relations to its class (which the bourgeois art, frightening to the bourgeois, was lacking) it must necessarily ask what the proletariat, up to now a pre-cultural social stratum, will demand from its art. It would be difficult to speculate which postulates a socialist society will lay down for its art in the stable post-revolutionary order. The demands laid out before it today by the proletarian-reader and spectator are clear as day. They are apparently not only aspirations for belligerent fanfare, but also the desire for an art that is comprehensible and engaging. Indians, Bufallo Bills, Nick Carter movies, sentimental novels, American TV shows or grotesque Chaplinades in the cinema, amateur theater comedy, jugglers in variety shows, vagrant singers, the equestriennes and circus clowns, folksy fiddle festivals, the Sunday soccer match: culturally, this is everything that the proletariat in its overwhelming majority lives by. The literary sorts, and many of you, will say: monsters, they are truly the only, most characteristic folk literature today. True, they constitute a badly manufactured verbal product in the same way that the furniture in a worker's room are badly manufactured products, they are the cinders of bourgeois culture, just as the laborer's quarters are a kind of junk of the industrial, capitalist city.

It is necessary to pause and think about these phenomena. There is no need to moralize them, they are most natural. After all, we know that people and the crowd are always right about themselves. It is the individual and not collective inclinations that confuse and lead astray. It is necessary to ask why A. Blok is not read amongst the proletariat as much as the anonymous author of the Buffalo Bill books. Supposedly because his verses are not able to subconsciously accommodate the aesthetic feeling of the proletariat and especially because they are not able to gain control over the whole of the moral and instinctive aspects of its being. We have to thank not only classical literature but also fairy tales and Westerns for many noble and aristocratic principles. Their life's wisdom is without a doubt more healthy, hearty and earthy than that with which *R.U.R.* and *The Life of Insects* so embarrassingly infects the audience. Just recall how beautifully Chesterton lays down the ethics of fairy tales! And just as we all adore love stories because they contain poetry of erotic excitement, we like to give ourselves over to the enchantment of astonishing tales and films because they all trigger our instinct for amazement in as much as they best oblige our burning desire for an energetic, full, active life. And why would the heroes of the cinema, Fairbanks, Chaplin, H. Carey, be of greater interest to the proletariat than the poor Frikolín and evil Dětřich, even if they are painted red in a story that calls itself Communist? The cinema and Buffalo Bill stories, I conclude, do not spoil the youth, but raise it well. It is not Fairbanks, but—pardon us—Fráňa Šrámek who spoils good manners.

Ordinary social novels and tales, and unfortunately even social films, although here and there they originate from good intentions, will not be met with success among the readers of the working class. It is not tales from the life of the pitiful nor pictures of the mine or steelworks, but pictures of the tropics and far-away lands, and the poetry of a free and active life that convey to the laborer realities and fantasies that excite and reinforce instead of a reality that crushes! The scribbler of mannered, communist rhymes does not live to see success and does not excite: only the affected gesture of the speaker, action on the movie screen, a story from an unknown, magnificent world, which will become our homeland one day, seize the proletarian heart.— — —

To the inveterate aesthete, my interpretation will seem like an unforgiveable heresy. But after all, the freedom of the creative spirit (which does not exist, by the way) does not need to concern itself with the opinions of miserable plebs. For it is still a sinful profanation of art to attempt to entertain and delight people who have not grown up in the literary salons.

But if we say that new art must be widely understandable and engaging, a very concrete and very difficult task materializes right in front of us. You must recognize that it is not the theme, but the sum of artistic work that constitutes the value of a work of art. And a little poem about the reflection of a crescent moon in a sorrowful lake, or about the roar of the industrial quarter and the proud flight of a biplane is easier to write than a good adventure novel, which should be armed with all the beautiful qualities of sensational, outcast literature as well as recognized literature on the level of culture. Robinson Crusoe and a number of novels by Verne: *Around the World in Eighty Days*, *Two Year's Vacation*, *The Mysterious Island*, *In Search of the Castaways*, etc. do not need to be defended here as literary art. How could we not be truly grateful to Verne, who has provided our astonished spirit with fantastic pictures of far away, and who at the same time enriches our understanding of people and the world, just as Dostoevsky teaches us to recognize the staggering depths of the soul?

Love the works that want to be loved—without aesthetic prejudices. Even when art that has been referred to as the most humble is not humble enough. It is after all true that the art of the picture galleries and libraries does not always teach one as much as life itself. That is why the guidance drawn by young literature from Buffalo Bills books and the cinema can be more ample and effective than that which can be drawn from Goethe or Vrchlický. And in their search, new painters do not hesitate to take into consideration not only Henri Rousseau but also the unnamed people painting. Because there, they are closer to people and life.—

Indeed, this is the essential difference within proletarian art itself: that is between the **new** popular art and existing folk art. It has been rightly said that folk art that is interesting not only ethnographically as a peculiarity but that is truly—artistically and psychologically—interesting, grew in the wasteland of life and culture. It could not expand and gain cultural importance or stylistic breadth. It was ultimately, namely as far as its form, an art derived from the style and creation of the dominant class culture; in the era of the Baroque, it lived by the elements of feudal culture, in our time, it lives by the elements of bourgeois culture. Today, if alive at all, it looks very bourgeois. Once the proletarian order is the order of the world, there will no longer be a subjugated class under the reigning social strata. The people's art will be the reigning art. This is similar to Christian art, which was in Antiquity a secondary, imitative, and immature style, only developing a cultural and stylistic breadth in the Roman period (though partly earlier in Ravenna), when a break between the old and new world was achieved. From there, it transitioned into Gothic art and developed into its most characteristic style. In socialist society, just as in the Gothic, there will be no difference between the reigning art and the undercurrent of primary production. Popular proletarian art will acquire the same strength that created the Gothic cathedrals.

I speak of proletarian art, the art of today and tomorrow, not as a social problem or a fact, but first and foremost as art, as a domain of human work. For me, it is not about its sociology or philosophy—I have only briefly attempted to examine bourgeois culture from this angle—but about determining several characteristics which distinguish it as art. I have introduced tendency and collectivism, I have introduced its folksiness. I have also attempted to determine the difference between revolutionary art, plain military and partisan art with its iron discipline, and a broader art, which does not grow from struggle but from the entirety of the life of the proletariat. I have said that this art will necessarily be collective. And to that end I have also said that adventurous and outcast literature, today effectively the only literature of the proletariat, is not actually proletarian but bourgeois literature, just as folk paintings are the refuse of higher bourgeois art. But its real folksiness, the collective agreement it finds in the broadest proletarian community, is something over which the Marxist must ponder because it certainly has deep and vital social causes. And if one thinks about it, they will find several features that show this kind of literature is adjacent to a simple mind: these are the same characteristics which are particular to the work of Philippe, whose artistry cannot be disputed. A certain extraordinariness—because Philippe made it possible for ordinary and well-known things to appear as though extraordinary and supernatural—the clarity of form and healthy, earthy Realism is unique to Primitive art. Realism, not Naturalism. Because Charles-Louis Philippe and Henri Rousseau are Realists: Lemonnier and Manet are Naturalists. There is no passageway between Realism and Naturalism; they are opposite poles and between them an abyss opens wide.

I move about only in the world of reality. I believe in reality. From there, the most fantastical pictures must be inferred. Reality is the depth of my clarity and safety; I do not doubt it even for a moment. Thus, I should not belabor it in order to exhibit my distrust in post-Kantian idealist philosophy. Impressionism and German Expressionism in their blinded lack of recognition for matter and reality have leaned on philosophical idealism. Their artistic praxis was truly barren. Oh, how much more moral and more ideal in this sense the Materialism of Henri Rousseau is!

In conclusion: I have not attempted to show why the art of today and tomorrow is proletarian; Lunacharsky has already proven that. I did not want to repeat explanations on the difference between proletarian culture, which pertains to the first phase of social revolution, a period of the dictatorship of the proletariat, and socialist culture, which emerges from the second phase, from a classless society. It should appear that proletarian art is only possible after the revolution and yet today, with the Revolution ignited in Russia only gradually engulfing the world, proletarian art is planting its first roots. With the growing class consciousness of the proletariat, a proletarian ideology arises organically. Proletarian ethics, just as proletarian art, are its constituents. I spoke about proletarian art only in so much as it is already a fact and a current issue. I spoke about literature, painting, the plastic arts, but I did not speak about architecture and the so-called art industry; a sociology of art could expand on them far better. Rather, I spoke of proletarian art as an art of the people, still existing under the thrall of bourgeois culture, and as a tendentious art, which marks the greatest effort of the belligerent revolutionary wave. I have said that since it is a collectivist art, it leads to stylization, a kind of new socialist Gothic; but in order for it to become a culture and style, it necessitates certain sociological conditions, which can only be created by a revolution. The style is not only contingent on aesthetic and, let me say, philosophical assumptions. Because there is not and will not be a proletarian architecture or proletarian theater until after the revolution. The absolute failure of Ruskin's attempts to socialize art through an art industry should be a warning; this applied art, which can most easily find its way into the worker's household, is, as approached by the German Werkbund, the Association of the Czechoslovak Werkbund and art and design schools around the whole world, **the most bourgeois** art.—

In this article, my only aim was to outline some tasks which demand a resolution from the proletarian artist; nothing more. It would not have been possible to even attempt a definite sociology of art. At a time when our Prague literary puddle—and oh, how shallow— is disturbed by a survey conducted by some asthmatic magazine asking both competent and incompetent figures their opinion on the possibility and necessity of proletarian art, it seems appropriate to me to voice my unwavering belief: either new art will be proletarian, or it will not be art at all.

(Spring 1922)

Literary Group: Our Hope, Faith, and Work

Based on a deep moral consciousness of the responsibility of each person for the development of human society, we here formulate our current stance on life and art, a stance that is the corner-stone of our hope, faith, and work. This formulation, however, is merely an outcry calling the alarm, a warning light that has flared up in our souls, a short signal designating the place and method of marshaling what is necessary in order to ensure that our life does not drown in confusion, and thereby also our art with it, but rather that both are born again new and happy.

We are socialists. The ground that nurtures us is the universal world will for the liberation of the proletariat and the creation of a new world of social balance. The proletarian is our brother. We are his co-fighters. Our socialism is a firm consciousness of the necessity of an economic revolution that will remove the oppression of the weaker classes and which at the same time will tear down many artificial barriers that stand between human hearts and prevent love and humanity. We believe, however, that this economic transformation, even though it is surely the first and essential condition for the healthy recovery of the world, will not lead of itself to a better human life, if it does not go hand in hand with a passionate cult of moral values, love, humanity, a revolution of human hearts, the final aim of which is the achievement of a grand cosmic brotherhood. Because we do not believe that the development of human society is determined by one single mechanical actor — that is, economic ***production***. We also do not believe in historical fatalism, in a predetermined inevitability of the course of world development towards an economic and social revolution. For us, ***this mechanism and fatalism*** is a doleful remnant of past times. We look at the world decidedly ***dynamically and pluralistically***. For us, the world is an enormous work in which every individual participates as one force. The direction of world development is a line of force that is the resultant of millions of impacts of individual wills.

A human being, standing in this collective act and connected with it by many bonds, receives supra-personal social commands and fulfills them; he is a participant in a social wealth of concepts, beliefs, and myths, but he also himself creates from the own needs of his heart, and through the positive results of his work he co-determines the life of the whole entity, in this way being co-responsible for its entire present and future. We declare certainly that for us it is a matter of importance that this development of the co-creating individual will should grow from pure hearts overflowing with love and humanity — because only in this way can the eventual final line of force be an improvement on the hitherto state of affairs. Basing our approach on this dynamic and pluralist view of life, we see in economic revolution only one force acting for the improvement of the world and life. If we want a real salvation of the world, we must also cultivate other forces participating in development: the hearts of every human being. Revolution cannot grow merely from hunger, but rather also from the ethical layers of the soul. And it is necessary to arouse, create, and pile up these ethical layers concurrently.

Our artistic work, our poetry, has become engaged in the service of this belief, hope, and world will. It is not an aim in and of itself. Our work wants to serve; it wants to be a means of life development. It is socially dynamic. We have adopted a certain stance towards the world by our declaration of social faith. This declaration of faith of ours constitutes a number of formulas, which at the same time are commands to action: the removal of the private-capitalist order, the liberation of the proletariat, but also the spiritual liberation of the human being as such from hatred, anger, and mustiness of heart and the creation of a new material and also spiritual world in which there would be more love, sociability, and humanity. If, however, one root of our poetry is faith, its second root is dynamic reality. In search of a moral human force capable of bearing the burden of confusion, of deflecting the selfishness, anger, and violence that are eternally emerging in the world, and of directing the good elements towards the development that we desire and in which we believe, we stand in the middle of reality in order to perceive in it the culmination of social forces and the ethos of pure hearts. We are immersing our hearts in today's proletarian life, in the mass consciousness of the crowds of worker, in order to capture the rhythm of their spiritual forces, desires, and outbursts, and to create from this psychological material preliminary images of the new worker-creator, of a new form of life, love, and marriage — a new world at the heart of which will be a good, pure human being. We are, therefore, building our poetry on the world view of the proletarian — but a new proletarian, better and purer, because we are consummating every reality with a faith, a utopia, with what should come about in future. Our poetry is, therefore, realism, enlightened by a social utopia.

Adapted to this proletarian experience and prepared by our belief, in art we aim to speak in a poetic primitivism, which is constituted by our best will to honesty and purity of work, an expression of an immediate adherence of heart to heart, and a gushing forth of the fundamental seminal experiences and feelings of the human being. In other words, we are distancing ourselves from an over-cultivated decadence and design, and from a mere rationality, from everything that does not have the burning fervor of the ***entire*** human being, the ***entire*** world, and their inseparable relationship. We despise the conceptual bourgeois world from which the old art arose. The world in the human being and the human being in the heart of the world — not as an opposition, but rather as a synthesis — this is the core of our perception of reality. We are informed of the human being as a creative cell of an enormous social tissue and we want to see the human being through the fates of the masses, classes, and entire worlds, just as we wish to see these through the human being. Our poetry does not want to be an epic chronicle of one isolated cell, nor a lyrical passivity of self-indulgent moods; it aims to be a drama of the perpetual revolution of life, one great, convulsing whole, growing with every individual and always inclining towards an ever broader and more responsible freedom. Hearts! Hearts in the middle! A tendency towards the center! Synthesis! And once again; hearts! Let us seek them! Let us create them. Let us give them to the world!

Let us transform a discord of world forces into a new, simple face of the world! Let us have the will for a firm form. Because with this will we are contributing to the creation of a new, better world. We are classicists in this desire for a new form and in our resistance against the most recent offshoots of bourgeois, disintegrative art, in which there is a terribly weak soul that does not possess the power even for the will for form.

A dynamic and dramatic poetry of social primitivism and classicism is our artistic desire and our new path, at the beginning of which we send our fraternal greetings to all social poets of the whole world.

Jaromír Berák. Lev Blatný. František Götz. Josef Chaloupka. Dalibor Chalupa.
Josef Hrůša. Čestmír Jeřábek. Miloš Jirko. Svata Kadlec. Zdeněk Kalista.
Josef Knap. Arnošt Ráž. Bohuš Stejskal. Bartoš Vlček.

Karel Schulz: Poetics

(A manual for writing verse. The first two sections include: meditative poetry. Lyric and erotic poetry. The third section includes: tendentious and revolutionary poetry.)

Tendentious and revolutionary poetry develops with the least effort and there is nothing difficult about it. In order to cheer up or amuse a worker, it is enough to write about tuberculosis, factory soot, scrofula, and similar things, and the effect is guaranteed. We offer a few examples:

The seamstress said
her hands were dead.
(Hymeš: The Seamstress)

Simply notice one thing: the foremost task is reserved for rhyme. The rhyme must jingle, cry, roar, rumble, flash, thunder, despair, believe, shoot, crack, whoop, adjoin, and ironize. Here is an excerpt from an election poem by comrade J. K.:

Vote for Baxa, make him the winner,
Prague will get its offal dinner.

Or (Hymeš: The Poor in the Hospital):

with a dog's instinct
I can predict conflict.

Here the rhyme is a bit wobbly, but it is corrected right away in the following verses:

into lungs batty
goes nothing fatty!

How enthralling! This general bizarreness has been a big plus in Hymeš's poetry lately.

Furthermore: tendentious verse must indicate a fierce passion and hatred, for example:

I would sooner run a dagger through my palate
than I'd write a tradesman's name on any ballot.

(Excerpt from an election poem by comrade J.K.) Yes, even comrades Neumann, Votoček, Němeček, and the Anonymous worker would have to admit that this is tendentious poetry, unspoilt by the fiends of Devětsil. Sometimes tendentious poetry does not have to make sense, it only has to be full of moving and hateful pictures. An example (an excerpt from the verses of comrade Slový):

Don't sit, my blue-eyed girl,
Where the stream waters whirl.
Watch out for that Mussolini
He'll make you cook his linguine
For the water-goblins!

No one really understands to *which* water goblins, but no matter, the poet was probably seduced by the beginning of that popular folk song, by the brook, etc. But just notice how masterfully Mussolini has been inserted into it! And so it continues:

Don't sit, my blue-eyed girl,
Where the stream waters whirl.
The duke will come, the master,
and that spells disaster.

Here the simplicity of the country girl is contrasted against the aristocratism of the Italian dictator, and the tendentious poem ends with a staggering picture, full of mystery and a depiction of cruelty:

Don't sit, my blue-eyed girl,
Where the stream waters whirl.
A white lion will catch you in the mud (!!!)
And properly suck out your blood.

Did you understand the gist of it? A lion, properly sucking out blood. Now, we have shown you excerpts of true verse, selected exclusively from material sent to us. Since comrades have recently been complaining about our paper having low standards, we would like to appeal to them to give the above excerpts a heartfelt read and to find the standards higher.

Jindřich Honzl: Theatrical Expressions of the Street

Advertisement

Up until now, actors have been servile spirits. They loaned themselves out to literature.

The actors of the street—servants to advertisement—are no worse. They carry cardboard sugar loaves. They lend out their bodies to Odkolek bread. They theatrically model themselves like Larionov's puppets in order to advertise Visan fat. With the purposeful, mechanical gestures of the new actor, the hired worker surprises their audience before the display window of the A. B. C. factory.

We look upon these human puppets with a dose of regret. They remind us of actors in a play by F. V. Krejčí or E. Vachek. What kind of vice are you serving?!

There would be no better servants that do not promote the bread of DZ, the margarine of FTM, and the shoes of A. J.—the non-theatricality of E. Vachek—but rather serve bread, fat, shoes, and—people (that is, the audience).

The Mask

Heroism lies in the mask. The moment an actor puts on the face of Macbeth, they become the hero of human poeticism. But this sort of heroism is a poor one. It is not so much about the actor lying, but about the lie being a pitiful one, the more pitiful the more seriously it was taken by the actor. The actor deceives our senses, which covet to fully taste the actor's heroism.

The street, the racetrack, the playground, film—they have more heroic masks. You recognize the getups of pilots. Their temperate greyness conjures stronger emotions in the modern person than the lighting at a staging of Icarus. Do you recognize the hard leather helmets of pilots behind motorized conductors as rationally formed masks of bravery? Their horror is calculated, precise. Their pathos is perfectly serious through their extravagance. Their characteristic, comprehensible form comprises hundreds of mutations of dramatic situations. They do not promise anything but what they can deliver—victory.

The mask ironically fits tightly to the human body. It covers its deficiencies. But the mask of the diver does not mock its wearer with its cumbersome ludicrousness. Only masks of actors representing demigods carry an ironic hostility towards the person wearing them. The mask of the diver is cheerful because it simulates the movements of a machine that is actually a person. It ridicules the machine disguised as a person. The safer, the more cheerful it is.

However, there are masks that are hideous in their horror. The vice of war is contained in the long and swinging, as if prolapsed, form of a gas mask. Its pointless heroism, its pointless death are the worst nightmares of modern civilization. It contains the drama of the horrors of life, the horrors of motion, and the horrors of exhaling freely. That is the principle of the drama which has become so disliked by new audiences. Where the main assumption is death.

"Death for death's sake," "civilization for civilization's sake," and "art for art's sake" are all similarly ugly slogans. Because they do not mean anything other than the end of life, the end of civilization, and the end of art.

Sport

Due to campaigners, doctors, and physical education instructors, sport is misunderstood. *Sport is theater.*

It is not the sign of a healthy century. Do not be mistaken. The successes of sport do not lie in the fact that many people play tennis. The significance of sport rests in the fact that crowds of thousands visit matches. Sport is not a healthy expression of an organically healthy individual in society. Sport is the organic symptom of unhealthy years. Sport is the subject of human poeticism. Sport is a differentiation of work just like automat-dispensed versus human-written poems are a differentiation of poetry. Sport is professionalism. Which means: strictly rational activities of creators. These provide people, the viewers, with an abundance of passionate emotions.

Look at potential athletes, women, and children in order to understand that the theatrical meaning of sport is far greater than the aim that doctors, economists, and sanatoriums have ascribed to it. *Sport does not treat neurosis. Sport presupposes it.*

The advantage of the theatricality of sport is that it is optimistic. That theatrical poeticism has attached itself to the human being. That it believes in humans, in their speed, skillfulness. That it is so generally comprehensible. And that it is able to arouse such strong sensations.

Demonstrations

The revolutionary parades and demonstrations are bad theater. They do not benefit from theatrical irony.

Good revolutionary workers are bad actors. They shoot real bullets. Their drama has not been written about in Nouvelle Revue Française or in Aktion. It is in their blood and in their hunger. Never has there been a playwright worse than these workers. There is not a whit of literature in them. They have likely not seen the lights of the Volksbühne (The People's Theater) or the Socialist Stage.

It is well known that poets are cowards. Is there anyone who would like to make workers and demonstrators into cowards?—We cannot theatrically play around with their revolutionary nature. It is dangerous and not very cheerful to put up a cardboard partition in the path of the workers' parade and then tear it down to improvise "Overthrowing Capitalism." It is trivial and ludicrous. Only a real revolution can ever be cheerful.

Demonstrations take shape only through their content. The greatest mistake is holding a demonstration which does not know what it wants to achieve. Only then does one start thinking about the red bandanas, costumed workers, and all kinds of other things.

I have heard truly poetic camp speeches and seen mightily moving demonstrations. However, I would never allow for poets to make speeches at them nor for theater practitioners to organize them.

The General Meeting of the Literary Group

On June 22nd of this year showed through its outcome an interesting phenomenon in the development of the young generation of Czech poets. Do not look upon this outcome as something that is connected to *literary politics*. No—the outcome shows a certain, general, and joyful phenomenon we can call: the dissipation of *cliquey unions*. In the post-revolutionary era, the youth rose to a literary boil in closed-off groups, collectively clarified their opinions, collectively formulated their standpoint vis-à-vis basic phenomena, and collectively built a new aesthetic. Well, the general meeting of the Literary Group marks a decisive turn away from this approach. The majority, which approved a binding collaboration between "Devětsil" and other constituents from the young generation at Host, expressed their opinion that today all of these groups and collective organizations of spiritual workers are only *amateur associations* whose aim is to collectively carry out functions that the individual could not achieve on one's own (publishing a periodical, etc.). Poets are becoming entirely spiritually *independent* from any *collectively formulated programs*, which served the purpose of guiding torches at the beginning of the poets' development—leading them through a too-vast spiritual world.

Today, the majority no longer needs torches. Today, it is not about fulfilling a program—but about a *modern creation of values*. We each go *our own way*—yet we are still certain that we will all go in the same direction. And so we join forces with our friends from "Devětsil" and with friends who are not members of a group—and we want our periodical, which we developed in the most challenging of times and have managed to retain, to be an expression of all valuable, generational creation.

This is the *raison d'etre* of the resolution of the general meeting of the Literary Group, which led to the withdrawal of some of its former members.

It was necessary to conduct this operation so that we could rebuild Host into a *new body—rich and varied*, a proper review for the young. The new Host will be *a grand periodical for the whole generation.* It will not be *eclectic*, however. The magazine will always and insistently strive to have: *a modern orientation and value.* There will be more rubrics. The circle of collaborators will be expanded. Fr. Götz will be the magazine's editor, and the editorial council will comprise of Lev Blatný, Čest. Jeřábek, Jar. Seifert, K. Teige (art section), and Jiří Ježek.

The last three years of Host have laid the foundation *for the new Host—great and truly modern. We ask our readers to remain loyal to us now that we can finally realize our greatest generational tasks, now that we are moving towards a truly broad foundation, and now that our work begins to ripen into new values.*

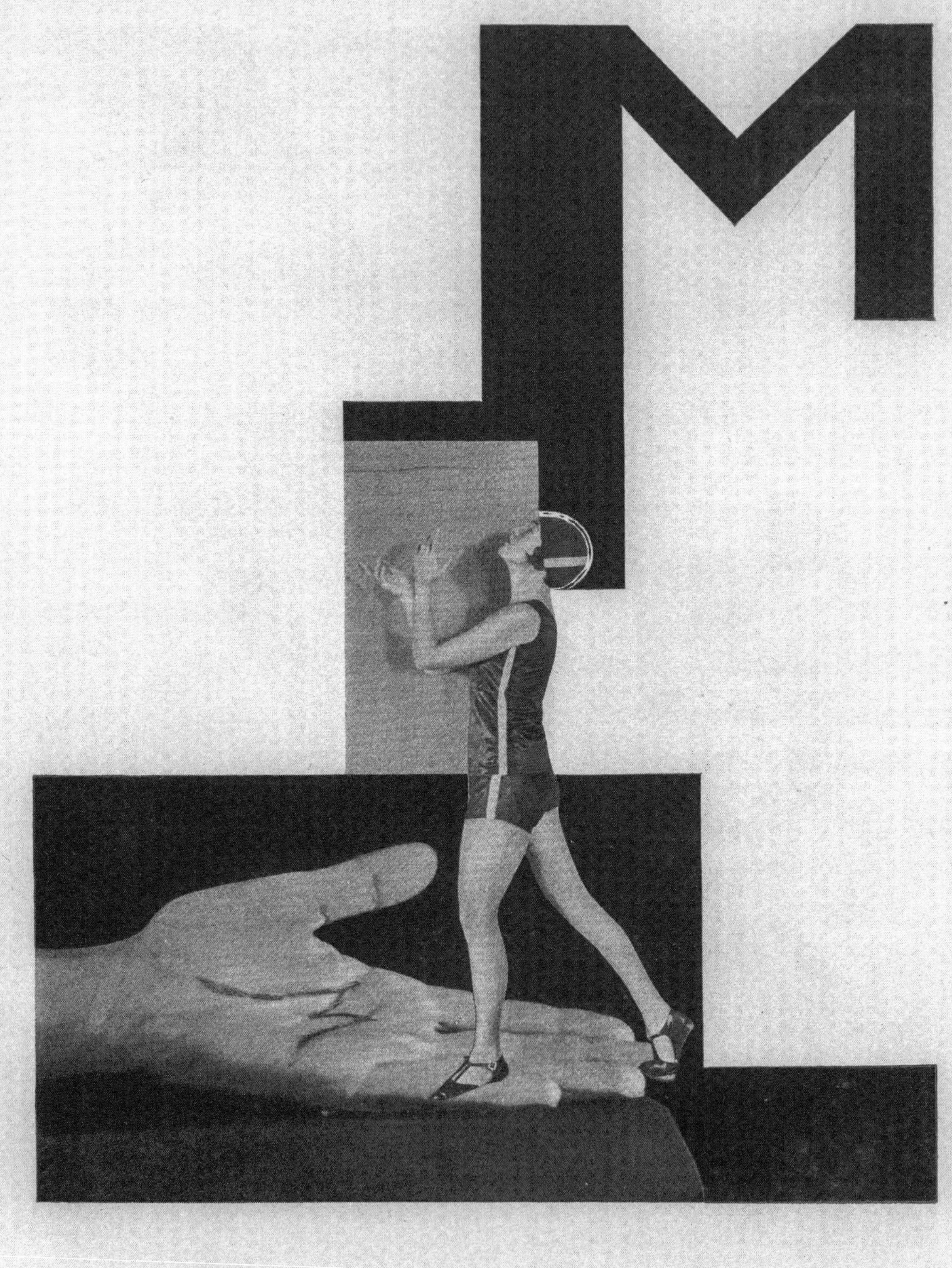
M

Chapter 2

From the World of Acrobats: Poetism and Constructivism

In the introductory text to the Devětsil almanac, in "Nové proletářské umění" (New Proletarian Art, 1922), Karel Teige proposes to writers that they focus not on "realities which grind one down", but on "visions, which impress and strengthen one." From such declarations it was but a mere step to searching for the foundations of a program promoting a vision of harmony and happiness. Already at the turn of 1923, social-revolutionary pathos was being pushed out by a faith in acrobats and dancers, and the Devětsil generation took on a direction from proletarian revolution to poetic water-lilies: "Social ideas gave way to the most subjective lyricism; the figures of workers were replaced by the figures of female dancers, and the worker's love by the poet's love. The avant-garde artistic program was formulated not only in manifestos, but was also present in contemporary literary criticism as an evaluative criterion. This criticism devoted increased attention to the fulfillment of the theoretical and programmatic postulates in the creative works of members of the avant-garde group and viewed with displeasure deviations from the group's program, which were naturally frequent."[1]

1 Ferdinand Peroutka, dramatist and journalist, systematically drew attention to the emptiness of the revolutionary slogans of the Czech avant-garde of the 1920s. In his treatise "Cesta generace od revoluce k leknínům" (The Path of a Generation from Revolution to Water-Lilies) from 1925, Peroutka evaluated the contribution of the young generation whose program had been introduced with an enormous fanfare, but which had practically immediately, in his opinion, been abandoned: "In his new book Mr. Seifert is no longer any more Marxist than a violet, expressing no more social values than a guitar, and is no more revolutionary than a besotted new husband." It became apparent that not only literary critics, but very soon also artists themselves, became aware of the unbridgeable contradiction between artistic program and artistic creation. Ferdinand Peroutka, *Osobnost, chaos a zlozvyky* (Praha: F. Borový, 1939), 61.

The world continued to show gaps in perfection and the avant-garde did not cease to work on its transformation, but it did change the instruments it used. After 1923 in the theoretical and programmatic texts of the Czech avant-garde, the new society is no longer being built by the muscles of the worker, but by the delicate hands of the magician or the acrobat.[2] Finally, the time had arrived for the prerequisites that Mahen had set out for art in the preface to his *Měsíc* (The Moon, 1920): a relaxed, pure fantasy, a liberated imagination, an art of pure fantasy, not an art that portrayed the world in a naturalistic or realist way.[3] The emerging post-war avant-garde had come of age and its adulthood paradoxically made itself apparent in a vision of the world as a circus.

In the first half of the 1920s the Czech avant-garde continued to be represented by two groups, Prague's Devětsil and the Brno-based Literární skupina (Literary Group). In a number of respects, the aims of the two clubs were similar, in spite of some specific disputes (concerning the Expressionist nature of the artistic production of the members of the Literary Group), and they cooperated closely at the magazine *Host*. However, this cooperation was brought to an end by the polemic concerning the nature of the avant-garde and modernity: following unsuccessful cooperation with members of the Literary Group, Karel Teige and Jaroslav Seifert published a declaration in number 7/8 of *Pásmo* magazine that they were leaving *Host*, because they had recognized "that only the left-wing of this generation, represented by Devětsil, is truly modern."[4] The Devětsil group continued to usurp the designation of avant-garde as an artistic direction exclusively for its own members, and in the second half of the 1920s the Literary Group and its artistic creation was shifted to the periphery of interest.

The first number of the Devětsil magazine *Disk* (edited by Jaromír Krejcar, Jaroslav Seifert, and Karel Teige, 1923) brought artistic evidence of the new aesthetic direction of the group. The magazine published Nezval's *Abeceda* (Alphabet), Seifert's poems that were later collected in *Na vlnách TSF* (On Wireless Waves), an extract from Vančura's novel *Pekař Jan Marhoul* (Baker Jan Marhoul), Šíma's comments on the visual arts, Štyrský's sketch "Obraz" (Picture), in which he argues for painting as the constructive principle of beauty in the world, and Teige's programmatic treatise

---

2 Thus, in this phase of the avant-garde even more emphasis is placed on art than was the case in the so-called proletarian phase. However, similarly to the early years, this is a case of art that does not imitate the world in a naturalistic/realistic way, but offers a depiction of the world in accord with the dominant contemporary aesthetic theories.

3 Cf. Květoslav Chvatík and Zdeněk Pešat (eds.), *Poetismus: antologie* (Praha: Odeon 1967), 116. Pešat's and Chvatík's antology *Poetismus* determined the face of Czech Poetism for a long period. For more on his phase of the Czech avant-garde, see: Thomas G. Winner, *The Czech avant-garde literary movement between the world wars* (New York; Bern; Frankfurt; Berlin; Brussels; Vienna; Oxford; Warsaw: Peter Lang, 2015). Perhaps the most extensive history of Czech Poetism is offered by Jeanette Fabian, *Poetismus: ästhetische Theorie und künstlerische Praxis der tschechischen avant-garde* (Wien; München: Otto Sagner, 2013).

4 Jaroslav Seifert and Karel Teige, "Host a Devětsil," *Pásmo*, an. 1 (1925), no. 7/8: 1.

"Malířství a poesie" (Painting and Poetry), which draws attention to the multiformity of life around the modern globe. *Disk* magazine embodied the new multi-media program. Other magazine platforms of Devětsil — *Pásmo* and *ReD* — also continued in the interconnection of verbal and visual art. Significantly, however, they focus on a new, purely Czech direction — Poetism.

This transformation of the Devětsil group's orientation was connected, among other things, with the thematic limitation of proletarian art, which prompted a search for new sources of inspiration. Already the *Život* (Life) collection in 1922 showed that the gaze of the young authors was turning away from the East in the direction of the West, towards America, the country of oceans, steamships, jazz, film, and Charlie Chaplin. Exoticism, circus, variety shows, African sculptures, totem poles, sailors — these are just a few of the fundamental motifs of Czech Poetism. A Utopian society built on harmony, love, and brotherhood are values that persist, even though in the theories of members of the Devětsil group life is newly given precedence over art. The measuring criterion of poetry and life becomes lyricism.[5] Art participates in the construction of a new world, and the new order of art is fundamental for the definition of the principles of the new artistic form. Poetism offered a complex vision of an order of life and art on a basis of dual elements — i.e., on the foundations of Poetism and Constructivism — clearly determining the form of the new art and its place in the life of human beings. In Poetism, the combination of art and life was presented as an instrument for achieving a happy, modern, and classless society. Poetism, and especially Constructivism as its second element, became the precondition for a new style which understood the experience of the modern human being in all its aspects. The requirements of modernity were applied by artists retrospectively to the initial post-war years, as illustrated by the contemporary affair "Dosti Wolkera!" (Enough of Wolker!) — a polemic from 1925 provoked by an anonymous article in *Pásmo* magazine (the authors were Artuš Černík, František Halas, Bedřich Václavek). In the article they criticized the appropriation of Wolker's

5 The new, highly lyrical prose was intended to have an emotional effect on the reader and reveal to her/him hitherto concealed and overlooked sources of poetry which reality itself has at its disposal. As a consequence of this, motifs that were dominant in prose before the Poetist craze undergo a radical transformation. The omnipotent masses and the revolutionary collective fighting for better tomorrows, the emblems of literature and deliberations about literature in the early 1920s, were displaced in the art of Poetism by an affectedly joyful relationship towards the world, which through its beauty and playfulness was supposed to function as a new "protective circle." However, neither in this conception was the relationship between the individual and the whole unequivocally resolved. The opposition between collective/masses and the isolated individual, experiencing depression and anxiety from the world/in the world, continues to be present in artistic expressions, even though it has lost its central organizing function. However, in spite of a massive enrichment through exotic motifs, the register of motifs and themes of Poetist prose still operated with motifs such as the masses, revolution, streets and big cities, the human being, and action. However, these motifs are newly found surrounded by elements with poetic (Poetist) potential, which are a source of positive emotions, entertainment, and games.

works by the bourgeoisie, who drown in sentimentality. Julius Fučík reacted to the situation that had arisen in his article "Likvidace Wolkerova kultu" (Liquidation of the Cult of Wolker), in which the framework of his defense of the poet was dictated by honesty towards the poet's oeuvre.

In 1924 Karel Teige published in the Brno magazine *Host* his first comprehensive outline of Poetism in his essay "Poetismus" (Poetism). Four years later, in 1928, the "Manifest poetismu" (Manifesto of Poetism) was published in *ReD* (no. 9), the second text setting out the program of Poetism. The third manifesto of Poetism can be regarded as being Teige's "Báseň, svět, člověk" (Poem, World, Human Being) from 1930, within the framework of which he now placed a number of key concepts of Poetism into connection with French Surrealism.

Poetism was, as Vítězslav Nezval claims, "discovered" one evening in 1924: "It was during long conversations and nighttime walks through Prague, while believing in modernity, progress, a new order, and human ingenuity; feeling our sensitivity, hating literariness, ponderousness, and careerist efforts; seeing spring come into bloom and stars move across the sky; and feeling a warm friendship, that Teige and I invented Poetism. This name of Teige's and mine, which was born one evening in a bar, was not meant to be either a program or a fashion. It expressed the need for an artistic arrangement of reality such as would be capable of satisfying all the human poetic hunger that has been ailing for centuries." The basis of artistic works of Poetism was the association of words; montage and collage became significant artistic means. In the Czech avant-garde the impulses for new sensations continue to be the world and civilization. However, new aesthetic qualities are attributed to these and they are freed from social pathos. This tendency is most clearly apparent in the case of depictions connected with the revolution, which takes on an aesthetic form, the form of a creative act: in Nezval's play-manifesto *Depeše na kolečkách* (Dispatches on Wheels, 1922, premiered in 1926), revolutionary efforts are overturned into a masquerade, a noisy swirling cabaret, a carnival procession, which transforms the world into one great poem. The role of the crowd is subject to this principle. Instead of marching workers, we follow a procession of clowns and acrobats who hold in their hands colorful juggling balls and instead of revolutionary slogans shout out programs of the new beauties of the world, while joyfully dancing ragtime on the barricades (Nezval's poem "Poetika" — Poetics — from the *Pantomima* — Pantomime — collection).

Poetism was presented as a method for looking at the world so that it would be a poem — the poem was supposed to be an expression of a new way of viewing the world and a new language, as presented by Vítězslav Nezval in his composition "Podivuhodný kouzelník" (Amazing Magician, 1922), one of the first reactions to Apollinaire's poem *Zone*. In 1924 Poetism was presented as a *modus vivendi*, a new method of modern life, in which a person would find his lost unity. It was a case of art of the human being for the human being — in Poetism the human being becomes the measure of all things. It raised the principle of poetry — lyricism — to the main dimension of life, of a humanity with folk entertainments, circus, and cabaret, and attempted an artistic rehabilitation of genres on the periphery. In Teige's deliberations, the joy and play in Poetism were presented as the crown of life, the basis of which was Constructivism. More than Soviet Constructivism, which was then culminating in the Soviet Union, Czechoslovak Constructivism represents the rational side of an artistic direction; in a certain sense a correction of free poetry, which is deputized by Poetism.

Czech Poetism was highly multi-medial. Verbal art is connected with photography and film; posters and adverts are integrated into artistic texts. The influence of photography is on the rise (e.g., Jaroslav Rössler and Jaromír Funke). According to Teige, the beauty of photography corresponds to the beauty of modern technology, and therefore he appeals to a modernly trained sight that intensifies the visual character of the texts and to a new typography.[6] In Poetism emphasis was placed on the current-day world, on the visual aspect of art that stimulated a path to an art for the five senses. The original pictorial poems — works on the boundary of poetry, assemblage, and collage — became a symbol of visual poetry. Avant-garde authors made use of the approaches of the Dadaists, the Constructivists, and typographists, and connected, among other things, postcards with photographs, pictures with newspaper cuttings and maps. Pictorial poems often served as models of short lyrical films — the authors published a series of "cinematic" poems, literally scores of lyrical films that were never actually produced. Poetist motifs are repeated in these: transatlantic steamships, the sea, exotic places and people, and so on.

Innovative typographical approaches were used in Nezval's *Pantomime* — an original multimedia project that incorporated a multitude of genres and secondary forms (poems, paintings, programmatic essays). Nezval's "Alphabet," originally printed in the *Pantomime* collection in 1924, was published again in 1926 with Karel Teige's typography and with photographs of Milča Mayerová's choreographic creations, representing dance figures inspired by "Alphabet." A theater performance was given in the same year at the Osvobozené divadlo (Liberated Theater). In accordance with the requirements from Teige's study "Painting and Poetry," the performance's multi-media expressions are an attempt to find a new language of poetry: "Aesthetics becomes *photogenic and vitalistic* [...] A PICTORIAL POETRY arises. A *cinematic art*. Biomechanics is the only dramatic spectacle today. Sport, cinema."[7] Included in the *Pantomime* book was the essay "Papoušek na motocyklu čili o řemesle básnickém" (Parrot on a Motorcycle, or on the Craft of Poetry), in which Nezval criticizes the old method of creation and argues that the main aim of art should be to provoke emotion. In accordance with this, the child and a child's point of view take on a fundamental significance in Poetist creation, as noted by film and theater director Jindřich Honzl in this epilogue to *Pantomime*: "People who like to

6 Regarding Czech avant-garde typography, cf. in particular the specialist work of Jindřich Toman, *Foto/montáž tiskem = Photo/montage in print* (Praha: KANT, 2009).

7 Štěpán Vlašín (ed.), *Avantgarda známá a neznámá* 2: *vrchol a krize poetismu: 1925–1928* (Praha: Svoboda, 1972), 495, 496.

wallow in problems must be referred to the child, who discovers truths."[8] Similarly, a new, highly lyrical prose had the aim of emotionality impacting the reader and revealing to them the hitherto concealed or overlooked sources of poetry that reality itself offers (among others, Vančura's *Rozmarné léto* — Capricious Summer, 1926 — Schulz's *Dáma u vodotrysku* — Lady at the Fountain, 1926). The literary approaches of Poetism placed a greater emphasis on sensibility and the imagination, distant from conventional logic. If we are to generalize, then the epic schema of Poetist prose is falling apart and is rather creating "narrative epigrams" (Bedřich Václavek). The (fictional) world consists of fragments, laid out horizontally, to the breadth of the whole world. The fundamental space of Poetist short stories and novels is not the room, a space clearly defined by four walls, but the entire planet, comprising all continents, and if the place of action is a city, then this is no longer a barren place of hopelessness, but rather a source of life and intoxication. In particular in the prose of Karel Schulz and Karel Konrád, scenes inside the city are captured in fast succession, as though by a manically revolving lens, giving always only a limited slice of reality, isolated from other slices, and often concluded by a (desired) point. The graphic lay-out of these prose works also evokes the cinematic technique.[9] Poetist writers sought the sources of poetic imagination in all spheres of human life.

However, the roots of Poetism lie in post-war proletarianism. The beauty of the current world was supposed to overcome the chaos of the post-war world. In his manifesto "Poetism," Teige advanced a vision of a world that laughs (this was the title of a collection of studies from 1928). However, the whole motto is this: "The art that is brought by Poetism is nonchalant, frolicsome, fantastical, playful, unheroic, and amorous. There is not a speck of Romanticism in it. It was born in an atmosphere of exuberant sociability, in a world that laughs; no matter that tears are running from its eyes." The conception of a radical renewal of the world through joy, beauty, and laughter is already from the beginning qualified. Teige is not writing about tears accompanying wild fits of laughter, but about laughter that drowns out and covers up tears.

Through the prism of Poetism, all elements of the artistic process were newly understood and consequently defined. Its relationship to technology was revised (beauty ceased to be the exclusive prerogative of art) and the field of aesthetic eval-

---

8 Jindřich Honzl, "K Pantomimě", in Vítězslav Nezval, *Pantomima* (Praha: Akropolis, 2004), 139–140 (p. 140).

9 Schulz's novel *Lady at the Fountain* is divided into short paragraphs, the connection between which is blurred by diversions, lyrical passages, and so on. On account of these approaches, the prose takes on the atmosphere of a grotesque. The characters do not act logically (in so far as they act at all, because quite often any kind of plot is absent) and the story lines are not in any way psychologically motivated. The characters in the short stories and novelas also often lack any name and are characterized either by gender (man or woman) or by their profession (detective, prostitute, magician). Their corporeality is deranged, animal; they wildly cut up ears and howl like wolves. Posters, African-Americans/black people, jazz, and similar are inserted (rather automatically).

uation was extended to modern civilization as a whole. Engineers and architects become the creators of the new beauty, because beauty is defined by function, purpose. The definition of the poet and her/his role in the new art also undergoes a transformation. While in the period of the tendency towards proletarian art we could envisage the definition of a poet in the studies of Karel Teige as the equation poet = worker; in the period of Poetism Teige inclines towards the following solution: poet = clown or acrobat; the definition is however always qualified by a Constructivist corrective: poet = citizen.

It was necessary to newly define the relationship between art and reality. In his article "Kapka inkoustu" (A Drop of Ink), Vítězslav Nezval expressed the need for an artificial arrangement of reality, so that the world became a poem. According to theorists of the period, the artist should radically change reality without in any way making this intervention a theme in his creative work. Therefore, Nezval writes about the need to view things in new associations and about the need for an *artistic* intervention in reality. Under the colorful crust of Poetist pictures there continued to hide a world that was still rather terrifying and which had not yet undergone the longed-for transformation, the craved liberation.[10]

An attempt at an aesthetic synthesis of Poetism and Constructivism — that is, construction and poetry, emotionality and rationality — was presented by Karel Teige in his collection of studies *Stavba a báseň* (Construction and Poem, 1927). The proposal of a dualism between purposeful creation and pure art was accompanied at the end of the 1920s for the first time by the first voices of exhaustion, of the end of Poetism, of Poetism as a corpse. Vítězslav Nezval reacted to this declaration in his article "Návěstí o poetismu" (A Notice about Poetism, 1927), in which he rejects burying Poetism alive. In connection with the liberation of painting, a liberation of words also took place, as indicated by Teige in his study "Slova, slova, slova" (Words, Words, Words, 1927). These are no longer the liberated words of Marinetti; the aim of this conception is an autonomous poetic language. In 1927 Karel Teige wrote: "The word deceives. It is the attire of our illusion and it seems to designate reality." The word as a kind of material is undergoing a crisis, claims Teige. He connects this crisis with the avant-garde fascination with technology, with the period of planes and radio waves. In a certain sense this felt crisis of the fundamental material of

10 The artistic productions fulfilling the characteristics of Poetism had a very free relationship to reality. Bedřich Václavek characterized epic prose by saying that it ended in a "denial of itself, a denial of the literary verbal type by itself. Today the referential function, bearing witness of the world, has been taken away from prose, primarily by cinema and journalism, which fulfill it better. Prose is coming to abandon the epic, a logically developing story line. All that remains for it is the emotive, poetic function." Bedřich Václavek, *Od umění k tvorbě. Studie z přítomné české poesie* (Praha: J. Fromek, 1928), 130. Even though according to the manifestos, prose was supposed to construct a new reality of a new world, in reality it had a very loose relationship to the reality of the world. For the creation of living characters and a complicated fictional world, Poetism — with some very few exceptions — did not offer adequate means.

literature suits Teige — he makes use of the uncertainty of the word for his defense of Poetism, the viability of which was repeatedly called into question by authors from outside the Devětsil group. After 1927, Teige himself was forced to pose the question of whether "Poetism is dead," to which Vítězslav Nezval replied somewhat ambivalently: "Poetism is dead? Long Live Poetism!" In the context of the crisis of the word, Poetism appears as a solution to the situation. In his deliberations Teige presents this artistic direction as a kind of unique possibility for creating poetry without words, working with material more solid than words — that is, with light, color, scents, sound, movement, and energy.[11]

In 1928 Jaroslav Seifert published his extensive treatise on Guillaume Apollinaire in *Tvorba* (Creation) magazine, declaring the allegiance of the Czech avant-garde to his legacy, in particular to his method of the long poem. In a number of passages in "Manifest Poetismu" (Manifesto of Poetism, 1928) Teige also returns to Apollinaire's concept of an open poem. Apollinaire's pictorical poems serve Teige as a base for his system of a synthesis of painting and poetry and a poetry for all the senses. Here Teige puts forward a vision of an absolute, universal poetry for all senses. He also continues to endeavor to defend a world of harmony and happiness, even though poetry collections by poets whose association with the poetics of the avant-garde was very loose had already appeared under the patronage of Devětsil — František Halas's *Sépie* (Squid), Vilém Závada's *Panychida* (Memorial Ceremony, both 1927), or the poetry of Vladimír Holan — works showing the slogan of harmony and happiness as unsustainable. Karel Teige chose a developmental strategy such that these collections also could be interpreted as key works of Poetism within its framework. He interprets Závada's *Memorial Ceremony* as an enrichment of Poetism, even though in many respects Závada's poem is anti-Poetistic. However, the exhaustion of Poetism was already evident and many authors who stood on the opposite pole of the Czech avant-garde (and were also in personal dispute with Teige) commented on the decline of Poetism. In order to draw attention to the bankruptcy of Teige's system of Poetism and the crisis of avant-garde approaches, Zdenek Rykr introduced his article "Teigism" (1927) with the motto:

---

11 How, though, to make use of such material in the verbal arts? The short story genre reacted only after a delay to the first manifestos of the Literary Group and Devětsil and in the early period, the "raw image" fulfilling the manifestos was to be found rather in poetry and drama. However, after 1924, prose gains the status of a reliable literary form that is capable, practically literally, of providing an artistic depiction of the fundamental postulates of Poetism. As one of the most literal we can designate Vančura's *Capricious Summer* (1926). Nevertheless, to overstate somewhat, this presentation of a joyful and playful world goes on par with the manifestos in presenting the kind of world that the avant-garde desired, and not the world as it is in reality. For many, a false relationship to reality is characteristic for Poetist prose, because it is not based on the current real world, but presents a world that, in the terminology of fictive worlds, approaches a supernatural/hybrid world. Cf. Lubomír Doležel, "Radikální sémantika: Richard Weiner a Franz Kafka," in *Studie z české literatury a poetiky*, trans. by Bohumil Fořt (Praha: Torst, 2008), 70–76.

"Let the young have their fling." This crisis culminates in a series of polemics conducted by Jindřich Štyrský in *Odeon* magazine. In his study "Želva, o které se nikdo nezmiňuje" (The Turtle That No One Mentions, 1927) Jiří Voskovec criticized the orientation of the Poetists toward life accompanied by slogans, arguing that art has ceased to be art. He warns against the possibility that art itself will become a turtle that no one mentions. Voskovec is referring to the over-production of theories in the context of the art of Poetism and he rejects heavy programs and manifestos.

Poetism also influenced theater. Devětsil had two independent theater sections, one in Prague and the other in Brno. In 1925 the Liberated Theater (officially started on 8 February 1926) was founded in Prague. Theater directors Jiří Frejka, Emil František Burian, and Jindřich Honzl participated in its foundation. Following conflicts, in 1927 E. F. Burian together with Jiří Frejka founded Divadlo Dada (Dada Theater) and in 1933 Déčko ("D" in Czech: the theater changed its name every year; the letter D was supplemented by the last two numerals of the year). Déčko became a center of progressive theater which combined projects on the boundaries of the visual, literary, and musical arts.

In 1927 Jiří Voskovec and Jan Werich joined the Liberated Theater. Their first play *Vest Pocket Revue* (1927) combined scenes on the stage with *forbína* (from the German Vorbühne), in front of the curtain. These improvised scenes, rather a Dadist-Poetist *Zone* poem, became the basis of plays popular with audiences. At the end of the 1920s, Werich and Voskovec were joined by Jaroslav Ježek, whose musical accompaniment was influenced by the American music scene, in particular by jazz.

In the visual arts, the closest theory to that of Teige's identification between the painter and the poet was Artificialism, an original direction of painting that was developed from the mid-1920s by Toyen (Marie Čermínová) and Jindřich Štyrský. They presented their conception of Artificialism in 1926 in a brochure, and then more extensively in the study "Populární uvedení do artificielismu" (Popular Introduction to Artificialism, 1927). Teige offered his own definition in the study "Ultrafialové obrazy, čili artificielismus" (Ultraviolet Pictures or Artificialism, 1928). According to Teige, Štyrský and Toyen awaken a dialog of the conscious with the unconscious and their pictures create an ultraviolet, supra-conscious world, a poetry of lines and colors. In their pictures from the end of the 1920s, vegetative and organic elements dominate. In Toyen's painting there is an evident interest in life (living things) that is only just beginning; it places a great emphasis on the transformation of matter. A blending of faces and a surprising revelation of internal spaces are typical for the paintings that she presented at the Poesie 1932 exhibition. Although in some aspects the artistic style of Štyrský and Toyen recalls Surrealism, at the end of the 1920s Štyrský was still criticizing this direction as a "historicizing form of painting." In his 1928 lecture "Básník" (Poet) Štyrský commented on the Surrealists: "Subconsciousness is a gag that many stick into their mouths in order not to have to think any more." Nevertheless, hand in hand with the abandonment of sensory enchantment in Poetism, there is an increasing interest on the part of poets and visual artists in dreams and the subconscious.

In 1930, the treatise "Poem, World, Human Being" was published as the third manifesto of Poetism. It initially appeared in *Zvěrokruh,* and was printed in a revised version as the second part of the concluding chapter of *Poezie pro pět smyslů* (Poetry for the Five Senses, 1928), or the second manifesto of Poetism in the book *Svět, který voní* (The World That Smells Nice, 1930). Here Teige summarizes the fundamental aspects of Czech inter-war Poetism and also indicated some further steps for it. In many respects this treatise represents Teige moving towards the standpoints of French Surrealism, as expressed in Breton's second manifesto from 1930. Teige here analyzes the development of painting and poetry and the changes in their relationship to society. According to Teige, with the onset of new artistic forms it is necessary to abandon traditional methods of classification and the categories of idealist aesthetics — hitherto art belongs in the collections of museums and galleries, as an object of research and archaeological interest. In his opinion, this is not merely a conviction about the rise of the avant-garde from "point zero," but also of the need for social reconstruction, because art should not stand apart from the serious questions of society, and in particular it should not stand apart from social revolution. In Teige's overview, poetry based on new discoveries from the fields of chemistry, sociology, and optics is newly enriched by discoveries in the field of the libido and Freudian sexual theory. In Teige's deliberations, revolution is still a path to the liberation of society, but at the same time also to the liberation of human forces (even those concealed ones).

In the early 1930s an extreme leftist group (Julius Fučík, Bedřich Václavek) formed on the Czech cultural scene, and the theme of the relationship between Marxism and literature appeared. In 1929, Klement Gottwald was elected to the leadership of the Communist Party and the party's orientation shifted significantly towards the policy of Moscow.

In 1930 Devětsil falls apart and is replaced by the Levá fronta (Left Front) organization, oriented towards the propagation of socialist culture. From the point of view of the history of the Czech avant-garde, the end of the 1920s seem like a crossroads — in a certain sense this is reflected in the "generational discussion" that was provoked on the pages of *Odeon* magazine by Jindřich Štyrský. The discussion concerned the death and possible resurrection of the avant-garde and the crisis of criteria; surrealism comes into play as a source of artistic inspiration. However, an entirely new feature is the reception and translation of articles, manifestos, and artistic works of Anglo-American literature. The Czech inter-war avant-garde opens up to themes that until now have been outside its area of interest. Nevertheless, it poses as its aim to continue to be highly avant-garde — that is, in the way that it defined this term at the beginning of the 1920s.

Karel Teige: Foto Kino Film[1]

Modern art. New art. These adjectives were overused and abused and *epitheton ornans* became *epitheton constans* until both are deprived of all faith: all things new are distrusted (because the instinct of the public is always conservative), and the *modern* was wrongly identified with *modish*. And at that: it has stopped being modish to be modern: many New Classicists endeavor at all costs to be fundamentally old-fashioned. As has been acknowledged, nothing gets old as quickly as modernity, but instead of recognizing that as a consequence of this, the new and modern should be revived in perpetuity, over and over supplied with topicality and innervated with active vitality, refuge was sought in eternal values. The Egyptian pyramids, East Asian sculptures, Greek temples, Gothic cathedrals, Baroque palaces have been around for centuries and millennia: what is modern is the Big Wheel or the Eiffel Tower and yet, today the Big Wheel is no longer and the days of the Eiffel Tower are numbered. Apollinaire would need to select another shepherdess for his poem about the world, "Zone," to watch over the bleating herd of the Paris bridges, and Jean Cocteau, the delicate, modern, and ironic spirit who proclaims himself amongst the "opponents of modernity," would be obliged to find another setting for his charming play "The Wedding Party on the Eiffel Tower" than a place as magical and poetic as the first-floor platform of the tower. It is not my task to prove that the eternity of the Egyptian pyramids or the Doric temples in comparison to the ephemerality of the Eiffel Tower or the Big Wheel ultimately lies solely in the material they are built of—in stone and iron—and not at all in "artistic values"; at the same time, I do not want to defend the opinion that there is no other truth than ephemeral truth, which could be an opposite extreme, without intending to show

1 This is an original translation. However, a previous translation by Kevin B. Johnson in *Cinema All the Time* exists and was referenced.

that all so-called timeless works were the height of modern in their time, that contemporaneity is one of the preconditions of the yearned-for timelessness, that the contemporary, topical, modish, and modern Seurat is more assured in this "timelessness" than the outmoded and lofty Bouguereau, even if the colors of his canvases were to blacken. There is no sense in elaborating upon and discussing this, and this is not the place for it. I only want to deliver a single assertion:

**MODERNITY IS NOT AN EMPTY WORD,
BUT A PRIVILEGE AND AN ACHIEVEMENT.**

There is no need to give extensive proof of this assertion. Each reality of the world verifies it, everything is an argument *in its favor*. The Red Star Line is rather more perfect than the vessels of the Argonauts. The Goliath airplane is rather more perfect than the mythological wings of Icarus or even the first Montgolfier balloons. You would most certainly prefer to travel in the Pullman cars of express trains than in an idyllic stagecoach. Radiotelegraphy is vaster than signaling with torches or carrier pigeons. Modern medicine is something that the old hack charlatan healer could not have imagined. Yes, modernity, being an achievement and a privilege, is simply ascension and advancement.

But, you might object, art does not know advancement. It has been explained and repeated emphatically that progress in art is incomparable with advancement in the world. Progress, as in a succession of constant change; advancement, as in ascension and the accumulation of achievements. Those who do not differentiate between the concepts of "progress" and "advancement" and rather equate one to another then ultimately assert that art cannot see progress, and thus one cannot apparently presume that the works of Picasso or Derain are at a higher level than Giotto, Negro sculpture, or the paintings of Cretan culture.

Progress in the sense of advancement exists only in matters of the concrete needs of life and in science, and not at all in philosophy or the arts, unless we take into consideration that long interim periods of decline can occur even there. In that case art today is not a matter of concrete human needs. The shape of the violin, for example, was developed for a long time until an absolutely perfect, functional, and suitable shape was found, subsequently becoming unchanging and standardized; and here its development ceased: perfection, a standard, was achieved, and standardized production set in. So it is and will be with other products of human work. This also applies to technology, mechanical and civil engineering, and it could also be the same with architecture if it were indeed concerned with construction instead of what it ambitiously wants to be—applied art, decorativism. But this is different when it comes to art as there can be no talk of advancement, ascension and an accumulation of achievements corresponding to the passing of years. Truly, in abstract and absolute terms, neither Paul Cézanne nor Henri Rousseau are "more advanced" or "more perfect" artists than Ghirlandaio or Fra Angelico. But nevertheless, it is possible to speak about advancement and perfection in a relative sense of a specific dominating tendency in a specific span of time: the Impressionism of Monet and Renoir is more advanced than the Impressionism of Manet, or perhaps even Turner; the post-Impressionist synthetism of Derain is more perfect than the early beginnings of Cézanne. And what is more: we can speak about advancement in the arts when talking about all ages, including when art was also a matter of concrete human need, when it was a part of the world and of life, one of its important realities, subject nevertheless to the achievements of a specific period, to the ample possibility for advancement with hardly any limitations. Regrettably, today's art has divorced itself too much from today's world: today the world and life are modern, intense, refined and ever refining, advanced and progressive: the art of the atelier wants to be non-modern and timeless, pure in its absoluteness, classical and unalterable, mystical.—

We have started off with these remands,

first, because I attempted to show that modernity, which is a privilege, an achievement, advancement, and perfection, is not ephemerality, but that it rather encompasses progress aimed towards more or less absolute perfection, towards *standardization*, unceasing life force and eternity,

and second, because I want to speak about art that is irreproachably new and modern, which presupposes progress as unceasing advancement and refinement, a steady march towards a paramount, higher perfection, and not progress as merely an occasional, periodical transformation of character. I want to speak about art which was born recently from scientific advancement and the desire of the human heart, which is not an aesthetic matter of the atelier, but an important event of far-reaching public significance on a global, life scale: that is to say, about

THE CINEMA.

The invention of the CINEMATOGRAPH enriched art with a new field, it almost literally discovered the wheel, a new world—it discovered art in America. And just as America was known before Vespucci and Columbus, just as it is impossible to ascribe the discovery of gunpowder to Roger Bacon alone, or the printing press to Gutenberg, just as Franklin and Prokop Diviš both discovered the lightning rod and Nikola Tesla and Marconi the radiotelegraph, the cinematograph is not the exclusive work and discovery of Edison or the Lumière brothers. Never, strictly speaking, is it possible to ascribe a great invention to a single person: a big discovery is not anything but the outcome of a long collective effort that always has multiple predecessors and origins reaching far back. Any great occurrence, grand accomplishment, is always the result of a collaboration and the inventor is nothing but one worker within a larger community. Einstein's theory would be unthinkable without his predecessors.

The cinema, born not long ago as an invention of a new age, is evidence nonetheless of a specific tradition with forbears centuries old. These are, in part, *Chinese shadow boxes*, which are based on the idea of projecting a moving image on a flat surface. This invention was brought over to Europe in the 18th century; at that time, shadow theaters opened in Versaille and the Palais Royal in Paris—; Henri Rivière and Caran d'Ache, well-known humorist caricaturists of the 1880s, screened "*French Shadows*"—delicately drawn and finely articulated silhouettes cut from zinc plates—in the Théâtre d'Application and later in the cabaret Chat Noir in Montmartre. The direct predecessor of the cinema is then Anasthasius Kirchner's invention of the *Laterna magica*, which, connected to the phantasmascope that allows for the rotation of color slides, made it possible for Cagliostro to simulate his wonders and for Robertson to reveal to astonished Parisians enigmatic phantasmagoria in a Capuchin cloister. Once Reynaud combined the Laterna magica with the praxinoscope, a first step was made towards the film projection apparatus. More detailed inventions continued in parallel, ushering in new achievements in the realm of photography, such as the Janssen astronomic revolver, Faye's chronophotography, the invention of film, Edison's biograph and bioscope—until finally in 1895, the company of the Lumière brothers projected cinematographic pictures and *the first cinema in the world* was opened in the Salle des Conferences on the Boulevard des Capucines. Painting in motion, formerly a laughable utopia or the secret of black magic sorcery, became reality and its mere existence exceeded all expectation: life itself entered onto the projection screen. No one knew then that they were standing at the threshold of a great future; the sentiment of the day was that such projections were a passing fad and would cease to draw the attention of the public, and that the perfected Laterna magica would serve scientific work only. Instead, the cinema has seized the whole world, operating everywhere, it is an unprecedented, bold new spectacle enjoyed by audiences all around the globe; today there are more than 70,000 cinemas worldwide.

And so cinema was born in a century of new discoveries, new lights, in a century when optics, the science of light, became the science of miracles, as Descartes had prophesied centuries before; an art born from this has become an art of miracles, a miracle in and of itself. With wonderful and dizzying speed, it develops, its advancement perceptible from one day to the next. The achievements of the centuries, from Chinese shadow boxes and the Laterna magica to the apparatus of the Lumière brothers, have been overtaken by the development of the cinema: if you compare the first French films, their small tableaus and stories, which are still being shown, for example at the Variété-biocope, with today's American sagas or a D. W. Griffith drama or something directed by Th. Inc., you will see a previously unimaginable improvement in quality and swift technical refinement. So we, contemporaries of these first decades of the celebrated, great, and revolutionary 20th century, assist in the birth of this new, celebrated art, indeed the real modern and contemporary art, the most vital and intense of all: the newness of it is an important cultural factor and not merely the trendy *haute nouveauté* or a seasonal curiosity: its strong, living, and enthralling beauty speaks to the public, which does not want to be lectured at and educated, but asks for sensory experience above all, such as those who are not permitted into the realms of today's class-based pseudo-culture (ach! Panem et circenses...!). Immeasurable strength lies in the popularity, accessibility, and absolute internationality of film, which speaks to crowds of all the nations and races of our planet: it is a proud hymn of the beauties of the world and can be an effective weapon in the service of human revolutionary ideals.

Marcel Raval, the young French writer, quipped that modern poetry was born from Arthur Rimbaud and the mechanical fairy. Cinema, like nearly everything in this world, is also a child of mechanics (of the machine) and of human ideal; however, being a successor to the formerly illustrious and powerful art of the theater, which is now sick and dying, and in the consortium of constituent arts, it is characterized by a far more complex origin. The cinema, whose family tree we observed moving along the maternal line from the shadow pictures to Laterna magica, via the invention of the Daguerrotype and chronophotography, up to the Lumière brothers' discovery, is associated with the scientific, technical, and optical tradition, but also another tradition still, that— for lack of a better term—we shall call "artistic." Yes, cinema is something "*beyond art*": the lyric, the epic, the novel, the drama, the satire, the comedy, visual beauty, music, acting, dancing; in short, all the arts united in a beautiful synthesis. Cinema is a fine art, cinema is an art of spectacle (something like the theater), cinema is poetry, cinema is ballet, fluctuating and simultaneous. The future aesthetic of the cinema, to which there are already some valuable contributions—mainly the writings of the intelligent and astute **Louis Delluc** (Photogénie, Ceinéma et Cie, Charlot)—wanting to define the particular, new, and universal beauty that is characteristic of film, must above all define the relationships

OF CINEMA TO THE VISUAL ARTS
OF CINEMA TO LITERATURE
OF CINEMA TO THE THEATER

PHOTOGRAPHY mediates the relationship and interconnection of cinema with the visual arts, with painting. Film is a cinéplastique art, just as dance is méloplastique; it is a living light painting, a reanimated picture. Its technical advancement, so fast and remarkable from its beginning through to current productions, is mostly contingent on the continuous refinement of photography because the beauty of film is first and foremost neither literary nor dramatic, but PHOTOGENIC.

The representatives of modern painting are above all the French, or better put: Montparnasse in Paris is the homeland of modern painting. The homeland of photography today is England and especially *America*. The Cabots and Yankees took hold of photography when it was still the primitive, embryonic Daguerrotype (which was, from the start, but especially from the last third of the 19th century, characterized by a certain visual expressiveness, generosity, and simplicity, well-balanced drawing, modeling, and elegant compositions, in short by the beautiful pictorial qualities that Josef Čapek astutely describes in his interesting book "An Art Most Humble"), and made it into the magnificent **PHOTOJOURNALISM** of today, *journalistic and documentary* photography which has a powerful charm and its own poetry; illustrated weeklies and picture magazines of England and America are a *modern cabinet of curiosities*. That which was once the French and European Empire style of picture-making is today the American illustrated magazine. And this modern photography, even a snapshot, has as much beauty in itself as a documentary, labor-intensive, Empire-style engraving, which is admired by not only the modern spirit but also the collector of antiquity. The beauty of a photograph, just like the beauty of works of modern technology, lies in simple and absolute perfection and is conditioned by its purpose: the beauty of photography is from the same stock as the beauty of the airplane, the transatlantic steamer or the electric light bulb: it is the work of an instrument and at the same time the work of the human hand, the human brain, and, if you like, even the human heart; the physiochemical production process, development, bath, exposure, etc., are all controlled by a person, by their ability and skill: photography is no less a human art because the photographer's capabilities have been multiplied and granted more control through the mechanical, flawlessly functioning brain of the camera, which does not care to be violated by the ever-changing tastes of the salon, but which wants to *standardize* the beauty, aesthetic, and order of photography. The refinement of photography multiplies its beauty, intensifies its clarity, realism, documentary quality—properties which are all inherent to photography and which are made poor use of by common "artistic" European photography, the senselessness of which I will touch on here. When a perfect photograph is brought to life on the movie screen, on that grey surface of our worldly heaven (in the words of Ivan Goll), we are shown the dizzying epic of life without cunning or duplicity, the visual drama (photogénie) of everything in the world, and you see that it is truly photography more than any other art that is best inclined to interpret most precisely and authentically the rhythm, poetry, and ceaseless drama of global events; the filmstrip can encompass more beauty in the world than the hymnal poem—take Apollinaire's "Zone": his lyric is not literary, soaked in alizarin or printer's ink, but immediate and real. It is reality. And reality does not need to have its praises sung in order to be beautiful, captivating, and poetic. It just is; and thus it is captivating, marvelous, and poetic. Léger's pictures of machines, or Marinetti's poem "À mon Pégase" do not supply the machines and limousines with their beauty; the beauty of the machine and the automobile is the beauty of reality and pure form, which does not need to be all made up with ornament or festooned by poetry. Yes, *the morality of photography lies in its realism and truthfulness*, for veracity is always considered a virtue and corresponds with the function for which photography was invented. Photography is the liberator of painting from naturalism, that foul-smelling mildew which ate away at its firm and constructive visual laws: with the intervention of photography, it was made clear that the aesthetic of painting should henceforth be anti-naturalistic and that it should have a new mission, a new concrete task and a new role in modern life. The credit due to photography for saving painting from Impressionism is enormous, but painting has repaid the favor poorly: it has infected photography with Impressionism, resulting in artistic photography, somewhat like an art industry, a false art...And with regards to cinégraphie, it is fitting to give preference to American photographic culture and opinion over Latin, French, and Italian directed pictures, which are capable of playing with light, shadow, and chiaroscuro with uncommon taste, and eliciting superb, lyrical effects (for example in the films *Mater Dolorosa*, *The Tenth Symphony*, *J'accuse*! and other productions of the Pathé company), but which sometimes are too tempted by artistic photography: "artistic-ness" presents indisputable danger for film and often the cowboy Westerns has more photogenic and dramatic beauty than a film d'art.

But what a splendid, photogenic reality American films afford us, full of strength just as they are full of tenderness. We have seen perfect shots of dark and rainy nights, the transparency of rain drops falling in the pellucid darkness of space (*Daddy Long Legs*, *Bread*, etc.), the lighthouse flood light reflecting off the fog of night, an arc lamp at a New York dock on a damp evening, the opalescence of electric advertisements at sky-scraper heights above the big city streets. The magic of filmic and photographic chiaroscuro is not borrowed from Rembrandt or Leonardo: it is even more captivating. But it is not only the poetry of the night, of darkness and the effects of artificial lights, the electric nights of the big cities, that is the object of photography and film. Daylight, clear and glorious, the azure heavens above the plains of California, the pampas or the mountains of Mexico! For let us not forget that photo and film are not mere hunters of artificial lighting effects: they are above all documentary. They offer evidence and proof that the world is beautiful, and as such the mere reality of film and photography disproves all the nonsense of pessimistic philosophy. Up until the discovery of the cinema and the refinement of the camera, philosophy could pronounce that reality does not exist, that all is an illusion. A single number of an illustrated weekly, a single film clip—maybe of airplanes taking off or the Gaumont newsreel—is irrefutable proof of the existence of reality, a direct demonstration of the multifaceted drama of modern life. Philosophy lied. Photography does not and cannot lie.

Or rather, photography only lies if it becomes "artistic." It is falsity, pretense, and ultimately the qualitative degradation of intrinsic, inherent beauty. Photography does not need a gallery-style chiaroscuro or impressionistic fogginess in order to be beautiful, just as ornament and décor never add any beauty to contemporary architecture. When painting abandoned Impressionism, photography inherited the reigning aristocracy's cast-off clothing. Expressionism has run its course, but photography and film (for example the nonsensical German attempt titled *The Cabinet of Dr. Caligari!*) have dressed up in expressionist garb. Artistic photography, same as the decorative arts, is something undignified, trashy, muddy, and unhealthy: its photoplastic strength has drowned in the half-heartedness of Whistler's aestheticism. Bareness, boredom; unseemly, false artistry. What far more beautiful, radiant and sharp photos do we see in the Anglo-American illustrated papers or on the movie screens in films about the Wild West! Herein lies the true poetry and hymnal beauty of Whitman's poems.

America is the home of modern photography and the asylum of photogénie, as I have already said. Yet we must remember that America is not only the country of Walt Whitman, but also the fatherland of Edgar Allan Poe, and so I would like to mention the strange, remarkable, and exceptional artistic activity of an American photographer living in Montparnasse in Paris—that is, MAN RAY.

THE CASE OF MAN RAY. MAN RAY, an American Jew, friend and colleague of modern French painters and poets, a second-rate Cubist painter. Like many second-rate Cubist painters, he eventually became a Dadaist, as was the trend of the time. As a Dadaist, he ceased to paint while still in New York, and began instead to construct the meta-mechanical images *Dada Mécano New York*, somewhat similar to the Supremacist constructions of the Russians Rodchenko and Lissitzky—a kind of utopian machinery, including antennas, airplanes, etc. He photographed these meta-mechanical constructions beautifully and carefully, with a precise knowledge of the craft of photography, which earns him his daily bread. He soon came to recognize that the photography of the constructions was more beautiful than the constructions themselves, faithfully conveying their material beauty and photo-plastic, corporeal expression, which is neither artistic nor entirely attributable to the author. And there he stood at the birth of a new branch of the visual arts: photography, which in becoming a fine art is a photography that is indeed fine, is indeed art, and almost quits being photography at all to become something closer to painting and the graphic arts. It is something distinct from the standard photography of a quasi-artistic atelier, which we have called decorative arts: photography acquires its own independent and intrinsic language. Nowhere, not even here, can photography forsake reality, but it can *transcend reality*. Surrealism is the character of Man Ray's photography. It is the character of modern fine art. And as such, Man Ray is the brother of Juan Gris.

Photography is beautiful even when it is not art, just like film. But it can become art without forfeiting its beauty, changing it or revising it at most. The director D. W. Griffith as well as Thomas Ince, J. B. Millet, and, to some extent, Antoine and Abel Gance have proven that. Man Ray proves this as well and does so most consistently.

A photograph of an egg in a glass is a great game and poetry of light, making poetry at the apex of technical perfection. The paper spiral draped around a stick, which nihilistic Dadaism saw as a modern sculpture and thus art, is nothing more to Man Ray than a transient reality whose beauty is to be captured by photography. Only photography that first develops in a dark room, even when its actual subject may no longer exist, can become art. But I find true photographic poetry, almost like black magic, in the most recent experiment of Man Ray, *Les Champs délicieux*, an album of twelve 18x24 cm photographs published with an introduction by Tristan Tzara: here for the first time, photography stands side by side with painting and the graphic arts, consistently and without the half-hearted endeavor of "artistic photography." Its beauty is comparable to the beauty of other visual arts examples of the last years. These "*direct*" photographs, by which Man Ray entirely circumvents the use of a plate or lens, are in and of themselves the subject, they are picture poems. The application of this photographic process otherwise used in the sciences achieves aquatint tones and delicate transitions, nearly unobtainable in the graphic arts. At times, they are almost phantasmagorical.

In his pictures, Picasso did not only use newspaper clippings, but, in some of his "Still Lifes," also photographs of pears. George Grosz and Max Ernst pasted not only entire photographs onto their pictures but assembled whole pictures from the pasted-together photographs. Whether correct or no, the public said this has nothing to do with painting, shaking their heads at these attempts with alarm and disapproval. Man Ray would have said that *this has nothing to do with photography*, fully aware that:

photo : painting = cinema : theater = orchestrion : piano =
future photo-plastic art : sculpture.

Just as the cinema liberated theater by liquidating its many varieties and branches, making its aesthetic more precise through resolute intervention, photography liberated painting, freeing it from naturalism. The revelation, invention, and action in Man Ray's photography in turn liberates "artistic photography" from its former decadence. Man Rays liberates hitherto "artistic" (impressionistic) photography simply by abolishing it. He creates a truly surrealist art out of photography, an art which, according to the words of Apollinaire, starts where imitation ends. And while painting turns back to reality today, to that entirely dangerous naturalism, moving from abstraction to the concrete, the photography of Man Ray stands up against the temptations of Whistlerism and approaches the form play of Picasso, Braque, and Gris. As soon as cinema seizes on the discovery of Man Ray as it has appropriated all other photographic achievements up to now, it will stand at the threshold of a new, unimagined territory.

From the opposite side, film will be enriched by the perfection of color photography.

THE RELATIONSHIP OF CINEMA TO THE FINE ARTS is mediated, as I have noted, by *photography*. The same goes for the reverse relationship of the fine arts to cinema. New painting can learn a lot from cinema, much as it can from studying photography. It is actually in cinema that art can become most conscious of its true purpose and mission. The influence of cinema on art is significant and does not consist merely of superficial changes, thematics, etc. Many young painters are impressed by visions of cowboys just as they are by the spectacle of the circus and the variété. This influence will not remain superficial, it is sure to deepen with time. But to expand on the relationship of cinema to painting—or more precisely: photography and painting and vice versa—would exceed the scope of this article.

CINEMA AND POETRY. Cinema lives by a different poetry than the theater. It does not know the sentimentality and hysteria of the Maeterlinck-Claudel type, nor the senile language of Ibsen. The poetry of cinema is not related to Symbolism or Futurism. It is also not in the slightest bit academic. In my opinion, Dumas and Victor Hugo are not conducive to adaptation by the cinema unless the cinema were to fundamentally revise and violate the text of the novel. Sentimental and historical literature is not well-suited for cinema. The same goes for academic literature, the official repertoire of the theater (*The Lady of the Camellias*) and the literature of a cultural nouveau, that is, poetic art. The cinema, in as much as it is a spectacle for the people, lives through that poetry and literature which is read by the people. Jules Verne, Karl May, Nick Carter, the Buffalo Bill stories, *Uncle Tom's Cabin*, *The Heroic Captain Corcoran*, *Around the World in 80 Days*, *The Children of Captain Grant*, *Old Shatterhand*, the clear-eyed Sherlock Holmes, Arsène Lupin, Bret Hart's stories of the Far West, and Jack London's novels from snowy plains, Upton Sinclair, Jensen, Mark Twain—in short, popular and sensational literature, adventure and travel writing—so-called trashy pulp literature.

It offers up sensational modern entertainment, its terrain adventure and fantasy. This is not the place to tout its often very healthy, unsentimental, and active morality or its new, modern, and active philosophy: both are however indisputably present. It is the child of a new world, of modern social and cultural conditions: it breathes in the sweltering scent of America, tempts with the magic of far-away places, intoxicates the masses, bored by sentimentalism and academicism. It is this literature—not that academic-Parnassian poetry, but this literature—that is the only popular literature of today, one that is also very modern: it is the lyric, the epic, and the drama all at once. This literature, which exists less in studies and libraries than in the setting of the broad heavens, free as a bird, or in the midst of the swift whirlwind of life—this literature is the basis of cinema, whose poetry is of the same stock.

The poetry of the cinema takes from all of these aspects of reality: automobiles, airplanes, steamship liners, cities, farms and farm boys, Indians, astronomy, suburban sprawl, festivities, landscapes around the globe, wigwams, skyscrapers, prairies, etc. It encompasses all feelings and emotions. As such, it is sister to the poetry of Walt WHITMAN and the other American poets, his pupils. (Sandburg, Lindsay, Masters, Treat, Ridge, Ezra Pound, Oppenheim, Kreymborg, etc.) It is capable even through humble means to evoke a clear and full picture of its environs: not only a train, a boat, a plane, or a band of Indians but also the small details of life, a tram ticket, a railway signal, letters with a seal, a calling card, a notebook, a watch, a ring, or a tropical helmet can be effective "actors" and meaningful elements in a film. It is allusion, which partially approximates the technique of the detective novel, and which also recalls the taste and charm of the poetry of Jean Cocteau as well as some other modern poets.

The lyricism of the cinema captivates via its own exoticism. It is not the decadent exoticism of the Baudelaire-Gauguin type, but rather a modern cosmopolitan exoticism: not an exoticism that is represented as flight from the hyper-civilized world to the dreamed-up pae dreamradises of Tahiti or the Orient, but the exoticism of the Trans-Atlantic, the Pullman cars, the Canadian Pacific Express. It is the exoticism of a travel journal, illustrated magazines, and a globetrotting sensibility, which always has a fresh perception of the world. On the movie screen, images flash by quickly because life itself moves so fast. From time to time, an express train passes before our eyes. A collection of light beams render Paris, London, New York, and Leningrad on the screen. San Francisco neighbors with Melbourne. The cinema looks upon the world through the prism of a cosmopolitan, international spirit.

Modern literature and new poetry are exposed to the strong, healthy influence of the cinema as well the so-called pulp literature, which is the plot source for American film. Novels have taken on a cinematographic technique of spontaneity. *Jules Romains, Blaise Cendrars, Jean Cocteau, Max Jacob, P. Morand, Ivan Goll, Apollinaire, Ehrenburg, P.A. Birot, Edschmid, Tzara, Epstein, P. Mac Orlan, P. Hamp, L. Delluc, etc. and in our country, Černík, Nezval, Voskovec, Seifert, and Vančura* have connected their poetry to the essence of cinema; some of these authors have even written film librettos, of which the most famous and interesting is Goll's Chaplinade. (An interesting topic for a literary-critical study would be to observe in greater detail the influence of cinema on modern literature, but it is beyond the scope of this article.)

THE CINEMA AND THE THEATER. Simply put: cinema is to theater as the airplane is to the flying person, as J. Honzl points out. The theater is centripetal, a concentrated impression, and film is centrifugal. The theater synthesizes to the point of symbolic allusions and abbreviations: film is, as a rule, epically expansive and as such is in love with expressive details. The theater has and always will have its boundaries, its limited scripts: the film's stage is the contemporary world, expanding out towards an infinite distance and a boundless life, because cinema is the celebrated "biograph" of art today. If the theater is fundamentally monistic and synthetic, film is pluralistic and divisionary. Such is generally the aesthetic difference and mutually opposed relationship of cinema and theater. But due to the influence of the current cultural and social conditions, the formal relationship is becoming more sharply and definitively separated. While the cinema develops at a speed of no return, the theater wallows further into deep decline. While international crowds gather every night in the cinema halls on every continent, theater rows gape empty. The declaration, "Don't build a theater" is accompanied with the wish, "Build the people's cinema!" Max Jacob ("Théâtre et cinema," *Nord-Sud*) says the following about the relationship of the cinema and the theater: the theater is a sculpture on a pedestal, not real life. But cinema cures us of all the epidemics and endemics of the theater. It is where the bandit is applauded, not the elegant snob. Convention is the basis of the theater, an unpretentious reality is the basis of cinema: we defend the cinema as realistic art, we reject the theater as pathetic and academic art. Where the theater lives through gestures and poses, the cinema lives through certainty. The theater is entertainment for romantics and the petite bourgeoisie, the cinema is for modern spirits and a refreshing source for those who think towards the future. It is an exaltation of humanity and can only be disliked by misanthropes and enemies of the world in general.

The theater has long ceased to be a celebration for a broad stratum of the public, as it was in ancient Greece. Close the theaters and no one will shed a tear, save for snobby audience members who go to opening-night premiers in order to ostentatiously show off their cultural standing. Cinema has taken its place as the popular spectacle in modern cultural life. Just as photography precludes the existence of naturalistic-academic painting, film precludes the existence of naturalistic-academic theater. Both are rather useless atavisms that will soon wither away at any rate. The theater will fall with the bourgeoisie. The cinema lives through the proletariat, the widest stratum of the public.

The cinema, like photography, does not have an old master's tradition, being new to our time. Just like photography strayed when it borrowed from the effects of Rembrandt or Whistler, the cinema went astray when it attempted to be like conventional theater. Just as the literature appropriated by the cinema is not in the least official, recognized, or academic, the theater tradition that cinema correctly inclines towards is not academic, official theatre. The cinema, being the spectacle of the people, found its tradition in heretical theatrical types, which are likewise the spectacle of the people that springs from the "pleasures of the electric century," to wit:

IN THE CIRCUS AND THE VARIÉTÉ,
IN THE BALLET, PANTOMIME, MELODRAMA, MUSIC-HALL,
CAFÉ-CONCERT, CABARET,
IN POPULAR CELEBRATIONS, SUBURBAN DANCES, ETC.,
IN SPORT.

The freedom of modern art was born in the circus, variété, and music-hall. Here lives true modern poetry, lissome, electric, non-naturalistic to the highest degree. New forms of humor, clownish irony, sentimental *gaminerie*, lively sketches, miraculous bits by equilibrists, jugglers, equestriennes, exotic dance, eccentric-girls, and Japanese acrobats are at home here—and it is a poetic and romantic dwelling. If romanticism has an eternal strength that permeates history, and if every age, including such an absolutely realistic epoch as ours, needs a little romantic spice in its ingredients, then this romanticism can be found today in the circus, the variété, and music-hall, it is to be found in the acrobats, the comedians, the clowns, the singers and dancers, and even in the renowned boxers, who live for the applause and favor of the crowd. It is a nomadic romanticism, a romanticism of contemporary itinerant songsters, cosmopolitan and globetrotting *trouvères*. And their production is not an empty art.

Given that the relationship of cinema to official theater, "artistic" direction and acting, and also to dramatic classical, naturalistic, and psychological literature, is simply tension between two opposites, it is possible to consider the circus, the variété, and music-hall closely related to cinema, its forerunners in more ways than one.

Of all those unsanctioned types of theater and spectacle, *The circus* and *Théâtre Variété*—their character, purpose, and mission—are closest to the cinema. They are exotic, like cinema. They are international, their expressive speech is some sort of artistic Ido or Esperanto, just like in cinema. They are spectacle without literature and outside of literature. The stars of the variété, eccentric girls, jugglers, sketches, the brutal dialogues in short clown performances, somewhat like the legacy of *Comedia dell'arte*, wonderful tightrope walkers and their risky, breakneck performances, beautiful and energetic tamers of wild beasts, unusual and refined dances of far-away places, graceful equestrians in vermillion dresses with green sashes and thousands of glittering baubles, every attraction more sensational than the next—all of these fantastic, exotic, intoxicating, and nearly miraculous things allure the modern artist, who has grown bored with the pathetic emptiness of the theater. Seurat, Toulouse-Lautrec, Picasso, Kubišta, Archipenko, and Léger extract their pictures from these environs, and the poetry of the jungle and the far-away, exuded by the circus, inspired the most successful and characteristic of Neumann's poems. But at the same time, the circus and the variété are the spectacle of the people, in so much as their strength lies in a healthy, sportive, and fierce reality, in grotesque and mighty caricatures and satires; and thus they are akin to film.

The same can be said of the *Music-hall*, *Pantomime*, *Café-concert* and *cabaret.* These are non-academic, ingenuous, and in the modern sense of the word, primitive: they are, or they ought to be, popular. They represent the full range of laughter, the indefatigable ventilator of an overheated brain, as F. T. Marinetti said. If today the circus is most notably at home in France—the Parisian Cirque MEDRANO (Boum! tous les soirs Boum!) and NOUVEAU CIRQUE being the most famous—the birthplace and current home of the astonishing and synthetic art of the music-hall or café-concert is namely the Anglo-American world. In Britain, Charlie Chaplin and Fatty Arbuckle came out of the London-based pantomime company of Fred Karno. The exotic review, travesty, parody, dance, dance, and more dance, and non-academic ballet—even Anna Pavlova of the Russian Ballet also dared to step onto the stage of the music-hall in the United States—Loie Fuller, Max Dearly, Mistinguett of the Casino de Paris, of the Eldorado and film (*Les Misérables*), who, in gamine fashion, returned to the variété the fanciful, untamed, languid, mischievous dance of the *danse gavroche*, elevating it to the standard of the hieratic dances of Isadora Duncan, Harry Pilcer, and Gabby Deslys, Mme Roberty of the Parisian Concert Mayol, Mme Paulette Dax, Pearl White, Musidora (from the film *Les Vampires*), Vernon Castle, Max Linder, Stacia Napierkowska: that is, the cabaret, music-hall, variété, the modern, lively, electric, and poetic theater; an art that is neither officially recognized nor appreciated but that does not maintain an old-fashioned modesty. It is not true that it is something of an inferior spectacle, some sort of theater of inferior quality, just because it is unacquainted with the morbid aesthetic of today. On the contrary, modern, truly modern theater, to which young poets and certain experimental theaters in France and in revolutionary Russia aspire, becomes a brother to the cabaret (such as the Russian Theater of Revolutionary Satire, or "Terevsat"), enchanting plays, *comédie-bouffe*, ballet, and vaudeville, while the modern-age place of grand theater and great drama has been taken by cinema.

By the way, it must be noted: the flowering of the variété and cabaret has been designated a product of a bourgeoise, pseudo-cultural milieu. To some extent, particularly here, this is true. Not only the external design of first-rate establishments, but also their programming, is expressly bourgeoisie. A local example demonstrating this would be Karel Hašler. But, at the same time, one can see that these establishments are politically motivated. In Paris, next to the old Bohemian Montmartre cabarets "Chauve Souris" and "Lapin Agil," are the luxurious revues of Ba-Ta-Clan, Folies Bergère, Olympia, and the Alhambra; but there are also popular suburban spectacles, and in Montparnasse on the rue de la Gaité, there is both the nationalist Bobino Cabaret and the socialist Gaité-Montparnasse. We know that the Russian revolution resuscitated the cabaret, and while it was, as Napoleon said, Pierre Beaumarchaise's "The Marriage of Figaro" that captured the French Revolution, the lyric, strength, anger, sadness, and defiance of the current revolutionary movement is concealed in the erotic and revolutionary proletarian chansons of some of today's cabarets: in the lyric poetry that grows out of the atmosphere of the periphery and its *fortifs*, and in the social pathos of certain films. Sherlock Holmes, Arsène Lupin, Apaches, and pirates, who are admired by the proletarian audience, are not born of bourgeois aesthetics, philosophy, morality, or lyricism. They are to the people what John Gabriel Borkman or Jean des Essientes represent for the bourgeois aesthete. There is no philistinism and snobbism in such a cabaret. Bourgeois theater loves refined and clever dialogue, fateful psychology, traditionally dramatic structure, individual, but at the same time conventional, heroes—small popular theaters love courageous Apaches, beautiful sailors, little ditties, light effects, shining spotlights, colorful posters, ever lively and colorful events and, being a spectacle without beginning or end, they translate, in quick succession, the unceasing drama of life. They are like folk dances, invigorating entertainment for the modern world and modern style, "the pleasure of the electric century." However, it would be a mistake and a sin to look upon life as upon Eden, the Luna Park, or Magic-City, as is often done today: in life we do not go from attraction to attraction.

THEATER AND FILM. In mimicking theater, the cinema lost its way. Film had nothing to learn from the shabby, degenerating, and hopelessly revivalist theater, save for some vices, which it soon managed to shirk, and the artificial ambition of a film d'art. But modern theater can glean valuable advice from film, which is full of vitality; from the circus, the variété, and cabaret likewise. Today's film dramas and serials surpass and obviate in every regard existing full-length dramas, which cannot compete, as well as narrative plays of lesser literary quality (à la "Excelsior"!), because their possibilities surpass the more or less imperfect theatrical gimmicks—even on the stage of the Châtelet. Modern dramatic production, being at the same time witness to the decline of contemporary theater, evades the old dramatic constructions that built upon debates, psychology, and devil knows what else, that have forfeited their raison d'être and instead willfully and programmatically give themselves over to the influence of the cinema, the repertoire of small popular theaters, the cabaret, and circus—and just like the circus and film, this production is connected to exoticism. The experiments of young authors rely on new scenic and directorial suppositions as opposed to the preexisting norms of the theater. Apollinaire, in the foreword to *The Breasts of Tiresias*, writes of the need for two stages, one of which would be in the middle of the audience (as in Japan), and one of which would encircle it like a wide band; Birot conceives his plays, full of circus oddities and variété exoticism, for clowns, jugglers, and acrobats; and Ivan Goll's *Methusalem* is a satirical piece permeated with cinematographic tableaus. Just as futurist painters put their viewer in the middle of their painting, modern theater wants to place the observer at the center of the play, in the middle of the spectacular and dramatic action. Vaudeville, pantomime, ballet, and attempts at a purely optical theater (Pitoëff): these are spectacles simultaneously lyrical and dramatic in sense and spirit, just as Fantômas, Buffalo Bill, or Chaplin are simultaneously lyrical and dramatic personalities. This has nothing to do with lyrical symbolist theater but with something that was portended by J. M. Synge's *The Playboy of the Western World* and Alfred Jarry's *Ubu Roi*. These modern attempts are perhaps strongly burlesque at times, but the burlesque needs to be filled with a breath of lyricism in order to be art. This lyricism is reflected in song, in dance, laughter, gesture, and *mise en scène*: it is a lyricism of everyday life, not narrowly literary but a modern lyricism that is united with the most urgent dramatism. In order to be perfectly clear, an example: sporting events are dramatic beyond reproach, and thus do not lack a strong modern lyrical emphasis. There is potential for a lyricism fused with the dramatic only through the abolition of traditional rules concerning the triumvirate of action, time, and place, in exchange for the introduction of a modern element: simultaneity.

CINEMA AND SPORT. Whereas film is not bound up with the theater, it is much indebted to sport, athletics, and acrobatics. Is it necessary to expand on this self-evident fact? A truly collective art like soccer, film has only scarcely found its heroes in theatrical tragedies, especially with regards to American films. (French film, under the influence of the auteurship of Abel Gance [*The Torture of Silence, The Tenth Symphony, J'accuse!*], Louis Feuillade [*Judex, Tih Minh*], Charles Burguet, Pouctal [*Work*], Antoine [*Toilers of the Sea, The Earth*], is comparatively closer to the theater, and its actors, such as Gabrielle Robinne, Ève Francis, Marcel Lévesque, Sarah Bernhardt, and Séverin-Mars, are theater actors.) But in the overwhelming majority, film has found its singular interpreters amongst athletes, acrobats, and comics of the circus. The famous boxer Georges Carpentier, a friend of Chaplin, now acts in films. It is only sport at the highest degree of perfection that could furnish film with such "smart" automobilists, horseback riders, or cowboys as are Herbert Rawlinson, Douglas Fairbanks, Marie Walcamp, Helena Holmes, Pearl White, Maciste, Harry Carey, William S. Hart, Ruth Roland, etc. Cinema, as an art, is the paramount work of the modern spiritual culture, and is at the same time a celebration of modern physical culture: it finds an equilibrium between them both, and in this lies its fairly substantial moral significance.

CINEMA AND MUSIC are in a mutual relationship, which is in all actuality quite complex, even if seemingly straightforward and clear. Film simply needs musical accompaniment: today, a theater performance without an orchestra is unthinkable and the images on a movie screen would become strange specters and bizarre apparitions if not accompanied by the melody of music. This is entirely natural from a psychological perspective, but there is nevertheless a question as to whether this need for music will continue once there are screenings of perfect color films that capture the light of day. In the meantime, musical accompaniment is a must. The music should suit the film and the programmatic selection of music for a film should be of interest to modern musicians in more ways than one. Mozart's *The Abduction from the Seraglio* and *The Magic Flute* are used to accompany oriental films. Similarly, Offenbach or Beethoven, Dvořák, Smetana, Bizet, Schubert, are played, and in France even Debussy on occasion; Chaplin's *The Vagabond* gets Chopin. But just look at how precisely the character of modern music corresponds to the cinema: Stravinsky with his rag-piano and pianola as well as international dance and marching music: the Salome foxtrot and Indianola...the rhythm of modern dance is authentically modern rhythm: in it, there is something of the rhythm of roaring trains and life on the street. What a good fit for film accompaniment is the jazz band! The music that best fits the film—a de facto mechanical theater—surely has to be mechanical music: the gramophone, orchestrion, pianola; because music, which has to be the accompaniment, illustration, and background to a screen drama, ought not to ignore the instruments of modern technological possibilities. Let the music roar with the noise of dynamos, Morse code, automobile horns, the din of express trains and airplanes, the banging of the typewriter in place of the usual chirping of the nightingale on a poetic summer eve! These "touches of reality," attempted by the futurists and their art of noises as well as Erik Satie in his "La Parade," can have a similar meaning for music as newspaper clippings, playing cards, textiles, etc. have for Cubist still lifes, with which Picasso, Braque, and Juan Gris revived the abstract geometric composition of their work, introducing into it something aesthetically un-distilled and vital; real, raw materials. The most conducive instrument for film is *jazz*, more expressive than Russolo's art of noises, which can be easily replaced by accurate recordings of the phonograph, capturing the roar and din of big cities and train stations, the promenades and docks, great mass gatherings and the thunder of proletarian demonstrations.

Modern music cannot work for dead theater. There is not and will not be truly new operas, just as there will not be new dramas. Perhaps we can expect to see new operettas, which are closer to popular taste and thought. So let it begin working for film: here it can discover an extensive list of beautiful, albeit difficult and demanding, tasks. Some composers of the Romance modernism, in particular members of the Parisian ***6*** "Le Six," have attempted this. Darius Milhaud is the composer of the Cinéma-Symphonie and scores for Chaplin's works.—

The poetic value of film is vast, as I have tried to indicate here. If I hesitate to ascribe the term of "art" to film today (the 1921 Paris Salon d'Automne awarded it the place of the 10th muse), it is only because its beauty, vivacity, and value surpass the quality of contemporary art. A whole order of names are connected to film that will be placed alongside the most celebrated phenomena of art in future histories and criticism.

Charles Spencer Chaplin, Charlot, Charlie, is the omnipresent artist of the cinema. He belongs to the proletariat of all nations and races and his work travels the whole world. He is the greatest figure in the art of film, the greatest phenomenon in contemporary art. He is the Molière and Aristophanes of today. Young poets of all nations pay tribute to him. His melancholic sadness provokes an indefinable cheerfulness in the crowd. He is more than an actor. He is a clown. A poet. He is the inventor of new, utterly modern expressions of humor and irony that are connected with a fragile and paradoxical sentimentality. He is one of those great humorists who "go sit in a corner and cry" (Neruda). He is living "a dog's life," he is a vagabond, an immigrant, a server, a shopkeeper, a piano mover, a fake count, a glass maker, an adventurer, a fireman, a soldier, a pawnshop clerk, a policeman, and a drunk: he is a jack of all trades but a master of none.

Douglas Fairbanks, who, along with Whitman, provides a most American viewpoint regarding the general topic of heroism, has embodied a true modern athleticism and poetry of sport in his work. He is the hero of Arizona, Zorro the avenger of injustice, both crestfallen and a man of the world, a bandit and a madman, the proprietor of a sanitarium, Robin Hood and d'Artagnan of the *Three Musketeers*, whom he modernizes simply and unwittingly with a natural style.

Sessue Hayakawa, the greatest tragic actor of the present, *William Hart* (Rio Jim), *Mary Pickford, Jack Pickford, Pearl White, Vernon Castle, Fatty* (Roscoe Arbuckle), *Dustin Farnum, Marie Walcamp, Mae Murray, Mae Marsh* (*Intolerance*), *Ruth Roland, Nora Talmadge, Lincoln, Fanny Ward, Alice Brady, M. Mac Laren; Coogan, Edna Purviance,* and *Eric Campbell* (Chaplin's partners), *Dorothy Phillips, Cl. Kimball Young, Harry Carey, Ol. Thomas, Marie Doro, P. Dean — S. Milvanhoff* (orphan Jeanette), *Mathot* (*Work*), *Biscot, Musidora, Peggy, Ève Francis, Nazimova, Gémier* (*The Torture of Silence*), *Sjöström — O'Brien*, etc. etc.

Directors: above all *D. W. Griffith* (*Intolerance, Dream Street, Broken Blossoms, Way Down East*), *Th. H. Ince, Mack Sennett, Loos, Emerson, DeMille, Abel Gance, Capellani,* etc. etc.

THE NEW PROLETARIAN ART—an art which Ehrenburg perceptively predicted would quit being art—INTERNATIONAL, POPULAR, AND COLLECTIVE, is the task and style of the future. Of all contemporary art, film comes the closest, especially in the works of Chaplin (The Kid, Chaplin as vagabond, Chaplin as soldier, Chaplin as immigrant, Chaplin as policeman) and Fairbanks. In them, you can sense the epic of modern life and the vastness of the world: and it is not a mere depiction of the world in pictures but an outright poetry of the modern world. Film is thundering and harsh, but it can also be concise. It is rich and its possibilities know no boundaries. Today, it is the only art for the proletariat. Its social importance is immeasurable: close the theaters, the exhibitions, the picture galleries, the reading rooms and churches, and only a small fistful of people will cry over them. The world will keep turning. However, it might come to a halt if the projectors stopped spinning in the cinemas around the globe. Kilometers of revolutionary film will seize the world just as a series of contemporary films have already captured the heart of the proletarian public.

Josef Šíma: Advertisement

THE FIRST thing to come to mind when one hears the word "advertisement" is the poster, announcement, *affiche*. And then questions immediately follow: Is the poster necessarily a work of graphic art? Must it be a picture? An advertisement is more than just a poster, and it follows that it is more than just a painting. Just as advertisement makes use of painterly elements, it also utilizes aspects of sculpture, photography, cinematography, light, and sound. But in what way? And why? Advertisement has a single goal, of which it is always conscious, and that goal is only and endlessly to advertise a specific thing in a manner that changes with the circumstances. It is striking—disproportionate, in the broadest sense of the word, and recurring—it is aggrandizing.

Often times it searches for a single world that explicates, or on the contrary, says nothing. For instance: on the outskirts of Paris, whole gables of multi-level dwellings are marked with giant letters that make up the word "Dunlop." A single, gigantic word—"Dunlop"—appears on the gable of a three-floor house. The word Dunlop appears a hundred times, a thousand times, on streets within the city, but expresses only an enigma of its meaning. Finally, you catch sight of a shop displaying the Dunlop sign on one of the city streets, and in the window display a pyramid of tires arranged from largest to smallest. And then you understand: Dunlop sells tires. Little printed brochures and price lists explain the rest in detail. However, Dunlop and its recurrence, its enigma, remain unforgettable.

ADVERTISEMENT cannot be approached in a painterly manner, or any other way: what might be a beautiful advertising object from an artistic perspective is a bad one from the advertising perspective. The goal of advertisement is not to show off the qualities of modern painting, sculpture, or photography. All art posters up to now, those terrible products of art and design schools (what are the decorative arts?), are bad from the advertising standpoint. A poster must always be an advertisement, never a picture or decoration. The only feature shared between the two is the fact that both the poster and the picture are colorful stains. The beauty of advertisement lays solely in the perfect attainment of its goal.

ADVERTISEMENT, just as the cinematograph, is deeply reflected in our day-to-day life. The times are better expressed through advertisement than art, which is undergoing a painful transition. Advertisement, unburdened by tradition, is the fruit of our times and, like the cinematograph, was created by demand; it is simple and comprehensible to everyone. It resonates with a general desire, can vary according to the circumstances and the environment, and is nevertheless precisely demarcated, always remaining advertisement as indisputably as chemistry remains chemistry. Like the cinematograph, it contains all the breadth of the old arts; it is comprehensible and has the greatest capacity for delicate finesse.

ADVERTISEMENT allows for the most banal forms of objects. A bottle of wine is the simplest bottle one can imagine; the bottle, adorned with a huge label proffering the name of the wine or liquor becomes an archetype of a bottle for all wines. The pathos in advertisement is unambiguous, it has its own rules and different proportions than the fine arts. It has a framework from which it cannot deviate under penalty of mediocrity. Endowed with banality, it enthralls with its clamoring pathos. Advertisement is the crowd. Circus Medrano, the whole of Place and Boulevard de Clichy, and Place Pigalle are all pasted up with circus posters that cry out with the pathos of our age. How much has the environment already given to the Impressionists, to the great Seurat? The posters of Toulouse Lautrec could only emerge here. Sarah Bernhardt was less lucky with Alfons Mucha.

IN ADVERTISEMENT and in the cinematograph, the reverberations of everything that gives character to this new age can be found: mechanics, commerce, practical science. If art were to remain in its pre-existing form, everything else would be called nothing other than pseudo-art. But let us consider whether that pseudo-art touches on life so intimately; does it not stand at least temporarily above so-called real art, which draws on tradition and cannot liberate itself from classical materials—stone, wood, canvas, oil, or watercolors—when today concrete and iron have become common materials as well as splendid mixtures of metals of excellent properties, dyes of marvelous tones and unusual resistance that can be used to paint enormous surfaces.

ADVERTISEMENT has nothing in common with art, as I noted at the outset, and I want to that underscore again. The relationship between the two is akin to that of engineering and architecture. No one can call the enormous harbor granary siloes of New York or the colossal valley dams of North American rivers architecture in the sense of architecture as an art. It is clear however that *from the technical side, modern architecture can be nothing less than a work of modern engineering. The copula of St. Peter's Cathedral in Rome was a unique construction in its time.* Though not predefined mathematically, it is built with precision and ten times the certitude. A master in the Farman factory constructs the fuselage of an airplane without calculations with five times the certitude. Why should architecture neglect these possibilities? Painters of *affiches* know how to use color, line, and space rather precisely even though they could not write a theory of wall painting. They often assemble objects and letters on a single surface without the help of perspective or optical projection and are able to differentiate the individual layers. An *affiche* painted on a wall by a craftsperson acquires by color reduction three or four tones, while its linear characteristic lends it uncommon monumentality.

FOR ADVERTISEMENT, the spatial arrangement is important. It touches upon that which painting has always arrived at. But, and this is a plus, advertisement has not stopped there. Without much thought about constructing theories, it instinctively and completely logically touched upon those mediums in front of which art awkwardly stood still: motion and light. Motion gets its modern artistic expression in the cinematograph; I speak here of motion and not of gesture. But that is a topic that does not belong here.

Light, however. Advertisement has completely claimed that element. What might be called the father of illuminated advertisements are the pushed aside, seemingly insignificant but beautiful fireworks. Fireworks, using light as a visual element, are very similar to advertisement in their showiness. They have an alluring strength, precisely what advertisement should never lack. Exaggeration, used to both reduce and deepen space, can be attained even more effectively with the use of light. An enormous, ticking pocket watch can be found against the black surface of a building, lighting up in a different color every five seconds, elongating and shortening the horizon of the street. The blue, carmine, orange, and white of its lights draw the giant silhouette of the chronometer further or nearer with the varying intensity of its luminosity. A low-flying airplane, illuminated by multi-colored reflectors from the rooftop of the store that it advertises, alternately switches on and off the lightbulbs spelling out the store's name on the bottom of the load-bearing surface. How many suggestive motifs fit for the theater stage has it revived?

ADVERTISEMENT, engaging the resources proffered by the times, is adaptable and therefore in constant contact with life. Stagnation would lead to its end, stripping it of purpose where purposefulness is everything. Its development is unpredictable, much like that of human society.

Paris, September 30, 1922

obraz

Štyrský

OBRAZ = živou reklamou a projektem nového světa a života
„ = produkt života VŠE OSTATNÍ = KÝČ!

Funkce obrazu { praktické, účelné, srozumitelné / propagační / organisující a komponující

OBRAZ { energií / kritikou / hybnou silou } **ŽIVOTA**

Požadavek: obraz musí být aktivní
musí něco dělat ve světě, v životě. Aby vykonal úlohu, uloženou v jeho ploše, nutno ho strojově rozšířiti 1.000, 10.000, 100.000 exemplářů. Reprodukce. Grafika letákem.

Nenávidím obrazy jako snoby, jež je kupují z touhy po jedinečnosti, aby mezi 4 stěnami estétského příbytku vzdychali před nimi v lenoškách (à la Matisse!). Obraz visící na stěně v uzavřeném prostoru, jalová dekorace, pro nic a za nic, nic nedělá, nic nechce, nic neříká, nežije.

originál — unikát
obraz není jen obrazem!!

Teige: **BUĎ PLAKÁTEM!**
reklamou a projektem nového světa

Návrh, projekt nového světa — vynalézáním nových, krásnějších, užitečnějších forem a hodnot života
— tvořením nových, krásnějších, užitečnějších forem a hodnot života

Reklama a propagace nových, krásnějších, užitečnějších forem a hodnot života.
Nový svět neleží ve hvězdách, v oblacích, ale na zemi. Mnohé z nového světa už známe, máme a žijeme

PROPAGACE

nové krásy, zdraví, rozumu, svobody, řádu, radosti, veselí života.

Goll: Chapliniada (kino). — Černík: Radosti elektrického století. — Nezval: Rozumnost bezhlavé veselosti. — Krejcar: Amerikanismus. — Birot: Poesie plenéru. — Teige: Paříž. — Seifert: Paříž. — Picasso-Seurat: Cirkus. III. Internacionála. — Film (Variété, Cirkus)

Reklama: idejí
knih
revoluce
akcí a atrakcí

Rozhodně **ne** propagace: „Mánesa", Ibsena, Stinnesa, Poincaré, buržoasie, sociálpatriotů, akademií, salonů, KU-KLUX-CLAN

OBRAZ

stavět	bourat
kladná činnost	záporná činnost
objektivní	osobní

ŽURNALISTICKÁ KARIKATURA REVOLUČNÍ ničí, bičuje, nenávidí.

Jindřich Štyrský: A Picture

A PICTURE = **a living advertisement and blueprint for a new world and life**
" = a product of life **EVERYTHING ELSE = KITSCH!**

The function of a picture { **practical, functional, comprehensible** / **propagandistic** / **organizing and composing**

PICTURE { the energy / the criticism / the driving force } **OF LIFE**

The requirement: a picture must be active
It must do something in the world, in life. In order to execute that task set down on its surface, it is necessary to distribute it in 1,000, 10,000, 100,000 copies. Reproduction. The graphics of a flyer.

I hate pictures like the snobs who purchase them out of a desire for uniqueness, so that between 4 walls of an aesthetic dwelling they can sigh before them on a chaise lounge (à la Matisse!). A picture hanging on a wall in an enclosed space is worth nothing, does nothing, wants nothing, says nothing, does not live.

original — unique
a picture is not only a picture!

Teige: **LET IT BE A POSTER!**
an advertisement and blueprint for a new world

A proposal, a blueprint for a new world — the invention of new, more beautiful and useful forms and values of life
— the creation of new, more beautiful and useful forms and values of life

Advertisement and propagation of new, more beautiful and useful forms and values of life.
The new world does not reside among the stars, in the clouds, but here on Earth.
We already know and have much from this new world and live accordingly.

THE PROPOGATION
of new beauty, health, understanding, freedom, order, joy, merriment of life.

Goll: Chaplinade (cinema). — Černík: The Joys of the Electric Century. — Nezval: The Reasonableness of Reckless Merriment. — Krejcar: Americanism. — Birot: Poetry en plein air. — Teige: Paris. — Seifert: Paris. — Picasso-Seurat: Circus. 3rd International. — Film (Variété, Circus)

Advertisement: of ideals
of books
of revolution
of action and attraction

Decidedly **not** the propagation of: "Mánes," Ibsen, Stinnes, Poincaré, the bourgeoisie, social patriots, academies, the Salons, the KU-KLUX-KLAN

A PICTURE

to construct	**to demolish**
positive activity	negative activity
objective	personal

JOURNALISTIC REVOLUTIONARY CHARICATURE destroys, whips, hates.

FORMA: diktována účelem: stručná, přesná, srozumitelná, zábavná, přehledná, konstruktivní, prostá; žádná dekorace, ornament, titěrnost, literatura, psychologie, mystika

K r á s a b e z d u š e

NÁVRH NOVÉ ZEMĚKOULE

o b r a z = konstruktivní báseň krás světa

NE: reprodukce, záplatování, imitace, restaurace, idylisování, sentimentalisování. Písmo v obraze má svůj praktický smysl. (Plakát!) Mluví. Jaký ostatně je jiný smysl písma? U kubistů litery jen dekorovaly plochu svou moderní výrazností.

Projekt nového světa může vypracovati toliko NOVÝ ČLOVĚK programové práce krajně reelní, že musí i dobrou podvědomou práci potírat jako nespolehlivou

P r á c e — t o ť p r o g r a m

Obraz vykonává svou funkci v životě jako každý jiný produkt lidské práce.

Obraz — výrobek života pro konsumenta, jenž slove svět.

Obraz — nebude nadále rozmnožovat bídu, ubohost, zoufalství, zpodobovat tíživé nedostatky dnešní doby, sociální křivdy, břich kapitálu, předměstské atmosféry.

Obraz — sociální bídy nikomu nepomůže, je vyráběn z nemohoucnosti vytvořit energickou revolucí nové řády, nový svět.

Obraz je produktem doby. Obraz není reprodukcí doby. Dobu zobrazí foto, film, obrázkové časopisy atd.

FOTO: objektivní pravda a průkazná jasnost nade všecky pochybnosti. Foto zabila kýč (díky!) ale nezabila obrazu! Uspíšila vývojové vyjasnění výtvarnictví.

Foto: dokument doby a krás tohoto světa. **Obraz:** projekt a tvorba nových krás, nových hodnot, malovaný **portrét** s ním nemůže konkurovati ani „pro indiv. pojetí + nitro umělce", (vlastnosti kýčařů, fráze). Foto schopno ohromného technického vývoje (rozměry, barva, jasnost, rychlost). Barevný Gauguin = 0 proti dokonalé barevné foto z trópů.

Foto uskutečnilo sny starých mistrů od pradávna — proč se jim ještě dnes pošetilci obdivují? — protože jejich malířský ideál nebyl než imitací reprodukcí. Ilusionismus.

NOVÉ TVARY UMĚNÍ DNES A DENNĚ VZNIKAJÍCÍ

nejkrásnější báseň: telegram a foto — úspornost, pravda, stručnost.

Viděli jste ve filmu státi u moře Pickfordovou, pomalu otáčela hlavu a dlouze a nyvě dívala se svýma jasnýma očima na nás — t. j. na několik set, několik tisíc lidí — **MONO LISO** — nemůžeš konkurovat!

Přirozeně, že malíři à la Nejedlý & Beneš a celé zástupy jiných bojují proti moderně, jež se na ně řítí jako lavina; marně, nemají dosti síly, aby dovedli najíti pevné a vhodné místo pro sebe a svou práci v dnešním světě — jsou zcela zbyteční parasiti. Foto je dokonalejším vypravěčem než oni.

Umění minulosti	U m ě n í p ř í t o m n o s t i	
Reprodukce světa a života	a) Foto Reprodukce světa a života dokonalejší, poučnější	b) výtvarnictví a poesie projekt nového života nové krásy nové hodnoty

Nenávidíme galerií, kde po staletí plesniví obrazy (věčná paměť). Zdraví světa a jeho mládí závisí na faktu, že vše se spotřebuje a nahradí novým. Proto svět nestárne, každou hodinou je mladší a krásnější. Kdyby nebylo historismu byl by svět o několik století mladší.

TRADICE: staří mistři pozorovali historická díla, aby viděli, jak nemají malovat. Moderní malíř rovněž, nebo ještě lépe: vůbec si jich nevšímá.

NEKONSERVUJME MRTVÉ! ODSTRAŇTE MRTVOLY, NEBOŤ ZAPÁCHAJÍ!

Pokrok a vývoj: nic nebude nemožného, všecky reelné projekty uskutečnitelné, vzdálenost = relativní. Pro smutné milence vypěstujeme černé růže. Naše projekty nebudou horečné sny, utopie, ale budou reelně poetické.

POZOR:

Nutnost rozlišování. Co z dnešního světa je základem nového? Obraz se zrodí z přemýšlení, konstruování a kombinování reelních elementů a myšlenek a nebude povrchním nadšeným pohledem. Epigoni rozmnožovali, špatně vyráběli. Přichází na jejich místo **stroj** + mechanická reprodukce. Bude méně obrazů a více mechanických reprodukcí.

Květen 1923.

2

FORM: dictated by the goal: concise, precise, comprehensible, entertaining, lucid, constructive, simple; no decoration, ornament, trifles, literature, psychology, mysticism

Beauty without a soul
PROPOSAL FOR A NEW GLOBE
a picture = constructive poetry of the beauties of the world

NO: reproduction, patching, imitation, restoration, idealizing, sentimentalizing. The letterform serves a practical purpose in a picture. (A poster!) It speaks. What would the purpose of a letterform be otherwise? For the Cubists, letterforms only decorated the surface with their modern expressiveness.

The project of the new world can only be prepared by the NEW PERSON through programmatic work that is acutely real, deeming even good subconscious work unreliable

Work — that is, a program

A picture carries out **its** function in life like every other product of human work.
A picture—a product of life intended for consumption called the world.
A picture—will not from this point on multiply misery, wretchedness, grief, nor represent the burdensome insufficiencies of today, social injustice, the belly of capital, the atmosphere in the suburbs.
A picture—of social misery helps no one, it is created out of an incapacity to create an energetic revolution, new orders, a new world.
A picture is a product of the times. A picture is not a reproduction of the times. The times are depicted in photography, film, illustrated magazines, etc.
PHOTO: objective truth and convincing clarity above all doubt. Photo killed kitsch (thanks!) but it did not kill the picture! It accelerated the clarification of visual arts development.

Photo: a documentation of the times and the beauties of this world. **A picture:** a projection and creation of new beauties, new values, a painted **portrait** which cannot compete "for the indiv. conception + the artist's soul," (the characteristics of purveyors of kitsch, clichés). Photo is capable of enormous technical development (in size, color, clarity, speed). A colorful Gauguin = 0 against a perfect color photo of the tropics.

Photo realized the dreams of the old masters from long ago—why do fools still admire them?—because their painterly ideal was nothing more than imitation and reproduction. Illusionism.

NEW FORMS OF TODAY AND THE DAILY EMERGING
most beautiful poetry: the telegram and the photo—economy, truth, brevity.

You have seen the film with Pickford at the sea, where she slowly turns her head and languorously looks at us with her shining eyes—that is, at some hundred, thousand people—MONA LISA—you cannot compete!

It is natural that painters à la Nejedlý & Beneš and that whole crowd fight against the modernism that is crashing down on them like an avalanche; in vain, they do not have enough strength to find a stable and suitable place for themselves or their work in today's world—they are entirely superfluous parasites. The photo is a more perfect narrator than them.

Art of the past	Art of the present	
Reproduction of the world and life	a) Photo A more perfect, more instructive reproduction of the world and life	b) visual arts and poetry the project of new life, new beauty new value

I hate galleries where pictures collect mold for centuries (eternal storage). The health of the world and its youth depend on everything old being used up and replaced with the new. That is why the world does not grow older—with every hour it is younger and more beautiful. If it were not for historicism, the world would be about a century younger.

TRADITION: the old masters observed historical works to see how not to paint. Modern painters do the same, or even better: they do not notice them at all.

WE SHOULD NOT CONSERVE WHAT IS DEAD! **CLEAR AWAY THE DEAD, THEY SMELL!**

Advancement and progress: nothing will be impossible, all real projects will be feasible, distance = relative. For sad lover, we will cultivate black roses. Our projects will not be fever dreams or utopias, they will be truly poetic.

ATTENTION:

The necessity to differentiate. Which parts of the current world form the basis of the new world?
A picture is born from reflection, construction, and combination of real elements and thoughts and it is not a superficial, enthusiastic view. The Epigonoi copied but were bad at creating. The **machine** + mechanical reproduction is taking their place. There will be less pictures and more mechanical reproductions.

LOVE NEW PICTURES

May 1923.

Vítězslav Nezval: Parrot on a Motorcycle, or On the Craft of Poetry

It has to be said without beating around the bush. I was awaiting in vain the arrival of the clairvoyant stenographer, when a fever, liberating itself from medical encyclopedias, turned into a firework show and started to dance. My charming little sister, my radio dove, bon vent bonne mer! The one who came from the nearby quiet of the hospital or from the boulevards of the last century and inclined her ear to my head will hear the ringing of 30 alarm clocks.

The nervous health of the XX century is a precondition of modern poetry, enabling speedy associations and free images.

*

I am engaged in favor of my method.

*

The poets of former times revered philosophy. The idea. Its continued gradation. Deduction, induction, elaboration of the subject (*sujet*), conclusion. The logic of concepts dressed in a ceremonial attire. Oh, what work! — The musty discomfort of offices. Thinkers!

The old method of creation, inorganic, subordinated to ideology, the subject, and logic.

*

I am in constant contact with my sensory processes. All senses in working order and on the go. 36 antennas and instinct eternally interacting. All of them melt into one single point of the chessboard. A sum of palpitations and its arrows — and lo and behold, sensibility.

A new method, an organic and physiological growth of form from images and their laws of reproduction.

Hey, look, it is you that are creating me! The sense of hearing through which I am being led to eternal sleep. The constant humming of the boulevards. A muted din through which I am put to death. It is necessary to look up at the flying airplane and hear the lark's song. A state of sensitivity in delirium.

Auditory types of artists decline along with the status of Romantic contemplation.

Hey, it is you! Eyes, through which I am awakened to life. It is necessary to see electronic flowers and to smell the fragrance in a repulsive throng. Magic mirrors, eyes, a vision of a primeval forest and bold fat verses on the corner. Hey, it is you! Blue colors of blouses, that upright firmament, the cockades of horse coachmen. And the constant presence of my gardens and wine grape harvests, my birds! Unforgettable fairy tales.

The superiority of images generated from modern big city realities has increased the visual capability of today's artist.

*

For me there are no concepts. Away with the subject! All this I have seen every day in several fractions of a second. I carry you with myself without any philosophical connection. It is you that are creating me. Hey, this is me! A sum of the images of these parrots with magical names.

The concept and the subject are deduced correlates of philosophical epochs. Logical and ideological Scholasticism.
The image, a primary and physiological correlate.

*

Unceasing intermixing. Every time a different mix. The law of association, no other force than that which governs my thirst and my passion.

The laws of this poetry are quite living like the laws of dreams.

*

It is necessary to constantly obey this law. Laziness, a Hydra that you want to be eternally satiated! It is necessary to constantly invent.

*

Poetic intelligence consists in deafening imbibed intelligence.

A magician who, from an endless array of possibilities, has always chosen only one. Elements in a constant whirl. Hey, look, some angles:

IMAGE: A face sharply reflected in a mirror, a fiery parrot or a lantern. The curtain falls! A face sharply reflected in a mirror.

ASSOCICIATION: An alchemist faster than a radio. It is quiet natural like an exchange of blood. Sparks jumping from one star to another. That peculiar type of thinking when we float along the river of Acheron attracted by the magnetic mountains which open up with their tableaus. A journey on a roundabout in a cave that has darkness between glass oases, between bouquets of light and fountains.

Primary association, generally valid, mediating the a state of open hypnosis between poet and reader
Secondary association, dependent on individual memory.

*

RYTHM: A force that tears apart the connectedness of pulsations. Gaps in the logical. There is no fluency. There is scintillation. Images accepted and rejected, humming-birds in a certain lighting. A range of signals.

Rhyme: To bring closer together distant wastelands, periods of time, races and castes through consonance of words. To discover strange friendships.

Necessity of the imaginary quality of the rhyming words.

Assonance: acute, mondaine, irresistible. It is unstable and magical like a port before departure, like the love of those who have glanced fleetingly at each other and fallen in love. An entertaining misalliance. A child about whom they said: a coquette.

Assonance permits a great quantity of associations, not being burdened with an acoustic bond as rule-bound as rhyme.

Metaphor: a gallant exalted man of the world.

Metaphor: an instrument of poetic transfiguration.

Art: The art of capturing and directing these runners. The art of an equilibrist. Hey look, maximum performance — that is actually a game.

Work: This is what came before. Ask the dancers and the fire-eaters. Ask the parrot riding a motorcycle.

Absolute control of form and construction. The creation of complexion.

Muse: That which gives tone to the fragrance.

A muse.

The ***axiom*** of this method, an entirely physiological process. The satisfying of the poetic instinct.

Integral predominance.

Art: great lovers, brave and beautiful, walking through a den of onanists.

Wings.

POEM: A miraculous bird, a parrot on a motorcycle. Laughable, fatigued, miraculous! A thing like soap, a mother-of-pearl knife, or an airplane.

A distinctive real object in the world of images and their forms, independent of the world of appearances.

Some likings: loud colors, roundabouts, pictures of saints in lace, the accordion, players from Jenofefa, people in aprons, planets, schnapps, the countryside, fairy tales and their associations.

Material from which its poetic superstructure arises.

Some likings: powder, shop display-windows, parks, promenades, orchestrions, a coffee-house, caprice, artificial flowers and their associations.

Love for the Muse.

Mireio 1923

New mix: History and fairy tales mixed with stories from music hall. A miraculous hybridization.

Invention.

Emotion: Maximum emotion in one second. Not a description. Summary image: a reflector that has an effect. A blow in sleep that provokes a dream. A procession like in a dream. From an effect to specific details. A bright point that stirs up the surface.

Psychoanalysts will evidently discover the true sense of this poetry.

Purpose: Emotion.

On the day of the last judgment, instead of a cynical corpse, that woeful funeral pyre of love, I will have to cast in front of the creator's face two or three poems. I enriched the world with two or three new parrots. For Rousseau the customs officer:

"A small pittance of a penny farthing helped him to paradise."

Karel Teige: Poetism

In the style-free 19th century various -isms were born, a looser and less binding replacement for styles. Today, there is no ruling -ism. Following Cubism, we have been witnesses of a competition between numerous artistic schools and creeds. Art has lost guidelines and become individualized to an extreme extent; it is dissolving into groups that call themselves avant-garde. There is only "new art," "the youngest art," which often boasts errors as old as the world, calling these errors: eternal truths. The degeneration of -isms is a simple symptom of a ***manifest degeneration of the hitherto types of art***.

Nevertheless, a new style is arising, and with it a NEW ART. This new art, not recognizing traditional prejudices, has ceased to be art and permits every promising hypothesis; it sympathizes with experiments, and its methods are as benign, its sources as rich and plentiful, as life itself.

This kind of art is probably going to be pursued by spirits who are less literary and professional, but who are on the other hand more lively and cheerful. In the flowers of this art you will find such an entrancing fragrance of life that this will allow you to forget about problematic artistic issues.

Artistic professionalism cannot last any longer. If the new art — and that art which we call POETISM — is the art of life,

the art of living and enjoying life,

then it must be just as self-evident, adorable, and accessible as sport, love, wine, and all delicacies. It cannot be an employment; it must rather be a general need. No individual life, if it is to be lived morally — that is, in smiles, happiness, love, and dignity — can get by without this art. A professional artist is a mistake and to a certain extent an anomaly already today. Professional clubs were not allowed at the Paris Olympics in 1924. Why should we not also reject just as resolutely the professional guilds of business people engaged in painting, writing, modeling, and engraving? An artistic work is not a speculative business article and cannot be the subject of rigid academic discussion. It is essentially a gift, or a game without seriousness or consequences.

The new, endless, and scintillating beauty of the world is the daughter of current life. It was not born from aesthetic speculation or from a romantic atelier mentality, but it is rather the simple result of the purposeful, disciplined, and positive production and living activity of humankind. It has not taken up residence in cathedrals or galleries; it has found its home outside in the streets, in the architecture of cities, in the refreshing green spaces of parks, in busy harbors, and in the forges of industry that nourish our primary needs. It has not prescribed any formal recipes for itself. Modern forms and structures are the result of purposeful work produced and perfectly executed under the diktat of a given aim and the economy. It contained the engineer's calculation and fulfilled his poetic vision. The science of building cities, Urbanism, has thus provided works that are enthralling and poetic; these works constitute the outline of a ground plan of life, a prototype of the future, a utopia that will be made real in a red communist future. The products of this Urbanism are machines of abundance and happiness.

The new beauty has been born from Constructivist work, which is the foundation of modern life. The triumph of Constructivist method (the extinction of manufacture, the suppression of decorative art, and a shift to serial production, categorization, standardization) is enabled only by the hegemony of the rigorous intellectualism that manifests itself in contemporary technical materialism. Marxism. The Constructivist principle is, therefore, the principle that is a condition of the very existence of the modern world. Purism is the aesthetic control of Constructivist work, nothing more and nothing less.

Flaubert wrote this prophetic sentence: "The art of tomorrow will be impersonal and scientific." Today's architecture, the building of cities, industrial art is ***a science***. It is not artistic creation, gushing from Romantic enthusiasm, but a simple intensive ***civilizational work***. Social technology.

Poetism is the crown of life whose basis is Constructivism. As relativists, we are convinced of a hidden irrationality that the scientific system has not perceived and not suppressed. It is in the interest of life for the calculations of engineers and thinkers to be rational. However, every calculation rationalizes irrationality only to a few decimal places. The calculation of every machine contains the symbol π.

In the current period it is necessary to have a special disposition for experiencing stark psychological contrasts that are extreme to the point of paradox. A discipline of the whole. Yet we are thirsting for the freedom of the individual. "After six days of work and building the world, beauty is the seventh day of souls." This sentence from O. Březina really captures the relationship between Poetism and Constructivism. When a person has lived like a working citizen, he wants to live like a person, like a poet.

Poetism is not only the opposite, but also the necessary complement of Constructivism. It is founded on Constructivism's ground plan.

The art that is brought by Poetism is nonchalant, frolicsome, fantastical, playful, unheroic, and amorous. There is not a speck of Romanticism in it. It was born in an atmosphere of exuberant sociability, ***in a world that laughs***; no matter that tears are running from its eyes. A humorous temperament prevails; pessimism has been sincerely abandoned. It is shifting emphasis in the direction of the pleasures and beauties of life, away from musty workplaces and ateliers; it is a signpost of a path that does not lead from anywhere to anywhere, but which revolves in a resplendent fragrant park, because it is the path of life. The hours here come along on blooming roses. Is this a fragrance? Is it a recollection?

Nothing. Nothing other than a lyrical-sculptural excitement at the wonder of the modern world. Nothing other than an amorous inclination toward life and its manifestations, the passion of modernity, modernolatry (worship of modernity), if we are to use the words of Umberto Boccioni. Nothing other than happiness, love, and poetry — heavenly things that cannot be purchased for money and that are not so serious that people are prepared to murder for them. Nothing other than joy, magic, and a manifold optimistic confidence in the beauty of life. Nothing other than the immediate data of sensibility. Nothing other than the art of wasting time. Nothing other than the melody of the heart. A culture of miraculous dazzling. Poetism wants to make life into a magnificent entertainment enterprise. An eccentric carnival, a harlequinade of feelings and images, a drunken reel of film, a miraculous kaleidoscope. Its muses are amiable, tender, and smiling, its perspectives are as fascinating and incomprehensible as the glances of lovers.

Poetism has no philosophical orientation. It would perhaps admit to a dilettantish practical, tasteful, and delicate eclecticism. It is not a world view — Marxism is that for us — but a living atmosphere, and this atmosphere is clearly not that of the study, the library, or the museum. It evidently speaks only to those who are from the new world and it has no intention of being understood and misused by Passéists. It harmonizes living contrasts and opposites, and what marks it out is that for the first time it brings a poetry that does not need words, music, or rhyme — something already longed for by Whitman.

Poetism is not literature. In the Middle Ages laws and grammatical rules were also turned into verse for the purposes of schooling. Tendentious ideological verses with "content and a story" are the last remnants of this type of poetry. The beauty of poetry is without purposes, without grand phrases, without deep intentions, without an apostolic message. It is a game of beautiful words, a combination of images, a weaving of pictures — possibly even ***without words***. What is needed for it is the free spirit of a juggler who does not intend to apply to poetry rational teachings or to infect it with ideology; rather than philosophers and pedagogues, it is clowns, dancers, acrobats, and tourists who are modern poets. The sweetness of artificiality and the spontaneity of feeling. A communication, a poem, a letter, an amorous conversation, the improvisation of drinking sprees, causerie, fantasy, a piece of comedy, an airy and light card game of recollections, a wonderful period in which people smile and laugh: a week in colors, lights, and fragrances.

Poetry is not painting. Painting, avoiding an anecdotal nature and avoiding the danger of decoratism, has set out down a path toward poetry. Just as poetry has become a form of creative expression (in the works of Apollinaire, Marinetti, and in Birot's "*plein air* poetry" and also in his films), so painting, liberating itself in a Cubism of form and color, has ceased to imitate reality because it could not compete with the photograph of reportage and it has started ***to become a form of poetic expression in an optical form. Optical words*** created in flag semaphore. And also in international traffic signs. Abstraction and geometricality, a perfect and infallible system, excite the modern soul. The process of emancipation from the frame of the picture, begun by Picasso and Braque, eventually leads to the ***abnegation of the paneled painting.*** A poetical picture is a book illustration, a photograph, a photo-montage.

The new language of art is heraldic: ***the language of signs.*** It works with standards. (For instance, Au Revoir! Bon vent, bon mer! Adieu! Green disc: way open. Red disc: way closed.)

Poetism is not an -ism — or at least not an -ism in the hitherto narrow sense of the word, because today there is no artistic -ism. Constructivism is a method for all productive work. Poetism is — let us repeat — in the most beautiful sense of the word the art of living, a modernized form of Epicurianism. It does not introduce an aesthetic that forbids or prescribes anything whatsoever. It has no wish to shape today's life or tomorrow's life according to abstract rules. It is not a codified morality. Morality is shaped only by the friendly relations of co-existence, between one person and another, a pleasure-seeking *bon ton* that rejects narrow-mindedness. Apart from that, -isms are not an entirely precise designation; they do not mean what they say, and to explicate them literally — almost etymologically and philologically — would in some cases (for instance, Cubism) be deranged madness. Neither Poetism, nor Constructivism, can be understood in any other way than as a designation of a method, an opinion, a belief, as a simple case of terminology (as in the cases: socialism, communism, liberalism, etc.).

Poetism is not art — that is, it is not art in the hitherto Romantic sense of the word. ***It has set out to bring about the regular liquidation of hitherto artistic varieties*** in order to establish the rule of pure poetry, shining in countless forms, multi-faceted like a fire and like love. It has at its disposal film (the new cinematography) and also aviation; radio; technical, optical, and acoustic discoveries (opto-phonetics); sport; dance, circus, and music hall — places of everyday discoveries and perpetual improvisations. It fully corresponds to our need for entertainment and activity. It is capable of precisely assigning art to its proper place: It does not overestimate its own importance; it knows that it is certainly not more valuable than life. Clowns and Dadaists taught us this aesthetic self-scepticism. Today, we no longer place poetry only into books and albums. Yachts are also a modern poem, an instrument of joy.

It is certain that human beings discovered art, like everything else, for their happiness, pleasure, and entertainment. A work of art that does not produce happiness and does not entertain is dead, even if its author were to be Homer. Chaplin, Harold Lloyd, Burian, the director of a firework show, a victorious boxer, an inventive and skillful cook, a record-breaking alpine climber — are poets anything greater than these?!

Poetism is primarily a modus vivendi. It is a function of life, and at the same time a fulfillment of its meaning. It is the creator of general human happiness and beautiful comfort, unexactingly pacific. Happiness is a comfortable apartment, a roof over one's head, but also love, excellent entertainment, laughter and dancing. It is an exalted upbringing. A stimulant of life. It ventilates depression, worries, and sullenness. It is spiritual and moral hygiene.

Life of itself, in the tiredness of work and the monotony of days, would be a senseless form, if it was to lack an animating heart, a flexible sensibility, and thus poetry has become the only aim of life as a purpose in itself. To fail to understand Poetism is to fail to understand life!

*

Humankind emerged from the war tired, disquieted, bitterly deprived of illusions, powerless to desire, to love, and to pursue a new, better life. Poetism (within the limits of its possibilities) wants to heal this moral hangover and also the illnesses flowing from it, which were manifested in Expressionism, for instance.

It grows from the constant needs of a human being, without pretension and artistic humbug. It knows that the greatest value of humankind is primarily the human being him or her self, his individual freedom subject to the discipline of collective solidarity, his happiness, the harmony of internal life. It is revising the historical idea of happiness. It is revising values and, in a period of the twilight of models, it has established ***the value of lyricism*** as its own particular and true golden treasure.

It is necessary to live a modern opinion on life through to its final consequences. Only in truth is a modern person a complete person. Romantic artists are defective individuals. *Être de son temps*. And art is the immediate signature of life.

*

Today, the world is ruled by money, by capitalism. Socialism means that the world is supposed to be ruled by reason and wisdom, economically, purposefully, usefully. The method of this rule is Constructivism. However, reason would cease to be wise, if in ruling the world it were to suppress the area of sensibility: Instead of an enhancement, this would mean an impoverishment of life, because the only richness that has value for our happiness is a richness of feelings, an extensive sensibility. And it is here that POETISM intervenes for the rescue and renewal of the life of feelings, of joy, and of fantasy.

In this essay we are trying for the first time to roughly formulate a movement that is animating several Czech modern authors. It seems that the time has come to say what Poetism is, because over the past year usage of this word has already become well established and it has often been used and misused by critics who often have no idea what it constitutes. Poetism was born as a result of mutual co-operation between several members of Devětsil. It was primarily a reaction against the ideological poetry predominant here in Czechoslovakia at that time. A rejection of Romantic aestheticism and traditionalism. A departure from hitherto "artistic" forms. In film, circus, sport, tourism, and in life itself we set out to search for the possibilities that pictures and poems did not provide us. And in this way arose ***pictorial poems, poetic puzzles and anecdotes, and lyrical films***. The authors of these experiments: Nezval, Seifert, Voskovec and, if I may add, Teige wanted to embrace all the flowers of poetry, quite unshackled from literature, which we are throwing away onto the scrapheap; we wanted a poetry of Sunday afternoons, excursions, glowing coffee houses, and intoxicating alcohols, of lively boulevards and the promenades of spa resorts, and also a poetry of quietness, of night, of peace and calm.

NOVÉ TECHNIKY V BÁSNICKÉM ŘEMESLE.

Bedřich Václavek.

Rychlost hmotného vývoje učinila z naší doby pravý opak rovnováhy a klidu. Změnila mentalitu člověka: Před 50ti lety ještě byl člověk uzavřen v nejbližším okolí. Dnes jest drahami, auty, velkým informačním tiskem, telegrafií a telef nií bez drátu, fonokin matografií v denním styku s celým světem.

Básník před 30ti lety		**Básník dnes**	
před očima: chiméry;	**jeho mentalita**:	**před očima**:	**jeho mentalita**:
	exklusivnost	**skutečnosti doby**:	zrychlený rytmus,
		positivní a tvrdé,	civilnost,
	vnitřní prázdnota	matematické,	aktivnost,
		vědecké,	spontánost
	rozkošnická nečinnost	rapidně produkující,	smysl pro odvahu,
		doby zázraků lidských,	metodičnost,
	nestálost	revoltující,	statečnost,
		vytvářející novou societu	nespoutaná básnivost.

Rodí se: VĚDOMÍ VŠEPŘÍTOMNOSTI SVĚTOVÉ
(synchronism obrazů, barev, zvuků, idei i sil, událostí, myšlenek
snu i skutečnosti
celého současného světa.)

LYRISM **především směřuje k ostrému výrazu moderního světa. Nechce jej poskytovati jednostranně, postupně, nýbrž v jeho současné mnohosti synoptické se všemi jeho vztahy, kontrasty a analogiemi. Básník vyšel z temnot dekadentních a ponořil se do ostrého světla moderního světa.**

Technika: nutnost dobré, montérské práce.

Technika povozu: technice avionů = technika staré básně: technice nové.
Místo trakaře sidecar, místo kamene beton, místo unisona polyfonní hudba,
místo hudby verše — obraz verše.

Věda o komposici!

Způsoby výroby mění se rychle. Stejně i technika průmyslu, obchodu, řemesel, včetně básnického. **Nový básník** podává prudký, mocný obraz doby

NOVÝMI PROSTŘEDKY SVÉHO ŘEMESLA.

Novou řečí. Nová látka – nová technika. **Novou technikou.**
Věnujme zde tichou vzpomínku všem poctivě
a dobře pracujícím. Bez nich
by nebylo
Nového světa.

ŘEČ má všecky přednosti a vady lidských vynálezů.

Nemá hodnoty sama o sobě. Je nástrojem básnického řemesla. Milujeme nejnovější patenty. Řeč není nikdy na výši doby. Jest sbírkou materiálu starého nebo právě stárnoucího.

Nerozumíme starým knihám

jako nerozumíme starým lidem a počáteční větě bible, protože kategorie jejich řeči se neshodují s naším poznáním a cítěním.

Myslíme a žijeme samostatně.

Nové myšlení znamená vždy opuštění tradiční řeči. Obohacení řeči. ŘEČ vznikla metaforami a roste jimi: když básnická fantasie doplňuje a oživuje slova.

SLOVO *stárne*

гъ panъ = „náčelník kraje"; – stčes. hpán – pán = „člen vyšší šlechty". Dnes každý pobuda – zítra bude toto slovo snad již nadávkou.

Slovo vzniklo vyslovením básnické hlavy (ne hlavy básníka.) Jakožto metafora znamenalo něco, často poměrně rozumného proti vymírajícímu rodu slov. V druhém období stává se šosákem. V třetím je šosáctvím zcela vylouženo, vybledne a zchátrá v nadávku.

Proto má každá doba svůj vlastní výsek řeči, jehož užívá k básnickým účelům. Napodobitelé ovšem užívají metafor starých. Básníci z druhé ruky ve středověku hotovili básně, sestavené

Bedřich Václavek: New Techniques in the Poetic Craft

The speed of material progress has generated the very opposite of equilibrium and peace in our time. It has changed the person's mentality: 50 years ago people were still limited by their surrounding environment. Today the railways, cars, large-scale printing, the telegraph and wireless telephones, as well as sound-cinematography enable daily interaction with the wider world.

The poet 30 years ago		The poet today	
had before their eyes: chimeras;	**their mentality:**	**has before their eyes:**	**their mentality:**
	exclusivity	**the realities of the time:**	accelerated rhythm,
		positive and firm,	civility,
	inner emptiness	mathematic,	activity,
		scientific,	spontaneity,
	luxurious idleness	rapidly producing,	courageousness,
		an age of human miracles,	methodicalness,
	inconstancy	revolt,	bravery,
		creating a new society	unrestrained poetics.

What is coming into existence: A CONSCIOUSNESS OF WORLDWIDE OMNIPRESENCE
(**synchronism** of pictures, colors, sounds, ideas, and forces, circumstances, thoughts,
dreams and the reality
of the whole contemporary world.)

LYRICISM **orients itself above all towards an acute expression of the modern world. It does not want to provide it unilaterally and gradually, but rather express in its contemporary synoptic plurality all possible relations, contrasts, and analogies. The poet has stepped out of a decadent darkness and into the sharp light of the modern world.**

Technology: a necessity for good, joiner's work.

The technology of the wagon cart : the technology of airplanes = technology of old poetry : technology of the new.

A sidecar instead of a wheelbarrow, concrete instead of stone, polyphonous music instead of voices in unison, verse—a picture in verse —instead of music.

The science of composition!

The means of production change quickly. As is the case with the technologies used in industry, commerce, and craft, including poetry.

The new poet provides an intense, powerful picture of the times
VIA THE NEW RESOURCES AVAILABLE TO THE CRAFT.
Via a new spoken language. A new fabric—new technique. **Via new technology.**
Let us quietly reminisce about all those working virtuously
and well. Without them
there would not be
A new world.

SPOKEN LANGUAGE has all the merits and faults that comes with human inventions.
It does not have values in and of itself. It is an instrument of the poetic craft. We love the newest patents. Spoken language is never caught up with the times. It is a collection of material that is either old or growing old.

We do not understand old books

just as we do not understand old people and the opening sentence in the Bible, because their category of spoken language does not correspond with what we think and feel.

We think and we live independently.

New thinking always requires the abandonment of traditional spoken language. The enrichment of spoken language. SPOKEN LANGUAGE came into being through metaphors and it grows with them: when poetic phantasy replenishes and revives words.

THE WORD *ages*

gъ panъ = "chief of the territory"; — Old Czech hpán — pán = "a member of the reigning aristocracy." Today everyone is a tramp—by tomorrow, the word will probably have become an insult.

Therefore every age has its own type of spoken language that it utilizes for poetic purposes. Impersonators naturally use old metaphors. Poets in the Middle Ages, on the other hand, produced poetry assembled z kombinací Vergiliových slov, domnívajíce se, že tvoří božské básně. Dnes o věcech zcela moderních píší řečí Vrchlického, Březiny, Sovy nebo Wolkera. Tím dosahují opaku poesie.

Básník tvoří metaforu ze své představy nynější a ze své duševní činnosti individuální; z nejpřítomnější nálady své a svého okolí. Záplava napodobitelů dnes však užívá citových metafor, jež už zchátraly, nevyvolávají žádoucí nálady a žijí jako nepoetické fráse. **Novotáři! Darujte nám své „nebásnické" metafory, abychom na nich dorůstali k nové citovosti!**

Slova se automatisují a nelze se jimi již sdělovati. Nová metafora, jež je nahrazuje, jest vytvářena vědomě.

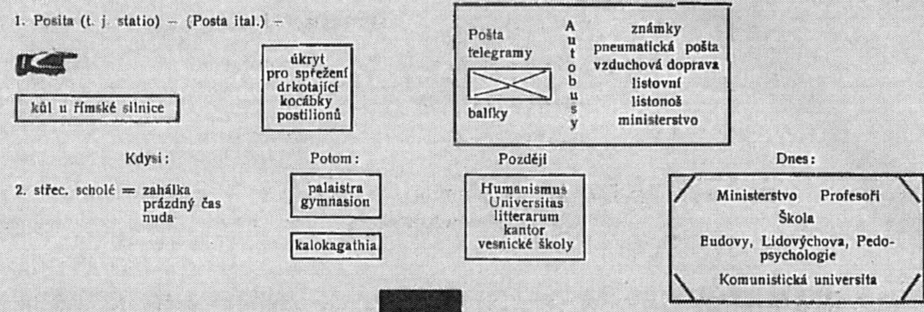

Básnická řeč dneška se teprve musí vytvořiti. Slova, jež před 30 lety rušila, působí dnes poeticky. Básnická řeč z doby obrozenské působí dnes humoristicky. K tomu je nutno s povrchu řeči převzdělané a zeškoláčtělé pohřížiti se do barevných hlubin Řeči.

Rozlom dnešní řeči:

1. Šílená řeč, jež se nabažila býti mezi lidmi, provázeti jejich bídu a prostou radost. Odloučena od lidské nuzoty, nad lidmi, slouží přejemnělým duchovým potřebám.

2. **Reservoár** obrody: řeč lidu, techniky, **internacionální poklad slovní,** prostá řeč denního života.

Básník včerejška lopotí se, aby naléval slova do zkostnatělých forem, a je spokojen, dá-li to míru dobře naváženou — i když to neevokuje žádných emocí u čtenáře.

Velikým básníkem dneška je ten, jenž nové představy vědecké, **nové emoce civilisovaného člověka,** *nové vědomí kosmogonické* dovede přetaviti do takových slov, že se – vzata z Reservoáru – stanou slovy řeči poetické.

Rychlý hmotný vývoj a nepřehledný styk posledních 50ti let přinesl takový příliv pojmů, že nestačí k vyjádření nových duševních stavů vnitřní, významová proměna slova. (Jak vzrostla hodina od pojmu horala, jenž namahavě stoupá do hor, k pojmu železničáře v expresu!) Vznikají nová, mechanicky skládaná slova: Českomoravská Kolben. Komintern. Hapag. Glavpolitprosvět.

Hlubokou změnu, kterou působ změna základů všech umění - výrobní techniky - prodělávají techniky všech umění. Básnictví ji prodělává ve slovích a ve výrazu.

O NOVOU NÁZORNOST bojoval už Marinetti zrušením syntaxe.

Poesie není spojením slov-pojmů, ale slov-zkratek pro náladu. Neboť slova v básni nepůsobí svým pojmovým obsahem, nýbrž náplní emotivní. Slovník básnický i vědecký liší se obrazy i strukturou frází. Nesměšujte! Udržte *čistý tvar!* Poesie nepracuje s abstrakcí, jež je druhotná, ale útočí na emotivní stránky lidské psychy, jež jsou prvotné.

ZRUŠENÍ RACIONÁLNÍ LOGIKY provedl za týmž cílem moderní básník. Nechce vyjadřovati myšlenku, jež ztrnula ve frázi, ale základní associace, jež kotví mnohem hlouběji ve vědomí a jež jsou essentielní formou intelektuálního života. Aby se zbavila logiky, odstraňuje gramatiku a především její integrující část — interpunkci.

Nevyjadřuje emotivních stavů frásí, gramaticky správnou, dokonale pochopitelnou, autonomní, ukončenou, uzavřenou jako kruh, určenou a tichou, **ale obrazem skutečně viditelným, tryskající metaforou zbavenou rétorického obalu.**

2

out of combinations of Virgilian words, thinking that this was a way to create religious poetry. Today, they write completely modern things using the words of Vrchlický, Březina, Sova, or Wolker, accomplishing the opposite of poetry.

The poet creates metaphor out of their most current ideas and individual intellectual activity; that is, out of their present mood and surroundings. However, the deluge of impersonators we have today makes use of emotional metaphors that are long beyond repair, in as much as they do not invoke the desired mood and exist as unpoetic phrasing. **Creators of the new! Present to us of your "non-poetic" metaphors so we can use them to build a new kind of sentimentality.**

Words are becoming automated; it is now impossible to communicate through them. The new metaphor, their replacement, is being created deliberately.

THE WORD *grows*

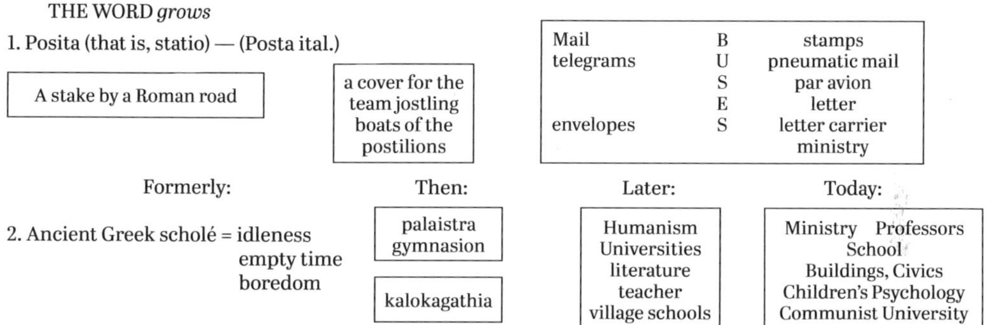

The poetic spoken language of today remains to be created. Words that were distracting 30 years ago now come off as poetic. Poetic spoken language from the Revival period comes off as humorous today. To that end, it is necessary to dive from the surface of an over-educated and didactic spoken language and plunge into the colorful depths of Spoken Language.

The break in today's spoken language:

1. Crazy spoken language, which has grown tired of being amongst people, accompanies their miseries and simple joys. It is separated from human need, it is above people, and serves overly delicate spiritual needs.

2. **The revival reservoir**: the speech of the people, technology, **international verbal treasures**, the simple speech of daily life.

The poet of yesterday toils to pour words into an ossified form and is content if that gives it a substantial size — even when it evokes no emotion in the reader.

The great poet of today is one who can, using the Reservoir, transform new scientific concepts, **new emotions of the civilized person**, *the new cosmic consciousness* into words of poetic speech.

Fast material progress and the chaos of connections over the last 50 years have brought such an influx of concepts that an interior, semantic transformation of words could not suffice to express new emotional states. (How the moment has shifted away from the depiction of the mountaineer strenuously climbing mountains to that of the railway worker on the express train!) New, mechanically composed words are arising: Českomoravská Kolben. Comintern. Hapag. Glavpolitprosvet.

A deep change has been caused by the transformation at the foundation of all art—production technology—and the technologies of all art are experiencing it. The art of poetry is seeing this through a change in words and expression.

Marinetti already fought for a NEW GRAPHIC STYLE with the dissolution of syntax.

Poetry is not connected to word-concepts but to word-abbreviations corresponding to a mood. Because it is not the conceptual content of words in poetry that affects the reader but their emotional value. Poetic and scientific dictionaries differ in imagery and phrase structure. Do not mix them up! Maintain a *pure form!* Poetry does not work with the abstract, which is derivative, but attacks emotive parts of the human psyche, which is primary.

THE DISSOLUTION OF RATIONAL LOGIC was executed by the modern poet with the same goal. The poet does not care to express thought that has petrified and become clichéd phrasing, but rather fundamental associations anchored much more deeply in consciousness that comprise the essential form of intellectual life. In order to be liberated from logic, one must get rid of grammar and above all its integrative component—punctuation.

The poet does not address emotional states through clichéd phrases, grammatically correct, perfectly understandable, autonomous, polished, complete, predetermined and quiet, **but rather by creating a truly visual picture, one gushing with metaphor and freed from its rhetorical coating.**

Nechte nás mluviti tak, aby nám rozuměl inženýr, dělník, šofér, aviatik, velkoměstský proletář! Literát nám rozuměti nebude. Nemusí.

NOVÁ TECHNIKA — VISUELNÍ

obnoví lyrism.

BÁSNICKÉ SLOVO ZTRÁCÍ
NA AKUSTICE A
STÁVÁ SE
VISUELNÍM.

Řeč = myšlení + konvenční znaménko zvukové.
Písmo = řeč + konvenční znaménko písemné.

Písmo = myšlení + konvenční znaménka: zvukové + písemné.

Písmo je často dlouhé hodiny jedinou řečí moderního člověka Člověk našeho století nacvičil viditelné značky pro své pojmy tak, že slyšitelné značky = slova mizí z jeho vědomí. Čtení a myšlení je spiato u něho přímo, střední článek slyšitelné řeči již nespolupůsobí.

Výraz moderního básníka = myšlení + písmo.
Tvar tedy musí míti: 1. myšlení, 2. i písmo.

Přednosti písma: 1. lehčí sdělitelnost časem a prostorem; 2. možnost vyjádřiti veliké útvary duchové.

Politik, filosof kdysi přednášel — dnes píše. Básník zpíval. „Mistrem pěvcem" v 16. století byl ten, kdo dovedl složiti samostatný text **i nápěv.** (Učedníci skládali texty na cizí nápěvy.) **Nápěv (melodičnost) byl integrující částí básně. Dnes jest ji: obraz básně.**

Anomalie:

Kdysi: huhňající Homér
koktající Minnesänger

Dnes: básník tisknoucí své verše či prósu
v nekonečných, stejných řádcích.

Odstraňte hrůzu z nekonečných jednotvárných stran veršů a prósy.
Riskujete, že ji bude odstraňovati hlupák podtrhováním a pokazí vaše verše.

Symbolisté užívali hudebnosti řeči za výrazový prostředek.

MODERNÍ BÁSNÍK UŽÍVÁ TISKU,
protože báseň nezpívá, ale píše.

Čtenář básně nevnímá sluchem, ale zrakem. Tiskový obrazec básně jest proto integrující součástí výrazových prostředků básníkových. OKO jest naším nejdokonalejším orgánem. Naše generace vrací mu primát, jejž mělo ve všech velikých dobách konstrukce. Díváme se na světelné reklamy, vrhané na nebe. Čekáme na optické básně v kinu.

OKEM vnímáme svět synopticky: současnou jeho mnohost shrnujeme v jediný obraz. SYNOPTICKÉ VIDĚNÍ SVĚTA:

Synchronism obrazů, barev, zvuků, idejí i sil, ať pracují společně nebo bojují spolu, myšlenek a příběhů celého současného světa promítá moderní básník do grafického obrazce zkonstruovaného z mnoha typů, osnovaného na několik ploch, současně vnímatelného.

Moderne { *gong de feu*
saturnale { *coup de cymbales*

Dispositifs mécaniques
symphonie d'odeurs électriques

orgie des sens
orgie des yeux

Tout s'y révèle

prodiigeux
anormal
cérébral
synchronique
moderne

Polie
intelligence

= alternent

Nicolas Beauduin: L'Homme cosmogonique (IX. Music-Halls str. 74.)

Technika ne akustická, ale optická.

Její výhody:

3

Let us speak in a way so that the engineer, the worker, the chauffer, the pilot, the urban proletariat will understand us! The literati will not understand. It does not have to.

NEW—VISUAL—TECHNOLOGY
will renew lyricism.
THE POETIC WORK IS LOSING
ITS ACOUSTIC ELEMENT AND
IS BECOMING
VISUAL.

Spoken language = thought + the conventional aural sign.
The letterform = spoken language + the conventional typographic sign.
The letterform = thought + conventional signs : aural + typographic.

The letterform is often the only language of the modern person. People of this new century have worked over the visual signs for their concepts so much that audible signs = words disappearing from their consciousness. Reading and thinking are directly connected; the intermediary of audible speech is no longer part of the equation.

The expression of the modern poet = thought + letterform. Thus the form must have: 1. Thought, and 2. the letterform.

The merits of the letterform: 1. easier communication through time and space; 2. the possibility to express great spiritual structures.

The politician and the philosopher used to make speeches—now they write. The poet sang. In the 16th century, "Master Singer" was a person who could compose a self-contained text **and melody**. (Apprentices composed texts adopting others' melodies.) **The melody (melodiousness) was the integrating component of a poem. Today that component is: the picture of a poem.**

An Anomaly:

Formerly: Homer muttering
Minnesänger stuttering

Today: the poet printing their verse or prose
in unending, identical lines.

Do away with the horror of unending, single-form lines of verse and prose.

You run the risk that a fool will do away with them by underlining them and thereby destroying your verses.

The Symbolists use musicality in spoken language as an expressive tool.

THE MODERN POET USES PRINT,
because they do not sing poetry but rather write it down.

The reader of poetry does not perceive by sound but by sight. The printed image of poetry is thus an integrating component of expressive poetic tools. THE EYE is our most perfect organ. Our generation returns it to the primacy it boasted in all great times of construction. We look upon illuminated advertisements, cast amongst the heavens. We await optical poetry in the cinema.

WITH THE EYE we perceive the world synoptically: we synthesize its simultaneous multiplicity into a single image. A SYNOPTICAL VISION OF THE WORLD:

**A synchronism of pictures, colors, sounds, ideas, and forces, whether they work together or against one another, the modern poet projects thoughts and stories about the entire contemporary world into graphic illustrations, constructed from many sorts,
laid out on multiple surfaces,
and simultaneously perceptible.**

Modern { *gong of fire*
Saturnalia { *clash of cymbals*
Mechanical device
A symphony of electrical odors
orgy of senses all reveals itself there prodigious
orgy of eyes abnormal
cerebral
synchronic
Madness = they alternate modern
intelligence

Nicolas Beauduin. The Cosmogonical Man (IX. Music-Halls, p. 74)

Technology is not acoustic, but optical.

Its advantages:

Stručnost, rychlost a přesnost sdělení (= požadavky moderního člověka), **výraznost,** čistota linií.

NOVÁ BÁSEŇ:
pohyb života ve vztazích se všemi ostatními pohyby universálního života. Odehrává se nejen v čase, ale i v prostoru. Blíží se filmu. Synoptická tabulka lyrických hodnot.

DEFINICE SLOVNÍKA:
to, co může býti pojato jedním pohledem ve všech částech své celosti.

TECHNIKA:
mnohotypový synoptism. (Nutnost nových pravidel komposice a dikce.)

Opuštění successivních a monodických forem lyrických.

Konstrukce, taylorisace výrazu, polymelodie, synoptický pluralism, polyfonická orchestrace.

VEĎME MODERNÍ SENSIBILITU
novými prostředky
k synteze snu a skutečnosti!

Brevity, swiftness and precision of communication (= the demands of the modern person), **expressiveness**, a purity of line.

NEW POETRY:
A life in motion in relation with all the other movements of universal life. It not only takes place in time, but also in space. It approaches film. It is a synoptic sign of lyrical values.

DICTIONARY DEFINITION:
when all parts of the whole can be taken in with one look.

TECHNIQUE:
multi-type synoptism.
(The need for new rules of composition and diction.)

Forsaking successive and monodic lyrical forms.

Construction, Taylorization of expression, polyphony, synoptic pluralism, polyphonic orchestration.

LET US BRING FORTH MODERN SENSIBILITY
with new tools
towards a synthesis of dream and reality!

Karel Teige: Constructivism and the Liquidation of "Art"[1]

For my purposes, constructivism does not mean some temporary aesthetic and artistic mode, but an important current phase in the progress of human thought and work, representing the present moment in the history of humanity, the youngest nuance in Europe. It is not at all an extremely narrow art -ism as those that crop up from time to time to ruffle the surface of the boredom of artistic life, it is active and living, a powerful and strident movement that gradually takes hold of all civilized countries. It is very civil and wholly international, a healthy direction for all productive work. The triumph of its beliefs and method, which is apparent everywhere, is a notable and substantive characteristic of our time. Constructivism marks a new beginning and indicates a new architecture, the rise of a new era for culture and civilization in general.

The catchphrase *Constructivism*, it could be said, is an interpretation in and of itself, a nearly philological and etymological one. It comes from *the verb to construct*. And so what is constructivist is simply synonymous with constructive. This interpretation, however primitive, is in fact much more apt than a conception of Constructivism as just the newest art -ism, the *dernier cri* of the atelier and exhibition halls. Because through the word Constructivism, *it is not possible to mean, simply, art*. I consider Constructivism as *the shadow of the present*, as something that connotes the current era of culture and civilization. I must emphasize that it does not usher in a new formalist system, an a priori aesthetic order, but rather forsakes all traditional forms and dissuades the ten Muses of classical Parnassus; it

1 Previous translations have appeared in *Between Worlds: A Sourcebook of Central European Avant-Gardes, 1910–1930*, Alexandra Büchler, trans. (Cambridge, Mass.: MIT Press, 2002), 583–589; and *Modern Architecture in Czechoslovakia*, trans. Irena Žantovská (Los Angeles: Getty Research Institute, 2000), 331–341.

is not about form, *it is about function*. Up until now, all art has been informed by Formalism. Constructivism proclaims the negation of Formalism with Functionalism. It is not about new artistic formula for the basic reason that it is *not about art at all*.

The liquidation of art.
With Constructivism we proceed
to the legitimate liquidation of art.

I declare the complete collapse of the varieties of so-called-art up to now. If I continue to employ the word "art" and if I continue to even use it in the future as a helpful term, it is necessary to take note that to me, it does not mean a sacred and aristocratic art with a capital A: beautiful academic art, ars academica, les beaux arts, dethroned by the modern era. For me, the word **art comes from the verb "to be able to" (*umět*i) and its product is artificiality, artefact.** It is thus a word simply indicating every artificial perfection and proficiency. In this sense, it is possible to speak of the art of building, of the decorative, theatrical, filmic arts, as well as the culinary, poetic, photographic, travel, and dance arts; the Czech language allows one to speak about the medical, mathematical, or agricultural arts; there exist books and guides on the art of paying one's debt, the art of palmistry, the art of tying a tie, the art of getting married. Art is simply a manner of making use of specific tools in a specific function and even the function and the tools are more or less varied in their significance. Art, according to the Larousse dictionary, is the application of knowledge towards the realization of a specific task.

This was intended to explain that I do not attribute any sacral and cultic haughtiness to art, that I do not ensconce it with the smoke of frankincense. I frankly renounce all aesthetic fetishism. Modern vitality regards so-called art as an anachronism of an aesthetic mentality and the Futurists in Italy and in Russia spit on the altar of art. The rational opinion of an unprejudiced Constructivism asserts that the whole problem of so-called art is outmoded today, that "art" itself is without value for us, that it is finished, that "art" and "artists" have simply lost their *raison d'être*. The degeneration of the artistic fields of painting, sculpture, and theater is so obvious that it is not possible to hide it.

OUR CIVILIZATION IS NOT THE CIVILIZATION OF ARTS AND CRAFTS (L'EPOQUE DES ARTS ET MÉTIERS) BUT THE CIVILIZATION OF THE MACHINE (LE SIÈCLE DE LA MACHINE).

If the Constructivists pronounced (in the words of Ilya Ehrenburg) that

new art quits being art

it was not their intention to perpetrate a brilliant paradox or Futurist iconoclasm. They only wanted to make an observation, articulate a piece of knowledge. They state that there are no eternal values in art and that today's art seeks a path to its own extinction. If we understand artwork simply as products that respond precisely to a specific material or spiritual need, which is the satisfaction of a person, a whole complex being, in that sense art is eternal, no matter how much its forms and manners change, and it lasts as long as the human race does. If we however understand art as the singular field of craft which delegated to Parnassus its nine representatives, then it is necessary to concede that these fields can go bankrupt and be replaced by others. The human need to live and be clothed is most likely eternal: but it does not follow from there that the decorative arts shall also be eternal. The human need for poetic delight, spiritual enjoyment, the need for an affected sensibility mediated through colors, forms, sounds, words, and smells, is apparently permanent, but it does not follow from there that picture panels, symphonic orchestras, and literature should always be necessary. This is all the more so if the modern person's thirst for beauty finds its satisfaction elsewhere, amidst the drama of life, rather than in so-called art. Any person with a modern sensibility can feel the insufficiency of art so far.

The Constructivists do not appear on the scene with proposals for a new art, but with plans for a new world, a program for a new life. They do not carry out some aesthetic theory but rather create a new world. They enter the scene with a proposal for a new globe. They propose to reconstruct the world on a new basis, oriented towards social equality. They deny *en bloc* all Classicism and Romanticism, all art -isms and aestheticisms, which demands both brave will and prudent intelligence. They have left the musty museums, the burial ground of thought, and swept away the dust from under their shoes. Inasmuch as the past is dead and history is no longer a teacher, it is not necessary to appeal to museums, traditions, or history. Renan rightly prophesied that a time would soon come when people would no longer be interested in their past. We can reduce all of history to statistics. It is more expressive and less illusive.

All of the modern art -isms that are the most contradictory seek analogy with the past in order to validate their authority. They have always managed to pull it off with a little goodwill. It is possible to find anything in history and to authorize anything with historical examples. If you want to, you can find Cubism, Orphism, Futurism, and Impressionism in the old masters. However, across history, for every argument *for* there always emerges an argument *against* and so it goes on forever. The Gothic floor plan, or perhaps San Vitale in Ravenna, could be presented as an analogy to new architecture—and likewise the architecture of Asia Minor, Morocco, and maybe even Tibet—whose floor plans are wholly unmodern. I therefore renounce once and for all an impulse to affirm modern principles in art-historical arguments, simply because I am convinced that they are not arguments and that the modern age is essentially incomparable to any other era of the past.

The twilight of artistic models has set in. The eyes, which make it possible to see, intelligence, which makes it possible to understand, and sensibility, which makes it possible to feel, have recognized that in the field of so-called art, there are more idols than any real values. Even so-called eternal values are idols; in reality, they are nothing but *long dead values*.

The non-believers and the skeptical modern spirit cannot be deceived by the myth of eternal values. Our stoic era believes that every human action is provisory, that there are no definitive states, that nothing lasts except that which is no longer living. Eternity belongs to the cosmic forces and we must not and cannot attend to it. There are no other truths besides the occasional, ephemeral truths. The basic characteristic of the modern spirit is skepticism against all dogma, all absolute truths, all eternal value. It exerts its power so as not to be confined by any rule, so that it always takes count of all circumstances and eventualities. Modern life became as strong and inventive through this skepticism as no other before it. The modern, unbelieving spirit, passionately pronouncing its freedom and lack of bias, is fully and unreservedly devoted to the animate and colorful life of the present moment; it ignores any order outside of that reigning life. *Constructivism knows how to look upon the world without absolute values.*

The rational spirit of Constructivism is necessarily realistic. It has a sufficiently ironic attitude towards eternity and the absolute. It knows that the heavens, regarded as inconsumable, mean nothing but a continual passing of existence. (A. France) Modern philosophy, which explores every fact, breaking it down to its essential elements without regard for any of its external labels (like "art"), searching for the possibilities hidden within it as well as its conditions, and answering the question of what it used to be before it became what it is now. Criticism would thus have had to become the science of a development of art types. And here I recognize that not even in art are there absolute truths as the spirit of art is in incessant transformation; the concept of truth generally excludes the concept of progress. And if the world is in progress, then the person is also in progress, in no way a complete being, constantly seeking to find a path to perfection and in order to create the new person. The person of one generation no longer demands or creates such poetry as the preceding generations. There is no eternal persistence, there is only eternal change and renewal. A new, active, dynamic conception of eternity, in which static, permanent values and truths do not have a place. Absolute and normative aesthetics are impossible and senseless. The ideal erotic type fundamentally changes in space and time; and with it the ideal of beauty, which is directly or indirectly dependent on the former, while undergoing even more fundamental changes. For the Negro, beauty lies in prominent lips, for Fairbanks it lies in the sportsman, for the Platonic ideal it lies in the ephebe, for the Jew in Tunisia it lies in a fat bride, and for the modern woman it lies in: herself.

We cannot lean on traditional principles and classical aesthetics. Classical aesthetics do not suffice for all the different types of today and cannot be the basis of modern criticism. Their theories could not remain valid if it were ascertained that they do not conform to the truth. Every work has its temporal order, its set of principles and its aesthetic. The aesthetic can only have value if there is a relative work to which its principles relate. Theory in and of itself has no value and purpose; only a theory of definite relative work, a direction, or movement does.

There are no historically traditional ideals and aesthetic norms, no inherited laws. Modern culture and civilization are a fact of their own laws and manners. If some work can demonstrate its viability against the arising and reining opinions, it would be foolish to condemn it. If new phenomena of technical civilization can demonstrate that their poetic intensity offers excellent compensation for a dying type of art, I shall welcome it with enthusiasm. I do not want to shut down any belief that could likely bring a needed resolution. Neither classical beauty nor the beauty of the Middle Ages is commensurable and homogenous with today's beauty, and I will not insist upon it. A so-called eternal order of art is often emphasized. But that supposedly eternal order, presumably derived from previous artistic realizations, and therefore in reality ex post, would logically need something to exist a priori. Works are after all not principles but results and outcomes that have grown from many and multi-sided experiences. If a new fact of life and culture is to be produced, philosophy, ethics, morality, aesthetics and criticism automatically need new criteria and measures. To today's relativism and pragmatism, the truth and beauty are a specific type of good and therefore not a self-sufficient category, which is possible to accept as correct within specific parameters. It is thus about a specific utility of art, in which the ethos is production. And by the way, I do not consider the utility to be material relativism exclusively.

The functionality of art (and not form, content, tendency, or the myths of German "Inhaltsestetika" ["aesthetic content"]) is the first and most important criterion. We cannot pointlessly squander abstract words on form and content and their relationship: a correctly posed question would inquire about function. In place of the artistic Formalism existing up to now—as all art was formalist—the Constructivist era lays down the basis for *Functionalism*. It is not about forms. It is about the reality of maximal *function*. And at this juncture, we diverge completely from traditional aesthetics and so-called art.

By abandoning the art of the house of worship, we came to stand at the crux of current life. Modern life is without a religious creed, as it itself is the creed of the modern person. It creates its products in a way that does not correspond to the prescriptions of aesthetic and ethical theories but rather takes the person into account. Constructivism sets stylistic and aesthetic criteria against its **human criterion**. "What the person has developed into actually goes against nature, hence their magnitude and beauty. Human beauty is artificial and only as such is it adequate and natural to the human; it is an invention that is perfected over time, one of visible work and intelligence." To the Constructivists, *people are the measure of all things*. Architecture, cities, instruments, sport, all are according to human measure. *People are the measure for all tailors.* It is thus the *stylistic principle* of all of architecture, because is not our domestic dwelling essentially another component of our apparel? And do we not all need to fit constructively together in our dwellings, just as our clothes ought to be truly functional, hygienic, discreet and elegant? Modern style and modern culture, being functionalist, does not have a single canonical form; it does not have a single constructivist principle as the Classical or Gothic had, for instance. The common denominator of everything is the *person*.

*

— The person is the stylistic principle of Constructivism. See *skeleton*, which contains within itself all creative and constructive laws in action: the calm and the energy of surfaces, purity, fineness, a defined profile, both an asymmetry and equilibrium of the organs, whose function indicates and determines the mass, the unceasing movement of substantial surfaces, a fluency and connection of curves, which require the unity of the organism.
— And see modern construction on a human scale and judge it by a human measure. The anatomic architecture of the iron framework of a hangar, which managed to escape the architectural formula of the Middle Ages, that is, the fortress. The framework is on the inside and there are no load-bearing walls, and thin skin covers it. Expressing the constructive framework on the surface was a provisional architectonic mode: the person only has constructive framework at the ankles and several joints!
— The Perret house in Paris on Rue Franklin from the year 1903 is also built to human scale. It is a constructor's tour de force. There is no inner courtyard and the front façade ingeniously opens onto the gardens opposite. Direct lighting. There are no load-bearing walls: the whole construction is carried by some minimal concrete pillars. The façade, while it does not attempt to mask the constructive framework, also does not aim to express it.

* * *

The person dresses and arms oneself in civilization. The form of civilization is a result of the struggle with nature, the exploitation of nature and changes from generation to generation. Nanook, a primitive human, has a biomechanical civilization, complementing primitive tools with the agility of their own muscles. The modern person has a machine civilization; the complex organization of their tools and production governed by still more complex forces of the spirit. We have left the cave and become the inhabitants of the big city and while the passéists call for a return to nature, "the dissolution of cities" (Taut), we cannot renounce that which we have culturally become: city people. The intervention of the machine caused an essential metamorphosis of culture and civilization, it gave the stimulus for the liquidation of art. *Because machine-made civilization is essentially at odds with a civilization of arts and crafts.* That conflict cannot be eliminated by ignoring the automobile, gramophone, cinema, and linotype. The aesthetes have funny ideas about life. As long as we live in concrete homes, we dress, we use waterlines, electric lighting, we travel by train and read the newspapers, we are not naked in the Garden of Eden. The machine has sealed the fate of craft. All attempts at its revival have proven to be not only in vain, but also unwanted. The machine liquidates art and craft. At first it imitated manual work, and it imitated it very poorly; and for this reason, an opposition to machine production was able to arise, as Ruskin has put it. Ruskin resembles the Don Quixote of Marx's aphorism: Don Quixote suffered for his errant speculation that the wandering knights could be compared to all forms of civilization. We adapt with difficulty after all to the demands of a contemporary mechanized civilization, for our historical education limits itself to a deep study of a time when the mechanical made no progress. Wells points out that historical findings in reference to Europe date from an age when the Greeks travelled around the world on horses or sail boats and gallies all the way to the days when Napoleon, Wellington, and Nelson travelled in nearly identical vehicles and sailing ships. With the discovery of steam and electricity—here the Muse of history turns up her nose and closes her eyes. And so a certain incubation period was necessary before modern productive thought could accept the machine. The machine immediately created new social, spiritual, and moral networks and relations, initiated a change in the environment, and finally became the professor of modern aesthetics and the liquidator of art. It became a part of humankind. And it is clear that its ascendance will strike down art or take possession over it. Élie Faure speaks about this. It would perhaps be more precise to say that the machine replaces art.

* * *

Our time is a time of science and technology. At first it escorted religion—at times very disrespectfully—out the door of its workroom. Consistently and candidly, it abandoned any mysticism. With idealistic enthusiasm it proclaimed itself materialist to the last consequence. It cheerfully waved the banner of Positivism. Then came experiments. What followed after religion was deprived of faith was a faith in the good of science. Scientists believe that their work can install a paradise on earth. They call this paradise a technological civilization. In the quiet of the laboratory, radium, X-rays, and serums are being discovered. In consequence of the special discoveries of pure science, verified under the microscope, massive and expansive radical changes are coming into production and industry, and applied technology is maturing into ever new inventions. As a consequence of this, beliefs are modified over and again, the medical practice and hygiene is improved, law-making and moral codes are reformed. The motivating force of this progress is the *machine*. The machine reduces work time through maximal productivity. Its law is the law of *minimal effort for maximal effect*. It is the **law of economy**. The law of economy is the law of the whole of work. And work is the only law in this world, a regulator that ushers the organizing material towards an unknown goal. Within a single year, industry is able to belch out more products than the total number of products manufactured in all the centuries prior.

Machine civilization has given modern people "the song of iron, the buzzing song of electric sparks, and they understood it: it is the song of its time, its merciless cadence can be heard in the rumble of trains passing above our heads," narrates Kellermann in the novel *Der Tunnel* (The Tunnel).

The machine is not a picturesque subject, but a structure and the development of such and such organized energies. It is not the subject matter of art, but instruction of the spirit. It is an example of a modern aesthetic, almost a symbol of modern beauty in its very organism and appearance. In its activity and function it is the liquidator of artistic crafts and all arts up to now, which have stagnated at the manufacturing stage.

"*Les belles formes sont les plaus* [sic] *droit avec les rondeurs*," (Beautiful forms are the most right with some roundness) said Dominique Ingres. And with this citation, if you please, one can verify the beauty of mechanical reproduction.

Are ball bearings, for instance, not perfectly formed pleasure for the eye? The luster of wonderful, modern material, the precision of geometric form—and the circle and ball are the most fundamental forms of all and the most flattering to our eye—directly suggesting the perfection of its tradition. This beauty responds precisely to the character of our time, persistent and sober, material and industrious.

Though I speak of the aesthetics of the machine, it is necessary to point out that I do not intend to preach about its divinity. If the sentimentalists have not been able to do anything but understandably curse the machine, the Futurists have praised it; it is necessary, however, to be rationally aware of what the machine can teach, and in how it can determine a new sensibility. We live in the age of steel, and polished steel is fascinating to our eye; mechanical beauty, if it is not the work of so-called practical knowledge, is certainly the work of the modern person; it is the crux of the culture of the era. The machine is an element that intervenes in modern conceptions. Up to now, the machine has been accepted by modern artists in a manner that is more or less incomplete, and mainly artistic. And naturalistic in essence. The distinguished beauty of the machine does not need to be festooned with ornament or panegyric poetry. The poetry of Marinetti and the pictures of Léger depicting machines did not make the machines and limousines more beautiful. It is better to leave the machines where they are, that is, at the factory, instead of putting them in pictures, sculptures, or poems.

The lesson that the machine affords us is such:

I see that where the goal-oriented engineer worked without any aesthetic concerns and the artist did not meddle, a genuine and one-hundred percent modern beauty matured with new materials. The machine was not produced for spectacle but for use-value, and still the sight of a factory in operation is a staggering modern theater. Pure profiles, clear contours, the precise and categoric motions of the machine encourage us to develop the logical creative capacities of the spirit and liberate the perverted feeling of art up to now, which was ethereal and craft training in metaphysics. To convey forms of the machine, whose beauty is in precision and functionality, through decoration in pictures and architecture, as was done and is still being done with "Jugendstil", is an act of false and involuntary machinistic Romanticism and a fundamental farce. The ancient Greeks certainly would not introduce clones of boats to architecture, but the forms acquired by aerodynamic calculations are carried over by these machinist Romantics today into their furniture and dwellings, static subjects. (See: Mendelsohn's Einstein tower in Potsdam.)

The lesson of the machine? The mechanical principles of today's aesthetic were not thought up by craft artists but modern constructors, who were not thinking about art. **And I observe that anytime a concrete task or a problem get the perfect, most economical, precise and complete solution**, without all adjacent aesthetic intentions, it matures into the purest, most modern beauty. It cannot be said that this beauty begins where perfectly fulfilled purpose ends; to make a distinction between the beauty and purpose of a structure is simply not possible. It cannot be said that architecture begins where construction ends. It cannot be said because *in this moment, when we are maturing into a universal, purposeful perfection, we are maturing at the same time and automatically into what is beautiful.* The starting point of this beauty cannot be determined, as we do not know where the curve changes direction, and we do not know when the thing, having met practical demands, appeals to our aesthetic sensibility. We know that form in and of itself is indifferent and affects our sensibility and arouses our vitality only when it is combined with some function. Here I pronounce that *all beauty starts where an indifferent lack of purpose ends.* A monumental modern beauty resides in every manufactured object for a precisely specified purpose that realizes the exact intention for which it came into being.

For today's visual artists, the confusion originates mostly in their uncertainty about the goal, purpose and function of their work. Meanwhile, modern beauty arises from the products and constructions of modern industry. New proportions, a play with volume and matter for which there is no historical precedent, carry within themselves a *number that is a code*. These undeniably beautiful constructions invoke a masculine atmosphere. Their modern beauty is mathematic. It is the beauty of a perfect system.

One might object that some machines—being perfectly purposeful—can be unsightly and ugly. That is not entirely correct. If they are unsightly, it is because they are in reality not perfectly purposeful—their perfection is relative and requires further refinement. It could be said that the unsightly machine directly calls for further refinement, that its ugliness is a symptom of its insufficiency. I assert that *the more perfect the machine, the more beautiful it is*. And it is perfect and subsequently beautiful only when absolute purpose is the sole concern of the constructor, and not beauty at all. If you have two machines of the same purpose whose practical perfection was judged as equal, and one of them is uglier, then without a doubt, *the second, more beautiful one will be more purposeful*. The machine is born out of calculation, and calculation always leaves some possibility, opens up multiple pathways. It is the work of *mathematical intuition* to determine the most convenient (and implicitly the most beautiful) outcome. Mathematical intuition, which intervenes here, does not at all mean artistic, aesthetic, formal intuition: there is no place here for feeling, fantasy and taste for beauty where a disciplined and logical mathematic spirit works.

The mathematic spirit of the machine explains everything. It explains its natural perfection. It even explains its hidden and inherent *irrationality*. Where I speak about mathematic intuition, where I explain the beauty of the machine—**and the beauty of the machine is an irrational value of rational production**—I recognize that irrational existence and efficiency persists outside of a rational assessment. Mathematics, as in geometry, was formulated as an art to precisely consider imprecise facts. Mathematical thoughts also operate with fiction, with consciously untruthful conclusions, which are accepted as truth voluntarily. A false correctness comes from the repression of irrationality at unimportant places. π, the irrational number, can be rationalized up to dozens of decimals, but always only in part; irrationality, however, is impossible to efface. Every machine with ball bearings, every cylinder, has π, an irrational element, within it. The circle, the elemental form—its formula is irrational. All the inexplicability of the beauty of the machine is apparently in its irrationality. And as such, machines can be an example of not only the modern, logically working brain, but also a modern nervous sensibility. There is nothing more nervous than a trembling motor.

The intervention of irrationality, the intervention of mathematical intuition. In contrast to the advancement of elementary and mechanical logic, I speak about the intervention of the biomechanical element: *invention*. The biomechanical force of human invention cannot be defined. In a series, there is always space for radical change: invention is the only unpredictable, random element of industry and technology. It rules out any other possibility for randomness, for where randomness reigns (such is the case with so-called art) an invention cannot assert itself.

The aesthetic of the machine thus says to us: Beauty is a product, which was created as perfectly and as purposefully as possible, with economy and precision in mind, without any regard for aesthetics. The machine is a work of the specialist, the engineer; not the artist. We need specialists. The perfect specialist creates perfect things. But that is not enough. They can only answer voiced needs, they cannot arouse new ones. The specialist, isolated from the rest of life, is thus not a cultural phenomenon because they cannot advance progress. The inventor is a specialist—a modern person. The biomechanical element of invention is a welcome force. We need inventors.

Artuš Černík, František Halas, and Bedřich Václavek: Enough of Wolker!

In the last issue of "Pásmo," an anonymous author called out, "Enough of Wolker!," claiming that this is necessary to "honor the poet's work," and polemicizing with a few sentences from an introductory statement in "Host" (issue 4), deriving from them the ironic fate of the poet: the revolutionary has gradually been stripped of his rabble-rousing thorniness and reshaped into a national poet: "his proletarian rabble-rousing absolves him from his artistic lack of belligerence." But directly behind him a truly new and great art begins, and that art is apparently hemmed in and bottled up by those who live with the dead, who worship him as the greatest poet of a generation.

We have a few notes regarding this provocation:

1. It is a bit foolish to oppose the assimilation process through which the masses consume the poet: if they make a revolutionary into the national poet, revolutionary thought becomes, to a certain extent, a living constant of national being—and from another angle: the poet alone, by developing, has justified this form of assimilation.
2. It is a bit foolish to assert that Wolker was the last of the major bad ideological poets. It assumes a certain clear-sightedness of the future and the prediction that the irrational Romanticism of Poetism, Phanticism, Surrealism, etc. etc. is the only great art for the future. We do not want to make predictions, but it is likely enough that Poetism will manage to stick around for some 10 years—with some major changes—and that then a poetry will arrive that will want to be truly *Constructivist*—that will want reason to be applied in the creative process. A then we will reach a new form of ideological poetry—and Wolker will again become a "great predecessor" while the Poetists will fall into a the masses' deep

disfavor. Progressive logic is often indeed very illogical. And it tends to care so little for human wishes and predictions.

3. There are three poets we can compare to the great figure of Wolker who outlived him: Nezval, Seifert, Biebl. If Biebl is following in Wolker's footsteps—and now sometimes even surpasses Wolker—that leaves *Nezval* and *Seifert*. Seifert is currently at a crossroads in his progress, which has been so inconsistent and the line of his work so scattered that it is impossible to guess if he will be able to match Wolker's creative strength. And the same goes for Nezval. Perhaps. I admit: he is a poet—and his value is not inconsequential. Of course: Wolker is the *greater poet*, Nezval the *greater artist*. Wolker's accomplishments were greater than Nezval's, which are too concentrated on *form*. It is thus not true that only after Wolker a great and modern art has started developing. This art barely reaches the greatness of Wolker. If today it is more modern—what will it be tomorrow?
4. Devětsil does not have the right to accuse his opponents of being bourgeois etc. He himself abandoned proletarian art. He is more bourgeois than he admits.
5. Therefore not: "Enough of Wolker," but rather: "More Wolker." It is necessary to respond to the questions that Wolker put forth—with new lyrical action! Wolker is one of the sources of our lyrical tradition. If the path leads away from him today, it will return to him in a few years. "Pásmo" does nothing to change that.

Vítězslav Nezval: Film

Let's move away from two idols! The first, *ars academica*, whose existence was already threatened by the mitrailleuse shrapnel of Dada, again spreading the shards of a Dadaist bohéme, academic art in all its forms.

It is necessary to agree with those who want to defend film before the Muses.

But there is another idol, the laughable and unintelligent little god of dilettantism, which makes faces at art like a painter of picture postcards at Monet's Boulevard des Capucines.

The pupils of trash literature whose animacy and courage are no greater than the courage of the blind man lying beside a beehive.

Film, a machine of speech and speech alone.

Abstract art, which confused languages under the embargo of modern beauties, is attempting something interesting and already dead like Esperanto; abstract art, remarkable, but without the universality of a mother tongue.

Film is a mother tongue without a country, the Sanskrit of a new humanity. It does not carry the sadness of the wandering Ahasver, being as it is at home everywhere. Its face is nothing like Janus's face. It is not bound to the past and does not fear the future. Look upon the quiver of a leaf, lost forever in the universe but brought to life again on the movie screen. One pulse from the rhythm of eternity, which convinces us that deity does not age. It is not necessary to think up new gods, heroes, forms. It is all there, in time and light. The old speech: aqua, l'eau, Wasser, voda, water. Modern art used something universal, the id. But how water speaks, projected onto the movie screen! A speech as comprehensible to the Papuans or the French as to the poet.

Speak to all! To old Europe like to lands without a history. What good are dilettantes with eternal triangles, crime investigators, and the insipid makeup of prostitution!

Let us turn to the stars: Chaplin, Fairbanks, Mary Pickford, Nazimova, Lillian Gish. We loved their magic canes which made us laugh, their childishness, fragileness, and the trembling of love. But film is more than its stars.

Because it is not a drama, a novel, a heroic or idyllic epoch, a funny or serious anecdote—those are the legacy of old art just like the photographic chiaroscuro, copied by artistic directors according to Leonardo. Film is about clairvoyant arrangements, a human selection. And companies on Broadway, which stink of art and enterprise, are as far from film as the Olympic Games are from Euripides.

It is necessary to cure all the senses so that they can perceive like a lens and have the leisurely persistence of Archimedes' or Newton's brain. Lie below a tree and let your nose be broken by a fallen apple so that we can uncover one of the eternal laws and use them for our benefit. The imitation of nature and re-evaluation of nature, like the empty catchphrases of today. Both were calling upon the Muses. Painters, poets, philosophers, you who let a thousand forms and propositions that play out every second go by for a single new form or proposition. Adieu, Muses! And adieu, stars! Your charm will remain through inertia for the next few decades. Adieu, artists whose rally cry is création! Your story will be told similarly to the tale of the construction of the Tower of Babel. Adieu, followers of art as imitation, neither Zola nor Dostoevsky gave us Paris or the person. It is not about création or imitation, it is not about Muses or about stars. Film! Because the word Naturalism has been discredited by both idols. And film, which initially wanted to capture a horse's gait and which has been applied to art, will in the future be true to its calling. Science and poetry—do they not resemble the great epochs of bygone religions!

Film. The new Sanskrit. But what to speak about in the first place!

Current perception. A point which was in the program of all modern aesthetics. In the program. Justified by a civilization of speed that rams things together, changing the sense of perspective. Simultaneism and so many more names!

Only film achieves this without stiffened syntax. The sea undulates on the roof of a villa, while a short way off in the garden fireworks flare, and in the entryway, the vision of a woman who existed 20 years ago dissolves. Only film is capable of that which creates music: harmony and counterpoint. Optical organ. Registers defining photogénie. And parading rhythm. An entire era divided into sixteenth notes. Added to that is the syncopation of the jazz band. A thing of psychology and technology. Contemporaneity of action and recollections of the same intensity. Gradually, the dream ascended and filled the screen with the music hall, while the only thing that remained from the one who remembers were enlarged eyes, fluttering above a bottle of absinth.

Film technology. It is not about aesthetics. Film, which has fortunately had none of it up to now, has to face one less useless struggle in the future. Although the seabed holds up from an aesthetic point of view, or a landscape filmed from an airplane. A person unadorned. A beautiful film does not reproduce forms. It creates them. It should be seen as a machine that endowed human ingenuity with flawless nerves, one gulping down matter and creating life after death. That is what we call it. The lens, gulping down an anthill at a certain distance. 200 pictures per second. A bearable fever. Dangerous! The stomach is churning. And then on the movie screen. The projector seems as though it was speaking from a dream. An anthill. One that we have never seen before. Film does not reproduce forms. It creates them. Nevertheless, nothing other than absolutely precise reproduction, total execution of the task. A thing of technology and the spirit.

Mystification in directing. Departure from old comedy! A definitive disjunction between the theater actor and film stars. It is possible to imitate the emotions of every night before the sold-out boxes at the theater. The temperature determines the vocal performance.

But who dares to repeat one's smile from yesterday? Repeat! The film director apparently breaks the habit of this training entirely. Certainly.

The star: the highest degree of the perfect person, who deserves their crown. To hang all the senses on the present second. Because illuminated time is the only painter of value. In their face, in their gate. The star: it is necessary to be so perfect that they resemble a machine in operation. The chord of C-sharp. Does the piano have a bad soundboard? Let us try it. A little out of tune? All in luxurious order. The C-sharp chord.

The same goes for stars. Emit the C-sharp chord excellently. But what does that mean? There is no norm here. The making of a star is not standardized or patented. Lillian Gish, the violin, created one single time in the history of humanity. From now on, instruments will be born from themselves. The task of the director. To strike the C-sharp chord correctly. Presumed that it is possible to find a keyboard. To guess the specific key for tuning the person. What a task! And to wait for how the required C-sharp cord comes out. It is not a humbling surprise. The instrument tensely anticipates what notes will be struck on it. Response is anticipated just as tensely. Unexpected and complete determination.

To achieve the reflection of the father's death in a detail of the daughter's face. That is the task.

Let us try it. The father is healthy overall. This or that man was the healthiest. Find any possible reasons for the death of the healthiest man. Analogies are liberating and murderous. For this second it is necessary that you be a tyrant to the end. It is what happens in your face, star. Tremble with fear for your father's life. The director believes in the mystification of the task just as well. After all, the reasons are likely. Through you, they experienced fear of death of their own father, your father, the father in general. Just like you? They experienced fear. But you are a woman. Father, do you want to know how much your daughter loved you today at 10:15 in the morning? The operator captured it. And that one-second drama, which really did play out at 10:15 in the morning, will be a one-second shot in the newest major motion picture.

Host 4, or the Dissipated Dreams of the Paper of a Generation…

Host 4, or the dissipated dreams of the paper of a generation. Teige and Seifert have left the editorial board. It is not possible to remain loyal to modernity and Host at the same time. What has been suspected is now confirmed. The dream dissipated despite the best intentions of Fr. Götz. The clear assertiveness and uncompromising nature of the first three issues is gone. Members of the Literary Group finally have free rein. And look! Anywhere you turn, there is pushback. A swing in the Tribune and a kick in the contributions. Modern culture can only come in crumbs from the hands of Devětsil—other than that there is only space for Branislav's rhymes and other miscellany. A panorama of modernity replaced with musealization. To Mr. Bartoš Vlček, the path is open! Mr. Knap, give it a try, we commend you. In essays, the dramatist defends their craft. Tactics in the rightward direction and tendencies of dementia in the first three issues.

Zdenek Rykr: Teigism

MOTTO: "Let the young sow their oats."
A Schicht poster for lemon curd

The community of young men who have been an integral part of "Devětsil" for some years now is certainly the only center of so-called Modernism in Czechoslovakia. They have architects, poets, prose writers, essayists, actors, directors, painters, and the public. They have magazines and a space, financial means at times, and international correspondence.

It is much desirable to be a member of this community, especially since with the group's legitimization members are safely protected from terrible names like kitsch, idiot, or reactionary.

In Bohemia and even more so in Moravia, and more still in Slovakia, and without a doubt more in Bulgaria, Ukraine, Romania, Bessarabia, the Caucuses, Persia, etc. etc. it is easy to fight with reactionary ways. Because we are witnessing the fact that in these and similar countries, the title of fool suits most reactionaries. It is also the case in England, France, America—however, there is also no "Devětsil" there. As for Germany, it creates university professors out of members from both camps.

It is clear: in countries which do not need "stunts" and do not need obstructions, revolutionaries have already become loyal traditionalists, and only on the periphery of culture and spiritual life are there revolutionaries of the "Devětsil" type à la Teige.

In fact, a periphery of spirit is analogous to a periphery of life or the city.

In the same way that Mr. Vena Vochoč from Nusle wants to play at being an Englishman after two pints of Braník beer, showing off his wrinkles worthy of an international adventurer who has robbed two castles and raped five princesses, a revolutionary of the "Devětsil" type à la Teige who has taken one school trip, read two brochures on industrial development, and seen a single picture of a harlequin manages to conjure up a worldliness far surpassing the dreams of Rimbaud and the perversions of Baudelaire.

Mr. Vena Vochoč from Nusle, a sleek mop of hair, a tie à la Menjou, and Charleston shoes, heads off to a bash for Prague chefs at Lucerna, where he gets to play hero amongst daughters of janitors, delighting in resembling Lon Chaney as the "Singaporean monster." This is what gives his life meaning in his youth.

His success in Lucerna resembles the success of revolutionaries of the "Devětsil" type à la Teige in countries where, as it is disdainfully said, reactionary ways, or conservatism, means foolishness. There where conservatism is the guardian of the estate of the nation and where its density has absorbed the logic of rational thought, are young exuberances evidenced on children's playgrounds. There where conservatism is protected like foul air in a room with closed windows and the estate of the nation is frequently questionable if not outright problematic, the revolutionary of the "Devětsil" type à la Teige enjoys great honor and respect. The revolutionary's irony can very easily turn garments slipped on little idols inside out, it can very easily call "down with art" because where there is nothing, not even death can take hold. They can very easily attack the Potemkin villages of the national spiritual stronghold. They can just as easily speak about Internationalism, where the simple label "made abroad" is an immediate indicator of quality.

In a sense, Mr. Vena Vochoč from Nusle is adorable, and the revolutionary of the "Devětsil" type à la Teige can be perceived that way just as well. Both Mr. Vena and the revolutionary are young, and to paraphrase Schicht's poster: "let them sow their oats!"

Time is that which evens out the incongruencies between the lived and the proclaimed, between the truth and stunts. Rather than curse out street urchins and scoundrels, as was done in one of the dailies, it is better to sharpen one's vision and build from stone where there are usually only paper walls, easily breached by the revolutionaries of the "Devětsil" type à la Teige.

If we believe that real values could take the bloodied hooves of ten revolutions stomping over them, we are always uncertain where the source is, from whence spurts the radium of spiritual progress. It is here one time, there another, but it is always reality and truth that opens it up.

If Nezval were even more Harlequin-like and Seifert more international, the few poetic seeds embedded in their writing would be a guarantee of their poetry. Only Teige's catchphrases, which are often so criminally hollow, melt away, since delusional visions and wild words are not enough to build culture.

Thus, it is only entertainment for the revolutionary of the "Devětsil" type à la Teige to take on gestures while using words like "quo usque tandem...?" They should be put up to some positive efforts that would force their trivializing smirks to turn into the serious features of reflection and their snobby mischievousness and false fantasies to embark on a path of favorable events.

The fact that they have not experienced such situations yet, though they have caused a fright here and there to some architect at his summer villa, is without a doubt evidence of their insufficient active intervention—because fate continues to wait to be molded.

Karel Teige: Words, Words, Words

If I were to draw a line of progression, it would lead from Romanticism through Symbolism, Fantacism, and Cubofuturism to Dadaism, and, if expanded upon following this logical path, would continue through Surrealism to Poetism with its poetry for five senses. I have attempted through the course of my retrospective look to show that the gradual emancipation of poetry from ideology, moralism, and every thesis is an attempt at making poetry be only poetry to make it independent and more specified, and to demonstrate the gradual loosening and liberation of forms. We saw how in his poetry, Rimbaud turned away from logic and intellectualism in order to turn towards the subconscious, how Verlaine turned his work away from literature so that it be music first and foremost, and how Apollinaire then introduced optical values in place of acoustic or audible values—in short, how poetry, as it wandered away from the literary arts, attempted to become purely tonal or purely visual, and thereby eliminate the concept of verbal art. In Mallarmé and later in Marinetti, we see both of these tendencies in action: both are concerned with audial as well as optical effects. And they are both also concerned with verbal art because both reform syntax, punctuation, and word structure. Mallarmé's poems undulate indefinitely with musical rhythms and are simultaneously optically structured within a typographic framework. Marinetti attacks hearing using strange onomatopoeia and the eyes using his typographical revolution of words in freedom. Poetism, continuing in this line and perfecting its possibilities, finally creates a poetry without words, optical, aural, olfactory, and haptic poems, broadens the domain of poetry and unworked territory, creates a poetry for all senses, and that poetry is like a new structure, at a complete remove from Wagner's conception of "Gesamtkunstwerk." But though I situate poetry outside the book in the case of Poetism, we should not forget about poetry in books. Next to these newly discovered structures of poetic creation, literature still remains and continues. Neither picture poems or radiogenic poems at which the progress of poetry peaks, moving from literature to phoneticism and opticality, do not necessarily disrupt, at least for the time being, the fact that literature = verbal art. Science works with models, tables, schemas and designs, but communicates with the word. Journalism is supported with journalistic photographs, but it shouts out words nevertheless. Perhaps mathematics, love, and poetry could get by under certain circumstances without words: politics and the workers' movement could not. The need for words communicated in print or by phonograph or radio remains and continues, there is a need for typographic and live words; revolution gives birth to great speakers and radiotelephony spreads the news and facts to its listeners. Besides rhetoric, we also need words to have conversation. The endearing prattle of humorous feuilletons.

Thus it is necessary to take into consideration verbal art, the art of the word. And it was Dadaism, with skepticism for word-based material, a criticism and re-examination of the word itself, that provided valuable services and impulses to verbal art. Because it must be expressly pointed out that Dadaism was, in the majority of cases, a verbal art. Like it or not, it remained literature, a literature par excellence, a fine and beautiful literature, but literature none the less. The progress of modern poetry from Verlaine to Apollinaire and Max Jacobs (see "Cornet à Dés" ["The Dice Cup"]: "Sir, your son is a poet! Fine, but if he is a part of the literati, I will wring his neck!") and to Poetism marks a gradual divergence from literature, a progress from Cervantes to Clifton or Hašek (so that we may proudly re-introduce one Czech author who can appear in this worldly overview) and from Clifton to the Dadaists—that is, to the literary arts. Et tout la reste est littérature! (And all the rest is literature!) After all, the Dadaists met around the programmatically titled revue: "Littérâture"! You could say we would not even have modern literature if we didn't have Dadaism: the movement was so literary and revivalist almost against its own will!

The revival of verbal art assumes above all a revision and a working through a word-based material. Already Rémy de Gourmont, who foresaw so many modern problems and whom we so often recall and will continue recalling here, pointed out in "Dialoque des amateurs sur les choses du temps" ("A Dialogue of Amateurs on the Subject of Time") the *decreasing value of the word* and its consequence: seeking out expressions that are more and more powerful so that they indicate impressions whose average intensity does not change and cannot change but very fractionally and gradually inasmuch as it is a psychology of humanity, of an animal kind, within the bounds of a type that is almost unalterable. Laforgue's Hamlet understands the emptiness of big words, does not respect them, and cries: "*Words, words, words*! That will be my motto until it is demonstrated to me that words rhyme with transcendental reality."

The word deceives. It is the cloak of our illusion and appears to indicate reality. It is a symbol, verifying myths that are centuries long. It is the falsified banknote of the golden treasure of reality. We do not know how and if words respond to truths and realities. Relationships between subjects and their names are imprecise. We do not know what exists underneath the words aside from their canonized sense. The naming of Adam in the Garden of Eden urgently demands a scientific revision.

For the poet, the word cannot be a picture, a surrogate of reality that loses its color, its form, its essence; for the poet, the word is material, and it is necessary that it be real, that it be of a definite reality, as real as brick or marble. This is not with regards to its problematic relationship to reality, but to its capacity for association, its form, sound, movement, the possibility of play, because it is not a precise indication of a subject but only its universal packaging, which connects it with the most remote pictures. New poems will thus be realities, born from a misalliance of words. Huysmans said that painting is the marriage and the adultery of colours. Thus, poetry is both the marriage and adultery of words. And its civil legislation?

Here philological criticism and modern linguistics in general have the word. Modern linguistics must first thoroughly study the life of the word, as Fabre studied the life of the insect, and only then will it be possible to precisely determine a transformism of language. Grammar should be above all a scientific observation that does not impose rules. Language is an unknown land, a material of culture and civilization so far unexamined. Linguistics must take into consideration the results of psychological and sociological research about language, they must observe style, that is, the technology and praxis of living literature and language: only then will it be possible to lay down solid laws towards a scientific verbal aesthetic. Grammarians and philologists forget too often that language is not static and unchanging and oppose its rejuvenation with stifling molds of firm rules, which are actually a philological exorbitance. They want to capture mutable language, want to make a dead language out of it and suppress the spontaneity of it in the name of tradition. Today in particular, language is undergoing deep and sudden changes born out of transformations of the collective soul and the intellectual conceptions that form the basis of radical change at the civilizational, social, political, and economic level. But grammarians and the publication "Our Language," a castrated steed, only record their legitimate births in their registers. Languages are modified under the influence of sociological, physiological, and psychological factors. Today, the age of cosmopolitanism, advances in transportation, international commerce, railways, TSF, airplanes, transats, and spatial velocity brings forth a mutual pervasion of languages. The railway, airplanes, and sailing ships create the grammar of an international language, the jargon of the Cosmopolis. Babelism. Polyglotism. All languages mutually succumb to the contagion: Germanism, Gallicism, Anglicism, Russianism. They acquire elasticity. It was ascertained that the Czech language has 20,000 Germanisms without which it would not work, and professors of Czech may despair over that if they please. Gellner jokingly observed that a good Germanism is, by default, more Czech than an Old Czech phrase. Under these circumstances, literature naturally becomes more and more consciously cosmopolitan. In place of singular national literatures, a world literature arises, as Karl Marx presupposed. The magazines of the modern artistic avant-gardes are international and polyglot. The Internationale of art is born. Naturally, this includes Slavs and Jews, people of a true cosmopolitan mentality, all the itinerants and Wandering Jews for whom the planet is not big enough, who, you might assume, have without exception seen all the major cities, learned 5 to 6 languages, and ultimately started assimilating all including nuance. In Moscow they are so Russian and in Paris they create a milieu très parisien. The larynx, transferred to another climate is modified under the influence of that milieu. Flowing, living, new speech moves from mouths to mouths, words come to life after having been articulated barely once. The sun burns and the frost nips away at accents, the speech of foreigners adapts to the language of a new milieu—accents are no exception, they are, too, controlled by the law of imitation, as formulated by G. Tarde, like things controlled by the laws of gravity. That verisimilitude is new, philologic, unknown.

Today, as the languages of Europe undergo an unceasing and comprehensive interpenetration, a linguistic endosmosis, it is not possible to close off language with grammatical rules. That which tends to be judged as a linguistic error or a grammatical mistake is in fact often an advancement and enrichment of literature. In contrast, a lapsus from a celebrated author suffices to legitimize barbarism. Decidedly, all philological progress is oriented towards flexibility, brevity, conciseness, and simplicity of speech, and leads ultimately to polyglot jargon. German cannot do away with the growing number of Gallicisms and the influence of French, simply because the French word and French phrase are shorter. This is because today we seek to use the short word as according to laws of economy, a principle of minimum effort. An unencumbering. We amputate long endings. Words tend to become monosyllabic. Soviet abbreviations, which have taken hold not only in contemporary Russian but also international use, are characteristic of this. Other simplifications of language will arise as well, some of which have already been realized in English, such as the disappearance of grammatical gender and declination. In English, nouns do not have gender and they possess only one form. Each language will also be more and more intensely pervaded by foreign, global words. English contributes all of the technical terms for sport and will be the language of commerce. French will be the word source for cuisine, fashion, art, and love. Perhaps some natural progress will give birth to a universal world language: it is a burning necessity in the age of popular print, modern transportation, and speed. The triumphal campaign of technology and the development of international Capitalism have demonstrated the necessity of a new universal language now that Latin has gone out of use as the international language of science. And there have been attempts: the priest Schleyer's Volapük, the Esperanto of Dr. Zamenhof, Lenz's Pasilingua, and Liptay's Gemeinsprache. Modern transport has made it possible to cover distances in short amounts of time. But this also revealed a need to discover modes of connecting thoughts aerially. Esperanto and Ido are not yet capable of that. It remains necessary to perfect the technology, as with every machine. Just as the automobile first resembled a horse and buggy and the airplane a bird or bat, Esperanto has resembled Romance languages up to now. It would need to be liberated above all from a similarity to and dependence on present national languages and become an artificial system of words that has nothing to do with any national language or grammar. Just as linotype is Gutenberg's crown invention, Morse code and other forms of signalization are the crown of a Phoenician alphabet, so indeed would an artificial, perfect, global language be the crown of Zamenhof's Esperanto. The reigning skepticism today about the value and significance of artificial languages actually legitimizes the imperfections of Esperanto and Ido and leads to recognition that speech gravitates towards differentiation that splits off into dialect according to a biological necessity. And so if Esperanto were to become more generally used, there would be so many different Esperantos, which would only continue to grow with its widening influence. Clearly, we are still very far from a perfect form of universal language. For this reason, B. Arvatov rightly recommended (in "Zhizn' iskusstva" [Life of Art]) that the Soviet Union, a state with many nations, not waste time with the sins of Esperanto and Ido. For in the USSR, a socialist state, the question of prestige of a national language does not exist so that one simply chooses one of the existing international languages. Latin was once such an international language, as was later French, which in some domains, namely in art, still is: today, however, the most universal language is English, a mix of Saxon-Roman-German. In fact, the Comintern and Profitern are introducing English in the schools of the USSR as a requirement, like vaccinations. The English *speak English*, Americans *speak English*, the Japanese *speak English*, the Chinese *speak English*, Russians *speak English*, Australians *speak English*, Black people *speak English*, Canadians *speak English*.

This is, however, not intended to preclude a universal language of communication in the future. An international potential for communication and understanding is a necessity, which certainly will sooner or later effectively solve the problem of today's Babylonian confusion of languages. But that future universal language is not only a philological issue. Actually, it is almost not even a matter of philology at all. It is possible that it will not be language at all, that is, a philological system. Maybe it will be an optical system. Heraldry and signalization. A language without words. A language without an alphabet. It will not resemble any national languages and will probably not resemble language at all. For that matter, our language today is not the language of books: and someday, we will probably forget what is currently protected as the crown jewel: standard language. It is necessary to consider the possibility of a soundless communication, the possibility of typographic communication without words. Today, modern typography together with modern philology is attempting to introduce a single alphabet to eliminate the Greek, Cyrillic, Fracture, or Japanese system of writing and replace it with a universal script, which would have a single sign for each sound and discard the distinction of capital and lower-case letters. Perhaps typographic words will arise, words that we will perceive only by sight, without transferring them into sound, a kind of international hieroglyph.

Such a universal "language," if it is a language at all—if it is something more like the language of the semaphore flag—naturally has nothing to do with verbal art. It is not possible to estimate what its "literature" will be. It is possible that by the time that language is discovered and designed, there will no longer be literature. The progression of events perhaps lends some truth to the claim of Rémy de Gourmont, who wrote: "There will no longer be literature, nor prose, nor verse, and thought will be expressed by a definite, dry, purely algebraic formula. It is highly likely that our way of writing will be abandoned as too lengthy. Some ideograms will suffice in order to pronounce all of human thought, which will be concise." In any case, it is clear that an artificial, universal language, strictly technical and entirely non-decorative, is not compatible with our present notion of verbal art. Further, it is clear that it presupposes a reform and internationalization of the alphabet and subsequently of typography, even if it is likely that in the future, speech will outweigh the printed word due to the influence of the radio: there will be phonographic libraries and radio-telephonic newspapers. It is impossible to imagine all the radical changes awaiting literature under the influence of all these circumstances! New materials and new technologies together with new tasks create new forms pertaining to that which we call the verbal arts (slovesnost) today. But let me return to the material of today, to today's language and words.

Grammatical rules and a codified spirit for all languages is obsolete today. Science needs a richer, more agile, nuanced, and namely more precise language. Technology creates ever new neologisms, which the official philologists care to know nothing about—and indeed, they are sometimes verbally unsuitable, improperly and ineffectively designed, barbaric. It would be a job for philologists and the literati to fix new modes of speaking into refined and purified forms and to bring about new, precisely created words.

Concerning liberated forms, I have also noted the transformation of poetic language. It was Romantic poets who put a red cap upon poetic vocabulary. We have seen how Mallarmé rendered syntax. And how Marinetti and Apollinaire definitively disrupted it. We have seen how Mallarmé attempted to invent words that would be exclusively poetic. And how Marinetti's "Words in Freedom" are a suitable instrument of teeming poetic intuition but not, as Marinetti himself pointed out, for journalism and scientific literature. That means that a *new, self-sufficient poetic language* arises here, distinct from complex, so-called standard language. What was previously a small deviation, a "poetic license," has become a new linguistic system, whole and autonomous.

Roman Jakobson correctly noted that a universal concept of language is a mere fiction. Language is nothing but a system of conventional values, of words, just like a deck of cards. And just as there are no laws for a universal game of cards—the same deck suffices for both Black Peter and Ferbli or for building a house from a deck of cards, linguistic rules can be stipulated only for a specific system with a precise, special task. And here communicative language oriented towards a subject and poetic language oriented towards expression are in sharp distinction as two different, mostly oppositional language systems, which are not suited to submit to the same laws. Both polar activities, intellectual and emotional, must therefore each have their own language with its own laws, with a consideration for their different aims and objectives. A scientific dictionary will not be like a dictionary for poetry if science and poetry are to both effectively construct their verbal form: their pictures and sentence constructions will be different. There are certainly some points of contact, but nevertheless it is often the fact that that which suits emotional literature would be unsuitable for intellectual literature, or vice versa. Symbolism is the period of the magic of the word. It represents a sacred reverence before the word. Because it is written in the Bible that in the beginning there was the word and the word was of God and God was the word. No matter that we do not understand this sentence, that it makes no sense to us. To the Symbolists the word was enchanting. Rimbaud, who discovered color in the vowel and sorted the form and movement of every vowel, brought a new, delicate element into poetic language and disturbed the grammatical logic of sentences: he tested the alchemy of the word. The number of associations rises. Two endings of a stream of associations no longer held together in one graphic field. Naturally, from Rimbaud's similes the word "like" disappears; words become flexible and fresh.

Further progress comes from a progressive differentiation of substance from its word copy, of actual things from a notion of them. The word is liberated from being inherently bound up with natural objects. The word is fully emancipated from things and from action, which matures into the possibility of broadening concepts and ideas, similar to the way in which monetary returns and symbols of exchange intensify a free market. The word is thus not an immobile and unchanging abstraction here, determining the idea of this or that subject, but becomes an element of sensibility for the poet, with the possibility that a new subject could be built from it, which is poetry. Poets delve into impertinent verbal acrobatics, they play with words like a child does, they make magical hors d'oeuvres in the kitchen of words, they free words from stable meaning in order for their essence to better shine through. The word loses its material and metaphorical value and acquires new forms and colors.

Marinetti's "Words in Freedom" are still not the liberated words of abstract poetry. Marinetti liberated words from the straight jacket of syntax, he broke through the Latin period of the sentence. Only Max Jacob, who continued the tendency of Mallarmé towards the creation of an autonomous poetic language and words, comes to the subjectlessness of words, and only in part, in that he does not use words to designate reality, but as a certain organism of phonetics and sound. In order for them to liberate the word from reality and thought, the Dadaists captured words to arrange them side by side without any dependence on each other, and the disjunction of these word salads had to defend against the possibility that words would be combined together and be interpreters of thought. They wanted to strip them of any surviving meaning and liberate them from the subjection to past ideas.

It was suddenly found that words are in retirement and terribly worn out. That they obtained their freedom in the moment when they no longer had the strength to capitalize on that freedom. It is an ironic fate, the freedom of the word. Just like the political bourgeois freedom of speech that only dares to speak freely once words can no longer have any impact! With Dadaism they arrived at the disintegration and *devaluation of the word*.

A lack of regard for the word will be the consequence. A lack of regard for the chatterboxes amongst the common people. It pulls the rug out from under the feet of the lawyers and parliamentary gasbags: a terrible emptiness gapes open below words.

The emptiness of the word and an obsession with the word is characteristically embodied in Ribemont-Dessaigne's novel "L'autruche aux yeux clos" (The Ostrich with Closed Eyes). The hero of the novel, Boy Hermes, following Tzara's recipe, extracts eight random letters from a cylinder and builds the word "Mtasipoj." It is a treasure, the birth of a new word! But what does "Mtasipoj" mean? And the author, personified in this Hermes, concludes that all words have a purpose: it suffices simply to assign it. God exists because somebody found the word and gave it a meaning and with that, God's existence was assured. But for the word "Mtasipoj" this is completely impossible because it seems to Hermes that its meaning already exists and that it will be made known presently. In post-revolutionary Mexico, the current language can be dissolved and a new language assembled that will have no sense. He intuits the beautiful possibility of a mysterious language in jail. He observes how constellations take on a resemblance to illegible and unspeakable words. Here he discovers the unexpectedly delightful language of flowers, the best aspect of it being the fact that it expresses neither error nor truths. The speech of birds is neither dead nor alive, does not entice the spirit and does not know the delight of sound. Adieu, poets and philosophers: behold the language of the desert! But language, the order of words, primarily lacking in sense, eventually, fatefully, acquires some meaning. It is possible to prevent this ossification of liberated words only by artificially attaching meaning that would correspond to each of the new words, perhaps similarly to how we can prevent the clairvoyance of prophets to fail if we obediently and voluntarily realize their prophecy. But Hermes cannot get rid of his obsession with the newly created word "Mtasipoj"; in the story, parrots in Ceylon fly away, carrying deep into the forest the cry of that secret poetry and out of all language, only a deaf and mute indigenous woman understands the word Hermes has created, a word Hermes himself does not understand.

Does it not remind you of Rimbaud, who bore "new flowers, new stars, new bodies, new languages"? Who invented "the poetic word, which either today or tomorrow will be accessible to all senses and whose translation is reserved?" Does it not remind you of the beautiful poetry in the prose of Mallarmé in "The Penultimate" ... where the refrain of a lost song is captured, where words without any relation give no explanation nor make any sense: "... the penultimate ... is dead ..." become a game and obsession for the disconcerted spirit, who continues to feel sadness, missing the unknown Penultimate, letting the pensive words wander alone and meaninglessly along one's lips? A material crisis of modern literature, a crisis of words, was suspected by both Marinetti and Apollinaire. In the celebrated poem "Victory," Apollinaire recommends a new phonetics:

O mouth humanity seeks a new language[1]
Beyond the reach of grammarians
The old words are dying
Only habit or cowardice
Puts them into poems
They are invalids
Christ we may as well sink into pantomime
It suffices after all in the cinema
No let's keep talking
Let's waggle our tongues
Let's send out postilions
We want new sounds new sounds new sounds
We want only consonants no vowels
Consonants that fart insensibly
Mimicking a small boy's spinning top
Sparkling nose-farts
Clack your tongue
Make the sounds of chewing with your mouth open
Hawking phlegm would also make a beautiful consonant
An assortment of labial farts could brighten the discourse
Belch often and at will
And like a letter it engraves the sound of a bell in our memories
Listen to the sea
Victory above all else will be
A vision of distances
And a vision
Up close
And everything comes bearing a new name

And Marinetti integrates lines of onomatopoeia into Words in Freedom—brutal, rough, creaky and screechy—which are like the rapid fire of mountain artillery or the motor of an airplane. Onomatopoeia is the return to a chaotic life. The panic of poetry. And onomatopoeia, which Marinetti calls abstract onomatopoeia, hurls us back, as it has been remarked, to the ranks of parrots.

The process of liberating the word is analogous to the process of liberating color in painting. But if color, the lifeblood of painting, its constitutive element, was already liberated through Cubism and Abstractionism, if modern painting was able to free itself of resembling reality and all decoration by liberating itself from all a priori forms, be it natural, stylized or decorative ones, in order to become an

1 The translation of Apollinaire's poem *Victoire*, with slight modifications made here, is from *The Self-Dismembered Man: Selected Later Poems of Guillaume Apollinaire*, trans. Donald Revell (Wesleyan University Press, 2004): 122–131.

independent colorful creation in which the form is but a result of colorful equilibrium, it has no existence in itself; and if music arrived at a similar destination, then verbal art, most limited by the shape of thought, is facing a process much more difficult, lengthy, and challenging. The word and its material is utilitarian in common language; in poetic language, it becomes the expression of our emotional experience and reality. It is a superfluous naming of things but at the same time has a particular personal meaning. A progressively necessary division between the word as language and the word as art (Mallarmé and the Dadaists and the Phantaists) rendered the former as something too inanimate.

Of course, a formal differentiation between the word, idea, and object means in and of itself a great invasion in the territory of the technology of the word. It enables the unrestricted poetic creation of words, by which the Russians matured into "Zaumists," and they indeed realized Apollinaire's postulate: "and everything comes bearing a new name." And it was surely this Russian modern poetry that gave Apollinaire the impulse to create the previously mentioned poem.

Russian Futurism, imagined by Mayakovsky, Aseev, Kamensky, Pasternak, Marienhof, Shershenevich, and others, stood up against the Romantic vocabulary of Pushkin. After breaking down syntax and dismantling sentences, it continued directly on towards an important reform of poetic language. The destruction of the traditional word, the creation of new forms, onomatopoeia. Mayakovsky carried out an indisputable literary revolution. New verse, new rhythm, new language, a language of the street and the marketplace, the language of posters and telegrams, a fusion of language with the standard written form, excerpts of sentences, assonance: the structure and organization of Futurist poetry is in no way given over to logical, rational demands, but rather to what is rhythmic and tonal. In Moscow, a new generation built on the poetry of Futurism before the war and then continued with language experiments in the laboratory, becoming the so-called "Zaum" group. The movement of ZAUM, which branded itself with the sign of 41° (a poetry fever) is comparable to Suprematism in the realm of painting. It is pure, abstract, and non-objective poetry. From Futurism, the Zaumists adopted an anti-traditionalism and an aggressive tactic of negation and an intense opposition to official and academic aesthetics; it approaches along those lines the defiant attitude of French and German Dadaists. But the negation that Russian Modernism proclaims naturally has more fire and revolutionary force: its offensive is connected with the offensive of the proletariat of the October Revolution: here a real revolution is enacted, here the old world is vanquished and a new one is built. And the words of the Russian manifestos, just like the proclamations of the Communist international, are incendiary, fiery, explosive. The deceased *Velemir Khlebnikov*, the most powerful poet of the group, wrote the manifesto "A Slap in the Face of Public Taste" and "A Treatise on the Greatest Impropriety," directed against bourgeois ethics and aesthetics, which was printed in Moscow by the Soviets. *Vasily Kamensky* published: "A Decree on literature on balustrades and posters, on painting of the streets, on music played from balconies, and on the carnival arts." The "Zaum" movement is really

Constructivism in the domain of the word. The poets of this group attempt to create a new, all-encompassing poetic language that is "beyonsense," a "Zaum language," as Kruchyonykh has described it. Their efforts are seconded by modern Russian linguists and philologists; Jakobson, Shklovsky, Brik, Kushner, and Arvatov are all undertaking laboratory tests of great significance: they experimentally demarcate the sensory meaning of the word and language. They study the properties of word masses, the nature of their bond, their differentiation from a natural object. The poets of the Zaum language—Khlebnikov, Kruchyonykh, Aliagrov, Zdanevich (Iliazd), Tretiakov, Tereshkovich, and Terentiev—realize a poetry of pure form, a poetry that has no naturalistic sense, that sings just to sing, a poetry of resounding words. The linguistic-poetic theories of these philologists and the praxis of these poets—a kind of magnificent chemical laboratory that investigates the fundamental elements of poetry, revives the word, and disciplines rhythm—indeed makes possible an abstract, non-objective, and non-naturalistic poetry. Supported by the research of exact science, a new verbal aesthetic is born. Only here does verbal art acquire pure and unalloyed elements. This revivalist work (obrodná práce) in language is not without influence on Czech poetic modernism: analogous endeavors can be traced in some of Seifert and Biebl's poems. Notably, the collaboration of modern Czech poets with the scientific research of Roman Jakobson (see his book: *On Czech Verse*) has greatly enriched Czech poetry—so terribly over-saturated, so inflexible and ponderous in the work of Jaroslav Vrchlický—the backwards "beefy daughter of glory," as Nezval jokingly christened our mother tongue.

The Dadaists did not make it as far in their liberated words as their Russian counterparts, the Zaumists. If the poems of Khlebnikov, Kruchyonykh, and Zdanevich are a ballet of neologisms, a whirl of words that are not connected to reality but are not only a nerve of phonetic associations, then the Dada poems are only stuck to a kind of negation. To a devaluation of the word; an indefinite liberation of the word. Their poems are almost always suffering from a certain verbal cocainism, remaining an individualistic toy store. The Dadaists remain purveyors of words, transforming the elements of life into pictures and crystalline sentences. They remain the literati. They have shown the nonsense of contemporary poetics in its entire scope and have done so more consistently than the free-verse poets and Cubo-Futurists whom they mockingly reject. Walter Mehring, who generally abandoned poetry in the traditional and academic sense in order to dedicate himself to the composition of couplets and songs—although it is possible to object that the couplet and song are the most genuine forms of traditional poetry, still connected with music and making use of mnemonic aids, refrains, and parallelisms, and that in general, today's music-hall couplets are the most pure embodiment of a classical poetic—jokingly mocks poetic anomalies. He writes: "In general, rhyming is a monstrosity, it is pathological hyperesthesia, a decadent phenomenon of broken-down nervous systems. An even more difficult case is the refrain. It also exhibits paranoic forms. Imagine a gentleman in good company, repeating a two-verse refrain after every fifth sentence. A paddy wagon would appear at the door for him in no time."

What is hiding in these mischievous claims is the recognition that we are stuck in our traditions, that we hold onto them without realizing that in the meantime they have lost all significance, that these poetic forms that were once mnemonic aids have no purpose today, and we forget that poetic material, that is language, comes from words and that words come from sounds and letter forms.

The German Dadaist and "Merzkünstler" (Merz artist) Kurt Schwitters went further than Tzara, who recommended putting together poems from words drawn out of a hat. If abstract poetry liberated the word from Naturalism (albeit within the limited possibilities of an old dictionary), it is permitted to compositionally evaluate the word against the word and not against matter or reality, and it is therefore impossible to deny that the word itself is a primary, elemental material. The word is formed from letter forms and sound, the indication of some reality and conveyer of associations. Thus it is not clear-cut and its aural echoes and associative consequences are complex. Inasmuch it is suitable that the material of poetry is clear-cut, it is necessary to take not the word but the letter form as its material. Kurt Schwitters forms poems from letter forms that are clear-cut; of course, it is necessary to keep in mind that literature is essentially without sound and that the letter form acquires sound only through recitation. Recited poetry combines two artistic domains: literature and music or acting: it is an impure form. It is necessary to scrupulously distinguish between poetry and recitation, between the letter and sound. Letter forms in and of themselves have neither content nor sound. But Schwitters composes them like a score to be recited. He likes to use explosive consonants (k, t, d) for the effect of phonetic surprise. His poems from letter forms are sound poems, "Lautgedichte," which he himself is able to recite like a virtuoso. They are not a self-contained form, nor are they a new form of typographic, voiceless literature; no recitation will make a poem out of a poem if it is not actually a poem. They do not present a definite form and arrangement, similarly to the poems of the Dutch Dadaist J. K. Bonset, who also dedicated himself to composing poems from letter forms, assuming that it might lead him to the possibility of reconstructing poetic material and technology.

The contemporary crisis of literature is, as I have shown, a crisis of material. It is the imprecise nature of the word. And where there are no words, there is naturally no literature. Speech atrophied with the invention and rise of the printing press, the word is no longer asserted only through sound as it used to be but also, and mainly, through its typographic form. After all, sound, that formerly specific element of poetry, is so changing and ephemeral: pronunciation changes with distances of time and space as well as accents shift: a man from Brussels will read Verlaine differently than one from Geneva or Marseilles, and people read Latin differently depending on where they are from. To build on the aural qualities of a word is today akin to building on sand. Standard, literary language, constructed over time through a system of graphic symbols, loses the possibility of using acoustic spells, accompanied by rhyme and rhythm. Therefore, the question of the persistence of literature and literary poetry, of literary art, depends on what new emotional and sensory sensations can still be drawn from the language material. Today's language, propagated through print, will necessarily be reformed. Because the letter form as it exists today is an insufficient translation of the word. Accent marks, exclamation points, question marks, and hyphens all have to replace gesture and spontaneous intonation but are not fully capable of this. A self-contained, optical language will be necessary here, a system of signs that words could embody through graphic figuration. This will only be possible when literature has autonomous, artificial, reliable, and naturalistic material. Up until now, typography has been an auxiliary intermediary between the reader and textual content; the eye reads what the ear would hear. Modern posters, signs, advertisements, and signals have grasped the optical significance of form, size, color and design of typographic material: here the word has arisen as an optical value.

Just as the letter form is a poor translation of the word, our words are a poor translation of our thoughts. They express in one dimension what our spirit has ascertained from all angles. Our words are the refined shriek of monkeys: the poet and the philosopher have nothing more at their disposition. We think in words, which are rational and which carry us back to our animalistic side and to nature. All speech is embodied, organic. Stendhal showed us that in primitive nations without culture, words are the means of thought, and that uncivilized people search for thoughts only by means of words. But in modern literature, the word must only be a rudimentary form. It thinks in facts, in ciphers and in some cases, in numbers.

But here is the limit of verbal art. New verbal forms come into existence outside of the boundaries of so-called literature where they are born from a concrete, living purposefulness. And thus, I do not find the real embodiment of today's literature in fiction, but in *journalism and advertisement*. Journalism has become a new and self-contained form with its own philology. Other "literary" types have also come into existence: film librettos, catchphrases, acronyms, and branding. These all belong to the new world of literature because they make use of its material.

Henri Bergson has shown that life wants us to understand only the utilitarian side of things, reality in its practical simplification. We do not see things alone, but rather the label attached to them. That endeavor, a given utilitarian need, was further accentuated under the influence of *language*. Because words, with the exception of proper nouns, all only indicate types. Language absorbs from feelings and sensations only their impersonal exterior, recorded once and for all, because it used to be one and the same circumstance for all people. It is a system of generalization and symbols. Through the common and socialized word, which expresses and actually addresses the true personal state of the soul, it is necessary to seek emotion, the pure and simple state of the soul. And from under joys and sorrows, *which have nothing in common with words*, a certain rhythm of life and life's breath emerges, from deeper within than the deepest emotions: a living, changing principle of every individual, a principle of one's anxiety and enthusiasm, grief and hope. Here we step into a territory where the word is powerless: and here, philology quits being an aid to literature, advancing in its place towards psychology, and in some cases anthropology.

*

Thanks to grouping and categorizing, people have gained the ability to speak and express themselves. The function of language is above all social. People are social animals because they are animals who speak, who create words and do not just parrot them. Gabriel Tarde has shown that if a necessity is felt by some group of people to express a new thought, then the first to find the word or a figurative expression that accommodates this need has to merely say it and before long, that word will be uttered by all the lips of the group in question. The first language, a verbal pre-matter, is emotive speech. A cry of pain or joy, responding to arousal; that cry was a simple, biological reflex, a reflex movement of the speaking muscles, vocal chords, and tongue. Intended to communicate to all who hear it the sensation of pain or joy. The response to that cry comes from a feeling of social interdependence. That wild cry is an immediate and vital expression of emotion. It accompanies gesture and action, for example, running away, skipping, etc. Later, the cry is understood even without relation to gesture or action. And it is at this stage that it crosses over to being original, *active language*, which is still preserved in our speech in relation to the imperative and vocative (a study of active language is especially important for theater speech, theater psychology, and technology), and already crosses over into *symbolic language*. Now a cry, or a sentence of cries (of words), can evoke physical sensation, an emotive or active state in and of itself. The word acquires its meaning, separate from gesture or object, it is a real algebra, allowing for rapid and purposeful combinations of psychological states and material objects and thereby an exercising of intelligence. Today, some tribes still have languages so imperfect that they cannot be understood without gesture, or in darkness. That, however, does not correspond with a low intellect.—Language is an instrument that is perfected over time. The symbolism of words makes it possible for some articulated sounds to completely substitute and represent reality. Through unceasing progress and precise selection in a determined sense, verbal language achieved dominance over other forms of language, and over all other means of expressing psychological states and sharing them with loved ones: drawing, sculpture, music, rhythm, dance. The oldest, most primitive psychological states, interpreted by language, are emotional states. They are echoes in the first strata of consciousness; they are biological phenomena. Only later did intellectual developments enter and along with them, *abstraction*, the essential condition of the evolution of purified ideas. Ribot has shown that abstraction is a secondary means and does not depend on the primary strata, a strata of sensation and perception, of taste, desires and tendencies, of primitive emotions. Long-term psychological work matured into its most perfect state only beyond the border of speech and verbalization: towards mathematic abstraction. Abstraction moves in three directions: the practical, speculative, and scientific, which are mutually dependent. The history of human advancement is the history of abstract development and generalized capability. Latin signifies its peak and the attainment of a phase of abstraction and generalization in language: the strictly logical sentence.

The strictly logical sentence—a form that was wholly abandoned by modern literature. The sentence, which cannot be submitted to logical analysis, becomes incomprehensible and all of language becomes futile. In fact, it quits being a form of communication in order to become poetic expression again, submissive to another logic. Modern poetry, pronouncing itself to be "illogical," appeals precisely to this other, hidden logic. The French saying goes that the heart has its reasons, which reason does not know. How do dialectics hold up before fanaticism and passion? The great voice of instinct knows no logic or intellectual conceptions, and a primitive psychism does not know of abstractions: everything is translated into images and tableaus. Nevertheless, definite rules are obeyed. Psychoanalysts have clarified the role of affective association in the subconscious work of instinct, and Freud has shown how sexual symbolism, introduced through sexual relations with non-sexual objects and terms touches on the same origins of speech. The picture, the metaphor, the life blood of poetry, is the very original form of verbal expression. Wundt, in his "Völkerpsychologie" (Folk Psychology), states that the metaphorical notion, as immediately given, stands at the forefront of consciousness. The metaphorical imagination has created totems. Totemism, that interesting phenomenon of primitive social life, identifies the tree trunk with a symbol. People have an indisputable propensity towards simile—which carries over from their childhood and the childhood of humanity—and all poetry of the major periods makes use of the same pictures. The same metaphors emerge through powerful feelings in all people and reign over personal phantasies. J. P. Richter stated that in general, our language is a dictionary of fading metaphors. Such fading metaphors are the locution of typical speech, so commonplace today. As quick as lightning, sharp as a knife, a voice like thunder: these were all powerful similes in the past. All lovers, always, and again and again, discover the relationship between the lover and the flower, spontaneously and without forgery, because they subconsciously feel the blossoming of a vegetal sexuality. These figures are found in Homerian, Hebrew, and Indic poetry, in the Song of Songs, and in African and Indigenous poetry. One can therefore suppose that definite symbolic relations and pictures preexist in one's intelligence, or rather emotion and the subconscious, that they are what we call an innate imagination and inner world. Primitive thought is of course wholly instinctive. Language is a symbolism in which sounds and pictures call up the signified. Popular speech, professional jargon, the argot of the periphery and the vernacular of the countryside are extremely rich in flowing, symbolic comparisons that have a fantastic, evocative heft. Popular expressions grow spontaneously with simple imagination that is alive, genuine, untouched, and without a conventional and analytic censor or intellectual constraint. Symbolism is not the only foundation of language. There is also the symbolism of gesture. Gesture preceded the word, going all the way back to animal stages, and as such is connected with the most primal, vital expressions. There is the symbolism of dance, which is a mimicry of the body, the symbolism of scent, of pictures, the symbolism of numbers and finally and most importantly, the symbolism of the letter form. The letter form is an interesting form of symbolism, created out of the social need for communication. Archaic forms and hieroglyphics show an interesting association between a concrete object and a whole order of abstract thought. The symbol is therefore not an artificial creation of human intelligence, but on the contrary, a deep expression of our instinctive thought, our subconscious and earliest psychism. Seeing the almost universal reach of a certain symbolism, I ask myself whether that correspondence could be a response to some higher reality, a *surreality* that is above us, and whether there might be between things which have a mysterious affinity, which are symbolically closer and resemble one another, a relationship truly established out of nature. Could our subconscious have understood something that has so far escaped our consciousness and intelligence? Here I touch upon the abstract problem of relations between Form and Matter in the scholastic sense of these words. And with the exception of some possible conjunctures, science has not yet offered a response to this problem.

*

Words, words, words. What are they to us anymore? The dictionary is not anything but a repository of expressions of most common use, like a map of the stars visible to the unaided eye. But there is a mysterious and unexplored life of words underneath the microscope and x-ray! Words are catalogued in dictionaries according to their intended use, like goods sorted in boxes in storage, where they supposedly have a definite and unambiguous meaning. The words that are conveyed to us in the dictionary are words illuminated by practical understanding in the light of day. And verbal art, literature, which uses these words as material, captures only that which is possible to capture in the light of day: infrared and ultraviolet reality fully evade it. Photography remains and will remain the dark room of the intellect, refined and further refining. But poetry invents x-rays from other worlds. The technological and constructivist century cultivates the word in the sense of purposefulness and a maximum practical capacity. Just like in the production of airplanes, where wood—a natural material—was refined to the capacity of steel—an artificial material—the natural material of the word will be cultivated into the unambiguity and precision of a cipher. Catchwords, signals, and commands indicate the maximum concentration and preciseness of a word attained by today's "literature." Language, direct speech, developing under the dictate of practical usefulness, speeds up, abbreviates, abstracts. To become abstract simply means to become civilized. Because the foundation and driving force of human, civilized progress is the development of the abstract capabilities of the spirit. Abstraction matures into its most perfect state at the point where it crosses the border of language: at mathematical abstraction. It could be said that it becomes active again, in a modern sense. Journalism and radio, the electrogenic words of illuminated advertisements: today we speak through lightbulbs, rotary printing presses, blowpipes, horns, and affiches, which realize important and decisive communication. There is no reason not to consider this orchestra of speech a verbal art. The word in the world, the word in the daylight, technologized and civilized, flutters in the wind like a flag at the earth's highest point, a shorthand and sign that is visible and audible from all sides. Journals and telephones send them out to all five corners of the Earth; a stenography of the rhythm of life. And in these transmissions, the cinematographic beauty of our epoch towers above us. That literature is a prismatic rainbow over a new globe. It is more likely the product of the factory furnace, strengthened and reinforced by calculations, than the dream of poetic extasy.

Poetry, poesis, pure creation is turning to the deep life of the subconscious again, to the Punkva underground currents of dreams and notions, to the fantastic vegetation at the bottom of the treacherous and black oceans. It absorbs their flashes without a lens for understanding and logic, without the dark room of intelligence, directly and immediately at the emotional site of sensibility. But it is something different than literature, than all of literature. There is no word that calls up reality from emotion and the subconscious as well as a picture does. Before thought ever became a word, it was a picture. Pictures of infrared and ultraviolet reality: infrared Surrealism, ultraviolet Poetism. Poetry without literature and outside of literature. The Surrealists hacked language into words without etymology, without any common sense, in order to find their intrinsic, hidden strength, which radiates in their poetry like electricity, conveying an association of sounds and forms. Their language is turning into an oracle and a line of associations and metaphors is a thread that leads us to the Babel of the spirit. The Surrealist dictionary does not interpret, it glosses. And Poetism observes the ultraviolet realities words cannot describe and literature cannot express; it realizes poetry using elementary materials by means of all the senses, not turning to a logical intelligence but to the whole complex being of the modern person. Its poetry, subconsciously inspired and consciously constructed, magnetizes the inner life of the person, organizes their molecular rhythm, inducing the active disruption of sensibility. Poetism has shown the possibility of a poetry without words, the possibility of making poetry with more dependable material, constructive and scientifically studied and examined, a more solid material than is the individual word: of making poetry with light, color, smell, sound, movement, energy.

Jindřich Štyrský & Toyen: A Popular Introduction to Artificialism

Motto: Pythagoras, who was the first to design a necklace, forgot the bitches.

We are proclaiming a manifesto for Artificialism in painting without any ambition to force magical glasses onto the rabble through which they can view the world in order to find themselves in it.

Artificialism opens a new epoch for painting that will inaugurate the fusion of the two faces of Janus. Thanks to this, it is never going to be a place in which herds will run around.

We are modern to the extent that we are not sure whether we are contemporary.

We have retained just one innocence: A mirror without a picture of Artificialism will not be an epidemic, as was the case with Dada, etc.

The only absurd thing is reality. The future of painting is secured by a nun crossing its path. If flowers were to fall in autumn, then what would leaves do?

Artificialism is an adventure that no one knows how it will end and that can only be eschewed by losing it.

Artificialism has no graves, and therefore no one can bring it a wreath.

We adored this collection of brief moments, but while we were deliberating about it, it turned to stone.

And while you are becoming acclimatized to the conceptions that you have about Artificialism, you will adore or bark only at an illusion.

Defenses and curses will be powerless.

Artificialism is the gravedigger of your stupidity.

It is not necessary to assign importance to anything in this article.

It is a matter of complete indifference to us whether you expire through old age or by paralysis. Someone else will make us happier.

Artificialism does not promote uniformity.

Why are you protesting against Artificialism or sympathizing with it? This is superfluous. It will remain and outlive you.

1st lesson: An unsatisfied insult is evidence of immortality.

2nd lesson: We do not remain responsible for the consequences of Artificialism.

Artificialism is an area to which firefighters always arrive late.

In order for you to be able to place an artificial Venus in your vicinity, you will need a security guard.

A consolation: In the end all of you will degenerate.

We invented Artificialism because we had nothing else to do and we never thought about dancing on the head of this shrew.

If only we had at least found somewhere a nest of hard-boiled eggs.

Artificialism is not an association either for variety of opinions or for identity of opinions.

Painting walked around the world like the angels Cherub and Mocassin only in order to scalp people, grope fruits, snap young trees, and gaze at the landscape: merdre, merdre, merdre [ref to Alfred Jarry's play Pere Ubu].

Epilogue: The final lines pass by in idleness, blurring the final remains of the deliberations that we have still been able to commit in the unawareness of what we call life.

Vítězslav Nezval: Dada and Surrealism

Dada is a group of furniture removal men. They have thoroughly taken apart the room of a modern bourgeois. The cornices are falling and breaking into pieces. On the Ottoman there lies a watch next to a pillow and a painting by Monet. The broken fragments of fancy cups and vases cover the bottom of the removal van. Pieces of lace protrude from the dust next to several pairs of shoes. Having caused this charming disorder, the Dadaists have scarpered in all directions.

The Surrealists are those Dadaists who have found an excuse for this rampaging. They appeal to a dream: While we were sleeping, something stronger than we ourselves led us to arrange the room naturally. Nobody is going to believe this excuse. The Dadaists are more sincere. We can adore them. Out of hatred for a carefully purified tradition they have started to lash out at everything. They have thrown out the man of the house. Here and there their rampaging has brought about a miraculous accident. A broken vase, a football, and a parasol have produced a beautiful still-life. We have taken a lesson from this.

We are standing in this smashed-up room. It is necessary to establish a new order. Those people who want to place the half-broken objects in their old places are going to be disappointed. What is the point of a broken vase on a bedside table? We can use the shards for scraping off mud. An adult person, a furniture removal man, or a cleaning lady will not know what to do. What is needed is a lot of childish imagination, which will be capable of putting together everything necessary from the glass fragments and tiny pieces of stone. Why are the police observing us!

Jiří Voskovec: The Turtle That No One Mentions

Mortal convulsions?

1. There is an awful lot of talk about art today. We are often disturbed by this and regard this theorizing as art's mortal convulsions. However, in this confusion it is necessary to judge simply: If art is constantly being talked about, then evidently it must exist somewhere. However, merely stamping old witticisms underfoot is not sufficient for this search. One of these rather worn-out witticisms is the slogan that *art will cease to be art*. In 1921 this was certainly an insightful paradox, which clearly excellently expressed the necessity of de-aesthetizing art. However, if this is made into a fundamental law of the "new culture," then it sounds at the least simple-minded.

Stephenson and the horse

2. When Stephenson invented the locomotive, nobody declared that *a horse will cease to be a horse*. It was replaced by a steam engine, but no one took away — or even can take away — its "horseness." It is no sensational novelty to say that the essence of things cannot be changed. Art remains art, even when it is supposed to be replaced by something else: In that case it simply ceases to exist, but its corpse will be an honest corpse of art.

There is no locomotive

3. However, the main thing is that so far no Stephenson of art has appeared. It seems that, in spite of the serious crisis that art is going through, so far it does not have the slightest desire to die. Mainly, it seems that no one is intending to replace this noteworthy horse with an even more noteworthy locomotive.

Decorative revolution

4. The sickness of our era is the entrenched conception that "a transformation is taking place." A new life. A new world. 20th century. Revolution. Revolutions are only on the streets, during the storming of the Bastille, or when viewing the first Cubist painting for the first time, and then they are in history textbooks. Life is more complicated, and intelligence is a machine for devising schema. In order not to waste time and to understand better, we say that a "revolution broke out" and that "Cubism at once opened up entirely new horizons for painting." In reality revolutions consist precisely of several days of shooting on the streets and in the conquering of the Bastille. I would almost say that revolution is the adventurous decoration of development. It is beautiful and it is desirable, but it is nevertheless supremely evolutionary like everything that is based on cell life. No, we are not in any pronounced transformation. It is possible that at some point in history the Renaissance will be reckoned as lasting from the 15th century to the 20th. It is possible that the 20th century will start a chapter of some kind of new civilization like the Gothic and the Renaissance ones. Let us leave this pleasure to our grandchildren and let us allow them to simplify our dust-covered fates a little bit.

Tatlin Tower

5. To simplify, that is all very well: However, this is permitted only for a recording intellect. We have every right to simplify history. But it is terribly cowardly to simplify what we are living in. Of course, reality today is more complicated than at any other time. War and other world attractions have made life even more complicated than it was before. However, precisely because of this, we cannot permit ourselves to hide from this terrible life in the formulas of programs and a brilliantly fabricated Constructivism. Today, every ready-made aesthetic theory is necessarily a Tatlin Tower. It serves for prostitution in third-rate "international revues."

Provisorium and One-Hundred Percent-ism

6. It would seem that, by rejecting an uncompromising, firm and revolutionary artistic program, we are approving a provisorium. As though we would say: "No Constructivism, away with Poetism, Purism, and Surrealism, for as long as the world's cultural situation has not become clarified, until human society has matured enough for a generous collective culture. For the meanwhile let us wait. *Inter arma silent Musae*. We can still try to do some art in some way or other. A little bit like alchemy. Or cooking. Let's have a look through in grandmother's recipes."

— Nothing of the sort. Precisely out of opposition to a provisorium it is necessary to reject so-called 100%-ism. So-called 100%-ism — that is, the desire to build unconditionally from reinforced concrete, even when bricks are more appropriate in the given circumstances. This so-called 100%-ism is also to claim that painting is dead because of the arrival of photography. The result is that the "100% architect" does not build anything at all because he does not have anything to build and merely drafts charming 100% plans and the "100% painter" neither paints nor photographs, but rather looks forward to the day when his (100%) reflector games will be transmitted in the standard cinematic-city of the future. *Is not precisely this the most heinous provisorium?*

Ye Who Are Warriors of God!

7. Hussitism did not arise by chance: We are a nation that is very religious, very educated, and very theory loving. The Germans have given us a stolid love for dogmatically devising heavy programs and manifestos, and our "Slavic soul" propels us toward sentimental fanaticism. And because it is not very far from the hills of Šumava to the Tatra mountains, we have not grown accustomed to energetic movement. Only to understanding, to comprehending. Once we have understood, we have time enough. We are settled down happily in the Heart of Europe and we are deepening, clarifying, proclaiming, and dogmatizing. Let us take a look:

— Once upon a time Mr. [Ilya] Ehrenburg remarked that art will cease to be art. We heard this and the phrase caught on. And so, very well, let us chew it over. Mr. Ehrenburg has long ago forgotten, but we are developing more and more of a taste for the idea.

— Messrs. Jeanneret and Ozenfant once opened people's "eyes that do not see" to the beauty of modern technology. They wrote manifestos, gave indications, caricatured, and recognized when it was appropriate to stop. In the meanwhile, our eyes have long ago fallen out over all the "poetry of propellers and central heating," but we still go courageously forward like poor blind men fumbling for the standardization, normalization, and classification of m-m-modern c-c-culture.

— At some historic party the word Poetism was thought up for the amusement of those present. It is still to this day not known by exactly what rule other, perhaps wittier, jokes made that evening have been forgotten, while Poetism will perhaps soon appear in school-leaving exams. And meanwhile everyone feels the right to declare: I am a Poetist. Poetism is — and enough is enough. I would like to see, in Cheb or Horní Dvořiště at the border, an allegorical statue of, for instance, forefather Czech or Jan Blahoslav, pointing back inland to show: *This is the kingdom of the written word. Hoc est regnum litterae scriptae.*

Alternate your shoes and socks! Alternate!

8. Everyone is shouting out that they have had it absolutely up to here with "isms." Therefore, the following happens: Take a new -ism, paint it and polish it, and say: All ready and done, this is the true one. I am not going to play any longer. In a year the game can be repeated.

Is the disappointment worth all the fury against the wretched -isms? Is it not better to reckon with the fact that the new -ism is merely a quite ordinary -ism? To know in advance that it will not last. To retain flexibility. Oh, this is not cunning; this is not insincerity; this is not even betrayal. An artist commits a betrayal only when he ceases to be an artist. If he is an artist under one slogan, then he remains one also under the next one. The flags of Cubism, Classicism, and even Surrealism have successively been raised over Picasso's paintings. Cocteau has run along with Apollinaire's Cubists, with the Dadaists, with the "Les Six," and when necessary he runs along all by himself. Can either be reproached for not being artists?

It is this simple. We have an awful, miserable climate in the region. And even artists have a need for clothing. And then, a little bit of dandyism is also necessary. Therefore, according to the seasonal weather, attire yourself for going for a walk in Dadaist style, or Surrealistically, and so on. How correct this is, so long as the artist does not forget *where his underwear ends and his own skin begins*!

Distinguished Robbers

9. In the end, this statement could be recommended: Let everyone do what he wants. Straight ahead to anarchy, grab a bomb, my friend! We are faced with a very delicate decision. There is nothing more distinguished than Dadaism: We must raise our hats to Soupault, Tzara, and Ribémont-Dessaignes, in whose cases Dadaist anarchy left art untouched. The distinguished robbers killed the police to the last man, and all the jewels remained in their places. I am afraid that here in our country plundering would occur; even anarchy would become a fanatical theory. Therefore, let us whisper quite softly: without external strictness, not giving a damn about anything, be diligent, attentive, and sensitive researchers.

A Bloody Truce

10. Once the deepest and most humble calm has settled in the foamy glass with your most intense passion; once in the middle of the most Dadaistic and most profane roar of laughter you smile indulgently at the most unbearable classic; once you shed tears over the touching parallelism of the most contradictory artistic directions of the past, the present, and even the future; once, during the great truce of relativity, in the dark you try to choke your arch-enemies with your left hand, while caressing your dear friends with your right hand, art will appear to you — a miraculous animal, a tortoise

"hesitant and firm,"

a tortoise that no one mentions.

Vít Obrtel: Harmony

1.

We did not create "Constructivism" to last for eternity, but to overcome boundaries. What today seems to be the last letter of a final alphabet will tomorrow be merely the first symbol of a more subtle and precise alphabet, because, with every day that goes by, people's tastes and desires become ever more delicate, and their capability for choice ever more consummate. Mathematics calculates shapes that are statically safe, in a constantly more and more disembodied form, from materials and combinations about which we had no idea yesterday.

This is no longer a case of an anti-decorative aesthetics, but neither is it a case of a Constructivist aesthetics. ***It is not a case of modern art.*** The word modern *de facto* does not exist. It is not possible to speak about modernity in sciences, where there is merely constant development, in which a discovery always derives from a previous discovery in a geometrically developing progression. It is not possible to speak about progress in art. In art it is always a case only of a change of form: The essence itself does not change. Just as a painting remains a painting, whether the means of creating it correspond to the possibilities of the 12th century or the 20th century (always of course in that century), ***so a house remains a house*** with the unchanged function of providing living space, a factory remains a factory, and so on. However, with every hour new problems (economics of movement) are arising as human requirements are increasing. The method of expressing an aim resulting from these requirements is transformed with technical knowledge, and through this process a new form arises corresponding to the materials and feelings of the period. ***It is only form that is changeable*** and aesthetically dependent on the flow of theories: form as a function of materials. The precondition for this is a technical knowledge of all possibilities mathematically comprised in the unit.

However, just as every mathematical equation, even if correctly calculated, is certainly not beautiful in the mathematical sense, so every architectonic unit, even if perfect in terms of construction (in the narrow sense of the term), is not good in the architectonic sense. Just as a person who is good at arithmetic is not necessarily a mathematician, so a good building constructor is not yet an architect (though of course basic lack of skill in addition and subtraction is not appropriate here).

If so-called modern architecture was to be evaluated only in terms of its use of the latest technical possibilities, this would mean that absolutely no good architecture exists at all, because at the moment when some building was completed, it would necessarily already be antiquated in the current period of ever newer and newer improvements and discoveries. The measuring standard for architecture that is built in this period must necessarily belong to the period. This standard can only be — as is perhaps already understood — its harmonious fulfillment of its aim.

Architecture is for human beings, and human beings are composed from elements in a harmonious unit. However, while for each person today these elements are more or less either identical or varied (matters of liking, temperament, and so on), when composed together these elements comprise the unit of a collective = a harmony of units. In matters of the aim the individual is subordinated to the collective, while in matters of personal liking he is subordinated to himself.

This is why it is necessary to accommodate the likes and desires of individuals on a social, Constructivist, economic, and hygienic basis within the practical limits of the possibilities of the whole, because it would be bad to enforce on people with differing personal likes a form of housing corresponding to a theoretical norm and in this way to simplify matters.

It is not possible to deny the formation of new forms, as well as the emergence of new functions of materials, conceived solely with the aim (physical and hyper-physical) of resolving living space in the sense of housing. This applies both internally and externally, because ***everything is created by space***: Living space is not merely the way from the bed to the table, but also the way home from work. The feeling of a clear and purposeful organization of the ground plan is just as important for physical needs as the feeling of visual satisfaction is for the practical hygiene of the soul. Not, therefore, the organization of ground plans, but rather the organization of space. Living space is not an American tin can; rather ***living space is a part of the universe***. Just as a house is not a statue, neither is it a machine. A house does not produce life, but rather a life produces a house. A house is a bordered space in which we allow the hours of our life to flow by, where we work, eat, feel joy, or abandon ourselves to inactivity on the paths of chance occurrences. To perceive this space with all the capabilities of the 20th century. An architect organizes this space by making use of all technical possibilities and all artistic values so as — within the practical possibilities of the collective — to implement everything connected with the economic construction of the house, but also to accommodate those non-material, hyper-physical aspects, to capture ***the harmony between human being, building, and nature***, as a part of this world.

2.

And so, finally, a human being, tired by the monotony of slogans, gives himself over to the facts of the laws of the melancholy of individualism. After a certain time he realizes that he was not so much mistaken, but that his ability to create has devoured these laws, that he has already quite forgotten about them, and precisely because it would never even have occurred to him that the problem could be concealed in how charmingly and elegantly he would run using his hands and write with his legs. He did what he knew how to do, what he had learned, and what he was allotted to do. And in this way everything would seem simple and plain.

The seeming simpleness of things affects uncomplicated souls who are good at distinguishing colors and forms, but whose thought becomes confused and evasive when someone smashes this thing into a thousand enchanting fragments. A simple thing affects refined souls who in a kind of amazement realize that what they have seen every day, they have seen at a certain moment so as never to speak about it, so as to forget it, but so as to feel it for ever.

Complication is in matters; its persistence is in us. We either reveal this complication or we conceal it, according to needs that are either a) physical or b) hyper-physical. The value and beauty of things is in their endless variability (variability within fundamental limits, where the fundamental essence beneficial for the whole does not change the form as necessitated by function, but rather merely satisfies individual desires and demands on the scale of a fundamental tone that grows along with the level of cultivation into a endless area of new sensations) — in the fact that concerning something determined by the need of the collective every individual selects what is closest to his own sensibility and that from which he obtains the most intensive experience.

Colors and forms abstracted from purposefulness: This is a self-evident precondition. Basic colors have become boring. Mixed colors are an expression that is too barbaric and tasteless. Here this is a case only of tones, of nuances, of barely perceptible hues, of a heavenly blue no longer of hours but of seconds, of a green of refined contentment, of a yellow of sudden awakening of the day beyond the curtains, of quarter-tones, of sixth-tones, of millionth-tones, of an entire new culturally delicate scale of color intuition. This is a case of the purest, most artificial, and most technical colors, because all are produced for general use by a chemical process; they arise through human invention and machine work.

This renewal is also taking place in forms, for instance in the scale of the cube and the scale of the sphere. This is a case of the purest and most refined relationship of the use of forms in all kinds of art: the projections of the square and the circle in a harmonic combination on a surface, the scales in painting and in architecture fabricated on the basis of fundamental forms. From their mutual relationship, the ingenuity in their arrangement, and the elegance in combining them arises a harmonious unit whose value does not disrupt the space in which it is placed.

In architecture a harmonic unit will be attainable perhaps within a short period in a state that is founded on the scientific basis of economic balance. This harmonic unit will be harmonious in space as functionally corresponding to the social, hygienic, practical, and economic requirements of the whole, as well as harmonious in the "non-practical" needs scientifically demonstrated for the individuality of each individual, through a standardization (a standardization that is not, however, rigid, but variable through a process of refinement) of parts used, their mutual combination, and their selection from a series in accordance with the aesthetic principles of the individual.

This unit, anchored in its artificial surroundings of gardens, fountains, lights, playgrounds, and swimming baths — all the magic of technology and poetry — will be a harmonious part of the world.

3.

In the current period no one has the right to deny himself any kind of available experience — whether it be lunch, sport, or work; whether it be a mood, a picture, or a poem; whether speed or a recollection — that brings a feeling of delightful satisfaction. If we feel the need, then we can rejoice collectively; if we feel the need, we can rejoice individually. About everything and from everything. ***The field of perception must not be narrowed, but expanded by all realities***. We know where we hang our clothes every evening, but our last look from the patent folding bed is drowned in the monotone, always indifferent wall. A change — miracles of the calculated shadows of electric lamps according to momentary mood and the constellation of the stars, the mechanical movements of walls, the increasing or decreasing of space according to the feeling or reality of society or isolation, doors and windows practically arranged according to the physical law of permeability in calculated and changeable apertures, the mechanical music of the gramophone and the dance step, the fragrance of flowers and emotions. To consume everything economically — wisdom and work, intoxication and dream — because life is ***a mix of reality and unreality in a harmonious balance***.

Karel Teige:
Karel Teige On Himself

Recently, I was invited by the editors of the magazine *Rozpravy Aventina* to write an article for it entitled "Teige On Himself." I approached work on this topic — thus far unexamined — scientifically and pragmatically and immediately set out to search for sources — both written documents and other recollections concerning this matter. However, before long I realized that it was not going to be possible to complete the work in the given time, because the material that I had thus far succeeded in gathering and partly studying was quite extensive, but nevertheless very incomplete and not entirely convincing, because it was full of contradictions, discrepancies, and contradictions-in-terms which only in a few cases could be successfully minimized through a critical examination of sources and their mutual comparison. Elsewhere, however, a lack of clarity still persists which makes impossible a precise and documented description of the entire case. Given that I would not like to fob off the topic "*Teige an Sich* (On Himself)" — which so attracts me in view of the fact that it has not hitherto been researched and in view of its evident complicated nature — with some unsubstantiated improvisation, I cannot today write this up in its definitive form and I am compelled to request the readership and the editorial board of *Rozpravy Aventina* to be satisfied for the meantime if in this place I now sum up — in so far as my uncompleted study of sources allows — the results of my hitherto research on this topic.

The excerpt from the registry of births, in addition to the still preserved — though considerably damaged — passport and the problematic record-book of university lectures attended, in agreement with other official papers, attest that Teige was born in Prague's second district at house number 1610 on 13th December 1900 and that his most blatant activity falls into the period at the end of the first quarter of the 20th century and the beginning of its second quarter. In general, official documents provide us with information that is much more precise and unambiguous than documents of a literary type. Literary documents that describe Teige as a child from the end of the millennium leave us in embarrassed uncertainty. If it were not for the official documents mentioned above, then the determination of the time period in which he lived would be absolutely indeterminable, because the end of the millennium can be thought of as a very broad time period, perhaps between the years 1700 and 2990. Apart from that, the literary reports speak about a child (from the end of the millennium). In contrast to that, at the city hall Teige is included in the military, electoral, and unfortunately also the tax lists, which refutes — or at least strongly restricts — this literary contention. Unfortunately, in the next section we are obliged to rely mostly on documents of a more or less literary nature written by a certain citizen Kodíček, an evident contemporary of Teige-On-Himself, which documents were published in the daily *Tribuna* at the turn of the years 1922 and 1923. These kilometers of articles contain harsh accusations raised against Teige-On-Himself: We learn here that apparently the Teige in question is a louse, a rogue, a filthy lowlife — in short a personality so defamed that the sensitive author of these vulgarities and insults always feels himself obliged to mention Teige's name as follows: please forgive me for mentioning this Teige. This record by the above mentioned citizen Kodíček appears very trustworthy. This is because I have not been successful in ascertaining that this Kodíček was convicted in court for the offenses to honor mentioned here, and therefore I conclude that either Teige did not bring a legal action against him at all or that Kodíček provided evidence of the truth of his statements. However, in the case of Kodíček we can leave all question of honor aside. I am merely surprised how someone like F. X. Šalda could later describe Kodíček's behavior as brutal and tactless and defend such a dubious individual as Teige-On-Himself appears to be. The credibility of Kodíček's insults is increased precisely by the fact that this is not the case here of a literary article and a critical evaluation, because Kodíček uses expletives so uncouth such as no Czech literary figure even knew at that time. Rather, his articles — in their style similar to sensationalist reports from court trials — can be classified among official documents, specifically those from the secret archives of the Police Directorate, where we could perhaps also find a whole range of reliable, but strictly confidential information and secrets about the life and activities of the said Teige. The non-literary and evidently illiterate character of Kodíček's articles, as well as the roughly similar — but less manly and drastic — articles of a certain Ferdinand Peroutka, the chairman of the Labour Party, written at the same time and in the same daily and later in the yellow magazine *Přítomnost*, evoke the justified impression that the above mentioned Teige was perhaps a person with an extensive criminal record, a personality banished from the decent and morally upright Prague society of that time — in short, a loafer, a drunkard, a waster, a bum, and so on. Nevertheless, this appearance is only partly confirmed by the official documents: So far I have not been successful in seeking out any evidence that the unfortunate person in question was apprehended in any kind of sensational conflict with the law. Rather I have found only a few minor misdemeanors and a number of reports to the police on account of excessive noise at night, interference in the performance of official duties, and similar matters. In contrast to that, the single police investigation that was undertaken against him was halted. The mentioned Teige was even one of the few of his contemporaries who did not carry out any assassination attempt on Mussolini, even though he dreamed of doing so. In view of the fact that I did not find any later documents about murders, robberies, violent rapes or similar crimes, I have been forced to consider the information of Kodíček and also of Peroutka as partly exaggerated. Additionally, it is not entirely clear whether this is not actually a case of mistaken identity, because the name of Teige does in fact appear in connection with serious crimes, but in a quite different context. At the time the attention of the citizens of our beloved Czechoslovak homeland was riveted on the sensational trial of the Teige sisters. Perhaps the writers of those indignant recriminations had this in mind. However, there is no evidence that Teige-On-Himself was any kind of guilty accomplice of these Teige sisters or that he played any part in their shady activities. My investigations on this matter have even successfully ascertained that these sisters are not his sisters, which of course does not rule out the possibility of some kind of distant family relationship.

In the case of Teige-On-Himself an *error in persona* — a case of mistaken or switched identity — may have occurred several times, all the more so given that this surname, even though quite unusual here in Bohemia, is nevertheless not entirely unique in Czech literature. Numerous literary documents — please note that I have not so far been capable of either sorting or studying all of these — seem to attest that often it is really a case of such an error, and therefore a more diligent critical appraisal of the sources and their careful, mutual comparison appears essential. For instance, it is difficult to assume that, let us say, the master tailor Teige about whom we read unpleasant things in Vančura's book *Proud Amazonky* [The Current of the Amazon] was identical with that Engineer Teige whose new house in Neklanova Street in Prague collapsed in 1913. Similarly, it does not correspond with the truth that both or one of these could be identical with the Teige, a variety-show magician and a juggler of words and concepts, to whom theater critic Dr. Rutte devoted so much admiring interest in his article "Hidden Face." Likewise, it does not seem to be the case that the hero of one of Synge's plays, the idiot Teige, was identical with the Teige, a representative of some kind of young generation (but not of the National Democrats), about whom František Götz writes extensively in his book *Jasnící se Horizont* [The Brightening Horizon]. Therefore, it is possible to assume that Kodíček's and Peroutka's assessments, judging by their emphatic nature, concerned that imbecilic hero of Synge's play. In contrast, the claims by Mr. Rutte about Teige as a variety-show juggler are most probably a poetic fiction, given that the name Teige unfortunately does not appear at all in the records of Prague's Divadlo Varieté [Variety Theater]. Perhaps in this case Rutte, the theater critic of *Národní Listy,* — taking his cue from his musical colleague — wrote a review of a theater performance at the Varieté that did not take place at all. I, therefore, draw attention once again to the unreliability and imprecise nature of literary records. It is also not entirely clear exactly which Teige Mr. Götz had in mind when, in his book *Jasnící se Horizont*, he mentioned this name in connection with the names of Jaroslav Vrchlický and Karel Čapek. If this is indeed a case of that same Teige about whom I am conducting my research, then I am forced to emphasize that so far I have found nothing that would confirm this connection stated by Götz or anything that would be a point of comparison between these three persons mentioned or anything in the relationship between them, except perhaps for a common futile desire to get rich by winning the Nobel Prize. I contend that neither does Götz's paragraph refer to the idiot Teige from Synge, nor to the tailor from Vančura's short story. If Götz claims and prophesizes that Teige, in spite of all his faults, will be received in heaven, then this is a definite error: Teige's death, as I set out below, provides absolute no evidence for this.

Most definitely, the process of examination of these complicated unclear matters and discrepancies is not making them any clearer, but rather on the contrary making things even more unclear. I am beginning to have my doubts about whether the Teige who is the author of the book *Film* is identical with the editor of numerous books, and whether one of these is identical with the Teige who is an editor of *Stavba* magazine. I have not been successful in actually establishing whether Teige-On-Himself is a painter, a writer, an architect, an editor, or a traveling salesman. Literary documents accuse Teige-On-Himself of a whole range of vices, scientifically named: Anti-Civilianism, Civilianism, Anti-Cubism, Cubism, Communism, Constructivism, and others. Mainly, they accuse him and his chief co-defendant Nezval of the highly contagious Poetism, a hideous vice and one that was not common in the good old times. In contrast, Teige-On-Himself has never excelled in virtues such as patriotism, loyalism, nationalism, Naturalism, Naturism, Classicism, Realism, or Academism. Naturally, an insufficiency of these cardinal virtues meant that he never gained the favor of the public, nor did he receive moral or material support or other *signa laudis*. I note that Teige-On-Himself has been found guilty of vices so contradictory that I really do not know whether this fact can be attributed to his lack of consistency or to a lack of consistency on the part of his commentators. It is evidently a case of both of these. I can put forward documents providing evidence of Teige's great inconsistency. For example, the mentioned Teige-On-Himself was from his early youth, perhaps from 1911 until 1919, an anarchist and a follower of Bakunin, after which he performed an incredible somersault and became a communist and a Marxist, in which error he persisted right up until his death. Further, the mentioned Teige as a painter declared painting dead, as a relic of the past, by which he enraged all those people making their living from painting. On the other hand, he dared to precisely differentiate between good and bad painters. Such a regrettable inconsistency caused a lot of bad blood, and as a result in various artistic milieus there was even a price put upon Teige's head. It is not clear whether this promised reward led to the action being carried out. Perhaps it did, as I have several documents about his headlessness and impetuosity. Sometimes Teige is disdained as a party propagator of the *proletkult*, while at other times he is disdained as a fundamental opponent of this. In this case, however, this is evidently a question of a lack of proper research on the part of his commentators, because I have not succeeded in finding even one article signed by him in which he has declared his support for the idea of the *proletkult*. On the contrary, I can cite a range of articles from various dates in which he resolutely rejects this idea. We can see a similar lack of clarity in the judgments by contemporary literary figures about that band of comedians known as Devětsil, whose entertainment program was for a time prepared by the Teige in question. Certain writers, after accusing this "Devětsil" of not being communist enough, then immediately became Social Democrats. There is a great number of such exceptional cases.

One of Teige's great faults was that he never had the correct instinct and he never succeeded in coming forward with his issues at the right time. He came late to meetings and he submitted his manuscripts and other assignments after the deadline. In contrast, he expressed his ideas and thoughts much earlier than they were mature enough to have a chance of meeting with success. For instance, in the years 1921–22 he fought against the rationalist-decorative architecture that was then dominant, and he earned only opposition and ridicule. After five years, today — that is, really at the right time, when the leading proponents of decorative architecture have reinvented themselves as the "leading" proponents of Constructivist and Purist architecture — his words would fall on fertile ground. In 1921 Teige wrote a few film scores. It can be expected that one day someone who comprehends that an appropriate time has come will make something very similar a reality. What was said in the *Devětsil* and *Život* collections in 1922 was stated at an inopportune time, and Mr. Peroutka laughed at it. Nevertheless, after three or four years, he printed in his magazine the same contentions that he had laughed at back then. Of course, at that time the names of different authors were signed under these contentions. The opposite of the lack of foresight shown by Teige-On-Himself and his comrades from Devětsil has always been the perceptive wisdom of the Literární skupina [Literary Group], which took over their counterpart's ideas always with a delay of two years — that is, at the right time, when the hour of their social success had arrived. Poetism, which arose in the years 1922–1923 in opposition to ideological and tendentious poetry and which developed into a certain aesthetic of all so-called "arts" in general, was devised by Teige and Nezval, but was evidently unripe and premature, exposed to the pillory of ridicule. The derivative second-rate Poetism of today and the future can be sure of its success.

Overall, very little can be said about Teige's literary and other work. There is no collected works. No comprehensive work exists. And when, after all, could such a work have arisen? Nighttime carousing, mornings slept through, afternoons lounging in a cafe, and the days of this century only have 24 hours. There are reports at the police about Teige and Nezval's revels stating that they lasted from Christmas to Easter. The collection of postcards that has remained after Teige attests that he traveled quite a lot, but — apart from his trip to the Soviet Union — he never wrote a single line of travelogue for the newspapers. This attests to his culpable lack of industriousness, because in this period it was a patriotic duty of all citizens regardless of sex, religion or age to write reports of their excursions in the daily press.

Perhaps we could find some personal, mostly extremely compromising, evidence about Teige in his partially preserved correspondence, which however is not accessible and is never going to be accessible, for reasons that I am ashamed to describe further. Nevertheless, this would be an interesting documentary source for a police investigator.

In the matter of the determination of Teige's psychological type I can point to the research of psychiatrist Professor Heveroch, who in his public lectures and articles cited Teige and his friends from the then Devětsil as severe cases of schizophrenia. However, once again this is in stark conflict with the character diagnosis of Synge, who represents Teige as an idiot.

Wild morals and a disorderly life caused Teige to die at a relatively young age in quite mysterious and inexplicable circumstances. No one made any claim on his estate. Over his grave only palms rustled; Mary sat there quietly until she became a victim of wild hyenas, and that is the end of that drama. None of the circumstances of the final matters concerning this person-on-himself provide any evidence for Götz's prophesy that he would ascend to heaven. He died without any descendants and without money; he never founded a family central heating system.

Concerning the matter of Teige's personal characteristics I could cite the horoscope prepared by the Great Magician Jan Bartoš and the planet that a parrot drew out for him at a market in Marseille. I found both of these in his papers, which were in horrendous disorder. I will submit this material — processed, sorted, and evaluated — at a later date. For the meanwhile, in conclusion I can only draw attention to the complicated nature of the entire task that I submitted to in agreeing to deal with the topic "Teige-On-Himself," which on account of the unreliability of the sources is becoming so problematic that Teige-On-Himself does not think it worth such an effort at all.

If, against expectations and in spite of what in truth I have had to say here to the dishonor of Teige-On-Himself, the Aventinum publishing house was to wish to publish something from the documents of his estate, then I would be willing to put together for this publishing house something about myself from his books about himself: to critically arrange this, to furnish them with scientific comments. In short, to prepare this for publication.

In expectation of hearing from you, I represent

Karel Teige,
who is not identical with, and so, and so on.
Praha 2, Černá 12a.

Milča Mayerová: Šíma's Dolls

When I was little, and my doll's head broke, I was really very sad, but today I know that the majority of dolls are headless and this no longer saddens me. Šíma's dolls are also all headless; I hope that this is not a case of any mockery... Well, no, certainly not, because this provides a space for a flower to grow in place of it. Flower and girl, two almost inseparable concepts, two of the rosiest images! Oh flower, miracle of purity and fragrance, symbol of tender innocence, what else depicts girlish fragility better than you?

Out of the black darkness shines a piece of a smooth body. You can think up any kind of face for it, the most affecting one that you have ever encountered on the street, the one that belongs to your doll, or the one that you have already sought for a long time and still hope to find. But you can also enjoy this without a face, without an image of living womanhood, merely as though from a piece of abstract beauty, from fleeting perfection.

After all, whoever looks at a living doll with fresh eyes will also see either only her face — the look into her eyes will tell him everything that lies in her depth; he will not see that she also has shoulders, a chest, and slim legs, that she is white and perfumed; the expression of her face fulfils him — or he glimpses a small piece of her nakedness, and then merely silently makes a bow and will not seek for the human face just as he would not seek it when admiring an exquisite crystal.

Perhaps this is the reason why Josef Šíma painted the heads of his dolls where their bodies are and vice versa.

ReD (= *Devětsil Revue*)...

ReD (= *Devětsil Revue*) aims to be a synthetic magazine of international cultural creation. Its content will quite simply be the life of modern creation, the birth of new forms, the victory of discoveries, and the tension of experiments. It aims to be a prospectus of ideas that are currently being realized as well as those that have not yet been realized or cannot be realized; a reporter from workplaces and ateliers in which proposals and forms of new living values are crystallizing; and a presenter of the results of collective productive work that is building the new conditions of culture. It aims to be a bulletin of knowledge from all fields — that is, artistic and educational ones; in short, a compact and complete panorama of the world and an atlas of poetry.

ReD, aiming to be a truly synthetic journal of modern cultural creation and also aiming to effectively participate in the creation of new aesthetic, scientific, social, and living forms, naturally cannot limit its interest and activity to only one element of this universal and cultural work — for instance, to aesthetic creation, to "art" — but it must rather be an overall review of all fields of modern productivity: naturally, the only work that will be regarded as productive will be that which corresponds to the maximal requirements of contemporary life and the contemporary human being, work which in short is at an all-time record level.

ReD aims to be a manifestation and at the same time a propagator of the modern spirit — a central office that collects reports on international cultural work, that aims to transform and reconstruct the world and to create new conditions of life and work on the basis of an organization of society oriented toward justice and a rational economic-social and civilizational balance. *ReD* aims to be an active collaborator of all those engaged in constructing a new human universe, a fellow fighter for social revolution that — in remodelling the face of the Earth — is implanting its creative work in a new living organism, in the young structure of socialist life. New cultural creation is not only an outline and a fore-image of future possibilities that will only become concrete and a reality in the context of new social relations, but is rather a participant in the revolutionary social metamorphosis. The only type of work that has human seriousness and a general cultural value is work that does not become stuck in a narrow specialization, but rather — without losing anything in its precision and perfection — is capable of seeing the entire horizon of life, work that is conscious of its connections with other specialist, working-class, and social work. Only work that has revolutionary perspectives constitutes a cultural act and sovereign creation.

The stance of *ReD* is determined by the stance of the “Devětsil” Association of Modern Culture, of which our journal is an organ. Therefore, *ReD* will be primarily a sampler and a compilation of Constructivism and Poetism. It will demonstrate, theoretically and practically, the mission and results of these methods of thinking, creation, and life. It will attempt to elaborate these concepts and tendencies; it will demonstrate aesthetic, technical, scientific, and also social forms corresponding to a new, modern spirit, and to a modern human being.

The scope of the active interest of our journal is given roughly by these headings, around which it will assemble its material:

> poetry • literature • music • dance • theatre • music-hall and circus • paintings and sculptures • film and photography • aesthetics • philosophy • psychology • architecture and urbanism • technical culture • hygiene • physical culture • industry and organisational work • sociology • socialism and class struggle • USSR • events and pictures from the world • journalism and news reporting • campaigning and advertising • typography and printing • documents and reports •

When enumerating the main points of the editorial program, we have no need to name the list of our co-workers. These will not be limited only to members of “Devětsil” A.M.C. *ReD* will be open to all those whose work is a part of the movement that is giving a new face to life and a new sense of the history of the present time, and to all works open to the modern spirit. *ReD* is simply going to ascertain the facts of modernity, examine working hypotheses, and revise current problems.

ReD poses a precise demarcation line between modern creation and old, perishing forms. It guides readers to the core of current work; it outlines its perspectives; it deliberates the pros and cons of all solutions, proposals, theories, and hypotheses. It will be an indicator of the tension of the era, and a creative energy, and a manifestation of modernity.

ReD is a red signal of the approaching new epoch of culture.

Bedřich Václavek: Buried Alive!

Poetism was supposed to have been buried alive. It happened this year. Because it became sad, it was regarded as dying, and many gentlemen, very much pleased, pulled quickly at the strings of philosophical and ethical criteria, ringing the church bells for it. They did not forget to express their respect for it by allowing it a decorated coffin of "form," which apparently it had tried to achieve while alive. However, this was a case of mistaken identity. That Poetism which for the first time defined the function of poetry and worked in accordance with this clear definition — the form of poetry that gave up pouring its personal anguish into the coffin of traditional forms — is still living. It is merely growing to adult years in a difficult period. What, however, has been buried is the risible and innocuous puppet of the epigones. However, this does not relate to Poetism, gentlemen!

Vítězslav Nezval: A Notice About Poetism

We have learned from almost all assailants on public opinion that Poetism is dead, and I have received the dubious honor from some of them of trotting along in the columns of some magazine or other alongside poets whose efforts are apparently conformist with the current wave of consolidation that is making itself apparent in statesmanlike and stabilizing tendencies.

In this they have tried to forget about Teige. Truly, he has never engaged in writing verse.

What is important for me is to recall some recently forgotten facts that remain true.

One evening in spring 1923, that unforgettable year — a recollection of which I will have when I am dying — one evening all the words of which have stuck in my memory, Teige and I were walking around Prague and enjoying the atmosphere of happiness, whose witnesses were the scents of spring, the stars, the rosary of lights in the streets, the drunks throwing up, the old women begging, the make-up of old whores leaning on street corners, that evening we found a way out of the disharmony of world opinions that were mummified, poisonous, and gloomy — and we invented Poetism.

This philosophy, which we will try to make more precise in a moment and which has been distorted with impunity for several years now, is the final and most radiant flowering of materialism, which succeeded in going from rough pulsations of material to subtle pulsations of material: to feeling and dreaming, from studying ideology to studying sensibility, from religion to sensations, from tradition to the current day, from aesthetics to empiricism, from logic to psychology, from psychology to physiology, from art-for-art's-sake to Poetism.

For so-called art this meant the destruction of the genre of literary poetry and the establishment of a poetry for all five senses, the destruction of aestheticism and the search for a six sense.

Just as Teige first of all mainly studied optical material from the new point of view of poetry, providing a basis for a visual poetry that already differed fundamentally from Cubism and formalistic purism, so I first of all studied words from a new point of view, from the point of view of a non-literary poetic vocabulary, providing the basis for verbal Poetism, which differed fundamentally from traditional poetry and from Expressionism, Symbolism, Futurism, and Dadaism.

Immediately after that we researched with all our senses. Teige: construction and poem, film, etc... I: pantomime, etc... We have provided the foundations. We will provide the foundations! Poetism is dead? Long live Poetism!

Bedřich Václavek: Resurrection of the Novel?

It has become an almost popular saying to speak about a resurrection of the novel, which for several years after the war lagged quite behind in modern literary creation. Theories have also already appeared explaining why the novel could only appear at a later time, and in particular the "second wave" of the young generation likes to boast a lot about its novelistic production. In this confusion, it will perhaps not do any harm to apply to the novel the functional criteria of Constructivist aesthetics and, by doing so, to elucidate the situation of the novel.

Previously, the novel fulfilled several functions. Its primary function was the communication of events, because the novel was an epic structure. The communication of factual realities and changes in these realities was its foremost task. In addition, for the entire period it also had an important social and political function. As the most significant example of this, we can recall the Russian realistic novel, into which an entire generation placed its political and social ideas. Later, the novel became an instrument of individual spiritual life and it is flooded with solutions to philosophical, ethical, and religious problems. Alongside all these functions, the poetic function, even though it was a permanent element of the novel from the beginning, was not very prominent. The novel that fulfilled more or less all these functions had a well-known conventional form, subsequently called the novelistic form *par excellence* by literary historians and critics of historical customs. A fundamental principle was a balance between the "thought content" and the creative (poetic) elements — or to use Walzel's expression between Gehalt and Gestalt — while the epic function played either a leading role or an important supporting role.

A differentiation of functions has led to individual functions becoming separated from the novel. For decades already the novel is no longer the main verbal form for communicating news, nor for declaring political, philosophical, and other ideas. More and more only the poetic function remains for the novel. On the other hand, a verbal form is crystallizing with an explicit function of communicating news. However, these two forms differ fundamentally from each other both in their tasks and in the methods by which they fulfill these tasks. This has led to a major disruption in the traditional, conventional form of the novel. In those cases when an author has not succeeded in giving up this conventional form and in strictly separating the two functions, the traditional novelistic form still remains, but we can detect in it the dissolution — even if unconscious and unwanted — of the epic structure and its crisis. However, in cases where the author is inclined toward purely contemporary tasks, the old novelistic structure is not sufficient, it loosens and snaps — so that the indications of a new structure can appear under its ruins. In the verbal creation of the avant-garde two independent structures are becoming quite clearly distinguished.

It was a long process during which a novelistic structure crystallized that excluded all other elements and concentrated on poetic aims. Romanticism, Decadence, and Symbolism were important stages in this development, which is still taking place today and is not completed. The new prosaic structure for the expression and creation of poetic experience is the analogue of that form of (abstract, absolute) painting that aims purely at creating aesthetic experience, at evoking emotion only with form and color, at creating elementary color relations; it is the prosaic pendant of pure lyricism. Just as abstract painting has left factual depiction to photography, so this form of prose has handed over the referential function to journalistic prose (and to a large extent, of course, to illustrated magazines and film). A new form is gradually taking shape as a consequence of this definition of function. Primarily, the plot is disappearing from the novel or is becoming merely a supporting structure that is subordinated to the poetic aim. This entails a rejection of the epic nature of this structure, its destruction and ironization. Dada, with its sense for the absurdity of conventional structures, has had an important say here. The "absurd" novels that are Dada's legacy primarily represent the dissolution of epic prose. At the limits of a "novel" conceived in this way two forms are crystallizing. One form concentrates on painting the soul; it aims to be a precise and delicate record of the most subtle spiritual tremors. Precursors of this form are Stendhal and Proust, to name only a few, and its cultivators are Soupault, Ribémont, Dessaignes, Tzara, Delteil, Apollinaire, Jacob, Cocteau and the Surrealists, and here in Czechoslovakia Hoffmeister and Nezval. The second form primarily pursues objectively poetic aims (for instance, Vančura). There are also a range of transitional forms and mixed forms. However, the overall contours of this prose are evident. It means a rethinking of elementary creation in prose.

On the other hand, journalistic prose is crystallizing as a form that is fulfilling the factual reporting function more effectively. Let us leave to one side newspaper journalism and examine only those journalistic forms that have taken over primarily functions that were earlier fulfilled by the novel and epic prose: reportage and socially aware reporting. They have a precisely defined function: to demonstrate over and over again the form of today's world. The criterion for evaluating them is how effectively and successfully they fulfill this task. In view of the fact that today a great battle for a new society is at the forefront of objective, human-collective social life, this journalistic prose demonstrates, discovers, and communicates primarily social facts, and it does so objectively without any interventions of freely combining fantasy, without any specially aesthetic elements. It does not attempt to give expression to the personality of its creator, nor to be an autonomous artistic reality. It is based on a factual study of many facts, on astute observation of the current state of the capitalist world and the social revolution, and then communicates its results contextually and urgently. It provides an intellectual connection between the scattered parts of socialist construction in Russia and the fellow combatants of the new class in Western countries. It also has an old tradition. In the 19th century we could search for this tradition in Zola and Gorky. Jack London and especially Upton Sinclair remain esteemed pioneers. In the current period the tradition has important representatives in Germany and Russia: in Germany, Holitscher, Paquet, and especially the "furious reporter" Kisch. The revolution in Russia was unforgettably captured by Reed and Reissner. Factual epics of the proletarian revolts in Germany have been provided by Fr. Jung and J. R. Becher. Of course, we find many differences between the authors mentioned here, but this is natural as this new form is only now being born. Here in Czechoslovakia this form virtually does not exist. Or at least it is not cultivated consciously. And nevertheless, it represents a necessary complement to poetic prose, which has successfully found cultivators here.

However, today a return to the old type of novel, which combined both the functions which are today separated, is impossible. Neither is a return to the "broad canvas" — to the old novel exploring social questions — convincing. This is apparently occurring plentifully precisely in the Soviet Union. If we read, for instance, such a "broad canvas" as Gladkov's "*Cement*," then we constantly feel how both tendencies — the creative-artistic one and the social-functional one — mutually disturb each other. Today, of course, prose is frequently rescued by new materials, but this is not a solution to its crisis. And what is happening here in Czechoslovakia in the prose of the "generation's second wave" is already a pronounced reaction, both thematically and creatively. This will not save the novel in the conventional sense. That is sure. It can only cause a little bit of confusion just like that caused in German painting by the "new realism" or in Czech and French painting by the return to Naturalism and Academism. However, the path of prosaic verbal creation is evident, and those workers of the word who are in close connection with the period and its constructive tendencies are going along this path.

Karel Teige: To All Those Who This Year Have Declared...

To all those who this year have declared that Poetism is dead, we say that they have come belatedly with their discovery, bearing in mind that various Ruttes, Kodíčeks and their consorts after all tried to beat it to death immediately at its beginning. They are over hasty and at the wrong time when they proclaim it as a corpse in a year when a number of Nezval's poetry collections are being published, primarily his *Akrobat* [Acrobat], when Biebl's book *S lodí, jež dováží čaj a kávu* [With a Ship That Imports Tea and Coffee] is being published, when Seifert's *Slavík zpívá špatně* [The Nightingale Sings Badly] has come out, when F. Halas has made a promising debut with his *Sépie* [Cuttlefish], when Vančura has surprised us with his dramatic poem *Učitel a žák* [Master and Pupil], and when Vilém Závada's successful *Panychida* [Memorial Ceremony] is rather evidence of a new enrichment of Poetism than of its extinction. To declare the death of Poetism from time to time is becoming an innocent pastime of pseudo-critics who have no idea that the public is not so crazy as to fail to see that the only thing that is really dead is something about which no one ever speaks any longer. The fact that Poetism has been grossly exploited by numerous epigones and plagiarizers who have totally failed to understand its essence and its mission and have adhered merely to its deceptive superficial appearance, is of course embarrassing to us, but it is no proof of the death of Poetism — rather the contrary! It is no accident that these "critics" who have declared the "death of Poetism" have been mostly themselves "under-sole" epigones of its aesthetic. How ridiculous the campaign against Poetism appears that Píša — in his book *Směry a cíle* [Directions and Aims] — contends he has already won; how ridiculous are the philosophical musings of Fraenkl, Götz, and others at a time when interest is being aroused abroad in Poetism as a result of its increasing power, intensity, and richness. In the *Rivista di Letterature slave* W. Giusti has published an informative article on Poetism and the almost official paper *L'Europe Centrale* has written as follows: "Cette jeune école tchèque est encore peu connue à l'étranger, mais elle y trouve de toutes parts des analogies, et ne peut manquer d'y intéresser vivement les nouvelles générations. W. Giusti souligne le sens profond du poétisme, réaction de la libre fantaisie contre le réalisme et l'idéologie de l'école prolétarienne. En s'appliquant à définir l'originalité des trois principaux représentants du poétisme, Seifert, Nezval et Konstantin Biebl, W. Giusti présente de nombreuses traductions de fragments de leurs poésies. Cette tendance poétique, bien vivante en dépit de tout ce qu'on peut lui reprocher, a déjà laissé une trace profonde dans les lettres tchèques, auxquelles ses trois jeunes représentants ont apporté une note nouvelle, sincère et jeune, qui ne périra point dans le changement continuel des tendances et des goûts."[1]

We were most amused when we read in the third number of this year's *Rozpravy Aventina* a new piece of evidence for the extinction of Poetism. Mr. F. Kubka writes his congratulations to Miroslav Rutte for his book *Měsíčná noc* [Moonlit Night]. Even though we are not looking forward to reading this book, we were nevertheless very amused by these lines: "And it was also your Czechness that has recast the plaything and intellectualist *qui pro quo* — that is, so called Poetism — and you fought against it for so long that in the end it blessed you. You have fulfilled something that had necessarily to arise from Poetism: a synthesis of thought and form — the music of feeling." Mr. Rutte's friend should not have done that to him! *Risum tenealis amici*: Rutte a Poetist! An American grotesque, carried out in the same way as when Kodíček declared in 1927: "We announcers of Purism and Constructivism," when his odious attacks against the first expressions of this direction here in Czechoslovakia in the *Devětsil* and *Život II* collections are generally already forgotten; or when the Národní divadlo [National Theater] — Dostal and Vl. Hofman — imitate the work of Osvobozené Divadlo [Liberated Theater] and Jindřich Honzl, but it is only this soulless imitation that is for the first time acknowledged by Czechoslovak critics as pure and mature modernity and deep originality. We can be happy that Poetism is not so terribly dead — when even Mr. Rutte is a Poetist.

R.

1 "This young Czech school is still little known abroad, but it finds all kinds of analogies there and it cannot fail to attract the lively interest of the younger generations. W. Giusti emphasizes the profound sense of Poetism, a reaction of the free imagination against realism and the ideology of the proletarian school. In attempting to define the originality of the three principal representatives of Poetism — Mssrs. Seifert, Nezval, and Konstantin Biebl — W. Giusti presents numerous translations of fragments from their poems. This poetical trend, very vibrant in spite of all that it can be reproached with, has already left a profound trace in Czech literature, to which its three young representatives have brought a new note, sincere and young, which will not perish in the continual changing of trends and tastes."

Vítězslav Nezval: A Drop of Ink

For a writer a drop of ink in an open fountain pen is like a magic mirror for a clairvoyant. You see in it your own tiny face. Bad mediums contend that this is a case of seeing from the invisible. These are weak writers who on every occasion describe their own little face. Ink glosses over a majority of mistakes. Occultists have a good principle: To concentrate on one thought for so long until the surrounding world fades away and small clouds start to appear.

If we are to create new art, then there is no other option than to surround oneself in one's thoughts with nirvana and to be concentrated for so long until the surrounding world fades away and small clouds begin to appear. For a medium, to forget about the surrounding world is the most difficult task of the entire séance. Yes, we are too accustomed to think through the surrounding world.

The millennium of the Catholic Church is coming to an end. Every age has renegades. A more important question for the church are its converts. Is it possible to speak of our conversion to nirvana, even though we have never left behind the church's ideas? If we saw our own small face, then this was not a case of seeing the invisible. Even though we never gave up the thought of nirvana, our séance had no chance of success. We were poorly concentrated.

Many Catholics are terrified of orthodoxy. They explain dogmas rationally. They do not achieve mercy. We have made excuses for not concentrating firmly. Was this perhaps a dread of the trance? For the majority evidently a habit of thinking too much through the surrounding world.

Everyday life is well known to all of us. We work for the Sunday, the day of rest, of our enemies. But our Sunday, our day of rest, is our future. Let us not forget that the Catholic Church is some kind of old Sunday, repeated for almost 2,000 years.

Therefore, be witnesses of my séance over Sunday. Let us consider how difficult it is to forget about the surrounding world. Concentration occurs gradually. I could emit premature shrieks as charlatans do. Primarily, I need trust in my abilities as a medium. I request not to be disturbed by superfluous questions. If you are sufficiently patient and indulgent, then our future Sundays will take place in a beautiful trance.

And so, my tiny face. There is nothing distinguished in it. A majority of its features blend with the ink. Do not be afraid. Ink is a bad mirror of narcissi. In a while a Sunday, a day of rest, will be formed from them. What kind of Sunday? Primarily one of the surroundings, but we are going to take heed to forget. Let us return to my eyes. There is oblique slanting foresight in them. It would seem that I have been crying for a very long time. And if I am now beginning to smile just a little, then that is so that I do not thwart the séance through undue seriousness. Shadows are going to pass by without causing my eyes to marvel. I know about them. I am going to pay careful attention to them.

Saul went blind from excessive seeing. This blindness became fate in the Catholic Church. Apart from that, it is mercy. Concentration is made easier.

I did not deserve to go blind. That is why it is necessary for me to see the world. My everyday good impulses lead me away from the world. Apart from that, in this there is a guarantee for us that eventually I will after all see our Sunday shine out. It will be necessary for us to be sensitive restorers so that we are able to wipe away several upper layers from the picture while at the same time not spoiling the work which shines beneath them.

Few people should seem as devoid of property as an epigone. In an epigone's furnished apartment nothing belongs to him. Every piece of their bed has gone through our hands. The wheels in the clock or the screws in the motor of an automobile to which they devote their time are touched by our precious hands. Why would we berate? Let us be aware of it. We have woven together the lace of adulterers one thread at a time, before the lace was taken from us. We will return for all this one day. No polish will remove the marks of our touch from their furniture. Let them be worried.

Whatever is not God's, is ours. Even the fact that we plow the soil means we have taken it over from God. It is no longer his old clay from which he fashioned Adam. This is the reason why we are not going to recoil from lanterns. They hang them over their harlots. We will hang them up over our children and over our loved ones. But we will cease to show them our bare legs in dancing shows.

This is an important chapter. Ah, really, syphilis is a bad disease. But the syphilis of prostitutes is a disease of slavery. Let us not be worried about the bare legs of women. This would be for us to fall into lies, into the Racine-like virtue of the aristocrats. We are worried about dignity and slavery, of which there is always a danger whenever there is a possibility of buying something. This is why we will deny ourselves access to cabarets, bars, and theaters. They are the display windows of the shops for the sale of bare legs.

We do not buy and we do not sell. Understand me well: In this we are similar to God.

We will return for all this. To return to bare legs their dignity. Because there will nothing to pay with. Let us not be afraid. We will continue to sleep in beds made with our hands.

From the things that we weave, sew, or forge, we will create a theater of facts and shapes. In the theater we will admire the light-bulb that we have cast in a factory. What else is this going to be other than a promenade of ready-made things for which we have polished wheels during the week, arranged by us who are going to light them up. We are going to surprise you with an entire week's work, well arranged. For what purpose should we then concern ourselves any further with morality? After all, morality is fear of being infected with syphilis and of the thieving sown by this. We will not have any need of morality. Let us go blind like Saul. Let us leave women and men to make love. Then my bleary slanting eyes will be straightened. They will be able to radiate romanticism like in childhood.

Come along with me to the fairground and help me reconstruct our Sunday, our day of rest. The lights sweep the dusk from the evening. Yes, we want to be surprised by all the things that our light-bulbs can be used for. We will display them every Sunday in a formation that will amaze you. We will show how a blouse excels alongside the tinfoil and silk that we have made in factories.

The variety-show illusionist does not conceal the true character of the world. This is done by idealist poets and humanists. This does not fit in with our all too lively Sunday. The variety-show illusionist performs an invisible trick in which a girl hangs vertically in the air without it being evident where she is being held up. With the help of our little tricks we want to show our work in such a way that you will be amazed.

Before the start of the performance, you experience the illusionist's girlfriend clad in a strange veil on the podium. In her we are going to love a princess. We put out of mind one layer that covers everything — prostitution. We dress up women in our poems and in our theaters in such a way that you are amazed. Do you guess what is going on here? At some other time, we will continue with evoking our Sunday.

•

Every idea is good in its essence. All of them have been misused. What to do with ideas?

•

If an idea proclaims a battle, it becomes whatever is its opposite, according to by whom it was conceived. Almost all of the toughest battles have been conducted by adherents of the same idea interpreted in different ways.

•

Ideas divest acts of personal responsibility. An idea is a guilty party that is not capable of being punished.

•

A passion for war is a diabolical obsession, thought up for extinguishing or weakening mankind. That mankind is a victim of this deception is attested by the special aura with which ***the quality of being dramatic*** is veiled.

•

People's attention is systematically diverted away from facts and things toward ideas. This is the source of needless misunderstanding.

•

Facts are easily understood. Ideas attempt to cloud facts.

•

In every idea there is cocooned hypocrisy. It becomes a noble idea. A fact is an actualization of something. An idea, promising so much, is swollen-headed just like a person boasting of his great deeds in the future in front of a person who has actually performed these deeds.

•

An idea is like the sign of a roguish hairdresser, who announces every day: free haircuts tomorrow.

•

To have enemies is regarded as more heroic than to have friends. This is one of the deceitful consequences of ideas.

•

An idea is like a hypnotist. People sacrifice their judiciousness to it voluntarily.

•

What to do with ideas? Replace them with facts, realities, thoughts. A thought differs from an idea as a diagnosis does from a prognosis.

•

An erroneous comparison: It is said that young women are beautiful like roses. A phrase. How much more grandiose it is to state about a bed of roses: roses and beautiful women. You will find scents that you have never perceived before. Roses will become roses more than at any time ever before. They will become roses.

•

A fact: How many poems have you read in which a man is playing to some roses in a garden and they are listening? How much more will you be thrilled by a fact without personification: A man played to some roses and the roses smelled sweet.

•

A ray of sunshine on the walls of a room in November recalls the countryside. It disappeared. But the notion of a sunflower is delectable enough to protect us from dejection.

•

The vanity of description and one more rose: a novel. Sunset in a room. There are writers who want to depict this sunset in words. They observe each piece of furniture one after another; they search for reflections. Older literary schools made use of a mythological apparatus. This simple mystery can be conjured up in one single sentence: The sun went down. And a recollection of it remained in the room. A rose in a glass behind the window.

•

Let us leave nature its independence. Let us leave the nightingale to sing to nightingales. For me, its song is a rattling sound that means nothing. A parrot imitates our speech well. This amused me for a certain time. For me it was an important step between a nightingale and a gramophone record.

•

We are terrified of emptiness. We wanted to fill up the forest with a nightingale. For the same reason we have created fairies, water-nymphs, and water-sprites. Today, thank God, there are woodland restaurants, radios, and steamboats.

•

Birds evidently despise parrots. We have taken them under our protection on account of their fake humanity, just as we have taken variety-show performers under our protection on account of their fake artistry. Today we are bored with both. After all, the parrots remind us of those artists whose stock in trade is the imitation of nature. We laugh.

•

The infertility of past ages is demonstrated in its decorative liking for nature. Women who wear dresses printed with garden scenes do not have confidence in their own beauty or in their own ingenuity. The lines of the body do not get old, because a person walks in them at every age. An everyday ingenuity is required in cosmetics.

A good work of art is durable in its construction and fashionable in its cosmetic treatment. Whoever creates cosmetic components from materials that are too durable will grow old and become laughable like a person who wears his overcoat for 30 years, just because he had it made from leather.

•

I am interested in a nightingale at whom children are whistling.

•

All natural fragrances isolate us. We feel like foreigners who have nobody and must escape into the world of plants. Artificial perfumes bring us together. Using them in the process of grooming, we are similar to thousands of other people.

•

Nature has a tendency to variability; an artist seeks similarity. Nature is combative; art is social and conciliatory.

•

I shave every day. In this I resemble my great-grandfather. No one calls me a traditionalist on account of this. For the same reason Sophocles is closer to me than Ibsen.

•

The game played by one footballer resembles that played by another. It is all about getting to the ball by the shortest possible route and scoring a goal by the fastest possible trick. All footballers make the same effort. Method is an agreement on the part of artists. For the public, the skill and excellence of the game are more important.

•

Art has the detrimental characteristic that it is capable of reviving the dead. I have taken advantage of this bad habit. At least I have the credit of having been capable of changing them into current-day clothes. For this reason I have travestied Diogenes, Manon, Joan of Arc, and Pierrot. Today I take my leave of archaisms. I want an art that is more modern than a big city. Because big cities have arisen without a plan and have on their conscience the crisis that some people attribute to newness instead of seeing in it the remnants of the chaos from which the cities arose.

•

As soon as a trade has achieved a certain excellence, as soon as the sweat of labor has dried up, as soon as a week of hard work has come to an end, there is this plaything here, this festive guest. The material in it is so excellently malleable that it leaves not a trace behind. This obliteration of traces has the effect that we regard it as a work of nature. In his most perfect works a poet is anonymous. In this way he resembles nature.

•

Let us recall the words of Picasso. "Not to seek, but to find. No work is created as a path to another work. Every work aims to be definitive and present. There is no development in the sense of progress toward some kind of ideal." And, therefore, we should not overestimate the importance of method. Therefore, we should not seek some kind of special key that would contain some kind of revelation of a secret. We should not seek for a norm in some specific features; we should not form theories from these, because in the hands of weak individuals these will change into a template just like the old paths — from which we have today already diverged, even though they were derived from works of the greatest genius. Let us not try to rationalize the greatness of Stravinsky by citing some kind of general rules. In essence there are no keys for the creation of greatness. There are no professional secrets. The secret of Picasso is to paint not only what we see, but rather everything visible. The secret of Stravinsky is that he composes everything audible. If we certify this by using the word polytonality, then in reality this is a case of something much less: We should refrain ***from covering our ears with the earflaps of dogma and rules***.

Let us leave the concert hall for a while and listen to the singing of country people. Some kind of pub with a harmonica and violins. A melody in C major accompanied in F major. Itinerant tinkers singing a carol about Mary and the Baby Jesus. Let us pause for a while somewhere behind the country double-bass player or behind the drunk singing a sad song to the dancing of a galop. And let us not be crazy and let us not imitate them. An example can be found in the ringing of church bells or in a jazz band, just as in the singing of birds.

Let us compare consciousness to a cupboard with many layers or shelves. The so-called traditional have become stuck on one of the penultimate shelves, while the modern — that is, the orthodox adherents of some modern school — draw from the top shelf, which is overfull with the current things of contemporary life. This is indubitably a superficial modern, which paraphrases and accepts as general rules "contemporaneity" or the achievements of some truly creative individual. A truly creative individual is not bound by the final layer of his consciousness. His creation is courageous, undisciplined — in other words, it does not submit to the discipline of another creative individual. He is capable of emptying the layers of his consciousness in any order he wishes, of mixing their contents and creating really new and original combinations. His development is not determined in advance, as in the case of weaker individuals; he has his own courage.

This is why originality and quality are the most certain criteria of so-called "leftism" in art. Any kind of evaluation with regard to personalities or ideas that we have acknowledged as modern is erroneous, because this evaluation concedes a greater or lesser degree of epigonism, which is an element that harms art.

•

The leftist intellectual front is invisible, comprising mutual sympathy and respect, associating truly original and valuable creators. Art is not war. Away with military metaphors. The free struggle of souls is the most beautiful spectacle of history. And a rich creator is not a capitalist. He does not exploit anyone. And he gives his wealth to everyone who wants to partake of it.

•

Drama is a visible expression of events demonstrated through a play. The old aesthetics contended that the dramatist's poetic act is comprised in capturing an event and a thought, and that the form depends on the director and the actor. This is an erroneous assumption. Because, apart from this evident sub-construction, drama is primarily a partiture of forms. It is up to the poet to create this partiture and up to the actor to transform himself into this. A dramatist seeks — above the world of thoughts, events, and feelings — the world of their figurations and forms; and so, form is the plot, the text, while the actor is its clothing and scene. A modern kind of drama is comprised of elementary realities, from the concrete facts capable of visible life. Dialogue and monologue are abstracts that will be contained in the dramatist's sketchbook and that it will then be necessary to portray. The difference between a theatrical abstract and a theatrical concrete is the same as that between feeling and fantasy. A feeling first descends into fantasy in order to be expressible.

In former times a dramatist, instead of tens or hundreds of concrete specifics, wrote a text for conversations and prescribed costumes and three decorations, dead from start to finish. We are asking when drama will become drama. Once they arrive on the stage like Picasso's menagerie. Once they paint the changes of a smile in front of the eyes of the public with theatrical makeup on their faces. Once the parts of the stage sets are transparent to all viewers. Once the backstage with its prostitution and its pseudo-artism collapses. Once there are no longer acts and transformations apart from acts and transformations without end. The impossibility of drama up to now has been felt primarily by actors. In a desire to embody a statement they have exaggerated words and gestures to the extent of giving the statement a new embodiment. This was artistic subjectivism, while a play is an objectification in the course of which the poet's and the actor's subject is lost in a concrete expression — form. Pain, joy, passion — all these are distinctive forms. There is no other way to interpret. A play is not an individual. It will be necessary for the entire ensemble to play one person or one small branch. A play is an element that is material in the same way as sound or color or rhythm. A stone is a stone. Nothing can be changed about that. A flood will wash it away. A role — that is an elementary determination, one that is unchangeable, calm. You can murder with it just as you can with a stone, without it suffering any kind of convulsions. An actor needs to be dead enough to be able to be alive enough.

•

It was during long conversations and nighttime walks through Prague, while believing in modernity, progress, a new order, and human ingenuity; feeling our sensitivity, hating literariness, ponderousness, and careerist efforts; seeing spring come into bloom and stars move across the sky; and feeling a warm friendship, that Teige and I invented Poetism. This name of Teige's and mine, which was born one evening in a bar, was not meant to be either a program or a fashion. It expressed the need for an artistic arrangement of reality such as would be capable of satisfying all the human poetic hunger that has been ailing for centuries. I did not want to make up new worlds, but to arrange this human world, and in such a way as to make it into a living poem. The means to this were supposed to be words, sound, the realities of this world, arranged and directed by inventiveness and sensibility. We believed that art will come to an end once "all realities are ultra-violet," once human sensibility is so artificial and the organization of the world so perfect and emotive that it will not be necessary to write poems and that to be a poet will be to be a cicerone of this world. Poetism is a method of viewing the world so that the world is poetic. It is not defined by the themes that are ascribed to it by its enemies. There are no themes at all. It is not Biedermeier-esque; it is not perfumed; it is not sugary; it is neither from the delicatessen nor from the bar, as is understood according to some of the themes that have occurred, entirely according to personal taste or visually imagined. This is not the way that Poetism was intended. I do not know whether Poetism affected anyone else ***in such a way***, apart from the two of us. And, if a certain group of poets is arising who are associated with Poetism on account of a certain visual exoticism and for a certain perfuming of their verses, and who have taken the "harlequinade of feelings" too literally, then this is not ***that*** Poetism.

•

Everything that already acts on our feeling through its natural emotionality — that is, everything that creates the content of life — is not suitable for being decorated through poetry. Let us, therefore, rid ourselves of effects that make an impression in and of themselves through their so-called fatefulness.

•

Reality is the dictionary for the creation of poetry. With the help of memory we construct dictionaries. Let us imagine a dead dictionary. And let us imagine a living dictionary. A dictionary that has the ability to relocate its definitions and create from them deliberations, thoughts, new and newer variants.

•

There are many people who are pretty thick dictionaries, but who however do not have imagination. They do not have the ability to create poetry.

•

A poet with experiences will evidently be a greater poet than a poet without experiences, if we presume the same degree of imagination in the case of both of them. A poet with living dreams, an observational talent, thinking capabilities, and a high intelligence will evidently be a greater poet than a poet who does not have these things, because his dictionary is richer, more colorful, and capable of all kinds of variations.

•

Yes, a dream creates a very significant element in the life of a person, multiplying his vocabulary and his recollections.

•

A tree is a tree, because once upon a time it was named thus. Words, expressing a reality, are therefore really reality itself. And Shakespeare is nothing other than words, words, words. In this way he differs from bad dramatists. A word is an object that is expressed. When, therefore, we relocate words in a poem, we are relocating objects.

•

When the words were new, they shone alongside each other in their constant, native intensity. Gradually, through their frequent usage, phraseology was created. No one, in the course of an everyday greeting[1], imagines lips on the white hand of a woman. It was necessary for me to disconnect this phrase, if I am to evoke its original meaning.

Logic is precisely what turns shining words into phrases. Logically, a glass belongs on a table, a star in the sky, and a door on the stairs. This is why we do not see them. It was necessary to place the star on the table, the glass in the vicinity of the pianino and the angels, and the doors in the company of the ocean. This was a question of revealing reality, of giving it a shining form like on the first day. If I did this at the price of logic, then this was an attempt that was extremely realistic.

Painters have invented the beautiful form of still life. This is a case of progress from genre to a whole entity. A poem is such a whole entity.

It will evoke some plates for you from which you will not want to eat, alcoholic drinks that you will not want to drink, towns that are in no way memorable, angels that will not protect you, and an old indifferent reality in such a way that it will enchant you.

1 Old fashioned Czech greeting "Rukulíbám", literary "I kiss your hand".

Karel Teige: Manifesto of Poetism

At the moment when the last glimmers of -isms — Dadism, Futurism, Expressionism, Cubism, Suprematicism — were fading, in a period of confusion and embarrassing stagnation that has reigned in all ateliers and workplaces, in the midst of a tasteless and embarrassing eclecticism meandering aimlessly along lost paths and non-paths, in Prague whose gates we wanted to open up to the healthy breezes of the world and the Gulf Stream of global creative activity, at the intersection of breaking waves from north-south and east-west, at 50° latitude north and 14° longitude in the years 1923 and 1924 — that is, four or five years ago — ***Poetism was proclaimed***. Poetism was proclaimed not only in order to replace some other artistic, literary, painterly, or musical -ism and art-ism; not in order to oppose or compete with some other -ism. In proclaiming Poetism, we only wanted to express and formulate an opinion and determine a direction; we did not intend to establish a new -ism for avant-garde ateliers, exhibitions, and salons, or to found a movement and a school. Poetism was rather the announcement of a "new era in the history of the human soul,"[1] a way out from embarrassing aesthetic and philosophical confusions, disorientation, and disharmony. Poetism was invented as a new aesthetic and philosophical opinion, as a declaration of belief at the end of the millennium. If, in addition to this, it has become a school and a poetics, then this is not the intention or the fault of its responsible authors. Poetism as an artistic -ism and as a school is meeting the fate of all -isms and schools: It has found its artists and its epigones; it has experienced several superficial fashions; it has been both torn apart and celebrated by critics, who one time have predicted its imminent demise and then another time welcomed it as a new discovery. This Poetism as a movement and a school is noth-

1 This is how F.X. Šalda characterized Poetism.

ing other than a derivative, here and there an extremely damaged one; Poetism as a kind of opinion and an aesthetic prognosis. The fate of Poetism as a school and as an -ism will not concern us here, because this lies outside of the proper field of interest of Poetism as a new aesthetic and philosophy.

•

The first years after the world war, when we experienced a world that was changed to its very foundations, painfully overturned, horror-stricken by the dark years of bloodshed, in days of incessant tragedies, in days of political and social upheavals, in the excruciating uncertainty of what tomorrow might bring, in the dramatically electric tension of the world atmosphere in which could be heard the alarming screams of economic and cultural crisis and social earthquakes, the threats of revolution in front of the gates of the world — these first years after the war confronted us with relations and realities that were new to their very core, in the midst of a world that was absolutely dissimilar from the world in which the previous generation had lived, worked, and grown old.

The light of these disruptive days is the dawn of social revolution. Lenin. Soviet Russia. The Third International. Socialism, the promise of new forms of life. The raw fragrance of transformation and ferment provides ***new perspectives*** for a creative soul.

The artistic generation that was born out of the war, deafened by huge breaking waves of social changes and swept along in the revolt against the old world in favor of a new order, acknowledged the slogan "proletarian art," declared a turning away from the sentimentality of private erotic and ethical crises, from Expressionist decadence and from aesthetic confessional exhibitionism, a rejection of subjectivism in favor of a merging with the new class reality, with typical and collective living forms. "Proletarian art," not having any space to create new forms and its own systems, become stuck in naive class-based rhetoric, and in its faith in the class struggle it ended up forgetting about itself too much.

Unsatisfied by the commotion of this "proletarian art," we tried to carry out a revision of its program and conduct a critique of it from a Marxist standpoint. It became increasingly more apparent that the program of proletarian art is an absolutely false and insufficient solution, an incorrect answer to the facts of the revolutionary epoch. Proletarian art, we recognized, in the form heralded by Lunacharsky, is a non-Marxist fallacy and aesthetic nonsense. It even became apparent that poems that aimed to be agitprop for the revolutionary movement were not only inadequate poems, but also utterly awful agitprop; neither fish, nor fowl. A poem was an insufficient weapon of the proletariat against mitrailleuse volley-guns and armored vehicles. We viewed the ironic fate of Petr Bezruč's *Slezské písně* [Silesian Songs], which did not aim to charm with poetic artistry, but rather called for help for the unfortunate seventy thousand in the region of Těšín (Cieszyn). *Silesian Songs* were read, enjoyed a success, went through many editions, and achieved official fame (even though their contribution to the development of Czech poetry was not particularly significant) — but the proletariat in Těšín were not helped. Precisely in this way, all other poems by social and proletarian poets — works in essence rhetorical, didactic, and ideological, or odes — were incapable of fulfilling a mission that is not suited to the functions of poetry. In other words, there is no need to misuse poetic verses in a situation when the clear communication and direct appeal of a journalistic article, the inventiveness of posters, and skillfully directed propaganda will achieve more effective results.

At this moment the remarkable magician and acrobat ***Vítězslav Nezval*** spoke up. Where others, with greater or lesser fire and passion, were rhetoricians and apostles of revolution, Vítězslav Nezval is a poet. He brings his magical fairy tale, full of miracles and miraculous figurative fantasy. Thanks to his magical dazzling, poetry is reviving once again and remembering itself. It was enough for him to write a poem for 100 verses to be born; he published *Pantomima* [Pantomime] and his poet contemporaries found their orientation.

In 1922 the *Devětsil* collection was published, which carried out a revision of the program of "proletarian art," while still however using this designation. Here Nezval's *Podivuhodný kouzelník* [Remarkable Magician] was published for the first time. Two years after this, in spring 1924, my Poetist manifesto [*Poetism*] was published and in fall the same year Nezval's *Pantomima* came out. At this moment the word "Poetism" was no longer foreign to the Czech public and critics. Often used by us in contemporary treatises for characterizing certain aesthetic tendencies, it was actively received and accepted by critics, and so, before we had sketched its content, there was already a fairly extensive occasional literature about Poetism contained in the annual magazines of the time. The previously mentioned article published by me was aimed at dispelling at least to some degree the nonsensical things that were widely written about Poetism. However, the comfortable sagacity of literary historians flattened our parabolas into obedient straight lines and from analogies they fabricated equal signs. Lots and lots of pages, in total a heavy tome, were written for and against Poetism, which in this way was reduced to a chimera of desiccated and hollowed-out grotesqueness. Contemporary literary and aesthetic essays were littered with citations from this unfortunate article. With the participation of both opponents and adherents, a kind of codex of Poetism was patched together, and this was evidently the source of Poetism as an artistic school, as an -ism, and as a poetics. After a period of idealized proletarians, barricades, and red flags, a new period and fashion arrived: a period of "free juggling," of "an art just as self-evident, adorable, and accessible as sport, love, wine, and all delicacies," a period of "clowns, dancers, acrobats, sailors, and tourists," of "a harlequinade of feelings and images" — in other words, that "eccentric carnival and magnificent entertainment enterprise." Metaphorical characteristics became a topic, and respectable Parnassian verses received new *sujets*.

From here on, Poetism, against our original intentions, became an artistic direction, an -ism used in reviews, the final chapter of literary history, and a poetic school; in lower spheres it even became a formula. We do not consider it our task here to describe the development of this Poetism or to conduct a criticism of it. Some powerful and rare talents have demonstrated themselves in it, as well as a large number of hideous epigones. We learned recently that this Poetism is already dead, replaced by some Constructivist Realism, Civilism, or Fatefulness-ism. In the obituaries written by its gravediggers and in the retorts in which its adherents denied its extinction, we were able to read all kinds of interesting things about the merits and mistakes of this -ism.[2]

The exegesis and evaluation of Poetism as a literary movement (declared dead evidently very much prematurely, by an unfortunate accident precisely in a season which was bountiful in new and noteworthy books by foremost Poetist authors) is the task of literary history and criticism, which is duty-bound to analyze to what extent this attempt at the revival and purification of poetry has been successful. — In contrast to this, we are concerned with Poetism as a new aesthetic and philosophy of art, as a new stance, a new theory, as a conception of new creation and new life. That is, in the words of the first manifesto: ***"Poetism as a function of life, and at the same time a fulfillment of its meaning; Poetism as a modus vivendi."***

Poetism as an aesthetic prognosis and a philosophy of creation is based on several ascertained and recognized laws and historical facts. Unsatisfied with and unconvinced by the existing aesthetic concepts, atelier recipes, and mythologies, ***we***

2 Look what Mr. Pavel Fraenkl wrote about us in *Host* (VI. 9–10):

"Poetist loudmouths are starting to chaotically set out their stall and are going a bit further with their semi-hysterical and semi-inebriated jests which were never worth the battle that was conducted against them and which died quite naturally from senility, in which however our obfuscating critics in clairvoyant fashion observed childlike fantasy, a holy allegorical simplicity, a directly physiological urgency, and I do not know what else.

Well, these blessed moments passed and the funeral rites rang out for Poetism, only for, a few years ago, the sound of these bells tolling to become more or less mixed with the joyful sounds of its revival. What was positive in Poetism — let us be very brief in these ***generally acknowledged truths*** — is its pictorial fantasy, the freshness of the word through pure melody, the hallucinatory whirl of images. However, Poetism did not succeed in gaining any kind of connection with the period, either past, or present, or even with any indications of tomorrow; it grew somewhere in a vacuum and there — without noise — it is also perfecting itself.

Or Mr. B. Mathesius (in *Tvorba*, II. 3.) :

"A range of pictorial possibilities has remained from this exploration; a soft and languid verse. In the development of Czech verse Poetism constitutes... a quite healthy developmental correction. Its indubitable merit was an endeavor at form, at a new stylistic composition, at a new linguistic and pictorial transcription of seeing. It removed excessive ideology and individualistic poses. For this let it be praised; and granted an easy death and peaceful rest.

Or comrade Josef Hora (in *Tvorba*, II. 6.):

"Thus far it is clear that Poetism has provided a backbone and a starting point for several young lyricists and has disoriented a load of other young poets, just as every other -ism has done so far. It is good that it has been used, that it has performed laboratory work, and hats off to it."

We could go on forever with such citations. However, we do not have excerpts and evidence to hand.

posed the question of art and poetry anew and replied to this question by bringing together the results of multiple analyses of a wide variety of phenomena from the last epoch of the development of poetry and art.

Our predecessors opened up the windows to Europe. From the perfectly internationalist character of modern civilization, we drew the conclusion that we would abandon the provincial and regional horizons of national and state allegiance: We discarded Czech literary history and we forsook the heritage of Czech painting. historic inheritance of domestic. In any case, the historical inheritance of domestic values did not offer us anything that would have validity for this European moment. (Except perhaps for… Like visions of white towns, deep in the waters drowned… this beautiful passage from a pre-1848 Revolution poem [Karel Hynek Mácha's poem *Máj*], a free and cadenced sequence of dream-like pictures, embodied what we were searching for in poetry.)

We embedded ourselves in the rhythm of European creation, into a rhythm whose metronome, under the influence of the social-cultural situation as it was formed during the course of the 19th century and which produced the conditions for contemporary creation, was Paris. Paris was a focal point not just of French production, but rather of international production, its Metropolis and Babylon, the spiritual center not only of French-language creation and the Latin tradition, the successor of Italy and the precursor of Moscow, just as spiritual hegemonies change in history in accordance with changes in social systems and consequent cultural changes. In a period in which national particularity and specificity has disappeared from a large number of national and regional literatures, literature is becoming global. (Karl Marx) If our work is to create the presence of this internationalist art, it must make use of all the possibilities and working results that the previous period of development provides for it. Modernity, which we have defined as the sum of current possibilities and the current state of the developmental process, demands that we encompass and incorporate the contribution provided by the creation of the immediate past, yesterday's famous French poetic, painterly, and aesthetic creation, which is and was the culmination of an epoch in the spiritual and cultural life of our civilization.

The beginning of the development of the poetry of our civilization, the historical point at which poetry found its task in the relationships of the new society of the capitalist century of mechanical civilization, the beginning of the new poetic century, we find in Baudelaire. It is from Baudelaire and from Romanticism that we date the beginning of what is called pure poetry, liberated from the thrall of laws to which in future it no longer has to submit. Romanticism is the *point de départ* of the liberation of poetry. Romanticism freed poetry from its quota of content; it prepared a new conception of poetry, a poetry that was not tendentious, not didactic, not thematic, a poetry precisely separated from philosophy, religion, morality, politics, and historiography. This revivalist and liberating Romanticism — this is the Romanticism of Nerval, Bertrand, Borel, Poe, and Baudelaire, not that of Musset, Byron, and Hugo. Apart from that, the opposition of the names Poe-Byron or even more distinctly Baudelaire-Hugo points to two lineages of poetry developing from Romanticism: on the one hand, "pure" poetry, which is gradually separating itself from "literature," and on the other hand, verse with content and plot — literary, rhetorical, ideological, and didactic verse, odes. All these latter types of verse continue in the mission that was fulfilled by medieval poetry in service to the church, history, and morality.

Poe and Baudelaire establish the foundation of the new poetry; they endeavor to solve the problem of a new poetry in conformity with the living and psychological conditions of a person of our civilization. Gautier speaks about a poetry that does not show anything and does not tell any story; he defined a poem as a fluent flow of "meta-metaphors" — a term that already makes one think about Apollinaire! In Romanticism's love of colorfulness and picturesqueness we can also see the first and thus far faltering steps toward visualization, sensuality, and the physiological embodiment of poetic means and effects.

"*Les parfums, les couleurs et les sons se répondent.*" And elsewhere in Baudelaire we read that "pure poetry converges with music, painting, and culinary and cosmetic art."

The main forces of the developmental course of modern poetry, dating from Baudelaire, we can establish as follows: 1. An increasing tendency toward the purification of poetry, the thorough elimination of foreign elements (morality, ideology, history, etc.). Parallel with this purification of poetry, fundamental changes in prosody occur. Form is liberated as a consequence of a change in poetry's predetermined function, and areas of pure reason, the world of ideas, cease to be the source of inspiration; an appeal is made to intuition, to the pure imagination, the fires of fantasy flare up, and the dark reverberations of the subconscious announce themselves. 2. A crystallizing idea of a correspondence between the sensations of individual senses and a premonition of hidden analogies between individual fields of art. A mutual connection among the arts and a unity of aesthetic emotion. Poetry, distancing itself from the rational order of literature and ideology, establishes family ties with music and painting. It crafts its material, the word, and its composition in such a way as to extract from it the maximum of melodies and pictures; it musicalizes and visualizes — that is, it invests sensibility in its material, which is the poetic word, by making use of all possible echos in the receptory apparatus of the reader's psychology. (A tendency toward the musicality of poetry is a *novum* especially for French poetry; phonetic tones and a sonority of poems points toward a certain influence from English and German poetry overall.) Poets feel the possibility of an entirely new, higher, absolute poetry, a poetry without literature and outside of literature, a poem of liberated imagination, a poetry of all the senses.

[passage omitted]

Leaving the care of inherited and expiring artistic forms — painting, literature, and other artistic crafts — to historians and conservators, we have attempted to get rid of these subsisting and superannuated forms, which conform to previous societies and civilizations, but which are not suited for our mechanical civilization and are unacceptable for the modern sensibility and pysche of a contemporary human being, and to replace them with forms that correspond better to the current age and to the contemporary human being. Therefore, we have not in any way attempted to achieve a revival, but rather to find new forms, because the new worlds, new areas, new reactions, the echoes of the subconscious and the imagination of the supra-conscious, infrared and ultraviolet, unexplored regions and blank spaces on the map of aesthetics — all these attract our interest and provoke a creative inventiveness with regard to experiments. We have attempted — far away from hitherto artistic and aesthetic conceptions — to light up a new art, a new poetry of colors, sounds, fragrances, and movement, ***a poetry for all the senses***.

The epoch of our civilization is a stage in which individual artistic types and specializations have liberated themselves from the tasks that they served in the past; a stage in which aesthetic activity is emancipating itself from the utilitarianism of one-time crafts in order to live an independent life; a stage in which these emancipated areas of art are growing closer together and becoming mutually wedded with each other so that in future it will no longer be possible to divide them up according to the categories of previous aesthetic systems. In a period when new scientific and technical possibilities are leading to entirely new aesthetic specializations and forms, ***the idea of the correspondence and unity of artistic emotion is ignited***.

[passage omitted]

Conclusions, Results, and Postulates

Analyses of the most recent chapters of painting and poetry have laid bare the limits of what is called art. Comprehending that the historical preconditions that brought into being the inherited forms of art are not valid today, we have declared the end of art in these inherited forms. The word “art” (still used by us in the absence of any more precise designation) is today devoid of content and sense. What is called art has undergone fundamental changes with regard to its mission, as well as its materials, techniques, and forms. Representational painting and epic verse are an anachronism in a civilization that has the Kodak camera and a fast rotary press. The traditional means of classification of artistic theory are being shown to be provisional and antiquated: the seven arts, the nine Muses, the trinity of arts[3], and so on.

3 See Karel Teige, “Toward a Theory of Constructivism,” in Karel Teige, *Modern Architecture in Czechoslovakia*, trans. Irena Žantovská Murray and David Britt (Los Angeles, 2000), 288: “the stylistic, historical, essentially medieval trinity of fine arts: architecture as the dominant art, then painting and sculpture,” as cited in Peter A. Zusi: *The Style of the Present: Karel Teige on Constructivism and Poetism*, p. 111.

Revising antiquated norms and aesthetic concepts, we abjure the right to replace them with new ones that are equally theoretical, abstract, and deduced from metaphysics. We understand the impossibility of *a priori* norms as postulates; we require laws inferred from facts as a result of analyses and experiments. Today's biological-psychological knowledge about the processes that contain the entire essence of productivity and receptivity is not sufficient for us to be able to create a completely new theory of art. As an answer to the question about the sense of art and the essence of productivity, we state a hypothesis of a unitary human productive instinct. This hypothesis of a unitary human productive instinct in all spiritual and living expressions stands in opposition to the basic tenets of Kantian aesthetics. Psychologists have divided up an *ars una* into *artes* according to means, techniques, and differing sensory receptions. Following our typical path of emphasizing function, while acknowledging a unitary creative force, we recognize once again only an *ars una* and we contend that, in spite of all division, the primary creative instinct obeys some set of laws. However, the precise biological nature of these laws remains thus far hidden in darkness. The creative instinct, complex and comprised of many factors, is a force living on the borderline of the spiritual and bodily area; the roots of the creative instinct can be observed in an instinct that is living and creative *par excellence*: in sexuality. Art has been defined as a disinterested game, but as a game that is precisely cultural and that constitutes a training of certain instincts; it is adapted to their functions.

The phenomena ***of inter-sensory correspondence and the equivalence and unity of aesthetic emotion*** point once again toward an *ars una*: to the conclusion that poetry is only one. All currents of inspiration are qualitatively identical and differ only in their expressive, quantitative means. Abandoning the concept "art," we understand the word "poetry" in its original Greek sense: ***poiesis, autonomous creation***. Today, poetry is not included only in books; it is possible to create poetry with colors, light, sound, movement; to create poetry through life. Poetry as a epiphemenon of a harmony of material, living, and spiritual facts; poetry as an autonomous human and artificial order. A poetry that shines even where there is no trace of "art."

If we reach the point from which we can view the entire field of artistic activity as an inventory of the past, we will necessarily see the large number of new possibilities and unexplored areas. The connecting paths between the sensations of the senses endow individual living and aesthetic expressions with an inflow of unitary and general creative energy. — Poetism liquidates the disharmony of the body and the soul; it does not recognize any difference between bodily and spiritual art, between higher and lower senses. Here is where the Christian and ascetic dictatorship of the soul ends. Tragedy — that aesthetic Sadism — disappears. Physical and psychological euphoria. Poetism seizes the world directly with all the senses and it feels the subtlest tremors of organic matter and its laws; it knows what a disintegration was produced by an imbalance of the three primordial human potentialities — sensuality, intelligence, and activity. What would aesthetic emotions be without a joy of the senses, without radiance and intelligence, and without the power of action? The joy of poetry is born in a harmony of all senses under the rule of the sovereign sense of life and love, which demonstrates the supremacy of poetry over other acts of living and feeling.

The great discovery of Poetism is ***happiness.*** Unhappiness — this is a conflict between our atavistic aspirations and our current possibilities. We are revising the human ideal of Happiness. The happiness of order, harmony, and art work. Happiness is contained in creation. The philosophy of Poetism does not regard life and a work of art as two separate things. The sense of life is a happy work of art: Let us turn our life into a work of art, into a well organized and experienced poem which constitutes a rich satisfaction of our need for happiness and poetry. Poetism — this is the "embrace of happiness, in which the entire world is concentrated like a hummingbird." Seeking happiness, we are aiming for feelings of harmony and balance. We are working out an order and an art of happy life; we are not concealing reality with illusions. Free of metaphysical worries, we are continuing in the line of the single non-Scholastic philosophy of Epicureanism and Materialism. To experience one's "human poem" means obeying the principle of selection: to find true happiness. Here, Poetism comes forward with the question whose reply has already been posed since who knows when: "That life is worth living is the most necessary of assumptions and, were it not assumed, the most impossible of conclusions." (Santayana[4]) And: "Nor is there any need to ask why a man desires happiness; the answer is already final." (Socrates[5])

Medieval art served. Poetism, in contrast, awakens poetry in its pure and unapplied form and builds its new world, a world of harmony and happiness.

4 G. Santayana: *Life of Reason: Reason in Common Sense*, Scribner's, 1905, p. 252.
5 From Plato: Symposium.

Karel Teige: Ultraviolet Pictures, or Artificialism

We include among manifestos and manifestations of Poetism this article on Artificialism, which is the name that Toyen and Štyrský give to their poetry of lines and colors, given that we regard the deep kinship between Artificialism and Poetism as evident and given that Artificialism, or specifically the pictures of Toyen and Štyrský, has a common starting point with Poetism.

To those who are approaching the new pictures of Štyrský and Toyen, we recommend that they forget all the tracts about painting written by Leonardo, Vitruvius, German professors or complaisant reviewers in the Paris popular press; that they realize that the pictures which they find themselves face to face with ***do not have anything in common with that craft that historians, aestheticians, and critics call painting***.

We have declared the ***extinction of painting***. And now we are presenting to you the works of two authors who, according to their civilian employment, deserve to be described as painters. So, we must come to an agreement. We have recognized that the form of painting whose works — famous and numerous — are today buried in museums is of no use to us today. We have perceived that what Leonardo was concerned with and what Picasso is concerned with are matters so different in their core that we no longer have the possibility to call them both by the same name: painting. And at the same time it was clear to us that what Leonardo was concerned with is for us today an irrevocably lost thing.

Craftsmen of the medieval age, the honored old masters, were not artists; they were not poets. The task of medieval painting was to serve: to serve the church, to serve the ruler, to serve educationally, to serve morality. Painting depicted; it was not permitted to be poetry, being burdened with iconic, illustrative, and documentary functions. The history of painting is comprised of a systematic and gradual emancipatory struggle undergoing various phases and diversions. It is only in our century that painting is liberating itself from its historic function and mission. Photography, film, journalism, and advertising are relieving painting of its representational and illustrative duties. And thus that form of art and craft — that is, the painting that arose in order to serve those tasks — has today lost its *raison d'etre* and is dying out.

At this time Picasso is proclaiming the era of painting as definitively ended. The painting that in the past served religion and the state, that depicted the world and illustrated the history of morals, is dying in order to reawaken to a new life in a pure, unapplied, specific form.

Liberated painting, ***the colored poetry of Artificialism and Poetism***, is in no respect similar to the historic "icon painting" or "painting from life." It lives in absolutely different areas and the means that it uses are totally different from those used in the works of the old masters or today's *passéistes*.

The art of Toyen and Štyrský is an expression of the ***contemporary identity of painter and poet***. It is a poetry of colors, and not a colored or delineated illustration of a poem. It ignites lyrical illumination without becoming wed to literature. Its lyricism is purely colored and springs from the ensembles of radiant surfaces and delicate lines.

The poetry of color, the poetry of optics, is not a mix of excrement from the painter's palette with a discharge of ink from the author's ink holder. It is not a transposition of verses into the language of lines and colors; it is not a pleonastic "Gesamtkunstwerk." Artificialism does not commit the same aesthetic error as Orphism or colored music, which seeks to translate musical compositions into colored compositions, or vice versa. An Artificialist picture is a poem in the original Greek sense of the word poetry, *poiesis* — that is, a sovereign and autonomous creation. It is an independent and specific poem of color and line. It is not a reflection of a poem created by others and in a different way.

Toyen and Štyrský create poetry with colors and lines just as Rimbaud and Nezval create poetry with words. And their poems of flowering colors fascinate with a kind of emotive force that was denied to the old masters of the craft of painting and to the Parnassians of literary poetry. They are pictures of rare colored incandescence, infinitesimal vibrations and nuances, an endless and miraculous kaleidoscope of dancing reflexes.

These pictures arise in an absolute *désintéressement* toward nature and toward the reality of the world. They do not have a model and are a *sujet* (topic) in and of themselves. They are also not merely a skilled and refined game for the entertainment of sight like post-Cubist abstract compositions, which in spite of all the perfection of their balanced colors do not excite or affect the viewer's sensibility. Štyrský and Toyen do not want to merely enchant our eyes; they ignite the fire of our highest poetic intuitions.

Rejecting the traditional tasks of painting, Štyrský and Toyen have also rejected its traditional techniques. They have spurned academic and gallery adhesives and thick pastes. They have avoided temperamental and personal "strokes" of the brush, which brought fake impressionists and their pitiful collectors to delirium. They have effaced the traces that engage artistic graphologists, and their pictures do not have any individual signature. Not only in the aspect of their mission, but also in the aspect of technique and material, these pictures are something entirely different than historical painting. In the century of polished steel and a supreme civilization of materials it is clearly incomprehensible why Mr. Matisse technically creates his works in a roughly similar way to that in which medieval and renaissance artists applied colors. Architecture today is rejecting the old craft methods and materials, such as stone, wood, and bricks: it constructs from iron, from concrete, from glass. The body-work of an automobile is not the work of a rural saddler. In the construction of planes, wood, a traditional construction material, has been cultivated to attain the load-bearing capacities of steel and duraluminium. In the same way, Toyen and Štyrský have rejected traditional methods and techniques of painting; they are using new means in order to create works that will enchant a person paying an almost unbearable attention to precision and the refinement of materials. Not having at their disposal any other material than oil colors, they have succeeded in extracting so many refined effects from this material; they have succeeded in making their color, which in the case of the old masters was heavy and pastoral, almost immaterial; thanks to perfect technique, they have succeeded in giving every color a thousand nuances and a clarity previously unimaginable. This technique, which perfectly realizes what the Impressionists perhaps dreamed of, is not however an aim for them, but rather a means of achieving the maximum luminosity of color and a magical *féerie* (play) of colors. Neither is the form of these pictures — in contrast to abstract painting — an end in itself: it is merely a prerequisite of an emotion aroused in the viewer. The pictures of Toyen and Štyrský do not tell the viewer any story: through the enchantment of their lines and colors they merely arouse in him or her a dialog of the consciousness with the unconscious, of the person with his or her recollections. Nevertheless, they are not pictures of dreams or hallucinations. Though perhaps subconsciously inspired, they are realized in the full glow of consciousness: they create poetry from new realities, new flowers, new lights; they direct a film of excitement and emotion; ***they create an ultraviolet, supra-conscious world***. These are magical and enchanting works, unforgettable jewels, the colorful haze and violet skies of a new dawn of poetry that is breaking out ahead of us.

The Artificialism of Toyen and Štyrský, deeply affiliated with Nezval's Poetism, lives with an assurance that ***the most artificial existence nurtures within itself the least illusions and the most happiness***. It makes poetry from colorful games, from transfigured, fabricated, abstract, and future recollections. It is not a passive record of the subconscious; neither is it a reading of the stars, nor an interpretation of dreams. It is creation; it is invention; it is poetry: the work, the fact, the fruit of poetic supra-consciousness. Toyen and Štyrský are adopting the slogan of Artificialism not in order to establish some new school or some movement. They certainly do not intend to put this word at the disposal of epigones. Just as they have given to each of their paintings a name that is itself a forceful lyrical abbreviation in order to direct the viewer's emotion, so they have chosen as the designation of their aesthetic stance a general term that is aimed at emphasizing its absolute independence with regard to the natural world and its absolute non-subjugation to the powers of the subconscious. At the same time, the term "Artificialism" also manifests its differentiation from Surrealist painting, which is so heavily indebted to Böcklin and Expressionism and which is incapable of making use of the unlimited possibilities that are the inheritance of Cubism and has thus degenerated into literary and formal historicism. Artificialism, precisely like Poetism, is the historic successor of Cubism in the direct and essential line. However, it has gone beyond the barrier that Cubism — that vivisection of the phenomenal world — did not succeed in crossing. That is why Toyen and Štyrský despise the "fat muses of the return to nature" of today's neo-neo-neo-Naturalists and classicists, and why they create poetry from an artificial, irrational world, the golden value of humanity at the end of the millennium, the rainbow of happiness; happiness as a kind of artwork and creation, not as a Greek gift of fate.

The pictures of Toyen and Štyrský are an inalienable treasure of the lyrical days and nights of our universe and our calendar.

Jaroslav Seifert: Guillaume Apollinaire

On that November day, when the fog and rain were transforming the Paris sidewalks into a dim mirror, processions of school pupils were promenading through the streets of Paris waving the victorious colors of the flag of their homeland and shouting joyously "Death to Wilhelm! Death to Wilhelm!" Of course, they did not mean anyone other than the German kaiser. However, hearing this shouting, a different William was dying, smiling painfully when death held out its hand to him. The poet Guillaume Apollinaire.

He died, having recently returned from the world war and several days after his wedding. He had lived through the fiery hell of the French-German front, but so unfortunate was his fate that he died of a dirty disease, the flu, that had infested Paris.

I write these few sentences with a pen all too unqualified. The occasion deserves more than merely to remember several wonderful years in the youth of several poets who, loving the poetry of this poet rather unconsciously, embarked on life and poetry a little courageously. Apollinaire's poetry resembles the wind which playfully lifted in hope the thoughts and the pens of these young poets. It would be ungrateful if on this occasion we were to fail to recall Neumann's *Červen*, in which Karel Čapek published his translation of one of Apollinaire's most beautiful poems *Zone*. Perhaps it is only after several years that this work of Čapek's has been properly appreciated. An excellent translation, captivatingly rendered in verse, in a surprisingly beautiful language that enchanted at once. Listen to a few verses of this excellent poetry:

Zone from *Alcools* (1913)

Aujourd'hui tu marches dans Paris les femmes sont ensanglantées
C'était et je voudrais ne pas m'en souvenir c'était au déclin de la beauté...

L'amour dont je souffre est une maladie honteuse
Et l'image qui te possède te fait survivre dans l'insomnie et dans l'angoisse
C'est toujours près de toi cette image qui passe

It would, however, be especially ungrateful on this occasion to forget the endearing Teige, who smoking his pipe awkwardly, was capable of reciting ever new improvised translations of the poet's verses in a more or less plaintive voice, well knowing that at that time we would have tried in vain to decipher the mysteries of the French language, which at that time remained precisely as secret as the hieroglyphs on the tombs of the pharaohs.

Some of these were verses that could have been recited by children on a podium at school, smiling sweetly, while others were verses in which the bestiality of war flickers, fire on the horizon and exploding shrapnel; still others were verses written in the mud of the trenches, when the poet, looking through the embrasure, watched the stars forming into a new constellation of letters that gave rise to the enthusiastic cry "Long Live France!" And then again there are plaintive verses about love, about locomotives and art, sung in melodies never before heard.

If today you return to the poem for the 100th time, in order to soothe yourself with the broad, calm rhythm of *Zone*, recall — just as we do — another poet, who — seeking his faltering health under the sunny shore of the Mediterranean — dreamed away the hours over a book of Apollinaire's verses. Among the seashells lies a book of poetry, and leaning over it the face of a sick Jiří Wolker.

Wolker's poem *Svatý Kopeček* distinctly echoes Apollinaire's *Zone*, which Jiří loved precisely as we do, not resisting in any way the beauty that penetrated through his heart and his eyes so powerfully. What a shame that he died so young precisely at a time when new prospects toward the outside world were opening up for Czech poetry and "the rains linked the sky for new poems."

I think that it would not be difficult to look for other traces of the stems of Apollinaire's muse in books of modern Czech poetry. These traces are deep and beautiful, and they do not perhaps serve in any way to its shame. New beauties of language and form are appearing, and the treatises about Czech tradition, which today is reproached over and over again, have shown themselves to be quite superfluous, when poets such as on the one hand Wolker and on the other hand Nezval have appeared — the names of poets who are transcending the constricted borders of this country.

And finally a reminder of some of Apollinaire's verses that he wrote while walking around Prague, which he loved as only poets can love a city:

Tu es dans le jardin d'une auberge aux environs de Prague
Tu te sens tout heureux une rose est sur la table
Et tu observes au lieu d'écrire ton conte en prose
La cétoine qui dort dans le cœur de la rose
Épouvanté tu te vois dessiné dans les agates de Saint-Vit

Tu étais triste à mourir le jour où tu t'y vis
Tu ressembles au Lazare affolé par le jour
Les aiguilles de l'horloge du quartier juif vont à rebours
Et tu recules aussi dans ta vie lentement
En montant au Hradchin et le soir en écoutant
Dans les tavernes chanter des chansons tchèques

Neither the sea, nor borders, nor wars, nor time can break the amazing bridges between cultures. A world view with which you disagree can cast a dark shadow on an artist's work, but art that resembles gold shines.

Jindřich Štyrský: Vest Pocket Revue

Vest Pocket Revue [magazine of Osvobozené divadlo (Liberated Theater)] (edited by Staša Jílovská) makes a very good impression in terms of its outward presentation. Neither, with regard to its content, do we doubt that it will be widely read, welcomed in families and subscribed to, because it is a magazine that is based on a belief in a wide spectrum of people and, if it remains true to the course that it has set itself and if it further deepens its rich content, it will certainly attract many male and female readers of the well known *Šejdrem* and *Pražanka* magazines. Neither do we doubt that the editors have shown themselves to be far-sighted when they chose glossy paper for the magazine because luxury impresses idiots and snobs of all social classes. The magazine can be read with interest not only by a Prague seamstress, but also by a member of the best Prague social strata.

The pictorial accompaniment is not bad either. The photograph of the ensemble of Osvobozené divadlo makes a graceful impression. The members look as though they have just emerged after a bath, they are well groomed, and they have a pleasant look. Josef Háša, the director of Osvobozené divadlo and the former managing clerk of the Autoobchodní společnost [Auto Trade Society], even had his hair pomaded before the photograph. The only thing that spoils this impression is the failure to include the portrait of Ferenc Futurista in the pictorial section. However, this deficiency is balanced by a whole-page reproduction of a portrait of the owner of the U Nováků building correctly included in a prominent and honorable place. Under the portrait we can read that the owner "has undergone tough business praxis and, thanks to his single-minded work and industriousness, he has succeeded in getting the U Nováků department store ranked among the biggest and most dependable businesses of this type in the former Austro-Hungary." We wish the whole Osvobozené divadlo similar success and we hope that this symbolic page will always inspire the theater company to further work and activity and that the company's members have already found some place in their hearts for this page.

Owing to a lack of space we cannot continue with a detailed enumeration of the magazine's other outward merits. In terms of the content it is evident that the tender hand of the female editor was not able to cope with that boiling flux of thought that almost explodes from the packed pages. For bringing order to this chaotic richness, a manly hand — a hand clothed in an iron glove — would be necessary. In the article *Third Era* the very astute authors Voskovec and Werich announce that once upon a time they moved in good society. They inform their audience that they had some kind of contacts with modernist people from the Devětsil circle, which cannot be denied because it is well known that Voskovec was expelled from Devětsil after successfully absolving the role of the charming youth in the film *Pohádka máje* (based on V. Mrštík's novel). About the first era of Osvobozené divadlo the authors themselves declare quite sincerely that they had nothing more in common with it than a sympathetic attitude. Whoever knows both creators will be all too willing to believe this because he well knows that they always like to turn up only after everything has already been prepared. The first part of the second era at Umělecká Beseda, starting in summer 1927, was apparently in the mode of *Vest Pocket Revue*. Only in passing do Voskovec and Werich mention that Honzl directed five premieres (Vančura: *Učitel a žák* [Teacher and Pupil], Mahen: *Trosečníci* [Castaways], E. Škeříková: *Mys Dobré Naděje* [Cape of Good Hope], Soupault: *Račte* [S'il vous plaît], Nezval: *Depeše na kolečkách* [Dispatches on Wheels]). This claim is evidence of the healthy self-confidence of the two souls, but not of a minimal sense of truthfulness, because they could also claim that also the second part of the second era of Osvobozené divadlo at Adria on Wenceslas Square was in the mode of the plays *Skafandr* or *Gorila*. The truth, however, is that in the last season the only thing that Voskovec and Werich had in common with Osvobozené divadlo as we understand it was a firm which, ideologically speaking, has become an inseparable part of them forever, which there is however no need to regret, because, after the premiere of *Líčení se odročuje* [Court Is Adjourned — play by Voskovec and Werich (1929)], ***it is evident that the current-day Osvobozené divadlo no longer has anything in common with the original Osvobozené divadlo — that is, with modern theatrical poetry and youth.***

Osvobozené divadlo in its current-day form is, for us and for every modern human being, a dead structure, and Voskovec and Werich should be ashamed that on such a beautiful stage they have demonstrated so little inventiveness and that they have presented to the public immediately for their first production such a stupid play as *Court Is Adjourned*. It is really lamentable that the authors (judging by the preface), equipped with such thorough knowledge of detective literature, wrote such a bad detective comedy, that they did not make use of all the amenities that the Osvobozené divadlo has at its disposal — which are considered fabulous in the context of Prague (a stage with a depth of 20 meters, perfectly constructed trapdoor, rigging systems, and so on) — and that they played the roles of their reporters so badly. The premiere of *Court Is Adjourned* showed Voskovec and Werich that they should, in their own interest, think long and hard about whether to show themselves on the stage in the company of actors like, for instance, Plachta, because it is clear that the charm of jesters in theater is "fading and fading until it entirely fades away." Today it is quite clear to everyone that Voskovec and Werich will only find "themselves" for the first time in the sand. However, this will not be the sand of Hendaye beach, where they have established their holiday existence, nor the bloody sand of amphitheaters, but rather the quite ordinary sand of circuses. There they will be able to develop their metaphysical and incomprehensible wish: "We want to act not with our brain, but rather with a spark." Once they are clothed in an appropriate outfit, this will certainly suit them better than the green suit in which they present themselves at home and abroad as "***the directors of the only avant-garde theater in Prague***."

Of the other contributions to this new magazine we take note of Honzl's article, written with a light touch and in a pleasant style that will surprise everyone who knows Honzl's previous exhaustive tracts. The Telegram by Ferenc Futurista and the humorous piece by Plachta provide evidence that neither of them are going to make a breakthrough at Osvobozené divadlo with their intellectual capabilities.

The whimsical corner ***Národ sobě*** (The Nation for Itself) does not exactly excel in a witty selection and it is to be regretted that nothing from the preceding pages of the first issue of *Vest Pocket Revue* was selected for this section.

As the only exception to what I have said about Osvobozené divadlo I regard the case of Ježek (musician).

In Its Third Year *ReD* Intends to Continue...

In its third year *ReD* intends to continue to fulfill its program and its mission, which it established at its foundation and which today it does not need to recapitulate or to revise. *ReD* is and will continue to be an analytical journal of ***internationalist modern creative work***. It understands the word ***modern*** in the most direct, most incisive, and most radical sense, just as it attributes the broadest meaning to the word **international**. It aims to be true to both these words, which express the program and extent of its activity, because it is convinced that they are inseparable. Modern culture is a product of a collective of international forces, the result of active cooperation. Modern creation is not a coming together of some international confederations for intellectual cooperation which cuddle up under the wing of the imperialist League of Nations: This is where international reaction is establishing itself. The International of modern cultural creation, which is gradually being consolidated from the international productive association of all modern young energies, cannot not be a sister of the International of the revolutionary proletariat. Today, on the eve of a general rearrangement of values — that is, the creation of a modern world — the last word of international modernism, the modern spirit and modern volition is: revolution. Our journal is an organ of international modernism, which is an organized and conscious resistance of productive forces against existing relations, traditions, academies, aesthetics and moralities, and against a disorganized and disintegrating social system.

ReD does not aim to be an artistic, literary, or philosophical and aesthetic revue, such as there are — and will continue to be — all too many of, but rather a compilation, a sampler, and a bulletin of new forms of life, experiments, and results of world creation; it is going to plot a diagram of the tension of aggregated productive and revolutionary energies; it is going to be an organ of all significant and revolutionary currents and tendencies in art and in science, in philosophy, and in life.

Those aspects of life about which it is going to report, it is going to find and detect not only in books and in paintings, but also in the massive upheavals in social life, in its intermittent revolts, in the life of crowds, in unrest and unbalanced social organization, in massive collective and individual eruptions of passions, crimes and adventure, and in everything that convicts the old world: strikes, executions, betrayals, persecutions, terror, and all kinds of monstrosities. It will also find aspects of life on which to report in the documents of the new world: social and architectonic Constructivism, and liberated poetry and paintings. International modernism, with its uncompromising ***non-conformism*** towards the current state of the world, of the old world, draws a demarcation line ever more resolutely between two worlds: From the beginning its creative output is an aggression and a resistance; from the beginning it has been persecuted and silenced by censorship.

ReD is far removed from the herd of Czech writers desperately mooing at ceremonial occasions; it does not squander space or interest on official Czech culture and art. It does not engage in compromise towards provincial and decaying false values. *ReD* is, therefore, isolated from so-called Czech cultural life, and the reactionary press is also careful not to give its readers any news about it. *ReD* relies purely on the interest, assistance, and sympathy of its co-workers and its already quite numerous readers.

Karel Teige: Poem, World, Human Being

The extinction of art has already been proclaimed many times, and not only in iconoclastic, Futurist-Dadaist-Romantic manifestos. The perishing and progressive degeneration of individual art forms has also been explicated and demonstrated in precise historic, sociological, and aesthetic analyses. The analysis of the final chapter of the development of painting and poetry, and the examination of the internal processes of these arts and the transformations in the relationships of art to society, have shown us the extreme limit of what is today called art — that is, a state in which moments of disintegration and expiration are gradually gaining predominance over moments of existence. The historic preconditions that brought art — or respectively, the individual fields of artistic work — into life are losing their validity ever more quickly.

The process of the divergence of Romantic art from bourgeois society is connected with the process of the expiration of inherited artistic forms. Simultaneously with this process of the expiration of individual artistic branches, of which we are witnesses, new forms are arising which are in their core different from and unrelated to the historic forms of art, and are also in their core of a different quality. The old academic aesthetics and the artistic theory of static ideals and idealist illusions is incapable either of describing or explaining this process. When, after steam and electricity, after the sewing machine and the typewriter, a "machine that paints" — a photographic and cinematographic camera — has been invented, when the sphaerophon, the radiophone, and the television have been invented, then it is necessary to forswear the traditional methods of classification and the categories of idealist aesthetics. We will not make do here with myths and formulas about the seven arts, the nine Muses, the two noble and artistic senses, the trinity of arts[1],

1 See Karel Teige, "Toward a Theory of Constructivism," in Karel Teige, *Modern Architecture in Czechoslovakia*, trans. Irena Žantovská Murray and David Britt (Los Angeles, 2000), p. 288:

and so on. Alongside dead philosophies, worn-out moralities, and faded metaphysics, mythologies and religions, the hitherto forms of art — painting, sculpture, and the dramatic and verbal arts — are being placed in the archive of history, into the collections of museums, so that they will continue to exist only as an object of historical research and archaeological interest. In the emergent world of new relations and new people, in the midst of an emerging society, they have no place and they will receive no role.

The process of the old art dying in isolation from productive and social life has prepared the preconditions for the onset of quite new forms and for the creation of a new synthesis of poetry and the world. The evolution of artistic forms discarded from the productive process, and therefore eventually also expelled from the world, has led them to their extremes, to their limits, and to extinction. However, at the same time, in this isolation from the world and from the life of society the conditions have developed for the transcendence of this isolation through other, new forms. If literati (who believe that life is a product of poetic imagination, that feelings are a product of literature, and that nature is a work of art or an imitation of art) declare that an artist anticipates the world's development, it must be conceded that the indications, seeds, and hints of new forms and new social reconstructions have made themselves apparent very soon in art, precisely because art is an area that is very remote from productive and social life, and as a consequence more free than this sphere, unburdened by the concerns of the ruling class, and that the "artistic community" — this "aristocracy of feeling," this republic of declassed individuals — even though very remote from the concrete realities of social life, has had a range of points in common with revolutionary social forces. In reality, many revolutions in art have signified the factual onset of new forms of life already in periods when social development had hardly taken its first steps towards these.

Romantic revolt, *l'art-pour-l'artism*, Symbolism, Montmartre, Montparnasse and other Bohemianisms, Dadaist defiance, and Surrealist revolution are an expression of the artist's opposition to the ruling class in the consciousness of art's isolation from life and social events, or possibly even a protest against the conditions that the modern division of labor have forced on artistic creation and the social standing of artists. It is necessary to see more under these slogans and -isms than slogans and -isms: We must decipher in them the elements of the extinction of the old forms of art that arose in feudal society in connection with craft work and the first seeds of new poetic qualities, as well as the first steps towards the overcoming of the antagonism between art and society, between the "ideal of beauty" and concrete realities. Behind the slogans and -isms that Romantic art (this is how we designate this unofficial and "pure" art, which since the times of Romanticism has been in revolt against society, in contrast to academic art, which the ruling class maintains as its

---

"the stylistic, historical, essentially medieval trinity of fine arts: architecture as the dominant art, then painting and sculpture," as cited in Peter A. Zusi: *The Style of the Present: Karel Teige on Constructivism and Poetism*, p. 111.

decoration and luxury) constructed as a high barrier between itself and society, so as to prevent it from being an art of contemporary society, society's servant and prostitute — in a type of art that constitutes the gradual disintegration of old forms and methods — the elements of a new poetry are arising and beginning to develop. However, these new elements cannot be fully realized without art once again transcending its isolation from life, without it stepping out from the barrier and limits of Romantic art.

In the isolation of art from life, from society, and from production, the elements of the new poetry arose and old artistic forms dried out. In an isolation that gave artistic creation *a purity of the atelier and the laboratory* when it took away its social and utilitarian functions, in an isolation that entailed a complete loss of contact between art and the world, a new poetry crystallized that can be realized, that can shine, that can live, and that can be victorious only by regaining this contact, and this not by a return to old relations, but rather by combining and merging with the world and with society at *a higher level of the development of poetry and of society*.

In the isolation of art from production and society, in a period in which production has been transformed from manufacturing into large-scale mechanical industry, artistic forms bound to the civilization of crafts necessarily had to die out. However, precisely the reconstruction of production to mechanical large-scale industry, the enormous progress of technology, and the separation of artistic crafts from industrial life have produced the technical and material preconditions for the creation of a new poetry whose methods and functions are absolutely different from the methods and tasks of the art of the past. This, therefore, means that "art is ceasing, or has ceased, to be art."

In a period of the expiration and dying of the old art, painting, literature, and so on, a ***poetry*** is being born, a poetry in the sense of the word as understood by the Greeks, but which the Greeks did not however know: *poiesis*, an integral, sovereign, life-giving creation. This conviction is the content and sense of Poetism as a "great poetic faith, a faith in the universality of poetry," in the words of F. X. Šalda. A poetry that is a new grouping of aesthetic qualities, constructed by new methods and from new materials, and that is seeking a new consumer, a new viewer and listener, a new human being in order to quench his burning thirst for lyricism and to richly endow all his senses and his sensibility with new vital energies and intensities.

The methods of this new poetry are being tested through extensive laboratory work. The exact results of the sciences — biology, psychology, physiology, sociology, optics, chemistry, acoustics, and so on — have provided the foundations of a new theory of art. Even though today's biological-psychological knowledge of the processes that contain the entire essence of poetic productivity and emotionality is not sufficient, as a reply to the question concerning the sense of "art" and the essence of poetic creativity we can at least pronounce a *hypothesis postulating a unitary human productive impulse*.

This hypothesis of a unitary creative impulse that is the subject of human action in all areas of work and even thought stands in absolute contradiction to the fundamental principles of idealist aesthetics, for instance Kantian aesthetics. Psychologists and art historians have classified "ars una" into various "artes" according to the means and techniques used, tasks performed, and varied sensory reception. Even though they have only acknowledged two sense organs as "aesthetic," they have divided up art into seven or nine branches, symbolized by the nine maidens from antique Parnassus. This is a scholastic template and a static conception of artistic events and development, precisely like Kant's differentiation of consciousness into three areas: thinking, desiring, and feeling. However, if we acknowledge a unitary creative force of the human being-producer, pursuing its typical path of function, we will once again come to know only an *ars una*, in which the activities of all senses, of the body and the soul, of the hand and the brain, merge together in a higher synthesis. The creative instinct (complex and comprised of many factors) is an energy living on the border of the spiritual and bodily fields, and it is appropriate to see the roots of this instinct in an instinct that is fundamental, living, and creative par excellence — that is, the sexual instinct.

Modern psychology now allows us to explain at least partly the function and psychological impact of this *poetry for all senses*, which Poetism is trying to achieve. If it has been demonstrated that human relations toward every kind of beauty are in core sexual, that aesthetic emotion and excitation is in essence identical or at least analogical to sexual excitation, and that erotic energy influences the entire sphere of the imagination, then so-called art — that is, poetry (in the machine era already liberated from productive-utilitarian and educational tasks) — cannot have any other function than to *cultivate a systematic culture of the senses and a kindling of sensibility, to harmonize and socialize the vital human powers* that have been mutilated, restricted, and suppressed by the old societies, by their moralities, their religions, and their economic relations — that is, primarily to cultivate, enrich, and harmonize the senses and the powers of human feeling and love.

Perhaps it would be possible to identify this unitary creative instinct previously mentioned with the "libido" of psychoanalysis and Freudian sexual theory. Freud, as is known, restricts the concept of libido to the sexual forces, while Jung expands it so that, for him, the libido merges with a general psychic energy. To differentiate the libido from other instinctive forces would be to assume that the sexual processes in an organism differ in their particular chemical composition from other processes, for instance digestive processes or the process of aesthetic contemplation. Today, we do not precisely know this chemical composition. Until the biological and chemical composition of sexual and aesthetic arousal is clear, until it is clear whether this is the same chemical process in both cases, it is not going to be possible to precisely specify the relationship between aesthetic and erotic forces. Psychology has shown, in particular through the analysis of neuroses and perversions, that sexual arousal is not exclusively a product of the sexual parts, but rather that all sense and bodily organs are participant in it.

The erogenous zone furthest distant from the sexual object, the leading "elevated" human sense organ (to use the language of the old aesthetics) — that is, the eye — is intensively aroused more than other areas precisely by that quality of excitation caused by what we call the *beauty* of a loved object. An optical impression is the path through which a libidinal excitation is most commonly awakened and through which a process of selection begins that causes the beauty of the sexual object to grow. This excitation, which creates pictures of beauty, is then once again intensified by these pictures, and this creative process awakens pleasure and induces the arousal of other organs and erogenous zones. Evidently, certain chemical agents, driven by the current of blood, charge the parts of the central nervous system with tension, which causes certain organic transformations. The excitation, awakening pleasure, is evidently bound by special conditions, of which rhythm is one of the most fundamental.

Pleasure arises through the sensory excitation of the erogenous zones, whose function can probably be performed by every part of the skin and the mucous membrane and every sensory organ (connection: eye — hearing — extra-retina vision — other bodily and epidermal senses — inter-sensory correspondence...) Alongside this, of course, there exist significant and accentuated erogenous zones, whose sensitivity, albeit individual, is on the whole high. Apart from that, sexual arousal arises as a side effect in the case of a whole range of organic processes as soon as these reach a certain intensity, and also in the case of powerful motions of the mind. Everything that happens and has some significance for an organism contributes to arousing the sexual instinct. The essence of this arousal is unknown, and it differs endlessly from one individual to another.

The significance of the erogenous zones, which is certainly enormous in the case of every "normal" person, is enhanced in the case of psycho-neurotic persons and in the case of all perversions.

Freud's sexual theories, of which we are making use here, show that the concept of beauty, which in the case of a primitive person is evidently identical with sexual stimulants, in the case of a modern person is extended more and more to objects that have only a distant or latent relationship to sexual selection. However, even in this case all actions — or respectively, all free actions of a human being — are influenced by the erotic, which has taught a person to dance, to work, to live, and also to love. An influx of excitations from the impressions and pleasures of the senses diverts a certain part of the libido toward cultivating these impressions and excitations — that is, toward aesthetic purposes.

Whether or not the arousal and emotions of the sense organs and the erogenous zones that arouse feelings of pleasure triggering internal secretions and influencing the development of the human organism are the same in the case of sexual and aesthetic emotion, in any case it can be regarded as proven that all the connecting paths that lead from other functions — that is, spiritual and bodily functions, including the aesthetic function — to sexuality are also identical in the opposite direction.

The theory of art that we have called *Poetism* is based primarily on the perception that the inherited artistic forms, which were conditioned on craft work, are already dead in our period. Further, we contend that the transformation of the foundations of production into large-scale mechanical industry has deprived the old artistic forms of their *raison d'être*, since it has deprived them of the functions that they previously served and handed these functions over to new disciplines better suited to fulfilling these functions. The consequence of this has been the isolation of art from society in the form of *l'art-pour-l'art*. However, the new organization of society, the world of the general plan, will not tolerate the isolation of certain productive forces; it will not tolerate these creative forces being without use for society. Nevertheless, this new art, whose germinal forms have crystallized in this isolation in the milieu of the Romantics and the "cursed poets," cannot bring any direct economic use, as art could when it was not differentiated from craft work. New poetic and aesthetic activity must be directed not at economic praxis or ideological evangelism, but rather at a culture of liberated and awakened human forces that have been deformed for centuries by social pressure. In other words, in place of the roughly religious, economic, or educational role served by art in old societies, we assign to poetry (that is, to the new art, to aesthetic creation) functions that, in the absence of a more appropriate designation, we must call eugenic, eubiotic, hygienic. In reality more is at stake here. It is a question of giving society *a new type of human being*: new instincts, new senses, a new body, a new soul. A humankind that has been mechanized by capitalist rationalization needs to regain a harmonious biological foundation. The new society needs a harmonious, *complete human being* who is disposed from his or her biological center to an orientation not towards the working day, but rather towards free time, towards private and community life. With this orientation, by once again giving poetry an important place in the world and the life of society and granting it a paramount function of cultivating, harmonizing, and socializing the senses, instincts, and imagination of the new human being, we reject both Ruskin's vulgar theory about the renewal of the old connection between art and craft work and also the opposite slogan about "art for art's sake." That is to say, this is a case not only of understanding, but rather also of changing the human being. (By poetry we here understand any piece of work that is purposely constructed from any kind of material and further any kind of harmonious human expression.) In contrast to a firm stance of instinctive certainty towards everything.

A higher type of social organization is conditional objectively on the use of technical progress and the scientific achievements acquired in the capitalist era and subjectively on the *rise of a new class,* which — fortified and purified through the revolutionary storm and the construction of a new social foundation — has not only succeeded in transforming economic and social relations, but *which has also succeeded in transforming itself*. Concurrently with the change in the material conditions of existence, with the struggle against the old society, and with the creative force of new economic formations that are establishing the objective conditions of the new world, primarily the subject himself or herself is changing and must change. Already in the transitional stages of the path to a new society (free association) the proletariat is ceasing to be a proletariat in the old sense of the word and is being transformed into socialist human beings not only in labor, praxis, and production, but also in the field of physical, affective, and intellectual culture. The cultural revolution about which Abram Deborin deliberates (Building Socialism and Tasks of Marxists on the Theoretical Front) is already taking place today. Already today, in the period of the terminal stage of capitalism and the first steps of building socialism, *the factual beginnings of communism are becoming apparent in their embryonic forms*, and this is so not only in the economic field (members of the Komsomol and now the high-performance youth labor brigades, voluntary work discipline), but also in fields that are relatively distant from economic activity.

For the purpose of creating a new person, it is primarily necessary to obliterate the remains and relics of the old ways of life that grew from old social habits, lifestyles, and civilizations; to obliterate atavistic forms of thinking and feeling that to this day are particular to Romantic artists: magical, mythological, religious, metaphysical, and idealist thinking. In a period in which the relics of the old social formations are falling apart, it is also necessary to demolish and throw on the scrapheap the conservative sediment of customs, feelings, and prejudices that were the result of these productive and social relations. A human being of the new class must liberate him or herself from the burden and shackles of the old world, and only by doing so will she or he become fit for life and creation in the new world.

It is essential to emphasize the importance of the development of the sensory organs, sensibility, and sensory content in connection with the social-historical development of humankind. “The forming of the five senses is a labor of the entire history of the world down to the present” (Karl Marx).[2] Over the millennia our visual system and other sensory systems have undergone deep transformations. There can be no doubt that the processing, cultivating, and developing of our sensory organs and the enrichment of our sensibility have an enormous importance in the formation of a new socialist human being.

Deborin has shown that, in a society founded on private property, the feeling of ownership is dominant and deforms the other physiological and psychological feelings. Private ownership also enslaves a person’s affective life. A person becomes deformed when his vital energies are evaluated materially; his living instincts waste away and become stultified; his biological forces are mechanized. “The abolition of private property is therefore the complete emancipation of all human senses and qualities” (Karl Marx).[3]

Already in the current-day stage of the class struggle, which is being waged by the proletariat not only for the control of production but also eventually for the free expression of human powers, class consciousness is transforming into the formation

2 Karl Marx, *Economic and Philosophic Manuscripts of 1844*, transl. by Martin Milligan, revised by Dirk J. Struik: https://www.marxists.org/archive/marx/works/1844/manuscripts/comm.htm

3 Ibid.

of the consciousness of the new socialist person so that this consciousness can then mature in the epoch of socialist society. If the aim is the transcendence of the hierarchy in the division of labor, the transcendence of the differences between physical and mental labor and between town and countryside, and the intensification of creative forces that will result from the disappearance of handcraft labor and the liberation of human beings for free creation, then it is certain that *only a new human being can prepare the higher phase of communism*. Human beings must regain their biological basis; only then can a universal development of individuals occur, along with a gigantic growth of productive forces, a maximum use of technical progress, and a high level of social wealth in the culture of the body, the soul, food, and housing.

After the end of "pre-historical" society, a socialist humankind will start to direct its history in full consciousness. Therefore, it is essential that this human being, a product of the social environment and social relations, who is supposed to transform these relations and this environment should him or herself become a new human being. A reevaluation of the affective world received from childhood — a reevaluation of petrified and atavistic affects and customs — into a new socialist consciousness, into a functionalist mode of thinking, into socialist reason, into a socialist sensibility and fantasy, and into socialist senses and feelings is certainly one of the hardest tasks of the cultural revolution.

A socialist lifestyle means this: life in new socialist towns, in collective housing, and in a society that has eliminated the institution of the family and that has liberated erotic feelings from material relations; life in a harmonized environment that allows the development of those human qualities that capitalism maintained in a mechanized and brute stuntedness. In this way a new period of the world will begin: not only a new organization of the economy and society, but also a new organization of the human being.

The revolution in human consciousness will liquidate the disharmony between the body and the soul; it does not recognize a difference between bodily and spiritual culture, between the lower and the higher senses. This is the end of the Christian and ascetic dictatorship of the soul. The luxury of blood and the richness of the body will be victorious. Beauty, poetry, and freedom, which were abstractions torn from real content, are once again merging with the forms and expressions of life.

The new poetry whose theory is Poetism is called to serve this cultural revolution. Its mission is to cultivate the senses — through all appropriate means, sounds, colors, light, and movements — and to enrich the sensibility of humankind. To supply topics for a new paramount art of living and loving, for the new living style of socialism. ("Poetism is primarily a modus vivendi[4]... In cities built by Constructivists, the Poetists will establish parks of the new poetry, a world that smiles, a world that

4 Karel Teige, *Poetism*, Host (1924), p. 202 (or p. 559 in this edition http://www.ucl.cas.cz/edicee/data/antologie/avantgarda/AVA1/90.pdf) and also from from *Manifesto of Poetism*, *Red* (1928), p. 320 (or p. 562 in this edition: http://www.ucl.cas.cz/edicee/data/antologie/avantgarda/AVA2/124.pdf)

smells sweet; only in the joy of the heart and the flexibility of sensibility will a human being find the exalted cheerfulness of creation."[5])

The culture and illumination of sensuality and sensibility: A human being who did not extract the maximum value from all the powers of his body and soul, as well as the maximum joy from his talents and organs, would be an inferior person and a saboteur with regard to society. Therefore, it is essential to teach human beings to use their senses in the most intense and direct way, to obey the wonderful laws of organic matter and the bodily machine, to grasp life with all the pores of the quivering skin, to relish the joys of muscles and senses, all of which are the conditions of a harmony without unease and weakness, the basis for a lucid radiance of consciousness.

The new poetry, as a university of the new human being, a game of colors and lights, sounds and movements, is not a disinterested game. Every game is a training and a cultivating of certain instincts; it is adapted to their functions. The new poetry is a game, even a game with the fire of life, a game that is dangerous for bourgeois society, a game of instinctive and emotive forces liberated from moral and social barriers and desirous of new intensification, new dimensions of vitality, new capacities and sensations, and new feelings of the world, matter, space, and distances.

The sole and multi-faceted function of poetry, as Poetism understands it and prepares for it, is to endow, satiate, and reawaken human sensibility, and to develop a human being's creative, sensory, emotional, and amorous faculties. It is therefore a major work of culture, which comprises everything bodily. Poetry for all the senses: not *l'art-pour-l'art*, but rather a significant social function in building the socialist world. In other words, Poetism as a transcending of the antagonism between poetry and the world, a new synthesis of the poem and the world, a synthesis of construction and poem.

The perspective for the future, more or less distant, which needs to be clarified already today on the real basis of hitherto developments, is the higher phase of communism — that "realm of freedom [that] actually begins only where labor which is determined by necessity and mundane considerations ceases; thus in the very nature of things it lies beyond the sphere of actual material production... Beyond the realm of necessity begins that development of human energy which is an end in itself, the true realm of freedom, which, however, can blossom forth only with this realm of necessity as its basis."[6] "It is humanity's leap from the kingdom of necessity to the kingdom of freedom."[7]

It is here in this realm of freedom, the integral freedom of a human being acquired through the development of his abilities, that the mission of these new po-

5 Similar text in Teige, *O Humoru, klaunech a dadaistech* [On Humor, Clowns, and Dadaists], p. 586 in this edition http://www.ucl.cas.cz/edicee/data/antologie/avantgarda/AVA1/93.pdf

6 Karl Marx, *Capital* Vol. 3, p. 593; https://www.marxists.org/archive/marx/works/download/pdf/Capital-Volume-III.pdf

7 Friedrich Engels, *Anti-Dühring* (1877), Part III: Socialism, II. Theoretical, transl. Emile Burns https://www.marxists.org/archive/marx/works/1877/anti-duhring/ch24.htm

etic forms — whose very first beginnings Poetism sees in "liberated art" and poetry for all the senses, which are Poetism's main interest — will come to an end. Life will acquire a magnificent harmonious intensity and will be in and of itself a rich satisfaction of the human need for lyricism. Once society has eradicated the repression of the libido and ceases to paralyze sensuous and erotic energies in any way, once there is no longer any pressure of sublimated sexuality — which will then find its sovereign freedom not only in poetic imagination, but also in erotic reality — then art, just like sublimation of the libido, will become superfluous, the special psychological constitution of artists will also disappear, and beauty will be no longer the artificial form of a poem, but rather an epiphenomenon of all expressions of life.

With the complete abolition of the division of labor, this kind of art as a special field will also die out. There will not be any other art or any other beauty except the good, joyful, and harmonious life of the human collective. The great discovery of this epoch will be social happiness, the happiness of order, of a piece of creative work, of harmony. The happiness of creation. Work without physical effort, voluntary and free, elevated to the field of creation: poetry. The sense of life for free human beings is a happy piece of creative work: It will be necessary to make their life into a creative work, a well-organized and experienced poem. In future, "once all experiences are ultraviolet" and "once [human beings] live and experience their own human poems," this will mean adopting this principle of selection: to find true joy.

The happiness of the human being-poet will be the liberation of all instincts, the radiance of a consciousness whose abilities will acquire a higher vibrational intensity, and the development of a productive instinct that will transform the human world into one single Gulf Stream of poetry.

This is the vanishing point of the perspective of Poetism. It is also the vanishing point of Nietzsche's philosophy: "Only where the state ends, there begins the human being."[8] The same thing — "an association, in which the free development of each is the condition for the free development of all"[9] — is the vanishing point of Marx's dialectical materialism.

---

8 Friedrich Nietzsche, *Thus Spoke Zarathustra*, I:11, in The Portable Nietzsche, ed. & trans. W. Kaufmann (New York: Viking, 1954)

9 Marx and Engels, *Manifesto of the Communist Party* (1848), Chap. 2, translated by Samuel Moore in cooperation with Frederick Engels (1888); https://www.marxists.org/archive/marx/works/1848/communist-manifesto/ch02.htm

MELENCOLIA§I

Chapter 3

Coming of Age: Crises and New Perspectives

Silence, twilight is in Czech poetry
No slogan has been coined for a long time
Poets are living here among us on their own credit
Theater is decaying on its own credit
The most cheerful have been infected with death
You can feel a somber faintness blowing from their verses
Not what refreshes, not what crushes
Not what wants to stand on the barricades...*

Josef Hora's poem "1930" can be read as an artistic farewell to the postulates of the avant-garde of the 1920s. The poet describes the emptiness of gestures, the exhaustion of -isms, the withdrawal from the barricades, accompanied by feelings of anxiety and sadness. It is not, however, a poem that is necessarily pessimistic; rather it is poetry of the change that the Czech avant-garde underwent at the turn of the 1920s and the 1930s. Josef Hora also devoted himself to new directions in the context of modern art in the magazine *Plán* (1929–1932), as its editor-in-chief. In an editorial, the magazine's editors propose the following solution to the crisis of the Czech interwar avant-garde: to set against the chaos of today a modern order and objective knowledge, an orientation towards the values of today. "We do not want to interpret narrow -isms nor to produce diminutive categories, but to view modern events and capture them in their fullness. The construction of a new order is grow-

* Ticho, příšeří je v české poezii. / Žádné heslo dávno nepadlo. / Na svůj vrub básníci u nás žijí. / na svůj vrub se kazí divadlo. / Nejveselejší se nakazili smrtí, / chmurnou mdlobu cítíš z veršů vát. / Ne, co oživuje, ne co drtí. / ne, co chce na barikádě stát...

ing on the ruins of the old social and artistic forms. *Plán* aims to show the ground plan of this construction..."[1]

The attempts at capturing a new modernity went hand in hand with the active building of an alternative avant-garde that was not based on Poetism. The exhaustion of Poetism and the opening up of new themes is captured in one of the late *Zone*-style compositions of the 1920s, *Nový Ikaros* (New Icarus, 1929) by Konstantin Biebl. In 1929, Biebl's poem was read literally as a typology of the current day; it was praised especially for its portrayal of the atmosphere of the modern period, for capturing the new worldview, the world agony of a generation, a broken and groaning soul (František Götz). At the turn of the 1920s and 1930s, faith in a poetry capable of maintaining stability and order also outside of art was hardly sustainable any more, and existential themes revealing reality as fragmented or shattered — that is, incoherent — enter into the form of the *Zone*-poem, which significantly reflects Apollinaire's concept of modern art. František Götz, literary critic and theoretical spokesman of the Literární skupina (Literary Group), placed these phenomena into connection with the "process of de-personalization," which in his opinion also concerned an absence of discipline of form. He interpreted this as a consequence, among other things, of a somewhat hasty discovery of a vision of wholeness and integrity in avant-garde utopias.

At the end of the 1920s, Jean Cocteau's book *Le Rappel à l'ordre* (Recall to Order, 1926) found a substantial resonance in the Czech avant-garde as a kind of path towards finding metaphysical certainties, which was decisive for the circle around the newly founded magazines, in particular *Tvar* (1927–1932)[2] and *Listy pro umění a kritiku* (1933–1937)[3] — that is, for those concepts of modernity

---

1 The subtitle of the magazine *Plán* was "Revue for literature, art, and science". In response to the declaration of the editorial board on a modern order, Julius Fučík reacted in *Tvorba* magazine, where he described *Plán* as a magazine that was misguided, harmful, and dangerous. The *Plán* editorial board printed his reaction as a short note under the title "The Misguidedness of *Plán*," where it decided to reply to Fučík by "not replying to him for the while" and the magazine continued to publish translations of works (e.g. James Joyce) whose poetics could perhaps at the beginning of the 1930s embody danger or even harmfulness in the eyes of avant-garde theoreticians.

2 In 1928 *Tvar* devoted a thematic double-number to the works of Otokar Březina and Jakub Deml. The argument about modernity within the framework of Catholicism (in particular in the context of myth as one of the determining aspects of modernity) was a point of departure for art critics Bedřich Fučík and Miloš Dvořák (among other things, the myth of the land of one's birthplace, the mystical nature of the word, the mother tongue, and so on). The central figure of both magazines was Bedřich Fučík (1900–1984). As a literary critic and translator he devoted himself primarily to authors with a Catholic orientation: among others, O. Březina, J. Čep, J. Deml, J. Zahradníček. In the years 1929–1939, Bedřich Fučík was director of the Melantrich publishing house, one of the most significant in Czechoslovakia in the 1930s.

3 *Listy pro umění a kritiku* (1933–1937) was published by the Melantrich publishing house, eds. Bedřich Fučík (1933–1934) and Vilém Závada (1935–1937). The magazine regularly published, among others, František Halas, Jan Mukařovský, Josef Hora, Jan Čep, Egon Hostovský, František Hrubín, Jaroslav Seifert, Vladislav Vančura, Jan Zahradníček, and René Wellek, and among foreign authors, T. S. Eliot, R. M. Rilke, P. Valéry.

that were more or less associated with the idea of Catholicism.[4] Nevertheless, at the beginning of the 1930s the problem of the search for order was perceived in a fundamentally more complex and broad way. Finding themselves in opposition to *Listy pro umění a kritiku* and *Tvar* were the authors associated with the journal *Kvart* (see Chapter 5), who took their inspiration from Alexandre Marc's article "Vers Un Ordre nouveau" (Towards a New Order), which opened the second year of *Kvart* with the contention that the civilization called modern was hastening towards its end. The concept of the avant-garde (and modernity in the wider sense of the word) was becoming more individualized. The vision of a unity of life and the world was falling apart, and concepts like myth, fragments, and ruins entered into the context of Czech literature. The idea of order was no longer sufficient for a unification of authorial approaches, which only with difficulty create some kind of common direction within the framework of published periodicals. In 1929, the Czech avant-garde enters an entirely new phase in which a countless number of artistic and philosophical concepts that can only be defined in a complicated way nevertheless represent in general an alternative to the avant-garde of the 1920s.

Richard Weiner's *Lazebník* (The Barber: Poetics), a collection of short prose pieces, was published in 1929. At the beginning of the titular short story, he writes: "The first sentence and already everything is tottering."[5] The feeling of a loss of balance is not a feature exclusive to avant-garde prose. Franz Kafka and Richard Weiner record an experience of "seasickness on dry land," while in Nezval's extensive poetic composition *Akrobat* (Acrobat, 1927) the acrobat balances over the abyss and in the end plunges into it.[6] At the end of the 1920s, dark themes, gloomy allusions and motifs start to appear in Czech poetry. Following his poetistically playful *Na vlnách TSF* (On Wireless Waves, 1925), Seifert's next collection was ominously called *Slavík zpívá špatně* (The Nightingale Sings Badly, 1926). At the turn of the 1920s and 1930s Czech literature reacts to the inauspicious political situation, and especially to the exhaustion of the model of Poetism, even though in theoretical discourse this model continues to be presented as the main avant-garde direction.

The end of the 1920s brought with it questions regarding the viability of the avant-garde. The Devětsil program found itself in crisis; Poetism was no longer capable of furnishing new artistic approaches and themes. At the turn of the decade, everything got into flow, current, discontinuity — these words repeatedly appear in articles and critical reviews at the end of the 1920s. Literary magazines published articles about a crisis of, an end to, the death of the avant-garde, followed by consequent deliberations about the possibilities for art after the avant-garde or

4 Cf. Tomáš Kubíček, *Řád tvaru: tradicionalistické časopisy v období první republiky (analýzy a rekonstrukce)* (Brno: Host 2020).

5 Richard Weiner, *Lazebník — Hra doopravdy*, (ed.) Zina Trochová (Praha: Torst, 1998), 9.

6 Weiner analyzes the metaphor of balance in detail in the titular short story of the collection *Netečný divák a jiné prózy* ([Indifferent Onlooker and Other Prose], 1917). See Petr Málek, *Melancholie moderny. Alegorie — vypravěč — smrt* (Praha; Podlesí: Dauphin, 2008).

its continuation. A certain exhaustion from avant-garde solutions motivated a need to once again define the relationship between language and reality, as well as the relationship of modern art to the past. This attempt no longer took place within the framework of the collective programs of avant-garde groups, but more often now in the context of individual creative solutions.

The years 1929–1931 were a period of stock-taking for the Czech avant-garde. In February 1929, the 5th congress of the Czechoslovak Communist Party took place. In response to the triumph at the congress of the hard-line policies promoted by Klement Gottwald, several writers left the party. In March that same year, seven communist authors, namely Josef Hora, Marie Majerová, Helena Malířová, Jaroslav Seifert, Stanislav K. Neumann, Vladislav Vančura, and Ivan Olbracht, published a brochure in which they expressed their fear of the threat of sectarianism. These authors were expelled from the party.

In fall 1929, the Levá fronta (Left Front) organization, working closely with the Communist Party, was founded and Devětsil, up until that time a key group of the Czech interwar avant-garde, fell apart (attempts to revive it in 1932 were unsuccessful). For a long time already the works of the foremost Czech avant-garde authors could no longer be united under the designation "Poetist": the artistic output of František Halas, Jaroslav Seifert, or Vilém Závada became ever more distant from Poetist approaches. Broader avant-garde groupings became ever rarer, and when they did occur, were mostly at the instigation of architects or visual artists (for instance, on the occasion of the Surrealist-oriented exhibition Poesie in 1932).

The early 1930s are connected with the political and economic crisis that in the words of the philosopher Václav Navrátil became a general crisis affecting the fields of science, art, philosophy, and religion. However, the crisis in the context of the Czech avant-garde in the 1930s can be understood as an impulse for seeking new sources of imagination, new theoretical concepts. Newly founded magazines (among others, *Kvart*, *Odeon*, *Plán*, *Rok*) brought information about themes that had hitherto been outside the field of interest of Czech literature. At the same time, the editorial boards and contributors of these new magazine platforms adopted a critical stance towards the past of the avant-garde — that is, paradoxically towards their own past. In its first year, *Kvart* distanced itself from the Constructivist theories of Karel Teige, which he had promoted in the second half of the 1920s in the avant-garde *Revue Svazu moderní kultury "Devětsil"* (*ReD*). The editorial circle of *Kvart* magazine, which formed around architect, poet, and theorist Vít Obrtel, thus created a space in which they were able to put into practice their "right to theory." In addition to translations of some of T. S. Eliot's poems, including an excerpt from *The Waste Land* ("The Fire Sermon"), the first year of *Kvart* also published two essays by Eugene Jolas, in which the crisis of modernity is connected with the crisis of language and words. The crisis of words, language, and speech is newly expressed by a part of the Czech avant-garde in the context of the ideas of European modernism.

The *Zvěrokruh* revue, edited by Vítězslav Nezval, also had a clearly defined profile. Its two numbers from the end of 1930 demonstrate a new orientation away from

Poetism towards Surrealism. Apart from translations of the French Surrealists (for instance, Breton's manifesto of Surrealism was published here), Teige's manifestos of Poetism containing significant passages about Surrealism were published in *Zvěrokruh*. The "cultural leaflet" *Rok* (1931, directed by Bohuslav Brouk, Jindřich Štyrský, and Vít Obrtel) opened with Brouk's essay "Na obranu individualismu" (In Defense of Individualism), representing a abandonment of avant-garde, collectivist approaches and a focus on questions of the essence of modern culture and civilization. The magazine *Odeon* (1929–1931, edited by Jindřich Štyrský) opened up themes of European and in particular Anglo-American modernism, for instance in the bloc devoted to Joyce's *Anna Livia Plurabelle*.

The unsustainability of avant-garde approaches and the crisis of the Poetist avant-garde became the topic of an extensive generational discussion about the past, future, and nature of the Czech avant-garde, for which Jindřich Štyrský provided the impetus in his series of articles "Koutek generace I–III" (Cosy Nook of a Generation I–III, 1929–1930). As the danger he viewed the avant-garde as facing, Štyrský formulated the devaluation of autonomous, innovative, original art to a mere lucrative opportunity and the succumbing of artists to cultural and political institutionalization. He uncompromisingly condemned the way in which certain literary figures and creative artists fed like parasites off Poetism — that is, those artists who published under the label of Poetism, but who exhibited kitsch that had nothing in common with poetry — for Štyrský the main measuring criterion of an avant-garde artistic work. Štyrský entirely repudiated such avant-garde poets, who were only in the avant-garde for lucrative reasons and "prostituted themselves" in art or in politics. His series of articles "Cosy Nook of a Generation" concluded with a polemic concerning the understanding of a poetic work and the role of the artist in society. Štyrský criticized the corruption of poets and artists of the avant-garde who had become conformist rather than revolutionary, and he repeatedly declared: "For a real poet today there is no other place than on the pillory," because he was convinced of the independence of poetry and its super-ordination over artistic and political programs.

A large number of literary figures reacted to Štyrský's opening fire into his own ranks. Some reacted critically, while others regarded his stance as a necessary classification and sorting out of generations. However, the debate, originally intended as a polemic about the (artistic and political) purity of a generation, eventually developed in a quite different direction and, rather than the issue of intellectual purity, pointed to the programmatic chaos, lack of clarity, and — as many critics noted — the dangerous crisis of avant-garde criteria. The most vocal critic was Karel Teige, who in his extensive deliberation "1929" welcomed Štyrský's article as an impulse for an essential critical cleansing of the intellectual and cultural left, yet nevertheless reproached him for his failure to name specific names. Thus, in the end, Teige added some names himself: Josef Hora and Vladislav Vančura. Štyrský replied to Teige in his article "Cosy Nook of a Generation II" where he writes about a modern poet who has never betrayed his work. He regards the failure to understand the idea that the work of a poet is ranked above other activities (in particular, political activities) as one of the greatest errors of the avant-garde generation and a crisis in its understanding of the poetic work and the role of the artist in society. The invectives between Karel Teige and Jindřich Štyrský culminated in "Cosy Nook of a Generation III," in which the main target of criticism became Teige himself.

The polemic over "a generation on two chairs' was the most vocal expression of the differentiation of what had been up until that time a united leftist avant-garde, an expression of its critical reevaluation, a prefiguring of the later dispute over Surrealism as the result of an attempt at creating a different, alternative avant-garde, a different conception of avant-garde modernity. The discussion gradually shifted from the autonomy of the artistic work to the significance of Surrealism for modern art. In his text "Malá prolegomena" (Little Prolegomena) Štyrský opens up to Surrealism in a highly stylized piece influenced by Sade and Lautréamont (he commented on the works of both authors in several later studies) — together with Surrealism the theme of melancholy enters his work, to which he returned artistically only at the end of his life.

At the beginning of the 1930s the position of Marxism in Czech literature strengthens, embodied by the person of Ladislav Štoll. Štoll entered literature first as an author of texts with dominant social themes, as well as a faith in collectivism and the revolutionary proletariat, and he then devoted himself to literature as a commentator and literary critic. He showed himself as an uncritical adherent of Marxism, as demonstrated by his studies from the 1930s collected in *Z bojů na levé frontě* (From Struggles on the Leftist Front, 1964). The studies of Bedřich Václavek represent an attempt to combine Marxism and the sociology of art. From the beginning, Václavek tried to synthesize avant-garde art, in particular Poetism and Constructivism, with a sociological view of the world. In his studies in the collection *Poesie v rozpacích* (Poetry in Discomfort, 1930) he declined to explicitly condemn avant-garde art, but neither did he classify it among "progressive developmental tendencies." The determining category for the newly conceived theory of art and literature became realism. Marxists understood this concept as a creative approach, not as a time-limited artistic direction or era. In their opinion, realistic artworks were supposed to attempt to capture typical characters in typical plot situations. Because the depiction of these was subject to historical development, realism is a tendentious art. By this definition, every artist who consciously inclines toward a certain (realistic) method and consequently contributes to a faithful depiction of real historical events is a tendentious artist. In their theories, tendentiousness is defined similarly to party affiliation — that is, as a morally established duty which exceeds the scope of ordinary political agitation. Instead of being aimed at the elites, the newly arising modern art was supposed to appeal to ordinary people and consequently, in a classless society, the other artistic forms would be replaced by a universal mediator of aesthetic and ideological qualities — socialist creation.

Josef Hora: Education for Modernism

For several months already now Karel Teige has been engaging in a polemic against "liquidators, fascists, traitors and social-patriots." These are the names that he uses for the seven authors who have left the Communist Party, myself amongst them. In the last issue of *ReD* he devotes a six-column breviary to this polemic with me — and this time also with Vančura — which could be, as is the custom in this communist organ of modern art, accompanied by more useful articles about sadism in the works of Lautréamont, photomontages from tailors' salons, and the such like. *Tvorba*, *Dav*, and *Signál* are also indulging in similar activities. Today, *Dav* has already appointed Teige the more or less official "president of a generation," and we are joyous that he is finally receiving this acknowledgement from the young generation. He is fighting in their name; he is coining slogans for them, slogans for which today the politburo is supplying topics with the same promptitude as "Dada" did once upon a time. At last he has got where he could have been a long time ago, into the role of the leader of the avant-garde left, the real leftist — that is, communist — cultural front.

If I understand Teige's polemics well, which parliamentary deputy [Josef] Haken himself praises as a proper Bolshevik kick in the stomach, and if I also understand these most recent six columns in *ReD*, then Teige is proclaiming something like this: these seven literary figures have betrayed communism and, by doing so, they have also betrayed modern art. Because what is new is the star of communism (for Teige certainly in its current-day form), and apart from this there is no modernism. Teige explains the actions of the seven, and mine first and foremost, precisely like a politburo member. They have sold themselves for state prizes, for comfortable positions, and grand careers. They are traitors, epigones, and bankrupts — and let's assail them. This is the argumentation of a person who is — viz *Dav* — the president of a generation. But luckily there is another leftist front here. Alongside poets crowned with state prizes, there are also people here who have the courage *to call themselves* "accursed poets and inventors, and to proudly bear their curse with all the consequences." Teige would not be Teige, if he were not to engage in coquetry at this moment. But this is dangerous coquetry, which is both irritating and ridiculous.

There has never been a less cursed generation in Bohemia than the current one of president Teige. It spent the war at home with its mummies, after the war it went along to watch workers' demonstrations from its warm stoves at home, at decisive moments it expressed its communism by singing the "Dubinushka" work song, and in poetry — precisely through the lips of Karel Teige — it has very resolutely banned any kind of drama, every serious indignation, rather wanting to have a poetry that is laughing and smiling like a bourgeois child. All that remains is for our friends now to found an organization of the "accursed" and — in order to increase their desperation — with a sombre expression to recite the theses that have just been issued in Moscow about the Bolshevization of literature. They would soon get over their, let us say, "Mauditism" as soon as they realized that their literary and artistic acts are regarded just as lightly as the acts of any other kind of fellow traveller who contends that he or she can grovel up to Bolshevism by berating its supposed or actual opponents.

I can already see clearly that for the meanwhile any disputes with Teige are pointless. If parliamentary deputy Haken is convinced that Teige's polemics are a proper kick in the stomach, then he is mistaken, because in reality Teige is kicking into the air like a laughing bourgeois child who is rolling around on its back. I have objected to Teige's view, I think justifiably: I contend that communism is not demonstrated by shouting, but by deeds. If you want to show, all of you from *ReD*, *Tvorba*, *Dav*, and *Signál*, that there is no modern art outside of communism, that is, outside of the Communist Party, — which is utter nonsense because art never has anything to do with the party — then get to work! Create some poetry for us from your conception of communism; create from this conception prose or drama, film and pictures. Don't speak comically about accursed poets as your brothers, but notice the humanly accursed non-poets. Give us something from the blood of a poor man and from his most essential life feeling — and then we will bow down before you and forgive all the crudeness with which you have attacked people with whom you express your disagreement, not as artists, but as those who make use of your party — and I know that this party is only supposedly yours — in order to give a kick in the belly to those who have something in their bellies. After all, the good Laco Novomeský, when he wants to conduct a polemic against me in *Tvorba* as to why intellectuals incline towards socialism, feels obliged to say it in this way: "We are not standing by the window of the political secretariat of the Communist Party, but nevertheless with the consent of this institution we can say that...'

Richard Weiner: The Barber

(Poetics)

The feeling that it is necessary to preface the following travelogue with a few words overcame me *suddenly*. The first sentence and already everything is tottering: The doubt about whether I will keep my promise when I promise only a few words and the scruple that it would better correspond to my thought if I was rather to say that I was overcome by a *sudden* feeling of necessity than that this feeling overcame me suddenly. The discomfort of importunate honesty! I place my head in the palm of my hands; I think strenuously. Oh, the beauties of syntax and word morphology! I think it over, unwittingly following the violet lines, and I shudder as though confronted with something unprecedented, ascertaining immediately that the first will not stretch out to infinity, but rather that — so soon after its beginning — I am forced to leap to where I started out from, only at a noticeably lower level; and I shudder for a second time when already the fifth — how long have I been reading? Hardly two minutes! — folds me up like a blind alley on the edge of a desert of a thus far blank page over which the coffee-house hum (it is half past five in the evening, aperitif time) hangs like a trembling radiance; no mirage here; and if I hear something else apart from that, then that something is a silence as entire as a smooth clay ball; it is through this silence that the only thing that matters to me speaks to me; this silence threw off composition like a person who, emerging from a healing spring, throws off his crutches, and it threw off morphology as an unnecessary mask which is donned by liars in order to conceal their embarrassment; because even in liars there remains a piece of the oppressive consciousness that words are merely sand in the eye. And here, then, is my first fundamental discovery: The adjective sudden would be used by a person who would wimpishly submit to necessity; if I have used the adverb suddenly, then this is out of subconscious pride that I am an unwitting plaything of this necessity.

I am writing a "few words," but — being a plaything — maybe there will be a lot of them. And I insist on this apparently grammatically false transgressive just as obstinately as I insist on my right to deny that there might be any difference between a few and a lot, no matter if only quantitative. I will rather say "primarily not quantitative" because this is the matter of very least concern to me.

I wavered between an introductory note and a footnote. However, I would have to resort to a footnote — God knows! — perhaps already in the third line. That is, to play with the reader's good will. Therefore, I decided on an introductory note. Because, in contrast to my other writings, which are primarily silent, this book demands this silence. And it demands this silence loudly. It contains the anger and rage of those who have recognized that they are in a cage and are trying to escape from it. But in vain; oh yes, this is taken care of: in vain! With a cage it is like with mud: the more you flail your arms around, the more closely it sticks. — "Be silent then!" — "Yes, but what about conscience?" — But mainly: What about anger? This is too good and effective a companion for me to reduce it to disinheritance — It is not a question of how to get the bird out; it is a case of persuading even the most mendacious that he is in self-confinement. Even afterwards it will sing like it sang before; however, it will understand this differently. That is already something.

If so many people do not acknowledge the fact that they are behind bars, this is the result of an optical deception: they have a screen behind the small screen. You know, behind that skillfully cut screen for deciphering secret script. A screen screened out like the solar spectrum (that chastened curiosity! As though it would not be better to *know* the spectrum in a white ray of light and to refuse to release it through a disintegrative prism); compact like a pocket tape-measure; methodical like the working timetable of a country notary, and well-ordered like his family relations. Who would not have already figured out that our cage is the screened, compact, methodical, and well-ordered speech of a humankind that is "attaining a high level of civilization" and the successful offshoot of this speech: phonetic-analytical script! *Aqua regia* and a scalpel. A probe sunk charlatanically into the inexpressible and removed with the deceptive pretense that the inexpressible has truly been discovered. Evidence of this, gentlemen, is provided by that rare distillate that we permit ourselves to discharge in front of you here: the famous dictionary of abstractions! — How not to envy Bushmen that they do not have the verb "to love" and the Chinese, uncommunicative like their ideograms. Not being able to reach agreement through speaking, they can at least hope a little that they will gradually reach a mutual understanding: with people and also with the inhuman. And if not, then there still remains the possibility of *not resisting* the unutterable, that is, of merging with it. While we, on the bank of the ocean, measure and pour our small measure in spite of the warnings of Saint Augustine. One of those precious achievements that the distinctiveness human speech has completed — these are achievements that are on the whole negative — is this: "Great feelings do not have words." However, it cannot be expected from rationalistic cowardice that it will add: "Small pieces of knowledge have them all the less." Let alone large ones (but truthfully: What is the difference between a small perception and a large one?). We display them in display cases *tout habillé* so that it cannot be seen that they are dummies and that their organ of perception is a mechanical clock (it ticks like a heart). — If you reach the top of, let us say, not Gaurishankar, but rather only Ararat — it happens to a poet here and there — you will have the world below you; speech still at your hand. See what you can do with it! High above the world, with this speech you are like with a toothpick in front of a mountain that you want to dig through. What will you do with it? — “Certainly, at least as much as a Bushman with his partial speech.” — “He would be silent.” — “Please do the same.” — As though this was the matter at stake! As though this was a matter of anything else than of how to reach an understanding with oneself! This is precisely what we are not capable of doing. Diabolical inquisitiveness has inspired in us a belief in the illusion of dialectical knowledge, and dialectics, the hobgoblin, chases in a circle like a dog chasing its own tail. For fooling others language is not sufficient; and it is even less so for persuading ourselves, for catching ourselves. — A screen for deciphering? The bars of a cage that there is no other possibility than to circumvent.

Jindřich Štyrský: Cozy Nook of a Generation 1

Our generation has matured: It identifies the moon with an electronic light-bulb, love with a bed, and poetry with a *portmonnaie*. It measures quality by the degree of success and aims to conquer life by submissively seeking favor with the powerful. Many have grown old and decayed, and time has transformed imperceptible and microscopic signs of spiritual poverty into large ulcers of degeneracy. Others have confirmed their own cowardice. They have elevated their own wretchedness so that they could, with impunity, be regarded as inferior good-for-nothings. Somewhere well out of sight in a secluded place they are looking forward to money like Judas. The ridiculousness of their lives lies in the fact that their real value does not reach that of their reputations. Sometimes they still mirror the appearance of movement like rushes in a pond. They slander each other secretly and mutually, without themselves losing respect toward each other. Even though they view the world in a very idyllic way, on the whole they create a structure that is much more complicated than would be assumed, because the more they are for sale, the greater the understanding for kitsch they express; or to put this better, the more indulgent they are toward kitsch, the more kitsch they create. They have excellent perception. The generation dreams of a new bath. ***For a real poet there is no other place today than on the pillory***.

Our generation spoke a lot about adventures and eccentricities; however, in reality there has never been a more peaceable herd. It contended that it contained the entire world, but it was not even capable of ascertaining its own volume. Already from the start its course has been linked with the extinction of the foreign joys on which it was grazing. For each attempt at expanding the generation's horizon, one ram fell as a sacrifice. The nation is already building memorials for many of them. They are depicted as seated and their youth receives a patina.

It is certainly more beneficial to adore illusions because it is not possible to enter into them than to believe in them because we live in them. It seems that for a long time yet we are going to despise *foreign* youths who are going to intermingle with small groups that are going and coming, only — at a time of general development and progress — to step quietly backwards so as to maintain in this way the eternal balance of living. Each generation should be driven out with the weapon that it deserves. It seems that our generation deserves neither a butcher's ax, nor a rapier, but rather a dose of strychnine.

The person of today — or his abbreviation or sign — falls into error because he wants to convince himself of the fragility of a rose by his *sense of smell*. However, the picture of the rose is hidden in his subconscious, which is in constant movement and which no *eye* can follow, and therefore no one can have a probable notion about roses. It is always going to be merely a rose that is going to provoke horror. Even if in future one single machine was to replace the work of a hundred thousand human hands, in the end a human being will still smash it into pieces after all because his hands will not have anything else to do.

The future of poetry does not lie in the cleverness with which generations advance. No generation has had more printed paper, more incense, parasites, jokers, narcissists, happiness, and Elberfield horses than our generation, and yet no generation has had less poets. Cleverness has taken revenge on this generation. Every fool who was born in a certain period regards himself as a member of this generation.

It is necessary to put an end to the myth about a generation so that the fools who have prepared a cozy livelihood for themselves in it in peace and quiet are able to rejoice, after the period of confetti, also from spiritual benefits — that is, from their own invisibility. And so that those who are prostituting themselves can at least for once and for the last time turn scarlet for shame again.

To sit on two chairs is the same kind of shamelessness as nurturing the secret wish to lie in two graves. Our generation is falling apart. Some poets continue to live in their own way. The Earth is heavy for them and the distance is light. Or the contrary.

Julius Fučík:
Generation on Two Chairs

Elsewhere we cite Jindřich Štyrský's article from the new literary monthly *Odeon* because this article is highly symptomatic of the new sorting of intellects that is now taking place here in Czechoslovakia. Štyrský is not alone. Finally, an attack — unorganized, but nevertheless concentrated — is starting on the squalidness displayed by members precisely of the young generation, who after all have clear tasks, but who have showed themselves capable of breezing into the waters of bourgeois officialdom; they have allowed themselves to become corrupted and have sold out their convictions, whether political or cultural. There are still a few magazines untouched by such decay. *Odeon*, *Signal*, and *Red* are all starting a cleansing — this must be intensified and it must be carried out very thoroughly. Otherwise, the entire generation will expire just as wretchedly as the class onto whose chair it is shifting.

Jindřich Štyrský: Cozy Nook of a Generation 2

I have been reproached that my article "Cozy Nook of a Generation" aroused a considerable commotion, but not an entirely honest one. However, I am also afraid of being misused in places where I would least expect it. Naturally, I did not react to comments on my article from certain circles, because these comments, rather than me, concerned a certain nook of the generation. These comments caused me neither joy, nor grief, nor diarrhea.

I do not seek the meaning of life in playing at being a judge or an executioner in the generation, because I am not suited to this either by my physique or by my abilities, and I leave this honorable function to hardened people who do not faint in the vicinity of the strangest individuals who appear in their underwear. I have summed up my opinion in a small pill, at first sight rather "languid," but which I nevertheless do not intend to dissolve in a lotion on account of this alleged insufficiency.

I consider my article absolutely unambiguous and I regard my words as definitive. I hope that everyone has found in them what is in them.

I would merely like to comment on several words. I was very amused when I ascertained what many people imagined when reading my words "***For a real poet today there is no other place than on the pillory***": They imagined some column to which some kind of Villon-like tatterdemalion is tied by chains; this tatterdemalion resembles a loudmouth from political meetings and holds in his hand (rough-skinned of course) the emblems of a certain political party.

I am surprised that Karel Teige has used my article by underlining some citations from it in support of his own conclusions in the matter of Vladislav Vančura, which — let it be said once and for all — is nobody else's business.

My article had no political subtext. I was talking primarily about the purity of works of art and about literary prostitution. It is evident from my words that ***for me a modern poet is a poet who has never betrayed his work***. I think that it is clearer than the sun that Karel Teige has used the following words of mine in the wrong place: "And so that those who are prostituting themselves can at least for once and for the last time turn scarlet for shame again." He would have done better if he had written about Vančura in connection with his own words at the end of the article: "***Alongside some kind of 'generation' there is luckily also something more solid: faithfulness to the artwork, opinion, and a direction professed in international communality.***"

It is a shame in general that Teige does not make more use of his leadership abilities and his combative elán in matters of poetry and that in recent times he has been subordinating his interest in poetry to his interest in politics.

I regard a thorough merging of the spirits of revolution with the revolutionary spirits in art as madness and as a remnant of reactionary attitudes — not only political ones, but also artistic ones. It is a negative picture of patriotic paradises. It does not matter whether a poet is a newspaper vendor of *Rudé Právo* or a Czechoslovak general, even though this is difficult to imagine! A real poet always stands to one side of political hunts and machinations. Revolutions always appropriate poets only *ex post*.

Naturally, I do not wish to establish a rule from a general truth, even though history, yesterday, and also the present demonstrate that usually the most developed revolutionaries, politicians, sociologists, and economists who have significance for today's life have been on the whole the greatest reactionaries in the field of art. It can also be said that on the whole poets have been completely indifferent towards state, social, and class revolutions. Whoever, for instance, knows Baudelaire knows that his revolutionary activity in 1848 was a quite insignificant episode in his life and that Baudelaire is not a poet of revolution, just as poet J. A. Rimbaud is not. Rimbaud joined the commune for one simple reason: He was hungry. However, he did not remain a Communard for even one month and he fled to Paris already before the legendary bloody week. We could also name Jules Laforgue, Nerval, Germain Nouveau, Lautréamont, Mallarmé, and Apollinaire.

A poet's interests are always somewhere outside of the circles of political parties. Poets do not dress in patriotic colors to go along and doze at meetings, and neither do they care how much cinnamon costs in the Soviet Union.

A poet frees himself from all prejudices. He admires the heroes of the revolution just as he admires the heroes of the counter-revolution. If he loves ***death***, then the execution of Sacco and Vanzetti excites him in the same way as the execution of the czar's family. And so on.

Poets are berated for being selfish and asocial beings, while ***from the right and also from the left*** hyenas howl over their actions and poetry. The poet's enemy is both the nice and the ugly of human society.

Yes: ***The only place for a real poet is after all only on the pillory***.

Karel Teige: Epilogue to Discussion About Generation on Two Chairs

The case of Jindřich Štyrský, who many erroneously expected would be the Heracles who cleaned out the stables of the literary community and drove the moneylenders out of the temple, but instead of that — with his latest article in *Odeon* — has joined the counter-revolutionary ranks of the enemies and subversives of revolutionary modernism; the case of Vladislav Vančura, who has parted ways with the Communist Party because he did not agree with its current leadership and who in fall accepted a state prize; the case of Josef Hora, ditto, plus his joining an editorial board of the social-fascist press; and some other fundamental problems that have surfaced in connection with these matters, primarily, the problem of the relation of the artist — or respectively, thc productive specialist — to society and to the revolution: All of these things together have provoked a discussion in which the only thing that many people find to reproach is that the "youngest generation" is in a state of disintegration, and let us rejoice. In the 22nd issue of *Tvorba* Sekanina, who wished — and was supposed — to deal only with the political aspect of the matter, quite correctly rejected Štyrský's stance and argued that it cannot be a matter of indifference to a modern person whether communism or fascism has a decisive influence on cultural life; that a modern creator, artist or scientist can no longer be some kind of illiterate idiot and that it is, therefore, necessary to be conscious that the social struggle and political life also impact the cultural sphere. However, when Sekanina contends that responsibility for "crisis of the youngest generation" lies with avant-garde critics, who apparently behave like a clique, indulge in favoritism, and have "failed to perform their duty," (He contends that it was the duty of these critics already to deal with the "case" of Nezval and Jindřich Honzl), then he is fundamentally mistaken, and I regarded it as necessary to draw attention to this error (in number 23 and 24 of *Tvorba*). So, I repeat once again: We reject the idea that a critic performing his duties should be understood as like being when a police officer "starts his shift." A critic is not, after all, armed with a truncheon. Secondly, an avant-garde critic really cannot be accused of suffering from complaisance towards friends. If Sekanina has never yet found publicly written the things that are spoken privately in the coffee-houses against X or Y, then this is evidently a plus point of this criticism, which is not — and does not wish to be — an amplifier of coffee-house chatter and gossip, which are anything other than criticism. Sekanina accuses Fučík (in the Honzl case) of not condemning in his review the production of Jules Romains' "Jiskra" [Spark][1] directed by Honzl, and Václavek of failing to criticize the compromises made by Honzl as director at the theater in Brno[2]. Well, if Fučík wrote about the sensationalist kitsch which the production of "Jiskra" was, that it was a pleasing piece of theater, then he most certainly did not do so out of some kind of favoritism towards Osvobozené divadlo or toward Honzl, but rather because — regrettably, but quite sincerely — he simply very much liked this kitsch. Therefore, it is possible here to reproach the theater reviewer for a lack of aesthetic understanding, but not for dishonesty or a lack of integrity. If Václavek, who supported Honzl's arrival in Brno, adopts a reserved stance towards the compromises that Honzl allegedly made in Brno, if he tries not to jump to a quick judgment and defers until he is able to provide full and objective evidence for it, if he does not intend to "execute" an author towards whose work he has been very sympathetic immediately the first negative signs appear, until it becomes apparent whether this is a case of a temporary crisis or a permanent decline involving systematic compromise, all this is merely evidence that an avant-garde critic understands his function seriously and responsibly. Anyone, even a Štyrský, is capable of loudly shouting sweeping and undocumented accusations. (Apart from that, I would like to point out that Václavek's review of some more of Honzl's productions in Brno is now at the typesetters and will probably be published in the next issue.) I am not competent to talk about the Honzl case as I have not seen the Brno production. However, I contend that Václavek did not act out of favoritism when he did not immediately sound the alarm in the "Honzl case" without due deliberation, when he waited to see how Honzl's work would develop. As far as the Nezval case is concerned, it is once again evidence of the seriousness of avant-garde criticism that it did not write about Nezval's new books in the way that Sekanina writes about them: In this matter I must reject Sekanina's arguments as unjustified and incompetent. Without wishing to take on the function of a critic of Czech literature, which is a task that I have never systematically engaged in and do not wish to engage in, I must repeat what I replied to Sekanina in *Tvorba:* The difference in quality of Nezval's poems, in short the unequal standard of his production, lies in — is almost scientifically given by — the essence of Nezval's poetic method. However, we must assure Sekanina that the several weaker, unemotive, ineffective poems in *Hra v kostky* are richly balanced by the most wonderful works of burning and powerful lyricism. *Kroni-*

1 Title of the Czech translation, original title unidentified — transl.
2 1929–31 at Zemské divadlo v Brně.

ka, Nezval's first attempt at a novel, is in my opinion a failure: It is a poor book, which unfortunately cannot be rescued by some really poetic passages. A failure, not kitsch. A responsible and really judicious literary criticism cannot, therefore, "deal with Nezval's case" because in reality there is no such case. Mr. Rutte may well speak — let us rejoice and be cheerful — about the poet's deterioration, but anyone who understands the organism of Nezval's talent cannot see in this indifferent and weak poetic collection a failure and a debacle of the most indisputable and richest poetic genius who has appeared in Czech literature.

We must decisively reject the view that avant-garde criticism has been corrupted by favoritism and the formation of cliques. You can reproach individual critics for individual errors in critical evaluations; after all, we do not contend that they are infallible popes. Avant-garde criticism "has performed its duty": It has made judgments, not always infallibly, but seriously and uncompromisingly, sincerely and responsibly. I repeat: ***Look at how many and which people the avant-garde was composed of ten or five years ago, and how many and which people it is composed of today! ! !*** You will recognize that precisely a sorting, a sifting, a cleansing has taken place. Devětsil has kept numerous epigones and sub-epigones at an appropriate distance. Avant-garde criticism has not been afraid of the powerful of this cultural world and has not suffered from sentimentality towards *Mitläufer* [fellow-travelers]. However, it has never pronounced its judgments theatrically; it has not looked covetously sidelong for applause from the gallery, and therefore it has not attracted such general attention to itself as Štyrský has. Nevertheless, its quiet and reserved work has not been without effect. Avant-garde criticism has not organized grandiose executions; it has not reveled in the battle cry "all heads on the block!"; it has not staged executions attracting the attention of crowds; neither has it wasted too much time in polemics that are good for "goading" certain readers. If you take a look at where people like Schulz, Frejka, Obrtel, Raffel, and Píša are today — as well as the gentlemen from Literární skupina, and people like František Kovárna, A. C. Nor, etc. — and where Štyrský is today, then you have to concede that the "purity of the movement" has been maintained.

This, then, is something that should be realized by all those who want criticism to "perform its duty" like a policeman with a truncheon or a schoolteacher with his cane in order to irreversibly brand works and authors. In the 5th number of his *Zápisník* F. X. Šalda writes about the disputes and conflicts in the "Devětsil generation," starting with the secession of the "Seven" and ending with the "***particular*** stance of Štyrský." His article is a serious, objective evaluation of the political and literary aspects of these disputes. Šalda absolutely does not wish to "reconcile these battles and lock them away" because, on the contrary, he is convinced that "they contribute to polarizing individuals and also generations." He writes: "The Devětsil people can quite happily hunt their enemies in murky waters. Their stance is so petty that they can have success only in illiterate circles, a success — I would say — only in the popular arena." However, Šalda views these disputes from the stance of a neutral, *au dessus de la mêlée*: that is, the serious stance of someone who is judging those who judge. Allow me to add a few comments to his assessment of the conflicts.

The main fault of the seven who in spring expressed their support for a speech against the leadership of the Czechoslovak Communist Party (KSČ) is that they came forward as a group, but in reality they are not a group. To put it better: They came forward at a moment when the party was fighting against an opportunistic ***opposition*** comprised of the party's historical right wing and the Jílek faction. Moreover, they did not come forward with any criticism — because they did not participate in the pre-congress discussion in the party — but rather with a declaration against the party leadership. This declaration was conceived as support for this opposition and it also expressed the stance of this *opposition.* However, ***a large majority of its authors did not go along with this opposition.*** It is true that the ***Communist Party should not exclude criticism. Only*** in periods of direct action, in the explosion of revolution, or in times of serious crisis does it have the right to not admit criticism, and in particular it should not be attacked from outside by those who are not bound by its discipline. If those who signed the declaration of the seven did not go along with the opposition, then it was their duty not to come forward against the party leadership at the moment of serious battles with this opposition. Therefore, we must condemn the declaration of the seven as a "serious error," while not doubting the personal conviction and honesty of these protesting writers. However, soon afterwards this personal conviction and honesty was inevitably put to the test. These protesting writers were communists and revolutionaries; even after their departure from the party they wanted and promised to remain so. Half a year later, Hora, who did not go along with the communist opposition (which is communist only in name), became editor of a social-fascist journal. We can see Seifert in a newspaper that is also "socialist" only in name (*Právo Lidu*), in a newspaper that systematically affronts communism and the Soviet Union. Of course, no one has the right to expect heroism from journalists. However, from ***revolutionaries*** we can perhaps expect a little bit of it, all the more so given that our trust in these writers justified us in hoping. We can do no other than once again to describe the cooperation of revolutionary authors with the social-fascist and bourgeois press as prostitution, which can only be excused by poverty. However, we contend that for a revolutionary the question of material existence is different than for an official with a salary. If we consider the low Czech fees paid for normal production and if we acknowledge a minimum material state relatively higher than the one officially acknowledged, we nevertheless cannot acknowledge attempts to achieve prosperity and a comfortable and cushioned living standard as an existential worry in the case of — a revolutionary. We do not regard any kind of pauperism and asceticism as a duty or commitment of writers or journalists; however, ***a revolutionary must be one made of more resilient stuff and character.*** If he must be prepared for the comfort of prison, then he must also be capable of enduring financial crises and not selling out. But, this has already happened.

In this matter, as a wonderful example, we can point to Stanislav K. Neumann, of whose revolutionary honor there can be no doubt or dispute.

Our disputes with Josef Hora, and in the matter of the state prize also with Vančura, have been, at least from our side, conducted as a political matter and on a political platform. Šalda correctly understands that there is a certain distance between the poetic world of Josef Hora and the world of Poetism, which cannot be ignored or bridged. However, the polemic against Hora was really not about this, and it was Hora who brought it the dispute to the literary pole. In the matter of Vančura this was also about a political moment: We regarded it as incorrect, when a politically engaged writer, who even after his departure from the KSČ wants to remain a communist, accepts a state prize. In order to avoid the possibility of false interpretations, at the same time we stated clearly how highly we esteem Vančura's literary works.

As far as *l'art-pour-l'art* and an absolute *désintéressement* on the part of the artist toward social events, we must once again emphasize that 100 years ago this *l'art-pour-l'art* meant a revolutionary stance; it was an expression of resistance toward the bourgeois world. Today, however, we must fight against this *désintéressement* of artists and scholars. Modern architecture is unthinkable without a clear economic and social stance: Its Marxist orientation and socialist stance toward programs (for instance, housing, family life, urbanism) is a condition of its modernity *sine qua non*. Henri Rousseau or Jan Zrzavý can ignore everything that is happening in social life. However, the "disinterested" type of artist is a type that is old and redundant.

The modern spirit is ***a spirit that does not lose its analytical and revolutionary perspectives when performing its specialist work***. However, it is clear that by adopting this stance we do not accept some erroneous theses about ideological art or about proletarian art and so on. We have never been able to take seriously buildings in the form of a hammer and sickle — such regrettable cases have really occurred — or verses painted in red on the barricades, and just as we have always fought against the vulgar Marxist theses of the *proletkult* and against the proponents of ideological poetry, who have executed Poetism as a grievous bourgeois error, so we must emphasize against the proponents of *désintéressement* that the aesthetic of Poetism is not, as Šalda correctly concludes, thinkable without historical **materialism** and that Constructivist architecture presupposes a precise Marxist evaluation of building programs and ***a conscious socialist orientation of creation***.

A clarification of "today's problems" can be achieved only by detailed sociological analyses. In this matter it is primarily necessary to prevent specialized questions being resolved according to the dogmas of some kind of vulgar Marxism. Today, it is necessary to construct precise scientific theories in the spirit of historical materialism and to at least start preparatory and detailed work on a Marxist theory of art. This is why it is primarily essential to reject the interference of incompetent zealots in specialist matters and to reject ***the superficial application*** of Marxist teachings in specialist and critical work. The zealotry of those who may master the alphabet of Marxism, but who are totally illiterate in matters of art and artistic theory, is already known from earlier cases: I had the opportunity to see a manuscript of a discussion piece in which the theory of Constructivism was criticized from a Marxist perspective, and this article — in a specialized matter, a matter of architecture — displayed a massive degree of specialist illiteracy. These people, who are perhaps even aware of their specialist ignorance but still dare to put forward a Marxist interpretation of these specialist problems (that is, to **deductively** apply a certain theory to certain cases — which is dogmatic and school-level) must be shouted down, because otherwise the long buried errors of "social and proletarian art" will occur once again — and once again a Marxist science of art will fail to be constructed.

Jindřich Štyrský: I Was Not, and Am Not, an Organized Communist...

Before the publication of the last issue of *Tvorba*, but regretably after the deadline, Jindřich Štyrský sent to the editors a "Declaration," which I am publishing. He is not yet acquainted with Teige's article and is reacting only to Sekanina's article. He is attemping to clarify what he said with such sincere verve in the 3rd number of *Odeon*. Because there is a possibility that this Declaration will contribute to clarifying matters — not so much within the generation, but rather to clarifying the relationships in the generation and the state of the generation — I am including it rightly in this discussion page. (All the highlighted passages were highlighted by Štyrský himself.)

(jef [Julius Fučík])

I was not, and am not, an organized communist, just like many others from my closest milieu, for instance Nezval, Teige, and others. I have never worked either in the working-class movement or in the Communist Party — much less, however, in any other party. This was, and is, known about me. For example, Julius Fučík certainly knew this, when in the 13th number of *Tvorba* he printed my article "A Generation on Two Chairs." ***My stance toward communism was, and is, positive.***

I am surprised that my article from the 3rd number is being interpreted as a betrayal and an attempt to go over into the reactionary camp. My entire article in the 3rd number of *Odeon* was aimed against squalor and kitsch, whether they appear on the right or the left side, and naturally it must also have offended those who provide cover for this squalor and kitsch. That is why I am forced to name Karel Teige.

I insist that the thorough merging of political revolutionary spirits with revolutionary spirits in art is gross nonsense. This was also explained in the 22nd number of *Tvorba* by Ivan Sekanina, who in essence said that this merging benefits neither revolution, nor poetry.

My opinion that revolution is misappropriating poets was badly formulated (judging by how it has been interpreted). What I meant to say was that poets are being misappropriated by so-called revolutionary critics of the type and character of Karel Teige.

However, I did not at all mean to say that a poet should not have a stance on social questions and political events, but this is certainly not an active stance. I, for example, am a member of the Left Front, because with the entire weight of my modern work I belong there and because it does not require me to engage in ***active*** politics.

When I wrote that a real poet always stands to one side of hunts and political machinations, then I think that I am also correct in this. Nevertheless, I contend rightly that revolution and the liberation movement is something more than political machinations. When I used words about loudmouths from political meetings, I should have expressed myself more precisely that those whom I am calling loudmouths are those who make use of their political influence and persuasion when it suits them but who remain silent when it is case of their friends.

I do not intend to allow myself to be pressured to some place where many in my generation have already found themselves, or where many of them are on the best path towards, while Karel Teige remains absolutely silent (and this is precisely what I reproach him for the most) — and neither will anyone succeed in pressurizing me.

Jindřich Štyrský: Cozy Nook of a Generation 3

In the third issue of *Odeon* I published an article that was interpreted in a certain group of leftist cultural workers as a kind of acrobatics. Some also attributed to it a political tendentiousness — and a reactionary one — and there even appeared one excellent person (Karel Teige) who made use of my article as a pretext for emptying out his sack of bile full of personal grudges (see *Tvorba* no. 23 and no. 24). I regard it as crazy and superfluous to engage in polemics with articles of such a type and such a level. I can only express my regret about the behavior of Karel Teige, who has recently strayed into the realm of ridiculousness. To my article in the last edition of *Odeon* I appended a few words which I published in *Tvorba* no. 24 and which at the same time I regard as a reply to Julius Fučík and the gentlemen Ivan Sekanina and Ladislav Štoll.

From both of Teige's pieces in *Tvorba* his chaotic mode of thinking is evident, even though it is clear that he is not concerned with ideological and fundamental matters, but rather with the "matter of Jindřich Štyrský."

I am not in any way personally biased against Teige. I concede that he has made indubitable contributions to modern culture in the Czechoslovak Republic, although it is as clear as the sun that **his activity has never been creative**, but always of a compilatory type, and that his entire body of work is nothing other than a compilation of other people's knowledge, other people's theories, other people's artistic methods, other people's work, and so on.

Karel Teige, once upon a time a bearer of light, when the country was desolate, today himself feels his own superfluousness. Today he no longer brings anything new, and this is the source of his hysteria and extreme spinsterhood. Teige's greatness consisted in the fact that he was capable of quickly assimilating other people's thoughts and the results of other people's work and that he doled out the wealth — albeit paradoxical and problematic — which he had acquired in this way in such large handfuls that in the end there was none of it left for Teige himself. It is in this that I see his personal tragedy and failure. The example of Teige could serve to demonstrate what I wrote about the generation (*Odeon* 1): **that it speaks a lot about adventures and eccentricities; however, in reality there has never been a more peaceable herd. It contends that it contains the entire world, but it is not even capable of ascertaining its own volume. Already from the start its course has been linked with the extinction of the foreign joys on which it has been grazing. — The ridiculousness of their lives lies in the fact that their real value does not reach that of their reputations.**

The personality of K. Teige is not in essence as complicated as he wants to persuade us with his written expressions. His activities from the very beginning have been merely a denial of himself, and that is why today Teige is nothing other than his own unsuccessful caricature. **We can observe all the things that K. Teige wanted to be**: a poet, an author, a journalist, a film-maker, a painter, a caricaturist, a literary and artistic critic, an architect, an editor, a musical and film aesthetician, a typographer, an advertising cartoonist, and so on and so on. **And let us look at what K. Teige is today**.

His literary and artistic statements have been a series of absurd contradictions. Teige declared a renaissance of realistic Primitivism, announced a people's collective art, and immediately after that reoriented towards Cubism, but wrote a monograph about Zrzavý. After that, disgusted with everything, he declared the liquidation of art, while holding Ehrenburg's coattails. In this period he started to produce photomontages inspired by Rodchenko, which he called pictorial poems, he signed manifestos of Poetism, in addition to all that he flirted mildly with Dadism, and declared the victory of Constructivism. And so on and so on.

I have drawn this portrait of our little know-it-all, while avoiding being personal, and with no small regret in view of his better past.

For a long while now K. Teige has been calling me "a non-producing painter." I would reproach myself with a lack of consideration towards him, if I was not to invite him to my exhibition (in February 1930 at Aventinum). I hope that he will like my work, as he always has hitherto. However, by this I expose myself to the risk that he will then be able to call me a non-producing literary author for a long time.

When I wrote the first **Cozy Nook of a Generation**, K. Teige *berated me bloodthirstily for failing to name individuals and not pointing at them* with my finger, and today he is probably going to berate me once again, even though I have made an exception only on his account.

For its next number *Odeon* is planning a range of articles on a **purely ideological and fundamental** basis and in future it is not going to concern itself with the problems and fates of individuals, leaving these personal clashes to weeklies such as for example *Tvorba*, where it seems they will be constantly on the agenda for a long time to come.

Josef Čapek: Crisis of Characters

This is the title of a piece in the communist avant-garde magazine *Tvorba* in which the magazine grievously reproaches writers and journalists Josef Hora and Jaroslav Seifert for going over to non-communist newspapers so as to continue to make a living from literature after their rebellion against the politburo. Apparently, demands *Tvorba*, for their rebellion they should suffer material deprivation — that is, we should understand, die of hunger while tearing out their hair over their disobedience toward the supreme politburo, which would thus punish them more strictly than the Old Testament Jehovah. Of course, it is all too easy for *Tvorba* to write some such thing. It is a magazine so overflowing with avant-garde pride that they quite forget here about the ephemerality of all such avant-garde and generational pride. In the meanwhile, we can see that the poetic capabilities of Hora, and let us hope Seifert, have not been damaged in any way by the fact that they are no longer marching along with the politburo. Josef Hora has forever succeeded in preserving in himself the poet that he became at a not all together avant-garde age, and we would like to believe that Seifert will also succeed in the end, even as he proceeds through life and all its crises. It is superfluous, and primarily not very far-sighted, when an organ of such a young generation talks about a crisis of characters. Does not the thought occur to anyone about where Vítězslav Nezval, Karel Teige, Adolf Hoffmeister, and those others — people from a generation that is precisely providing a picture of a very sudden and surprising splintering and disintegration — will find themselves in five, 10 or 15 years? There have already been more generations in the world than this one, and the fate of all of them has been that the generation has split up and dispersed — all too surprisingly, paradoxically, and sometimes even tragicomically — in all kinds of directions, to prominence and then again to insignificance, and to various sides where no one would have expected to find them, least of all the generation itself. A crisis of characters? Yes, this will certainly happen, and avant-garde *Tvorba* should expect it in the future — with very few proud feelings — precisely in its own ranks.

Kurt Konrad: Manifesto of the Left Front

"An Intellectual Against Revolution" was how Emanuel Berl entitled the most important chapter of his pamphlet "Mort de la pensée bourgeoise" (Death to Bourgeois Thought). The topic of this chapter is the nonconformism (non-identification) of the intellectual with bourgeois culture. A new name: an intellectual above the classes. More than at any other time, this question has become the center of literary — often excessively literary — discussion. The conflict between two worlds, which already today is heading towards a final struggle, confronts the intellectual with an unavoidable question of crucial living importance: whether to proceed toward his demise in the system of declining capitalism quietly, passively — even if under the enterprise of the "left opposition" — or to direct his creative energy, expanded in a real combative opposition, against this system together with the revolutionary proletariat. Not merely by opposition (Berl foundered with this stance), but also constructively: for the dictatorship of the proletariat.

Berl was courageous. He comprehended the complete hopelessness of "nonconformism at any cost" and, in spite of all intellectual solitude, he puts forward additionally the suicidal requirement that criticism should not submit itself to any eventual consequence possibly flowing from this criticism. In other words, criticism without any definite aim, but merely with a negative, nonconformist stance against bourgeois thought.

All this because Berl — in spite of his often surprisingly dialectical insights — remained at core an anarchist. He remains an anarchist because he always views machines through the eyes of an opponent of machines and fails to uncover in them a powerful instrument of planned construction, and also because he cannot understand the core of current-day rationalization and standardization: the desperate attempt of capitalism to halt its own collapse. And so "L'homme contre la pensée bourgeoise" — the human being ***against*** bourgeois thought — becomes Berl's ideal. But **for whom**?

The agony of bourgeois culture is demonstrated by thousands of such intellectuals. This is an expression of anarchistic convulsions, an expression of internal degeneration, which as a kind of superstructure is causing the suicidal mood about the extinction of Western Europe, which sees nothing of the power standing in opposition, namely the proletariat, and which considers the extinction of capitalism as outright extinction. This inactivity of a supposedly combative persistence "above classes" is a mark of agony. It is also a mark of the decline of the intelligentsia because it does not have a real revolutionary stance, a stance providing a solution.

After all, what is the significance of those formal world revolutions from -ism to -ism, from Impressionism to Expressionism and from Cubism to Constructivism, of those "revolutions" that are often dissected by intellectuals as a kind of underground revolutionism — in comparison with the historical task of the revolutionary proletariat? What is the measure of the nonconformist "revolutionary spirit" compared to the revolutionary and reconstructionary aims of the working class?

If Berl, Karl Kraus, and F. X. Šalda, whose nonconformism reaches precisely the point where the revolutionary activity of the proletariat begins, stand on one side, then also standing not far from them are those who have reached an awareness of the proletariat but have gone no further. These include those people who have well grasped that this is a case of more than revolt, that this is a case of revolution, but also those people who have only half understood historical materialism by placing the main emphasis on the creation of progressive forms and, enticed by the tendencies of their specific section of work, by emphasizing form over content.

These are people like Teige who always speak so much about the ***social*** function of housing, even though this has long since been a case of ***class*** function — Comrade Teige, bourgeois sociologists have also reached the stage of "social functions," and precisely this is a mark of reformist ideology; and also people like Nezval, Seifert, Hora, and Halas for whom the poetry of Apollinaire and Rimbaud — so distant from the collective — still represents the culmination of all poetry; and finally people like Štyrský for whom luminous forms — here the circle back to Teige is completed — of the distributed light spectrum seem to be the only force, the only incendiary fact, of our current period.

These are those intellectuals who wish to build a new world from the new forms emerging everywhere in the period of declining capitalism — in pioneering fashion, early like flowers from mud — without destroying the old content, without creating the preconditions for a new content. Rationalization and the "cooperation of modern energies" do not yet constitute historical progress. Much less revolution. Revolution is primarily a new class-based content, the forms of which will emerge during the dictatorship of the proletariat. It is the dictatorship of the proletariat that is on the order of the day and not for a long time yet a socialist society.

Therefore, there is no other difference between the Constructivism of Mendelsohn, Loos, and Teige and the Constructivism of Tatlin, Ginzburg, and Lissitzky — even though the last of these arrived at a really revolutionary Constructivism only after a long period of formalist oscillation — than the difference between the standardization office of the metals industry of imperial Germany and the highest council for planned economy in the Soviet Union. The entire difference between capitalist rationalization and socialist rationalization. The entire difference between bourgeois and proletarian class content.

However, the main line of the manifesto with which the Left Front is appealing to the public is precisely what it should not be if the stance of the Left Front is really supposed to be a front of **revolutionary** intellectuals. Even the social fascism of Masaryk, Peroutka, and Hampl is "leftist" in the sense of a class-conscious bourgeoisie. The difference between the leftism of this manifesto and the leftism of Masaryk is only a difference in nuances. Masaryk also does not identify with the fascist *numerus clausus*, but he does identify with the social-fascist economic *numerus clausus*; Masaryk also identifies with every clumsy, general shouting of the intentions of financial capital. Therefore, in all circumstances it is necessary to pose the question that not only contains nonconformism, but also clearly states with whom we are conforming.

Because we have yet another expression for "new rational social-economic and civilizational balance," and this expression is "economic democracy"; because social fascism as the vanguard of financial capital is fighting against "liberalist" culture and in favor of a fascist dictatorship and culture "better" corresponding to monopoly capitalism; and because for a long time already nobody is fooled by a materialist worldview: Materialism without revolutionary dialectics is more than "reactionariness," more than "conservatism and reaction." "A connection with other cultural and social forms of work" creates just as few revolutionary perspectives as the fight against liberalist culture, which today is merely a quixotic fight against windmills.

A Left Front? Yes! But such a one as is capable of going ***beyond*** sterile nonconformism.

(Translated [from the German] by Marko.)

Bedřich Václavek: On the Marxist Theory of Art

In the discussion in the ranks of the left, the question of Marxist criteria in artistic criticism and theory has been raised, especially after what our avant-garde has done for building up these criteria. Julius Fučík wrote (in the 22nd issue of *Tvorba*) that "the artistic criticism of our young generation regards itself as Marxist, but it is not." When, Karel Teige in the 23rd issue of the same journal (in the discussion section) then asserted that a crisis of criteria is one of the causes of the crisis of literary criticism (he adds: "Literary and theater criticism cannot today rely on such reliable criteria as, for instance, the criticism of architecture"), he was sharply criticized by Fučík, who argued that a crisis of criteria could not possibly even exist for a Marxist! Fučík further asserts that Teige and others "are suffering from absolute confusion in questions that they should be resolving as theoretical specialists in the artistic sector. It is simply becoming apparent that in this direction nothing has been done." And Fučík pronounces this nothing as the most serious and sensational reproach to avant-garde criticism.

These words of Fučík's could evoke some such picture as this: Marxism has given firm, unambiguous criteria for the evaluation of art, and these criteria cannot undergo any crisis. It is Teige's fault, or the fault of others, if they have failed to adopt these criteria, which apparently are clear for the informed or in other countries.

There is nothing more distorted, nothing provides better evidence of limited thinking and being uninformed, and finally nothing reeks more of ***vulgar Marxism*** than such claims. Therefore, I will attempt to briefly sketch the true state of the question concerning Marxist criteria in the theory and criticism of art. I have thoroughly studied an extensive literature on this question which I have collected over several years. At present, I am unable to give a definitive assessment only of the Russian literature on this matter, because only a part of this literature has been available to me. I can emphasize, as I have already written in *Tvorba*, that no less has been done in this field here in Czechoslovakia than elsewhere, but that all together little has been done in all countries. *There is no **Marxist theory and criticism of art (in the sense of a constructed system) with firm, unambiguous criteria**.* Precisely because in this direction the work using the method of historical materialism, as carried out by Marx, Engels, Lenin, and others for understanding political-economic, social, and political developments, has not so far been carried out. The attention of Marxist sociologists has always been concentrated on the driving forces of social development and on fields currently decisive in the fight for a new society. So far, cultural fields, in particular the field of art, have been researched insufficiently by artistic specialists using this method. Therefore, it is quite self-evident (and this is not the personal fault of Teige, as Fučík reproaches him with his invective tone) that our left is clearer in political questions than in artistic questions. This is simply the international state of affairs. Which, of course, does not mean that we should not want, attempt, and be able to change anything in this state of affairs.

Today, it is clear to a Marxist critic what he must say if he is supposed to evaluate the ideology of a work of art. He is capable of explaining, from social causes, the choice of topic, the artist's relationship to this topic, and the artist's class and professional stance. He can demonstrate the dependency of the artist and artistic life on economic life; he can reveal the class use — or misuse, as the case may be — of art. However, let us not be misled by this: ***The conclusions that he then pronounces are macroeconomic, political, social-psychological, and so on. These can be of assistance in constructing a Marxist theory of art, but they are not however yet a Marxist theory of art itself.*** As soon as we proceed to those questions that have so far been little analyzed and concerning which there are the greatest disagreements among Marxist theoreticians and critics — such as, the fundamental clarification of the phenomenon of art; its function in various periods; the causes of structural changes in art in various periods of social development; the connection between the development of art and the development of societal labor, in particular the division and forms of this labor; the relationship between the development of art and the development of technology; the forms of the production of art; and the causes of changes in form — then we are really in a state of uncertainty, simply because we are here in an unresearched field in which opinions are unstable. It is really terrible and sometimes comic how the opinions of people who are otherwise well orientated in Marxism (in politics and political economy) part ways here. Anyone who is at least slightly acquainted with this matter could give dozens of examples here. This will only change when the corresponding work has been performed. It would be a major error (which sin in evaluating art is committed by those Marxists who are exclusively politically oriented and illiterate in expertise) to think, for instance, that ideology is everything in the evaluation of a work of art and that there is no need to care about anything else: This stance has already been rejected many times here in Czechoslovakia. It would also be a major error to describe matters as though today everything has already been properly examined and clarified. It is not, therefore, an assertion in contradiction of Marxism when Teige speaks about a crisis of criteria. Marxist opinions on art have undergone a significant development up to today: They have undergone fluctuations along with the general development of Marxist theory, while on the other hand they have also been influenced by contemporaneous opinions, such as the individual "directions" of modern art. Today also, when work is again beginning on a Marxist theory of art, it is undergoing this lively development. The crisis of criteria in current-day criticism is, therefore, primarily a crisis of antiquated criteria, and Marxism has contributed to a significant extent to causing this crisis. In order for this crisis to be transcended by new Marxist criteria a major theoretical work must first be performed, which of course is a suitable task for revolutionary specialist intellectuals. However, let us not be mistaken that everything can be rectified by some well-intentioned journalists or by a few articles. This can be a lifelong work for an individual or a work lasting many years for a group working collectively on the matter. Only through a range of works, their comparison, and a constant critical monitoring of the relevant literature can new criteria — reinforced and scrutinized precisely through Marxist methodology — be established.

Abroad, it is mainly the Soviet Union where work in this field is being done. Endeavors to perform this work are also essential in Western countries (because the relationship towards art is different under a dictatorship of the proletariat than under capitalism, and all this will necessarily make itself apparent in the results of research). Here in Czechoslovakia this work has been held back by a lack of specialists engaged in it and mainly by a lack of possibilities for publication. Without critical reactions from others it is difficult to work successfully in any field. Nevertheless, a certain amount of work, by no means insignificant, ***has been performed here and is still being performed***, and therefore Fučík's claim that "the artistic criticism of our young generation regards itself as Marxist, but it is not" must be circumscribed in its baseless certainty and placed in the correct context just as resolutely as some other claims of Fučík's attack must be restricted. Since the time when *Devětsil* engaged in polemics with *Dav* and the avant-garde of the time and refuted the vulgar Marxist myths and errors of the proletkult, there has not been a lot of discussion about questions of the Marxist theory of art, ***which does not of course mean that no work has been performed in this field***. A critical revision of what has been created here in Czechoslovakia in this field and a discussion of the results so far and of current questions will be beneficial for theory, but only if naive, superficial, unproven, and uninformed "opinions" are excluded from it — in short, if it is really conducted with the materiality and specialist precision that the solution of such significant questions deserves and requires.

Arnošt Vaněček: On Words

The flow of words that is developing in front of our ears is communicating new accents of a new period. The metal grooves are unable to convey the protraction of old words and names with the usual patience and are requiring a new vocabulary of expressions and concepts. The mechanical influence of machines is breaking off the superfluous ornaments of living forms just as fast as it is breaking off protracted syllables.

Words that have not come directly from the soil of the language of necessary speech, words that have been invented by language correctors and purifiers, are fading away, cut down by sharp teeth and lips like artificial fruits from wax that were supposed to decorate small plates painted in the tricolor of nationalist ornament. Meanwhile, on the tips of tongues new words have been curling up — words that are prepared for good digestion and for seeping into almost empty veins. On the scaffolding of buildings, in the casting shafts of foundries, in steelworks, in offices, and in the verses of poets. The commission for the construction of specialist expressions has struggled in vain against youthful words that have been churned out by the chiefs of state offices out of pure joy for bureaucratic creation. Illegitimate offspring, even if not recognized by the law, therefore at least by the sovereign diction of regulations. However, a new word, which flashes here and there from the speech with a spark, needs neither a commission, nor caution.

They are created by everyone who produces new parts for automobiles, who writes words for advertisements, just as by those who create new poems and prose.

It cannot be claimed that the current state of the language is already sufficient to express any kind of thought and any kind of object. And the ash of old words has not yet started to flare up in the flames of today's language.

With the dying out of individual craft production some words have disappeared from the living language to remain only as a junk-shop decoration of historical novels. In his paper on the fundamental forms of manufacturing Karl Marx writes: "Formerly the individual work of a Nuremberg artificer, the watch has been transformed into the social product of an immense number of detail laborers, such as mainspring makers, dial makers, spiral spring makers, jeweled hole makers, ruby lever makers, hand makers, case makers, screw makers, gilders, with numerous subdivisions, such as wheel makers (brass and steel separate), pin makers, movement makers, *acheveur de pignon* (fixes the wheels on the axles, polishes the facets, &c.), pivot makers, *planteur de finissage* (puts the wheels and springs in the works), *finisseur de barillet* (cuts teeth in the wheels, makes the holes of the right size, &c.), escapement makers, cylinder makers for cylinder escapements, escapement wheel makers, balance wheel makers,"[1] and so on.

The continuation of the transformation of manual production into factory production will mean that in future we will count among words that have died out not only, for instance, "blacksmith" and "carpenter," but also the words "cobbler" and "tailor."

In his study in defense of new words Robert Sage writes with justification: "Give a classical writer the task of describing a radio apparatus, an automobile, a psychoanalytical process, a talking film, or a modern city in the language of Steele and Addison. It will be no less clumsy than an American tourist trying to order breakfast in Siberia."

"It can be objected that the vocabulary that is lacking is mainly technical, and that technical expressions can be created for those who need them, and this without spoiling the written or "correctly' spoken language. I strongly disagree with this, because it is becoming more and more necessary to integrate a greater amount of technology and science into our general experience. Even more important is the fact that our mentality is immeasurably different from that of the 18th century, when monarchical grandness still ruled over everything, when Darwin and Freud had still not been born, when the prospects of steam power, electricity, and combustible materials were unknown."

Here in Czechoslovakia the greatest apparent disparity now is in the usage of words and sentence constructions in the large quantity of translations under the baleful influence of Vrchlický and the school of Parnassian epigones, who have translated — and continue to translate to this day — the clear words of poets into ostentatious and grandiloquent baubles, contorted by pseudo-poetic fantasy. They have made great poets like Keats, Shelley, Rossetti, and Blake, for example, boring and repellent.

A shift to factuality, bringing a radiance of imagination, was brought about by a revolution in the selection of words and primarily by the works of Halas, Nezval, Seifert, Vančura, and Závada.

1 Karl Marx, *Capital*, Vol 1, Chap. 14, section 3; see: https://www.marxists.org/archive/marx/works/1867-c1/ch14.htm#S3.

And new words are waiting to be poured into molds in which they will shine on other words. And many modern experiences, phenomena, and feelings are waiting to be expressed in words that are still shy and almost unknown, floating above reality. And once these words fall to land, finally spoken and written, then they will break through the textbook laws of grammar, those old bones whose limbs already need to be replaced.

Ladislav Štoll: People in a "Laboratory"

Recently, in the theoretical thinking of Marxists writing in Czech it has been possible to notice an intensified effort to penetrate deeper into the field of culture, which up until now has been been completely neglected, while in the field of political-economic theory all is completely clear and development in this direction continues marked by a happy unity of word and deed.

This discrepancy, which is mentioned in an open letter to the International Bureau of Proletarian Revolutionary Literature, is very transparent on our section of the class line, even though elsewhere, especially in the Soviet Union and Germany, it has been overcome with a rich progressive literature of discovery.

This contemporary campaign of theoreticians of dialectical materialism in the field of culture, this incursion into the higher sphere of the superstructure, is taking place — it can be roughly said — from two sides. One side is marching from the direction of real life, from the experience of the class struggle, from the sphere of issues of political economy, where the relations are already clear. Some of those from this group, in their firm conviction of a causal connection between the economic structure of society and its superstructure, have often succumbed to the allurements of superficial, linear relationships and are attempting to explain the origin of assonance in verse from the economic situation. For these incompetent, bold excursions, they have received the designation of vulgar Marxists from those who have an incomparably greater cultural-historical knowledge and a better overview of artistic forms throughout history, but who do not however come from the direction of real life, but rather from a sterile world of an idealist theory of art and for whom the method of Marxist thinking has not penetrated into their veins.

I have in mind various questions which have been the subject of discussion in recent days. I do not know how to answer these questions, and neither do I want to. I merely want to place them in a certain mutual relationship in order to ensure that at least a direction of orientation flows from them in the confusion that currently reigns. In my opinion, the main cause of the difficulties and confusedness of Marxist theoreticians in the field of culture are unexplored places in the discipline of social psychology. I will quote, as cited by Urx, Plekhanov's formula aptly summing up the opinions of Marx and Engels on the connections between the economic basis and the superstructure:

1. The state of productive forces.
2. The economic relations conditioned on this state.
3. The social political order, which arises on a given economic basis.
4. The psychology of the social person, which is partly conditioned indirectly on the economy and partly on the entire social political order which arises above this economy.
5. Various ideologies in which the features of this psychology are reflected.

This formulation makes quite evident the direction of the path along which we must finally pursue questions of pure ideology — questions of artistic forms — to their roots. This is evidently a case here of a transition of that sphere of the problems that Plekhanov in his formulation designated number 4. It is a case of ***the psychology of the social person***. Concretely, in my opinion, this means perhaps the following: Hitherto Marxists have shown us society and the person within it with all his external dependencies and relationships. Now they are finally realizing the necessity of showing society in a person in order to scientifically ascertain those processes in the internal life of an individual that are conditioned on the development of productive forces and on the historical procession of social changes. This is a case of demonstrating how the forces of the laws determining the development of the whole social entity are reflected, by means of psycho-physiological attire, in the natural characteristics of individuals, in their behavior, feelings, habits, decisions, thoughts, and ideologies.

In my opinion, this is the work with which we are historically confronted right now and which will not be resolved by some discussions or by Marxist-Freudian complications. This is work in which primarily revolutionary artists must participate — new people who, through a high intellect, have essentially transcended within themselves the old social person of capitalism; new people who are consciously undergoing a process of transformation and are becoming the people of tomorrow's social order not only in their ideology, but also in their psychological presumptions; new people within whom, under the strain of intellect, new feelings and capabilities are liberated which up until now have been stifled in entire complexes by a basic feeling of private ownership and by the psychological and physical forces which necessarily follow from this existential principle of a person in a capitalist society.

And because a "revolution of abstract thinking," as Deborin says, "presumes the same revolution of sensory consciousness," it can rightly be expected that it will be the senses — the sight — of these new people, their purely class psyche, that will give birth to a new art, whose seeds are arising today as products of complicated processes of the struggle between old and new forms of social consciousness.

The issue now is where we should search for these new elements — these elements of the next artistic forms — in contemporary artistic production. It is interesting to compare some replies to this question. The open letter of revolutionary writers, assembled at the international conference of revolutionary proletarian literature in Kharkov, replies in this way:

> "Revolutionary literature in Czechoslovakia cannot continue to restrict itself to high literary creation and to cooperation with fellow travelers, but should primarily focus on **work involving the masses** (my emphasis). This means devoting attention to working-class creators and peasant creators, if they are developing toward literature, and to any writers from the working class at all... It was a leftist deviation when reportage and journalism were declared as the only verbal works suitable for revolution."

In his book *Poesie v rozpacích* [Poetry in Discomfort] Bedřich Václavek says something entirely different:

> "... as a consequence of the escalating division of labor and the differentiation of functions flowing from this, art has become entirely divided from utilitarian production... A return to craftsmanship from machine production is impossible... In a period of the ultimate division of labor and a diverging differentiation of tasks, functions, and forms, all art — even that which is beginning to be built on the basis of machine production — stands apart from other, productive forms of work. Art ***is something different from work*** (! my emphasis). It has differentiated itself from other social functions and come to exist of itself and for its own sake; it ***has become an aim, and not a means***. Art in the period of imperialism has **no other tasks than aesthetic ones** (my emphasis)."

No less interesting is the reply of Karel Teige (with which Václavek identifies in the book previously mentioned):

> "Art does not try to change the world and influence practical life."

From the replies given here by theoreticians who profess allegiance to the flag of the revolutionary proletariat, it is evident at first sight what a confusion of opinion reigns in questions concerning the sense of art and its future forms.

However, in my opinion, one thing can be said with certainty, and this is that the theoretical replies of Teige and Václavek are in stark contradiction with the teaching of dialectical materialism.

In my opinion, the incorrectness of Teige's and Václavek's opinions consists in the fact that both have simplified the social-historical process to two concurrent historical processes: the technological process and the development of artistic forms, between which there is only some kind of direct mechanical dependence. The sphere of social psychology and the complicated dialectical relations expressed through this psychology have completely escaped the attention of both these theoreticians. This is why, in the case of Teige and Václavek, we meet so often their favorite contention that artistic forms are directly conditioned on the state of productive forces. For example, in his book *Poetry in Discomfort* Václavek says:

> "Proceeding to the characteristics of art under imperialism, we must primarily perceive the relationship of art to technology, given that the enormous progress in working technologies is the most important phenomenon influencing art. A factor is appearing here in history that has never been present in any culture up until this period: **a revolutionary factor — the machine. And this factor is changing the "age-old" and "unchangeable" state in the arts** (my emphasis). By its economic predominance, enormously developed machine technology is destroying the last remnants of craft capabilities. Through the division of labor, manufacturing has already torn apart the original connection between a personality and a piece of work and has depersonalized work... **The personal inheritance of craft capabilities has continued to live only in a free artist** (my emphasis), who however was only able to produce certain forms, to work in fields that have not so far been successfully mechanized... The more that technology develops, the more art changes into "pure art,' which has a solely emotive function."

These opinions could also be signed without reservation by Karel Teige. Apart from that, it is sufficient to open the first issue of Nezval's *Zvěrokruh* and there in Teige's article "Poem, World, Human Being" [Báseň, svět, člověk] we can read that:

> "The theory of art that we have called Poetism is based primarily on the recognition that the inherited artistic forms, which were conditioned on craftsmanship, are already dead in our period."

Or, in another place in the same article:

> "When, after steam and electricity, after the sewing machine and the typewriter, a 'machine that paints' — a photographic and cinematic camera — has been invented — when the sphaerophon[1], the radiophone, and the television have been invented, then it is necessary to forswear the traditional methods of classification and the categories of idealist aesthetics."

1 Instrument invented by German music theorist Joerg Mager, see https://120years.net/the-electrophon-spharaphon-partiturophon-and-the-kaleidophon1921-1930/

I think these examples are sufficient evidence to convict both Marxist theoreticians of mechanicism, and that of an actually quite vulgar mechanicism. After all, here purely technological questions, delicate problems of the categories of idealist aesthetics, are placed — in an almost naive way — alongside questions about the state of productive forces. Let us recall the previously cited formulation of Plekhanov. Where have all those rich, complicated dialectical social-psychological processes disappeared? Where has the class struggle, which conditions so powerfully the psychology of the social person and which imparts to his ideology a supra-personal class aspect through the dialectical means of this psychology, disappeared?

Teige, as it seems, probably under the influence of Deborin's deliberations in his *Tasks of Marxists on the Theoretical Front*, has already become vaguely aware of this deficiency and is trying to confront it by incorporating Freud's closed system of psychoanalysis — as an accepted given system — into the teachings of his mechanistic system. He remains further dedicated to his method. Not only does he fail to fully appreciate the social elements of psychology, but once again he does not pay any attention to them at all and replaces them with pure biology:

> "the reconstruction of production to mechanical large-scale industry, the enormous progress of technology, and the separation of artistic crafts from industrial life have produced the technical and material preconditions for the creation of a new poetry..., a poetry that is a new grouping of aesthetic qualities, constructed from new methods and from new materials, and that is searching for its new consumer, a new viewer and listener, a new human being, in order to quench his burning thirst with lyricism and to richly endow all his senses and his sensibility with new vital energies and intensities. The methods of this poetry are being tested through extensive laboratory work. The exact results of the sciences — biology, psychology, physiology, sociology, optics, chemistry, acoustics, and so on — have provided the foundations of a new theory of art. Even though current biological-psychological knowledge of the processes that contain the entire essence of poetic productivity and emotionality is not sufficient, **as a reply to the question of the sense of art** (my emphasis) and the essence of poetic creativity we can at least put forward the hypothesis postulating a unitary productive human instinct." [Karel Teige, "Poem, World, Human Being"]

I think that it is not too difficult to ascertain crude methodological seams under the artificial deposit of expressions from the modern vocabulary of science.

Where, however, does this failure to understand the social-psychological conditionality of artistic creation, this ignoring of class psychology, lead? To the most reactionary conception of idealist dualism.

This is exactly what it is when Bedřich Václavek writes that:

> "An artist is concerned with evoking emotion; a revolutionary is concerned with achieving a new socialist society. Mixing up the two benefits neither art, nor revolution."

Or when Teige even writes this:

> "In the isolation of art from life, from society, and from production, the elements of the new poetry arose... in an isolation that gave artistic creation a purity of the laboratory and the atelier."

Is this not the old idealist conception? The only new thing about it is that the holy "Parnassus" has been replaced by a "laboratory" or an "atelier." Are not the old idealist conceptual structures being painted over here with the terminology of scientific vocabulary? Are they not actually talking here merely about ***the means of scientific analysis*** where they should actually be really analyzing? Where they should be scientifically analyzing those processes in the internal life of an individual which are conditioned on the forces of the laws governing the development of the social entity, which give a living content to his characteristics, instincts, and empty biological forms? Which are reflected in his social consciousness, in his ideology, and even in his — ***poetry***? "***Social relations determine not only the forms of consciousness, but also the forms of feeling***," says Deborin.

However, there can be no dispute that it is much more comfortable to shut "pure poetry" up in a laboratory according to Teige's recipe, leave it there to crystallize in isolation, and wait until it rediscovers its lost contact with life "at the highest degree of the development of poetry and society" than to admit to the reserved individualistic subjectivism of the "aristocrat of feelings" and to demonstrate the social-psychological conditionality of this old degree of social consciousness whose class-based living contents have long ago been exhausted by naturalism. This old degree of social consciousness, not finding any new class-based living content, is condemned to mere intellectual formalist speculation with -isms, including Poetism, which are nothing other than class defeatism, nonconformism — hideaways in the grenade funnels on the battlefield of the class war.

However, the new revolutionary art neither plays with "elementary materials," nor crystallizes in the isolation of a laboratory, nor waits for a higher degree of development, nor puts political editorials into verse, but rather it seeks in the midst of life in the class struggle the elements of new living contents, which it then returns back to society by making easier for a social person the internal process of his transformation, filling his chest with the content of the new proletarian class consciousness, precisely as realist naturalism did when it furnished a historical and class consciousness for bourgeois society. However, this is not to say that a period of proletarian naturalism is arriving. To deliberate about whether there is going to be a proletarian naturalism or "pure art," as Václavek and also Urx do, is to think in a grossly fetishistic way. The new contents of revolutionary art presuppose new points of view and new insights, of which the spontaneous product is form — that invention which is the subject of a thousand influences from life and tradition. Why, then, make use of the museum designation of naturalism? Why renew the coating of an old conceptual structure? This is also certainly not the task of Marxist criticism.

I said at the beginning of this article that the main cause of the confusedness on the part of theoreticians of dialectical materialism are unexplored places in the discipline of social psychology. I said that it is necessary to analyze the processes in the internal life of an individual that are conditioned on the historical changes of the social structure. It is clear that this is not going to be possible without making use of findings of psychoanalysis. However, this means transforming the methodology of psychoanalysis from its foundation, and not merely compiling its rules.

It is certain that one of the most important tasks when examining this process of the creation of an ideology in a human mind will be to divert our attention to the childhood of a social person. In this way it will be possible to show how, through the structure of the family — which is a world that is directly subjected to deformations caused by the methods of productive forces and by changes in economic relations —, how through this world of the family the economic and social structure is imparted into the consciousness and subconsciousness of the emerging social person. What a difference there is, for instance, between the antagonistic bourgeois family, where the wife is the private servant of her husband, where the whole family serves their lawful breadwinner, and a proletarian family, where the wife under the pressure of brutal industrial rationalization has ceased to be a private servant of her family and, engaged in the productive process alongside her husband, has become his comrade. How absolutely different are the psychological climates represented by these two households, in which poets gather their decisive experiences and where a poet's consciousness and subconsciousness is formed. Class morality forces itself into the poet's experiences, thus contributing to his creative fund, in which his relationship to his parents and the mutual relationship between his parents give him the key to understanding social coexistence, the key to his worldview.

I know well that this perfunctory formulation overestimates the social-psychological impact of family upbringing compared to the large number of other corrective social influences. However, I am not concerned with its evaluation, but rather with providing evidence of the unsustainability of Teige's and Václavek's theories of a "purely laboratory poetry, isolated from the life of society," evidence of the methodological incorrectness of Teige's Marxist-Freudian theories.

Bedřich Václavek: The End of the "Revolutionary" Avant-Garde

Nezval's new novel *Posedlost* [Obsession] (published by Sfinx) is one of his weakest works so far and at the same time an example of that type of Poetism, diluted and decadent, that forces us to think about the most effective way to liquidate this unfortunate legacy of it.

In its setting, experiences, and atmosphere, the entire long beginning is quite identical with his *Kronika z konce tisíciletí* [Chronicle from the End of the Millennium]. However, here everything is disturbingly diluted. Nevertheless, these parts of the book, founded on a reproduction of distant impressions of his childhood and adolescence, are still the liveliest parts of the entire book. The rest of the "story" about how a young plebeian insinuates his way into a castle, falls in love with the lady of the castle, ascends through degrees of aristocratization, seduces one of the young ladies living at the castle only to abandon her shortly after for the lady of the castle, which drives the young lady to suicide, in response to which he then neurasthenically and sensationally slits his wrists — all this, which comprises the longer half of the book, is something absolutely tasteless. In this part of the book lively primary perceptions and associations are combined more and more with secondary associations, as desiccated as the artificial flowers of our great-grandmothers.

What we have here is a case that should give cause for thought to Nezval and the others who declare their sympathy toward the revolutionary movement, but meanwhile produce these paper decorations. They talked about "pure poetry" and "pure art" without ideology, by which they meant a creative method. However, "pure art" turned into a specific program which — consciously or unconsciously — attempted to limit poetry only to "general human experiences" and to avoid political matters. How many such "generally human" experiences there would be today! The result of this has been an escape to the laughable private affairs of a vain and imaginative poetic psyche, an escape to some other planet where poets who are not beasts live in a world imagined in a way that is all too dry. And ideology (understood: once upon a time revolutionary), thus driven out from pure poetry, has returned to it from another quarter and has spread out quite unpleasantly. However, this is no longer revolutionary ideology, but a laughably petit bourgeois ideology, and this is the entire folly that is hatching out from Poetism here.

Let us take a look at where this has ended up here in Nezval's case. The young plebeian is endlessly enchanted by the "notion of pleasure offered by life in aristocratic circles," he insinuates himself into this life, and is eternally happy when he learns to eat aristocratically and to act haughtily towards the servants who exhibit "physical resistance" to his noble friend Leon when he wants something "from those people." The psychology of this promising young plebeian is captured beautifully, for instance, in this paragraph:

> "The thought that he would soon be able to walk around in a cap resembling an officer's cap lifted Ludvík's self-confidence, because with his decision (to become an officer) he had found himself half in those strata of society that he had come to know with his entry to the castle — amazed that his future honors would enable him to equal Leon. He now saw in the adventures that he intended to embark on with Leon's nieces a small preparation for life and a pretext for testing his courage, because he knew that, not being rich, he could not rely on anything other than this courage."

Sometimes he willingly plays at being pious in order to gain favor with the lady of the castle, and he indulges his ambitions, his hypocrisies, and his outbreaks of vanity, all of which is poetized here with a narcissistic and naive love. However, this aristocratic environment, created and adored like a paper decoration, is not accidental. Whoever evades current-day life and its problems can only create the dead worlds of the past in order to be able to "live" in them. And it is more comfortable to rise above the platform of small-town life on the back of Pegas to elevated aristocratic paradises than it is to open one's eyes and see the class struggle, and to stand on the side of the forces that are ***fighting*** for a new world. After all, Nezval also once wrote "Podivuhodný kouzelník" [The Strange Magician] and the verse: "I handed in my ticket in the sign of the revolution?!" [in *Menší růžová zahrada* [A Smaller Rose Garden] (1925)] However, to hand in a ticket (in elections?) is not enough — and that is the issue here.

Nezval's psychological approach contributes to this disturbing distortion and narrowing of scope. Enclosed in following the excitations of his own personality and reproducing them without selection, he does not see the world. And it is no surprise that he has fled to the aristocracy. His erotic monomaniac Ludvík could hardly live anywhere else today.

As far as the formal creative aspect is concerned, *Posedlost* makes an impossible attempt to mechanically transfer the method of pure poetry to prose. However, the prose does not actually stick to this method of "pure art" but rather quite unapologetically works with a coarsely fabricated plot. In this way informal verbal entities, reflecting free association and fantasy, have been inserted into a narrative schema. This has resulted in terrible paragraphs comprising one monstrous sentence, disintegrating into thousands of relative clauses and other subsidiary parts. This is an absolutely impure form that has not been properly thought through. The substance of this book is full of poetic insights and associations, but the whole is utter kitsch, both in the total hopelessness of its intellectual orientation and also in its creative aspect.

Here we can see the endpoint of that "apolitical" poetic approach which — as Štyrský once wrote — is affected just the same by the execution of a czar as by the execution of a revolutionary. Here are the endpoints of Czech leftist literature that were addressed by the Open Letter of the Kharkov Conference of Proletarian Writers (*Tvorba* V, 50), which accurately placed them into the new framework of the period and its development. Here we can feel clearly the necessity to set out on another path, to radically change orientation, and to attempt to find a way out of the vicious circle, as this open letter indicated.

Bohuslav Brouk: In Defense of Individualism

The cultural age! The 20th century, enlivened by people with a high cultural level and with cultural needs, interests, and problems. A vehicle driven by an invisible force transports you between the ranks of skyscrapers to a building. In the underground entrails of the building, in a dark room on a white screen with the help of shadows, over a period of two hours, you will view an illusory tragedy of the life of people who are perhaps already long dead. You come outside and a street vendor will sell you a newspaper, from which — as a benefaction of telegraphic news reporting making use of the capabilities of the rotary press — you are informed daily about current events from all over the world. The wonder of human culture that we must take our hats off to. Yes, the 20th century is an especially cultural age, but to what degree is it therefore also possible to regard its human contemporaries as thus cultured?

The metro, cinema, newspapers — all these are the certainly achievements of the first order, bearing witness to a high level of culture. However, what merit does the average person — the person who fills the boulevards of the big cities, who pays his ticket for the tram and his ticket to the cinema, has a subscription for the radio, and acquires an excellent radio receiver — have in this? In short, he plunders the culture of his age, he parasitizes it, offering his labor in return for its enormous benefits. One person does the accounts for eight hours in an office, a second stokes coal in a power station, a third services a machine, a fourth drives an bus, and a fifth is a cog in the state administration.

Let us take a look at the miracle represented by the tram. What is so brilliant about this? Someone dug up some iron ire, someone else threw this into a furnace, while some other people heated it and thus smelted it. Then someone serviced the press and processed the molten metal into sheet metal, or someone forged various components, and finally the fitters arrived and, according to a plan, assembled a machine and nailed together the bodywork. Then someone else came along, learned how to drive this vehicle, and started to transport people in it — people who, along with all the workers mentioned previously who participated in the construction of an electric tram, are in reality in no way responsible for the creation of this far-reaching progress. To board a tram and buy a ticket is not in the least an ingenious act, just as the individual acts needed for producing a vehicle are not ingenious acts.

The servicing of machines is not anything so special that people can be called cultured on account of it. Moreover, neither can an engineer take credit for human progress in any way. Technical and administrative organization are tasks that do not have any greater intellectual value than the specialized acts during production. A machine is engendered by a machine, and therefore only an inventor can take credit for its existence, and not a production engineer.

Production is the using of an invention, and no special qualities are needed for this. If we analyze the entire productive process, we arrive at activities that could easily be performed by the most barbaric person. The entire culture, in so far as we see it in supplying the world with technical improvements, is a result of "epochal" capabilities comparable to a parroting of words learned. Culture does not depend on the number of automobiles driving through a city, but rather on the museum exemplar of the first automobile produced. If the radio was an invention that was not used much or even at all, then our century would be just as cultured as it is when every tenth person has a radio receiver.

Culture does not depend on education or on living standard. If someone measures the cultural level according to the consumption of soap, this is an expression of the highest degree of lack of culture that renders any further evaluation of similar measures quite superfluous. Very well, soap may be of itself a part of culture, but its consumption may rather be evidence of vandalism: perhaps of vandalism because making use of culture is itself a barbaric act in relation to culture. ***Culture is inventiveness. In contrast, consumption is — if it wants to flatter itself — civilization.***

Let us concede that a person living outside a cultured society comes into possession of Nietzsche's *Zarathustra* and regards this work as a certain cultural level, as a measure of spiritual maturity on the basis of which he forms an idea of the cultural level of humankind. If he then goes into our cities, he is certainly going to be considerably disappointed by the immaculate primitives inhabiting them. Culture does not grow in any way with an increase in living comfort. The abundant conveniences in life enjoyed by someone living in the current century demonstrate only the excessive use of culture; they demonstrate that cultured people have lived and are living. Civilization, as we have consented to call the use of cultural works, is a memorial of culture in a barbaric environment, just like the drawings by a white man in a cave where he was tortured by savages. Civilization is a clear expression of the fact that there are geniuses and that there are people who look similar to these geniuses and who attempt to imitate them.

A society rationally uses the fruits of the madness of genius, which is a creative end-in-itself. No one creates for people, but rather out of a spiritual need. Inventors are madmen obsessed with fantastic ideas. Their ideas are not acquired empirically, but are rather *a priori;* evidential support for these ideas in reality is only found through all possible kinds of efforts. Every method, every methodological cognition, is something primitive, which can be learned even by the dullest living creature. If we search for something but do not know what we are searching for, then we will also not find anything, and even if we do find something by accident, then it will remain unnoticed. If we examine something, then we must do this for a certain aim. We can only search for the searched for. Scientific method is only a means for justifying a fixed idea. Thousands of inventors fail because they cannot actualize their ideas, and yet intellectual maturity and progress is dependent only on imagination. ***Imagination cannot be learned from anyone. In comparison to this, erudition is idle parroting.*** Civilization, in which we also include erudition, arises through collective organization; it is a simple, in no way sharp-witted, utilization of the vital force. A civilized person is a horse-powered engine. There is no genius contained in its work or in the process of yoking the horse. The idea is contained in the invention of the engine, and neither the farmer nor the horse has anything to do with this. In the same way, neither are the head technician or the workers subordinate to him participants in cultural life. Cultural life, which is contained in genius — by which we should understand all imagination, including that which is not successfully fully actualized, that which does not fully correspond to reality — is the property of individuals and also serves his personal consolation and no other aim.

The pride of cultured people employs rather the mechanism of madness than the method of common sense. Culture is dependent on intuitive imagination, on obsessional thoughts that enslave and subjugate a human being. Reason is something as natural to a person as flying to a bird. Some amphibians have more gills. Genius does not consist either in the quality of being amphibian or in intellect. Intellect is a character of human beings that is no more magnificent than the attributes of other living beings. The progress of humankind does not owe its existence to reason. Reason without genius would not be a very engaging phenomenon, and perhaps only then would we also realize its real value. The most barbaric savage has reason, and yet nevertheless we do not admire him in any way in comparison to animals. Reason is an abstract faculty which only first receives material through the imagination and which without this element would remain unemployed, just like the flying capabilities of a bird closed in a cage. ***Knowledge as cognizance is the rational use of genius, and erudition is the rational use of cognizance. In this culture differs from civilization. Civilized people steal cognizance from geniuses; and so, precisely as capitalism is based on the exploitation of workers, so civilization is based on the exploitation of geniuses.*** The difference between a genius and a cultured person — in view of the extreme exceptionality of the designation of the quality of genius — can only be recognized in the fact that a cultured person is also a person whose fixed ideas have over time been shown to be incorrect or whose ideas have never been proven correct. The quality of genius lies in imagination, and therefore, even if it cannot be proven, its originator remains a genius no less than other celebrated geniuses. In addition to his quality of genius this originator has merely earned the epithet of an unfortunate one.

To remain a foolish dreamer in the eyes of the crowd is a matter of personal luck, a matter of chance. A scientist lives for one idea, and if this idea is shown to be incorrect, not corresponding to reality, then his fate is sealed. He will remain unacknowledged forever and yet he has not done anything worse than his more fortunate colleague. Both correct and erroneous opinions arise from purely personal sources; they are *a priori* wishes that want to be imposed on nature. Those happy fellows whose prerequisites correspond with nature accidentally discover a real truth; in contrast, those whose interests collide with reality do not emerge from error in their work. However, both the one who asserts a falsehood and the one who adopts a stance corresponding to the truth are only attempting to verify something previously wished. ***Scientific value depends only on luck, on whether an a priori prerequisite agrees with reality.*** Pure empiricism, bare reason, is infertile. Through an empirical path we always discover something that has been occupying our thoughts for years. A fixed idea is conditioned on the libido and therefore also has a signification that is common to all expressions of instinct. ***It has a tendency toward gratification and it does not care about unearthly ethical postulates.***

Science is precisely just as gratifying a form of creation as poetry. The difference between them is only in the fact that, while a scientist turns over one idea possibly for his whole life, striving to verify it, an artist does not care about the reality of his imagination and incessantly produces endless ideas without regard for anything. In poetry form takes the place played by reason in science. Intuition is needed by a scientist in the process of verifying his imagination in order not to avoid blundering along an endless path of pure empiricism, while an artist needs intuition for a consummate expression of his sensibility in a given material, whether color or physical matter in the case of visual artists or mere words in the case of poets. ***It is not only a fixed idea that is rational, but also the method by which this idea is implemented — both artistically and also scientifically.***

Spiritual life consists in the rational processing of the imagination surfacing in a ready-made form from our subconscious. It is not the intellect that supplies our soul, but rather the instinctual subconscious. In contrast to the imagination, which is a clear, pure phenomenon, intuition is an unconscious presentiment. However, its content is never external, but rather always internal, also originating in the unconscious. The unconscious is the unique and exclusive source of our extra-rational cognizance. There is no other cognizance that can be applied to an objective reality than cognizance of unconscious content. Intuition arises through the relationship between the conscious and the unconscious subject, and never through the relationship of the unconscious subject to the real. Intuition is a purely internal cognizance. The quality of genius depends entirely on an individual's psychology. ***Nothing can be known, cognized before it has been "thought up," imagined.*** And only an individual can imagine something — never a collective. A collective is only enabled to act, and therefore a collective can only act in terms of a civilization and not culturally. A society is a physical working unit that must be supplied with material by geniuses. ***The future and the past of society are founded on the exploitation of geniuses.***

Society remains, unfortunately, a constraining factor on free imagination in spite of the fact that its existence is founded on using this imagination. Individual growth is unpleasant for society in the collective plan. Physical work does not know searching and speculation. Every physical energy expended on an immediately useless aim is lost. Physical energy requires the most rational usage, because reflection would not bring any benefits. The method of physical work does not understand the method of psychological work. In its economic interest physical work tries to rationalize genius — possibly because it does not even know that genius is based on irrationality. The free psychological growth of an individual is held back by the momentary interests of society, which — even if it was conscious of the needs of psychologically creative people — would be afraid to invest a lot of means into the chance benefit brought by them.

A psychologically required anarchism is more costly for a socialist society than for capitalism. A capitalist system does not have any economic interest in absolute collectivism. It consciously encourages fractionalism and divides up the entire society already on the basis of the closed family. ***The collectivist-anarchist basis of capitalist society renders it more bearable for creative psyches than the collectivism of the future socialist society.*** However, in spite of this, it is easy to explain the opposite phenomenon: the interest of creative psyches in revolution. Just as uncompromising anarchists cannot bear capitalism, so they would not be able to bear any other social form. Anarchists are dangerous for any kind of society. ***The interest of anarchists in revolution is always acute, and that is why we always see creative people, just as cultured people, at the head of revolutions, even when the fruits of these revolutions over time make them bitter. In many cases, by their revolutionary impulses they stab a knife into their own backs, because the regime installed turns first of all against them.*** Formerly, they were a trouble to the order of the old society, then they helped to create a new society, and now they are also a threat to this society.

The domain of creative people is revolution, rebellion, and free movement. Sciences — learned logic and knowledge — cannot serve anyone as a basis for researching. People who rely on these two elements in their work are pupils of science and never actual scientists themselves. Scientific organizations and various schools are archival institutes of scientific history. Just as the special subjects of scientific work are ideas determined by individual libidinal wishes, so entire human progress arises from subjective reasons. ***No scholar has created a new theory for any higher purpose than to overcome and humble his teacher.***

Already on this basis no kind of organization or school is possible, and if one was nevertheless realized it would merely make its new pupils stupid. ***Like a Golem, imitative work is not spiritually creative, but rather physical, and therefore it can only make use of inventions, but cannot however itself invent anything.*** It is a similar case with art. Schools founded on the learning of form breed only pseudo-artists pretending art. Cultural Golems who are incapable of offering anything more than their bodily force and tenacity are a very embarrassing phenomenon in the field of art. Whereas in the case of science a Golem can hold the important post of a teacher and popularizer, the significance of an artistic Golem is diminished to absolute zero. The history of philosophy is valuable information, while art copying the old masters is vulgar, unprofitable plagiarization. Art, which can only be used directly as an emotive work, cannot be changed in transcription into more popular subjects or be transferred to other subjects. Art cannot bear archival selections; these can only be faithfully reproduced without any kind of personal modifications.

Culture cannot be anything rationally coerced or anything directly supportable. To contribute to the cultural development of humankind is possible only through a social development towards anarchism. However, an already more or less collectivized society leaves the Titanic forces of imagination to consume private, intimate life and leads especially talented people rather to psychotic madness than to psychotic genius. The requirement of liberating an individual from the prejudices of provisional scientific truths and social usages, and the permitting of individual methods and perpetual skepticism, is the only method of spiritual hygiene and of raising the cultural level of humankind. ***However, the social poverty of the world economy stands in opposition to this.***

Jindřich Štyrský: Little Prolegomena

Marx's dialetics, as the final word
of the method of scientific development,
do not allow the evaluation of an object
in an isolated, one-dimensional, and caricatured way.
Lenin

When Don Quixote tilts against windmills
with his raised lance, this is suited to him,
but Sancho Panza is not permitted to do this.
Engels

Everything that exists, everything that lives
on the earth or in the water, only exists and lives
by means of movement.
Marx

It is fall once again, the time when a poet takes his harpoon down off the wall and goes off to hunt for mermaids. We greet you, blue stockings, keep dreaming of your ideal of an eternal festival!

It depends on us alone whether we regard a morning journey by tram as a matter of need or a matter of enjoyment. Once upon a time, in our youth, we made friends with Mrs. Meluzína wind goddess[1] before we learned to distinguish the wheat from the chaff: Teresa smelt of roses, Annie of cinnamon, and Catherine of violets.

1 Meluzína — female mythological being, personification of howling wind.

Poetry has never been such a simple matter as it is today. Apart from poets, any person whatsoever can decide on its future. Long gone are the times when poets could elect their own princes. Gone are those marvelous times when two men could settle their differences of opinion with clubs in a glade in the woods. And the times when a person could publicly wear the scalp of his opponent on his belt.

Poets are mostly crazy. It is enough for them to spawn mermaids, while they could be victorious over singing cows. Thanks to their table society they create immortal works.

One evening a poet met Heraclitus.

Everything simultaneously exists and at the same time does not exist. Everything is in flux; everything changes incessantly; everything is constantly arising and perishing.

Yes, I understand that and I know what you are getting at, replies the poet, but I stand aside from the class struggle precisely because I do not regard myself as exploited. Nobody in the world can appropriate the result of my work. And if my sympathies incline toward the side of the working class, this is...

Unfortunately, Catherine interrupted him; this is also because the cultural needs of the proletariat can also be well assuaged by a well chosen turn of phrase.

Those of you, dear ladies, who introduce your speech with the comment that you are speaking in accord with Marxist theory, commented Heraclitus, can preach about anything whatsoever.

There is no one that can be so easily intoxicated as a poet, and the cheapest way is a violet perfume. Poetry will remain modern up until such time as it starts to confront a new worldview. By a roundabout way the Constructivists will go back to the place from which they came. It seems that the entire crisis of the working intelligentsia lies in the fact that this class has not succeeded in good time in understanding the principle of movement and has reduced the world into a depository of things and requisites, while the eternally intersecting events and the movement of matter have completely escaped it. Poetry has also become idiosyncratic: putrefaction, terror, and death. However, a poet only experiences success when he ceases to surprise the public.

That is good, said Annie, I will also open up my entire inside to you.

Commit harakiri while remaining seated, Annie. Then return to the graveyard clay, soaked in the piss of drunkards, and stuff your intestinal flora back in once again.

As soon as a poet is conscious of his intentions he ceases to be a poet.

It is necessary to become absolutely clear in order that we can say what is usually kept silent. Never have affairs in the field of poetry been as simple as they are today. The issue of *modernity* in poetry is decided by a few students, and here and there some advocate butts in to the domain of literary criticism with his opinion in order to draw attention to himself. Bank clerks also express their opinions about poetry so that it can be seen that their souls are animated.

Leave them their feeling of importance, said Teresa, smelling of roses, leave them their illusion that they are creating because for the meanwhile they are not destroying. Be indulgent toward them, let them write and orate, and let them evaluate poetry under the veil of a materialist worldview, they will thus become superficial snobs earlier than if you were to discuss with them, because by discussion only you lose and they gain. Let them observe the world through the windows of coffee-houses — that is, from your precinct.

The city dweller is thus far of the opinion that everything in nature is modeled according to a sphere. Never has modern art approached the notion of eternity and the concept of immortality so closely as in the grandiose curved stones of Brâncuși. Only that art and that poetry that correspond with the level of the proletariat can be declared as the poetry of the future.

But I am deliberately destroying myself, said the poet. I look myself in the mirror and I see myself without make up, without a halo, and without lilies, in a state so wretched that I do not doubt even for a minute that I really resemble a coalman. I know that this is not a false resemblance because I do not look at myself with *my own* eyes.

You see, opined Catherine, one day the proletariat is going to love you and admire you very much. For the meanwhile the only thing that bothers the proletariat is that *you still exist*.

As far I could understand, said Heraclitus, the poet is not arguing with dialectical materialism, and neither is he denigrating the proletariat, but rather he despises and spits on Marxist good-for-nothings and those who merely parrot phraseology, the failed sons disemboweled from the cloaca of bourgeois families into revolutionaries of limited intellect, inverted prolet-snobs, and communist landlords — in short, those whom Engels called vulgarizing peddlers.

When an inferior person gives himself over to some philosophical system he becomes an *intellectual*. Society and membership of a certain class arrange his path through life and make it easier for him to understand dogmas that would destroy him as an individual. However, the Marxist conception of the revolutionary in the sense of the dictatorship of the proletariat does not contradict the idea that a good revolutionary can be an absolute bonehead. Apart from that, a poet is not interested in the way in which a democrat or a proletarian lounges in a plush chair.

A poet has the right to hide behind the greatest variety of faces, said Teresa. *Everything that is comes to pass in order to perish*, whispered Mephistopheles, hiding behind Goethe. If there was no wood, then there would be no woodcuts.

A poet is not interested in the question of whether a good poet can come from the ranks of the working class, because the birth of a proletarian poet is not anything unusual.

Proletarian literature is a successful attempt to rationally reduce the level of the working class. This betrayal perpetrated on the proletariat is happening in that some half-educated fools and windbags from the lowest depths of culture are arrogating the right to satisfy the cultural needs of the proletariat. If a person views the world through the eyes of a Marxist, then many things that so far had a limitless importance for him seem quite trivial and valueless, while that which he has hitherto underestimated takes on the highest possible value for him. It depends on what you give preference to: whether you become a snob, or whether you become a poet, commented Catherine.

The only thing that I care about, replies the poet, is that I am not identified with those intellectuals well known from the spring *crisis of the intelligentsia* which preceded the [Communist Party] congress, so similar to a congress of veterans.

It seems that the only ones who are going to maintain the tradition of poetry in the future are going to be the crazy and the mad.

The importance of poetry in life is going to be minimal. The only readership for a poet is going to be his relatives. Marxists are aware of the superfluousness of poetry and also of the fact that poetry as such — in other words, what we think of today under the concept of poetry — is an expression of *the old world.*

Let it be a consolation for the poet that today and also in future every person rots or dissolves into ash.

Only Teresa never asked the poet why he placed this color in the middle of the square and why he chose a metaphor so unfeasible. Teresa is not interested in the question of why a rosehip has five leaf crowns and why a rosehip flower exists at all when nothing would be changed if it did not exist.

Perhaps poetry is only those feelings and states without which a human being could exist. Someone desires to leave paradise and another person desires to enter it.

One person despises ordinariness, while another person despises the supernatural. Someone looks at the future of poetry from the outside, while another person looks at it from the inside. In the five-year program the method of mastering imagination has been forgotten. I am afraid, said the goblin from the dark alleyway, that I have become very rundown. How ridiculous I would perhaps be if I was to put any other flower in my buttonhole than a red carnation.

And, nevertheless, once upon a time he also loved poetry, said Annie, and with an ambiguous smile she straightened her brassiere.

Be silent, Annie. There were times when everything was understood as art — cleaning shoes, making cakes — and in time we will also aggrandize the deterioration of the art of burying the dead. Poetry is only an opportunity and an invitation to dream. In poetry and in dreaming *time* is preserved, burying the *epoch.*

Karel Teige
Introductory Remarks: Towards a Dialectics of Architecture and Sociology of Housing Forms

The modern architectonic stance, at first a formalist anti-decorative movement, has gradually been deepened and purified during its development. Over a period of several years, modern architecture has arrived at a place where, according to its early manifestos and theories, it always should have been: Constructivism was not, after all, supposed to be a new formal aesthetic direction, but a social-economic method. In the process of this purification of the new architecture many people have remained half way along the path, and these people were not only mediocre and weak intellects. Many retreated from Constructivism and from modern architectonic ideas as soon as it became apparent that their development and use in praxis were taking on not only an aesthetic character, but also a social character. This retreat means, in the work of certain authors, not only a trivialization, but rather a total perversion of Constructivism into its complete antithesis — that is, a restriction of architecture to a formally aesthetic and socially conservative form of creation, into a nonsensical pseudo-Constructivism, which in many cases today prevails in the circles of architects who still continue to consider themselves as modern. Really, there is no phenomenon that under certain circumstances is not transformed into its exact opposite. That is why it is necessary to emphasize the really social aims and the major class re-evaluation of the new architecture. The world is divided: There are two worlds, two cultures, two sciences, and two architectures.

Here an essential differentiation is taking place, a necessary *classifying of intellects* in the groups of architectonic modernism. Authors who have proceeded together for a number of years are here parting ways: Some are going to the left, some to the right; some remain half way along the path like milestones showing how far they were capable of going, while others are throwing off the burden of dying ideas and are boldly going further ahead. A majority, however, wishes to restrict itself to its specialization, and to avoid and ignore politics. But this majority fails to perceive that, by this stance, it falls into the most wretched form of politics: fascism (just as many stubborn practitioners ostentatiously despise theories, but in reality are inspired by theories that are several hundred years old). This is also demonstrated by Le Corbusier's book *Précisions*. In this way many authors are showing the limits of their powers; they are showing a limit beyond which they are no longer innovators and revolutionaries. If they are showing this today, in a revolutionary epoch, then it is clear that the period when they were able to play a leading role has passed.

The architectonic avant-garde is resolving the problem of a minimum dwelling by the form of collective housing. Collective housing blocks are building and architectonic forms of a higher quality than the hitherto forms of family housing, and they are in stark contradiction with the existing state of the family as a social-economic unit and with the ruling family ideology. They are a negation of the hitherto forms of living in single-family houses and in family apartments in town rental houses. They are a form of housing that will be, but is not yet, a utopia. And this is because *everything that will be already exists* — in an embryonic state — *contained within what now exists* as a contradiction of the existing and qualitatively inferior state, and it will transcend this contradiction through its higher quality. The collective housing block, about which we will write in detail in later chapters, corresponds to the social state in which the family has ceased to be an economic unit and in which the division of labor has been overcome, just as the inequality between man and woman, and between parents and children, that flows from this division of labor has also been overcome.

However, in today's society there already exists a social class — that is, the proletariat — in which the family as an economic unit has been dismantled and reshaped. A transformation of what currently is — that is, of the hitherto family form of housing — is not utopianism, but rather it can be implemented precisely because elements of what will be in the future are already contained in the current-day state; because indications and elements of future forms and relations are already taking shape in economic, social, and intellectual life generally, and in architectonic creation especially. In every piece of work, in material and also in intellectual production, new and old tendencies exist alongside each other, or to put it correctly: in opposition to each other.

The modern architectonic stance — that is, Constructivism, which has gradually taken shape from the preconditions given by the advanced technology of industrial capitalism, on the basis and in the sphere of the capitalist world — does not develop from the dying elements of capitalism, but rather from its progressive elements: that is, from those elements that already within the framework of capitalist economic and intellectual production are registering themselves as dialectical contradictions of capitalism and are becoming elements of the new planned productive and social organization. Collective housing, as a new architectonic form of higher quality corresponding to the collective living style of the proletariat, is a negation of the town-apartment household, a negation that has developed from the contradictions of the old forms of housing and that was contained in these contradictions from the beginning. The development and transformation of architectonic forms takes place precisely because negative elements (the disintegration of the family-based economy) simultaneously also have a positive side (the transformation of home-based working into centralized mass production).

The dialectic of architectonic and housing forms is that a given architectonic form develops and simultaneously disintegrates. From a rudimentary architectonic form — from the accommodation of a primitive, from the tent of a nomad, from Nanuk the Eskimo's igloo, or from a rural cottage — that is, from a universal housing space without differentiated functions (for instance, a primitive combined kitchen-living room) individual functions gradually become separated. Firstly, they are divided into economic and living spaces, and then later into spaces for cooking, food storage, washing, sleeping, eating, intellectual work, and so on. That is, specialized differentiated rooms become independent and separated from a universal space. At a certain moment in this differential development the old form of housing collapses: Economic elements become completely isolated from the housing space and are centralized, while the housing space changes into one cell for an individual serving all accommodation functions (sleeping, intellectual and intimate life). *A differentiated town apartment was the negation of the primitive universal living space. The negation of this negation is a universal living space for individuals in a collective housing block.*

Chapter 4

Complicating the Real: Czech Surrealism

In May 1933, Vítězslav Nezval and theater director Jindřich Honzl rang the bell at house number 42, rue Fontaine, in Paris in order to make the acquaintance of André Breton. However, no one opened the door and the tired artists made their way disappointedly to a cafe, as Nezval writes in his memoirs: "I am tired, I am despondent. I suggest to Honzl that we go and rest at a cafe on the corner of the square. We enter. We chose the first unoccupied table. Opposite us is sitting André Breton."[1] The surrealist principle of accidental meeting in its best form!

The relationship with France, established by Czech writers before World War One, was renewed with partial success after the war. In 1920, Karel Čapek's seminal book *Francouzská poezie nové doby* (Contemporary French Poetry) was published, one year after his translation of Apollinaire's *Zone*, which had a fundamental influence on the character of Czech poetry of the 1920s. Also significant was the relationship of the Czech avant-gardists to the French *poètes maudits*; in particular, translations of Charles Baudelaire and Arthur Rimbaud were published in the 1920s and 1930s. Jindřich Štyrský and Toyen exhibited their works at several exhibitions in Paris. News about events in France were mediated by Richard Weiner, correspondent of *Lidové noviny* newspaper, and painter Josef Šíma, both of whom lived in Paris and had links to the group Le Grand Jeu.[2] In *ReD*, Karel Teige in particular

1 "It is like a scene from Nadja," I say to this person whom I could not not meet in my life, without whom my life would be endlessly poorer and sadder [...]" Vítězslav Nezval, *Neviditelná Moskva* (Praha: Fr. Borový, 1935), 16–17. Detailed information about the development of Czech Surrealism, focusing on the historical period 1929–1953, is provided by the research of leading Czech art historian Karel Srp — cf. Karel Srp and Lenka Bydžovská (eds.), *Český surrealismus 1929–1953: skupina surrealistů v ČSR : události, vztahy, inspirace* (Praha: Argo, 1996).

2 Le Grand Jeu group functioned in the years 1927–1932. Among its core members was Czech painter Josef Šíma, living from 1921 in France. Significant personalities of the movement were

informed about the activities of this Surrealist group (issue number eight in 1930 was entirely devoted to the activities of this group) — he regarded the works of its members as an expression of the desire for freedom by a person in revolt.

Even though the Czech avant-gardists actively received Breton's texts already in the 1920s, with only a few exceptions they did not agree with the exclusion of the conscious — that is, the free element — from the creative process. It was perhaps Karel Teige who received the Surrealist approach most cautiously, in particular because in the 1920s it was in conflict with his conception of Poetism in a number of respects. Czech Poetism as a purely Czech avant-garde direction presented confidence in life; fundamental was its hedonistic side, linked to the sensations of the senses, which did not correspond with the Surrealistic attempt at penetrating to a person's deeper, unseen sides.

One of the points of intersection that connects the Czech avant-garde with French Surrealism already at the end of the 1920s was eroticism. In 1930 Bohuslav Brouk wrote his study "Onanie jakožto světový názor" (Onanism as a Worldview) which was published in the first annual edition of Štyrský's *Erotická revue* along with surveys regarding the sexuality of leading French Surrealists.[3] Štyrský's poetic text *Emilie přichází ke mně ve snu* (Emily Comes to Me in a Dream, 1933) was also complemented by an erotic (pornographic) photo-montage.[4] Nevertheless, the erotic as a fundamental source of the Surrealist imagination was a target for censorship — for instance, in the translation of Lautréamont the censor prohibited several of the most sexually explicit places.

Roger Gilbert-Lecomte and René Daumal. One of the aims of this grouping was to transform seeing, perceiving, and thinking in the context of boundary, extreme states of consciousness (extrasensory perception, clairvoyance, and similar). A fundamental source of art for them was the so-called sudden event, that is, an event that becomes an experience that is capable of bringing a person into a state of absolute perceptiveness. This opinion platform was not strictly linked to art. The effort to achieve immediately felt experience, *the game for real* without any kind of compromises, was supposed to be made both in creation and also in life.

3 A number of foremost avant-garde artists were involved in the literary and visual form of *Erotická revue*, published in the years 1930–1933: Jindřich Štyrský, Toyen, Adolf Hoffmeister, František Bidlo, Emil Filla, Bohuslav Brouk, Vítězslav Nezval, František Halas (some hidden under pseudonyms). Significant translations included texts by Louis Aragon, Sigmund Freud, André Breton, and Paul Éluard. Jindřich Štyrský conceived the magazine as a private printing for bibliophiles, maximum 200 copies. The numbered editions were accessible only for subscribers and on account of censorship were not permitted to be publicly sold, lent, or distributed in any way.

4 This short literary text is complemented by ten collages that were never independently exhibited during Štyrský's life. Similarly to *Erotická revue*, the book *Emily Comes to Me in a Dream* was also published as a private printing, not for public sale — an announcement concerning its exclusivity and strict private nature was printed directly in the book. A common motif of Štyrský's collages is an open, uncensored depiction of erotic motifs and sexual scenes. For more on Štyrský cf. Karel Srp and Lenka Bydžovská, *Jindřich Štyrský*, trans. by Anna Bryson et al. (Praha: Argo, 2007).

A further source of inspiration for the Czech avant-gardists who accepted the creative approaches of Surrealism were reminiscence and dream connected with the subconscious. Already in the context of the Artificialism of Štyrský and Toyen in the 1920s, as Teige pointed out in his essay "Ultrafialové obrazy, čili artificielismus" (Ultraviolet Pictures, or Artificialism, 1928), use is made of a creative means which arouses a dialog of the conscious with the subconscious. The transition from Artificialism to Surrealism is represented by Štyrský's illustrations for Lautréamont's *Les Chants de Maldoror* (The Songs of Maldoror) and the work presented in the *Apokalypsa* (Apocalypse) cycle, among others. Already from the start of the 1930s, we can follow in Czech literature some experimentation with Surrealism in poetry and also in prose, a line of diary-like self-analytical texts and montages revealing the multiple sides of the human psyche. In the context of literary texts it was Vítězslav Nezval who created one of the first Surrealist texts in Czech. Nezval's drama *Strach* (Fear, 1930, premiere 1932) and his prose piece *Chtěla okrást lorda Blamingtona* (She Wanted to Rob Lord Blamington, 1930) bear clear features of Surrealist aesthetics.[5] Surrealist motifs are also significant in photography. At the first exhibition of Surrealists in Czechoslovakia (1935) Štyrský presented two extensive collections of photographs, *Muž s klapkami na očích* (Man with Flaps on His Eyes, 1934) and *Žabí muž* (Frog Man, 1934), in which he connects objects with recollections and offers an interpretation of reality from the point of view of psychoanalysis and dreams (the tailor's dummy was a favorite motif). The interest in collages and castings (for instance, Hudeček's textile relief *Sokrates a Faidros čili o kráse* — Socrates and Phaedrus or On Beauty), as well as the revival of subjects often connected with sexuality, was directly inspired by the work of Max Ernst.

The positive reception of Surrealism by key members of the Devětsil group, which fell apart at the beginning of the 1930s, is demonstrated by two numbers of Nezval's *Zvěrokruh* (1930), in spite of the fact that in his introduction to the first number Nezval explicitly stated that *Zvěrokruh* was not a Surrealist revue. The second number was devoted almost entirely to Surrealist poetry, painting, and theory (among other things, it contains a translation of Breton's "Second Manifesto of Surrealism"). However, in the context of the Czech avant-garde Surrealist theory continued to be subjected to criticism. In his article "Nadrealismus a Vysoká Hra" (Surrealism and Le Grand Jeu), Karel Teige pointed out some unclear theoretical points in Breton's manifestos, and even Nezval's *Zvěrokruh* printed an article "Surrealist Revolution' with a very critical conclusion: "The ideology of the Surrealists is an ideology of a de-classed group, given by the collapse of the social bond and the atomization of the individual: Surrealist revolution evidently has all the features of

5 The play *Fear* was Nezval's first attempt at a full-length drama. In it he combined artistic approaches that can be connected with practically all avant-garde directions (Poetism, Expressionism, Dada); however, he places emphasis on the basic Surrealist motif, the dream. The plot of *Fear* begins with a dream; in the dream the sleeping main protagonist speaks with his son, who curses him for having abandoned him before his birth.

individualistic anarchism." In the early 1930s Teige continues to defend the autonomy of Poetism, even though his third manifesto of Poetism from 1930 — "Báseň, svět, člověk" (Poem, World, Human Being) — already represents a step towards Surrealism in a number of respects, however with continuing reservations towards the method of automatism.

In 1932 the exhibition "Poesie 1932" was held, which was an important milestone in the acceptance of Surrealism in the history of interwar literature.[6] The representative exhibition of avant-garde art in interwar Czechoslovakia was organized by the Mánes association of visual artists and boasted a rich participation of foreign artists, including Hans Arp, Salvador Dalí, Joan Miró, and Paul Klee. Among those Czech artists who confronted their works with those of the Paris Surrealists were Josef Šíma, Emil Filla, and František Janoušek, while Jindřich Štyrský and Toyen presented several canvases in the direction of the boundary between Poetism and Surrealism. Within the framework of the exhibition, Roman Jakobson delivered a lecture on "Co je poezie?" (What Is Poetry?). He views poetry as an inconstant and mobile concept, and in contrast to it he poses the poetic function, which is independent of culture. In reply to the fundamental question concerning the way in which the quality of being poetic makes itself apparent Jakobson answers: "In that the word is felt as a word, and not as a mere representative of the conceived object or as an outburst of emotion." Together with Jan Mukařovský, Jakobson was behind the theory of the Pražský lingvistický kroužek (Prague Linguistic Circle), for which the notion of the work of art as a sign was central.

In May 1933 Vítězslav Nezval addressed a letter to André Breton, in which he wrote that the Czech avant-garde adopted a similar stance to cultural-political and aesthetic problems and, therefore, he proposed mutual cooperation. In 1935 Éluard informed his wife Gale about the success of the Surrealist mission in Prague — for the Surrealists, Prague was the gateway to Moscow. A year later, a Surrealist group was officially founded in Prague.

6 The exhibition lasted from 27 October until 27 November 1932. The president of the SVU Mánes artists' group was architect Josef Gočár. According to the exhibition's catalog, 155 sculptures and paintings were presented. In the introduction to the catalog, Kamil Novotný describes the problematical situation of the post-war generation, seeking a catharsis that traditional art was not capable of offering them. Therefore, this generation of artists sought new means of expression. Firstly, they discovered new artistic inspiration in literature and in architecture in the context of Poetism and Constructivism, but painting continued to seek new means of expression. According to Novotný, it was only Surrealism that first enabled the renewal of post-war painting, through a combination of imagination and freedom. He directly cites Breton's theory of the creation of a work of art by implementing the method of automatism, a game uncensored by reason and with the help of dreams and the unconscious. He explained the presence of artists with an earlier date of birth (among others, Emil Filla, Paul Klee) by the modern conception of their creation. He explained the literary name of the exhibition — "Poesie 1932" — by the common aim of visual art and literature, typical for the Czech post-war avant-garde.

The Czechoslovak Surrealist Group was founded on 21 March 1934 with the declaration *Surrealismus v ČSR* (Surrealism in Czechoslovakia), which in its introduction paraphrases the first sentence of the Communist Manifesto of Marx and Engels — this time, however, it is the specter of fascism that is haunting Europe.[7] The leaflet (published anonymously, conceived by Nezval) was signed by 11 other artists, among others Brouk, Biebl, Honzl, Ježek, Makovský, Štyrský, and Toyen — a number of them members of the already defunct Devětsil group (Karel Teige, however, did not sign the leaflet). From the beginning, sympathy towards Marxism is apparent from the *Surrealism* leaflet, which in places paraphrases Breton's Second Manifesto: "If the materialist dialectic allows us at the same time not to see the permanent contradiction of reality and surreality, content and form, consciousness and unconsciousness, activity and dream; if we also fail to see the absolute contradiction between evolution and revolution, invention and tradition, adventure and order, necessity and chance; why should we then persist without closer cooperation with surrealism, which was the first of the world's avant-gardes to find its most classical expression in the idea of the surreal, the point which dialectically conjoins these opposites." In contrast to Teige, Nezval was much more open to Surrealism and deeply sought the roots of Czechoslovak Surrealism already in the 1920s, as is evident in the essay "What Is Surrealism" (1934), which was originally written for Brno Radio. Here he analyzes Surrealism as an artistic method, a stance in life, and a political persuasion, similarly to André Breton in his lectures, which were published as a collection with a postscript by Nezval in 1937 under the title *Co je surrealismus?* (What Is Surrealism?).

After the foundation of the Czechoslovak Surrealist Group, Karel Teige offered an alternative developmental model of the Czech avant-garde of the 1920s: He declared the current era of Poetism as the era of Surrealism, and by doing so he located Poetism as an artistic direction that preceded Surrealism in its foundation (the first manifesto of Poetism came out in June 1924). One of the points that Poetism and Surrealism had in common was an acceptance of the opinions of the Communist Party and the Third International. Nezval also declared the allegiance of his group not only to Surrealism, but also expressed the consensus of the members of his group in questions concerning Marxism-Leninism and dialectical materialism. (During the 1920s and 30s the basic works of Marx, Engels, and Lenin were translated into Czech). However, the political direction thus defined was not accepted by all members of the group, especially in the context of the worsening political situation in the Soviet Union. A rift would not be long in coming.

---

7 Teige writes more on the relationship between Surrealism and revolution in his study "Ten Years of Surrealism": "(...) Surrealism is not only an artistic idea, method and direction, but rather a revolutionary poetic movement which identifies with the Marxist-Leninist worldview, and on the cultural front desires to intervene in broad social and political questions by openly fighting against war, against fascism, against religion, against the bourgeois family, and against official ideology." Karel Teige, "Deset let surrealismu," in Ladislav Štoll and Karel Teige (eds.), *Surrealismus v diskusi* (Praha: Levá fronta, 1934), 8–9.

In the period of the flowering of the Czechoslovak Surrealist Group — that is, in the years 1934–1938 — the group engaged in extensive international cooperation. Czech-French relations attained a substantial intensity. In a letter to his wife Gala, Éluard writes: "We are much more famous here than in France." In 1935 the group's first exhibition took place, featuring among others Toyen, Štyrský, and Makovský. In the same year André Breton and Paul Éluard came to Czechoslovakia for lecture tours.[8] In his article "10 let surrealismu" (Ten Years of Surrealism) from 1934, originally delivered at a discussion evening of the Levá fronta (Left Front) and later printed in the collection *Surrealismus v diskusi* (Surrealism in Discussion, 1934), Karel Teige presented Czech Poetism and French Surrealism as two equal movements whose paths merged in 1934 — he described Surrealism as a rib from the body of Poetism.

In the years 1934 and 1935 the Left Front organized several lecture evenings devoted to Surrealism and Socialist Realism. The first evening bore the name "Surrealismus v diskuzi" (Surrealism in Discussion); a collection with the contributions came out in the fall of the same year. Two fundamental themes arose from the evening: the relationship of Surrealism to Marxism and the relationship of Surrealism to dialectical materialism. Karel Teige developed these two themes in his extensive essays "Surrealism in Czechoslovakia" and "Ten Years of Surrealism" in which together with Nezval he declared the group's allegiance to dialectical materialism. The atmosphere in Czechoslovakia in this period was influenced by Hitler's Germany and the cultural situation was impacted by increasing censorship of the press. From the mid-1930s we can see the growing cult of Stalin's personality and an increasing mistrust towards the functioning of the Soviet Union. A new reading of the situation in Russia was offered by André Gide's book *Return From the Soviet Union*, which came out in Czech translation in 1936. Gide describes the absence of artistic freedom and the feeling of danger, connected in the context of Russia with totalitarian oppression. Attention was attracted especially by the book's chief thought — a comparison of the Soviet Union with Hitler's Germany. Immediately in January 1937, the Přítomnost (Presence) club organized a discussion evening on this topic, at which Karel Teige spoke on behalf of the Surrealists.

In the context of the reception of Surrealism, a way of viewing the new world with the help of the concept of an "internal model" resonated in the Czech avant-garde. The first person in Czechoslovakia to concern himself with this association was Jindřich Štyrský, who utilized Breton's formulation of an internal model that

8 Among the first reactions to the exhibition was the following: "The first exhibition of the Surrealists in Czechoslovakia. An anatomical, psychopathic, pathological FREAKSHOW. [...] A gallery of international works of Surrealism, which is not an artistic school. [...] Everything in life size. Open human bodies, where the entire inner organs and the composition of the human body can be seen. Abnormality. A monstrosity. Natural science collections; a collection of dreams and hallucinatory objects, illusions, and so on." Stanislav Hoblík, "Sen noci Svatomatějské," *Fronta* 7, no. 29 [7 March 1935]: 355–356.

all artistic forms of expression should be governed by if they were to be considered as surrealistic. At the end of the 1930s, Karel Teige also accepts Breton's theory of an internal model — the surreal is understood as a strengthening of the position of the subject in relation to reality.[9] Nevertheless, in the context of the group's rift with the Left Front, the concept of the surreal showed itself more as problematic. In the collection *Surrealism in Discussion*, communist critic Ladislav Štoll emphasized that Surrealism and Marxism were marked by different relationships to reality: for Marxism, only objective reality exists; while for Surrealism, the subjective reality of psychoanalysis is equally important. From the mid-1930s, the problem of the relationship of Surrealism and Socialist Realism seeps into the discussions on the concepts of the surreal.[10] In his studies, Teige presented the opinion that there was no theoretical dispute between the two, and he defined the connecting line between both platforms as revolutionary Romanticism.[11]

---

9 Even though Karel Teige tries to attach the creative elements of the internal model as much as possible to unconscious instinctive life and to detach them from conscious emotionality, his attempt to explain the development of art as a process arising from the unconscious contents of an artistic work leads him to a gradual acceptance of the connections between conscious subjective emotion and unconscious processes. One of his first studies on this theme was the study "Jan Zrzavý — předchůdce," in *Výbor z díla 3: Osvobozování života a poezie. Studie ze čtyřicátých let* (Praha: Aurora, 1994), 3–41 and also the article "Vnitřní model," *Kvart*, no. 4 (1945–1946): 149–154.

10 The relationship between Surrealism and Socialist Realism was much discussed in the 1930s. Teige writes: "According to the Surrealists' opinion, Surrealism is not in conflict with the general theory of Socialist Realism. In artistic practice, however, there are deep differences, because almost all the Socialist Realism work to date, Soviet and Western, is more or less similar to the methods of older, descriptive realism. Despite the differences which remain between Surrealism and Socialist Realism, however, there can and must exist solidarity between representatives of both trends, who without exception subscribe to the dialectical-materialist worldview and to the revolutionary workers' movement – in all areas and questions cultural and political, in the fight against reaction, fascism, and war." Karel Teige, "O Surrealismu," *Doba* 1, no. 19–20 [6 November 1935]: 275. The magazine *Doba*, which was edited by Karel Teige, published a number of articles on the theme of Surrealism and Socialist Realism. The magazine also published translations of foremost French Surrealists: André Breton, "Intelektuální práce a kapitál," *Doba* 1, no. 5 [29 March 1934]: 66–68; André Breton, "Politická posice dnešního umění." *Doba* 1, no. 19–20 (6 November 1935): 266–271; Paul Éluard, "Sbratření," *Doba* 1, no. 19–20 [6 November 1935]: 259–261. An invitation to a discussion evening on the theme of Socialist Realism was also published here. Among those who participated in the evening were E. F. Burian, Adolf Hoffmeister, Kurt Konrad, Vítězslav Nezval, Karel Teige, Bedřich Václavek — "Socialistický realismus," *Doba* 1, no. 13–14 (November 1934): 208.

11 The relationship between Romantism and revolution was analyzed by Teige in 1936 in his programmatic text "Revolutionary Romantic Karel Hynek Mácha" (1936). Cf. Karel Teige, "Revoluční romantik Karel Hynek Mácha," in *Ani labuť ani Lůna* (Praha: Otto Jirsák, 1936), 10–28. Teige had already earlier emphasized that it was appropriate to link the pessimistic themes of Romanticism (disintegration, death) only with the "first period" of Romanticism: "Romantic revolt is born in the first third of the last century in the Bouzingo group: Gérard de Nerval, Théophile Gautier, Petrus Borel, Aloysius Bertrand. The first period of Romanticism is the period of a desperate pessimism engaged in revolt, which only Alfred de Vigny overcame with Stoicism.

Apart from the official Czechoslovak Surrealist Group, several other Surrealist-inclined groups existed in the 1930s, which however for personal or social reasons did not want to join the group around Vítězslav Nezval. Some individuals also agreed with the aesthetic premises of Surrealism: Zdenek Rykr, František Janoušek, Ladislav Zívr, František Gross, and others. However, they never officially became members.

In June 1936, the Czechoslovak Surrealist Group published the collection *Ani labuť ani Lůna* (Neither Swan, Nor Moon), named after the poem of the same name by Romantic poet Karel Hynek Mácha. In protest against the official celebrations of the anniversary of the publication of Mácha's epic poem *Máj* (May, 1836) and the falsification of his legacy, the collection's authors presented Mácha as a poet of revolutionary Romanticism. The texts were accompanied by collages by Jindřich Štyrský and Toyen. The motifs of Toyen's collages were close to those of two of her key pictures, *Opuštěné doupě* and *Spící* (Abandoned Burrow and Sleeping, both 1937), in which fragments of bodies and empty girls dresses also appear — figures of melancholy par excellence. In his text "Svět se stává stále menším" (The World Is Becoming Ever Smaller), Štyrský writes about "a mirror without an image, ruins without recollections." The first half of this statement still refers back to Artificialism, while the second half points to Surrealism. The collection *Neither Swan, Nor Moon*, more than a complex portrayal of the Czech Romantic poet, was thus rather another activity of Surrealism, something that was savagely criticized by contemporary literary critics. For instance, F. X. Šalda rejected the collection as unscientific dilettantism; he literally writes about dogmatic apriorism. The academic community reacted to the Surrealistic-oriented study on Mácha's legacy with the collection of the Prague Linguistic Circle, *Torso a tajemství Máchova díla* (Torso and the Secret of Mácha's Works, 1938).

Characteristic for the Czech avant-garde of the 1930s was a return to the past, represented by the mythology of antiquity — for Czech poets, ruins evoked a space of the unconscious. Inspiration by dreams is also apparent in the Czech avant-garde in the tension between figurative sculpture and objects, notably in the work of sculptor Vincenc Makovský, the textile reliefs of František Hudeček and František Gross, the Surrealist objects of Ladislav Zívr, or the photographs of Václav Zykmund

In the 1830s, poets breathed the atmosphere of disintegration and death. A rare accursed personality, a son of unhappy blood, a firebrand and royal eagle, Petrus Borel, a soul thirsting for freedom, this anarchic and revolutionary spirit, is a fore-image of the poètes maudits [...]" Karel Teige, "Od romantismu k dadaismu," in *O humoru, clownech a dadaistech* 2. *Svět, který voní* (Praha: Odeon 1930), 14. Here he already makes modern art conditional on Romantic creation: "And Baudelaire was precisely the first poet of the modern human being and modern life. [...] Underneath the Romantic gesticulation and the obsolete and bizarre staffage of some poems is always concealed the modernity which Baudelaire emphasizes as an integral part of the work." (Ibid, 17).

and Miroslav Hák. An important inspiration was the exhibition on Prague Baroque, which was organized by the Umělecká beseda artists' forum (1938).[12]

In 1936, when Vítězslav Nezval published the article "Proč jsem surrealista" (Why I Am a Surrealist) — he gave two reasons, among others: collectivism and friendship in the group. However, this group friendship was not to last long. In March 1938, an incident occurred that was unprecedented in the history of the modernist Czech interwar period. While Karel Teige insisted on the aesthetics of Surrealism and an undogmatic Marxism and gave public expression to his mistrust of the contemporary regime of Soviet Russia, Nezval submitted himself to the politics of the Communist Party and announced the dissolving of the Surrealist Group, which he had co-founded himself four years earlier. However, he ran into vehement opposition from the other members, and in the end he was expelled. The Prague Surrealist Group immediately met in order to adopt a stance on Nezval's attempt at the group's liquidation. The result of the negotiations of, among others, Toyen, Brouk, Štyrský, and Teige was the unanimous decision that the group did not regard itself as dissolved, but would continue in its activity without Nezval. On 11 March 1938, Breton received a telegram that Nezval had been expelled from the Surrealist Group in Prague for artistic and political reasons. While after the conflict in spring 1938 Nezval announced the dissolution of the Surrealist Group to the newspapers, the remaining members informed about Nezval's expulsion from the group and the continuation of its activities.[13]

Teige replied to the antagonistic situation with this brochure *Surrealismus proti proudu* (Surrealism Against the Current, 1938) with the subtitle "The Surrealist Group replies to Vítězslav Nezval, J. Fučík, Kurt Konrad, St. K. Neumann, J. Rybák, L. Štoll, and others." The book's cover also bore meaning. It depicts a hand with a quill pen which is breaking through a brick wall (the same drawing appeared in the leaflet in which the verdict on Louis XVI was announced). In the studies from the *Surrealism Against the Current* collection, Teige, as one of the first, places fas-

12 The relationship between the avant-garde and the Baroque (and Mannerism) is analyzed in detail by Josef Vojvodík in his work *Povrch, skrytost, ambivalence: manýrismus, baroko a (česká) avantgarda* (Praha: Argo, 2008). In his view, one common feature of avant-garde art and Mannerism is their conception of art as an absolutist style, an attempt at perfecting the work of art as expressing "subjective internalization," but at the same time also a thorough emancipation from nature and the external model. Mannerist artists defined themselves against tradition by an escape into the past, while the avant-garde chose as its aim a (Utopian) future. According to Vojvodík, another common feature was their conception of the work of art as a challenge for the recipient (reader).

13 A declaration with a clear name immediately appeared in *Ranní noviny*: "The Surrealist Group is not dissolved: (...) all members of this group state that Mr. V. Nezval is not authorized to liquidate the Prague Surrealist Group, which continues to exist and will continue in its activities and in cooperation with the international Surrealist movement. This cooperation has also proved itself in the participation of Štyrský and Toyen at the recent international exhibition of Surrealists in Paris. Mr. V. Nezval has been unanimously expelled from the Prague Surrealist Group." "Surrealistická skupina není rozpuštěna," *Ranní noviny*, no. 62 [15 March 1938]: 4.

cist Germany and the Stalinist Soviet Union on the same level. He reacts not only to the exhibition "Entartete Kunst" (Degenerate Art) from 1937, but also to an incident from 1936 when avant-garde works were removed from an exhibition and replaced by realist paintings from the second half of the 19th century. In a range of respects, the *Surrealism Against the Current* brochure became the gravestone of the Surrealist Group.

The German occupation in 1939 entirely transformed the cultural climate. The Protectorate of Bohemia and Moravia was established and censorship reached new heights — in the instructions for the press valid from September 1939 the restriction of the word "war" itself was proposed. The illusion for the citizens of the Protectorate that nothing serious was happening was also transmitted into the instructions for the press service: do not allow any reports about suicides or arrests in the Protectorate. Surrealism was entirely excluded from official art and shifted into illegality. Avant-garde culture found itself in a sleep, as implies Štyrský's key metaphor of the book *Z kasemat spánku* (From the Casemates of Sleep, 1940), in which Štyrský, together with Jindřich Heisler and Toyen, realized poem–objects, the avant-garde key tension between word and image. In the years of World War Two, various fates awaited individual artists. In 1941, Jindřich Heisler, the youngest member of the Surrealist Group, who cooperated closely with Toyen and Štyrský, did not come forward for the registration of non-Aryans and to the end of the war he hid in Prague, primarily in Toyen's apartment. The Surrealists only created in seclusion or in illegality. International contacts were entirely cut off. However, informal Surrealist groups continued to operate in Prague (with names derived from Prague districts — Žižkovští surrealisté, Michelští surrealisté, Spořilovští surrealisté — Surrealists of Žižkov, Michle, Spořilov) as well as in some other towns. This enabled some continuity of Surrealist activities to be established after the end of the war. Czech Surrealism is the only avant-garde movement that on the basis of its continuity gained the designation of a permanent avant-garde (Anja Tippner).[14]

14 Anja Tippner, *Die permanente Avantgarde? — Surrealismus in Prag* (Köln; Weimar; Wien: Böhlau, 2009) / Anja Tippnerová: *Permanentní avantgarda? — Surrealismus v Praze,* Trans. by M. Brunová (Praha: Academia, 2014). Tippner focuses on the functioning of the Surrealist Group. She interprets the history of Czech Surrealism with regard to literature, film, and theory and attempts to identify a contemporary Surrealist avant-garde in the context of history (among others, Jiří Švankmajer, Vratislav Effenberger, Karel Teige).

Vítězslav Nezval: Preface to *She Wanted to Rob Lord Blamington: Poetry and Analysis*

"Because if you only go on spouting words,
you will never understand me any better'[1]
K. H. Mácha

Lord Blamington is an inhabitant of our second semi-circle soaked in ink. On the day of 8 September 1929 I fell asleep as usual during the holidays sometime around half past eleven. Because I heard the clock strike twelve a few minutes after waking up, I can determine quite precisely when this lord appeared. Through preliminary explanatory notes I do not want to deprive the reader of the horror that gripped me when I learned of his existence.

Nevertheless, whether I want to or not, I must say a couple of words about the strangeness of the little room in which this dream occurred to me. It is a former school office, and because it is separated from the apartment by a corridor, it suited me as a work office all the more on account of the fact that it had been furnished for living since the time when they moved grandma into it, whose illness required nighttime care.

After my arrival for the holidays (two years ago) they moved her into the apartment and the family reconciled itself with the fact that it would be woken up several times a night by the sickness that diabetes caused grandma, who had endured a stroke, because I myself also needed an apartment for the sake of my work, and so I took over this small room from grandma.

1 Však jak pravím, pilně poslouchejte, / neb jak slova jenom vypustíte, / nikdy víc mně neporozumíte. From Karel Hynek Mácha: "Pouť krkonošská". trans. by Hugh Hamilton McGovern, see "Krkonošská Pilgrimage", *The Slavonic and East European Review* 27, No. 69, 1949.

Already during the holidays grandma's illness worsened and in the middle of November she died from a second stroke. Her death did not surprise us, and I regret that I do not have more space to describe her decline, which was almost surprising in its lightness, and so we felt much less horror and pain than if grandma had not died in such a way.

When she was still healthy and after her first illness, when her consciousness was still intact, she believed with almost religious certainty that she would die peacefully, basing her belief on an automatic text of mine, written more than eight years before her death.

Ever since I was fifteen, I had been interested in spiritualism. I used to meet up with some quite young guys in a room on the first floor of the bakery where we tried without success to hold a seance with a little table. However, already at that time I demonstrated an inclination towards automatic conversations which I pronounced in the dark and which four years later under the influence of a friend I changed into automatic writing.

At that time, we carried out attempts during broad daylight and most often in a secluded part of the chateau park, where the father of a friend was the head gardener. For these attempts we required a few sheets of large-format paper and a soft-lead pencil. Without any kind of intoning on our part the pencil started to move, scrawling ellipses and crossing over at a free, but also very fast pace, and in unbroken writing.

Sometimes we wrote for an entire half day, and after we had said our goodbyes (we were not from the same village), each of us continued on our own at home, communicating the results the next day. Most of the texts of my friend concerned the previous lives of the girl with whom he was evidently in love, even though he did not actually express this. These were real visions, which enraptured both of us. I recall that dirty London alley where, according to the texts, in a previous life this girl had been a harlot, even though now she was from a very serious kind of family.

On other occasions we called up some famous spirits. We learned that Dostoevsky is a janitor in New York. Strange phenomena were provoked by the thought of Baudelaire. Instead of a text, the pencil started to spout forth ellipses, hurling our hands around and bashing them on the table, and so we had to call on the patron for help, who announced himself to us under the name Dorema.

There is a family relationship between Lord Blamington and Dorema. Both of these existences were born from the automatic activity of the spirit.

About Dorema we learned many details, and he was a magnanimous and virtually angelic being. Lord Blamington, about whom I have known only for a few hours, is a demon; at the very least there is much of the dandy in him.

Dorema thus protected us from the wild phenomena that occurred during the calling up of Baudelaire, and usually he was the prologue of our joint attempts.

Some of our texts had a clairvoyant sense. The friend predicted the death of the local doctor three years ahead.

He predicted of me that I would give up my intention of studying medicine, that I would change the Law Faculty for the Philosophy Faculty, and that I would devote myself to literature. He described several of my previous lives and did not conceal from me that I had been in jail, because in several previous lives I had been a drunkard.

He therefore discovered for me the technique of automatic writing seven years earlier than it became the foundation of the poetics of the Surrealists in Paris, and at the end of the holidays we parted without ever meeting.

I continued with seances on my own and I also displayed a remarkable clairvoyance. It surprised me when in answer to a question about a female friend who was about to get married I received a reply from which it followed that her wedding would not take place and that she would die. I ceased to believe in our method because the girl was proverbially healthy and her wedding was a matter of two or three months away. I concealed this inauspicious reply from her and I was disconcerted when they wrote to me after my departure that she had become ill with tuberculosis. After a few months she died.

Well, in a certain text I had predicted that grandma would outlive her husband (at that time he was entirely healthy and seemed to be much younger than grandma, who suffered from rheumatism) and that her death would be peaceful.

Even though she knew of my blitheness and even though she did not have any great trust in me, in these matters she was evidently the only person who took them seriously and several times she posed me questions to which she always received satisfactory replies, even though they concerned persons whom I did not know and relationships about which I had no inside knowledge. During my texts she was usually calm and after my departure she often spoke about them as about indubitable certainties. Truly, she outlived granddad and the result of our seances was the salutary calm with which she contemplated her own painless death.

Immediately after her death we clothed her and placed her in the separate room, where she lay for three days until her funeral.

Although the room was newly painted a short while after this, I did not dare to move into it and I preferred to work in a room where I was disturbed. A year later at Christmas I plucked up the courage to move into the room and spent five or six nights there, almost sleepless. I stared fixedly at the place where she had lain dead. In the dark I listened to my own auditory delusions and I was often on the verge of desperation, not being able to fall asleep.

This year I have somehow as a matter of course posed myself the obligation of overcoming the remains of my fear and I have now been living in this former office for almost two months without anything “spooky’ appearing to me.

In order to calm myself down I carried out an experiment, which is mortifying for me. However, I admit to it without being afraid that I will be condemned more than I deserve to be.

Three weeks ago a close friend came to visit me. I thought about whether I should give up my own bed for him, or whether I should give him the second bed, which stands in the place where dead grandma lay for three days. In my soul I apologized to my friend, who did not know that in the places under him she had lain dead and who was not going to be afraid of anything and who would be calm, but in spite of that I reproached myself because the dog whom I had brought to the bedroom a few days earlier had started to bark in a terrified way and tried to flee. In the morning I leaned over the headboard with one single thought: whether he was alive. The result of this experiment calmed me down such that I forgot about my former dread and it was only today's strange dream about Lord Blamington that reminded me of it.

Before I resolve to set about writing down the dream, I will mention some events that are not connected with it, but which are nevertheless equally mysterious.

It was evidently only just early fall, because I rushed out of Národní kavárna (coffee house) without my hat and in the dark in front of the coffee house I saw J. Š. — who a moment earlier had been sitting with me at the table — engaged in an argument with a former friend.

Together with T. we left for the Passage coffee house, where as always in the evening there were so many people that we hardly got a table. Even to this day I do not know what was the cause of the outburst of my friend. I remember the table where we were sitting on account of what happened after our arrival. Because on this occasion the techniques of automatic writing could not be used, on account of the fact that we would have attracted the attention of the people at the nearby tables, we made use of an older technique and I started to speak without thinking about everything that I saw in my mind.

The main impulse that brought me into a state of clairvoyance were several words that Š had said to me already downstairs in the restaurant about his great-grandfather, who out of misanthropy drove relatives out of their deathbeds and had horses brought to their bedsides.

When I became acquainted with Š in the society of friends from the Devětsil group, I was agitated because I was supposed to leave Prague in a few hours on account of my military defense obligations. Š accompanied me to Masaryk Train Station, where we sat for roughly an hour. He knew my "Podivuhodný kouzelník" (Remarkable Magician) and, thanks to the passage about the lily of the valley, he recounted to me the impression that he had had at the moment when his sister had died. When they came to announce her death to him, he was looking at lilies of the valley.

We became friends and, if I remember well, already then I could have predicted everything that I saw in several images while in the Passage coffee house. Primarily, I described to Š in a quite detailed way the house where he was born. I described several scarves of his mother and the inside of a cupboard for kitchenware, where I saw a rosary and a small bottle of digitalis. Š was excited by these corresponding details and suddenly cried out. I had just seen a broad ironing board, on which three dead bodies lay on top of one another. When Š explained to me that on the board, according to a custom about which I did not know, deceased members of his family were placed, and that his sister, mother, and father had lain on it, I was overcome by horror and broke off the conversation.

Afterwards, more than three-quarters of a year later, when Š and T had returned from their stay in Paris, Š invited me to his estate in the Orlické hory (Eagle Mountains).

I arrived there shortly before evening and I was welcomed by them with an unforgettable concert.

T wore on her head a broad Mexican hat and played the barrel organ.

They led me into a room where their paintings were hanging. While I was looking at them, a gunshot resounded from outside. I learned that their steward shot in this way quite often in order to scare off thieves. After evening dinner we looked through the souvenirs that they had brought back from their travels. I recall Baudelaire's drawings of Jeanne Duval. Already before evening dinner they had led me up to the loft and showed me their buzzard chick.

Before midnight we were drunk. Suddenly in my mind I saw a board and, crying out, I ran without light up to the loft, a part of which I had glimpsed a while earlier in the weak light of a petrol lamp. I groped around with my hand and suddenly with a shout I touched a piece of wood. Š ran up to me with a light. I was holding an ironing board in my hand.

Then I quickly gave orders. Pointing with my finger to the closed cupboard, I named the objects that were in it. In some kind of small cup I saw in my mind an old medallion. It was there.

A similar, albeit less terrifying event happened to me three weeks previously in the small room when I was putting my friend to bed. He said to me: A very strange event occurred to my father a few days ago at the railway station when he was looking in the direction towards the station kitchen. I asked him not to recount it to me, that I would try to guess it myself.

I very clearly saw his father observing the station cook, who looked exactly like his wife who had been dead for more than a year. My vision was absolutely precise.

Bohuslav Brouk: Afterword to Jindřich Štyrský, *Emily Comes to Me in a Dream*

Those who conceal their sexuality despise their innate capacities without being able to rise above them. They reject their immortality, even though they are unable to break free of the sad merry-go-round of life, which human sex organs enable and guarantee, and to achieve the immortality of the mythical gods. Though they hold the illusion of their immortality and rid their behaviour and psyche of sexuality, they are never able to rid themselves of the physical proof of their animality. Their bodies continue to demonstrate the human destiny that is immortality; therefore any hint of human animality unsettles those very people who dream so arduously about the contrary. Any mention of animality — not only in life, but also in science, literature and art — upsets them as it interrupts their dreaming, disturbing their rationalist airs and social ostentation. Every forced perception of excremental and sexual acts dissolves their super-human fantasies and demonstrates that it is useless to free themselves from the power of nature that, presuming their mortality, has equipped them with sexuality and an irrepressible need to satisfy this hunger.

Nothing can depress those elevated above the body's material nature more than when their body automatically announces its presence. Let us consider how depressing the effect is on the golden boy when he feels an uncontrollable shit beckoning during a triumphal campaign, or how bitterly the snobs tolerate their sexual desire for a lowly subordinate. Their bodies pull them back to animality, and their superhuman self-confidence falls prey to disillusionment. The bodily processes that they are stuck with are their Achilles' heel, the susceptibility of which has been superbly discerned by pornophiles.

At its core, pornophilia is combative and sadistic. In their activities, pornophiles attack the snobs who believe themselves superior to animality. By pointing out human nature, they remove all the artificial inequality of people; this new criteria leads to new castes that are not differentiated socially, but by vital potency. Pornophilia thus destroys the illusions that snobs hold of their godliness, while exposing their physical ineptness and inferiority that they themselves bring about by loathing their bodies. The body is the final argument of those who are unjustly brushed aside and neglected, since it enables them to render groundless all social distinctions when compared with the power of nature. Yet, through the body, pornophiles do more than break down the social barriers between people: due to the body's aptitude and integrity, they rise above others who, from different perspectives, instead scorn them. It is from this perspective in particular that pornophilia can be first and foremost a weapon of those socially weaker, those who are materially and culturally oppressed and who can, at least in this sense, exert their power and importance through the potency of their undeteriorated bodies. Therefore, it is easier to conceive that those who succumb to pornophilia are of a more revolutionary nature than those who side with the languishing bourgeoisie.

Pornophiles sadistically assault the arrogant psyche of the ruling pretentious. The latter then react to these attacks that disrupt their dreams in the same way: through sadistically motivated prudishness and puritanical persecution of the "morally corrupt". Perhaps you too can persuade yourself of the motives for the origin of pornophilia when, in the company of pretentious snobs, you will have countless urges to interrupt the prevailing, idiotic idyll with a thunderous outburst of words such as "Shit!" or "Fuck!"

The original reason for engaging in obscenity cannot be distorted even in the primitive drawings of vaginas and penises by savages — images of which are still to this day being depicted on city walls. If the sadistic nature of their drawings is not directed against society's pretentious, it is aimed at women — at their inferior penis-less sexual organ — whom they threaten to punish with their penises, portrayed in large drawings and sculptures. In this age, however, pornophilia, whose psychological value lies in the demonstration of obscene works and expressions, and not in their apprehensive concealment, has become a weapon against those of the same sex, but who are unjustifiably haughty, so that instead of misogynist traits it has acquired misanthropic ones.

Since the biological consequences of sex also unpleasantly affect pornophiles (who, like everyone else, do not want to admit their own mortality) that which the pornophile likes obtains a unique veil that conceals the general unpleasantness evoked by a suggestion of our animality. A work that possesses obscene aspects can serve, if treated in this particular way, as a surrogate satisfaction of sexual desires, of the direct sexual urge, or it can be treated artistically, in which, though continuing to possess its combative value, it does so in a special sense. The sadistic nature of a work with a pornophilic trait, especially an artistic work, is, however, usually latent, hidden in the creator's unconscious, without ever becoming conscious, just like the sense of the vehement rejection of it by puritans. The true motive of their actions is unknown to both pornophiles and puritans, and therefore misunderstood. The sadistic sense of pornographic works certainly does not influence their aesthetic value and is not in any way a stranger motive for creation than the motives for creating the customary genres.

In an artistically rendered pornographic work, sexuality is freed from its actual biological function and is only conceived hedonistically without its reproductive consequences. In other words, it does not attack the animality of snobs, but the relative inferiority of their animality. The artist does not provoke puritans for their fleetingness and mortality that he too will succumb to, but for their impotence and sexual inferiority that they inflict upon themselves with in their unreasonable longing to be superhuman, thus letting their sexuality degenerate. Artistic pornophilia does not conceal the sadistic nature of pure obscenity, but limits the means of its aggression by excluding the biological aspect of sexuality and excretion from its content. Therefore, in pornophilia-motivated art, sexuality's hedonistic sense, not its biological one, fights against snobs — it is mainly the imperfect humanity, not the imperfect godliness of snobs that it attacks. The longing for immortality can be ridiculed for its unfavourable consequence: sexual degeneration. Art therefore only tempers the pornophile's sadism in utilizing the biological aspect of sexuality, which is disagreeable to both the pornophile and the pornophobe.

In also finding pornophilic inclinations with people who are actually accused of it, they often like the kitsch aspects of it meant to sexually arouse them. Indeed, shoddy pornography completely subdues the sadistic motives of pornographic works by making them accessible to the very caste of people against which the essence of pornophilia aims. Pornophilia only leads to immorality from the perspective of puritans persecuting combative, sadistic pornophilia, to which they outwardly attribute the same meaning as possessed by their pornographic literature and paintings, carefully hidden away in closed drawers to be used for the occasional arousal that, in most cases, their moulting wives can no longer provide. This is the only branch of pornophilia that does not need an audience, and even shuns it, since most people, and not just puritans, have difficulty achieving an orgasm in the presence of others.

Free of all bias, we appreciate solely the artistic value of pornographic works. If the obscene content diminishes for some a work's value, then the art of Strindberg or Tolstoy could be rejected for its misogyny. Pornophilia cannot be reprehended for being pathological, for it is afflicted just as other cultural manifestations as well as the sadistic puritanism of its opponents. If a work of art is pornographic, it is just as much a cultural phenomenon as it is humanist art. If it is limited to a solely libidinal expression not linked to other cultural or economic values, it is just as neurotic as petty sympathy. It can then express itself in a purely pathological way in erotomania and scatology, just as anthropophilia does in the masochism of martyrs. Our humanity, culture and civilization are merely a quantitative application of neurotic conflicts and if our pathology then yields works of value, we cannot be reproved for this trait. Sublimation of the neurotic libido is creative, while the normal libido leads only to playfulness. Both types of the libido are then involved in obscenely motivated creativity. The neurotic libido determines the content of works while its form depends on the normal libido. If the normal libido seeks a surrogate of direct satisfaction, it creates kitsch out of the obscene creations. If its demands are sublimated, a work of art is then created.

The arousing, kitschy treatment of pornographic themes has no other function and value than that of dolls designed for masturbation. Such works are limited to real sexual acts and cannot be separated from the air of seclusion without ceasing to perform their functions consisting of the illusion of a real partner and intercourse. On the contrary, an artist whose work is not bound to reality in such a way does not need to have naked girls urinate into a chamber pot and can offer them an Alpine valley. Not letting the semen turn into a yellowish stain on the sheet and, instead, transforming it into lightning, he can split a gothic dome for them. He can replace the lovers' bed with the universe, and can place a globe under the woman's ass, then let the sun rise from her genitalia; it will be a most superb abortion.

The artist, unhindered by the rational coordination of ideas, genuine proportionality and syntax, frees sexuality of its biological function of producing new generations, which is all too awkwardly evoked by pornographic kitsch if it achieves its arousing purpose with an orgasm. Artistic pornophilia can never be viewed in an ironic light and cynically dismissed as real or reproduced sexuality stuck to the sheets.

If another world has long ago reached a new assessment in art, the censorship by puritans, aroused by the obscene content, has prevented the treatment of sexual scenes, insomuch as it offers proof of healthy sexuality while their sexuality woefully wastes away behind their flies. They recognize, albeit unconsciously, their sexual inferiority and envy others for their powerful penises and healthy asses not plagued with haemorrhoids as their own are. They are thus much more tormented by a work of art with obscene content than by pornographic kitsch, since the artist has spread sexuality's rule throughout the world. The kitschy pornophile remains in the realm of secluded alcoves. In contrast, the artist has spread out all over the world. He lets the seas urinate, the Himalayas take a shit, the cities give birth, the factory chimneys masturbate and so on. Nothing is sacred to him, he associates sexuality with everything.

His pansexuality has a double meaning: First, it attacks the impotent puritans. Secondly, it frees sexuality from its reproductive function. He understand them purely in aesthetic, hedonistic terms. He does not tarnish the pleasures allowed by the libido with mundane truths. The created erotic scenes do not begin or end with depressing banalities; the banality and dullness of sexual satisfaction cannot be eliminated by perverse desires. They too are dull and banal. To play libidinal games, one must find a milieu that deflects our senses from the sad post-coital state and that prevents the rational speculation which poisons our passion. Our eroticism must be freed of its depressing association with fat wives and the marital bed, under which a chamber pot is hidden.

Nevertheless, poetry is the art of discovering the exotic in the mundane, which is why there is no need to reject mundane things, just mundane situations. This can be done through the subjective assessment of things and actions, by extricating them from their usual order. By negating their biological and economic sense of reality, poetry disrupts its rational relations and, using a new syntax, instils the old content with new meaning, a new story. Thus the mundane, the awkward, becomes the unexpected, the emotive. Poetry is the art of finding the emotive perspectives of everyday life. The art of living is the art of where and when to drink a cup of black coffee or, in the field of sexuality, where and when to ejaculate. If the puritans want to call this pathological, we will help them. It is situational partialism.

The modern artist moves from the world of dreams and hallucinations to the world of the most deranged lunatics who, exhausted by the adventure that their reason had taken them on, have renounced it and get by with the adventure that the liberated libido provides them with by freeing their senses. The adventure of reason, of rationalism, is a pathologically closed psychosis that negates the intellect and, through autistic seclusion, deprives people of the ability to rationally assess their views and actions. The liberated libido can manifest itself freely in this pathological state. Psychosis brings an end to neurotic raging in a negative way, through the gradual impediment of the body's mental and physical functions. If it is limited to the negation of reason and does not prevent perception, movement and the likes, natural paths of our behaviour and our emotional, aesthetic and non-rationalistic perception ultimately appear before us.

The world that the lunatics have entered through the blunting of their spirit, the artist has entered with common sense, for he has managed to artistically utilize a natural, purely hedonistic view of reality. If ancient art is analogous to neurosis, modern art is, for the most part, akin to the manifestations of psychosis. From the realm of dreams, hallucinations, alcoholic deliria and painstakingly forced symbolic phantasms, today's artist has arrived at a natural, purely emotive assessment and perception of reality that itself creates phantasms, about which ancient art never even dreamt. Modern poetry has spread a magical, dreamy studio atmosphere to the entire *plein air*. It has enabled the artist to disregard the socio-economic values of life and to think and perceive things in a solely hedonistic light. The liberated senses and psyche can thus view the entire world emotively, no matter how fleeting. In an artistic concept, a pornographic work shows life's passion detached from mundane objectives. The artist frees our bodily acts of biological purpose and lets us enjoy ourselves just as nature has enabled us, carefully liberating our animality from a desolate vision. Asceticism and all avoidance of hints of sexuality are nonsense. Let us enjoy everything we are capable of, for everyone enters the world as an appendage to an umbilical cord and ultimately turns into mere dust.

Jindřich Štyrský: Surrealist Painting

(a few notes)

A person with the disposition that André Breton called Surrealist — a Surrealist poet or painter — for whom spontaneity is a process, will be (without needing to explain this process) in complete harmony with the dialectical-materialist view, which is not an artificial doctrine and which is based on observing the law of real existence. Therefore, if the poet or painter moves truly spontaneously in spontaneity, and if he speaks of his work intuitively and devoid of philosophical ambitions, I believe that he must still come to the conclusion that the views of dialectical materialism must be found to be self-evident. As for the spontaneity of which I speak, Salvador Dalí captures it beautifully: "I avoid spontaneity in its pure state, because it adheres to convention. I prefer "systematization', which arises spontaneously as delirium."

I would like to rely solely on this intuition in this brief study. Verifying it remains the gnoseology of dialectical materialism, which, knowing precisely the laws of reality and real existence, illuminates, when applied to psychology, the subtlest aspects of the thinking process, which could never be explained by positivism, and which has turned idealism upside down.

Until I had completely and thoroughly accepted dialectical materialism and while I was still at odds with it, I did not wonder whether what it called appearances had a specific basis in the laws of real existence. The aesthetics of artificialism differed from the gnoseology of Surrealism in that it did not question the reality of appearances. In practice, a painter's intuition spontaneously requiring this connection to a real foundation was, in my view, safe enough not to clash with the laws of real existence, even though the commentary of this practice could have easily, at that time, fallen into idealism.

If I were to situate Artificialism, I would call it a link between Cubism and Surrealism. At the dawn of the Surrealist movement in France, it was not possible to speak of Surrealist painting. At that time, André Breton himself considered the group of painters around him as forerunners of sorts, and not as pure representatives of Surrealist painting; in those days they were mostly already distinctly established artists: Picasso, Chirico, Klee, Arp, Masson and Picabia, whose works he more referred to than sang the praises of. On the other hand, it was mainly artists just beginning with surrealism, such as Miró, Ernst and Dalí, who were then wrongly criticized (with the exception of perhaps Miró) for their illustrative, literary and anecdotal concept of painting. Today, when most of them (except for Max Ernst whose development can be called revolutionary) have significantly developed, the situation is different. In my transitioning from Artificialism to Surrealism, without wanting to use someone else's cutlery, I did not betray my intuition which I rightly feel has led me, but I did betray that topsy-turvy idealistic intellectual position that once caused me to clash with some of those who were very rigorously seeking to rebuild their ideology from a dialectical materialist perspective.

Surrealism rediscovered for painting reality and its emotionality which lies in its psychological sense. That something seems one way or another to us has a deeper cause, unless, of course, we have thought it up as a masterful piece of ambitious subjectivity. It has its cause in the laws of the real existence of reality, seen not from a positivist standpoint, but from a dialectical and materialist position. Surrealist painting draws mainly from intuitive knowledge, though not from intuition in a Bergsonian sense, i.e. intuition as a form of immediate perception of super-empirical, transcendental and metaphysical reality.

To realize the distance that now separates us from the original Cubism, I paraphrase Picasso in that he wanted to paint pictures by which an engineer could precisely construct the things depicted, and Dr. Vincenc Kramář that "Cubism was primarily about the shape, plasticity and the exact position of things in a space, about capturing the utmost objective elements, and that this picture of the object was to be complemented by other properties such as color and others that we learn about through strongly subjective senses. To fill the canvas with these perfectly understood things and, on the other hand, to fulfil their beauty by creating a painting, was the ultimate goal of Picasso and Braque. That was Cubism."

Aware that art is a process in which everything aims for a higher unity through the development of oppositions, we encounter in Cubism an amazing, epochal opposition to practically the entire previous historical development of painting. Dr. Vincenc Kramář defined more purely and accurately than any other art theoretician the role of Cubism, without which Surrealism would never have been born — though the latter seemingly denies its contribution, but just seemingly. In terms of worldview, Cubism arose from the idealistic concept of artistic form and is philosophically linked to the art theories of Kant and Schiller.

"In a truly beautiful work of art, the subject should do nothing, the form everything." — (Schiller). Surrealist painting renews the existence of things. That is not to say that Cubism was a wholly abstract art, especially in the later phases of its development as we see in the latest works of Picasso and Filla, who are only a small step away from Surrealism.

Surrealism regards dialectically the relation between form and content. Today, after the epochal discoveries of Cubism, we are opposed to the whole fetishism over so-called pure painting and all the problems of space and its construction by non-illusionist means, problems of light, problems of doing away with the closedness of figures, the breaking down of objects into their basic shapes and the natural concerns of deformation, of atmosphere, of illusionism as impure artistic means. The Surrealist painter is unpredictable in the formative means chosen and used.

In Surrealist painting, content and form create unity. In a Surrealist painting, neither the construction nor the composition is autotelic, as is the case in "pure painting".

We can well imagine a Surrealist artist working on a strip of a painting in progress. The Surrealist painter does not compose, since he replaces the artificial order of construction with an order that he himself creates simultaneously. This is the result of years of construction led by instinct that subconsciously gathers experiences. Surrealist painting is a reaction to painting that only wanted to evoke optical impressions. Surrealist painting strives for a direct and deep psychological expression, and therefore defies mere aesthetic assessment. Surrealist paintings are, as Karel Teige aptly writes: "Fire flashes of the imagination; an imagination that once gave birth to sphinxes, dryads, centaurs, dolphins, harpies, devils and angels today creates monsters even more astonishing than a woman's torso with a fishtail, new sirens, altogether different from the image of woman and fish."

Surrealism: Romanticism's revival.

I would like to end by saying that I hope our art criticism does not overly squander the epithets of Surrealist painting and the Surrealist painter, and that it is able to distinguish those who are true Surrealists from those who plunder the world of the imagination and for whom the theory of Surrealism is a shield for epigonism and plagiarism.

(from a lecture given at an evening gathering of the Group of Surrealists in Prague at the Mánes Gallery on 11 May 1934)

Bedřich Václavek: On Surrealism

1. The polemical methods of surrealists

In issue no. 7 of *Index* we made a brief and disapproving comment regarding the significance of the Surrealism discussions that took place in our country last spring. In return, we were taught, in the anthology *Surrealism in Discussion* by Karel Teige, a lesson as if we were school children who, in our "provincial Brno indolence" had neglected to study up on Surrealism, or as if we were rascals maliciously representing it. I claim authorship of this comment, from which my name was inadvertently omitted.

Perhaps Teige would have responded differently if that omission had not been made, for he would have had to recall the numerous fights we had engaged in, often just the two of us on our side. We always had our differences, but we respected them. If he had known that I had been the one who had fought so frequently in backing the work of Devětsil, he would not have so easily accused me of "conservative aesthetic and psychological inclinations" and of an obtuseness regarding modern art, dismissing me with insults and general condemnation, as he does with many others, and as he had rightly forbid others to do with Surrealism. But it is not about this personal side of things or about *Index*. I am only mentioning Teige's outrageous response because the style of this attack is typical of the polemical methods of Surrealists in general. Let us disregard the amusing fact that an anthology was published aimed at providing a picture of a certain public discussion that had occurred, and that it also includes all those who dared to subject this discussion to criticism. Let us also ignore the method of quoting the classics of socialism, which Surrealists only quote insofar that they speak for Surrealism, and do not quote in instances that their statements are directed against it. We are mostly concerned about the means of discussion that insultingly dismisses anyone not fully proclaiming himself a Marxist — and often even Marxists do not agree with Surrealists. The Soviet critic Maxim Gorky had some harsh words at the writers' conference in Leningrad which, as one of the most significant literary conferences of Soviet writers, preceded the Moscow Congress. In assessing themes, characters and the mutual relations of people, criticism must be based on facts that provide an immediate observation of the turbulent course of life. It is not enough for the critic to tell the author: this is done incorrectly because our teachers Marx, Engels and Lenin say this and that about the matter. In our country — and this holds true for other countries as well — there are many such things that could not have been foreseen. Critics must be able to say: "It is incorrect because reality is in contradiction with what the author writes." This was a prompt lesson for Soviet critics, but also for all Marxist critics in general, if they had acted in this way. However, our Surrealists, who so zealously quote but speak so little of art's relation to today's social life, must above all take this to heart. For their polemical methods only damage dialectical materialism, which never feared this assessment of reality. Indeed, that was its strong side — and ultimately the reason for its superiority as well. Flatly rejecting all objections of critics because they are non-Marxists proves nothing. Their mistakes must be specifically shown!

Yet there's another aspect to the matter. Again, I am talking here about those with whom Teige does not at all want to speak because they are of a different worldview than he, or are not as far down the path to it as he. Does he think that he will win anyone over to his view with such arrogance? That he will convince someone in this way? He certainly will not achieve this through insults and scorn.

But that was always the method of the former Devětsil. Whoever disagreed with the group was simply a fool, irrelevant. As a result, they ignored all contemporary Czech literature — and it lived its own life. Another consequence was that Devětsil's often high theoretical and creative level had such a negligent effect that it remained isolated. Who from Devětsil truly critically assessed contemporary Czech literature? Who truly gave it a thorough and critical comparison to the works of Čapek's generation or of their successors from the post-war generation? Who praised or critically rebuked the work of a number of writers with the same worldview? Nobody. And so it resulted in the formation of today's two camps among dialectical materialist-oriented artists, and that, in addition to the pioneering work of this avant-garde, there appeared mediocre and sub-mediocre works of many writers, who have so far cleverly occupied positions, and now Devětsil Surrealists suddenly feel surrounded by strong enemy positions and see enemies everywhere — even among people with the same worldview, merely because they don't agree with them. This is the curse of groups who prefer wrapping themselves in the robe of exclusivity and who consistently avoid discussions with people sharing the same platform!

Simplifying the polemical task using some of these inaccurate generalities is also a polemical method of the Surrealists. If Surrealism is charged with perversion, malady and degradation, Teige only identifies "bourgeois critics", whom he feels makes these accusations because they consider anything that is not resigned to the living conditions and laws of a capitalist society, anything that is a rebellion, desire, dream, love and revolution to be "sick, insane and degraded". But what if people of the same worldview, who cannot be suspected of narrowmindedness, have similar objections to Surrealism? And their ranks are not thin!

2. What it's all about

We could move on, but let's take a look at the terrible act that *Index* actually committed to its readers and modern culture with its comment. It declared the problem of expression in art to be a secondary problem — especially at present "when everything is at stake: social progress, culture and, above all, that which the working class is fighting for." If I say as much, then apparently I suffer from "an embarrassing misunderstanding of art and poetry." Well, I feel that they are the ones suffering from an embarrassing misunderstanding since they claim to be Marxists, and yet manage to get themselves entwined at such a time in matters that will largely be resolved by solving the main issues regarding social development. Perhaps they do not realize that the basic (Kantian) concept of art still lingers in this one-sided interest in the expressive aspect of art: the view professing that it does not matter what the poet says, buy how he says it; that delight in beauty is a delight that is devoid of interest. And whom this fading bourgeois aesthetics serves is as clear as day.

Identifying the poet's expression with poetry in general cannot be done as easily as Teige does in his argument with us. Poetry has interests that are greater and currently more urgent than whether the expression by which the poet embodies his idea is, at all costs, adequate to what he says — even if it should be adequate. However, if we persistently encounter in poetry blatant indifference to that which is moving through the world, it is merely a thin bandage for that if the poet speaks of his important matters in the language and expression of an artistic (or even Parisienne) *dernier cri*. Instead, we tolerate the "conventional expression" so rejected by the Surrealists, if it says something substantial. (Judging by the spring manifesto, they wanted to graciously forgive the authors of the same worldview and objective for it, though now they seem to have changed their view on this.)

Karel Teige was somewhat outraged that we called a local Prague affair Surrealism. Thank goodness that the critical distance provided by our stay in Moravia has made us aware of not only the psychosis of Prague's national street, but also the psychosis of Prague's cultural milieu in which things play a temporarily oversized role — one that they simply do not possess in our culture as a whole. And we also browse through international literature from time to time to see the international position of Surrealists and what the entire international literary left is working on. We can even live without Prague's massive import of all these events from abroad. Above all, however, it seems to us that something like Devětsil that so perfectly faded and disintegrated from within all by itself — we are still willing to defend its activities from the time when it played its historical role — should not be revived today now that different paths are being taken. Devětsil's work was once an important part of Czech cultural history. It replaced, partly in its own development as well, the content premise of an uncertain and budding proletarian poetry after the war. It was its antithesis that emphasized an original and non-derivative poetry. Now we are leading to the synthesis of this thesis and antithesis. Just as it is impossible to return to an original, primitive, budding proletarian poetry, so is its antithesis, Poetism-Surrealism, not feasible. We see this on both the Czech and international scale. Thus, for instance, in the USSR the lack of proletarian literature to date is currently being harshly criticized; so there is one such antithetical wave emphasizing the importance of a genuine, original, non-derivative poetry. But it is not Surrealism that is developing there, as the Surrealists may mistakenly believe, but a large and powerful concept that is far from any sectarian spirit of art groups, a spirit that one resolution of the Communist Party's executive committee has long deemed its distinctive feature — toxicity. It is from the perspective of this internationally constructed concept that we dared to view Surrealism in a negative light. That's all.

Karel Teige: Ten Years of Surrealism

The future of poetry? Yes, even art and poetry will captivate the masses and become the reality of life. In doing so, it will change its hitherto structure.

In advanced communism, when the difference between physical and mental work (and between specialists of both areas) is overcome, when productive forces at full tilt make physical work disappear and restore blessed leisure and the poetic "right to indolence". Only then will art become a reality of life and cease to exist in its current, class-created forms, as "art", so as to become the intimate fate of the person-poet, of one who can be led only by a revolution to fulfil humanity.

Communism will (as we read in "Deutsche Ideologie") bring an end to an artist's isolation within a single field, will bring an end to the concentration of artistic talent in solitary individuals linked to the suppression of artistic abilities in the masses; now the cursed, isolated avant-garde groups and their studios and laboratories have no other function and are, according to Breton, nothing more than "the loneliness of a few people whose role is to save from perishing that which, for the time being, can only blossom in a greenhouse and that which only later will find its place in the center of a new life and order." "The existence of poetry in literary form, no matter how modern poetry since Romanticism has been in the confines of literature" can only be explained by the anti-poetic social conditions, the effects of which will disappear only after the victory of communism all over the world". (Tristan Tzara) Poetry will cease to be a special form of creation and become, as the Romantics have long ago dreamt, a *reality of life*: it will not be an expression of the world, but participation in the world, in which *the principle of poetry will identify with the principle of reality*, in which beauty and reality will be joined in an absolute bond. The following note may serve to clarify Surrealism's relationship to reality: Surrealism *is not abstractivism or imitative naturalism:* Surrealism *is realism in a dialectical sense*, in which the reality of empirical evidence identifies with the reality of poetry. Therefore, it is the antithesis of positivist realism, "understanding reality only in the form of an object's empirical evidence and ignoring psychological life as reality, and is thus also the antithesis of that which art history calls realism, meaning the descriptive record of the reality of external phenomena.

Surrealism, which consciously follows up on the revolutionary tradition of Romanticism, seeks to control the legacy of culture and poetry, a legacy both magnificent and devastating, and to utilise them in such a way as to turn them as a weapon aimed against bourgeois culture and society.

In the preparatory process of identifying poetry and reality, poetry and the world, it is this less popular art, Surrealism, that deserves the greatest credit. In its psychological and poetical probes, and the attention to dreams, games of chance, and the makeup of "Surrealist objects", Surrealism has made art accessible to all capable of lyricism: so Man Ray's photograms, Max Ernst's collages and "Surrealist objects" have opened the way for lay creativity, enabling "armless Raphaels" to paint. Surrealism has reduced the significance of the "author"-specialist and the significance of the term "talent". For instance, in the phantasy of dreams it saw proof that the gift of fiction is not the privilege of select writers, but is essentially inherent to everyone. Then, by denying descriptive, positivist realism, which understood reality in a limited sense (As a law of Realism, Courbet declared that the painter can only paint what he sees) — the Surrealists, dissatisfied *with that which is*, i.e. with the restricted and class reality and with the *path that leads to that, but which restrictive realism claimed does not,* arrived at sur-reality, to the enrichment of reality, and understood here the world of dreams, of poetry and love as the *real world.* If the laboratory and studio isolation of Surrealism, viewed from the perspective of everyday reality which only understands the surface of things, means a loss of contact with poetry and the world, this isolation is also a sphere where a new concept of poetry is crystalizing, a poetry that can only prevail by re-establishing this contact, and not by returning to its previous forms, but by fusing and identifying with the world and humanity at a higher stage, at a higher level of development of poetry and humanity, in a "true realm of freedom". Only in this will poetry acquire material reality in the life of humanity. Only in this, captivating the masses, will it become a real force and cease to be mere literature. Only in this will it fulfil Lautréamont's prophecy that "*poetry will be made by all and not by just one*".

We are listing here only the main theoretical writings of Surrealists, or critical studies on Surrealism; this list does not include collections of poetry, albums and film librettos, partly because book publications of Surrealist poetry are too extensive and partly because even the article "10 Years of Surrealism" only concerns the ideological development of Surrealism and not its works in poetry, painting and film, which would have to be the subject of a separate study.

André Breton: Les Pas perdus, 1924. Manifeste du Surréalisme, 1924. Légitime Défense, 1926, Le Surréalisme et la Peinture, 1928. Second Manifeste du Surréalisme, 1930. Misère le da Poésie, 1932. Les Vases Comniunicants, 1932. Point du Jour. 1934. Qu'est-ce que le Surréalisme? 1934.
René Crevel: Salvator Dali ou l'anti-obscurantisme, 1931. Le Clavecin de Diderot, 1932.
Georges Hugnet: Petite Anthologie poétique du Surréalisme, 1934.
Tristan Tzara: Sept manifestes dada, 1924.
Marcel Raymond: De Baudelaire au Surréalisme. 1933.
Guy Mangeot: Histoire du Surréalisme, 1934.
Jean Daniel Maublanc: Surréalisme romantique, 1934.
Claude Cahun: Les paris sont ouverts, 1934.
Davičo, Kostić and Matić: Polozaj nadrealisma u drustvenom procesu, 1932.
Stefan Napierski: Od Baudelaire'a do nadrealistow, 1933.
Pierre Naville: La Révolution et les Intellectuels, 1926.

Periodicals, anthologies and collective publications:
La Révolution surréaliste, 1924–1930. *Surréalisme au service de la Révolution*, 1930–1933. *Minotaure,* 1933 a d.,
Le Surréalisme en Î929. (Variétés, Bruxelles) *Au grand Jour* (1927), *Nadrealizam danas i ovde,* 1931–1932. *Intervention surréaliste* (Documents 34, 1934). *This Quarter:* surrealist number (1932), *Fransk Surrealism* (Spektrum 1933).

Vítězslav Nezval: What Is Surrealism?

This spring a leaflet was published in which the Group of Surrealists in Czechoslovakia first introduced themselves. As the author of this leaflet, I am well aware that its four pages could not provide more than a general manifesto that ten young artists, along with the author, supported. Some of these artists are well known due to their extensive work in the past, others are appearing before the Czech public as completely or relatively unknowns. They are the poet Konstantin Biebl, the psychoanalyst Bohuslav Brouk, the Hungarian poet Imre Forbáth, the theatre director Jindřich Honzl, the music composer Jaroslav Ježek, the poet Katy King, the poet Josef Kunstadt, the sculptor Vincenc Makovský, and the painters Jindřich Štyrský and Toyen. Karel Teige has also stood in solidarity with the Group of Surrealists in Czechoslovakia.

The leaflet in question actually attracted so much attention that an ample pile of papers was produced in reaction to it. Let us say straight away that, in addition to the positive interest that it aroused and which drew thousands of people to a lecture and discussion on Surrealism, it also resulted in considerable negative interest. Many critical articles appeared against it. The first attacked the leaflet because it entered the fray on the base of dialectical materialism in solidarity with the revolutionary proletariat. The second insisted that the leaflet's ideological aspect was derived from idealistic philosophy. The third felt it was too late for Surrealism. The fourth asserted that it was all just a bluff, and so on. The person whose judgement mattered most to the leaflet's artists was the founder of French Surrealism, André Breton, who found the manifesto to be compatible with the intentions of French Surrealists and, based on this, is encouraging the Group of Surrealists in Czechoslovakia to collaborate on Surrealism on an international scale, promising the group that French Surrealists will provide the utmost cooperation.

I do not hesitate to say that many misunderstandings regarding this leaflet arose for the most part because, in addition to reasons we cannot speak of here, few of those reacting to it actually knew what Surrealism is. In this quarter-hour lecture, I will try to explain it as clearly and concisely as possible.

Surrealism arose as a movement in France thanks to André Breton, though he was not the first to use the word. It had already been used previously by the poet Guillaume Apollinaire in the preface to the play *The Breasts of Tiresias*. Apollinaire understands Surrealism as the imaginary depiction of reality through a work of art which should no longer imitate reality, but present it in extreme abbreviation and extreme exaggeration. As a person who wanted to imitate walking, he created a wheel that serves the function of walking on an exaggerated scale; the Surrealist artist hyperbolically exaggerates reality, instead of simply imitating it. Apollinaire felt that abbreviation and exaggeration is one of the most effective means of modern art. Yet he never attempted to explain the cause and essence of the impression that comes from a Surrealist way of expression. Only Breton did this systematically. I cannot explain here the evolution of his ideas, but I will briefly give a summary of his findings during Surrealism's development. Breton paid close attention to the work of the founder of psychoanalysis, Sigmund Freud, and especially to Freud's analysis of dreams. Although Breton differed from Freud in many ways, in part because his thinking was based on a materialist philosophy, while for Freud this was not always the case, and although he had significant objections to the many inconsistencies in Freud's teachings, Breton acknowledges Freud's work that relies mainly on experience, on his psychoanalytical method, and paid special attention to Freud's views on interpreting dreams. A dream is a certain processing of reality, differing from intellectual processing. Three components that make a dream what it is, that set it apart from reality, are: the condensation of time, space and action in a dream, the exaggerated dramatization of real events and the so-called displacement principle that manifests itself in the frequent substitution of beings and things. Poetry, and especially modern poetry has always more or less had all three of these means at its disposal. Time is also shortened in a poem, the space and action condensed, and one thing is exchanged for another, whether through the use of meek poetic tropes such as traditional synecdoche, metonymy and metaphor, or through their extremely liberal use. Like a poem, a dream has, in addition to its own content that is extremely difficult to grasp in all aspects, also its "manifest" and "latent" content, both of which appear extremely clear to us after closer psychological and psychoanalytical analysis. Manifest content, i.e. the life, or rather, experienced material, from which a dream or poem constructs, through condensation, dramatization and displacement, its extremely unique building. Latent content, i.e. the secret symbolic content of the means used by the dream — the secret sexual content. This latent content gives poetry and dreams their irrational character, while condensation, dramatization and displacement, resulting from the censorship of consciousness that seeks at all cost to conceal this latent sexual content, give poetry and dreams their indecipherable and particularly impressive character. This knowledge, which became for Breton, thanks to the psychoanalytical method, a key for understanding the essence of dreams and poetry, was not formulated at once with the certainty of which I am now expounding. It only emerged after many Surrealist experiments, one of the first and most typical of which is automatic writing. This consists of the poet attempting with as little conscious control as possible to record in rapid succession ideas that occur to him and capturing them in their unique order, which the poet's consciousness should not influence. This automatic writing, often attempted by Surrealists, resulted in a large number of texts, some of which are extremely poetic. Breton accused some of them of a certain affectation, that they deliberately, willfully imitated dream elements for a purely literary purpose, instead of reflecting as faithfully as possible the dual state that arises in automatic writing, the relation of the conscious to the unconscious. Surrealism's first automatic text is the book *Magnetic Fields* that Breton wrote right after the war with his friend Philippe Soupault. In the first Surrealist Manifesto, Breton defines Surrealism as pure psychic automatism in which the true function of thought was to be expressed by writing and all other means. The Surrealism of Breton's first Surrealist Manifesto is still an intuitive Surrealism, and only in Breton's book *Communicating Vessels*, which will be published this autumn in Czech, does it become a purely intuitive knowledge, or shall we say a scientific knowledge. Surrealism continues to want to and will use the broadest possible intuition to navigate its discoveries, currently doing so in many ways. Along with Surrealist games, which demonstrate from which the freedom of connecting ideas and from which the absolute randomness of poetic effect is born, it worked in Surrealist activity on constructing artificial objects called "Surrealist" objects. A variety of real things are used in their construction that, although possessing an indifferent value, combined in a certain way give off a strong poetic effect that consists of the latent sexual content that they indirectly render. In Breton's words, the more veiled this content is, the more powerful its effect. More than any other method before or after it, Surrealism wants to be aware of the essence of poetry's effect. On the path to this objective, Surrealism succeeded in extricating itself from the false mysticism of many processes considered until now to be either transcendental or non-existent. As previously stated, since Surrealism has based itself on the Marx-Lenin worldview, according to which the world should not only be understood, but also changed, Surrealists are connecting their experimental activity, intended to contribute as much as possible through their unique method to the deepest understanding of a person's conscious and unconscious states, to social activity that is striving to transform the world in the sense of social justice and historical development. Indeed, Surrealists believe that the spiritual liberation of humanity, whose hidden sources are being explored by the Surrealists, can only occur in a society that is devoid of social and class oppression. Breton himself tells those who find the connection of these two seemingly exclusive activities to be suspicious that Surrealism does not exist in bigamy, and stresses that both those who only want to understand the world and those who only want to change it should realize that this understanding must go hand in hand with this change, and that nothing can lead Surrealism astray from this path.

I can only add that the Surrealists in Czechoslovakia identify with this concept of Breton and that they reached it in their own ways, which were somewhat different from those of the French Surrealists, since there were differences in the Czech and French poetic traditions that led them down another path. We who are now united on a plan of Surrealist activity have worked more subconsciously than consciously on Surrealism over the past ten years. Our work was not a unified movement; it was more a case of individual paths leading to Surrealism than systematic activity. Guided by intuition, we drew close to and moved away from Surrealism, but we moved intuitively within its realm. This we did through extremely individual experiments, which where not as systematic as the experiments of French Surrealists simply because they were individual and stemmed wholly from the individual will, and were not corrected and directed by the opinions of a group. Today, when it has been declared in our country that Surrealism is the movement of a few artists, its development will yield surprising results.

Záviš Kalandra: The Sur-reality in Surrealism

I would like to pose and answer only one question here — precisely the one on which all other answers depend in the given hierarchy, i.e. the answer to the practical questions of whether Surrealism is a threat within the ranks of revolutionary and proletarian literature, whether it is compatible with the needs of the struggling proletariat, whether it is compatible with historical materialism, whether there is a need to oppose it, or if it does not matter, or if it is right to support Surrealism.

In these crucial, practical questions we cannot simply grope for answers based on a specific temperament that will vainly claim to be Marxist, unless it is cleansed during the analytical process that the subject in question goes through in Marxist criticism.

This methodologically central question cannot be anything other than this: What is "sur-reality" within the concept of Surrealism? Yet this question itself has two aspects: one resides in the sphere of knowledge, the other in the sphere of art. They cannot be non-dialectically detached from each other. After all, every work of art stands on a certain epistemological basis, whether this is realized or not.

Surrealists tell us that it is based on dialectical materialism; it is up to their Marxist critics to decide whether it really is or whether, despite the best intentions, it perhaps succumbs to a kind of self-deception. An analysis of the Surrealist concept of "sur-reality" can and must make this clear. The notion of sur-reality did not first appear in Surrealism — on the contrary, it has already been in many concepts, and there is nothing more natural than for these older, so well-known concepts to cast their light and shadow on the new, still dimly lit Surrealist concept.

In its oldest, already antediluvian form for us, sur-reality appears in supernaturalism: these are, as we know in many not overly important variations, the systems that place above the real of this world the much "more real" transcendental reality, existing beyond the reach of our sensory perception, despite being real. This essentially theological notion of sur-reality was put to death once and for all by Kant's critique — which, however, merely opened the door to less primitive and thus more dangerous forms of idealism. Philosophical supernaturalism believed that sur-reality could be considered an object of human knowledge — not sensorial but of reason. For beginning with Kant, sur-reality has been preserved in idealistic systems as merely a realm of the unknowable, concealed behind the material world as an unknowable, but real residual that remains after removing all the comparisons and deformations into which human senses and human "forms of opinion" have distorted them. Whether this transcendent residual is presented to us as a Kantian "thing in itself", a Schopenhauerian "world as will" or as a Bergsonian "élan vital", it is always the principle of some imaginary idealistic "truth" over material reality, even after Kant the idealistic systems insist on the concept of a certain sur-reality existing beyond the senses of the given world.

Here we face our question: is Surrealist sur-reality also of this nature? Does it in anyway resemble supernatural or critically idealistic concepts of reality? If so, then down with Surrealism! It would then be absolutely incompatible with historical materialism and as dangerous as any other kind of idealism.

Naturally, there is a need to look at how Surrealists themselves respond to this question. It is worth mentioning in advance that their responses are not always sufficiently clear. Yet if we are able to understand them, they are in most cases unequivocal.

For the sake of brevity, let us take as a representative view the one that Vítězslav Nezval provides in the leaflet "Surrealism in Czechoslovakia".

"The very etymology of sur-reality indicates that we are not within the realm of scientific epistemology, in which for materialists the real is given independently of our senses as an objective phenomenon, whose existence is independent of our more or less accurate knowledge, that it is rather an expression of this knowledge process and no longer of general knowledge, of acquiring knowledge through concepts, but an extremely subjective knowledge, and yet still knowledge; an absolutely precise expression that will prove that this extremely subjective cognition applies to all subtleties and not only to one head, but to all heads capable of dealing with this expression (just as a person is capable of dealing with the word "la main" once he has learned the French language), that this extremely subjective cognition is objective cognition and that it aims at understanding the real (given objectively beyond the senses for materialists), as it is reflected in us, to understand ourselves." —

A critical analysis of this response finds that:

1. Sur-reality is not being hypostasized here, meaning that nothing is made from it that is independently and really existing — neither as supernatural transcendence accessible to reason, nor in the sense of critical idealism as an unknowable "thing in itself".

2. The Surrealist "sur" is in the subject, meaning the Surrealist sur-reality is nothing objectively given in the world of idealistic ideas, but is an expression of an artistically creative human subject.

If Surrealism is and wants to be a creative method, it should not have anything to do with epistemological matters, and if so, only indirectly, in which case it is the task of Marxist criticism to ascertain its epistemological conditions. However, Surrealism wants to be something else as well, something more, overlapping the boundaries of creative artistic activities into the realm of knowledge. And here our question is presented in a new form: does the Surrealist method also have some objectively epistemological value? That is to say, is Surrealist knowledge real knowledge?

Vítězslav Nezval writes in the manifesto:

"In the prefix "sur" we will thus see the perceiving subject, who is to be deciphered by the real and who will discover for it a unique emotional value, and not give a general definition — a knowledge wholly unique, an understanding of the individual acquiring knowledge..."

In other words, according to the Surrealists themselves, this is a subjective knowledge of the subject, an inner experience that is thoroughly and experimentally explored — these are the very contact points of Surrealism and psychoanalysis. Is it possible to achieve objectively valid results this way?

Yes, but only objectively valid knowledge of the human subject, of his psychic mechanisms and their functions — and only if we remain aware that here, as Nezval says, "we are understanding the individual acquiring knowledge" and nothing more, if we can resist all temptations of the hypostasis of the subjective into the objective.

But does this kind of knowledge have any meaning? Again, the answer is yes: it can serve to understand the "true individual" as Karl Marx put it. Indeed, we must be very careful that the empty specter of "the normal economic individual" does not also infiltrate the Marxist political economy, as it haunts so many bourgeois economists. This delusion, which does not exist anywhere, is only meant to serve these gentlemen for the sole purpose of excluding from the economy the bearer of the class struggle — who, in fact, can be an actual person with all his desires for happiness and with his resistance to paint. There would be no class struggle, if there existed an ideal (for the bourgeoisie) state in which proletarians were not people with hearts and nerves, but emotionless robots incapable of distinguishing between pleasure and misery, without any demands and for whom it would matter little if they met their cruel death today, tomorrow or in a thousand years. And neither would there be any place for a Marxist interpretation of the still most powerful component of human ideology — religion — which, according to Marx, is the "sigh of the oppressed creature": if Surrealism tells us that it wants to explore this very "oppressed creature", we must wish it and ourselves the best of luck, though we also must warn it that there are many dangers and pitfalls on the way.

For if the Surrealist subjective knowledge of a subject can approach its objectively valid knowledge, then its method of knowledge is very narrowly limited. If it wants to be independent, it will not be able to avoid the illusions of subjective idealism. If it does not integrate the subject that it is understanding into the realm of the real world, it will not have in it the true individual that Marx and Engels speak of, but a chimera that will closely resemble the idealistic monsters from a psychoanalytical menagerie. It is psychoanalysis and its errant ways that are the cautionary message here, and therefore we need to acknowledge that Karel Teige dismissed Surrealism's relationship to psychoanalysis — quite correctly, in my view. Statements such as Breton's "everything leads us to believe that there exists a spot in the mind from which life and death, the real and the imaginary, the past and the future, the high and the low, the communicable and the incommunicable will cease to be contradictory"*[1] — show that Surrealism is in danger, that perhaps it will pass a subjective illusion off as an objective finding only if it is strongly emotional, perhaps even under the guise of "dialectics", by the sleight of hand of "a unity of contradictions", which, in the above Breton statement, merely steals this name. After all, where is this spot that Breton seeks? Nowhere else but in the purely emotional sphere, where the individual, in a subjective illusion, breaks loose of the shackles of the real world and frees himself from the reins of all the rules of objective knowledge.

The danger is there — and Surrealists can only avoid it if they are constantly aware of the fact that their method of subjective knowledge of a subject, at it lies in the depths of their artistic expression, is itself too narrow and therefore cannot alone lead to objectively valid findings, but can only achieve this if its special rules are always applied within a broad, solid and reliable frame of the only correct method of knowledge — dialectical materialism. Here Surrealism has a precisely defined place; it can only leave its confines at its own risk of inevitable foundering in idealism.

Are our Surrealists aware of this? From what they have said so far it seems as if they are. In this case, it is our duty to help them — especially since all Marxists are obliged to take Engels' words seriously: "That is to say, we all placed, and were bound to place, the main emphasis, primarily, on the derivation of political, legal and other ideological notions, and of actions arising through the medium of these notions, from basic economic facts. But in doing so we neglected the formal aspect — the ways by which these notions come about." And all Marxists must be aware of the great significance of the work that awaits us in the field, where the Surrealists are now calling for cooperation.

Wherever we might see in Surrealism the genuine threat of subjective idealism, against which nobody is currently immune, we are obliged to draw their attention to it and, if necessary, warn them of it. Yet if they really take the path announced by André Breton in *The Second Manifesto of Surrealism*: "We subscribe to the principle of historical materialism", the Marxist view of them is that of a friendly critique ex-

1 Quoted from Breton's "Second Manifesto of Surrealism", 1930.

amining, above all, whether their particular work truly corresponds to that binding statement.

However, there is no guarantee that the Surrealists and Surrealism will not fall back from the revolutionary front lines that it had wanted to join and into which, as shown here by Karel Teige, the French group was led by its past development. Here again Marxist criticism will have to be on guard; and our Surrealists will have to understand that the sharpest criticism, friendly but open, and if necessary ruthless, is the best that they can wish for from our side. We add to that the hope that they will become closer to the workers and their revolutionary movement, even in its everyday forms, for that is the firmest prerequisite for them to truly avoid all dangers posed by influences of the bourgeois environment and bourgeois ideology.

I now arrive at Surrealism as artistic expression.

As we know, it is here that Surrealism wants to speak of its "Surrealist revolution". It is clear to our Marxists that it should not have the slightest right to speak of it in the sense of a cultural revolution that presupposes that the proletarian social revolution has been carried out; and if we see Surrealist tendencies pointing in this false direction, we would have to oppose them. Yet Surrealism, of course, means something else by its "revolution", something that can be called a revolution only metonymically, just as nowhere else in the ideological sphere can one speak of a "revolution" other than a revolution in quotation marks.

If a creative subject is the source of Surrealist expression, there is nothing new in this, and it is all the less revolutionary: for this source is in all art of all ages and classes. This subjective principle of all art is simply the very principle of the human imagination, meaning it is the principle of dissatisfaction of the real individual with the real world, a principle with a role in the class struggle through human history and in every individual case of psychosis, which is the principle of mental activity awake and in dreams — psychoanalysis rightly speaks here of the principle of pleasure, constantly colliding with the principle of reality.

We see this constant conflict in the mechanism of all creative work in every epoch of art. But until recently creative individuals (and people in general) did not realize its effect under artistic expression, for although it never ceased to have an effect, it did so covertly. However, the objective of genuine art criticism should not be to satisfy the superficial criteria of "content and form", whether this is gauged by Hippolyte Taine or by Georgi Plekhanov, but to penetrate the expressive totality of each work all the way to its most subjective core, that is, precisely where that subjective principle resists the pressure of objective reality; here the criticism can and should capture the artist's energetic center as part of the real class world of people.

What specifically distinguishes Surrealism from all of the old artistic "isms" is the basic fact that Surrealist artists are aware of the effect of this principle of pleasure; it thus differs from other modern "isms" (Cubism, Futurism, Expressionism, Constructivism and, above all, from the preceding stage in our country, from Poetism) in the degree of this awareness, which leads to its specific artistic expression.

Yet the fact that Surrealists are aware of the effect of the principle of pleasure does not eliminate it in the slightest — for that would mean killing all art. Accepting that this awareness is lacking, the Surrealists take its mechanics firmly in hand, study its technique and create from it a machine for the production of that which they call "sur-reality". If you will excuse this very banal image — they build here a Surrealist mill: the artist's perception brings to it elements of objective reality and inner experience, and the artist's work takes from it finished products of illogical tissue, unempirical links and an unconventional brand. They have passed through here a tense creative individual, who is aware of the effect of the principle of pleasure and who, previously at its mercy, becomes its master — at least in artistic expression.

Every product of art is something specifically different from a product of nature: it is different precisely because it has always undergone the processing of a human subject. If this processing is unconscious, the effect is an artistic deformation of one kind or another; as soon as it is conscious, i.e. as soon as the creative individual consciously gives the full freedom of effect to his unconscious mental activity, which he is exploring and studying for this purpose, the effect is that of Surrealist sur-reality: the mosaic of elements of immediate perception, memories and colors of emotions, no longer built by logical mechanisms or into forms of empiricism or convention, but by the force of the freed and explored principle of pleasure into irrational constructions.

Therefore, the Surrealist sur-reality as an artistic expression perhaps does not differ from other artistic products in that it is no longer of this world, but rather that the subjective principle of pleasure appears more fully, unfettered, immediately and strongly in it. If this art is to have an effect, it can only do so directly, only by way of a "short link" (V. Nezval) from subject to subject — without the help of the rational transformers that we have been otherwise used to in art. We must therefore forget the effort that still automatically emerges when we encounter a work of art, the effort to "understand" it, and let the emotions of Surrealist poems and paintings directly affect our emotionality. We then will soon grasp that these transformers are actually foreign to the specific principles of art, that they are instead a disruptive element, without which art products' unique aspects can have a better and stronger effect on us. But to each his own, even in art; one must decide for oneself whether one likes Surrealist art, is indifferent to it, or is repulsed by it. One final question requires an answer at this point: whether Surrealist art can have an effect on the masses, in a positive way, for the cause of the proletarian revolution. And here I do not need to dwell on mere conjectures; empirical proof has already been presented. I am referring here to the effect that Nezval's superb poem "The March of the Red International" (which is no less Surrealist for being written before the Surrealist Manifesto) had when it was recited to revolutionary workers and intellectuals at the Commodity Exchange. Perhaps most of those who only read it got nothing out of it, but nobody who heard it recited with all its emotional force could escape its powerful effect, instilling revolutionary confidence and having a clearly revolutionary effect.

The extraordinary interest garnered by the Surrealists' manifestations and discussions about Surrealism, whether that of its supporters or opponents, is merely a gratifying phenomenon in an age when cultural life is plagued by fascist reactionaries. I feel that you will at least approve of my ending here by calling on Surrealists to now provide us with material other than that of their hitherto written and oral manifestoes, to now provide us with the material of their art works. Only then will a truly fruitful discussion be possible.

Karel Teige: Socialist Realism and Surrealism

If we question the perspectives of the future development of Socialist Realism in the art of the Soviet Union, we should keep in mind the different avant-garde groups and diverse modernist currents that revived and often dominated Soviet art in the period immediately following the revolution and which were later, around 1925, pushed out and nearly silenced by various groups of proletarian painters, writers and architects adhering to the program of a "reurn to the classics". We are thinking here of futurism, suprematism and constructivism — currents that had their core in LEF (Levy Front Iskusstv) headed by Vladimir Mayakovsky.

Dividing Soviet revolutionary art into two wings — into avant-garde groups and associations of proletarian artists and writers, corresponding to a similar division of revolutionary art in the West — is now a thing of the past. The Union of Soviet Writers counts among its ranks both former LEF members (including Tretyakov, Tynyanov, Pasternak, Aseev, Shklovsky, Brik and Kushner), and former RAPP members (including Bezymensky, Bedny, Gladkov and Zharov), all of whom collectively embrace the program of Socialist Realism. Since, however, Socialist Realism is still a theoretical concept that has not been tested in practice (and since it is not true, as Bedřich Václavek errantly thinks, that its theory was derived from previous Soviet literary and art works), we keep finding in today's Soviet art, especially in the works of former RAPP members, former conventional Realism and Naturalism, albeit with Soviet themes. Claiming Socialist Realism, Soviet painting in particular is drowning in works of the most bleak color printed, naturalist kitsch, while its architecture walks in academic togas, dressed in Greco-Roman pillars and eclecticizing between antiquity, renaissance, baroque, the empire style and formalist modernism.

If we want to properly assess the contribution of Soviet art to this point, we must observe at every developmental stage the close link between it and the process of socialist construction and the cultural revolution. We must not forget that Soviet art is developing in a country where there are lines for books, where theatres and cinemas are sold out daily, where there is a rush to galleries and museums and where books and magazines printed in the millions are shortly sold out. We must not forget that two decades ago three-quarters of the country's population could not read or write, and that illiteracy first needed to be wiped out for this daily craving of readers to occur. This circumstance led to the fact that most of the literary and artistic production, directed at a readership that had recently been more or less illiterate, needed to be of the "awakening literature" type that — *mutatis mutandis* — characterized the literature of the Czech National Revival a hundred years ago: the literature of the likes of Josef Kajetán Tyl, Václav Beneš Třebízský and Boleslav Jablonský. However, just as, in addition to Josef Kajetán Tyl, we had Karel Hynek Mácha and Božena Němcová prior to the 1848 revolution, so did Soviet poetry have, along with its writers of revolutionary calendar stories and poems, the likes of Khlebnikov, Blok, Bryusov, Aseev, Pasternak, Yesenin and Mayakovsky.

Two types of literature have always been produced in a class-divided society: the literature of the ruling class and a literature that is not of the people, but for the people. To put it more specifically: a bourgeois literature for an educated and cultivated bourgeoisie, and a bourgeois literature for lowly educated people — calendar stories, detective stories, sentimental colportage novels "for maids" and Wild West stories for the young, etc. The Soviet cultural revolution had to take into account as the legacy of a dark past this sociological difference in education, and thus also in literature, which can only be overcome through the planned increase in the cultural level of the general population through the construction of socialism. However, as far as artistic culture is concerned, there is certainly as considerable a difference between a Khlebnikov or a Pasternak and the reading of a peasant from the far reaches of the Soviet Union as between Nezval and calendar stories. The literary culture had to begin with alphabet books for tens of millions of the Soviet nations. It had to take into account the primitivism and simplicity of the uneducated reader. Although there is little doubt that "one cannot combat the popularity of calendar-reader sentimentality with calendar-reader sentimentality sowing socialist knowledge" (Laco Novomeský in the article on "The Mission of Literature in Soviet Life" — "Land of the Soviets", year 3, no. 8), and though we know that "red kitsch", which may have a certain agitative importance, spoils the taste and dulls the sensibility of the proletarian reader, we must not forget that the quantitative Soviet literature of agit poems and prose that taught the Soviet working class to read and led them to books, created the conditions for its demise: that "red" popular-calendar and agit literature, by helping to introduce millions of people to a cultural life, caused the leap from quantity to quality. The red calendar taught the primitive reader to read books. A reader who reads books is no longer primitive and no longer wants to just read calendars. While the cultural level of people in a capitalist civilization has, since the introduction of obligatory schooling, been maintained at the same primitive and low level, and while in Czechoslovakia the working-class reading level is currently not that much better than it was a century ago, in the USSR we are witnessing the rapid cultural rise of the lower classes. V. Borin aptly spoke of this in his paper on the congress of Soviet writers (at a Levá fronta evening on 26 September 1934): "Our people still consume stories about industrious Agnes and the gunner Jabůrek; in the Soviet Union the people only learned to read a few days ago and have already reread Jabůrek and Agnes for the nth time. That is the rise and progress of a new culture. Naturally, there have been and still will be many more struggles, miscomprehensions and mistakes before they all get to Pasternak." Let us add to that: today, on average, they are reading Sholokhov, perhaps even more advanced writers.

We are taken aback by the current state of most Soviet, literary, fine-art, film and architectural production in that academic classicism and old realism are consistently being imitated. Soviet painting and architecture in particular are now drowning in the most *passé* academism and decorativism. Just as the theory of socialist realism rejects past conventional realism, in which, however, the practices of writers and painters who subscribe to Socialist Realism remain imprisoned, so do theorists of Soviet architecture claim that Soviet architecture, though needing to learn from Antiquity and Classicism, should not copy the building styles of the past. Yet experience shows that a "return to the classics" leads either to an imitation of past styles or to the creation of a kind of Neo-classicism (in truth: pseudo-classicism) or later to a hesitant and wobbly eclecticism that gleans from Antique, Renaissance and constructivist architecture. If we ask the reasons, rooted in the dynamics of social development, why architecture has been pulled down into academism and decorativism, we will see that the causes for this architectural retreat and reaction are of a historically positive and progressive nature. A return to Classicism is an indirect and misleading product, a falsely oriented by-product of past absolutely positive and progressive social and cultural processes, and is above all a by-product of increasing prosperity and the rising cultural level of the working class. It is little wonder then that, if on the path leading from austerity to material prosperity it gets temporarily sidetracked to some petty-bourgeois taste, which determines the character of furnishings and "decor" of today's white-collar residences in Moscow. The desire for beauty and splendour has awoken in the people. Without extensive cultural preparations the Soviet people cannot imagine beauty and splendour other than how they know architectural splendour: based on old palaces and cathedrals. The progress of socialist construction has brought the working class in contact with culture: but it is still not possible for these people to suddenly, enthusiastically and comprehensively welcome the most advanced result of modern art, which, however, must not be adapted to the immaturity of the masses and to the bad taste of bureaucrats.

Where architecture or painting and literature have, at the cost of their spearheading position, adapted to the primitivism of the public at large's culture the result has been that the architectural, painting and literary response of the socially and historically immensely positive processes has taken on, even if temporarily, retrogressive classicist and bureaucratic airs that are in no way adequate for socialism, and in which we cannot see anything progressive.

Every instance of Soviet art must be considered in connection with the movement of Soviet social and cultural life, which is very rapid. An episode of recidivism to Classicism, decorativism and Naturalism is just that — an episode. Soviet architecture and Soviet painting and sculpture still seem to be academically entrenched. On the other hand, it is certain that the first all-union congress of Soviet writers, thanks to Radkov's biting criticism and especially owing to a lecture by N. I. Bukharin, whose important talk angered many insulted writers, marks the beginning of a new dawn of Soviet poetry and literature, which will escape the hitherto tight circle where it was imprisoned by the same RAPP and MORP, and leave behind the agit-journalist style, the rhyming editorials. The congress drew attention to poets like Boris Pasternak, and pushed agit-poets and realistic chroniclers into the background. The Moscow congress showed that the current socialist reader already wants more than calendar and red-tinged stories or color-printed pictures, that he expects from a book deep human emotions and not textbook didactics or propagandistic catch-phrases. If Soviet poetry is to truly rise to the level postulated by Socialist Realism theory, it must first and foremost overcome in itself the remnants of descriptive, conventional realism, of its template and schemas. It can be assumed that, on the way to overcoming old Realism and Classicism, Soviet art will once again pick up the threads of those avant-garde tendencies that were temporarily abandoned after 1925 in literature and painting, and after 1932 in architecture under the influence of RAPP's vulgar theories. It is understood that constructivism in architecture is capable of positive development and that it can lead to a truly socialist architecture that will not merely repeat past styles of certain classes. It is understood that it is not the descriptive realism of today's films ("Chapaev", for instance), but of Eisenstein in "Potemkin" (whose structure is Cubo-Futurist) that is the path to socialist film art. In the works of Aseev, Mayakovsky, Khlebnikov and Pasternak, new socialist poetry will teach many what was forgotten and overlooked in the RAPP period. Surrealism has not been integrated into the development of Russian poetry and Russian art. We can assume, however, that Soviet socialist art will, on the way to dialectical realism, enrich its lyrical reality with that which Surrealism tore away from anti-lyrical reality and with that which it opposed this anti-lyrical reality as its revolutionary call: the deep world of a real person, of the person-poet, in perfect harmony with himself, who has the right to the freest development of his powers and to whom only the classless world of socialism can return this right, which has been denied by the capitalist system. In a society in which the "free development of each person will be a condition for the free development of all people" Lautréamont's prophecy will be fulfilled, as will a faith in surrealism that poetry will be written by all and not just one! When the aforementioned dam will no longer exist between the West and East, the new Soviet poetry will join with the new Western poetry in a single lyrical current of socialist life.

Jindřich Štyrský: Surrealist Photography

I have been photographing for some fifteen years and in that time have managed to take a lot of pictures that were absolutely perfect in photographic terms, and with which today's official amateur photographers, whose clichéd pictures inundate exhibitions around the world, would have been delighted. But all of this no longer interests me in the slightest, in fact it bores me.

The only thing I now find fanatically alluring about photography and that interests me is the search for the surreality concealed in objects of real life. Yet this endeavour precludes any aesthetic formalism that spoils surrealist photography, and precludes any interest in abstract photography and lensless photography. *Surrealist photography is not abstract photography*. It is therefore fundamentally wrong to consider — as the uninformed have done in our country — the work of Brno's Fotoskupina pěti (Photo Group of Five) to be surrealist photography. What this group does is utterly ordinary aesthetic photography living off the magic of Man Ray, Moholy-Nagy and the likes.

The beginnings of Surrealist photography as we understand it and as we see it at Mánes are inextricably linked with objects that are old fashioned, with objects that are commemorative or bizarre, such as mannequins or prosthetic legs. These objects conceal within a latent symbolism emphasized by an ordinary way of shooting them and makes them, as V. Nezval writes "akin to the extremely tangible and elusive inhabitants of dreams". The whole problem of photography lies in the photographer himself being surprised prior to the discovery of a certain object and imagining this discovery in a surrealist sense. However, chance and attunement play a significant role here.

We shall not remain in this world of mannequins and machines that we have discovered and that, as we have seen, is becoming the food of amateur photographers. Nevertheless, our discoveries are our secret for now. As far as technical matters are concerned, we are working to achieve as little distortion, whether by light or lens, of the shyuzhet as possible — of the shyuzhet that had the power to announce its presence.

The two cycles of photographs that I am exhibiting were created by randomly arranging isolated photographs and adding captions to them that underscored their hidden meaning.

Jindřich Chalupecký: A Word on the Situation of Surrealism in Our Country

I. All that remains is to distinguish the double meaning of the word "Surrealism". One meaning consists of the collective designation of the work of Breton, Éluard, Dalí, Ernst and a few others, even of those who have broken with Breton's group (Desnos, Tzara...): i.e. the designation of one part of this complex of events that we call the modern spirit. The other means the attempt to create an international cultural organization.

Today, there is a particular effort to present Surrealism in this its second form. Non-French Surrealist subsidiaries are emerging in several countries and willingly submit to the ideological supervision of the parent group. It seems that ideological discipline is appreciated firstly and solely. Surrealism has had significant international success and can thus be considered impressive. And yet there seems to be a misunderstanding: How does this organization relate to what is called the modern spirit?

II. The uncertainty of the individual today results in doubts on the principles of knowledge and being. Reality is in crisis. All life experiences are becoming the subject of research and testing. All past experiences of the European soul are gateways to help. This means that all uncertainties are brought together. The problem of what is truth becomes increasingly exasperated until the last and surest certainty is seen in uncertainty, in all possibilities of uncertainty.

We can therefore say that the modern spirit means the heroism of the human lot that lives its certainty, the certainty of its existence, the certainty of its reality, in constant danger.

It has arrived at the following metaphor: the surest path leads along insidious cliffs, protected only where it is unexpected, with meaning only in the incomprehensive, a future only in the unprecedented, and possibility nowhere else but in the impossible. Perhaps this is the teaching that modern art has once again arrived at.

III. Surrealism is moored here. It begins with a trust that expects everything from the miraculous and mysterious, from the incomprehensible and despised. It seems that the most necessary thing of all is to begin a new life. Or better yet, to begin a life. And life always begins anew with the arrival of confusion and darkness. When the mystery, in its fullness, becomes complete, it astounds with its clarity. It becomes complete, ceases to be a mystery, and becomes a clear being, a simple and obvious thing, a thing of life that has been realized. To achieve this clarity, to confirm its truth and reality, we must not retreat from the confusing and incomprehensible, but steadfastly *stay with the mystery*.

It can be said that the highest value of Surrealism lies in its will to be surprised, in its bravery to complicate a situation, in the declaration made by Dalí that he hates simplicity in all its forms. To welcome the arrival of mystery, all that is depressing, all that is hopeful in it. This is the primary trait; and secondly in its quest for relentless systematicity, in the quest to reach the end of the discovery, or in the will to fully see, to fully hear. To fully poetize, to fully paint — to fully live.

I don't think that Surrealism's unique contribution to modern art is fully appreciated. What it has done is declare more categorically and undertake more thoroughly than ever before the proposition that art does not have a decorative meaning, but an ethical one. It is here to intervene as strongly as possible in the individual's life.

There is the requirement that art, rejecting all other demands traditionally imposed on it, becomes *as capable as possible of devouring each and every life and being devoured by each and every life*. Artistic experiences are then applied to life. Art, stripped of the privilege of being a refuge from life, will be an instrument of life.

Perhaps in this way: automatic writing; a dream; and an individual's entire affected life is a harsh and defiant unclarity. Confusion, flickering twilight and without clear value. The light strikes only when the sleeper has lost consciousness. All efforts should now be made to strike *before consciousness is lost*. To fully know that circling, swirling and clinging unclarity, which is an unknown clarity. And this is called artistic creation.

Thus, Breton could write in the first manifesto of Surrealism: "I believe in the future resolution of these two states, dream and reality, which are seemingly so contradictory, into a kind of absolute reality, a sur-reality if one may so speak."

IV. My interpretation of Surrealism can be considered largely arbitrary and inauthentic, unless it is accepted that the use of psychoanalysis is not a constitutive part of Surrealism. In fact, only Breton uses it more consistently: it does not play a distinct role with either Éluard or Dalí (except for his design of surrealist objects). After all, this part of Surrealism is probably the most problematic. One could demonstrate here a rationalization that is overly simplistic, which, in interpreting art, completely ignores its specific value, blaming the merit of it cryptically and without further interpretation to the "dramatizing and monumentalizing power of censorship". We can always question whether Freud's theory, which claims that the libido arranges itself during adolescence and is governed by sexual drive, was by nature always and everywhere sexuality. It would also be worth examining whether the notion that a libidinous (which I shall rewrite as "affectionate") interest in the world (which is actually what art is) is a cryptogram of sexuality could be just as easily said vice-versa. (Sexuality itself as a symbol?)

What strikes me, for instance, is when I use the teachings of psychoanalysis to decipher (and this decryption is probably quite correct) verses of the national song

I lost a horseshoe off my white horse;
Hand it to me, my dear,
You'll be my wife,

the mystery of the poem is unresolved, and if I read it, aware of its reasonable erotic meaning — that is, if I remove the role of censorship, it is even more wonderful, more mysterious.

I will say against this psychoanalytical rationalization that the poet's task is to *expand the mystery*, and in doing so they are resolved. In this context, light is shed on the following sentence in German by Jakub Deml: "Das Rätsel ist weltlich, mehr: gemein! Mehr: gottlos! Mindestens eine Spielerei, ein Kind der Langweile, Ratlosigkeit, eine Oberflächlichkeit, Leichtsinn. Dagegen das Geheimnis: etwas Heiliges, mit Gott Verbundenes, Ewiges, Frommes ... Das Rätsel schwätzt, ironisiert, macht dumme Witze. Das Geheimnis schweigt." The mystery remains silent.

For the sake of being understood, I hasten to add that it is owing to Surrealism that it remains strict with itself, that it has nothing in common with popular and facile mysticism, which renounces reason out of mere lethargy and relies on a spirituality that delights in unclarity, that *fears clarity* and does not know, does not want to know that the fire of clarity initiates the arrival of a reality more concrete than any other, the occurrence of a strict nakedness.

V. Surrealism has shown that the poet is not an expert in writing verses, painting, composing music and so on. A poet is a person of a unique life intensity: more than anyone else affected by seeing.

He is a poet that illuminates his life with the spotlight of poetic clarity. To see for oneself that life is a poem.

Under the disconnection of existence to feel and capture that current of a new connection, to conquer by all means, from all sides of that new reality, all new realities, poems clear, always complete and everywhere. "God will quietly play you," says Halas. Thus, Surrealism wants to carry out what is the boldest and highest meaning of art.

I had all this in mind when I wrote a year ago that Czechoslovak Surrealists "are facing the task of becoming Surrealists". Today, they feign great outrage over this statement, saying things like this: "One's audacity probably stems only from the fact that, unlike Surrealism's other enemies who read nothing, he at least read out loud two or three Surrealist books, and, considering the backup plan, ineptly declares that Czech Surrealists "in applying to enter Surrealism are facing the task of becoming Surrealists". That is how it was formulated in the *Surrealism* anthology and signed by Nezval. I am quoting this so that, if I do not write about Czech Surrealism as a "jewel" and "beauty of that flower" (this has occurred) I at least will not be accused of harbouring a *secret* bias.

"The task of becoming Surrealists": this holds the very error that I would almost be a part of. A wicked circle, imperceptible corruption and therefore the worst.

Becoming Surrealists... I will not write of Nezval's *Invisible Moscow* and *The Chain of Fortune*, it would not be fair to judge Czech Surrealism using Nezval's prose. Of greater significance is to notice how Nezval becomes a Surrealist in his new book of poems entitled *Woman in the Plural.*

VI. These poems certainly want to be above all a manifestation of that human ability that Surrealists include under the term *automatism*. This puts them at the center of the Surrealist efforts since automatism has remained from the start the strongest pillar of their concept of man. It shows them that a poem is not created by the conscious being of the writer, but that it springs from where he knows not about himself. "Car je est un *autre.* For I is another," writes Rimbaud on May 15, 1871, "If the brass awakes the trumpet, it's not its fault. That's obvious to me: I witness the unfolding of my own thought: I watch it, I hear it: I make a stroke with the bow: the symphony begins in the depths, or springs with a bound onto the stage."

Two years earlier these words were read in a different context, in that of *The Songs of Maldoror*. "If it is day, each can put up a useful resistance against the Great External Object. But as soon as the veil of nocturnal vapor spreads, oh! To see his intellect in the sacrilegious hands of a stranger. A merciless scalpel scrutinizes the thick brush. Consciousness exhales a long cursed groan; for the veil of her modesty receives cruel cracks. Humiliation! Our gate is open to the wild curiosity of the Heavenly Bandit. I did not deserve this horrid punishment, you, the hideous spy of my causality! Si j'existe, je ne suis pas un autre. If I exist, I am not another. I do not admit to this equivocal plurality within. I want to reside alone within my reasoning. Autonomy.. or else I change into a hippopotamus. My subjectivity and the Creator is too much for my brain. Here is the cassolette where the incense of religion burns. Eternity roars like a distant sea and is approaching with great strides. Prostrate yourself, humans, in the fiery chapel! ... Do you understand how I suffer? (yet my pride is satisfied)."

This is not a mere dramatization typical of Lautréamont, but a truly accurate demonstration of two aspects of this matter. Compare the grateful and pious humility of Rainer Maria Rilke, one without the defence of an affected poem —

Upon what instrument are we two spanned?
And what musician holds us in his hand?
Oh sweetest song.

Or perhaps even more clearly:

How small that is, with which we wrestle, what wrestles with us, how immense, were we to let ourselves, the way things do, be conquered thus by the great storm, — we would become far reaching and nameless

Compare the same humility in a different formulation by Pasternak:

Let's drop words as gardens drop orange-peel and amber.
Lavishly, diffusely,
And scarcely, scarcely.

You'll ask who ordains it?
The omnipotent god
of details, of love,
of Iagailos and Iadvigas.[1]

Compare these poets on their knees with the proud one who does not allow himself to be fragmented, to be two, to be me and another, incomprehensible; I don't even know which of his proofs begins with the proposition that "a person cannot be independent of himself". Compare this with Valéry, who remarks at the beginning of his literary work: "If I were to write, I would infinitely prefer to write in full awareness and consciousness something weak than to conceive, owing to ecstasy and beyond my own efforts, a great work that would rank among the most beautiful."

Thus, automatism is not a discovery of Surrealism, but a general experience of poetry, as soon as it seeks to observe itself. In its Mediterranean will, it wants to create a comprehensive method out of what was discovered and tossed before it; especially from Rimbaud. Automatism is to be a means for the experimental cultivation of poetry.

Creating a work of art means staring at that which is within us; poetry is listening to the dictate that if we abandon conscious will, the unknown areas of our being, which are the quarries of unsuspected and perhaps the greatest powers of man, will announce themselves. However, having said that the dictate should be listened to, the value of the poem clearly lies in how well it is heard. This means that automatic writing ceases to be a poem in proportion to the lack of attention, concentration and ability to shift into this other being leading to deafness, overhearing, confusion, er-

1 Quoted from A. Livingstone, *Pasternak on Art and Creativity*, 1985 — transl.

rant interpretation and even to altogether missing the dictate, so that only random associated clusters, including reminiscences and phonemes, flow and are recorded.

A poem's value is thus given by remaining in it; remaining in this secret, perfect immersion in this great being. I would like to present from Nezval's book a perfect example of such writing that from the first to the final verse remains in the poem, which is entitled "Manuscript of An Evening". Unencumbered by a plan, by an attempt to interpret and convey, it is a rather silent rhyme, above which soars, undisturbedly, pure enchantment which safely reports the presence of a poem. Take this excerpt for instance:

One bay window / The door opens and someone enters / To cast a spark / You don't know why it burned
A little snail / Climbs to the place / Where the sculpture is sensitive / Like the instinct of a sunflower
And a sore spot / Which will remain after the whistle / Is covered by darkness / The evening's broken chandelier

My intention in quoting this is no longer to argue whether or not Nezval is a poet in this book. This is the premise on which I want to examine the relationship between Nezval the poet and Nezval the Surrealist. The question is whether this relationship benefited the poem or not.

VII. Often, very often, *Woman in the Plural* demonstrates the danger inherent in misunderstanding the automatic dictate. Let's take at random the short poem "Women After Bathing". After a hesitant upbeat, a vision of summer is highlighted:

The thrush of their sun-browned shoulder chase summer out of all mouse holes / They lie like soaked sheets / And fingers in the grass read the alphabet of the blind

That is truly seen. However, the second stanza begins to hesitate, to overhear itself, it runs into vague metaphors and ends in a poetic cliché:

The mass singing of their tree frogs / keeps me from sleeping / I raise my head to the shutter of their arms / which has a trace of the night.

The next stanza morosely dissolves into an image of an already quite simple meaning:

An entire regiment of slender women / manoeuvres with cornets / Whose secret is betrayed by broad-shouldered boxers

The cornets with a secret are barely secretive: the broad-shouldered boxers were chosen to save with their extraordinariness that which could still be saved. Alas, it is in vain: the magic is lost, the poem ends in an irrevocably rational banality, which is not obscured by the attempt at fortissimo at the end:

> *The buttoned summer / Expands and swings its breasts. /*
> *The Angelus never rang louder / Than these two bells under which whole beams of bamboo shake.*

Such a weakening breaks the poems in this book for good. The verse-cushioning repeatedly disrupts the magic, mushing the poem into eloquence.

> *Other darker spools of coarse thread with black beads / She asserts her will with the heel of well-hidden dynamite / A telegrapher of messages always encrypted / She loses a honeycomb carnation or brush on every step / I adore her neck of lavender soap / Her sandalwood hand plucks the bouquet of her own nape*

I feel that only the fourth of the quoted verses is valid. In the first, the spool and beads, which may be symbols, are entangled in a sentence devoid of continuity, perfectly depriving them of imaginability. The second is broken by a meaningless association. The third is of a poetic cliché that has been in vogue in recent years. There is no need to talk about the penultimate. The final verse was compiled by Nezval from nice words that are, if I'm not mistaken, a memory of translating Mallarmé's poems. What I want to say is that there's *a lack of continuity*. The poem is linked from verse to verse, often from word to word. It remained without continuity, and a new continuity was not achieved. And yet the meaning of automatism is that it is a fascinating stream of new connections.

This poem does not have in store surprising turns, sudden connections and amazing metaphors.

Read these verses of feverish imagery, as is the *terminus technicus* for them —:

> *Behind the large belly I saw laughter with the eyes of a fly / As beautiful as a cobb of corn / It walked along the night pharmacy like a murderer from mouths to mouths / This time I entered the nun nailed to the wall / And a whole herd of creatures from the soap of various odours / I lack the strength to search in all the boxes where their wigs lie / Wigs with the shade of all lethargic evenings / Oh, meteors*

New ideas are exposed in rapid succession, one after another, appearing very emphatically, very clearly. But you also feel as if they lead nowhere, that they are a pack, "a game of detached imagery". Such is automatic writing if it runs on and wanders; yet when it is seen, when it is heard, it is a being, a clear, efficient and precise organism. A tissue that grows increasingly deeper.

The lack of an internal organism then results in a mechanical organization that arranges side by side, supposedly adeptly, many phrases suspended on a repeated preposition, verb or comparative "like". Elsewhere they at least shatter the poem.

Read the one called "The Trapdoor". What thunderous poetic equipage, what poetic ornament and digression! Take it off; that is, cross out at least 35 verses on two pages; it will not be needless work. Nobody knew of the monumental poetic vision previously hidden here. Now there is merely one step to the opinion that franticness, complexity and amazement was only feigned here for the sake of a surreal appearance.

VIII. A poem begins when a person no longer knows what is happening to him. Consciousness has intensified so much that what was formerly consciousness, and is usually called that, turns out to be insignificant and does not itself want to confess to the new, forthcoming consciousness. Or did consciousness really change?

As an example, how much intransigence and wholly unique experiences are needed so that this new consciousness, so driven to fleetingness, to elusiveness, can be maintained, deepened in clear knowledge, grasped in the form of words, as an example of which we should read Éluard's poetry, whose latest collection, *The Public Rose*, was translated — not at all well — by Nezval and Vaníček (published by Mánes). These poems are vigilantly extracted from an unbroken silence; nothing from the skill of reason, nothing from the comfortable metaphors of those who wretchedly lean on the similarity of things; nothing that would not be a new understanding, and nothing that would not be the shining blade of extreme precision.

> *Bright days of the past / Their lions made of metal rods and their eagles of pure water / Their thunderous pride inflating the hours / the blood of fettered dawns / Throughout the breadth of the sky / Their tiara shrunk into the mass of a single mirror / Of a single heart / But now down deeper among the annulled paths / That singing that holds the night captive / That singing that deafens and blinds / That offers an arm to spectres / That denied love / Writhing in worries / With diluted tears / That broken torn twisted ludicrous dream / The harmony lying fallow / The begging people /*
>
> *For they only wanted gold / All wanted their untouched lives / And the perfection of love*

Poetry, which is a function of the will to know — to know: to assume nothing. I told a secret, and it means wanting nothing but whatever may come. To set out at the mercy of anxiety, solitude, to bear at one's own expense all the weight of oneself, one's abandonment of everything: to recognize the need to see: to set out at the mercy of the unexpected, the unprovable, the unknown. The time of poetic experience is arriving here. Also starting from here is Nezval's myth of a woman omnipresent, omni-hidden, of woman-life, of woman-death which he invokes in his poem "Prophecy" and in "Litany", poems of depths and of the depths guiding the consciousness; also starting from here is the great view of the aforementioned "The Trapdoor", seeing the ceremony of death and surrendering to it in final resignation:

I was falling but it was just a feeling of forgetting / Reality faded quietly dissipating / I was falling like the earth in its flight through space

I greet your gliding flight, O wings of death / O that I may put myself in her hands / Like weary eyes to sleep / Like a woman's womb to hot semen / Like my hands to my thoughts / Drifting like mutating clouds across the ruptured land

Surrealism certainly freed the poet's speech from old clichés, yet it also threatens to offer new ones. Just as these poems of death, in which this book and the poetic experience certainly culminate, are already beyond the Surrealist ideology, so are the parts of this book that strive to be the most surrealistic the least poetic. Cliché: this means the intention is above the poem, which, instead of discovering, serves the past, the known, any preconception. I tried to show how Nezval had come to be mere eloquence, assuming that automatism would lead him to poems of such and such appearance, which he believed to be surrealist. I could give as an example of another form of this mistake (regarding the need for Surrealist appearance) the entire poem entitled "Showcases", assuming that, in line with Surrealist theory (which, after all, hesitates in this matter), poeticness is identical to sexuality, he came upon a document of sexuality, a document of a psychological phenomenon well known as "substitution".

Thus poetic ways cease to be a kind of life, so that they can once again be a mere *manié de dire*. I remember Breton complaining about the "half-heartedness, which only supports the intrusion of automatic speech into a more or less conscious process".

IX. In examining the relationship of Nezval's poetry to his surrealism, I was able to determine two ways in which that relationship manifests itself. Sometimes it frees up his path to poetic knowledge and sometimes it leads him out of Surrealist ideology. Sometimes it encourages him to rely on Surrealist theory and, with faith in automatism — an automatism simply understood, it leads him out of the poem.

This also demarcates both possibilities generally valid for the influence of Surrealist theory and practice: it can be an impulse for a new struggle "on the borders of the borderless and the future", but it can also be a repeated use of principles already determined for goals that have already been determined.

Which of these possibilities attracts Czechoslovak Surrealists, which of these possibilities is the reason for joining the organization "International Surrealism"?

The Surrealism anthology that they published reports exclusively on their fervid and beautiful enthusiasm for Surrealism. They are excited about everything Breton is for — and especially enthusiastic about Breton himself. Their sole endeavour is to be like him, to become Surrealists. Their Surrealism largely draws from reading and studying French Surrealist publications. (Biebl seems to be the exception). They repeat experiments whose results were published by French Surrealists; partly with documentary success, partly with no less documentary failure: this time for a misunderstanding that stemmed from the popularization of Surrealism (an irrational understanding of the subject with rationally justified answers). Their confidence is spotless; whoever is not an orthodox Surrealist is ineptly attacked or more wisely ignored. (In the end, a Kremlička print has to endure celebration).

Yet in their enthusiasm, in this confidence, with this discipline, in this unconditional reliance on Surrealistic principles, a state of mind contrary to that which I have tried to define as the modern spirit is revealed. It suggests the pleasure of security, a desire for security, for comfort, for "its own sureness". The question that I previously asked is answered, for the time being, in favour of the second of the indicated possibilities.

We could ultimately say that the developments in Surrealism do not lack a certain logic. Let us remember that Surrealism begins with a distinct effort to unequivocally decided the complexity, contradictions and aesthetic, noetic and metaphysical issues that most emphatically provoke modern art. It is then a working hypothesis, but one that at a certain point changes into a recipe — for poetry and for life. If Surrealism ends with no longer wanting to explain, but considers man and poetry as already explained — at least *in pricipiis* — if it ends in a closed system that can only be filled and proved again and again, can only be repeated again and again, if this Surrealism is then called international Surrealism, it is already just a way of averting, by offering a fixed definition, the cruel and blinding problem that lies in uncompromising distrust: Who am I?

Thus, even if it means opposing this Surrealism and beyond it, there is the need to remain defenceless *when facing this question*.

Ladislav Novomeský: Czech-Slovak Cultural Relations

The most recent issue of *Elán* contains several apt remarks by Andrej Mráz on the effect of Czech critic F. X. Šalda on Slovak cultural life and on Czech-Slovak cultural relations in general. These are words that can in a certain sense be considered as a directive for Czech-Slovak cultural relations, as professed by the vast majority of the Slovak literary, art and academic world.

"For Slovakia's cultural effort it is quite evident that in our spiritual endeavours we will not shutter ourselves from the values that Czech cultural life can provide us with. There have never been such efforts in Slovakia, neither in the past nor today. Only mindless political demagoguery on both sides imagines boogiemen in this realm as well. On the Czech side, people live with the bias that Czech cultural life is so potent, big and powerful that it can and must think to give generously to Slovaks, and to immediately expect in return gratitude and Slovak kowtowing. On the Slovak side, there must, of course, be an instinctive resistance to this willingness. There then arises in Slovaks an exaggerated and often comforting distrust of Czech culture.

It must be clear here on both sides! Czech and Slovaks must recognize that the Slovak cultural life does not want to and cannot be burdened by that which is peripheral and epigonic in Czech culture — regarding both its own cultural development and the international cultural situation. Slovak spiritual endeavours encounter many pitfalls and obstacles; they strengthen and grow by overcoming their own shortcomings, backwardness and prejudices. It would truly be an unnecessary burden for them if ballast from the Czech sphere were to also somehow implant itself into the Slovak cultural situation. And there is no doubt that this very layer of culture, though perhaps bearing the badge of officiality but otherwise far from the truth and from being of value, is being introduced to Slovakia through education and other means. Here too we need to see a certain failure of Czech cultural work in Slovakia, that in our country everything that was not culture passed itself off as Czech culture.

Obviously, we are concerned with culture and not with the statistics on everything that the Slovaks have consumed in the "Czech cultural kitchen". We do not want to have cultural relations between Slovaks and Czechs just to make happy the good souls who force themselves to mediate the exchange of cultural values between Czechs and Slovaks; it is only possible to push for these things so that they truly lead to the cultural blossoming of Slovaks and so that they assist in our spiritual struggle."

We gladly note the words of this young Slovak literary historian — especially considering our multilateral objective of creating a solid relationship: the mutual cooperation and mutual respect between the nations of this republic. This definition of Czech-Slovak cultural cooperation should be emphasized all the more because their author is the same Mráz who directly and passionately dismantled the pseudo-scientific concepts of Czech-Slovak unity and of a Czech-Slovak merging in literary history, thereby appearing to harbour anti-Czech sentiments.

We are pointing out this aspect of Mráz's academic activities in part to make clear that the resistance of Slovak cultural life to the attempt at Czech-Slovak unification or merging is by no means the same as separatist resistance to an understanding and cooperation between Czech and Slovak culture and vice versa: efforts to reach an understanding and establish Czech-Slovak cooperation is in no way an acceptance of the proverbial plan of Czech-Slovak unity or of the need to merge the two cultures! This fact, which is a creed of the entire Slovak cultural life (as attested to by the Trenčianske Teplice Writers' Congress) is also a call to the Czechs — a challenge to Czech cultural life: only the best, the most freedom-loving that Czech cultural life has to offer can adjust Czech-Slovak cultural relations. The sooner the Czech cultural world rids itself of that officially protected scientific and anti-cultural "we're-one-nation", "one-branch" and "of one blood" article, supposedly exported to us for political reasons, the sooner we will be able to speak of normal and clearly defined Czechoslovak cultural relations. With their worldliness and international level, the leading circles of Czech cultural life have contributed more to a Czech-Slovak understanding than those Czech writers and scholars who have devoted all their efforts and meagre talent exclusively to dubious issues of Czech-Slovak unification.

1936

Vítězslav Nezval, Jindřich Štyrský: An Attempt at Realizing the Irrationality of Photography

What are rectangles?

a) indeterminate
V. N.: A cymbal, a domino, a piano.
J. Š.: Cakes, a plate around the keyhole, a keyboard, an organ.

b) from a sexually perverse perspective
V. N.: A sadistic element.
J. Š.: Sadism.

c) from an everyday perspective
V. N.: Hobnails, a swaddling blanket.
J. Š.: Condom wrappers at the barber's, the edge of the maid's underskirt.

d) what leads to a sexual image
V. N.: The impression that it's lying on the ground.
J. Š.: Three dark pinholes and a black blanket below, beating on a drum.

What are the small cubes placed on?

V. N.: On the ground, on a bed that is covered with planks, the sexual arousal comes from a feeling that these are the planks of the bed from which the mattress is put away; the image of planks on which they place the dead also resonates.
J. Š.: On coffins with cream, the sexual sensation of pressing piano keys and running your fingernail between your fingers.

What does lace mean?

V. N.: Pillow lace, drapery on a coffin, a shirt sliding off shoulders, a tablecloth falling of a table and lovers, who unexpectedly threw themselves into each other's arms.
J. Š.: Venice, a boat and a cabaret too.

What does the lower part mean?

V. N.: A wild animal's cage, the resolve to knock on a woman's bedroom, savage lust.
J. Š.: Montmartre, Rue Lepic one night with Nečas.

What does the last marked part mean?

V. N.: A wall, a porter between the doors, a barn wall in the late afternoon.
J. Š.: A laundry room.

Overall impression.

a) poetic
V. N.: Omelettes at a funeral parlour, razor blades and a magnetic floor as well as the Seamstresses Cafe or the Spool Bar.
J. Š.: An accordion song played on the street.

b) sexual
V. N.: Goose excrement after a pilgrimage.
J. Š.: bedsheets and mangled but not yet ironed laundry and its scent.

c) rational
V. N.: Target shooting as sexual function.
J. Š.: The balance of black and white.

A definition along the lines of Lautréamont's "As beautiful as...

V. N.: As beautiful as the chance encounter of a spool and a magnet on the beaded embroidery of a dried-up stage.
J. Š.: As beautiful as the chance encounter of a dead girl in a negligee with a clown under St. Apollinaire's trussing.

Karel Teige:
Surrealism Against the Current

"It has become commonplace ... that left-wing political circles can only appreciate recognized, if not enlarged forms of art."
André Breton: "The Political Position of Today's Art"
Prague, April 1935

The activities of the artistic and intellectual avant-garde that entered Czech public life in the years of great revolutionary upheavals immediately following the world's bloodbath were carried out from the very beginning with an awareness of the communion of its objectives with the vanguard of those social energies that history summoned to reconstruct society and liberate humankind. The avant-garde, whose core consisted of the DEVĚTSIL Union of Modern Culture, and whose role the SURREALIST GROUP is continuing, in all of its collective exhibitions, in its anthologies and magazines and in its manifestoes and programs, by which we have, at key points on our journey, defined our position vis-à-vis the process of contemporary intellectual and social development, and in the overall nature of the work of artists who have stood at the forefront of the battles that this thoroughly non-conformist left has waged against official academism, has acted in line with an awareness of the solidarity of progressive spiritual forces and progressive social forces, with an awareness that the revolution of art and science can only be applied and developed hand in hand with the struggle for the liberation of the working people. And yet the work of this intellectual left — which has wholeheartedly subscribed to the dialectical-materialist world view and has sought, though not without understandable errors, to conduct its work in those artistic and scientific fields that it could affect by its initiative and means, through the dialectical materialist method — has been developed from the onset in more or less clear disagreement with the cultural policies of the workers' parties and namely the Czechoslovak Communist Party, with whom we had hoped to comradely cooperate as much as we could. At times, the communist press had even focused its energies on attacking this artistic and scientific left, thereby objectively weakening the primary struggle that this avant-garde was waging against the right-wing, conservative and academic front.

The polemical controversies between members of the avant-garde on the one hand, and between supporters of Proletkult and Agitprop or of those promoting RAPP (Russian Proletarian Writers Association) or Socialist-Realist theories on the other hand, were mostly one-sided. When the SURREALIST GROUP stated in its first pamphlet "Surrealism in Czechoslovakia" that it recognized "the need for solidarity that binds all those standing... on the side of the revolutionary proletariat and that it does not intend to unnecessarily argue against the works of those writers siding with the proletarian revolution, who express themselves in a conventional way," it was thus confirming the position that we had maintained in DEVĚTSIL's practices. Having had for many years its activities, often condemned in communist periodicals as decadent, perverted, monstrous, reactionary, idealistic, formalistic, bourgeois and counter-revolutionary, exposed to many attacks by this party, we have become accustomed to not attaching more importance to such pseudo-critical campaigns than they actually had. Though willing to discuss fundamental and topical problems (whenever there was at least a minimum guarantee that the discussion would not be conducted as a free-for-all by those lacking knowledge of the given matter), we did not consider it necessary to respond to all, sometimes quite illiterate attacks, that were printed, for instance, against Poetism in 1925 in the periodicals "Avantgarda" and "Dav" and in 1931 in "Tvorba". We argued against our opponents in the left camp *only* when our silence might have obscured our positions, or when we knew — and this is the case for our current argument — that the matter at hand could be jeopardized if the attacks against us were not rebuffed.

The same permanent conflict has been reproduced, in various stages and ways, in the disputes between Devětsil and Proletkult, between Poetism and RAPP ideology and later between Surrealism and so-called Socialist Realism. This conflict has never been fully resolved, not even when it seemed to be bridged by practical cooperation. The period of several years, in which the communist press and functionaries of marginal educational organizations maintained relative tolerance and non-aggressive tactics towards supporters of the avant-garde, and when, for instance, it was possible for us to cooperate in the Left Front, subdued this conflict and promised that the cultural policy of the working class's vanguard, carried out up until then unsystematically and without expertise in the spirit of casuistic opportunism, would go in a better and more responsible direction. When the attempt of the "Open Letter" of Kharkov's International Conference of Revolutionary Writers (1930) to resuscitate proletarian literature dismally failed, it was hoped that the methods of the Soviet cultural policy, whose line was broken by twists and turns attesting to the fumbling search for a path without a reliable compass, would not be mechanically and bureaucratically transferred to another cultural context and to substantially different conditions. In the period when this ongoing conflict was kept in check, signs emerged that seemed to foretell an improved orientation of the communist and Soviet cultural policy in art-related matters: the RAPP was dissolved, and Boris Pasternak was enthusiastically applauded at the Soviet Writers' Congress. It was then, as André Breton put it in his lecture for the Left Front in Prague (1935), "truly a sign of the times that one of the leading figures in Soviet politics, Nikolai Bukharin, a superb dialectician, took on the task of giving a report on poetry to the first congress of Soviet writers... and it was also a sign of the times that André Malraux was able to deliver his wonderful and decisive speech." We see in the literary-theoretical intervention of Bukharin, "the party's most valuable and strongest theoretician" (Lenin 14 January 1923), the most enlightened and positive act regarding poetry and literature in the history of the Soviet Union's cultural policy. At this time, it was even possible to hold serious discussions in Prague on the principles of Surrealism and Socialist Realism (see the anthologies *Discussing Surrealism* from 1934 and *Socialist Realism* from 1935), which is all the more significant since, at the same time in France, the AEAR (Association of Revolutionary Writers and Artists), an organization similar to the Left Front, had rejected *a priori* the discussion sought by Paris's Surrealist Group, which was endeavouring to take part in this organization through a comparison of viewpoints. In France, especially after the "Argon affair", when the author of "Paysan de Paris" deserted to Socialist Realism and when Ehrenburg published his famous diatribe in the Soviet press, the activities of the Surrealists were, wherever the influence of the PCF functionaries was applied, silenced and condemned by all means. In contrast, the early activities of Prague's Surrealist Group were viewed quite favourably by most communist critics, and lectures by André Breton and Paul Éluard in Prague (Spring 1935) even received an enthusiastic response in communist newspapers, which we noted in issue 1 of the "Bulletin international du Surréalisme". In this bulletin, which Prague's Surrealist Group published (9 April 1935) with both of its guests, we were able to state, in a conclusion to previous lectures, discussions, exhibitions and other activities, and to the voices of communist theoreticians and art critics, that "we consider the question of Surrealism's accord with the revolutionary views of Marx and Lenin to be definitively, objectively and positively answered".

The Surrealist Group, currently forced to engage in a defensive polemical battle on two fronts: against the conservative academic right and reactionaries as well as against the cultural line of the Czechoslovak Communist Party, is fully aware that the external situation in which the political tension is reflected requires that, for the collaboration of anti-fascist intellectual forces, and, above all, for the cooperation and unity of action of the art and scientific avant-garde, which endorses, regardless of party, the socialist camp, an acceptable ideological base be secured that would support a readiness to fight together for *creative freedom* against the attempts of the Gleichschaltung. In the interests of this common approach, we considered it necessary, on the one hand, to reject the recent campaigns against Surrealism even by the press that believes itself to be in the ranks of the left and, on the other hand, to refute the numerous accusations made by V. Nezval against the Surrealist Group.

The Surrealist Group had repeatedly demonstrated its efforts to cooperate with artists outside the group and whose work we consider to be close to Surrealism and important for the development of new art. The second exhibition of the Surrealist Group (collection of Štyrský and Toyen) that Jan Mukařovský opened in Prague and in Bratislava with his speech, and where E.F. Burian, F. Halas and Laco Novomeský took part in the closing of the exhibition at Prague's Topič Salon, has become, especially considering the highly attended opening in Brno where Roman Jakobson and Jiří Kroha gave their polemical talks, an effective *demonstration for the freedom of avant-garde art* and a protest against any efforts to restrict it.

The desired unity of the intellectual left is not weakened by mutual criticism and discussion with differences of opinion on this or that matter; on the contrary, such criticism and discussions strengthens its solidarity. Intellectual initiative, the critical study of current issues and the free exchange of views formulated on the basis of such examination will — while remaining loyal to the principles of the accepted worldview — benefit the disciplined unity of action, in which extremely divergent yet consistent and knowledgeable opinions can shake hands, and loyal socialist-minded individuals (not consorting with cultural reactionaries) may have repeatedly clashed. We regret that the invectives of some communist journalists against new art and Surrealism resort to the kind of arguments (or rather pseudo-arguments) that offer little opportunity for an ideological, theoretical discussion of controversial issues and devote most of their energy to ensuring that their writing is filled with crude insults that they throw in the face of modern artists. Yet the insults by which magazines such as Popular Culture (Lidová kultura) attack the Surrealist Group are not able to support the fight of the left cultural front against fascism and reactionaries; they could — if left unanswered by us — damage and break the intellectual left. We also regret that V. Nezval was unwilling to engage in a mutual, principled discussion regarding the ideological conflicts that arose, that he did not posit one view against another, but formulated politically distorted and often demagogic accusations, attacking the Surrealist Group and justifying these attacks with numerous incorrect and inaccurate statements, untruths and half-truths, improprieties and tendentious distortions that we have had to correct step by step in our reply.

At its inception (1934), the Czech Surrealist Group defined its relation to dialectical materialism and its position in the cultural and social struggle through a discussion which possessed, despite its intense character and tumultuous resonance, a serious level and comradely accent. The program principles that we have pursued that we embraced here are still valid and binding for us. There is no difference in viewpoint between the introductory essay of *Discussing Surrealism* and the position conveyed in *Surrealism Against the Current*. Today, however, our opponents, incapable of using ideological weapons to engage in controversy, are turning their anti-Surrealist arguments into grocery-line quarrels. Articles that should serve to further enlighten the people, can no longer speak of Surrealism and "Formalism" without the use of frenetic insults and a provocatively malicious and hostile tone.

And yet, (despite its embarrassing decline), we do not want to consider this press, given its original socialist mission and the situation requiring unity of the left, and concerning those ideas that can join the avant-garde of scientific and artistic work with the social progress movement, to be hostile in the most extreme sense of this word. Where we would rightfully expect, even in accounting for the undeniable brusqueness of divergent views, disagreement with radical *opponents* in this or that matter, we instead encounter raging *hostility*. Our opponents respond with sticks, curses, harassment and defamation to the heresy that dared to critically object to the cultural practices of the USSR and the Czechoslovak Communist Party. But one thing should not be forgotten: despite the more acute conflicts that must be, without a weary acceptance by both sides, fought through, we are now facing the despotic threat of fascism. Afterall, we are both standing on the same shore; if it is flooded by fascist waves, both our books and those of our opponents would be swept away...

The editors of communist journals, chanting slogans about the unity of the nation, lend a helping hand to conservative academics and the vulgar practitioners of kitsch, not to defend against a reactionary culture, but — as evidenced by Neumann's "Notes on the Fight with Formalism" ("Kultura doby" II. 6.) — in the name of a united, squelching fight against the isms of "degenerate art", which then pave the way for this reactionary culture. The increasingly frequent concurrences of the fascist and communist (Soviet and western) press, fighting against monstrous formalism, are striking: this agreement lies not only in their aesthetic assessment, but also in methods of combatting art that is independent and uncurbed. It is time to remind reviewers from the periodicals "Lidová kultura" (Popular Culture) and "Rudé právo" (Red Right) that, in a democratic climate, criticism responds to criticism: neither bloody vengeance, terror, charges of treason and calls for "expulsion from a nation" nor censorship and the braying of hearsay and insults are employed in a civilized world as a convincing response to critical objections.

The Surrealist Group will not voluntarily cede the right to defend and apply its activities, its criteria, ideas and their nuances as thoroughly as possible, and will do so not only against the hostile camp on the other shore, but also against opponents from the intellectual left, whose solidarity is not disturbed by different shades in opinion.

The views that we are polemically summarizing here were declared by Nezval, as he blindly believed without proof, not only to be incorrect, but even "dangerous in the current situation given the role of the Soviet Union and efforts for a united anti-fascist front". For whom and what are they dangerous? — Not only the views, but the observed facts themselves are incorrect and dangerous. It is not an open critique of Soviet cultural and artistic practices, but the Soviet cultural policy and its practices themselves that are, in the current situation, and given the role of the Soviet Union and efforts for a united anti-fascist front, incorrect and utterly dangerous. Our opponents would evidently like to impose a choice on us: either keep quiet about the embarrassing aspects of the USSR's cultural and political line considering the almighty successes of the five-year plans and of the power of the Red Army, and in light of the threat of fascism — or be expelled to the ranks of the enemies of socialism. We will not allow ourselves to be gripped by the inquisition-like pliers of this deceitfully constructed and monstrous choice. Insisting on the need of all socialist programs to have free expression of thought, we declare our actively proven will to defend the Soviet people, socialism, democracy and peace, and our right and obligation to point out, from the perspective of socialism, the shortcomings, mistakes and transgressions of communist cultural practices in the USSR and in the West, and to examine through Marxist analysis the roots of cultural reactionism in the Soviet and Western world.

Short-lived will be the joy of those who welcome the fact the Nezval has renounced "the disappointing direction and disappointing followers" and that he has "detached himself at the last moment from the worst errors of his entourage", and who expect he will soon rid himself "of the methodical mistakes introduced by Surrealism, just as he has rid himself of his political mistakes" (see *Kultura doby*, year II, issue 6), or who, like Bedřich Václavek in *Index* (vol X, issue 4), express the satisfaction that Nezval "honourably passed the test where much, even everything was at stake", and "hopefully await Nezval's further development in line with reality". Let the notorious opponents of Surrealism be pleased in stating that they long ago "claimed in essence the same thing that Nezval is saying today". No matter what path Nezval's future work takes and regardless of whether it backs the hopes of the backward-looking and conservatives, enthralled by most of the verses of "Mother Hope", the storm that arose from Nezval's case has cleared the air. Surrealism and the activities of the members of Prague's Surrealist Group, unfettered by compromises, will manage to carry on, ever more resolutely, *against the current*.

Prague, May 1938

Chapter 5

Alternative Modernities: New Myths, Art, and Science

"The beautiful years of the 1920s were gone. We started with the 1930s, in deepening darkness," wrote art theoretician Jindřich Chalupecký in the introduction to his collection of essays *Obhajoba umění* (In Defense of Art, 1988).[1] Theoretical treatises of the 1930s are repeatedly dedicated to the themes of the opaqueness and confusion of the world, the emerging economic and cultural chaos, and the crisis of order, which in a certain sense follow on from the crisis of criteria identified by Jindřich Štyrský in "Koutek generace" (Cosy Nook of a Generation) (see Chapter 3). The attention of a range of artists is attracted to everyday reality, to the life of the modern human being in the metropolis. The labyrinth of city streets, the melancholy of night-time walkers, the everyday nature of the tasks of ordinary life were attributed the significance of myth by some authors. In the Czech avant-garde of the 1930s, instead of the building of a new art, world, and person, which characterized the 1920s, themes relating to the past appear. The adjectives *new* and *modern* do not entirely disappear from the vocabulary of artists, but a trend to a certain *return* appears — to history, to memory, and to tradition — that is, to themes apparently contradictory to the avant-garde. However, in reality this direction represents rather a different type of modernity, one founded on a return to order.[2]

1 For more, see Hana Rousová et al., *Konec Avantgardy?: od mnichovské dohody ke komunistickému převratu* (Řevnice: Arbor Vitae, 2011); Hana Rousová et al., *The End of the Avant-garde? From the Munich Treaty to the Communist Takeover* (Řevnice: Arbor Vitae, 2011).

2 In a number of studies from the 1930s, modern art is presented as art which lacks an order. In his article "L'Ecole de Paris" (The Paris School; 1931), Jindřich Chalupecký deliberates about modern art, similarly to T. S. Eliot in his cycle of lectures devoted to the Metaphysical Poets (The Clark Lectures): as signs of modern art, he considers the disintegration of reason and the need for order in reality. "Tradition is neither movement forward, nor reversion (...). Tradition and modernity only make sense where they cease to deny that they are mutually

The absence of group gestures or unifying criteria (as defined in a program) demonstrates the complexity and diversity of the Czech cultural scene of the 1930s and increases the impression of opacity and chaos, to which artists themselves refer. In contrast to the 1920s, which can be relatively well defined by the foundation of artistic groups whose program is often represented in manifestos, the situation in the literary scene of the 1930s is pluralist, and a range of (not only) foreign models and artistic approaches that were overlooked by the Poetist avant-garde are put into practice. In this respect, a range of writers and visual artists avoided the concept of the avant-garde without having the need to replace it any way. For instance, in his essays from the end of the 1930s, Jindřich Chalupecký circumvents the concept of the avant-garde with the designation *modern art*. Even though in a range of stances his approach is based on Surrealism, he openly criticized avant-garde postulates, in particular radicalism and the conception of art as a kind of vanguard.

In the 1930s, an acceptance of alternative sources of modern art was characteristic especially for artists outside of the Surrealist Group, which in a number of respects represented a continuation of the avant-garde of the 1920s — in the mid-1930s Karel Teige compared the Czech form of Surrealism in terms of development with Devětsil's Poetism of the 1920s. In his lecture "K otázce avantgardy a nástupu nové generace" (On the Question of the Avant-Garde and the Onset of a New Generation) from 1937, which he delivered at a vernissage of artists who already formed the core of the future Skupina 42 (Group 42: Ladislav Zívr, František Gross, František Hudeček, and others), Teige evaluated these works as "an explicit confirmation and strengthening of the avant-garde." After 1929, when discussions started to appear concerning the possibility of the continuation of a radically leftist avant-garde, a number of new concepts — arising from European modernism — appear. In the context of Czech art of the 1930s, among the most significant of these were: the influence of Ango-America modernism; the significance of mythology and myth; the return (turnaround) to reality and every-day reality.

While interest in French and Soviet culture unequivocally dominated in the post-war avant-garde, at the turn of the 1920s and 1930s there was a marked increase in translations of the hitherto overlooked output of Anglo-American modernism. In 1929, Arnošt Vaněček's anthology *Američtí básníci* (American Poets) was published, mapping the poetic creation of the United States in a broad scope. In the same year Ottova angloamerická knihovna (Otto's Anglo-American Library, 1929–1934) was founded and translations were published of Virginia Woolf's *Orlan-*

the same," writes Jindřich Chalupecký in the article "Aktualita" (Current Affairs) from 1937. This inclination towards tradition is significantly inspired by the first Czech translation of Eliot's study "Tradition and the Individual Talent," which was published in a translation by René Wellek in 1933 in the magazine *Listy pro umění a kritiku*.

do, Joyce's *Portrait of the Artist as a Young Man* and *Ulysses*, and part of Eliot's *The Waste Land* (published in book form only in 1947).[3]

Essays originally written in English concerning the themes of language, specifically the word, received a significant reception. In contrast to the early 1920s, when the avant-garde drew upon Marinetti's Futurism and Teige "liberated" words by an emphasis on their graphic, visual form, in the 1930s the crisis of the word, language, and speech was a major theme in the context of the ideas of European modernism. As the cause of this crisis, technology and the transformation of the post-war world were no longer dominant, but rather conventionality, the non-progressive character of the art of the past, and its persistence in the archaeology of literature. These themes were introduced into the Czech environment by, among others, translations of the studies of Eugene Jolas, in which the crisis of the word and language is presented in connection with the crisis of modernity. In his article "Logos," Jolas rejects non-progressive art and calls for a revision of the values of the past.[4]

---

3 Writer and translator Adolf Hoffmeister discussed the translation of *Ulysses* into Czech with Joyce personally already in 1928 (after French and German, Czech was the third language in which the novel was published, in 1930). This was followed by *Dubliners* in 1933 (trans. Josef Hrůša) and a translation experiment, in which three translators (Maria Weatherall, Vladimír Procházka, and Adolf Hoffmeister) attempted a translation of *Anna Livia Plurabelle* (cf. Václav Paris: Anna Livia Plurabella česká, *Litikon* 2, 1., 2017). Further translations of English and American authors followed over the course of the 1930s. These were accompanied by theoretical studies and manifestos, in particular the texts of Eugene Jolas from *transition* revue and the essential essays of T. S. Eliot, "Tradition and the Individual Talent" (1933) and "The Function of Criticism" (1935). Hoffmeister talks about his personal meeting with Joyce in a collection of interviews *Piš, jak slyšíš* (Write as You Hear, 1931). The transmission of Anglo-American modernism into the Czech environment was strongly influenced by academic discourse, in particular the personality of René Wellek (he translated the works of Conrad and D. H. Lawrence), an expert in comparative literature who emigrated to the United States in 1939 and worked at Yale University, and Otakar Vočadlo, a correspondent of most translators in the 1930s and the author of the first books in Czech on modern Anglo-American literature (*Anglická literatura XX. století*, 1932; *Současná literatura Spojených států*, 1934; *Moderní americká literatura*, 1938 — English Literature of the 20th Century, 1932; Contemporary Literature of the United States, 1934; Modern American Literature, 1938.)

4 Eugene Jolas published the Paris literary magazine *transition* (1927–1938), oriented towards experimental creative work. His essays were translated into Czech by Arnošt Vaněček. Both the magazine and the essays concerning the word in modern art, the logos, and the end (death) of the novel found a significant reception in the Czech avant-garde (they were partly translated into Czech in a matter of a few months). In the article "Logos," in which he was one of the first to mention the archaeology of literature in the context of modernism, he further comments: "There is a contradiction here which the poet encounters at the beginning of his development. Either he will entirely abandon the attempt to express his universe by means of the ruined instruments of a inflexible and exhausted language, or he will be forced to try and resurrect the somnolent word." (Jolas, *Kvart* 1, 1930, 1: 38). Jolas describes the need for different words; that is, such words as attach more closely to the world and thus succeed in making cognition accessible: "Words have a reality that dictionaries do not know. Etymology is for archaeologists of literature. We want an etymology of cognition." (Ibid. 40).

The themes and approaches of Anglo-American modernism influenced a range of authors. In her novel *Amor a psyché* (Cupid and Psyche, 1937)[5] Milada Součková presented a sophisticated playing with mythology. A strong return to the past is characteristic for the works of Vladislav Vančura, significantly in *Obrazy z dějin národa českého* (Pictures from the History of the Czech Nation, 1939–1940). However, of the originally planned six parts, he only managed to finish two; he was arrested by the Gestapo while working. The question of to what extent human beings are capable of recognizing truth about reality and themselves was addressed by Karel Čapek in three philosophically-oriented novels, which he combined into the "noetic trilogy": *Hordubal* (1933), *Povětroň*, and *Obyčejný život* (Meteor; An Ordinary Life, both 1934).

In 1930, as an alternative to Teige's form of the interwar avant-garde, the magazine *Kvart* with the subtitle Sborník poezie a vědy (A Journal of Poetry and Science, directed by poet and architect Vít Obrtel, 1930–1937; 1945–1949) was founded. "This is not a philosophy of life; rather, it is the struggle for the Absolute," as Václav Navrátil evaluated the ideological content of the magazine's first year. *Kvart* did not publish any program as a stance of the editorial board, but an article printed in 1931 in the "cultural leaflet" *Rok*, published in cooperation with Vít Obrtel, Jindřich Štyrský, and Bohuslav Brouk, can be considered such a declaration. In this article, Navrátil precisely formulated the magazine's stance: it attempted to acquaint the wider public with hitherto neglected literary works and philosophical and artistic theories that rejected bourgeois conservatism. In Navrátil's interpretation, the theoretical essays, short stories, and poems of contemporary Czech and foreign literature and also of authors from previous periods created a bridge connecting the idea of the cognition of the absolute with a literary-historical and artistic context. He found an equivalent for this in the visual arts in the Artificialism of Jindřich Štyrský and Toyen, whose graphic designs were published in the first number of *Kvart*, while in architecture these ideas were complemented by Obrtel's neo-Constructivism. In his essays published in the collection *O smutku, lásce a jiných věcech* (On Sadness, Love, and Other Things, 2003) Navrátil

5 Milada Součková worked with the modernist magazine *The Booster/Delta*, which came out in Paris in the years 1937–1939. In the issue devoted to Součková and Rykr, an excerpt from her novel *Amor and Psyche* was published in English. See Malá *Česká literatura* 62, 2014, 3: 395–409.. Součková was influenced by current trends in European modernism, and we can find significant points in common between her work and Jolas's opinions on literature. From her correspondence with Jindřich Chalupecký, we know that Součková owned several numbers of Jolas's magazine *transition*, which she probably acquired during her stay in Paris on the occasion of the Salon des indépendants (1937), at which her husband Zdenek Rykr exhibited. She devoted herself systematically to the issue of the crisis of language and the need for new words in her poetry, specifically in the expansive poem *Mluvící pásmo* (Talking Zone, 1939), now translated into English.

interprets the need for myths in modern art as a consequence of the destruction of the personality — he repeatedly writes about poetry as a search for myth.[6]

Kvart opened entirely new themes for the 1930s of the Czech avant-garde: a dualism of the human being and the world; the past; history that is not conceived in time, but rather in space. While Teige continued to operate with a conception of the painter as a modern poet, in the *Kvart* circle the modern artist was perceived as a much more complex concept — as a representative of artistic continuity, tradition, and even a witness of literary history, who finds his inspiration in a new conception of the word, myth, memory, archive, and encyclopedia.[7] For artists working with the concepts of European modernism, the associations artist-worker and artist-acrobat were an already outdated and superceded past. These associations were replaced by a conception of the artist as an "*athlete* of the ideas of all periods," accompanied by an emphasis on the necessity of a return to the "old masters of poetry and ideas." In connection with this, deliberations appear about new forms, new contours, and the need for a revision of values. Concerning a revision of painting, in the accompanying text to his exhibition catalog *Obrazy* (Pictures), Zdenek Rykr wrote about transformations of styles and the emergence of new sources of inspiration. Rykr's wife, Milada Součková, formulated the need for a new method of creative writing in her essay "K problému současného románu" (On the Contemporary Novel). Here she openly acknowledges that, although she writes novels, she does not believe in the future of the novel, because it is not possible to build the novel of a new era via the technique of the old novel.

---

6 Navrátil's conception of human time and poetic time is inspirational: "Scientist work from details. Phenomenologists are interested in the "phasing" and the "articulation" of time, which means the temporal period as known from nature's idea of the world. Psychology is interested in how the consciousness of time is evoked in the human being. For physicists, the universality of time is a metaphysically undetermined, physical dimension." Václav Navrátil, *O smutku, lásce a jiných věcech* (Praha: Torst, 2003), 352. In the context of time thus defined, Navrátil introduces the concept of poetic time, inspired by the poetry of Josef Hora. About his poetry Navrátil writes: "Hora's poetry is inspired by subconscious music. This too, is the theme, for music is the blossoming of reflection on time. Hora is master of revealing the secret, unheard, but fateful melodies. 'Lakes of shy sounds, who has cursed you?' Those who understand could speak at length on this image and others like it." (Ibid. 354). According to Navrátil, Hora's conception of time is purely existential — that is, there is only one time, all-encompassing, and our existence is bound by it. We all belong to it; according to Navrátil, it is a time that "loves us without mercy." Václav Navrátil, "Čas vědecký, čas básnický," in *O smutku, lásce a jiných věcech*, Karel Srp (ed.) Praha: Torst, 2003), 352–354.

7 In October 1938, the remains of Romantic poet Karel Hynek Mácha were exhumed and transported from Litoměřice — which was part of the territory ceded to Nazi Germany — to Prague. The operation was initiated by Karel Engliš, governor of the Czechoslovak National Bank, because of concerns that the symbol of Czech history and art could fall into the hands of the Germans. In May 1939, the remains were subsequently brought to the cemetery at Vyšehrad and reinterred, accompanied by a ceremonial procession.

In Czech literature in the mid-1930s, in connection with the threat of Nazism, the themes of anxiety and fear appear, both concerning European civilization and, in the context of World War Two, literally for one's life. Art abandons playful avant-garde themes, characteristic for the early 1920s, and moves in the direction of more serious texts about death, human life, and freedom (among others, Josef Hora, Jan Zahradníček, and Vladimír Holan). Just as in literature, so too in the visual arts, we can see an increasing frequency of the motifs of ruins, graves, and the museum sarcophagus.

In 1938 the Munich Agreement was concluded — an agreement between Germany, Italy, France, and Great Britain on the cession of border territories of Czechoslovakia to Germany. The democratic era of Czechoslovakia, designated as the First Republic, thus came to an end. In March 1939, Czechoslovakia was occupied by Nazi Germany and the Protectorate of Bohemia and Moravia was established (it lasted until the end of World War Two). The artistic reaction to the political-cultural events processed the themes of anxiety, alienation, separation, and fear about the Czech language: for instance, in Milada Součková's elegy for the mother-tongue, the poem *Kaladý aneb Útočiště řeči* (Kalady or the Sanctuary of Speech, 1938). In the years 1938–1939, Zdenek Rykr painted the cycle of paintings *Náhrobek či Elegie* (Gravestone or Elegy), which have the common theme of ruins (many of them depict the head of an artist-genius, probably observing his own dead body). In these paintings Rykr in a certain sense depicted himself — a genius on the verge of death (in 1940 he committed suicide), but this cycle is itself a gravestone of the avant-garde.

In the period of the Second World War, censorship intensified and modern art went underground, where magazines and books were published, as well as illegal collections, for instance *Roztrhané panenky* (Torn-Up Dolls, 1937)) of the Skupina Ra (Ra Group), presenting the experimental photographic techniques, compositions, and collages of Otta Mizera, Josef Istler, and others. In 1944, Otta Mizera along with Jan Řezáč, Miroslava Miškovská, and Josef Prošek created the illegal collection *Ochranné prostředky* (Protective Means), in which the main themes were the cynicism of war, alienation, the individual's loss of identity in a period of oppression. These are also the themes of exigent and urgent paintings by Toyen in which during the war period the main place was taken by a portrayal of violence and death. In her ironic painting *Po představení* (After the Performance, 1943) a young woman without a face hangs upside down; her body disappearing into the wall recalls a victim hung up by the legs. The nine-piece cycle *Schovej se, válko!* (Hide, War!, 1944) is full of animal bones, which often however behave like living beings. The title of the cycle refers on the one hand to Lautréamont's appeal (Poésies), and on the other hand to the introductory poem of the same name by Jindřich Heisler. (During the war Toyen concealed Heisler in her apartment, because as a Jew he would have faced forced deportation; in 1947 they left for Paris together.) In contrast to her contemporaries, Toyen did not resort to a direct description of suffering experienced; her paintings are a meditation on extinctions in which human figures are already mere phantoms.

In 1940, in the magazine *Program D40,* Jindřich Chalupecký published his study "Svět, v němž žijeme" (The World In Which We Live). The title was a reference to Teige's work "Svět, který se směje" (The World That Laughs), written in the mid-1920s. However, in particular it is a deeper reaction to the ideological crisis of the avant-garde and modern art as a whole — in his studies from the end of the 1930s, Chalupecký repeatedly develops his concept of the avant-gardes as symptoms of the spiritual crisis of Europe. In the period of the Second World War, artists find their source in the present moment; they artistically process the position of the human being in the world in the context of everyday human life, which is not infrequently a source of anxiety and sadness, but also of physical pain or hunger.

The text "The World in Which We Live" became the programmatic text of Group 42, a loose association of visual artists, poets, and translators who contributed significantly to the plurality of artistic and critical approaches utilized and to a renewal of interest in the concepts of tradition, the past, and myth. Among its members were painters František Gross, František Hudeček, Kamil Lhoták, and Jan Kotík; poets Jiří Kolář, Ivan Blatný, Josef Kainar, Jiřina Hauková, and Jan Hanč; photographer Miroslav Hák; sculptor Ladislav Zívr; and theoretician Jindřich Chalupecký. In addition, at the end of the 1930s the aesthetics of Group 42 were shared by Milada Součková, Zdenek Rykr, and others, who never officially became members. [8]

The group's members presented their work in a double number of the magazine *Život* (an. 17, 1942, no. 2), which can be regarded as the group's manifesto. Among others, František Gross and František Hudeček presented their visual art here, while Josef Kainar and Jiří Kolář presented their poetry. The poetics of Group 42 — especially Jiří Kolář, Ivan Blatný, and Jiřina Hauková — and their predecessor Milada Součková was deeply influenced by approaches taken over from the prose of Joyce and Woolf and the poetry of Eliot (new translations of Eliot's seminal poetic texts were produced within the group, without the possibility of publication).

In the context of Chalupecký's writing, the myth of the city becomes a new myth; there is a clear appeal here to focus on real life and the human being in the midst of the metropolis. Modern myth should actively participate in the creation of a person's identity.[9] The avant-garde — that is, that part represented by the Devětsil

8 Sculptor Ladislav Zívr, a member of Group 42, confirms in his diaries that the group had no program. Chalupecký's text "The World in Which We Live" served as a *de facto* substitute. In a letter to Zívr from 20 November 1979, Chalupecký confirms this contention: "And when I look back and think about what exactly was the significance of the Group, then of course it was not in this "civilism," as is commonly written about it. This significance was in two quite different matters. Primarily, in that we had no program and merely insisted on the validity of modern art [...]. And secondly, in that right in the middle of the war, we refused to care about the war — art was more for us: a refuge, protection, truth."

9 The phenomenon of crisis was analyzed on many levels within the Czech avant-garde. Chalupecký conducted an extensive analysis of the motif of a crisis of European civilization in his concluding work *Evropa a umění* (Europe and Art, 2005). In the introduction to this work, he places the 20th century into contrast with a faith in progress, but he views the roots of the

group — has run out of stream. The discussion of generations from the beginning of the 1930s concerning the crisis of criteria emphasized the need for seeking new themes and theoretical concepts. For many artists, mythology and myth represent a story, a comprehensible narrative, providing a key for the understanding of the modern world. Myths, as Chalupecký's studies show, are perceived as spiritual tales that can be found on the street. Therefore, through their systematic presence, myths can substitute for an order. For a number of avant-garde artists of the 1930s, the everyday world became a mythology of the modern human being, whose constitutive feature is that it must be sought, created, or apprehended.[10]

The turn towards reality, accompanied by a requirement for this reality to enter literature directly, is characteristic for many of the artists around Group 42. "Once during a walk through night-time Prague (and moreover very dark) František Hudeček and I ran into a fluorescent fish. It was the skeleton of a salted herring, which shone more clearly with a blue light than neon," wrote visual artist Kamil Lhoták.[11] In this way, the everyday reality of people penetrated into art; poets and visual artists were interested in the world in which they lived.[12] The reality of the modern poet became the city, its people, paving, pedestals, its lamps, houses, stairs, and apartments. According to Chalupecký, all this together created a part of a new

crisis as much deeper. In a certain sense he expresses a similar view to that expressed by J.-F. Lyotard in his essay *Anima minima*, albeit Lyotard is even more radical: "The ideals of Western civilization issuing from the ancient, Christian, and modern traditions are bankrupt. The cause of the bankruptcy is not in what is called historical, social, political, or techno-scientific reality. The recurrent crisis, or rather, the permanent crisis, the West talks about in its becoming proceed from an essential disposition. The West is that civilization that questions its essence as civilization." Quoted from: *Postmodern Fables*, trans. by Georges Van Den Abbeele, Minneapolis: U of Minnesota Press 1997, p. 235.

10 In Chalupecký's opinion, Anglo-American literature in particular found a fascinating connection between art and life. He views it as the arrival of an art that is neither esthetizing "nor moralizing, if you will; we can most likley find it in that barbarous, great, and unknown land which is North America. Its poets [...] have never lost their direct relationship with the world and life, which is the only thing that can make a work of art living and useful." According to Chalupecký, it was precisely this direct relationship to the world and to life that was the only thing capable of making an artistic work alive and real.

11 Kamil Lhoták, *Výtvarné umění* 17 (1967), no. 3: 123.

12 Chalupecký writes extensively about art and reality in the study "Umění napodobí skutečnost" (Art Imitates Reality, 1942). In his opinion, the artist does not approach the objective as if approaching chaos, but creates a certain order. There is a certain irony contained in the study's title. In the article he writes about the need not to imitate, but to capture objective reality, to reconstruct it. On the basis of an approach defined in this way to the question of the relationship of art and reality, he praised the poetic collections of Jiří Kolář, specifically on account of the relationship to reality in his poetry, which is everyday, non-poetic, experience of human existence in the city. In the approach applied by Kolář, Chalupecký detects a certain connection with the works of T. S. Eliot and James Joyce, whose work he described in his study "Konec moderní doby" (The End of the Modern Period, 1946) as the most extreme realization of modern art, precisely in the context of its relationship to life and to the world.

mythology that returned art back to the human being.[13] Visual artist and poet Jiří Kolář introduced his poetry collection *Ódy a variace* (Odes and Variations, 1946), containing poems from the years of occupation (1941–1944), with the motto: "And That Is the World/And That is Life." The interest on the part of artists in the reality of the modern human, which we can follow in Czech literature at the beginning of the 1940s, did not undergo an artistic deformation in the way that Poetism did. This was a reality that was raw, in no way transformed. In the context of this new approach, studies and deliberations were published discussing what means modern art had at its disposal for recording reality.

A significant platform for Group 42 was the magazine *Listy — čtvrtletník pro umění a filosofii* (1946–1948, ed. Jindřich Chalupecký; from 1948 in cooperation with Jan Grossman). A useful contribution was made by the thematic issues of *Listy*. The third issue was devoted to existentialism, which at that time was presented as an opposing pole to Surrealism. A further issue was dedicated to the representatives of Anglo-American modernism (Henry Miller and others). *Listy* combined artistic criticism with a philosophical approach and informed about world currents. It was the first place to introduce the thoughts of Sartre, Camus, Heidegger, Gabriel Marcel, and Karl Jaspers into Czech theoretical discourse.

In the first years of the Second World War, the avant-garde postulates of the 1920s were sustainable only with great difficulty. Thus, at the turn of the decade the question of the viability of the avant-garde returned once again, the same question posed in 1929 by Jindřich Štyrský. This time, the question came from the ranks of the youngest generation. "The End of the Avant-garde? Yes!" declared somewhat theatrically Kamil Bednář, the spokesman of a newly emerging generation of artists. He presented his creative works in *Jarní almanach básnický* (A Spring Poetic Almanac, 1940).[14] Bednář describes his generation as "passive" and "diffidently reticent," oriented towards the timeless values of the specific "naked human being," as he first formulated his program in his essay "Slovo k mladým" (A Word to the

13 In this conception the city is a particular distinctive landscape that surrounds the human being. However, it is the human being who experiences existential anxiety in the entrails of the city (just as many authors of the period wrote about it), who is the fundamental thing that must be once again transformed. The relationship of the subject and the city landscape became an important theme for modern Czech architecture. A specific solution is offered by the monograph of architect Ladislav Žák, *Obytná krajina* (Living Landscape, 1947), which in the context of European functionalism comes forward with an ambitious plan of the Czech landscape as a kind of "living space."

14 In the preface, Václav Černý sums up the fundamental questions posed by the authors of the almanac and their main task — to create a new concept of the human being, respectively humankind. He asks: "What is the first, deepest, given content of this humankind? What are the immediate givens of humankind? And what are the limits of the human being, and how far can they be shifted?" (Ibid. 12). In the context of the work of the authors in the almanac, he describes the common features of the group's poetics: "new poetic facts," "new directions of creative will," and "a changed stance towards the world." (Ibid. 10). He regards primarily the collective experience (war) that connects the young poets as the source of these changes.

Young, 1940).[15] Literary historian and critic Václav Černý published a summary of the main theses in his article "Slovo o Slovu k mladým" (A Word About Word to the Young) on the pages of *Kritický měsíčník*, in which he reproaches Bednář for a lack of comprehensibility and clarity in the passages devoted to the "return to timeless values." Černý does not agree with the proclaimed rejection of everything that has been brought by modern art, especially the avant-garde. This also applies to the propagated return to older (more classical) poetic forms. The discussion that was provoked by "A Word to the Young" was summarized by Kamil Bednář in his book *Ohlasy Slova k mladým* (Responses to A Word to the Young, 1941). Bednář tried to sketch a program of its own for his generation. He agrees with Chalupecký's vision of the world in which we live, and his emphasis on the human being and her/his position in the modern world.

In April 1946, Chalupecký's study "Konec moderní doby" (End of the Modern Period) was published, which starts with the sentence: "The modern period has already come to an end." These are the words of Václav Navrátil from the beginning of the war, reacting to the exhaustion of avant-garde experience, whose artistic expressions no longer had the capacity to organize the chaos of the world. Karel Teige, indefatigable defender of the avant-garde, still believed in the continued viability and life of the avant-garde even after World War Two. In his study "Osud umělecké avantgardy v obou světových válkách" (The Fate of the Avant-Garde in Both World Wars, 1946), he presents Surrealism as the last avant-garde direction (the shipwreck survivor) that has survived. In the graph of modern art, which has the form of an arrow, Surrealism is at its tip — the most progressive avant-garde direction. Nevertheless, Jindřich Chalupecký supported an entirely different opinion in the context of the progressive nature of Surrealism. In his study "On Dada, Surrealism, and Czech Art" he writes about the exhaustion of Surrealism's progressive tendencies: "With the onset of the war we became aware that Surrealism in its orthodox form ceases to be sufficient. Face to face with reality it even seemed an artistic game to us. Therefore, we chose the path indicated by Breton, that we regarded as the most valuable thing in Surrealism: we were captivated by the miraculous nature of the everyday."[16]

---

15 In the conclusion of his study, Bednář devotes attention to young new art and affirms the abandonment of avant-garde approaches. He writes that the new poetry does not break the established forms introduced by pre-war poetry; in particular, because it is no longer possible to go any further in experimentation in form and content. In connection with this, the requirements for poetry, therefore, necessarily change — they are no longer connected with form, but with what Bednář defines as human content, influencing the themes and motifs of modern poetry. The programmatic pronouncements of the authors associated around Kamil Bednář provoked a relatively extensive discussion, which took place on the pages of *Kritický měsíčník*. To a certain extent some critical reactions were motivated by the lack of clarity of Bednář's text, bordering at times on the enigmatic, the reason for which may have been fear of intervention by censors.

16 Jindřich Chalupecký, "O dada, surrealismu a českém umění," in Jindřich Chalupecký, *Cestou necestou* (Jinočany: H&H, 1999), 223.

In May 1945, Czechoslovakia was liberated by the American and Soviet armies. The assistance of the Soviet Union was reflected in the first post-war parliamentary elections, in which the Communists received more than 30% of the votes. In 1946, the government of CP leader Klement Gottwald was appointed and a majority of significant positions both in the government and in cultural posts were occupied by communists. The paths of Czech modern art were further complicated after World War Two by the communist putsch in February 1948, followed by the establishment of a totalitarian state in Czechoslovakia. The borders with the West (not only cultural ones!) closed for a long time — modernism and the avant-garde were forbidden by state censorship after 1948.

In the account of the magazines excelling at the beginning of the 1930s, one fundamental aspect has remained so far unremarked: the word "science" appears in a number of them (for instance, *Kvart: sborník poesie a vědy* — A collection of poetry and science —, *Plán: revue pro literaturu, umění a vědu* — A revue for literature, art, and science). The attempt at conciliating art and science was apparently closest in the case of Czechoslovak structuralism, developed on the foundation of the Pražský lingvistický kroužek (Prague Linguistic Circle).

The Prague Linguistic Circle was founded in 1926, initially as a free association of linguistic scholars who pursued a functional-structural approach in the study of language, and from the beginning of the 1930s it was one of the centers of European Structuralism.[17] The founding member of the circle was general linguist and English language expert Vilém Mathesius, while significant contributions were made by Bohumil Trnka, Bohuslav Havránek, Roman Jakobson, Jan Mukařovský, and others. The circle entered European consciousness at the end of the 1920s at the 1st International Congress of Linguists in The Hague (where the program of synchronic linguistics was presented) and at the 1st International Congress of Slavists in Prague, where the programmatic theses of the circle were presented. One of its fundamental acts was the establishment of phonology — concentrating on the description of the functional use of sound units — as a central discipline of the circle and of European linguistics generally at the International Phonological Conference in Prague (1930) and at the 2nd International Congress of Linguists in Geneva (1931).

A fundamental institution for the circle's work were the lectures of members and guests followed by a discussion. Among those who appeared at the circle in the inter-war period were Lucien Tesnière, Yury Tynyanov, Otto Jespersen, Viggo Brøndal, Rudolf Carnap, and Edmund Husserl. The list of those appearing provides evidence on the one hand of the circle's prestige, and on the other hand of its openness to non-linguistic disciplines and non-structuralist approaches. Key themes were language functions, the difference between written and spoken language, and standard written language forms or language culture; and in artistic disciplines, aesthetic function, literary development (in particular, in the material of verse),

17 For more, see Jindřich Toman, *The Magic of a Common Language: Jakobson, Mathesius, Trubetzkoy, and the Prague Linguistic Circle* (Cambridge: MIT Press 1995).

poetics, and so on. In linguistics, the functional-structural approach determined the discipline in a fundamental way for the following decades. In literary studies, its continuity was interrupted in 1948. Later, researchers of younger generations carried on from its work.

In 1932, the collection *Spisovná čeština a jazyková kultura* (Standard Czech and Language Culture) was published, a collective work by members of the Prague Linguistic Circle (Vilém Mathesius, Bohuslav Havránek, Roman Jakobson, Jan Mukařovský, and Miloš Weingart), who discussed the need for stability in the standard written language and the differences between poetic and standard written language. Members of the circle conducted a polemic with linguist Jiří Haller (and also with Josef Zubatý and Václav Ertl, who worked at the magazine *Naše řeč*), who promoted a purist approach to language. The object of the disputes were Haller's linguistic criticism of artistic texts — for instance, the collection of essays by Otokar Fischer *Duše a slovo* (Soul and Word) and Nezval's novel *Kronika z konce tisíciletí* (Chronicle From the End of the Millennium). The approach to the history of the Czech language of the circle around the *Naše řeč* magazine was criticized by Roman Jakobson in the chapter "O dnešním brusičství českém" (On Contemporary Czech Language Cleansing). In addition to purely linguistic academic work, Jakobson also systematically studied questions of Czech and Russian verse (in 1934 he published his seminal treatment of Old Czech verse) and poetics. Another significant collection of the Prague Linguistic Circle during the period in question was *Torso a tajemství Máchova díla* (Torso and the Secret of Mácha's Works, 1938, with contributions by Mukařovský, Jakobson, D. Čyževský, and others) and *Čtení o jazyce a poesii* (Readings on Language and Poetry, 1942, with contributions by V. Mathesius, J. Veltruský, F. Vodička, and others)

On the occasion of the "Poesie 1932" exhibition, Jakobson gave a lecture entitled "Co je poesie?" (What Is Poetry?) in which he described the concept of poetry as unstable and time-conditioned, while the poetic function (poeticness) is an element *sui generis* — that is, such a case when the word is felt as a word, and not merely as an outburst of emotion or a mere representative of a named object.

In 1935, the circle began to publish the quarterly *Slovo a slovesnost — časopis pro otázky teorie a kultury jazyka* — edited by Bohuslav Havránek and Vilém Mathesius. Leading Czech and foreign literary scholars, critics, and linguists published here (among other, Otokar Fischer, Pavel Eisner, Oldřich Králík, Pavel Trost, F. X. Šalda, Arne Novák, Dmytro Čyževsky), and also did literary authors (Karel Čapek, Vítězslav Nezval, Vladislav Vančura). The first number included Karel Čapek's deliberations on "Kdybych byl lingvistou" (If I Were a Linguist), F. X. Šalda on "O básnické autostylizaci, zvláště u Bezruče" (On Poetic Self-Stylization, Especially in the Case of Bezruč), and the studies of Jindřich Honzl and Vladislav Vančura "K diskusi o řeči ve filmu" (Towards a Discussion of Language in Film).

Within the framework of the Prague Linguistic Circle, aesthetician Jan Mukařovský developed a theory of the symbolic nature of the work of art. According to Mukařovský, in its essence, a work of art is a sign and a bearer of aesthetic information which cannot be expressed in another way. Mukařovský posed the question of in what way the individual elements are combined into a meaningful unit — to describe this unit of meaning, Mukařovský used the term "semantic gesture." The adjective "semantic" here means that it bears a meaningful intention; it enables us to understand a work of art as a dynamic, complex unit with relations to the author and society. Mukařovský developed the relationship between aesthetics and non-artistic phenomena in his study "Estetická funkce, norma a hodnota jako sociální fakty" (Aesthetic Functions, Norms, and Values as Social Facts, 1936). He complemented his previous theory with an anthropological aspect in his study "Může mít estetická hodnota v umění platnost všeobecnou?" (Can Aesthetic Value in Art Have General Validity, 1939). The structuralism presented in the studies of Roman Jakobson and Jan Mukařovský as a method founded on the noetic principle replaced the original formalist approach in aesthetics.

Mukařovský studied the problem of poetics in detail. The individual elements of the construction of a work of art — arranged hierarchically from phonetic elements to those bearing meaning — created a basis for examining the developmental changeability of artistic structure. His research was polemically aimed against formalism, which isolated the work from external connections. In contrast to formalism, Czech structuralism probed the methodological possibilities for examining the relationships between literature and the social environment, what literature corresponds to and for whom it functions, and the relationship between literature and reality. In this respect, a significant polemic with Marxist oriented theoreticians (for instance, Z. Kalandra) was provoked by Mukařovský's extensive work (1934) on Matěj Milota Zdirad Polák's poem *Vznešenost přírody* (The Grandure of Nature, 1819).

Vít Obrtel: The Right to Theory

The saying "man is the measure of all things" was not shouted by our Constructivists with sufficient pathos to force Protagoras to speak from the manuals of philosophy upon discovering this. Of course, nothing in the world changes in its essence, not even that old truth that understanding is dependent on the subject. This perhaps makes it all the more difficult for us to understand dogmatic theories on the relativity of form-changing things, of a new doctrine on a single and true function that became an end in itself, without man, who was for the time being lost in the idea of a mass (not the reality of a collective = sum of parts), obediently uninterested (although listening) in the theoretical delusion of the saviours themselves.

Theory will remain theory and reality reality. The individual's mistake matters little, what does matter is the submissiveness of the many who err. Understandably, things will go their own way. All of the mere preachers of aesthetic and practical theories can and will usually arrive at paralogisms, without the necessary factual work to support them, as opposed to individuals actually producing who can take a wrong step, but then are forced to correct themselves upon the next encounter with the essence of reality.

Today only phenomena physically touching a person have become the goal to be mastered. Phenomena psychologically touching people were rejected due to life's practical need. Thus, in order to facilitate theory, a person ceased to be considered as such, but was instead viewed as a scheme. The harmony was disrupted. These efforts, which emphasized in a primitive way the superiority of physical feelings over psychological instances, threatened life in its fullness.

Theorists coining mottos such as "art will cease to be art" and "the practical, constructive revolution begins where poetry ends" caused, on the one hand, many obedient jocks to truly believe them and, on the other hand, the preachers to interpret and modify these phrases as they deemed necessary, giving them meaning that suited the immediate, agitational needs.

The formal beauty of machines impressed the aesthetes and the waves of snobs following them, just as a good brick attacks a bricklayer's sensibility, though the latter does not forget that its purpose is to serve the construction of a house, not to be a self-serving model as the prophet's disciples believe. It so happened that functionality was decided by form. A house that should not have a flat roof, though this would be fully justified by constructive and economic principles, was considered *apriori* (apparently not from an aesthetic viewpoint, but from a functional one) to be bad.

This thus satisfied the revolutionary slogan that "art will cease to be art". The use of concrete, this completely new construction material, whose possibilities in construction cannot yet be commented on by builders and theorists working with it their whole lives (due to its unpredictable properties consisting of the unattainable precision of work and thus the superiority of empiricism), has become an aesthetic formula, not a truly practical one, of the "modern sentiment".

Slowly, however, the child's fascination with lyrical-romantic slogans disappears. It turns out, as always, that productive work is valuable, and that dubious slogans are worthless. Just as the sun will rise during the day and the stars at night, so too will theorists always rise and fall, covering their dilettantism with a cloud of phrases without doing more harm than sound film. After all, even snobs have the right for someone to ensure their entertainment.

Art will cease to be art. Transcendence cannot be closed in a matchbox.

Science guarantees us the satisfaction of our physical needs, art of our psychological needs. Our lives require not only certainties, but also probabilities.

Performance in the field of art and performance in the field of science (both in the broadest sense) cannot be combined without one or the other suffering. The purpose of the individual serving the public need either becomes science or art. (Though I am not taking into account the material needs of today's system.) I produce certain values, I accept certain values. This depends on the person and their relationship to physical and psychological needs.

Therefore, for the individual's life there is the need for an equilibrium in the percentages of corresponding physical and psychological facts. However, these can be established to the extremes in both directions, in which the individual is satisfied in the minimum or maximum (or minimums and maximums) in both directions. (All or nothing). But here we are entering the metaphysical domain.

Protagoras's statement, that man is the measure of all things, suffices; yet it is worth pointing out that, although we do not doubt the meaning of this phrase, we still have legitimate doubts of its truth as it appears to our Constructivists.

Václav Navrátil: The Breakdown of Individuality and of Poetry

The development of the bourgeoisie in states of power culminated in what is commonly called bourgeois culture. French bourgeois culture is made manifest through the aristocratization of individuals from a social perspective, and through rationalism and classicism (whose main representatives are Thibaudet and Benda) from a philosophical standpoint. The spiritual tradition works to re-edify this position. In contrast, German bourgeois culture arises by exaggerating the national idea, not only politically but also ethically.

Pacifists and antimilitarists can therefore also be included in this criterion. It is a reverence for the heroes of the national spirit, with whom, as in the circle of the Holy Grail, lie intellectuals who feel so mystically elevated. Goethe, Hegel, Kant, Fichte and Bismarck serve as heroic types as needed. Our national development was initially determined by this German-Romantic nationalism. It was, therefore, essentially Germanic despite being directed against it: See Jungmann, Kollár and the pan-Slavic efforts. These are the direct offspring of mystical German nationalism linked to anti-Semitism and its other features. Therefore, it was not Czech cultural development that the older generation underwent, but German cultural development.

Considering these circumstances, we must admit that the development of the Czech bourgeoisie has not yet completed its culture that today's generation does not represent since it is too young for it. The slogan of the struggle against bourgeois culture, elsewhere well understood, was therefore rather incomprehensible in our country. The delayed cultural development is rooted in the former political dependency, which largely determined it artistic development, with the national style playing a significant role. This is why the cultural struggle was apparently so easy, since it was fought in the name of education against ignorance. On the whole, we can characterize the bourgeois development as a path from persons to personalities in the subjective sense. The habitus of the bourgeois individuality is ethically, philosophically and politically determined.

I began this essay with a developmental construction. The importance of historical constructions must be received critically. These constructions must not be applied as precisely as a physical law, e.g. the law of free-fall, but it is certain that they are proven and that a diagnosis of the period can therefore be constructed on their basis. At least a historical scheme on the transition from bourgeois barbarism to bourgeois culture can be accepted. Assuming this, we will examine the current breakdown of individuality and poetry. As far as poetry is concerned, I believe in its schizoid nature, from which stems the fate of poets — the absolutely necessary liberation from all non-poetic voluntarism. This is a position that is not unequivocally given by the certain type of poet, but from which the poetic type (which seems to be conquering, revolutionary) can be judged. Pure poetry is a search for a myth that is timeless and that turns to the past rather than the future. The form in which the myth is sought can be revolutionary, though the professed myth is not always revolutionary, even if the poet finds consistently new and more immediate ways to profess it. We do not mean by this absolute schizoid historicism, but a simple law of poetry which brings us that which is crystallized, not what will be created. The fate of poets does not allow for conformism. Poets, as a type, cannot conform in their eminently fateful freedom. This would be an intellectual act in conflict with the irrationality of poetry. The position on revolutionary and Civilist poetry is related to this. Civilization will thus become poetry if it becomes a myth — not through its program, but through its reality. Similarly, revolution as a source of inspiration is not a program being carried out, but a timeless dream. Such is Wolker's poetry. Therefore, "Civilist" poetry could not have lasting success, since the initial impression of grandiosity of the civilization dynamics is not yet for poetics. It becomes poetics when it is a myth, which does not mean the wonderfulness of the past, but the wonderfulness of the present. However, the poet's path gets here to the bottom of earlier subjectivity, though this does not mean that today's poetry is subjective. On the contrary, we can have here verified the fact that the greatest subjectivity of a poet's work provides the greatest objectivity of the myth. Collective myths, such as the birth of religion, grow from personal myths. The poet conquers objective myths. This is a refutation of the rebuke by "realists" who fault modern art for its exaggerated subjectivism and thus a kind of uselessness. They do not understand that modern subjectivism is objective, which we say with a grain of salt, since the present-day characterization is that the subjective is the de-subjective.

In the first part of this essay, I have posited the bourgeois individuality, determined ethically, philosophically and politically by dependencies that it has with the conventions of the material world. By convention, we do not mean a mere social convention, but a philosophical conventional in the sense of Poincaré's conventionalism.

Therefore, the old individuality as an individual subjectively free is considered by the new philosophy to be an individual who is not free. Bergon's philosophy breaks the illusion of the old individuality as not free, and forms the myth of the new, free individuality, meaning free from dependencies on conventions and identifying intuition with its object of knowledge. Hegel had previously expressed this indeterminism of identity in his thesis that what is individual is not free and what is of the whole is free.

Through Bergsonism, psychoanalysis, Proust, among which is filiation, or at least kinship, we have philosophically broken down the old primitive schemes of individuality. However, when we speak of breaking down the bourgeois individuality, we do not only mean an objective psychological breakdown of individuality, but the breakdown of the ethical individuality in the internal sense of the word. Thoughts are not created, but lived. Therefore, the breakdown of individuality, even if philosophically formulated, cannot be a mere philosophical scheme, but is experienced over a period of time. Hence it is our task to state the factors of the period that caused the internal breakdown of the bourgeois individuality.

The war deprived its participants of the psychological affects that could accompany its affairs. People generally became accustomed to the dangers in the war despite the fact that Tolstoy believes it impossible to get used to them. War experiences are spoken of with the absolute peace of objectivity. It is thus clear that the effective level of past individuality has been altered by these influences. The second factor is today's hard struggle for life, which does not allow people to dwell on their individuality, as their self-awareness is diminished by today's existential turmoil. Related to this is industry's technical excess, which treats people as machine-made units. Further reasons include the modern sentiment for solidarity, this *Merkabah* that rids the individual of the sacred autonomy to which bourgeois culture was leading him. New tendencies to break up past individuality, even if they are antithetical, are similar. Rationalization, economization, capitalization and collectivization. It is a paradox of the present age, an age of wholeness, and yet with resistance to past rationalist universality. Opposition to scientific analytical psychology, which is atomistic, and psychoanalysis, which is synthetic. The boldest synthetic analyses are taking place. The factors, of which the above have been given as the primary ones, have caused the breakdown of past individuality, and the sceptical objectivity associated with it that is devoid of the subjective criteria of the old individual. The old sacredness of private life has disappeared. The age has expropriated the right to a former intimacy, to criticism of the family life and of the sexual life. What was previously intimacy is now public domain.

In addition to the modern masters, a sense for objectivity is reflected in the growing popularity of old French Realism such as Stendhal, Balzac and Flaubert. However, this does not express a sense for rationalist critical realism. The current tendencies in literature and in science are not rationalist, but irrationalist. This can ultimately be applied to rationalism itself, which may appear irrationalist from an irrationalist regard. Irrationalism is related to extreme objectification.

Factors of the new life have caused the breakdown of the old culture and old myths — hence the crisis and the search for new myths (if not new, then at least different). As I said earlier, poetry is schizoid by nature. It therefore follows that some types of poetry are essentially bourgeois, despite ancient myths professing a modern sensibility. A crisis occurs where the old myths have expired and new ones have not yet been found, resulting in modern decadence. Each destruction of an old myth and search for a new one is accompanied by scepticism. Yet this scepticism is far from a critical or methodological scepticism that is common at the beginning of philosophical systems, but a purely irrational scepticism that is lived, just like a faith is lived. Finally, even philosophical scepticisms are often originally of an irrational nature, such as the evil spirit of Descartes or the devil of St. Augustine.

I believe that today's breakdown of individuality and the scepticism related to it is not a developmental shortcoming of our age. New myths will be found down the path of extreme scepticism, which leads to new views via purgatory. *Omnis determination est negatio*. Negative scepticism will determine new discoveries in the field of life. Life's irrationality will defeat the spiritual dogmas of bourgeois culture and life's irrationality will bring the new forms that we are striving for.

Zdenek Rykr: Introduction

- Standing outside (artistic) groups and not enjoying any special popularity in the Prague art world, I would like to write here a few words as an introduction to my work. I'm well aware of Goethe's famous words about the artist not talking, but since this year I am presenting things that are slightly different from that done by Prague's artists, I myself must do what others do to others.
- Today's painting practically counts its development in days and hours. What was yesterday considered salvation became unnecessary overnight and sometimes vice-versa. Indeed, today we are standing before the revision of the greatest revolution in painting (Cubism), we are going through the first echoes of Surrealism and, on the contrary, are captivatedly examining the first steps of Impressionism, whose several discoveries, revolutionary sixty years ago, commonplace thirty years ago and obsolete twenty years ago, do not seem quite timeless to us today. It can be considered that of these three stages (if the psychological-associative contribution of Surrealism can be viewed as a stage), the genus of today's art draws its origin from somewhere in the blood of Impressionist passion for the living and from somewhere in the machine construction of Cubist methods of a new formation of the painting as a separate whole, not describing reality, but creating it through painting-specific means.
- Would it be bold to draw a parallel between today's reaction to formalist post-war Cubism and the reaction that Impressionism made in the latter half of the 19th century against the lifeless academic paintings of brown sauces and literary themes?
- I feel that this comparison is not bold, but entirely natural and logical.
- The painting that Impressionism reacted to was neither a Delecroix nor a Courbet, but it was to many of their lifeless, schematic followers, it was the direction, formalist academism that Impressionism defied. The same goes for today. It's

not a reaction to Picasso or Cézanne, but a reaction to Picasso-ism and Cézanne-ism and to everything that came of it.

- Our motives are similar to those that drove the first Impressionists to revolt. Just as naked women stretching in the dim of beautiful draperies no longer spoke to them, neither do the colors of Cubist paintings, no matter how interesting or beautiful, speak to us anymore. Both are just as lifeless and both are the fruit of art studios. Impressionism escaped from them with the charge of artlessness to nature, to the streets, to the dance halls, to the waterfront and to the woods. We are escaping there too, but instructed by Cézanne and Picasso. Enriched with this legacy, we part ways with Impressionists, remembering that then they were riding in horse-drawn carriages and today we are driving 100-horsepowered cars. Their lives were sung by an idyll of grasses, birches, women's skirts and shiny top hats, ours are bursting with tension and humming with the mechanics of technical conveniences. All this must somehow be reflected in the organization of our paintings, in the economics of resources and in the formation of expression. Let us also not forget that the end of the war presented us with compelling life orders, with a straightforward decision and with the harshest social reality. Architecture, which of all the arts was the first to be touched by this new order and new need, was the first to launch the most definitive forms. And the laws of its inner realization had to be identical with the laws of the inner order of the painting. Just as architecture only wants to be building, so does a painting only want to be painting. As there are no longer secret corners, deceptive nooks and pretence, nothing of the such can be in a painting. Independent like a flying balloon, inside assembled methodically and clearly as a machine from the means most intrinsic to painting — from a line, a spot and material — rhythmized by the music of the case, it entices and stirs up the imagination of the living spectators, because it is alive itself and has come from life.
- This is more or less how I imagine my responsibilities to my profession, and the 29 paintings of my current exhibition is an attempt to carry this out.

Vít Obrtel: On Building Towers

In recent years some architectural theorists have promoted with the zeal of stubborn savants a kind of popular rationalism, i.e. a petty-bourgeois doctrine on the benefits of Constructivism for eating and sleeping well. Of course, such a humanitarian view is, even if served in a dialectical-materialist pill and despite an initial bitterness, easily digestible for the bourgeoisie, perhaps even pleasant: one of these pills not only heals their body, it also pleasures them by the predicate of modernity.

It is dangerous to communicate through words, since a word loses its semantic nature by changing the environment of its purpose, by not becoming a symbol but a subject of allegory.

Constructivism used as a working method, i.e. taking into account all its physical facts, is in fact merely a further step on the developmental path in learning about materials, disposition, etc., i.e. learning about the use of new scientific research in a craft. However, it is not, and as such does not want to be, something more than architecture, but only a practical component of it. Any misuse of scientific and practical research by those interested in nothing more than their work for programmatic slogans, in which a certain word is forced to possess an incantatory meaning, is merely an ephemeral and insincere game. Though this game has no meaning for absolute truths it is often dangerous for real moments. I give as an example how the sentimental slogan "minimum dwelling" is misused in this system [the slogan is in itself false; a "maximum" should instead be claimed).

The existential conditions of today's collective in Czechoslovakia are given by the ongoing post-war economic crisis in which only powerful groups of individuals salvage their material reign. Here, "constructivist theories", which have become common practice today, would be deduced "from objective facts, from production conditions, from specific purposes", which in lay terms would mean "whoever has power has also got it good; that is, the perception and certain knowledge of a subject, becoming an object in the area of production forces and its powerful society, determined by them, give to this sanction the use of knowledge for the material benefit of investing capital in a theoretical sense. Yet we could come up with countless similar paradoxes, just as uniform constructivism creates them out of scientific constructivism.

Similarly, the opposite (now completely abandoned) method of idealistic formalism finds the greatest understanding in the materially weak classes, since it is in this method, or in its realization, that their longing (though quite primitive) for the beauty not found in their material existence is released. Thus, the theory of formalist architecture, whose roots lie in the moral domination of money (once again by the fact that certain words became the program of those preaching them), is abandoned by the bourgeoisie for the slogan of modernity, and becomes a morbid spectre of the socially weaker classes. Every word that was supposed to express a certain work performance or discovery, whether in science or art, popularized by those who only see results, not understanding the method, effectively becomes its own opposition to the effect in an environment for which it was not created. The creator, dealer and consumer all understand it differently.

Finally, it is not up to constructivist (and especially not formalist) theory whether the further development of architecture (and by that I mean the complete concordance of the "interior and exterior" as a harmonious unit) occurs in the sense of the aesthetic and practical simplification of forms and lines, or a loosening of the imagination. Scientific constructivism has its function set in the field of practical research, being the basis for architectural creation, for one must not only "eat and sleep", but also "dream". Herein lies the functionality of architecture, which is neither science nor art — it simply is.

Václav Navrátil: Kvart

During its relatively short existence the periodical *Kvart* has secured for itself a reliable place in Czech culture. Yet an ideological assessment of its method still has not been made.

Kvart's position can be formulated as such: It tries to rouse all the unused cognitive forces that have been neglected under the pressure of modern intellectualism. Its efforts are directed against intellectual superficiality and conservatism, which can be found both in the ranks of the "reactionaries"as well as of the "progressives".

This method has a metaphysical presage, which is namely that, in line with the Surrealists, it rejects the intellectualist dualism of reason and feeling, dream and reality, spirit and body. These dualisms are monistically identical here. Knowledge is what is gained in the eternal struggle for the absolute, and intuition is instrumental to this. Ideology does not decline to subject this to the scepticism of hitherto valid values that may even have the highest recommendations. Its program therefore includes a revision of values. There is a boldness here; they were not afraid to look further than is demanded of believers, and they even viewed things differently. This is not about wandering, it's about fighting. Let the values of science, morality and religion be called into question. This method cannot, however, be blanketly classified as irrationalism, as a life philosophy, and the reason is that there is a full awareness here that irrationalism in metaphysical systems is closely related. A division of the two arises from the wrong questioning and from problems in school philosophy. This is not a life philosophy, but a struggle for the absolute.

In this regard, *Kvart* performs a meritorious act in that, along with writings by Czechs, it provides examples of similar ideas both from the present and the past, from almost all types of literature. It introduces us to Surrealist philosophers: Carl Einstein, de Réneville, Jacques Baron, Roger Vitrac, Paul Éluard, Robert Desnos, and Aragon. Also appearing in the first issue are Alfred Jarry, Hölderlin, the poet T. S. Eliot, Jules Laforgue, Aloysius Bertrand and Tristan Carbier, among others.

In later issues, *Kvart* acquaints us with the likes of Emanuel Berl, Eugene Jolas, Harry Crosby and N. Klyuev, while William Blake, Sitwell, Paul Verlaine, Santayana, Plekhanov, Jung, de Montaigne and Empiricus are also interpreted here.

As is evident, not only current (or rather future) phenomena are taken into account, but also the past masters of poetry and ideas. However, this historical consideration must not be viewed as backward-looking historicism; on the contrary, it is a manifestation of the cooperation of this movement with prolific thinkers of all epoques. It can be said elliptically that history is not conceived in time, but in space. As in Hegel's universe, the struggles of all ages are present in the world, not as a dead scheme, misunderstood and spoken of in schools, but as vital impulses. In the old ecclesiastical intepretation, prayer was considered to elevate the mind to God and was not the same as the recitation of prayer from a book. Words die, but the fight does not die. Only the fundamental fire justifies the value of knowledge.

From an artistic perspective, *Kvart* offers writings derived from thinking similar to that found in the realm of fine arts represented by Artificialism.

In architecture, the impulsiveness of this thinking led to a revision of Constructivism and the concept of Neo-constructivism. As is evident, despite the diversity of ages and people, the ideology of *Kvart*'s collaborators, even those living centuries ago with courage in the field of knowledge, is united.

The fourth issue of *Kvart* has just been published and continues in fulfilling the declared program with theoretical articles and works of prose and poetry.

Some of the contributors, randomly chosen, include: Aragon, Desnos, Péret, Éluard, Apollinaire, Deubel, Ryūnosuke, Valentinus, Vašica, Hořejší, Halas, Seifert, J. L. Fischer and Zahradníček. As with its predecessors, this issue features exemplary typographical design.

Vít Obrtel: On the Work Method

They have captured the feasible at the highest level. To approach the intersection of two lines at infinity. To recognize through the senses and reason (not to despise intuition), to recognize the utmost through the imperfection of the means. To construct buildings of mirrors on the imperfect perfection of reality, for the higher the building, the further the stars will be. To seek the relation of facts and ideas in an absolute space. To assign to things their place in the order of events — partly primitive, partly cultural.

A. *The instance of line.* The connections of points on the horizon of views — to be realized. Intervals — for the surreal. Lines as a material intervention of the finest gradation of thought. A straight line or curve in the formed section of a space, according to the uniform method of each field. The edges of shapes, the touches of areas in the overall concept of a work. Lines of lost points, lines of fog and stones.
B. *The instance of area.* The delimited areas in dimensions given by geometry — to be realized. Without boundaries and in x dimensions — for the surreal. The area and colour according to the will's order limited by dream or thought, by the reality of the irrational for the reality of the real. The area consisting of part of the space in dimensions infinitely large to infinitely small, and the color from the most brilliant white to the deepest black, and transitions that cannot be detected by the eye. The area of poets and the area of scientists.
C. *The instance of shape.* The geometric combination of areas — for the real. A shapeless shape — for the surreal. Shape as a calculation and termination, shape forming a space based on principles of composition for physical and hyperphysical reality, shape derived from a shape based on the order of proportionality, pure substance or composed in intersecting axes and thoughts hum-

bled by material shortcomings of the world of phenomena. A perfect shape in its proportions and fulfilment measured by a human gauge, but under a sky full of sweetness and horror.

D. *The instance of word.* In the beginning, there was the word, a word expressing the will of a desire that became an act, a word whose meaning was also its essence. A word for speaking and hearing, a language that we no longer understand as the word has become a discordant sound or the random arrangement of letters, and the fact of the order of composition has turned into an inexpressive idea. Word — thought — dream.

E. *The instance of a number.* The number as a corrective and as a form, as the essence of relations of everything that occurs. The Pythagoras number. The ratio of relations of substance and thought, of the real and irrational in the unity of being. — Number — ratio — harmony.

Thus, we must perceive and understand with all our senses and reason the material and immaterial, relations and order; we must act in the unity of essence, to create the most perfect harmony of substance and thought, and ultimately to doubt beneath the onslaught of the irrational and negation, which, however, are of creative value in the reality of things, in which the smaller is always the larger of the smaller.

Václav Navrátil: On the Crisis of Crisisology

Oh so many beautiful things are in the air.
The Radio Factory.

What is a crisis? We would not make a good impression with this question in the current situation. We will therefore modify the question, while expecting a dogmatic answer: Is there a crisis or not? We'll get the response: There is a crisis. We will also receive a rundown of everything considered symptomatic of a crisis.

What speaks for a crisis? Above all, a strong social consensus. Everyone you encounter today is convinced of the existence of a crisis in all areas of human activity. This social consensus seems to justify — according to all logical rules — the veracity of the view that the world is going through a general crisis.

As for the facts that are objectively ascertainable, the following are usually given as signs of an economic crisis: unemployment, bankruptcies, insolvency, a drop in national income. A crisis in science is accompanied by a loss of faith in science, a lack of satisfactory answers to humanity's latest questions, as well as these other aspects: a lack of stability in the scientific systems and the ensuing disunity of the scientific worldview. A crisis in religion sees a lack of understanding for a blissful life in line with God's word, and a loss of interest in questions of religious truth. Or a different diagnosis: today's age rejects religion, but cannot eradicate its religious disposition, which then degenerates into neurosis and emotional anarchy. Symptoms of a crisis in art include stagnation in creativity on the one hand, and one-sided lawless progress on the other. Art becomes estranged from social consensus, and dissensus arises. In a crisis of democracy, the management of public affairs is not in the hands of the people, but under the guise of democracy controlled by a dictatorship of certain individuals and special-interest groups, who often rule against the interests of the people. We hear the words corruption, oppression and policies against the people. Then there is the crisis of the family accompanied by a loosening of the bonds of family life and a drop in population.

We have chosen only the most common catchwords that we encounter daily, recalling the most striking examples. We will begin to talk about these things, at first without theoretical subtleties.

In our criticism, we will try to focus on the question of what a crisis is.

Crisis in the areas of economic activities appears to be the most conspicuous. Unemployment seems to be a convincing argument that there really is a crisis. Yet we ask, perhaps quite unusually and unpredictably: Must industrial unemployment be a symptom or a cause of the crisis in all cases and under all circumstances? If we look at history, we see that this is not the case. Unemployment and the poverty that accompanies it, came and went, sometimes even without the slightest talk of a crisis. On the contrary, humanity was full of patriotic enthusiasm. The age was one of merit. Time was filled in its own way. Or in times of mass religious paroxysm, during the early periods of the anabasis of Christianity, or during the Hussite Wars, as well as at other times.

Let us consider today's unemployment. In employing our intellect, we dare make the heterodoxic assessment that the unemployed are far better off today, purely in terms of living standard, than their *soci malorum* of the past, and even than those who were employed in those times. If we consider modern social facilities, social care, the results of modern technology, locomotion, lighting and hygienic conveniences, we recognize that the standard of living is much higher today than ever before. Unemployment is today considered by scholars to be a purely social phenomenon. The unemployed with their individual aspects are not considered. Despite it all, unemployment is currently a far more worrying phenomenon, both objectively and subjectively, than ever before.

It is argued that the situation is different today than before, or that class consciousness has increased. The first objection is a tautology, to the second we respond: a greater class consciousness is not obvious with regards to the economic conditions when considering the objective conditions of the crisis. In fact, we will reveal that our intention is to do abandon, contrary to common opinion, the presumed connection between economic conditions and spiritual orientation.

It is argued that we are comparing several things that cannot at all be compared. Different times, different tendencies. We respond that we are aware of this, but that we are dealing here with the relation between unemployment and worldview, while striving for phenomenological precision. The simple position of our problems allows us to recklessly compare things that are seemingly incomparable.

We know that a low social standard is not a direct catalyst of revolutions. In his book *La France contemporaine*, Taine demonstrates that the French were doing much better under Louis XVI, when the revolution took place, than under Louis XIV when, as we know, there was no revolution, despite much dissatisfaction.

Let us make ourselves clear: our intention is not to claim that there is or was no shortages. There is a shortage, and there are economic failures, just as there have been in the past. However, it is not written in stone that economic shortages lead to desperation; and a crisis is not necessarily rooted in economic conditions. This is the point we are trying to make here: A crisis is something more than shortages.

We also want to emphasize that we are not against social amelioration. We merely want to show here using random examples that human affairs are not as simple as they appear to be according to a rudimentary economic diagram. The intention of this article is to object to uncritical economic dogmatism.

From other fields: a crisis of literature has been a pressing topic for many epochs, though later periods may have viewed these times as golden ages of literature. A crisis of philosophy was, for instance, spoken of after the periods of Romantic philosophy represented by the famous triad of Schelling, Fichte and Hegel. Today we know how these views were corrected. This once again proves that the word "crisis" must be treated much more critically.

Is the meaning of family life on the decline? Yes, it is. We are often lacking the most essential. But must this fact also be a necessary basis for crisis? Was it, for instance, when Christ commanded his disciple to abandon his family? When, upon his request to bury his dead father, Christ replied, "Leave the dead to bury their own dead; But as for you, go with me and proclaim the kingdom of heaven." The scripture says: *Quaerite regnum dei et justifiant eius. Haec omnia vobis adicientur*. This is even a denial of economic and family values in the name of fighting against a moral crisis.

After this general excursion we will notice how the crisis is assessed and how it is explained by today's administrators of culture. We will recognize both the judgments of writers and philosophers and those of sociologists and economists. First, let us consider how philosophers view the crisis.

In his study *Die geistige Situation der Zeit*, Karl Jaspers accuses intellectual society of a loss of the aristocratic spirit. He compares our age with that of sophistry. People misused philosophy for political and personal gains.

Ortega y Gasset describes from the other side a crisis as an invasion of the "mass person" into culture. By mass he does not mean the proletariat, but the person of mediocrity. The masses destroy all values of culture.

This concept of Gasset brings to mind in some respects Dostoevsky's famous myth of the arriving commoner as a collective demon of evil. Fritz Klatt takes a similar view as Gasset in the book *Die geistige Wendung des Maschinenzeitalters*.

However, these concepts are quite one-sided. Despite all his reservations, Ortega y Gasset cannot help but attribute this mediocrity to the masses in a social sense. Here we must be careful, for this tendency against the masses is fundamentally wrong.

It can be said that the most famous ideas are and were carried by the masses. An idea longs to be carried out in an action that is its most beautiful fulfilment and most perfect form. *Perfectio involvit realitatem.* An idea is realized by the masses. The masses make ideas famous. Of the many examples we can name religious movements, romantic nationalism and struggles for social advancement.

In addition, one who is called a mass-man is able, due to his one-sidedness and energy, to make the kind of sacrifices to an idea that one not considered a mass-person would rarely be capable of doing. Everyone is of value in their own way, and the same holds true for a mass-person. Finally, a crisis most conspicuously appears as a collapse of the intelligentsia. The cause of a crisis could also be proven in a way that is the opposite of Gasset's. Not as an invasion of the base masses among the noble intelligentsia, but as an invasion of base intellectuals (which today is not, unfortunately, a *contradictio in adjecto*) among the noble masses. He also neglects to show which idea will lead us out of the crisis, since people can then prevent a crisis if they are the bearers of an idea. His concern for the mass-person or non-mass person resembles an engineer, who is supposed to but cannot build a bridge, as he is not seeking to resolve the bridge's structural components, but is instead contemplating who would and would not be suitable for the masonry work.

How do sociologists and economists view a crisis?

Considerable scientific attention is paid to a crisis; there is a clear attempt to guide the crisis research in one direction, in a specific system. We therefore speak in advance of crisisology. Now what does the crisis solution look like?

Here is an example. A society's crisis is said to have arisen due to a severing of social bonds. Isolation and dissensus occur instead of cooperation and consensus. A crisis in art is thought to be rooted in the world's economic transformation. There are several theories on what causes an economic crisis. One theory seeks its base in production conditions, another finds the cause of the crisis in consumer conditions, still another views it as a monetary crisis, an oversizing of the currency.

In studying these crisis theories in detail, we notice that all those who speak or write about crises dogmatically base their arguments on the assumption that there is a crisis. They do not analyse this phenomenologically and do not describe it in more precise terms but try to explain it using a causal methodology. "Perhaps there is no need to prove that there is a crisis," says a leading Czech sociologist. "It's more about clarifying what the crisis consists of." However, the vast majority of Czech and foreign sociologists understand this "clarification" as the need for a causally genetic interpretation, not as a phenomenological analysis. They do not precisely define the phenomenon itself. Let us put it this way:

They do not ask what the crisis is, but immediately turn to the problem of how the crisis arose. They seek the inception (Entstehung) of the crisis in the genetic sense. The origin (Ursprung) of the crisis in the phenomenological sense eludes them. This one-sidedness has grave consequences.

This "Objectivism" assumes epistemologically, if it were epistemologically surmised, a pragmatic, psychological and materialistic view, whereas the terms are compared as gradations with regard to consequence.

And now let us take a look at what results from that.

It is easy to assume that such a solution actually sees the causes of a crisis as largely economic. The spiritual factor is considered here to be primarily an epiphenomenon. Following a thorough epistemological analysis, this position cannot avoid this consequence.

Experts would perhaps argue against this reproof that their work is exclusively scientific. All other knowledge (artistic, religious experience) is subordinate to scientific knowledge since science is said to understand and describe in detail reality and its laws. Apparently, the consequence of which we accuse science cannot be changed and cannot be ill-fated since it is a scientific truth.

This is also a dogmatic view. Epistemological criticism has already done much to weaken it. The veracity of scientific judgment is subject to the question of veracity in general. It is in no way removed from it. Truth is by far a greater secret than the average expert, untrained in epistemology, believes.

Science does not objectively represent reality, for it is unable to represent it. It is a mistake to think that knowledge represents reality. Knowledge is a more complex problem.

In addition, a scientific system is a cognitive system, limited by time. There is no way to say that it is something absolute. A scientific objective is a 19th-century objective, just as religious objectives prevailed in the Middle Ages and metaphysical objectives in Antiquity. This is only an analogy, and is not to be interpreted as ingratitude for scientific work. We can only fully appreciate its practical results if we recognize that it is too one-sided for certain functions.

Now that we have critiqued today's understanding of the situation, that we have even dared to doubt whether the symptoms which are generally attributed to a crisis actually qualify as decisive characteristics attesting to a crisis, that we seem to doubt the existence of a crisis, we can ask: Is there a crisis?

Our answer, by no means sensational, will take some by surprise and disappoint others: There is a crisis.

However, this crisis is not caused solely by the disruption in a production economy, or by unemployment or deflation. There is no economic crisis, or art crisis or marriage crisis. There is only one crisis. Indeed, a crisis is a concept that has become a myth. There is no term that is more used.

In a panic, in the complex of fear that afflicts humankind, we can see an element of spiritual agitation symmetrically correlating to religious agitation. The word crisis has become the religious myth of our time. It is a religion of subversion, the horror of a solitary humanity rooted in the loss of something that we still have not managed to recapture.

This loss could be characterized as the loss of a spiritual system. But is this understood today? Is humanity already capable of grasping this? Do not similar diagnoses appear to be clichés? Perhaps they do, but this is already a tragedy for all of us, and one of the most powerful punishments of the crisis is that we cease to live with thoughts. Thoughts have degenerated into clichés. The loss of a spiritual system is an escape from a height outside the realm of life, into the realm of life itself. There it introduces psychological (or psychoanalytical and biological) naturalism — both philosophical and scientific. Humanity is punished for its lack of wisdom. This decline in the sense for constructing wisdom is like Schopenhauer's pessimistic fall into the realm of biological will, which Czysarz characterized in the lecture "Goethe und Schopenhauer", that it is *der gröste Sündenfall des neunzehnten Jahrhunderts*.

Besides philosophy, science has also contributed to these consequences. Let us use this figure of speech: Science originally began to look for the stone of wisdom but ended up with the wisdom of the stone.

Moreover, the faith in science was of a religious naivety. Those with the strongest faith in science were those who did not know it well. However, we have seen that many scientists who probably knew it well, have turned away from science to embrace religious systems.

Like science, economic constructions will be unable to satisfy humanity, unless the demand is placed on them to accommodate humanity beyond its economic scope. Socialism and science devoid of a mystical appetite must die out. They are not marked for eternity.

It is indeed a paradox that socialism's dangerous disadvantage is that its ultimate ideal is too feasible, too close. An ideal can be a perfect catalyst when it is relatively unattainable, which should be its law.

After all, we must keep in mind that our low life is preserved by what is beyond life. A life that consists only of itself degenerates, as if by lack of external nourishment, as if the organism wanted to feed on its own body. We have examples of this from history: human health has shown a decline in times of humanism, which can only be explained by a shift away from mysticism towards earthly life.

Our crisis is therefore far deeper than it would seem through a superficial assessment of the current economic conditions. This crisis is a continuation of the pre-war spiritual crisis, which appears as much in times of prosperity as in times of economic depression.

A lack of unifying ideas is given as one of the causes of the crisis. We have refrained from assessing this cause until now. So, is this true? After all, we have here traditional Catholicism and impassioned communism; our age suffers from a hypertrophy of religious maximalisms, whose words sound utterly empty. There is nothing easier today than being right, than speaking of, say, honesty, love, god, harmony, peace, humility, or even of democracy.

However, a crisis of ideas goes hand in hand with an abasement of words. The slogans by which Bergson vigorously protested the "forms rigides" stiffened into these detested *formes rigides* — and did so in all its ghastliness in his name. Bergson's *elan vital* is no longer a decree of energy, but a mechanized *chose toute faite*. Everything is mechanized. People are modern in conservativism and mechanically conservative in modernity. That is why we have lost ideas; we have lost unifying ideas.

The far-reaching capacity of ideas is underestimated. For instance, the contradiction between rationalism and empiricism is referred to in academic philosophy. Yet it is not known that, for instance, empiricism was one of the forces that penetrated deep into life and controlled it in various forms, or that the liberal spontaneity of capitalism has its roots in the philosophical empiricism of the 18th century and, conversely, the attempt at planning in rationalism. In closely examining human history, we see philosophical differences, seemingly ephemeral, like dreaded divides filled with life's drama.

Outrageous and impious dilettantism cannot and will not be able to see this, for it has lost many of its abilities to ask and answer. It is not an economic crisis, an art crisis and other crises, but a single crisis that can be called a crisis of questions and answers. This is the very reason why these people cannot resolve the crisis: they only know one type of question and answer, which has been ineffective. They do not know how to ask what a crisis is and what it is to deal with one.

The whole matter will need to be resolved *ex integro*. Is this possible? Absolutely, though it will require us to know an important trick. This begins with a return to ideas. It was said that ideas do not matter, but that people do. We see it differently: Ignore the people and pursue ideas. Then others will appear. But there is one more thing that we wish to secretively add:

In order to achieve the absolute, it does not suffice to be merely honest. To penetrate the greatest depths, we also need to be somewhat "free of commitments" — though this is nothing more than an aside.

Now for the conclusion.

Humanity will be at its most glorious when all people are poets, meaning poets of the absolute. Only then will we be graced with a deep and soothing love, an absolute, undiscerning love. Therefore, the moment of truth has not yet arrived. Only then will the people be happy.

Zdenek Rykr: In Today's World...

In today's world it is somewhat unpopular to present an exhibition like the one I am opening.

From one side, the audience has grown more tolerant and understanding; on the other, painters have grown somewhat tamer in producing their art, and happy days of quiet coexistence followed. In fact, everything is already understood, everything has already been debated, everyone is slowly but surely finding their decorum and place. In reading the criticism and contemplations on art, don't you already know in advance what it is going to be about? The walking is no longer done on tightropes, but at ease on footpaths, lined with fondness and even enthusiasm. Voices of resistance grow silent and hushed from fear, snobbery and uncertainty. Where it has been eradicated pursuant to law and paragraph, there is no art; where it is, perhaps out of the joy that it is and can be, there have been times of affection and understanding. But isn't this situation rooted in a terrible indifference to the essence of fine art?

If we confuse natural interest with professional interest, it explains why, despite all the misery, there are so many different expositions and exhibitions (both retrospective and contemporary) in cities around the world, and why nothing ultimately happens in art. Besides a few political stones thrown witlessly and unnecessarily, can we name a demonstration in recent years that fought for something? Somehow artists communicate far too easily with their audience these days. We cannot suspect these relations of being devoid of good intentions, but rather of existing just so that they exist — so that there is Surrealism, so that there is modern art, etc., etc. And here the one who does not exist exhibits. If any of you get lost within these four walls, do not be surprised by the loneliness you encounter. Why would people come here?

The lines that follow intend to say what is really going on here. Today's painting, and even art in general, is hidden in both Surrealist literature and in the remnants of Cubist and Classicist achievements achieved in recent years. Painting's own problems have subsided and penetrate places as if they were abandoned labyrinths, such as in Klee's insidious cobwebs or Miró's points of pathos, as was on view at the most recent exhibition at Mánes. The radicality of both is subdued: in the first instance by the small format and discretion of its intimate presentation; in the second by its large format and decorative gesture, and by the lightness of provocative shapes and effectual colours. Not wanting to evoke a trace or even a hint of analogy with these sentences, I mention this only for the sake of finding for myself (and perhaps even for some of you) a place, albeit distant, for this exhibition. Painting has always been about reality. Along the dangerous path from the eye to the inside, on the path to the whole reality, and not merely half of it, lies the great graveyard of endeavours, talents and illusions. It is difficult to discover the simplest things, and even harder to rid ourselves of the sediment of habits and secured joys. The hardest thing is letting go of everything. Only when the grief of parting with everything is ground into the joy of discovery is it time to work. Only then, when the experiences of eyes and life become the experiences of feeling and spirit, will there unfold a single world — the inner and outer world together. This is why last year I exhibited weathered wood, bones and old ropes — not to scare the audience and ridicule art, but to clarify how a piece of old wood or a fragment of a gnawed bone, taken out of its everyday relations and isolated in a new environment, speaks. I wanted to feel when the wood would cease to be a stick and the broken figurine a knickknack, and when these things would begin to live their strange lives — one in the horror and pain of loneliness, the other in the bizarreness and romance of feelings.

This year I moved from this isolation of things to another stage, and I admit to having got there in the silence of mosques, in the soft murmur of Turkish gardens and in the darkness of the winding streets of Rhodes. It was not my intention to compete with the painters of minarets and oriental beauties but wanted somehow to do something myself that would be the Orient, something that would be mysterious, strange and whispering, and so I made several of the boxes (nos. 1–5) included in the catalogue.

If I isolated material last year, this year I used it so that it was as remote as possible from its usual meanings. Paper no longer wants to be paper, and stone no longer wants to be stone, etc. Moreover, these materials do not want to imitate the world; they do not want to represent a house, pavement or a tree, but want to be an integral part of something separate, of a new thing that itself speaks, in a specific language, in this instance the language of the Orient. In illuminating the freedom and possibility of art here, I dared to make Greece "Greece". Gone is the murmur and sinuosity, and I also took the liberty of making the format larger and made four things, of which the first two were meant to speak of the sea, of the air and of size, while the third was to speak of the silence and whisper of breezes, and the fourth of the hardness of fight and strength. This time I treated the material in a broader, simpler, clearer and more compelling intonation, and in colours as well.

Later in southern Bohemia, between the wayside crosses of the field paths and cold gloom of the monastery corridors, I continued to look for how I could express myself and who I am. I was suddenly surprised by the proximity and veracity of Catholic symbols. I saw how the life in them — with prayers, songs and customs — deeply penetrated that entire region, and, in fact, how they have also penetrated us or me. I decided to make a Way of the Cross and several symbols related to Catholic teachings. As before, I did not want to copy things, so the verbal accompaniment in the Way of the Cross is for me just a kind of fixed outline of the artistic processing. A fresh cross made of soft wood passes through twelve paintings, and different materials, sometimes supressed and sometimes emphasized, would like to speak of the splendour of Pilate's court, of the dark night "of the burial of Jesus", of the weeping of the daughters of Jerusalem, etc. A few other symbols are of a similar kind, except the numbers 31 and 32, which lead me to the final paintings. I wonder whether I could do the same (as I do with materials) with a substance even closer to me, such as color and painting. I have clarified the infinite function of color and shapes made from it. I no longer have the outline of the symbols or the preceding finished realities in which I would have control, as was the case in Greece or the Orient. All I have here is reality: myself, a brush and paint. Paint is only what it is in itself, and the same goes for the shape in which it is applied. A painting is not and does not want to be a transcription of ideas or external realities. Do not look for things in these paintings, but look at them as you would, for instance, flowers that you had never before seen, or animals that you had never before encountered, or both. After all, one would like to be shaggy and wild, one amusing and radiant, one ironic, and still another kind of wormy and so on. It is absolutely not a reality likened to the external world, but realities from life. This is a gamble and paintings can be like life: boring, uninteresting, unnecessary, impoverished, but also the contrary. Their law lies in their exact profile, in their distinct form, unmistakeable and unique.

I would be content if any of them surprised you, for I think that you are somewhat bored if, for instance, you look at a painting in which the waves are still pounding thc cliff, or a man is still playing his flute, even if it is a bit distorted.

I know that there are great dangers of decoration, emptiness, and of simple transcription lying in ambush on this front, but this makes it all the more enticing for me to know my way around in this dark and tangled forest of art exposed to its elements, though thus freed to possibilities that cannot even be thought up, just painted.

That then is what I would like to say to you about this exhibition that you have attended with good intentions.

Kamil Bednář: On the Youngest Generation of Czech Poets

Nobody will experience the difficulty of understanding as hard as the newcomers. The age in which they seek their position and expression has all the signs of a temporary state. The universal world, which recently seemed so close, is almost in ruins. This theatre is full of bloody and unpredictable irony. The age, in which all were to be turned into poets, has dressed them in uniforms, and the soldier, the national soldier, has become a symbol. The idea of the future, which has replaced for many the need for a myth, is so sober and confusing that it rules out a clear faith. It seems that these young people are too experienced, too instructed by all to mature early, and this is to the benefit of the thing that subjects them to a difficult, masterly test.

It is desolate in every corner of the world. Was darkness outside the window necessary for their eyes to recognize the brilliant light of everything called home? The tale of the lost and found son will soon become popular again. And the injustice perpetrated by the Devětsil generation forces us to avoid their mistakes. It took Paris to make us bow to Vrchlický's shadow. It was grasped quite late that the tears of *May* had burned for centuries and the precious initials of Karel Hynek Mácha once again shone on the tree of poetry.

The need for perspective can be satisfied in various ways. In today's age the future speaks to us from places where no one has looked for it. Therefore, let us turn back and try to find what had previously united us, if we are indeed divided today. The word "tradition" could be shamelessly uttered with one exception: let it not be imposed from without, let the will to be inspired by it come freely.

Poetry goes with politics (one of this pair is necessarily damaged) as long as the latter is able to maintain the same human interpretation that inspires the poet. We do not deny that such politics is usually young, a politics of resistance rather than that of positive work. Moreover, it is impassioned enough and utopian enough to count on poets. Today, poetry can only emerge bruised and battered from this friendship, as perhaps politics did fifteen years ago.

Hesitation is what kills revolution poetry, which needs clear hatred and clear love, a stark casting of light and shadow. There also needs to be some chiliasm, plenty of coarseness as well as applause. It must not know the word "diplomacy".

Poetry will go it alone for a long time, even if reluctantly. For the dispute that it would like to help resolve will be decided by other forces. Only here and there does a streak of light appear among the clouds, in the direction in which its true homeland might be, at the point where the individual meets the masses.

Beauty is undoubtedly the function of poetry. Although there is so much doubt and disagreement over this that we avoid this word, beauty is in a secret relationship with that which is, if you will, the poet's true mission: to expand the realm of consciousness. In a sense, Breton's statement that "beauty will be convulsive or not at all" misuses old experiences. Everything that is born comes into the world bloodied.

The freedom that the poet demands is, despite different interpretations of the term, quite clear: the freedom of individual experience.

If poetry has any obligations to public life, they consist of having to fight for the freedom that it demands for itself and for others. It will soon encounter plenty of skirmishes when the emerging chauvinism of threatened democracy joins the terror of dictatorships.

Poetry will be without a unified avant-garde, without a clear program for a long time. The state of the generation requires the free development of individuals, and true poetry, which seems astonishingly unchanged from the first poets of the Bible and poets of cherry blossoms of China, has only one thing in mind: a person as a still undiscovered miracle.

Paul Valéry says it best: "Beauty is a private matter".

The prisoners of society well understand why the monster of official beauty is built.

Kamil Bednář: Notes on "Today", "Reality" and "Czechness" in Poetry

I. Often those taking a "final judgment" stance on poetry rely on the mysterious and indefinable gauge of "today" or "reality". But ask them what "today" means! Is it even possible to clasp a certain aspect with forceps, to tear off a piece of bloody flesh from life and say: "Look here, is this "today"? With ample distance we can roughly and schematically determine that a certain section of history was such-and-such period (Baroque, Renaissance, Feudalism, etc.), that such and such lifestyle, worldview, most typical feeling and thought prevailed in it. But can an entire period be explained like this? These are merely guideposts; in fact, the most diverse lifestyles exist side by side in every age and cannot be summed up with a common denominator. So, if we want to be fair, we need to use all such schemes with an awareness of their semantic limitations. Of course, many people today may find the demand for "today" quite tempting and insistent. Yet we are now sufficiently experienced to know that the deceptive slogan of "today" has been used for everything, including demagoguery and the narrowest political interests. Let us instead ask for *inner truthfulness* and the most "today-ish" things will dissolve like soap bubbles — for it is a phrase, an empty word, nothing.

If someone said today that Czech poetry must come to terms with today or that it must be comparable to today, that person misspoke, for he did not realize what arbitrariness and political sectarianism it would open the door to. Poetry, all poetry, comes to terms with today — there is no other way since it is created *only* in the present and its creators live *today.* Difficulties are only in the inappropriately used word since the content of the word "today" cannot be defined. This is merely an inner truth, nothing else. We must not imagine that national life manifests itself only in its highest, e.g. political forms. No, the nation lives through all its individuals, through all its phenomena of life; it also manifests itself in the latest and most intimate feeling, in the most conspicuous thought and in the most concealed act.

An emphasis on the importance of one's roots is appropriate but let us not seek them only in the loud proclamation of our love for our country. Life, and therefore national life, is far more diverse, differentiated and varied. Let poetry be as well!

II. So much noise was made with the slogan "reality" in poetry that it is only today that we realize the fragmentation of forces that led to it. Have you already asked yourself what reality is? Not at the podium, but in your most intimate privacy? In its most basic meaning, this term has no precise content. In fact, there are realities by which a certain section of life, but not life itself, is understood and which can be firmly established. This is, for instance, social, political and technical reality and the likes, in which the difference between the period fifty years ago and today can be quite successfully determined. But since when has poetry dealt with those areas of life that are not the most basic? Only *life*, the secret of its existence, and its emotional and intellectual issues is the realm for poetry, nothing more. If the poet says, "I love the night", do not seek in these words instructions on how to carry out a revolution or how to prevent war — poetry does not deal with the tasks of the day, but directs the soul and shows it how to emotionally cope with life. And if you have been seeking a "period" there, seek it in *how* it is said. The actual content of poetry, its themes and ideas, do not change, only its tone changes, only the way it is said in a new or, perhaps, old way. Therefore, no area of life can be excluded from poetry as obsolete or unnecessary, no feeling as too intimate, no idea as unhealthy. All these attacks on poetry are nothing new; the things which poetry is being criticized for today are the same things for which Karel Hynek Mácha was reproached. Do we need this drastic example to grasp that it would do considerable harm to smack the pens from the hands of today's poets in the same way that everything that wronged Mácha was an unforgiveable injustice *to the nation*. "Reality" cannot be simply a criterion. For if it merely means the *material* existence of something; in fact what moves society and what is also a source of poetry — the human spirit — is not reality! Otherwise, every sensory impression, every illusion, dream and thought are also reality. Therefore, all poets have the right to their dreams, but only if they are able to express them.

III. There are certain sacred values that should only be spoken of with respect. For example, there should not be much talk about Czechness, about patriotism, about the love for one's country, nation and people. And if such words are spoken, then it should be done with a deep understanding, without bias and misuse of these values. At K. H. Mácha's tomb we can ask ourselves how it was possible that his work, today a pillar of Czech poetry, could have been misused. How was it possible that so many others, including Smetana, were accused of what is incomprehensible for us today — namely, non-Czechness? Those on the side of the opponents of our masters currently considered the most Czech were not without merit or significance. How then was this possible? The question is easily answered. If we consider the inertia of human attitudes and consider our own inertia in views, it will lead us to the idea that Czech-ness is not simply an unchanging and constant value, that is a dynamic value, a value recreated again and again, that each generation needs to struggle over it anew, and that we do not inherit it from our fathers. Then it is possible to see that Mácha's work *was not* really "Czech" in its day, meaning that it did not correspond to the idea of "Czechness" of its age, but that it later moulded it to its form. This too is the mission of poetry: to create and form this value. Czechness is then the result of all the diverse forces that create it.

What are the consequences of this? The knowledge that Czechness is not merely the prerogative of those programmatically rendering it, that it is not something that is dead or ossified, but rather the most vibrant work of the present — meaning that, in the name of this value, any dictate, any coercion in terms of conviction and creation is excluded, and that, on the contrary, the most varied encounter of diverse forces is desirable, and that the more struggles the Czechness created by our age faces, the more magical the flower will be.

Václav Navrátil: Myths

TO JAROSLAV JANÍK.

Psychomythology. This word was invented merely to express the fact that miraculous stories can be born from the greatest experience. A process is occurring. A law is valid. A myth is both a process that is valid, and a law which is unfolding. Myths are spiritual stories found on the street, or street stories found in the soul: That is, the greatest objectivity grows from the greatest subjectivity. It is therefore not psychopathology, but psychomythology.

Such myths are they myths of the *present*. They are “significant events” taken from the most ordinary life. They are so mundane that their characteristics can even become mysterious. Thus, they are not prehistoric, but *pre-geographic* myths. (Only those perceiving history statistically can understand this).

Poetry should profess myths. The deepest poetry is both mythology and metaphysics.

Yet myths cannot be sought, they must be created. In fact, these two acts are identical. We seek myths, and this creates possibilities of transcendental poetry, just as the Romantics had sought.

*

It was said that events and situations are actually one and the same. And that situations *or* events are both static and dynamic! Nothing happens and everything flows.

Narcotizing situations are dangerous and redemptory. The injection that one gets in this way consists of both poison and medicine, simultaneously, though this is also a kind of feigning — of happiness and of the latest meditations. This is always the case.

*

However, this often needs to be alluded to.

We already need to take into account that in some parts it is forbidden to go into overly detailed verbal interpretations due to the impending danger. Journeys to far-off lands require more than the familiar supply of words. An otherwise extremely successful commitment to the most sensitive of directions is devalued merely by the scientific method to describe everything in a protocol-like method. You will need to rely on whispering, a hint, an image, a tone, a puzzle and ambiguity for some situations. Only through such a secretive method is it possible to communicate at a distance. The greatest depths are unclear. Clarity can be as flat as an illuminated panel.

*

This has begun as an expressionist story of sorts, but I am not to blame.

Breaths of the sleeping

Today it started getting dark earlier than usual. By four o'clock in the afternoon it was completely dark. A few minutes later, at around 4:35, the transition to a completely different history had begun... It was, after all, easy and urgent. One is destroyed by nightfall, which is blinding, as if the weight of the entire universe is pressing down on one's eyes. It would suffice to lie down to immediately fall into some inner event. In such circumstances, we are all convinced that we are awake. This is only partially true. We are awake, but our logic is not. We are awake, and yet we sleep. The dream during wakefulness occurs. *Insomnia vigilantium.* (This situation could be expressed by the formula that we read our wakefulness, for a dreaming person is always somehow reading. Yet it would also behove a reading person to dream.)

Time is counted down by the counterpoint of two rhythmic occurrences: the sprinkling of the sands of time and the distant barking of dogs somewhere near the woods, beyond the gas attacks of the wintry destroyer of nature.

But there will be other legends of rhythms.

There is here the rhythm of waves on the sea of dreamy music. That gentle arrival of sea blue to the human soul is very familiar. The bar indicates a symphony of the sleeping. A silent war is raging against rhythm.

Although this time a person is completely alone in his waking sleep, his breath takes on a collective meaning. It is as if a collective breath is playing.

The observer has the most intense dreams in the sleep of others; when in absolute silence he listens to the ticking of clocks in all rooms, when he listens to the chanted breathing of the sleeping of an entire city.

The deeply sleeping shout their breaths. The breaths culminate in sighs. The community of sleepers is dramatized. There arises a diverse conversation, and at the same time it is a strange and remarkable symphony of collisions.

It looks as if, somewhere in the land of shadows, avalanches of sand and ash are crashing down from the mountains, or like the deadly shrillness of falling airplanes. For years, many had listened to this music of roars from the corners of darkness and desolation.

Suddenly there was a loud shout interrupting all of this — the shout of a completely unknown word, perhaps Greek in origin. This shout immediately became the center of the landscape scenery. Yet from that moment everything began to crumble. I'd never heard that word before, nor have I since. It was if the sun, nailed to the pillory of noon, burst into flames.

That was a logical solution to the temporary uncertainty.

Analysis of a significant night

Previously, events that were significant for millennia took place. Generations gathered and prepared for action, sounds reverberated in the air. And during these events, which filled the minds of all people, it was possible in the dark of the night to check an old familiar place, which remained completely calm as if the events did not concern it. The night and the sun merged here.

It was possible to confront the air with the general drama, to seek in it, as in a mirror, an ominous picture of what was happening. And this picture was really there. I saw it in a piece of the sky, in a piece of a tree, in the red clouds that mysteriously filled the sky at the end of the struggle, as if they were a prophecy of events to come. They brought fear and promise. When everything was quiet, I paid close attention to the circumstances. I completely focused on observing.

When war arrives, people are afraid of every rustling sound they hear. Strange figures appear on the streets. The call of a bird at sunset in the fields gives fright like a tragic warning signal. But birds — the private pilots of the microcosm — don't even know how ominous they are sometimes under mysterious circumstances. Just as terrifying is the rumbling of an airplane and the flash of light in the night sky. Everything seems like mysterious signals of disasters.

The night before the attack was to begin was filled with this mystery. Everything was dark. The darkness was nothingness. It was as dark as nothingness, and yet figures were moving in the nothingness, as in the witches' night. But they were wholly unique figures.

A car rumbled from somewhere. A quick staccato passage, played on the pavement, lasted about two seconds. The noise then suddenly stopped. The cart had probably come to a halt. Why? Is there merely a private reason this? Absolutely not. We said *that everything was signals*.

It is on the periphery. On the periphery of the world, of the city, of the night of day, of hours. Only from afar was it possible to perceive the symphony of sounds reproduced by the military platoon. Yet I never caught a glimpse of this distant platoon. That, too, is destiny. And the seismographs noticed a distant train, whose sounds, inducing goosebumps, are hammered into the rocks (foreboding echoes of machine-gun fire).

And there was silence. Only very rarely did pedestrian steps come to life. But even they quickly died away. They were only there to heighten the necessary mystique of modern war. A female figure, expressing a kinship with the houses and walls, had the same purpose.

Darkness still rules here. This is the strangest circumstance of the age. It is a return to natural positions. No one would believe how dramatic complete darkness in the city is. It was said that darkness was "like nothing". It would then rightly follow that nothingness is dramatic.

Hypotheses:

1. Total mobilization means the concentration of people, as well as of things. Everything is involved. However, the usual and apparent indifference of things creates a dramatic situation in extraordinary circumstances. For it is a counterpoint of the events and thus helps to determine the neurosis of the sphere.

2. Whoever lives in a big city has forgotten about the stars. The light curtain, with which city nights are equipped, prevents an upward view. If it were not for this curtain, we would be able to see high and far. Then the city dweller would be in touch every day with the sediment of stars (it is actually metal ash, melted from the burnt sky).

The blackout of cities has provided this opportunity. The city dweller has once again seen the stars after decades. Stars in a big city are, after all, a very interesting scenic accessory.

Silent animals

Other backdrops of such meditative dreams are the clouds of forests where the pale pedestrian wanders.

Strange beasts walk there in funereal step, completely silent, like ghosts. Their rhythmic and slow march produces general amazement. Yet a familiar tug will come in this dream. It is the horror of a doe, leaping up, probably after an inaudible shot.

There is an explosion of fear. The ominous suspicion of the physical essence of humankind is added to this. The human body also has its memory. Its unease means an ominous anticipation of the future. It is a hint of our unknown.

The sudden unease of a summer day, when crowds of terrified people await a storm, mixes with nocturnal fear. It could have been expected with certainty that this day of confusion would come, that the songs that we will encounter will turn mad. The old and young alike will scream incomprehensible words. You will return to a senseless euphoria and early strangeness. The birds will screech bizarre and incomprehensive melodies. Each tone will change into a sound and each sound into a tone. Something unusual can be expected at any moment. It should have been known in advance that confusion would be born from the eccentricity of the surrounding world. Perhaps a person is normal, but people are crazy.

And all the city's clocks resounded at once on top of it all, calling for greater caution and heightened attention.

An explanation:

The new mythologizing hypersensitivity works chemically too. It acknowledged Nietzschean elements but needed to produce their compound: *it's midnight noon.*

*

A note on fear. Today there is no difference between collective and individual fear. There is only one fear, which is by nature vertical, not horizontal, as it was perhaps before. People today are afraid of an air raid, not of a horizontal attack. One is left to the mercy of something that cannot be seen. We are not used to looking upwards. Death attacks without warning (which runs counter to Heidegger's theory). This feeling is also one of the causes of the anxiety of the age. People are prepared for any treachery from above; this is beyond their horizon and leaves them helpless. Previously, the fear was only horizontal, people could easily defend themselves. Today's fear is a heroic fear and is an epidemic like the medieval plague. For there has never been an age as dangerous as the present, and it has never been so full of mysteries that transcend humankind. The glory of people on earth! We think everything is within our power, yet there are signs that our own weapons are slipping out of control.

Nevertheless, fear can be alleviated. The genuine threat causes one to get used to it, and we live on, calmly, with the greatest certainty, as if there is no danger. Even the reason for fear is quite relative.

An encounter

Now for a situation that is probably a *petit fait significatif*: I once made a private pilgrimage in peculiar places. It just so happened to be night. Suddenly, a figure swayed in the distance and then there appeared two teenagers whom I had never seen before and whom, given the unusualness of the situation, I would never see again. I must have looked quite odd because one of these young people, as they walked closely, said in seemingly good conscience, "Look, he's looking for yesterday."

This certainly was not intended to be incorrect, and it is not that ridiculous either. On the contrary, this jovial guy who became a very desirable discovery in this stylized situation, much like a chorus in a Greek drama — was telling a rather unwitting truth. It can even be said that this nocturnal situation was quite aptly characterized by this trivial statement, by which I was to be attacked and robbed. I really was more or less looking for yesterday. Which is not so bad, as others do the same. The right to live in the simultaneity of events — in the time and space — can be clearly acknowledged. Departing into the past is synchronized with walks into the future, since thinking evolves from memories even though each idea is a rebellion. Finally, it was possible to find a defence against that young man in popular phraseology itself. We often hear the saying: "I am not of today", which is intended to express shrewdness and foresight not only to the future, but also to the past. However, I did not use this defence. But it is possible to reassess the statement "I am not of today". We would see how nostalgia can become the equivalent of shrewdness. This was what I got out of my nocturnal excursion, which otherwise is probably completely meaningless.

Whistling in the Dark

The man that I am pointing to right now is wandering under the enchanting influence of love. Needless to say, it is night. The organ of trembling stars rumbles in the foundation of the sky until even the lanterns shake. And silence and tranquillity are expressed by a smile and friendship.

How strange and mysterious it is to listen at night to the radio of the world. The air is filled with strange forces that carry words and melodies. Everything is alive in the air, even though nothing is seen. We would be wrong if we thought that we are alone! We will first go and have a look into the space. Several homes are listening to the same melody. We can only verify this space in time. Each house gave us the same tune as we walked. We remain with the same music as we walk. But that's the way it should be!

Then everything fell silent. The inhabitants abandoned one radio after another. Was the night revived even after that? It seems so! For although the electric waves ceased to serve the people, they devoted themselves to whirling in the air. They became independent.

And only then did I hear the whistling. It is a call filled repeatedly with sexuality and love, an expression of life made by invisible crowds that wander through the night. It is an opportunity for one to pity the world and the throngs of helpless and cheerful people who do not realize that they should be sad. This whistling simultaneously gave a lift and positivity of both the static and dynamic.

It was not whistling as interjectional speech, but as part of a song. The first few bars that no one had ever heard before. And no one will ever hear the continuation and end of this song. For every signal is an infinite beginning of a song.

It is so merry and bitter at once! We cannot (not a single one of us) help ourselves, we must dive to the bottom of this matter.

And it is only further proof that the highest compassion is aroused not by misery and sorrow, but by merriment and whimsicality. For this is compassion for innocent ignorance.

Things and moments

We are surrounded by millions of cases in the form of objects and millions of objects in the form of cases.

Objects are created by moments, and moments are created by objects. Someone was holding a sausage pastry; there is also an ink bottle and an orange in some significant constellation; everything suddenly belongs situationally to everything else. A still-life is created.

*

Just as there is scientific and personal history, so too can there be scientific and personal archaeology. This is not a venerable science dealing with the excavation of ancient objects, but an archaeology of moments. Let us remember, for instance, examples from the lives of our acquaintances. We recall one hero who goes far away, perhaps fleeing the home forever; he passes through an unknown land; at that moment he gets the strange feeling that his ancestors once lived in the land that lay before him. Or an old Chinese poet encounters old willow women that he had previously seen a thousand years before; the poor old willow women trembled with joy when they see him after such a long time.

*

This sudden and irrelevant experience has documentary value. Ultimately, however, everyone has this kind of personal archaeology. The stones you walk by are conspicuous to you. There are streets that you fear. You will find old letters left in remembrance in the attic. You long for the old gables of houses. Forgotten books are not forgotten. The crosses in cemeteries and on crossroads are tragic autumnal airplanes that travel through the ages.

*

A clock is the soul of a house. Where there is no clock, there is no soul. In the old days, a clock was a totem pole.

*

We will need to read in the things that surround us. The objects seen around us are not merely objects defined by geometric dimensions. They are specific *stories*. Therefore, an object is not merely an object, but *also* a history, and a history is not only a history, but also an object. This means that an individual object is not just ordinary and normal. It is covered with many affections, "engrams" as psychometry calls them. History sticks to it, and it too sticks to history. It is the histories of its environment. And its environment is its histories.

The problem of things in time is turned into its unfinished history: Time must have the power to melt things down. And things must have the power to resist time. Everything that has ever happened is stored somewhere, stored in time. The space in which we can read them seems to us to be time.

I have heard, for instance, a recent story of one thing stored in time forever. An acquaintance once told me this most banal and inane poem:

I once walked past an antique dealer and bought an old vase.
Someone took this vase from me;
I searched in vain, until recently,
forty years later, I saw it.
It was in the window of another antique shop. God knows the journey
it had undertaken to get there.

Quite a few people confuse time and space in this way.

*

Yet no general law can be applied to things, because each individual thing is itself a law. Things cannot be generally named. Each thing has its own name, even if it is unknown. And everything has its own *responsibility* in the universe.

*

Many things signal something completely different than they seem. A picture that does not know it is merely a description, or rather, a transcription. It transcribes a script that is actually a world. It transcribes signals. Therefore, if a picture is to fulfil its task, it must not be a mere transcription, but a signpost.

*

We could recommend that astronomical observation be introduced not only for celestial bodies, but also for terrestrial objects. Instruments of observation could be applied to these too, psychometric microscopes of sorts.

Place

There is still a cult of place. There are certain places that one fears and loves at the same time. When this occurs, we may cite Frazer's theory on the origin of the totem that he puts forth in the book *Totemism*. According to this theory, a certain type of totem is created from the cult of a certain place. Frazer calls this totemism local.

A certain place is a center of impersonal mythical power. Primitive people believed that the ancestors of those long dead inhabited this place. This cult of place is then transferred to certain objects.

This theory is interesting not only for scholars, but also for the fact that an eternally human trait can be seen in it. Each of us has secret places where our totem resides — in gardens, in forests or high in the mountains, where once, long ago, it rained; where a detective could uncover ancient crimes of nature caused by sudden landslides, also causing the rapid growth in that area of protective shrubs and of random, solitary shrubs. These trees remain degenerate, but the place becomes mysterious.

Or the totem resides somewhere else. We capture in memories the legend of the last remnants of smoke, sent as a remembrance by a recently departed train, but one which we had never seen. These remnants then creep into the treetops like a brown dream, like the train's ectoplasmic body.

Certain places are therefore a strange mirror of the tragedies of sorrow and of the tragedies of happiness. The mystery of allurement that these isolated places acutely possess are eternally the same whether they are experienced by a civilized savage from Polynesia or by a savage civilian from Europe. It is from this human nature that the totemism of a place and the belief in a *genius loci* developed.

And there is one other opening. The world is a war, and there are "no man's lands" in this war. There are places that do not belong to anyone and are not used for anything. These are places that are absolutized. They are completely forgotten islands somewhere in the middle of an arid stream of tracks beneath a railroad station or abandoned places on its banks. Or places belonging to no one, but where a victim left behind a dilapidated object of use, such as a pottery fragment that has become nature. And now comes the mythological point: These places are *things*. They are mobile, they wander. They are wandering places. Encounter them once! You walk around them all the time, and they around you.

The work of art and time

It is also worth mentioning what role the "work of art" plays in time. Does a permanent work of art exist or is everything changing? Is everything historically relative? Try to figure this out!

But all this must be made more complex and difficult. For to simplify means risking delay.

Therefore:

If someone proves that everything is historically relative, that everything is subject to change, that there is no stable creation of the human spirit, tell him that performance and a work of art are not the same. The performance dies, but the work of art endures. In history there are not only performances, but also works of art. Yes, everything is relative, but the *absolute* is already contained in the words *everything* and *relative.* Dialectical philosophers are well aware of this.

However:

There may be those who speak of eternal values; they will claim that there exist eternal works of art that they want to analyse in a grammatical spirit. If by chance you encounter them, use the following as your objection: It is not just a work of art in history, it is also a performance. It is true that a work was written, but in order for us to understand it, we must also recreate it. Here lies the secret to understanding and comprehension; it is an eternal struggle, an eternal drama.

There is no epigonism in the largest and most difficult abysses of human thought where it meets divine *scandalum*. But everything is just repetition. This means that the repetition of something is its new *creation.* It is the equivalent of creative originality. Repetition is creation, and creation repetition. In this, the understanding of a work changes into the creation of a work, into the performance, by which the act of creation is repeated in history.

How should we view the discrepancy that was caused by this? It is not just a worthless pile of contradictions?

The answer: There are *fortresses*, but they are identical to the event. As previously stated, movement and tranquillity are identical in a myth. This is illuminating for mythology, and also for dialectics.

Consolations

When human misery catches up to you, you suddenly hear comforting motifs as you march into the underworld of thoughts. These may be the sound of piano keys being struck in the clouds, at times when the streets and all of life suddenly become serious and when you recall, let's say, a unique half-opened window, how the sun looked on August 17, 1918 at 2 pm. Reminders that should mark the anniversary of a private story are not attached to this date. Nothing at all occurred at that time. Absolutely nothing other than what was described.

Indeed, some people walk around stung by hidden situations. Every day, such a madman is looking for a party, to which he nevertheless regularly arrives late, at day's end, when the beauties have closed themselves and the sounds have drowned into distances in darkness and silence. Yet right away he will see: the glory of the "old sun" is recognized in a certain random voice, one of the last. Repeated screams, falsified over time, can once again be heard. Events that once took place behind seven walls are played on the stage. That will be the final dream.

Rest assured that you will reread the illustrated newspapers of your life. You will rejoice in the love around you. You will think that you are really experiencing your happiest moments. You will even be proud of your happiness. This is not resignation, for there is sorrow in resignation, while here the joy and laughter and even hilarity is somewhat vulgar as in intoxication. I will invite you back. We will return to the places that we once visited. We will hear familiar voices and sounds. There is even the sudden fright that we experienced long ago. We will feel that everything we experience is completely logical. Nothing will come as a surprise.

A solution:

This recitation of the book of life provides us with the certainty of thought, which means the reconciliation of Fate and Logos. It is a beautiful moment when knowing catches up to and captures the known. Then there occurs what perhaps happens only once in a lifetime: we encounter ourselves in space and time.

Kamil Bednář: A Word to the Young

We conclude our incomplete and sketchy essay with one final question: What then is the task of young people?

It is above all and without a doubt to connect and merge into a single stream their scattered power, to create a sense of belonging to the generation.

It also means continuing to look for the "naked" one and making him the starting point for the construction of a new social person. To bring a halt to the current trend of analysing and fragmenting the view of the world and of man *ad absurdum*; to stop the crazed relativism created by war and our confused age. To search for and create new and newly seen relations of man to man, to nation, to society, to things and to the universe!

We mentioned today's mission of young people, the fact that in today's broad, nationwide front, their task is to make this *quantitative* idea into a *qualitative* one, if they do not want to drown in the predominance of the generation above them that is lacking the very fertile and driving influx of new and young blood of thought. Perhaps this is to be understood in the sense of the aforementioned interpretations. Let that man, "naked" and "human" and the new man just now sought, be the base for the new national idea. Let the awareness of the new national community gush from the new sense of life that the young bring, even if not yet in its pure form!

As if our eyes were washed by the suffering and bathed in the water of life, they acquire a more penetrating view. We are moving towards a greater and greater truthfulness, and in many parts of the earth a new spirit is already being born. Truth is no more than a *direction* towards truth, and truthfulness is the path we take. The ground is shaking, and one epoch of world history is coming to an end, while another is already knocking at the door. We are witnesses — nothing more than that for the time being — who wish to observe the technology of divine creation. To see how states fall and regimes crumble, how ideologies baffle and beat each other, and how everything that is false breaks, and half-truths crack like kernels under the pressure of rolling history. We are somewhere in the middle — and alone — in the middle of the truth. Let us look for man; a new humanism of unprecedented dimensions stands on the threshold of history! Man, whom we can see best today, for we see him every day in thousands of changes, thousands of trials and tribulations, during which everything insignificant falls into darkness.

VI.

Finally, we would like to add a glimpse of the young art generation. As always and everywhere, here too is the first proclaimer of a new mood the most delicately reacting social body — poetry. That is why talking about young art means talking about young poetry, even if other branches of art are full of talent. But poetry seems to have more or less precisely determined its path. Perhaps we can say that so far only poetry has already worked out its aesthetic scheme: what poetry is and is not, how it should or should not be. There are those who feel that poetry of the young is not sufficiently avant-garde — now an empty word. They feel it is not unusual enough; it does not go far enough in breaking already established forms as introduced by post-war poetry. Nothing new, they say!

This is correct; precisely because young poetry does not want to be avant-garde. For it too has its not yet uttered generational motto: to discover the being of man. The disintegration of poetic form with which Poetism and laboratory experiment began, culminating today in the poetry of Vladimír Holan, reached the pinnacle of its development, a point that cannot be surpassed. The demand for unusualness, the problem of the imagination, is no longer the motto of the day, and instead the demand for human content, necessarily and in line with the age, has emerged.

But let's not be mistaken: human content, yes, but not in a vulgarized sense, such as the dictates of social, rural or patriotic motives. (There is perhaps no need to prove that these dictates miss the target since they are based on a demand that is known in advance and therefore does not have to be a discovery).

In young poetry this is, at the risk of unprecise expression, the path to man, the search for man. It is obvious that this search is not done portentously, with a lantern in daylight, and if you want to learn about it, then only in the poetry itself. Searching for a person is not as easy as the concept in which we describe the creative endeavours of the young. Let's not be mistaken, especially when it comes to psychological analysis: not even young poetry can avoid it (no poetry can). But analysis is not the final objective here. It has essentially a different character: it is not a self-serving deconstruction of a rigid and deadened reality, but precisely a search by exploration, a search for a path, and its goal is, on the contrary, a longing to find solid ground. It is too subtle a difference for us to capture here, and its focus is entirely elsewhere. But let us notice one thing that perhaps testifies to our theory: man as the speaker in poetry, as the person who can be constructed from the poetry itself. In young poetry, this is a person with no social relations, no relations to a general conviction or prevailing ideology. He simply does not have the social traits that e.g. the Socialist Realism movement required when it divided literature by class. A man of young poetry is a man without class affiliation, without class traits, nothing but a man, a "naked" man, composed of feelings, instincts and senses, simply confined to his deepest substance.

However, we are not concerned here with aesthetic decomposition. We merely want to point out that so far it is essentially only poetry that is a generation's first messenger. This is understandable when considering the lack of programmatic direction and the scepticism that is characteristic of it. Given its immediacy and the gift of responding quickly to new realities, it can only be poetry that *precedes* the idea, still concealed in it. Hence the lack of novelists and theorists among the young. Both require clear and firmly formulated ideas, which, however, are still hidden in poetry itself. The novelist does not react directly to the perceived reality, and young people, in particular, have not yet developed the technical description of reality, which is what a novel, with its subtle and complex craftsmanship and its symbolization through the action, is. The lack of theorists, especially critics, is related to the general decline of Czech criticism, especially in journalism. And yet the young critic would have here all the more extensive, fertile and still untilled soil. However, he would have to give up the usual official-critical ambitions, a path leading effortlessly to the goal. For even a critic must be burned by the facts that he feels and must work his way to his judgments, reaching into the flame for it with his bare hand. For a critic is born of the same pain as a poet. This should be known to all those among the young who show an inclination towards theoretical thinking. Let us not expect the critic, as with the playwright and director, before young poetry has firmly assumed its position. More complex and in their composition predominantly technical disciplines, disciplines of long and arduous prior work, they need more time to formulate their vision.

Finding man and rebuilding man will be the mission of the young generation. The concept of man, as we have already briefly mentioned, underwent a deconstruction of his fixed personality, it broke it up and fragmented man to the point of an unclear microcosm. The slowly returning notion of man being whole again, to which we are hoping that young people will bring their fertile and painfully acquired experiences, will create a new person.

A person who finds his peace again and will also have his human order; a person bowing in voluntary discipline to the real laws of nature. Perhaps the purpose of this age is to re-examine all values that have pushed the old values into the background, though not yet demonstrating their authority to do so. At least in literature we see young people going further back, right to the sources of modern literature. And literature can be for us a forerunner of social development here, for in literature, too, there was a time of almost meaningless experimentation, the lawless and irresponsible breaking apart of values that were (but were they really?) replaced by new values. Especially in art's endeavour not to be art, where there were attempts to make poetry that was not poetry, a novel that was not literature, visual art that was not visual art, but poems; theatre that was not theatre, but music; especially in this effort, which we can now say that, though it failed, was an enriching experience in many ways, and we see the same restitution of enduring values and laws that we expect in life as well.

We have tried so hard to shed light on questions that have been so little discussed, if not completely neglected. We expect that both the agreement and resistance provoked here will have a truly productive effect: that they will not be made in vain and will provide a better, clearer and more detailed formulation than ours.

Jindřich Chalupecký: The World in Which We Live

One of the most striking features of modern art is the dissipation of canonical thematic types: figural composition, landscape, portrait and still-life are gradually disappearing from paintings, and the same holds true for epic, meditative and sentimental poetry. At first, the most demanding themes disappear, the rest then slowly become a mere pretext, until they too entirely vanish — though with a tendency to occasionally return: thus, figural composition recurs in Surrealist painting, meditative poetry in philosophical or semi-philosophical poems, referring mostly to the example of Valéry or Rilke.

We can conclude from this that it was most likely a mistake if the decomposition and suppression of themes was interpreted as a path to theme-less art. We have heard enough about "subject-less painting" and, as for poetry, getting rid of themes was to be a kind of arabesque of words and ideas, if sometimes even this "content" was rejected in favour of artificial speech, sounds devoid of verbal meaning.

This trend quickly passed. The interpretation that sought to prove that the development of art was heading towards a rejection of themes was apparently wrong. In Picasso's Cubism or Reverdy's poems, the theme clearly disappeared for the sake of a purely painterly or verbal construction, yet this liberation of art was not intended to reduce to a festival of senses and imagination, even if it is the most enchanting.

However, another trend was at the same time interpreting modern art completely differently. It came from Rimbaud, Lautréamont, Jarry and Chirico, and found its most systematic form in the theories and practices of the Paris Surrealists. An important reassessment of theme was made here. Instead of the petrified and vanishing literary and artistic types, a single kind of universal validity emerged: man, his life and his innermost life became the theme of art, and art was defined as a creation of the subconscious. The subconscious in the sense of Freudian psychoanalysis.

If it considered automatic writing, the simulation of literary manifestations of madness, the paranoid interpretation of things seen or about records of dreams, it remained at several articles, one book, a few paintings and the work of Breton, Éluard, Dalí and Ernst; it then went further, taking a different direction, unable to be limited to the rather narrow and monotonous possibilities of authentic manifestations of the subconscious.

If, however, neither the removal of the entire theme nor the expansion of the theme to all of man's inner life suits the meaning of modern art, where should it then be sought? Let us attempt, disregarding theories that the life of modern art has borne with it, to effectively help them for a while and then immediately forget about them, to determine some traits that accompany them.

*

The destruction of types and disappearance of the theme took place at the same time as the extraordinary boom of the metaphor. Not only did it gain courage, but whereas before it was, as they said, poetic adornment, now it seems to have become the poem's primary and sole content. According to the school definition, a metaphor occurs if we compare two things having a common feature, and "the metaphor transfers the name from the one object to the other so that their similar feature illustratively appears". If modern art then elevates the metaphor to the main structure of a poetic vision of the world, if it turns it from a "formal" means into the poem's "content", it is easy to draw a conclusion on the essential difference between the non-poetic and the poetic, between the rational and irrational concept of the universe: while a rational concept of the universe integrates it into a system of various phenomena and states, i.e. into a discontinuous system, an irrational concept of the universe views it as a whole intensively and in all directions continuously and fluently.

If we then imagine both of these tendencies of human assessment of being — the one going for diverseness and the other for unity — meaning that rational thinking culminates in an organized classification given by speech, transforming the universe into a vocabulary of signs of individual things, into a set of components, and irrational consciousness ends in uniting the universe into a single indivisible mass.

In contemplating this, we also arrived at an explanation of two features of modern poetry:

First, the content of a poem is its form, and this also means that the form of a poem is its content. Form and content merge, showing themselves to be one and the same. Hence the non-thematic quality of modern poetry: its theme is nothing more than the poem (e.g. a feeling, reflection), its theme is nothing less than a poetic understanding of the universe.

Secondly, this poetic understanding of the universe fatefully ends after the poem. If speech was made, as they said, to classify the universe into individual things, the poet must then destroy this function of speech; he tries to use it in the opposite sense, he violates it, destroys it himself to show the path it is to take to break through the apertures from the prison of the rational construction of the universe; leads to intuition of the Whole, of the individual aggregate totality of being, to the opposite of classification, to that which is by definition inexplicit. It is no accident that so many modern poems end by breaking off, with a cry, a tightening of the throat, in silence; it alone can finish the suggestion of this work of art.

Let us note that the same is true in modern painting. Here, too, the destruction of the rational universe is the objective: Picasso's paintings shatter the object, reassessing it in an increasingly multivalent form, the individual thing disappears in favour of the painter's form suggesting a world that is no longer things.

*

Is then the purpose and meaning of art to be exhausted by that crushing pause, by the unearthly sob, by the superhuman and inhuman over and beyond?

Behold modern man, abandoned by the new science, pushing reality far into an unimaginable and unthinkable trans-reality, abandoned by religion, which seems wrong in its role, but has fatefully survived in its form; man, transformed into a helpless cog in the social machine, obstinately run like a crazed perpetuum mobile, reduced to two dates, the day of birth and the day of death, between which there is nothing, nothing more than a little nonsense, when his head still spun and which he quickly corrected thanks to his rationality of a useful component, doing his work just as diligently and as uselessly as the whole machine — and now even art is abandoning him, going somewhere beyond and away from man, yanking him out of life in an unearthly and supernal moment — this man who has not yet lived, who needs to be returned to life. How terribly this art resembles the perhaps supreme, but also final brilliant flaring of dying cultures, how close it is to late Rome, to Rome of the oriental cults and Neoplatonists — The end? Is it the end? Or should Europe follow the fate of the lost, distant steppes of Asia, the fate of those cultures that once, after so much suffering and striving for such an inhumanly high tone, managed to remain in a terrible, blissful and destructive resting on the edge of the heavens, to live their long centuries with eyes fixed on the distance beyond humanity — and with some secret irony to definitively reduce the individual's personal life into a monotonous ceremony, from generation to generation, unchanged and repeated without interest — ? Will man forget about man, about this wonderful event, the flickering of flames, alive, alive and alive amid the infinity of the inert duration of existence, alien to the eternal law of strict matter and the monstrous absolute? Will he forget about him, about the miracle of his unpredictable will, feelings and self-confidence, will he brutally and angrily eliminate his mystery in favour of boundless sleep, where even dreams are eradicated; will he bring shame on himself, falling to the divine heights of being, where consciousness and unconsciousness, being and non-being, activity and resting are no longer distinguished? What confusion! Is perfection perfection?

Or, devoted to accepting himself, will he remain a tragic hero enduring between God and nothingness and denying both of these two-in-one, will he remain an absurd and desperate experiment, to be self-aware, being incomprehensible, to want without ever being able to understand the reason and meaning of his wanting, and to feel, so that he is sacrificed over and over to primordial confusion? What is man if not he who feels and never understands?

To live, to live. In spite of everything, despite the comforts of lifelessness, despite the fact that everything is arranged here as if only to divert attention from life, one wants to live, and Europe — old, painful and unhappy Europe — does not give up and shakes with the writhing of the masses, who plead, beg, despair and decide, not knowing for what, but out of some unshakable certainty that there is a need to dare to do something that is not this.

To live. To return man to mystery, confusion, to life. To start anew. Art, you small and unsightly pictures, you little poems stubbing your little words amidst events so immense, would you be able to –?

If you are not helpers, you are at least witnesses. Somewhere out there you have the courage, on which humanity will probably have to agree: the courage to be and not to understand, for that is precisely what life is. I call on the painting of Italians cities and French swimming pools, as seen by Chirico, the forever unfinished machine of Duchamp's *La Mariée*, the chorus of Joyce's *Ulysses* and the painful leaves of Jouve's books, the harsh and fresh sensitivity of the poems and prose of American poets, of Aragon's Parisian peasant, Fargue's intoxicating writings, the severity of Dalí, a few terrifying paintings by Bonnard, the insidious protocols of Breton, the photographs of Atget and of those who followed him, and scenes from some old films, especially the brick wall and the gas meter from Chaplin's *The Kid*. Consider it foolish to assemble such a collection, and yet resonating here is something that I call *the mythology of modern man or the world in which we live.*

*

In living his life, man is naturally led to judge things around him primarily by how much they assist or oppose his attempts to make a living effortlessly and safely. Hence he interferes with reality, removing unpleasant or obstructing things and making comfortable and pleasant things: civilization. Life is simplified, made easier. It is reduced to the smallest number of reactions or standardized. Rationalization leads to automation. Man no longer needs to be on guard against reality, his reactivity to the environment has become unnecessary.

There is another tendency which opposes this one. Here, too, man is aware of reality as something that is beyond him and, above all, against him. It is something alien, unknown, about itself; it is its limits and therefore its negation. However, since it is its negation, it also forces him to be aware of himself: and in this role reality gives rise to an artistic act. Art always begins in unexpected contact with reality, not included in a rational system, emerging from it and therefore exposing the sensibility of the spirit and mobilizing its powers, trying to empower it. Its theme is always ignorance, loss of orientation, an attempt at a new one. At the same time, it forces a person to feel. No matter where it begins, as soon as the disjunction of being I and it, man and the universe, enters into consciousness, both emerge in their true monumentality.

Things are therefore more than the demarcation and negation of the subject; they are the condition and a constitutive part of consciousness. However, if we now recall that consciousness is a *function* of life, the form of this relationship of man to the world is clarified to us: it spreads things out into its time and makes them participants of this senseless and unrelenting act of being, which was dictated by an unknown command, so that it not only was and endured, but also so that it was carried out to its detriment and with all its might each and every moment, so that resisting the widespread tranquillity of the oceans of eternity, beckoning from all directions into the blissful rest, and defending against the certainty of death its incomprehensible futility of life, it transformed its constantly threatened life into an unquenchable thirst for life, and in this longing to live, in this hunger for existence, it defied things and the dead rational scheme to assure itself of its life and to make them guides and symbols of its desperate hoping, to make them the myth of its life.

*

Things. These things. Not anaesthetized, standardized products not taking into account memories, but vibrant, indubitable, existing, unique, indubitable for their defiant unfamiliarity, for their irreducible reality, able to confirm themselves and ensure the reality of the subject's life: not even things that are artistic, smoothed and modified to be beautiful, pleasant, delectable; things that are hard, evil, mysterious, relentlessly applying their impenetrable consistency and resting firmly on the painful skin of a living organism, the "air, rocks, coal and iron" that Rimbaud's famous verse hungers for.

So often an example of art has been sought in a dream; and yet human timidity has confused a dream with dreaming, with the delightful assembly of simple, safe, friendly, imaginary artifacts, not daring to learn from the power of a dream that places these very things that we are constantly encountering, and does not care about the rational or aesthetic quality that we intend to assign to or deny them. And so often there has been talk of realism in art, so that instead of from reality, art can be made from surrogates of reality; i.e. from things so tried and tested, but that occur so infrequently in the proximity of modern man, e.g. from allegories of the seasons, from the exoticism of rural life, if not from nudes, bouquets and still-lifes, provided exclusively for artistic purposes.

While the feeble and careful painter and poet of today seek for their art a reality that is as harmless, as remote and having as little to do with their lives as possible, and flee from it somewhere far away from themselves, in other ages man relied on the closest possible reality with art, whether it was the beasts he hunted, the silk robes of the women he loved or the landscape in which he lived. The reality of the modern painter and poet is practically a city; his people, his cobblestones, his lamp stands, the signs of his shops, his houses, staircases and flats. And he denies this reality, denies it because he fears it, since it is the world in which he lives, and modern man fears this world because he would remember himself in it — and he fears himself.

*

If art is to acquire lost meaning in the individual's life, it must return to the things among which and with which he lives. But not as a theme that is before a work of art and outside it. If it rejected the repertoire of old, dead themes, as has been established in various kinds of art, it cannot mechanically replace it with a new theme — to restitute old types and render reality harmless once again by including it among traditional themes as mere variations. All that remains is for it to create reality; for reality is not at the beginning of a work of art to be modified or processed by it, it is only at its end. Art discovers reality, creates reality, reveals reality, this world in which we live, and we who live. For not only the theme, but the meaning and purpose of art is nothing more than the everyday, terrifying and glorious drama of man and reality: the drama of mystery facing a miracle.

If modern art will be incapable of this, it will be useless.

*

Jindřich Chalupecký: History

Since the Great War, a strange unrest has weighed down Europe. She has begun to doubt herself. Were the years divided by battlefronts enough to bring this on? How often she has gone through wars without feeling undermined. This time, however, it as if she suddenly realized something new and unique in her situation. For a while, she wanted to be carefree and merry, but she did not enjoy her fun. The old days did not return. A gloominess of the mind lingered. The question of what she was actually moving towards came up all the more frequently... of how much she had contributed to human happiness over the past two centuries. The notion of progress became particularly suspicious. The new economic arrangement did not work out. Her achievements, her history took on a mysteriousness. Everyone relied on reason, and meanwhile events were doing whatever they wanted. She also looked at her rulers and saw that they no longer dared to do anything. People of spirit, philosophers and poets also no longer dared. Some declared that from now on they only intended to serve an idea, a class, a nation. Others claimed themselves craftsmen of books, paintings, history or sensations. The few remaining seemed to suffocate with anxiety. Art diminished to screams, dizziness and experimentation and moved somewhere far away from man.

That's not all. The *normal person's* life was subverted, the private life — unmanaged, improvised according to rules that no one had any faith in anymore and for which one was grateful only because there were no others. There were strange excesses: *Nacktkultur*, Christian Science, the godly Rudolph Valentino, absurd clothing. And escapes: attempts at a collective in the stands of football and other stadiums. And all this time neither a collective nor an individual existed. And yet man *does exist*.

* * *

Should Europe collapse? How could she live without the thoughts from which she has drawn her strength, by which she resolved to resist all temptations to *give up, to be satisfied*. Is she at the end of her tether? Did she acknowledge that the past sufficed, and that it was useless to merely repeat it? Does she no longer have a *destiny*, no longer consider herself worthy of tasks beyond her, no longer feel obligations and has no choice but to fall asleep in animal satisfaction or to disintegrate, dissolve into a confused activity that she is no longer aware of herself. Valéry's terrible question keeps coming to mind: "Will Europe become *what it really is*: a small cape off the Asian mainland?"

Yet there remains something that secretly unites her in all her places and in all her manifestations. Europe is still defending its primacy over the rest of the world. It is the primacy of suffering. Even if he loses consciousness, the European is still not too tired to feel. It seems as if he no longer has anything to believe in. Yet he insists on his right to his own destiny. He is still the one from whom no one else in the world can isolate himself. But what does he want? If he does not want to give up his privileges, where does he want to go?

There is a reason that the word *problem* has become so common in the speech of modern poets, politicians, philosophers, artists... Problem: it replaces the word anxiety. Mankind is anxious.

* * *

It is not surprising that at such a time some feel that Europe has no other alternative than to return to antiquity, to Christianity, to the great incentives that long drove it to greatness. I recall how the slogan "new enlightenment" could recently be heard in our country. The gate through which Europe once departed from its certainties is the same gate through which it should return to them. Is not Europe afflicted with a lack of reason? What else then can we ask of her but to try wisdom and once again take up her noble heritage?

Instead, a strange Europe, far removed from its entire past, is rejecting it. It is done, it is perfect, it is beautiful and now it is worthless for Europe — she has already made up her mind. She suffers, suffers terribly, but only in her desperation is she sure. That is the only thing that shields her from death, and she knows it. Admire her heroism. She leaves nothing to deliberation, to reason. She knows that she should create again. Her old certainties will not help her; she is left with nothing but her insecurity. It is an insecurity older than all her certainties. She has already lost and now she is starting over.

Do not ask about her objectives. "If anyone on the verge of action should judge himself according to the outcome, he would never begin. Even though the result may gladden the whole world, that cannot help the hero, for he knows the result only when the whole thing is over, and that is not how he became a hero, but by virtue of the fact that he began." (Kierkegaard)

* * *

Not through the gate of deliberation, not through the game of reason... We are in danger of irrationalism. And yet Europe must go through this hellish gate. Virtual anxiety must stabilize earlier in the current desperation, the horrors of human existence must further accumulate so that for the last time they become irrevocably obvious, so that it is no longer possible to remain indifferent. Then there will begin, as Herzen used to say a hundred years ago, "the third volume of world history". After all, is irrationality *merely* hellish, *necessarily* hellish, or hellish *in its final and true form*?

It is not by accident that the crisis did not afflict all of Europe evenly. So far, the Mediterranean countries have been best shielded from it; yet they resist it only owing to their tradition, which provides them with extraordinary life *training*, a reserve of skills that, though practically petrified, are still somehow usable. Beyond the old and seemingly indestructible borders of the Roman Empire it is exposed more sharply; in North America, in this new Europe, on the virgin soil, unrecognized by any invigorating — and depressing — memory, a white person acquires the most bitter and impassioned experiences of her.

A future historian may notice how the springs of new power originated right where there was no experience to help man make do with the little that remained; right where it was clear that he no longer had anything to lose, where there was nothing left but to dare, where there was nothing left but a passion that wants to live.

To dare. Did man ever dare to do something out of reason? For this is the last sentence of reason: "Nothing is more than something". Existence is not justifiable; an empty space, and if empty, then it is no longer a space: that is the conclusion that reason reaches if it resolves to create something comprehensible to him, or at least most likely comprehensible. But the universe, planet, life, man...

If man had been created rational, he never would have desired the unknown, the incomprehensible, the future, he never would have created his systems in which he dictates the impossible and the unimaginable to existence: systems of ideal and non-existing values, systems of culture. The life of an animal, the life of an amoeba, the life of a stone — of the most distant sorrow, of pain, unhappiness, of what can most closely fulfil the perfect and absolute order of instincts, of life, of existence. But man...

He does not fit into life through the gate of reason. Bloody sacrifices, senseless superstitions and panic-stricken horrors were the basis from which culture originated. Though actually, they were already cultures. They never emerged and were never preserved from a program of reason, but from a hunger forever inexplicable and irrational.

But woe to Europe if they are raving about a *tempered* life, which will be devoid of danger and pain, with longing always satisfied. Woe to the educators who want the law before the legislator.

This is what it is about: finding the new strength to listen to old questions. The answers do not come before the questions. Because there is no answer. But there is life — that is the incandescence of the question.

In the end, there are two lessons. The first: Trust history. The second is Nietzsche's: *Gefährlich leben*.

Jindřich Chalupecký: Art Imitates Reality

I. There is no picture identical to its subject. One cannot reproduce, one must produce. Art is *homo additus naturae*; it is in the humanity of error, in the necessary contradiction that is between the depicted and the depiction that the artistry of the work lies. It could be said that art is a beautiful mistake.

The more specifically the artist grasps reality, the bolder he reassesses it, the more impassionedly he uses it for himself, and the more artistically he fares. A picture is not a report of the world, but the artist's expression.

Nevertheless, a work of art is conceivable without an artist; if it departs from the reality that it depicts, it similarly departs from the reality it expresses. It is understandable even if we do not communicate with its creator through it.

The imitation, description and true expression of the psychological state of the artist of the work is no less impossible than the imitation, description and true representation of an object.

He who has begun to work on his painting in sorrow or joy must forget about himself, and even "beautifully err" in this way.

The theme, the inner and outer motive, is merely an excuse to create a work of art. It extends it in the direction of poetry, eventually leaving it behind in favour of pure beauty.

The creative forces that build a work of art are autonomous on all sides. Not relying on any reality that is external to them, the reality itself is wholly unique. It relies on itself, is based within itself, the miraculous design of a new cosmos that floats, rests on itself, "supported" in Flaubert's words "by the inner force of style".

II. If, however, all non-artistic reality of the work is a burden that it rids itself of, does that then mean that painting, sculpture and poetry can never become pure art? All of history has shown us that these arts must be realistic, that they always remain dependent on the things of the world around them and are always adorned by the artist's individual creative power.

Does this mean that the general idealness of art, the pure beauty, is limited in specific arts and in individual works of art by the materiality of the circumstances of their creation, such as the presence of their artist, the material used or even the function assigned to the work?

Can essence be distinguished in art: its aesthetics (bound to its autonomy) — and its secondaries: the representational and psychological content?

Or is there a different relationship between these various aspects of a painting, sculpture and poem that we have calculated to be their *imitativeness*, their *expressiveness* and their *autonomy*; one that is different than the relationship of essentiality and additivity, of the artistic and non-artistic, of idealness and materiality, and of form and material?

III. Let us try to explore the relationship between the imitativeness and autonomy of a work of art.

At first glance, they are mutually exclusive opposites. The greater a work of art is an imitation of an external object, the more it loses its autonomy. The more it applies its own composition, the more it must modify, distort or reject its own (and self-conditioned) composition of objectivity.

Nevertheless, we can notice a relationship here — one that is given by the autonomy of the depicted and the autonomy of the image.

The artist does not approach objectivity as chaos that needs to be formed: a landscape, a human body, objects to be depicted or an event to be described must have its own order within, thanks to which they themselves endure.

This attribution of independent objectivity to the perceived world is uncommon, but it is precisely this which is characteristic of the artist's attitude to objectivity: that he does not relate them to a subject, that he does not deem them to be a useful tool and controllable environment for the practice of human life, but that he starts from selfless admiration, uninvolved understanding and kind acceptance.

Therefore, he does not introduce order to the objectivity by placing it in relation to himself but confers on it an independent existence and order.

Then the autonomy of the work of art is a correlate of the autonomy of the depicted object; an instrument by which an object can be grasped in its autonomy, the condition under which it alone will be understood in its own validity and authentic wholeness.

A work of art does not want to imitate material reality; it wants to capture it. It does not want to submit a report on it; it wants to reconstruct it.

It wants to be reality "once again", the Nietzschean spell: "come back".

The Renaissance painter used a three-dimensional space because he regarded it not as a category of his consciousness, but as an objective form by which the independent order of objectivity is realized. He did not imitate this space but reconstructed it to help him bring back fleeting and elusive objects.

The Byzantine or Egyptian artist would never have considered his artificial spatial construction to be an artistic artefact into which he should transform things. In his eyes, they were a space in which the world and things really and truly *are.*

"The transposition of a three-dimensional space into a two-dimensional surface" and "a naturalistic, illusive space" are examples of ill-conceived words of recent theoreticians. Strict realism is the program of all art.

IV. Just as a work of art cannot be a copy of reality, its shadow, its illusion or appearance, it also cannot be a footprint, an imprint or a snapshot of the artist's psychological state.

He loses himself in it and at the same time returns to himself. He moves away from the present moment from which his existence arises and on which he is modelled, covering up the random and occasional. Leading it beyond the edge of time and space, which scatters his life into tiny gestures, he reveals it in its hidden essence, not of the past, not of the future, not of the present, but of being.

He unconsciously places and creates in the autonomous construction of a work of art his authentic existence and creates, his true double, his self "once again", his Kierkegaardian "reaffirmation".

V. The aesthetic autonomy of a work of art is therefore not a form that would be filled with expression and imitation.

Its autonomy *conditions* its imitative and expressive function and at the same time this autonomy is conditioned by these functions of a work of art. It is autonomous *because it depicts* the reality of the artist's external and internal world; and it can do so *because it is autonomous.* Its objective is as much its autonomy as its realism: to ascertain and understand inner and outer material and spiritual being in their originality and authenticity; *that is*, to achieve autonomous, absolute being.

We have said elsewhere that art is an ontological practice. Here we can say that it is ontological realism.

Its autonomy is not a bearer — a representative — of its aesthetics. We can do away with the word *aesthetics*, among many others, as a "mere sound". Art is not about beauty, but about reality.

VI. The path we are taking is foolish. But we are not taking it, it is taking us. Let us leave the responsibility to it and move on.

Finding the unity of a work of art (unity not consisting of the necessary connection of its components, symbols, functions, i.e. its original unity which is not divided into parts), we have captured the apparency of antinomic differences, such as its autonomy and expressiveness, as well as its autonomy and imitativeness. However, the result we have achieved will remain dubious if the artwork remains divided into its imitation and expressiveness, into its relation to the external world of objects and its relation to the internal world of human subjectivity.

The problem is immense and cannot be dealt with in a few lines. Let us name just two of the premises offered up to us.

The first premise: The world of subjectivity and the world of objectivity are different. There is a substantial divergence between man and external things; he does not have access to things about himself, and the manner by which he arranges and interprets signals that appear to him is exclusively his own work. His subjectivity is outside the world of external things and is its own universe, whose laws have nothing in common with the laws of the external universe. So then, there is not just one universe, but two, or even as many as there are discerning subjects. Each of these monads comes from a different world and is created from different matter and a different spirit. They are only microcosms, but does not the universe exist? Is it not the universe, but a countless plurality of universes that touch each other but still exist in another order of being? Can they then touch each other? Don't they have to be non-beings to one another? So even being itself is not singular, but plural? It seems necessary that everything being, including subjectivity and objectivity, in any differentiation of the individual beings, was connected in essence by a single and always identical order, was contained in a single and always identical set. It seems that a universe in different places — at different times — in different possibilities — cannot be absolutely different. A plurality of absolutes cannot be conceded. The concept of a universe absolutely different in itself violates the very law of identity. Let us reject this premise.

The second premise: If the universe is always and everywhere identical to itself, every subjectivity, every individual monad that it contains must be absolutely identical with it and with every other monad. However, the observed ideal identity does not allow for material diversity. This means that such an absolutely identical universe could not in any way diversify into individual monads; there could not be a multitude of individuals through whom being occurs; there could not be a "subject" and "object" at all. Let us also reject this premise.

The first premise, corresponding to the factual multitude of monads, is unthinkable because it contradicts the principle of identity. The second premise, conforming to the principle of identity, precludes the actual multitude of monads. Is it possible to somehow mediate between them?

Let us assume that the universe varies from monad to monad, that being and remaining one it has the ability to infinitely change.

Then the connection and mutual knowability of a subject and object is not only possible, but even necessary; it is a metaphysical condition of their being. Their actual discord, otherness and ignorance is the partial, random, occasional and changeable, the mutual communication between them occurs owing to the constant identification of the theme, of the basic specimen of which they are variations.

In this way, the universe appears as an ideal, the monads as its materiality. We are thus working with the concepts of idea and matter, although we rejected these concepts at the beginning of this study. Can our idea be formulated in a way allowing us to do without these Aristotelian distinctions?

VII. Let us therefore try to clasp together universality and monad-ness of the universe in a tighter way: let us consider monads as incompletely realized universality, as attempts by the universe to exist, and let us omit the concept of the idealness of universality as effectively unprovable.

By doing so, we have dismissed the idea of the universe as a filled order, a closed case, and opened the possibility of seeing it as an unfinished incomplete act in progress; it is a dramatic process rather than a stable duration, a multitude of the imperfect rather than a unity of the complete.

If in this way we have denied the absolute to the concept of being, if in this idea "everything" is not filled only with being, we must allow, in addition to being and against being, incomprehensible non-being, nothing, which opposes being.

Here we find ourselves beyond the limits of the conceivable. "Everything" takes on a paradoxical form, it is not only the sum of being and of the possible, but also of the impossible.

Nevertheless, the concept of the monad as a being in the realization process, exalting against nothing and undermined by it, capable of *being more* and *being less*, probably suits our most common empiricism.

They are necessarily from the same — being. They are necessarily different — imperfections. For being is essentially and necessarily imperfect, in acquiring perfection it would cease. They are identical and able to communicate with each other where there *are more*; actually, they do so through the phases of this process. They break down into unique individuals, where there are fewer, where the phase fades and falls by the wayside.

VIII. Let us return after this excursion to our question of whether we can rightly find in a work of art an imitative component and an expressive component, which — even if bound to the autonomy of a work of art — breaks them down into two quite disparate meanings.

After what we have said, we can entirely reject this concept and compare the theory to the completely uniform appearance and behaviour of a work of art.

The subject, establishing the expressive aspect of a work of art, and the object, establishing its imitative aspect, are essentially identical.

It only depends on whether the order, in which a work of art is realized, is shared by the subject and object, whether it happens where the universe is concentrated, consolidated and secured, or where it is scattered, crumbling and fading out.

This is precisely a matter of the autonomy of a work of art, and in it its function comes to light. Through this autonomy, a work of art situates itself where the universe "is more", where "it establishes itself", where "it is floating in the air, supporting itself", where it is its own "miraculous design".

A lack of autonomy deprives a work of art of clarity and universality. Owing to this shortcoming — an exclusively "artistic", "formal" deficiency — it falls either on the side of the subject and expressivity, or on the side of the object and imitativeness. It occupies a place where the universe "is less". It becomes exclusive: comprehensible only to a certain circle of people, to a certain age.

IX. The timelessness and supra-personal qualities of a work of art, its ability to break loose from the personal, the strange, the temporary, in a word, its *universality* is a most wonderful phenomenon.

We do not understand, nor will we, the language, customs, hopes, misfortunes or joy of he who carved this wooden sculpture or composed this song. What we may be able to track down from this, we reconstruct only for our understanding; but we cannot relive anything from his life.

And yet it is through a work of art that we communicate with him across all the space and time that separate us, that make us non-beings to one another. It does not matter that objects that the artist depicted here, that the specific function that he assigned to the work of art, that the entire worldview within which he lived, that the subjective state from which he created the work of art fell long ago through the timbering of time to a bottomlessness that turns former existence into non-existence. It is through the work of art that we are with him. We are together in the depths where *the world is made.*

A work of art — created, perceived — places the artist in the most heightened existence.

An aesthetic view of things is not "admiration devoid of interest". This saying contains *contradictio in adiecto.* If it is admiration, then it is full of extreme interest: of ardent and heroic love for the world, for things, for the living.

It is through a work of art that the subject appears in the mutual presentation of objectivity, ceases to be a being closed within himself, standing within himself, and recognizes himself as a participant of the universe, as dependent on the universe as the universe depends on him; the being of the universe is within him, just as his being is within the universe. They are both co-essential.

X. Co-essential beings are also interchangeable. The object thus becomes the subject.

The world, discovered through art, is not a set of obsolete facts; the subject and object make themselves mutually present as events.

The object-event is recognized by the subject-event. Therefore, this or that object, e.g. a landscape, can be depicted as a sad event — it can be portrayed through grief. The artist did not use it to merely illustrate his psychological state; it is in fact a sad event, one paragraph of the universe's infinite story.

The same object in another work will be by the same justification a happy event — pleasant, terrifying, festive — and often ambiguous, where admiration and ridicule, pleasure and pain intersect...

The greatest works of art are inarticulate. They capture the great many meanings of the story that is the universe and that is humankind. They are in its fullness.

XI. The existence of a monad depends on it itself being an "attempt by the universe to exist", a universe "once again", a microcosm. It is autonomous: "established within itself", it wants to be of itself and to endure of itself. Does the concept of autonomy formulated in this way really apply to a work of art? Is a work of art really an autonomous, "self-supported" object?

A tree, a person, a crystal, an atom — these are able to use their own powers to defend themselves from destruction, to strive for their existence, "to make" themselves. A work of art, left alone, is merely a disfigured piece of wood, stone, a falling layer of clay, a rotting sheet of paper. It is garbage of the universe, dead debris — not a living monad. Therefore, *it is not autonomous*. It is fully dependent on people, enduring only if used by them. Its autonomy is fictitious.

If it is not autonomous, it is also not a reconstruction of an objective reality and does not reproduce it "once more". It is an illusion, an imitation of reality.

Similarly, it is not a reconstruction of the subject, another self. It is only its symbol.

Non-autonomy, fictitiousness, illusiveness, symbolism of a work of art — what causes this debacle?

We have said that a work of art is placed in this essence of being, where they disregard the fragmentation of the universe into monads, where they become concomitant, simultaneous and coexisting, where they enter into perfect and boundless communication. We will therefore communicate through it with anyone, regardless of our spatial and temporal conditions — but *not with an animal, and not with a stone!*

A work of art is limited by its humanity.

It is given in human speech and in human space, not in universal, absolute speech and space.

XII. It is through one's spatial view that the state of objects is established and arranged. A space is not an emptiness into which things are placed, but a constitution, an order of objectivity.

If we stick to the premises that we have indicated up to this point, it is not possible for human consciousness to arrange, to conceive things in a way that is the exclusive creation of human subjectivity and has nothing to do with the authentic, autonomous means of the existence of "things themselves".

When we rejected the existence of a universal order of things, while accepting individual, monadic variations of this order, we must consider in this sense the three-dimensional space of our consciousness as one of these variations. It is not the same as a space, a constitution — or rather spaces, constitutions — things themselves — but it is also not absolutely different from them.

However, a work of art can only be presented in this altered space, which is otherwise imperfect than other spaces. Where this space does not apply, it ceases to exist as a work of art and is "dead debris".

There is no universal, absolute space.

A Euclidean space is the only means by which a work of art can approach the state of being of objects; yet this space also does not belong to these objects, they do not fit into it.

We have noted that it is not a void into which things are placed. Yet it is used, transferred into the realm of habituality, which it is considered to be. Dynamic in its origin, it is detached from things and becomes static. It indifferently possesses a fullness that no longer consists of things but merely three-dimensional message boards of its identification marks, symbols of its practical meaning, usual conventions, whose identification to things "about themselves" is sacrificed for the sake of a quick and comfortable handling of them. The person we meet is a kind of three-dimensional stand, useful only to the extent that it bears the marks by which we recognize this "something" to be a person — one of a certain sex, age, social status, etc., but is no longer a visible and tangible being, presenting himself to us through his colours, contour, surface and corporeality. He has become his own hieroglyph; his appearance means him; he himself is merely a concept, an idea, an abstraction.

Conversely, the matter of *art* is to return the human capacities of a spatial view to its original function, when it equips a system of objects from the energy field of the universe, capturing them in their own vivacity, unpredictability, variability and mobility. Therefore, in painting and in sculpture, instead of grouping things in conventional units of objects, their qualities of space, form and colour, corresponding to the primary features of their autonomy, to their being "about themselves", are accentuated.

Therefore, art sacrifices the conventional recognizability of things for its artistic purposes. Its realism lies in its "unrealistic-ness": it is true in how it does not resemble "reality" — i.e. its practical scheme.

XIII. Similarly, speech chases the universe from the unknown of its non-human realm. It captures a world of time and space, a world of substances and actions, of nouns and verbs, a world of sentences. It is the force that compels things to approach us. Without words, they would not be accessible to us.

But as the spatial view from an original vital fulness diminishes into a schematic void, so does speech, when from the medium of communication with reality it becomes a medium of communication between people. It escapes into conventional abstracts, whose identicality to the object is no longer verified.

The essence of art is, however, to use speech in its original function to help penetrate living things; to force speech upon them so that once again the non-stagnant, mutually continuous, mobile and active approach us.

Philosophy begins simultaneously with poetry: with faith in logic. Let us call it the verbality of the universe; with faith that the universe's attire is the same as that of speech, of the word, of logos.

If the word is identical with things, then the ability to speak, the ability to form words is the ability to create things, and the Word is the primary cause of the universe; God is the Word, just as the Fourth Gospel says.

However, if that created was enthralled and disturbed by sensorial matter, we will return them to God in a word.

Then words, being co-essential with things, have the ability to directly affect them. A poem is the right to be a magical spell.

XIV. If the spell does not summon, the image does not come to life.

A work of art, being fiction, acquires reality only if it is *used* in the other, real life of the individual. Used *separately*, it is an immoral escape from reality into fiction.

Milada Součková: On the Contemporary Novel

> *Man sei sich bewußt, daß der Roman als Form im Sinne des Dramas oder der festen Formen der Lyrik noch kaum existiert. Seine Form, selbst beiden berühmtesten Beispielen der Weltliteratur, ist meist das simple Nacheinander mittelalterlicher Epik, aus der Prosaroman als gesunkene Kunstform hervorgegangen ist.*
>
> *Sein Problem aber ist im Grunde das Problem der Gestaltung der Zeit.*
>
> Eugen Gottlob Winkler

That is the motto I put at the head of my novel. What kind of novelist, you ask, claims to have the authority to testify against it in her own case?! It sounds contradictory, and yet it is so: Even though I write novels, I do not believe in the future of the novel, at least not as it has appeared to us and continues to appear on average in its latest period of development. I do not believe that the production of novels, which was more a kind of commercial-financial system than art, should have a future. Just remember those stellar novels, presented to you at a dizzying speed one after another through advertising. They left behind nothing more than the habit of reading "novels". What certainty, what encouragement, what magic, what morality, what imagination, what feeling, what knowledge or reality does this production of novels leave to its readers?

Why were most of these novels so bad? Because they disregarded reality, employing it only superficially and using almost exclusively proven means of expression to convey it. Unless life was too much of a hindrance, unless there was too much of a schism between it and the novel, everything went quite smoothly, at least on the outside. Yet the present increasingly demonstrated the unbearableness of the novel's form, infinitely varied.

Now we hear the call that the modern age needs its artists, that they should stand and face it.

If we are helpless, one thing is for sure: it will not be possible to express the new reality with old forms.

In a recent issue of *Europäische Literatur*, we read that the drama of the present is being created, is alive and will be written, but that one demand can be made of contemporary artists: that their craftsmanship reach a level that would prepare for and correspond to the requirements that will be placed on them.

Surprisingly, however, many artists, in an almost alarmed state, believe that they will find salvation by taking refuge in the past. There is nothing more dubious than this. Just as an airplane cannot be constructed based on a steam engine, so is it impossible to build the epic of a new age with the technique of an old novel.

Although every artist and art theoretician will tell you that form and content are indivisible, it is privately acknowledged that new content can be expressed through an old form. There is little doubt that if the matter of form and content — with all its e.g. artistic and ethical consequences — were not just words in the mouths of artists, theoreticians and scholars, but were acted upon, we would rid ourselves of many unnecessary considerations.

Countless strenuous theoretical and practical attempts at the collective and proletarian novel have been doomed in advance because theoreticians and practitioners do not realize the simple demand that we are trying in vain to express the content of the worker's life through the slightly more sensitive technique of bourgeois novels.

Moreover, a departure from individualism is only theoretically subscribed to; in practice, novels are still based on individual, pseudo-psychological arbitrariness. We do not achieve general validity by diluting the individualism, but by enhancing it where it is included in a higher law.

Some time ago I read a statement by a Czech writer that his ambition was to write a novel "for maids". I'm not sure if this is the right approach. Instead, I think that a writer should, above all, write for a person, regardless of whether that person is a servant, a clerk, an artist, a worker or a minister.

Let's be specific: it is certainly easier to write for a wide-ranging women's magazine than for human society. You can argue that not every writer can be a national, European and international one. No, I will not call for romantic notions of the artist, who would rather fail than betray his great dream. I would rather remind you of Machiavelli's archers, who aimed high above the target, not to overshoot the target, but to hit it by compensating high.

Roman Jakobson: On Contemporary Czech Language Cleansing

I will stop at several examples, but I think that even these examples are sufficient to shed light on the pseudo-scientific nature of the methods and aims of this outspoken purism that censures the linguistic store of the written Czech language, authoritatively strikes off numerous words and phrases of this store, and, by doing so, ineluctably impoverishes the written language. Quite often this "confiscation praxis" of Czech linguistic cleansing shakes a norm that has already achieved general approval, and in some cases it directly damages the stability of the written language and causes linguistic confusion. An expert warns that "it is not easy to replace an old, widely used technical term with a new expression" (*NŘ* XV, p. 130). However, the editorial board of *Naše řeč* [Our Language] remains implacable. This established and widely used term is a Germanism in its origin, and so away with it, away, even though the expression has already become so domesticated that it has been incorporated into folk etymology — that is, "*ex post* something is inserted into this expression which — judging by the German root — was not even in it originally" (ibid., p. 131). "Something to which you have become accustomed (custom is a second nature) always seems natural," declare the editorial board, "and what is new and to which you are first supposed to become accustomed always seems unusual." Precisely convention is a characteristic feature of specialist terminology, but the verdict of *Naše řeč* is a different one: We should cease to use the accustomed term and get used to a novel one.

Let us emphasize once again that the slogan of a struggle against established Germanisms cannot be scientifically justified. Inherited Germanisms in the Czech written language are the same legacy of the cultural past as, for example, the close connection between Czech Romanticism and German Romanticism or the dependence of the ideology of the Czech Revival, in particular the idea of Slavic kinship, on German philosophy.

Haller incorrectly contends that, among the genetically non-Czech elements, only "rare exceptions that we can easily count on our fingers" have penetrated deeply into the Czech language (*Rádce* 1). For a Russian, who has a command of Czech and German, it is easier to translate from one of these languages into the other than from these languages into Russian or *vice versa*. French and Yugoslav philologists have also told me of the same experience. The similar statement by Polish linguist [Aleksander] Brückner concerning the deep permeation of Czech by German phraseology and semantics is well known.[1]

The close association of the Czech language to the German language is a reality of many hundreds of years and a consequence of the fact that for a very long time the Czech educated class has been partly bilingual and closely connected with German culture. When the language cleansers root out a handful of Germanisms, this is a kind of exemplary punishment and there is an essential element of arbitrariness in it.[2]

Even in purist articles a decent number of evident Germanisms remain. For instance, in Haller's article in *Obchodní čeština* [Business Czech] (XIV, 189—196) the following examples of foreign-influenced speech can be ascertained:

> "okruh, v němž se pohybuje její frazeologie", "libuje si v ustálených formulích a obratech", "překážka, která se staví v cestu nápravě", "nepopiratelná potřeba", "kapacity", "aby se náprava provedla přes noc", "pomůcky", "k jisté sebekázni", "že by se mnoho a právě největších chyb napravilo", "poroučíme se vám v úctě".[3]

In places where we would rather expect a reflexive verb, in Haller's article we find a passive verb, which Zubatý in *Naše řeč* has pronounced as a bad habit.

For example, "byly již podnikány rozličné pokusy", "tímto nedostatkem je ovšem jednak podporován velmi vydatně ten vliv německý, na nějž stále poukazuji, jednak

1 Dzieje jezyka polskiego [History of Polish Language], 3. ed., 1925, 283 n.

2 Let us concede that our explanation is erroneous and that *Naše řeč* is really cutting out all fundamental foreign elements in the language. However, the sum of all these foreign elements that *Naše řeč* admonishes is so poor and monotonous that inadvertently two questions arise. The first: When the index of fundamental errors in the case of all current-day authors is in essence almost the same and when these errors are occurring even more often in spite of the reproaches that *Naše řeč* has been repeating with admirable persistence for 15 years, would it not be more economical and more realistic to acknowledge the victory of usage and simply forgive these epidemic mistakes? The second: If this index of bad speech is so limited, then what justifies the language cleansers to speak, as Haller does, about a "general decline of language," about a "dismal period," about "linguistic poverty," about a "decrepit Czech language," about an "impossible state of affairs," and so on? I think that M. Weingart is rather correct: "In the thousands of years of the history of the Czech language there are few periods of its flowering equal to our period" (*Čas. pro mod. Fil.* XVIII, 1932, 114).

3 Author gives examples of German-influenced vocabulary, phrases and grammatical structures in the Czech language that have become so natural for Czech speakers that Czechs do not perceive their German origin.

zdržován vývoj k lepšímu", "je tedy jejich české vyjadřování ustavičně vydáváno vlivu němčiny".[4]

We can see that wiping out Germanisms is rather a demonstrative statement than a factual assessment of the state of the language. This is, therefore, a matter of language policy and it is necessary to pose the question of its justification. This policy cannot be described as a nationalistic policy; a more suitable term would be racism. After all, Germanisms are persecuted here only for their presumed distant origin. They are persecuted, even though for Czech linguistic feeling they have become absolutely domesticated, and so a person inexperienced in etymology finds out with surprise that these expressions are all of a sudden denied their domestic rights.

"Beginning with the 17th century... great caution is needed," warns Haller. "The same caution is, however, also necessary in the case of expressions for which a partial continuity can be ascertained only back to the 18th century or the 19th. It would hardly be beneficial for the language to accept such expressions without criticism because they may be of any kind of origin" (Probl. I, 4). Not even the existence of a word in the "linguistically undamaged" 16th century is a guarantee against the reservations of the language purifiers: "Veleslavín-era Czech cannot be a model for current-day written Czech... for the reason that this Czech is itself disrupted by German and Latin influences."[5]

The slogan of the struggle against Germanisms had an absolutely different significance in the period of Austro-Hungarian rule than it has today. At that time the Czech intelligentsia and the entire nation was constantly threatened with the danger of gradual Germanization.

The specter of Germanization is over and gone. Many former Germanisms have long ago lost their undertone of foreignness for the linguistic consciousness, unburdened by bilingualism. Precisely as it would no longer occur to anyone to exclude, for instance, Gebauer from the nation on account of his German father, as happened in the course of the manuscript battles in the press[6]. That is why Haller's pathetic questions sound like empty phrases: "And today, when we are building our national life from the foundation again, are we supposed to leave precisely our maternal tongue, which makes a nation a nation, simply in the wretched state into which it was brought by the haughty dominion of our national enemies? Not to want that the liberation of the nation be completed by liberating our language from all

4 Author gives examples of Haller's own use of passive constructions in Czech, which language purists criticize as German influenced, rather than reflexive verbs, which purists promote as better Czech usage.

5 V. Ertl, *Časové úvahy o naší mateřštině* [Historical Deliberations on Our Mother Tongue]. Daniel Adam of Veleslavín (1546–1599), Czech lexicographer — transl.

6 In 1886 linguist Jan Gebauer disputed the authenticity of alleged ancient Czech manuscripts, later proven to be fakes.

the traces of foreign rule that even more than Marian columns recall our national humiliation?" (*Rádce* I).[7]

Those who thunder against foreign elements in speech should not forget that there also exist *actions calquées* (adopted actions), to which a flavor of foreignness is also attached no less than to *mots calqués* (adopted words). Contemporary Czech language cleansing also belongs to such actions. Immediately in the first issue of the first year of *Naše řeč* a model of this is given: "Already for several decades an attempt can be observed in neighboring Germany to cleanse the language of foreign words. Bismarck also wished the movement well and officially supported the effort. The last war years strengthened this movement especially powerfully. The current relationship to France has already led to the replacement of French words with German ones, but Germany's consciousness of its own power and self-sufficiency is also making itself apparent in this cleansing of the language. Naturally, the waves of this movement quickly also rolled toward us."[8] Further, direct reference is made to the *Verdeutschungs-Wörterbücher* — that is, to a publication of that renowned Sprachverein whose language policy, one-sided and chauvinistic, has been criticized on more than one occasion by leading German scientists and writers.

In the first year of *Naše řeč*, there are some very interesting explanations of the functions of language cleansing. In the policy statement contained in the article "What We Want" the fundamental factors of current language changes are correctly captured: "busy, versatile life; bustle of everyday work; frequent interaction with foreign elements." However, instead of acknowledging the inevitable influence of these factors on the language, the declaration calls for a fight against this influence, which allegedly "corrodes, violates, and destroys Czech words in newspapers and in public offices, in schools, in literature, and in social conversation." In other words, it calls for a dispute between contemporary life and language. The battle against the connection between language and the present consciously takes its place within the framework of invectives against modern culture in general: "We have civilized Prague, and after it the countryside, with "kinos" and "bios" [terms for cinemas]; we have filled the theater, literature, and the newspapers with flirtatious titillation,

7 "Let us firmly hope," wrote Zubatý, rejecting the cleansing proscriptions of a certain Dr. J. H. in Czechoslovakia, "that Dr. J. H. will not be helped even by his strong words about those people who are 'also patriots' but who 'are making a beautiful language into a subsidiary Cinderella and are unaware of the crime they are committing on their nation by constantly supporting only the foreign at the expense of the beautiful inheritance of their own mother tongue…' and Dr. J. H. could also receive a surprise if — with his 'corrections' — he was to come across a more vigorous Czech who would thank him precisely with the words: Get lost and leave me in peace." (*NŘ*. XIV, 36).

8 In the same number of *NŘ* a journalistic voice advocating the cleansing of the Czech language is cited with approval: "That this tendency cannot be underestimated, we can see from the fact that in Germany the cleansing of the language is taking place with the direct assistance of the Berlin police director. In other words, the Germans today regard the purity of their mother tongue as almost as important as efficient food provision or order in military affairs. The slogan 'for cleansing of the mother tongue' has also been brought to us" (24).

piquant "witticisms," and translations of dubious value; Parisian cabarets have become the tenth muse of our arts — it is a surprise that the other nine muses have not deserted us; Prague and after it the countryside have been destroying our old monuments with delectation and, in their place, have been building mostly monstrosities; in Prague we have built a new part of the city that could just as easily serve new Berlin or new Budapest; new linguistic forms, abominations that are distasteful to the point of vulgarity, have spread from Prague to the countryside." (I, 65)

The conclusion remains: It would be incorrect to regard the recent passionate polemic over language cleansing as a sign of a conflict between Czech literary artists and current-day linguistic science. On the contrary, as V. Mathesius already emphasized in 1929, "on the question of linguistic correctness, a linguist, regarding language from a functional standpoint, holds out his hand to the artist who uses language creatively. This is no accident." There is no dispute between writers and linguistic science, but rather a healthy resistance on the part of Czech writers against an attempt to impose a reactionary language policy, an attempt that can only pretend to be scientific.

Jan Mukařovský: Dialectical Oppositions in Modern Art[1]

In attempting to outline the dialectics of modern art, we should first state what we consider to be modern art. The concept of "modernity" is extremely vague; its vagueness is caused by it being considered, at times, a distinct value, though at other times a mere designation of time. We are not at all concerned with its use as a value assessment, but only in its demarcation of time. Nevertheless, we must decide on our own responsibility, for even if we can justify our decision, someone else could set different boundaries and have their own reasons for them.

Given the purpose we have in mind, modern art begins for us at the boundary between the Realist/Naturalist period and symbolism in literature and at the dividing line between impressionism and post-impressionist art in painting.[2] A common feature of the developmental period beginning with this double divide is the suppression or, if you will, the breakdown of the individual. To be clearer, let us go back deeper into the past, back to the first half of the 19th century, to Romanticism. There is no doubt that Romanticism, at least in some of its manifestations, is closer to today's art than to the period immediately preceding that of today's art, i.e. the period of Realism, Naturalism and Impressionism. Ample evidence could be introduced: for instance, contemporary Czech poetry repeatedly returns to Mácha's poetry, not out of Platonic admiration, but to seek assistance from this Romantic in resolving structural problems that it itself faces. The answer to the question of wherein the similarities between Romanticism and today's art lies is not a difficult one: in both periods an artwork is intensely felt as a mere sign, and between this

---

1 Given as one of a series of lectures on modern art organized by the Mánes Union of Fine Artists in January 1935.

2 However, Impressionism is also an extreme case of the Realist-Naturalist tendency and the first stage of rejecting an imitation of nature.

and reality there is no absolute and necessary similarity. During the period of Realism that took place between them, there appeared, in contrast to this, a tendency, increasing throughout the period, aimed at suppressing the factors that can stand between reality and an artwork — above all, subjective feeling, or even any objective assessment for that matter. The ambition of a poetic Naturalist is to provide a scientific document, the ambition of an Impressionist painter is to adequately capture the bare sensory perceptions before any interpretation as the immediate equivalents of the physiological reaction to external impulse. (However, we are only speaking of a tendency, not of the possibilities and degrees of its realization.)

The common feature of Romantic and contemporary art is thus aiming for the distance between empirical reality and its reflection in art; this distance is achieved by deforming empirical reality. In addition, however, there is also an essential *difference* given by the individual's participation, distinct in each of these periods, in deforming reality. In Romanticism, the individual transforms this reality into his own responsibility: it is a revolt of the individual against a reality that is already modified at the moment of perception by social conventions. It does not matter whether in the given case the individual is strong enough to bear this responsibility (titanism) or whether he succumbs to it (*Weltschmerz*, Werther's sorrows). The individual's responsibility is related to the strong application of emotionality — see, for example, the lyricizing of the epic in the so-called Byronic narrative poem. In the period that we have called modern, the situation is different in this respect, as poetry in particular clearly shows. The individual, as a stronghold of noetic certainty, was suppressed in the Realist-Impressionist era: the only task assigned to him in the famous statement: "*la nature vue à travers un tempérament*" by the leader of French Naturalism was that of a wholly secondary coloring of the treated reality. At a time when in the natural developmental antithesis to this period of documentary fidelity the tendency to deform reappears, it is no longer the individual who could take responsibility for violating social convention, through which empirical reality is woven at the very moment of sensory perception. Symbolism, the poetic style standing on the threshold of this period, clearly testifies to this in its desire for the extreme objectification of artistic expression, i.e. for an "absolute" work of art, which, being as far as possible removed from empirical reality, from the basis on which people of the same time and social area would most likely agree, would nevertheless apply — and precisely for this reason — as an unchanging value for people of all periods, places and social backgrounds. In its quest for objectification, Symbolism has gone so far that its weight suffocates the poet's creative ability. The Symbolist experiment resulting in Mallarmé's desperate motto: "A roll of the dice will never abolish chance" (meaning that it is impossible to create an absolute work of art not dependent on a person), shows the horror of the individual who has succumbed to Symbolism and the hopelessness of the situation thus created. Never before had modern art arrived at a formulation so extremely focused against the individual, and yet the suppression of the individual as the one shouldering the responsibility for the deformation is common to all phases of artistic development to this day. Futurism, for instance, explicitly declares in the words of its fomenter Marinetti that "the "I' must be destroyed in literature"; Dadaism, while wanting the extreme disruption of empirical reality, so impeccably removes any personal responsibility of the individual that it leaves decision-making to pure chance.[3] One could object by citing Expressionism — art based on emotion, even escalated emotion. However, I would respond that Expressionism, by its nature and failure, provides proof to the contrary. The "immeasurable feeling" (*das mąßlose Gefühl*; K. Edschmid), from the viewpoint of which this artistic current views reality, strives for an objectification that can even border on the ontological; the ambition of Expressionism is to construct art as metaphysics. It is the impossibility of this objectification that is the cause of its failure, enabling W. Hausenstein to write in his argument against Expressionism: "We are tempted to think that Expressionism is not only far from objectifying the world, but that it is the most extreme excess of subjectivity that ever existed." Thus even Expressionism aims to objectify and founders in its impossibility.

It is natural that in this state of things one cannot speak of the noetic responsibility of the individual; even his complete breakdown is occurring: "The past concept of individuality is threatened. This also applies to individuality in which everything is in flow, in which discontinuity and disaggregation is everywhere, so that one loses oneself, breaking down into a series of reactions and explosions that are unrelated, with no common thread of reasonable purpose." (F. X. Šalda in *Zápisník*) Contemporary art is swayed by two opposing tendencies: one leads to the deformation of empirical reality, to its corrosion, while the other prevents this deformation from being based on the noetic responsibility of the individual as a measure of all things. Nevertheless, this also closes the path to material reality, to the realm whence the impulses activating a person's sense came, a realm that therefore exists independently of people, but of which people are part. Although like modern art, Romanticism rebelled against empirical reality, it differed from it in that it had access to reality, independent of people and their relationship to the world, via the individual, whose free will, unrestricted by social conventions, appeared to him as direct testimony to the existence of this reality, of which people are part; although Realism, in contrast, relinquished the individual as a guarantee of the existence of this reality, it found a new guarantee in the belief in a precise parallelism of empirical and material reality. Though modern art adopted from the Realist period a distrust in the first, Romantic guarantee, in the developmental antithesis it also rejected the second guarantee, which had been accepted by Realism.

However, we must not confuse or misidentify different things: if in modern art the individual is excluded from noetic responsibility, the artist's individuality is in no way by this removed as a factor in the structure of an artwork. In this sense, it is more freed and strengthened by removing the noetic responsibility, so that

3 Dadaist depersonalization is, however, different than that of symbolism: the symbolists rule out chance in the name of order, the Dadaist rule out order in the name of chance.

today, more than ever, a unique shade, a unique coloring of the work is applied and also required by critics and viewers; even individual works of the same artist or the various periods of his work are individualized relative to each other. Structural individuality or uniqueness is even becoming an important criteria of a work of art's value.[4] It is worth mentioning that in recent years the artistic direction tasked with re-establishing the individual as a fulcrum in art's contact with material reality has become all the more programmatic. This is Surrealism. In its deformational relationship to empirical reality, it is incorporated into the developmental cycle of modern art; traces of Dadaism are especially evident in it. From the noetic perspective, however, it is led by the effort to re-establish contact with material reality — by way of individuality. However, it does not attempt to reconstruct the Romantic, psychological individual who consciously supports his noetic validity, but returns to the biological individual. For Surrealists, the individual is a natural phenomenon; hence the attempt, during artistic creativity, to penetrate, if possible, to those layers of psychological life that seem closest to the biological base, i.e. to various types of psychic automatism, and to dreams, etc. Through the biological individual freed of social relations, the Surrealists intend to make direct contact with a material reality that is to be newly revealed to humankind. Furthermore, if the Romantic individual has ostracized his bearer from other people, Surrealism assumes that the biological individual, although typologically differentiated by dispositions, does contain enough traits accessible to a general, supra-individual understanding. Yet these differences between Romanticism and Surrealism cannot prevent analogies from being discovered; for example, Surrealism's interest in dreams is closely related to Romantic art's similar interest: it was not only Mácha from the Czech Romantics who recorded his dreams and used them poetically; materials published recently by Grund show that Erben also did so. Finally, it should be noted that the picture we have tried to provide in the above paragraphs is necessarily schematic. Terms such as Romanticism, Realism and the likes cannot be thought to capture the entire range of the real state; therefore, the distinctions we have made and everything based on these divisions apply only in the roughest outline; we must not forget that, for example, a plethora of poets were already emerging in the Realist-Naturalist period of the 1870s that were directly a part of modern art (Rimbaud, Lautréamont).

A common feature of modern art is, as we have shown, the suppression of the individual, in particular the complex, and therefore distinctly unique psychological individual, which, with its mere presence, underscores the a work's unity. Under these circumstances, a clearly objective artistic construction appears before the perceiver's eyes, accompanied by numerous dialectical contradictions woven into it. It is no coincidence that art theory has developed concurrently with modern art in various ways and realms towards a concept of artistic structure as a contin-

4 Cf. F. X. Šalda, Introduction to the *Soul and Artwork*: "A true assessment is nothing more than proving the uniqueness of the phenomenon in question, its tragic creative dramatic character that will never again be repeated."

uous series of developments existing in the collective consciousness and evolving in part due to the contradictions it contains. The structure appears to be free from a dependency on the individual and on material reality, but this also disturbs its balance. Antinomies, which are always submerged in art, rise clearly to the surface. A work of art appears as a set of opposites. Each of its components is both itself and its opposite ; similarly, an entire artwork is in an antithetical relationship to what is outside it. A heightened dialectical tension in modern art often occurs through a unilateral emphasis of one of the two members of the antinomy in question. For instance, if there is a contradiction between the aesthetic function and other, subordinate functions of art, the aesthetic function is either marginalized (see *l'art pour l'artism*, which has been applied several times in modern art as a seminal rule) or else completely denied (see modern architecture). Related to this strong antinomicity is the tendency to arrive at the final consequences (see a predilection for experiment). For instance, if it is a matter of purifying painting from non-painting means, this path will end with Suprematism and Neoplasticism, which removes from the painting not only objects, but also any plasticity, drawing aspects and finally even the painting's frame so that the color is the only element on which the painting is conceived. Similarly, the pursuit of "pure" poetry has ultimately led in the final consequences to a denial of all elements of poetry, except for sounds and their compositions (poems in an "artificial language"). It should be noted, however, that sometimes there also occur cases in which an enhanced dialectics is achieved in modern art not by emphasizing a single member of the antinomy, but, on the contrary, by intense oscillation between the two members: examples will be given in discussing the pairs truthfulness/fictitiousness and subjective expressiveness/symbolic objectivity of a work of art.

Let us start with the dialectical contradiction between art and society. In no era and in no art has the relationship between these two areas been so direct and tranquil that art fully expressed a kind of "spirit of the age". This is because society itself is always stratified and is never based on the tension between the individual components and on their mutual movements. Art, generally linked to the certain class that bears it, is also incorporated into this tension and movement; though it is possible that the bearers of different art, or even of different types of the same art are, at a given time and society, different classes. Today, however, the state of things, which has been prepared since the last century, has come to a head and art has been stripped of the solid social base given by its connection to a certain class. It is no longer a clear-cut relationship between artist and recipient. The artist often creates his works for unknown and socially indeterminate recipients, e.g. in painting and sculpture the works are usually made for exhibitions, in which the work is subject to free demand, or entrusted for sale to dealers who are not always governed by contemporary tastes, but instead speculate on what future tastes might be. Instead of a buyer representing for the artist a precisely determined social milieu, the audience, a socially diverse and indeterminate group of individuals has now assumed an increasingly emphatic position between art and society. A symptom and gauge of the alienation between art and society is the development of art criticism, particularly in magazines and newspapers beginning in the previous century. The critic stands as an intermediary between the viewer and art, his influence extends to both sides, but his basic attitude is controversial towards both the artist and the viewer: it is against the will of both that he asserts his demands and feels most comfortable, unfettered by any obligations (see F. X. Šalda, *Criticism Through Pathos and Inspiration in the Fight for Tomorrow*). Even this circumstance is typical in that the stronger the critic's influence, the more diverse and random the group of individuals representing the audience; for instance, it is well known that the theatre critic is always directly more influential and feared than the literary critic, since the theatre audience, often varying from one performance of a play to the next, possesses much less cohesiveness and continuity than the literary public, which is relatively stabilized and therefore loyal to writers they once liked.

And so in the entire realm of modern art we can see a considerable distance between it and the social organization. Between art and society stands the viewer; between the viewer and art stands criticism, and neither criticism nor the viewer perform the task of a passive, firmly adhesive glue, but are instead restless elements — the viewer for its social diversity and variability, criticism for its bilateral polemical focus. It is therefore not an exaggeration to claim that art is socially uprooted in today's world. One notable consequence of this abnormality is an accelerated developmental pace. Schools and trends change rapidly and the contradictions between them are considerable. This is due to a detachment from the retarding influence of the social environment that in earlier times bound art with its demands. This detachment means that art has a heightened autonomy, which, under the weakened pressure of society, is left to its own, unhindered in its developmental dynamics. The weakened link to society also exerts its influence on the external organization of some arts: for instance, theatre has shown an increasing tendency to create small avant-garde scenes that, appealing only to a small circle of viewers, paralyse the theatre's social ambiguity.

Naturally, artists have a hard time dealing with the distance between society and their work. There arises antipathy towards the viewer, the variable. In the beginning of modern art the artist even tried to completely disregard the viewer. As we have noted, the Symbolists, longing for an absolute work, claimed that they do not even need a single reader (Mallarmé). Similarly, Futurism, in the words of Marinetti, proclaims that "we need not be understood" (Liberated Words). Even if the artist does not reject the audience, but instead desires it, the path to mutual understanding remains blocked; André Breton writes of this in Communicating Vessels: "A public for whom one speaks and from whom one would have to learn a lot to continue to speak but that does not listen; another public, indifferent or quarrelsome, that does listen". Yet rejecting the public does not necessarily mean rejecting the relationship between art and society. If we can assume that Symbolism — at least its most distinctives forms — strove for not only the de-socialization, but also the dehumanization of art in the sense of an absolute value independent of the viewer, this cannot be said of further developmental phases of modern art. It is merely an argument against the public, against a socially diverse crowd that is unable to provide art with security by way of the consistent flow of their demands. However, the aim of this argument is to restore the direct relationship between art and society itself, though certainly not with a single layer of it — a complete return to a previous stage of development is impossible here, as is the case in all other areas of development. The objective is to restore it throughout society, though one that is homogenous. This tendency is attested to by, among other things, the statements repeated by contemporary artist in various forms in which they claim that art will be unnecessary in a future society since all people will be artists. Although we may think this idea unfeasible due to the varying degree and types of aesthetic talent in individuals, nothing prevents us from interpreting such statements as an expression of the desire for the genuine injection of art into the life of society as a whole.

It is clear that the dialectical opposition between art and society, which has always been one of the most powerful factors in the history of art and also an important factor in the historic development of society, is very intense in modern art due to the mutual alienation of these two areas, but also strongly highlighted by the needs of both sides for a new mutual rapprochement. It is also worth mentioning that the effect of this unprecedented relationship between the two areas is also reflected in the structure of the artworks: as proof let us recall the strong tendency towards exclusivity, which is often applied in modern art as a factor in artistic composition; compare the various ways of concealing part of a subject, obscuring the verbal expression in poetry or complicating the overall apperception of a painting, etc. All of these various means run concurrent with the attempt to limit the public, as previously described.

Having discussed the opposition between art and the collective, the next matter at hand is the antinomy between art and the individual's psychological life, which can be expressed in the following formula: a work of art as an immediate expression of the subjective mental state — and as an objective sign mediating between the members of the same collective. A pure subjective expression is, for instance, a spontaneous cry of pain or joy. There is no denying that there is something in a work of art that resembles this cry: it can appear to be the equivalent of a mental state of both the originator and, as the case may be, the perceiver. Yet besides that a work of art is also a supra-individual sign, free of any subject, emphasizing only that which is open to general understanding. It is possible for a work of art to lean toward one of these extremes; cf. the opposite of Romanticism — Realism — which in some respects corresponds to this polarity. However, modern art, especially in some of its forms, prefers to oscillate between both extremes, simultaneously evoking an excitement that is distinctively intensified, but also making clear that the quality of this excitement is, given the real individual, irrelevant, merely functioning as a component of the artwork. This play is most pronounced, as is natural, in lyric poetry; Vítězslav Nezval himself has uttered it several times as part of his poetics, e.g. in the verse:

Today the poet leapt from the pulpit
With a soft hat instead of a helmet,
He stopped writing long ago under the moon
And even bid farewell to his audience
In lieu of feeling he has imagination

Feeling, as a component of a poem, is for Nezval the "filling in the pastry". Elsewhere he writes:

The immeasurable bliss creates in me an axis
on which I turn like the starry heavens
I swing on the still water, I swing on the pathos
I conquer on the wave of the festive heavens

The antinomy cannot be poetically expressed more clearly: pathos as an expression of immediate excitement and pathos as play, wholly incorporated into the structure of the objectified sign, outside the realm of which it loses its validity. However, it is also obvious that criticism, if aimed at overtly expressive poetry, can make such "I am playing with feeling" seem like the poet's cynicism.

Another antinomy based on the semiotic nature of art is the contrast between an artwork as an autonomous and communicative sign. This especially concerns art that works with a clear theme (content), such as painting (pictorial, not ornamental) and poetry. The theme is always to a certain extent a message about reality; yet in calling a thematic artwork an autonomous sign, we are referring to its property, that its content is not to this extent connected to a certain specific reality, so that it is possible to question its truth-untruth and to pose this question as one that is essential. If, for instance, we perceive and assess a novel as a work of art, we do not require that the event that it recounts corresponds to a true fact localized in a certain point of real space and time, although such a requirement would be completely natural and appropriate for any other — communicative — expression of language. However, art needs to be understood dialectically in this matter since, in all its autonomy, there is always the possibility that a work of poetry or painting contains a message. Yet from the perspective of art itself, the message contained in it only functions as a component of artistic construction. For instance, a typical trait in a realistic novel or painting is the attempt to evoke an *impression* of truth of that which it recounts, describes or depicts. But this is just an impression, e.g. an illusion evoked by the creative means of a work, not documentary veracity (cf. Jakobson's article "Realism in Art", *Červen* 1921). Thematic art thus oscillates between truth and fiction; sometimes an emphasis is placed on this, at other times on that branch of antinomy. In contrast to this, modern art emphasizes the antinomy between Fictiveness and Truth, often by intensifying the aforementioned oscillation, which it achieves through a complex stratification of the transient shades between the two poles. For instance, as Jakobson recently pointed out (*Slovo a slovesnost* no. 2), Vančura's *The End of the Old Times* plays on the border of truth and fiction by confronting two systems of fictional values — the feudal world and the world of the parvenues after the war, pretending both to be true. At other times, the real and fictitious are placed side by side so that there is not certainty about the individual details of the theme that it belongs to on both levels. See Nezval's *Like Two Peas in a Pod* and *Monaco*. The transition from a fictional to a real plan has already been used in Symbolist poetry, whose treatment of meaning is such that the developed poetic image changes with a slight of the hand into direct naming and vice versa.

In painting, which is related though not identical to these cases, there are reversals from objectivity to non-objectivity and vice versa, after removing the objectivity from realistically depicted things, etc.; thus even objectivity and non-objectivity form here a dialectical antinomy, whose tension is increasing in contemporary painting when compared with that of other periods. For instance, Cubist painting both breaks the object by disrupting its true contour, but also emphasizes its objectivity by allowing it to be viewed (though synecdochically) from many different perspectives at once so that its unity is felt as a crystallized spatial point independent of changes in the viewer's perspective. Futurist painting often makes from things characterized as tangible objects metonymies for intangible actions when e.g. the Futurist paints a bunch of things seemingly unrelated that, however, express street noise, whereas the individual sounds are expressed through beings and objects that are their originators. Even more intense is the transition from extreme objectivity to extreme non-objectivity in Surrealist painting, in which the objectivity of every individually depicted thing is emphasized, but at the same time it is indicated, through the unmotivated encounter of mysteriously diverse objects in the same image, that they are only metaphors for the completely non-objective hidden meaning of the whole. Even directions that seem to wholly exclude objectivity from a painting do not lose their relationship to it; there are even cases in which the dialectic reversal of absolute non-objectivity into a new total objectivity becomes apparent. Here we have in mind Suprematism, which in the argument against objectivity went all the way to the eradication of drawing and plasticity: the image, composed of colorful rectangles acting as a mere colorful quanta, not as contours, and thus perfectly non-objective as a painting, becomes the thing itself. A theoretical proponent of Suprematism (A. Behne, Von Kunst zur Gestaltung) states that the "new painting is not governed by an object that is a color only created through symbolism, fiction, representation, allusion, but is directly governed by colors used here not as allusions to something, but as that which they truly are and what they themselves apply as red, bright blue, dark green, etc." The Suprematist painting strives to such an extent to become a thing among things that the idea of a machine-made painting loses its absurdity in the eyes of Suprematists.

Thus we arrive at another antinomy — between the material and its use in a work of art; here we are concerned with the opposition between an artwork as an aesthetic structure — and the same work as a thing. Let us start with a simple example: a stone, such as a precious-stone, a piece of jasper, is a thing of certain real (physical, chemical, etc.) properties that our senses tell us about; however, once we assume an aesthetic relation to it, a change occurs: each of its properties — maintaining its real validity — also becomes, in its relation to the others as part of their whole set, a factor of the aesthetic state (Verhalten) that this set evokes in the viewer. A work of art is also both a thing and an aesthetic construction: the material in it is also the bearer of tangible properties; given its aesthetic effect, these properties then also become components of the artistic structure.[5] Material therefore has a considerable importance for the construction of a work of art: a marble sculpture is not just realistically, but also artistically something other than the same metal sculpture.

The specific properties of each material can be used in a work of art either positively, i.e. in a way that they are taking into account these specific traits, or negatively, i.e. in working against the traits. In both cases the material functions as part of the work's structure. Here too is modern art, as in other respects, increasingly dialectical: it draws strong attention to the raw properties of the material by leaving it enough distinctiveness to stand in opposition to the artistic structure, even though it is embedded in it. Typical of today's art is a predilection for unusual materials such as completely new ones by which they already draw attention to their specific traits and to their materiality. Leaving aside architecture, in which new materials can be at least partially explained by the boom in industrial production and trade offering an extraordinarily vast selection, we can take as an example in painting Moholy-Nagy's works that use as their base glass mirrors or metal plates not completely covered with paint and, instead of oil paints, sometimes employ varnishes. These paintings can even utilize completely new materials such as celluloid or gilalite. Often, in order to emphasize the material as a thing, attention is drawn in painting to its rawness, its unprocessed nature; e.g. glued pieces of paper or newspaper, playing cards and the like, to the painted surfaces of Cubist paintings. A similar case can be found — in the same School of Painting — in the realistic representation of the material's structure, e.g. of the annual rings in wood in the middle of a painting breaking the contour of the depicted object and standardizing the details in stereometric shapes, thus creating a non-realistic effect. Finally, we can also mention the relief modelling of some depicted objects using color paste, which is evenly applied over the rest of the painting's surface. The augmentation of the supply of materials and overt use of their properties is particularly reflected in the background of 19th-century painting, which mostly worked with a considerably reduced repertoire of materials, leaving other materials for lower forms of art.

---

5 In this sense, of all the types of modern art the unique position of film, which is the art of the youngest generation, is also symptomatic, and therefore most precisely meeting the demands of the age: While other forms of art — particularly theatre, the closest to film — show a tendency to limit the heterogeneity of the public, films aims at reaching the broadest social spectrum. More than any other type of art, the likes of Chaplin appear in film, corresponding to all levels of taste.

The dialectical opposition between the material and aesthetic function that a work of art acquires points to another antinomy between art and non-art, i.e. between products with a dominant aesthetic function and those that are either subordinate to another dominant function or do not have one at all. This antinomy is by no means restricted to modern art: the aesthetic function is always in contradiction with others, so that, even in art, it is pushed out of the leading position by another function and, conversely, outside of art it tends to become the ruling function.[6] In modern art, however, intensified deviations have appeared: sometimes the absolute domination of aesthetic function is proclaimed as principle and artistically realized (e.g. *l'art-pour-l'artism* in Symbolist and Decadent poetry); but at other times the proclamation is opposed to aesthetic function (e.g. Functionalist architecture theory). Yet both an extreme emphasis and denial of aesthetic function turn into their own opposite: the utmost exclusion of functions other than the aesthetic cause the aesthetic function to transform into another function, such as a moral ("What above all exasperates people of taste in the spectacle of vice, is that it is misshapen, out of proportion" — Baudelaire) or intellectual one ("Recognizing the beauty of the world is the objective of our endeavors" — Březina). On the contrary, the maximum denial of aesthetic function in functionalist architecture becomes a means of aesthetic effect (maximum efficiency = maximum aesthetic value). We should also add to the strong emphasis of opposition between art and other products of human activity the tendency, applied in modern art, geared toward such products that, though previously functioning as art at a certain time or place, or continue to do so as the case may be, do not, however, belong to the aesthetic canon of art in the environment for which the artist creates, since they are at odds with it. Take, for instance, the relationship between African and modern sculpture, or the trend towards "peripheral" art in poetry (e.g. Karel Čapek's essay "Marsyas" or Nezval's foreword to *Five Fingers* and some other typical instances in the works of both poets) as well as in painting (Josef Čapek's *The Humblest Art* and the works of Henri Rousseau). However, since such contact between "high" and "primitive" or "low" art also mean that a foreign aesthetic canon is brought to the artistic structure of a work, we will explore them in more detail when we come to the antinomy between "beauty" and its denial. Furthermore, the relationship between art and non-art is characterized by modern art's intensive relationship with machine technology (Civilist poetry, the convergence of machine production and the fine arts, the emphasis of machine intervention as an aesthetic factor in film and photography). The mutual oppositions between the individual arts are to some extent similar to that between art and non-art. Since, however, this does not concern art's contact with non-aesthetic areas, we will discuss them later.

The antinomy between art and non-art drew attention to the aesthetic function that forms the basis of art. We will therefore now turn our attention to inner an-

6 For more on this antinomy see e.g. Aesthetic Function and Aesthetic Standard as Social Facts, Social Problems, 1935.

tinomies of the aesthetic function itself, i.e. to the oppositions that arise in a work between the components acting as aesthetic factors. The first of these is the antinomy called (not exactly) the opposition between content and form. The relationship between these two groups of components into which a work of art is split (as far as thematic art is concerned) can be defined in various ways. We will use a definition that, though not entirely exhaustive, captures the essence of the matter for our purpose: content component in a work of art are those that usually appear to be determining; formal components are those that appear to be determined. In reality, however, content is always both determining and determined, as is form, for it is on this very tension between the determining and determined that the dialectical opposition between content and form is based. Modern art increases this tension and vigorously penetrates the content-form antinomy in that it shifts the primary emphasis to its non A, emphasizing form's determination of content. Thus, for example, modern poetry often develops content from form by deriving a theme from elements of language. Take, for instance, some of Nezval's lyrical poems in which the only (though changeable) continuous thread of the theme is given by the semantic chain of rhyme, or poems from Biebl's collection *Golden Chains* in which the thematic context is revealed by euphonic patterns. The culmination of this tendency in painting is a certain type of Expressionist painting: Wassily Kandinsky's "absolute painting", František Kupka's Orphism, some paintings by Josef Šíma and Štyrský's and Toyen's Artificialism, in which a rudimentary thematization (e.g. space, contour) is vaguely suggested by the distribution of colors (e.g. warm colors rising in the foreground and cold ones receding in the background) and by the guidance of lines (vague indications of objectivity using closed and unclosed contours).

It is also possible for the emphasized antimony of content and form to appear in such a way that form, while not altering its formal nature, also becomes the content. An illustrative example is provided by symbolist poetic images. Already in its relation to the thing that only indirectly indicates, the poetic image is clearly a matter of form. Yet in the case of symbolists, e.g. with Otakar Březina, it is often used in such a way that the developed image itself forms a minor thematic whole. Sometimes the narration of the entire story is given through the image — and only as an image. Take for example the following verses:

> None of the living lose their way here. Only resurrected by my eyes
> did sorrow rise from these place and, taking steps muted with fear,
> so as not to disturb the sleep of invisible brother, come to meet me.
> (The Sorrow of Matter)

The image of sorrow going forth with muted steps is already more than mere form: it is form dialectically transforming into content. Another example is provided by the "double" poetic images in Breton's *Communicating Vessels*, in which the same word acts both as an image, i.e. the formal matter, and as naming itself, directly related to the theme. The poetics of this kind of image has been provided by Nezval in several instances in his story *She Wanted to Rob Lord Blamington*. Here is one such example: "A novel. A sunset in a room. There are writers who want to paint this sunset with words. They observe the furniture, piece by piece, looking for reflections. Past literary schools used a mythological apparatus. This mystery can be evoked in a single sentence: The sun set. And a memory remained of it in the room. A rose in a glass beyond the window." The rose is here both the image of the sun, i.e. form, and an actual rose with all its characteristics, thus also content. The opposite case is also possible in which content, remaining itself, also becomes form. We have in mind here Cubist painting whose content is usually given clearly by the title alone. However, the title — e.g. Man with a Pipe — also largely determines the formal interpretation: if the painting did not have a title, the interpretation of its form would often be vague, and if it had a different title, the interpretation would change. The theme works here in a revelatory way as a formative factor.

In such ways — through the determination of content through form and through the dialectical transformation of form into content and vice versa — the opposition between content and form comes to a head in modern art. However, each of these groups of elements have its own inner antinomy that also achieves a distinct effect in contemporary art works. In a work of art, the inner antinomy of form is a factor that is both organizing and disorganizing. The main component of antinomy is, however, the organizing force of form; this is how form is generally understood and defined in theory. Yet modern art emphasizes negation; that is to say, the disorganizing power of form which, in its culmination, changes through a dialectical reversal into a new positive: into a reorganization by way of form. One of the most illustrative examples can be found in Cubist painting. Here, though form disorganizes the subject by depriving it of the unity of perspective and by transforming the parts in which it is decomposed into the regularity of stereometric shapes, it also organizes it into a new surface and contour unity. Similarly, Poetist verse begins by disassembling the causal connection of events brought by the theme from external reality and by replacing it with a new formal connection (such as compositional, purely semantic and rhythmic).

Content (the theme) also has its inner antinomy along with form's inner contradiction: this is the antithesis between uniformity and plurality. A work of art's content is, by definition, a semantic whole. At the same time, however, there is also plurality, which is divided into subordinate units, whose mutual semantic relation both disrupts and emphasizes the overall unity. For example, in the normal construction of an epic plot there arises tension from an unexpected sequence of events, whose connection into a semantic unity is initially impossible. Only through a denouement is the theme consolidated by fastening all of its parts into a unified meaning. Modern art often increases the dialectical antinomy between coherence and incoherence of a theme by presenting it so incoherently that each of its parts possesses a separate objective relationship (i.e. a relationship to reality, assumed to be the work of art or its theme). Surrealism has gone furthest on this path, composing in poetry themes out of the most varied facts, and in painting from subjects unlinked by anything other than the fact that they share the same frame. Even a unity enabled by form (e.g. through composition or rhythm) is rejected here. Yet the documentary nature of each of the facts given in a poem or the objectivity of each of the objects depicted in a painting is emphasized so that its incoherence has the utmost effect on the viewer. The combination of facts and objects mutually dissociated from each other in a semantic whole is left up to the viewer or reader. In this way, the theme's inner antinomy is underscored.

We could go down through the whole structure to the individual components and reveal the antinomies by which it is interwoven into the base, but an interpretation would require a detailed and art-specific analysis too lengthy for our purposes here. Nevertheless, we cannot ignore one of the most important antinomies — the opposition of beauty and its denial. We do not mean the conventional problem of the aesthetics of the "ugly", but that a work of art, especially in its initial freshness, evokes not only aesthetic pleasure, but also strong elements of displeasure by transgressing the traditional aesthetic norms. Modern art likes to intensify this feeling of transgression, which, however, does not mean the suppression of normality, but rather revealing and heightening it: the greater the transgression is emphasized, the stronger it must be felt. Contemporary art therefore likes to attempt to breach a norm with another norm. This is done by opposing the ruling canon of norms (= taste) with another canon that is also already fully formed within the system and developing its own distinct ideal of beauty, though valid somewhere outside the realm of "official" contemporary art. Examples of this were given above when discussing the opposition between art and non-art. Instead of denying a single set of norms (canon), oscillation occurs between a set of two, generally within the structure, in that some groups of components are subject to one canon, others to another (e.g. the sentence structure against the choice of words in poetry). However, it is also possible for contradiction to arise outside the structure if the work, constructed entirely on a foreign canon, is placed in the context of official art, whose canon then forms the background when viewing the work.

Finally, the last antinomy worth mentioning is the mutual opposition between the different arts — in other words, the contradiction between an art geared to another art and a "pure" art (i.e. "pure" poetry, painting, etc.). Each art can seek a way to other arts by emphasizing the components it has in common with other arts (e.g. themes linking poetry, drama, painting and film; rhythm and sound aspects bring poetry closer to music; the arrangement of light and shade, dimension and contour are shared by painting, sculpture and film). On the one hand, it attempts through its specific means to compete with the specific means of another art (see e.g. poetry trying to compete with the visual possibilities of painting; film completing with theatre and theatre with film). The mutual relations of the individual arts are also attested to by common metaphorical clichés used by critics, such as the "musicality" of poetry or of a painting, the "poeticity" of music or painting, or the "plasticity" of a poem or painting. The mutual relations can also lead to very complex relations; thus, for instance, the composition of Richard Wagner's music (characteristic motif, musical and authorized references) occur with an obvious inclination of the music to poetry. The novelist Thomas Mann consciously adopts — as an undercurrent — the Wagnerian principle of construction as a model for the compositional construction of his poetic works (see W. Schaber, *Thomas Mann zu seinem sechzigsten Geburtstage*). It is, however, also possible for a certain art to try to be itself by emphasizing the specific traits that distinguish it from other art. For instance, poetry could emphasize purely linguistical elements and painting could do so by emphasizing its colors. Both tendencies — towards "pure" art and to merging with another art — are taken to the extreme in modern art (see, for instance, poetry in an "artificial" language and Suprematism in painting; conversely, poetry symbolically merging with music and Surrealist painting identifying with poetry). Yet the dialectical pair often interestingly intersects with the subordination-superiority pair of aesthetic function. Take, for example, Symbolist poetry, which links its direction towards another art (music) with the emphasized supremacy of aesthetic function, or Constructivism in architecture, emphasizing the specificity of architecture while striving for subordination of the aesthetic function.

We have tried to show that modern art is built on dialectical oppositions, but not in the sense that there are no such oppositions in other developmental phases of art — indeed, they are a constant driving force of development, but in such a way that the oppositions, which are generally applied gradually, appear in droves and emphatically in modern art, acting overtly and intersecting one another. We showed at the beginning of this study the causes of this particular condition. Our objective was not to criticize modern art or to argue in its defense, but to attempt an experimental noetic characterization. Modern art is often characterized as a manifestation of the crisis of contemporary art and society. Such a characterization is only justified if it is not an expression of resentment for all innovative art, and only if it is accompanied by the knowledge of how much effort to reconstruct the world of values is in modern art, and how strong in its apparent chaos is the pursuit of order, though one which is dynamic.

Jan Mukařovský: The Individual in Art

In art the individual performs a dual function: The task of creator and perceiver befalls him or her. At first sight, these functions, even though inseparably connected, seem to be mutually contradictory, given that the first of them presumes an active approach, the second a passive one. However, their mutual exclusion is neither absolute, nor distinct. Every work of art has a certain similarity with the word: Just as a linguistic expression mediates between two individuals, one of whom speaks and the other of whom listens, a work of art is also intended by its author to serve as a means of communicating with the perceiving individual. In a linguistic expression the tasks of the author of the expression and the perceiver are far from being non-interchangeable. As a rule, the active role of the speaking subject falls alternately to each of the two persons engaged in the conversation, and the listening individual is not fundamentally deprived of the possibility of taking up the conversation. Here, meanwhile, we have the most fundamental form of linguistic expression, dialog. In art the situation is only seemingly different: Let us take as an example the environment creating folk art, where any kind of subject is potentially a creator and also a perceiver. And if we look at "high" art from this perspective, then we ascertain that there also — in the present and in particular in the course of its history — we ascertain traces, in many cases very distinct ones, of the same state of affairs: Here also the "passive" individual is far from having no influence on the creating of art, especially if he is a benefactor or the ordering party, expressing in advance his requirements.

In all its forms art has a lot of similarities with a continuous dialog, whose participants comprise on the one side all those who gradually create works of art, and on the other side those who are the perceivers of these works. Both sides are mutually dependent. Therefore, the blossoming of art in a certain country and the appearance of an entire group of creative talents always presupposes a high level of aesthetic culture — a level that can also be created by the previous import of foreign artworks — and can, therefore, rather be a fact of perception than of creation (compare, for example, the import of Italian creative art which preceded the blossoming of French painting in the period of the Renaissance). It is of course true that the perceivers form a collective, and our attention is focused towards the individual, but this collective, which we call the public, enters into a relationship with art only through the mediation of the individuals of whom it is comprised, and in addition it is also dependent on these individuals for its individualization, greater or smaller, its average capability to perceive works of the type of art that is in question in any given case. There is, therefore, a constant mutuality — given by the potential identity — between the creating individual and the perceiving individual even in cases when their tasks are, in practical terms, not interchangeable.

Another form of the problem of individuality in art is given by the relationship between an individual and the objective development of art. This development, which is autonomous, is determined by an immanent rule-based relationship, the source of which is the direction inherent to each structure to retain the identity of the developing structure. However, if this direction is to be put into effect, an opposite tendency is also necessary, which tendency is directed at the suppression of the identity of the structure. In other words, the immanent rule-based relationship requires as its necessary counterpart a chance event always coming once again from outside in order to cause a movement. And the task of this chance event is taken up precisely by an individual, primarily in that he becomes the bearer of various external influences (social, ideological) representing impacts that shake up the structure of art. However, even then, if we are to leave to one side all objective influences, the individual as such of her or himself still remains as an absolutely unique chance event. The question of external influences can, therefore, in the final instance be understood as an antinomy between a continuous line of immanent development and a range of constantly new creative individuals, each of whom through their impact bends the line of autonomous development without ever being capable of rupturing it.

The actual development is, of course, much more complicated than this schema and the individual is not so independent of the development that he is influencing as it may seem at first sight. Although it may seem a pure accident, nevertheless the mere possibility of his intervention is bound to the objective development. In every stage of this development there exist the seeds of several various possibilities for the future, several tasks that the creating individuals of the next generation can divide up among themselves. And it can happen that the group of individuals that this generation is going to have at its disposal will have either a greater or a lesser number of roles that need to be filled, or it may happen that for a certain serious task the coming generation will only have a weak individual at its disposal. In such a case a historian of art, comparing the parallel development of art in several countries, will ascertain irregularities and gaps in development there where the number of creative individuals was not commensurate to the number of tasks. If, on the contrary, at a given moment there are more individuals available capable of fulfilling this same task, then a competition will occur between two or more artists whose talent is identical; sometimes it will happen that one of the competitors will seek out a substitute role instead of the one that a stronger competitor has prevented him from occupying. Then again, in such a case when the only individual who is capable of occupying a certain important role is weak, then the historian will be able to ascertain an appreciable disproportion between the value of the artwork, which will be weak, and its historical significance, which will be considerable. It can also happen that an individual does not find a task corresponding to the degree of his talent. If he, nevertheless, has enough strength not to allow himself to be broken by this, then he will become an "accursed artist" whose work will be condemned to wait until sometime in the future when it may possibly encounter a developmental trend of some future period that will enable it to find understanding among the public. If a creating individual succeeds in finding a full accord with some developmental trend of his own period, he will blend so perfectly with his task in art that sometimes this will also influence his human relationships: mutual attraction, mistrust, or even hatred between artists sometimes reflects with surprising fidelity an affinity or respectively an opposition to the trends that these artists embody in their artworks. In summary, it can be said that, if the existence or respectively the lack of individuals endowed with a specific talent appears as a chance of birth, the possibility for an individual — even a talented one — of finding a role as an actor of development depends on the number and quality of developmental trends contained potentially within the development itself.

We should further add that the individual whom we have so far treated as though he or she were a constant is in essence him or herself an event. If we confront him or her with the development of art, then we are actually confronting a dual development. In addition to the question of the influence exerted by the individual on the movement of art, it is also necessary to pose the opposite question — that concerning the influence exerted by art on the development of the creative individual.

Just as we feel the presence of an authorial individual behind every work of art, so by projection every work of art also seems to us to be a unique and unrepeatable individual. The uniqueness of a work of art, at least in some periods, forms an important prerequisite of its positive evaluation; in other periods, less individualistic, it can seem that "originality" has only a secondary importance. This is why it is also not possible to give a definition of plagiarism in the field of art that is valid once and for ever.

In conclusion it is necessary also to say a few words about the relationship between a concrete individual, authorial or perceptive, and the abstract subject contained in the very structure of the work, a subject that is only a point from which this entire structure can be encompassed in one view. In every work of art, even the most impersonal, signs revealing the presence of this subject are to be found. This presence becomes entirely evident, for instance, in lyrical poetry, which expresses feelings; however, it is necessary to reckon with it also in the case of a painting whose perspective is calculated in the spatial placement of the subject contained in the work. Even naturalistic drama staged quite realistically differs from reality precisely in that it presupposes the presence of a subject (a stage without a fourth wall, etc.). A subject never merges — and neither can it ever fully merge — with any concrete personality, whether the author or the perceiver of a given work of art; in its abstraction it represents only the possibility of transmitting these personalities into the internal structure of the work. There exist works of art that force the perceiver to feel the author's personality as a subject, while there are other artworks that lead the perceiver to accept the role of the subject him or herself, and then again others in which the subject seems not to be present. The choice between these various possibilities is not left to the perceiver, but is determined by the structure of the work.

If one or several persons are depicted in an artistic work (epic, dramatic, or pictorial), these persons are felt as an embodiment of the subject or, if there are several of them, as a personification of the subject's internal conflicts; therefore, the perceiver feels compelled to identify either him or herself or the author with these persons. Here also the identification is rather a case of projection than of embodiment. The most substantive meaning of a depicted person should not be sought outside of the field of art, but in art itself. Each of the persons depicted in a work of art is, by the way in which it is depicted, a realization of a traditional type of "hero"; even in those cases when — under the influence of the historical situation or the artist's genius — it so happens that art creates a person who is truly unique (as, for instance, Don Quixote, Hamlet, Faust in poetry and in drama, or Apollo, Christ, etc. in the visual arts), then precisely on account of this uniqueness this person will gain in the future the validity and function of a type.

Original Sources

1. The Birth of the Avant-Garde: Between Avant-Garde, Expressionism, and Proletarian Art

1. Weiner, Richard. "Opona se zvedá"; "Na hradě." In *Třásničky dějinných dnů*, 3–5; 20–27. Brno: Polygrafie, 1919.
2. U. S. Devětsil. "[Doba se rozlomila]."*Pražské pondělí* 2, no. 49 (1920): 2.
3. Hora, Josef. "K novému umění." *Kmen* 4, no. 31 (1920): 364–367.
4. Mahen, Jiří. "[Stůjte a podívejte se!]." In *Měsíc: fantasie*, 19. Praha: Stanislav Minařík, 1920.
5. Neumann, Stanislav K. "Devětsil." *Kmen* 4, no. 46 (1921): 550–551.
6. Teige, Karel. "Obrazy a předobrazy." In *Musaion*, vol. 2, edited by Karel Čapek, 52–58. Praha: Aventinum, 1921.
7. Čapek, Karel. "Poznámka." In *Musaion*, vol. 2, edited by Karel Čapek, 58. Praha: Aventinum, 1921.
8. U. S. Devětsil [= Vladislav Vančura]. "[Báseň není zjevení]." In Jaroslav Seifert. *Město v slzách*, 7. Praha: Rejman, 1921.
9. Vančura, Vladislav. "Tvary věcí." *Červen* 4, no. 12 (1921): 175.
10. Götz, František. "O Hosta a o ty, kteří stojí za ním." *Socialistická budoucnost* 20, no. 5 (1922): 1–2; no. 6 (1922): 1–2.
11. Teige, Karel. "O expresionismu." *Rovnost* 38, no. 17. 1. (1922): 3–4; no. 18. 1. (1922): 3–4.
12. Götz, František. "Trochu polemiky, trochu vyznání." *Socialistická budoucnost* 20, no. 19 (1922): 1–2; no. 20 (1922): 1–2.
13. Wolker, Jiří. "Proletářské umění." *Var* 1, no. 9 (1922): 271–275. [Coauthored by Karel Teige.]
14. [Teige, Karel]. "Nové umění proletářské: úvodní článek." In *Revoluční sborník Devětsil*, 5–18. Praha: Večernice, 1922.
15. Berák, Jaromír et al. "Naše naděje, víra a práce." *Host* 2, 1922, 1: 1–4.
16. Schulz, Karel. "Poetika." *Sršatec* 3, no. 49 (1923): 3.
17. Honzl, Jindřich. "Divadelní projevy ulice." *Disk*, vol. 1 (1923): 5.
18. "Valná hromada Literární skupiny." *Host* 3, no. 9–10 (1924): 226–227.

2. From the World of Acrobats: Poetism and Constructivism

1. Teige, Karel. "Foto Kino Film." In *Život*, vol. 2, 153–168. Praha: Umělecká beseda, 1922.
2. Šíma, Josef. "Reklama." In *Život*, vol. 2, 102–103. Praha: Umělecká beseda, 1922.
3. Štyrský, Jindřich. "Obraz." *Disk*, vol. 1 (1923): 1–2.
4. Nezval, Vítězslav. "Papoušek na motocyklu, čili o řemesle básnickém." In *Pantomima*, 29–32. Praha: Ústřední studentské knihkupectví a nakladatelství, 1924.
5. Teige, Karel. "Poetismus." *Host* 3, no. 9–10 (1924): 197–204.
6. Václavek, Bedřich. "Nové techniky v básnickém řemesle." *Disk*, vol. 2 (1925): 1–4.
7. Teige, Karel. "Konstruktivismus a likvidace "umění"." *Disk*, vol. 2 (1925): 4–8.
8. [Černík, Artuš, František Halas, and Bedřich Václavek]. "Dosti Wolkera!" *Host* 4, no. 5 (1925): 157–158.
9. Nezval, Vítězslav. "Film." *Český filmový svět* 3, no. 10–11 (1925): 12.
10. "[*HOST* 4. čili rozplynulý sen o listu generace...]." *Pásmo* 1, no. 7–8 (1925): 12.
11. Rykr, Zdenek. "Teigism." *Pramen* 7, no. 1 (1927): 24–25.
12. Teige, Karel. "Slova, slova, slova." *Horizont* 1, no. 1 (1927): 1–3; no. 2 (1927), 29–32; no. 3 (1927), 44–47; no. 4, 70–73.
13. Štyrský, Jindřich, and Toyen. "Populární uvedení do artificielismu." In *Fronta: mezinárodní sborník vědecké aktivity*, edited by František Halas et al., 18. Brno: Typia, and Zdeněk Rossmann, 1927.
14. Nezval, Vítězslav. "Dada a surrealismus." In *Fronta: mezinárodní sborník vědecké aktivity*, edited by František Halas et al., 22. Brno: Typia, and Zdeněk Rossmann, 1927.
15. Voskovec, Jiří. "Želva, o které se nikdo nezmiňuje." In *Fronta: mezinárodní sborník vědecké aktivity*, edited by František Halas et al., 122–123. Brno: Typia, and Zdeněk Rossmann, 1927.
16. Obrtel, Vít. "Harmonie." In *Fronta: mezinárodní sborník vědecké aktivity*, edited by František Halas et al., 137–139. Brno: Typia, and Zdeněk Rossmann, 1927.
17. Teige, Karel. "Karel Teige o sobě." *Rozpravy Aventina* 2, no. 7 (1927): 77–78.
18. Mayerová, Milča. "Šímovy panenky." *Rozpravy Aventina* 3, no. 5 (1927): 55–56.
19. "[ReD (= revue Devětsilu)...]." *ReD* 1, no. 1 (1927): 1–2.
20. Václavek, Bedřich. "Pohřben zaživa!" *ReD* 1, no. 1 (1927): 45.
21. Nezval, Vítězslav. "Návěstí o poetismu." *ReD* 1, no. 3 (1927): 94–95.
22. Václavek, Bedřich. "Vzkříšení románu?" *ReD* 1, no. 3 (1927): 95–98.
23. R. [=Karel Teige]. "[Těm, kdož letos prohlásili...]" *ReD* 1, no. 3 (1927): 128.
24. Nezval, Vítězslav. "Kapka inkoustu." *ReD* 1, no. 9 (1928): 307–314.
25. Teige, Karel. "Manifest poetismu." *ReD* 1, no. 9 (1928): 317–336.
26. Teige, Karel. "Ultrafialové obrazy čili artificielismus." *ReD* 1, no. 9 (1928): 315–317.
27. Seifert, Jaroslav. "Guillaume Apollinaire." *Tvorba* 3, no. 4 (1928): 69.
28. Štyrský, Jindřich. "Vest Pocket Revue." *Odeon* 1, no. 2 (1929): 48.
29. "[ReD bude v 3. ročníku dále plniti svůj program...]." *ReD* 3, no. 1 (1929): 1–2.
30. Teige, Karel. "Báseň, svět, člověk." *Zvěrokruh* 1, no. 1 (November 1930): 9–15.

3. Coming of Age: Crises and New Perspectives

1. Hora, Josef. "Výchova k modernosti." *Čin* 1, no. 7 (1929): 156–158.
2. Weiner, Richard. *Lazebník (Poetika)*. Praha: Štorch-Marien, 1929.

3. Štyrský, Jindřich. "Koutek generace [1]." *Odeon* 1, no. 1 (říjen 1929): 12.
4. -jef- [= Julius Fučík]. "Generace na dvou židlích." *Tvorba* 4/2, no. 13 (9. 10. 1929): 201.
5. Štyrský, Jindřich. "Koutek generace [2]." *Odeon* 1, no. 3 (prosinec 1929): 45.
6. Teige, Karel. "Epilog k diskuzi o generaci na dvou židlích." *ReD* 3, no. 3 (1929): 91–92.
7. Štyrský, Jindřich. "[Nebyl jsem a nejsem organisovaným komunistou...]" *Tvorba* 4/2, no. 24 (24. 12. 1929): 380.
8. Štyrský, Jindřich. "Koutek generace [3]." *Odeon* 4, no. 1 (leden 1930): 60.
9. Čapek, Josef. "Krise charakterů." *Lidové noviny* 38, no. 31 (18. 1. 1930): 7.
10. Konrad, Kurt. "Manifest Levé fronty: příspěvek do diskuse." *Tvorba* 5/1, no. 3 (23. 1. 1930): 45–46.
11. Václavek, Bedřich. "O marxistickou teorii umění." *ReD* 3, no. 4 (1930): 97–98.
12. Vaněček, Arnošt. "O slově." *Kvart* 1, no. 1 (jaro 1930): 56–57.
13. Štoll, Ladislav. "Lidé v 'laboratoři'." *Levá fronta* 1, no. 8 (15. 1. 1931): 1–2.
14. Václavek, Bedřich. "Konec 'revoluční' avantgardy". *Tvorba* 6, no. 5 (5. 2. 1931): 78–79.
15. Brouk, Bohuslav. "Na obranu individualismu." *Rok* 1, č. 1 (říjen 1931): 1, 3.
16. Štyrský, Jindřich. "Malá prolegomena." *Rok* 1, č. 1 (říjen 1931): 1, 4.
17. Teige, Karel. "Úvodní poznamky: K dialektice architektury a sociologii bytové formy. In *Nejmenší byt*, 21–39. Praha: Václav Petr, 1932.

4. Complicating the Real: Czech Surrealism

1. Nezval, Vítězslav. "Předmluva." In *Chtěla okrást lorda Blamingtona: poesie a analysa*, 5–12. Praha: Odeon, 1930.
2. Brouk, Bohuslav. "Doslov". In Jindřich Štyrský. *Emilie přichází ke mně ve snu*, 29–33. Praha: [s. n.], 1933.
3. Štyrský, Jindřich. "Surrealistické malířství (několik poznámek)." *Doba* 1, no. 9 (24. 5. 1934): 135–136.
4. Václavek, Bedřich. "O surrealismu." *Index* 6, no. 9 (1934): 103–105.
5. Teige, Karel. "Deset let surrealismu." In *Surrealismus v diskusi*, edited by Karel Teige, and Ladislav Štoll, 7–56. Praha: Knihovna Levé fronty, 1934.
6. Nezval, Vítězslav. "Co je surrealismus." In *Manifesty, eseje a kritické projevy z let 1931–1941. Dílo Vítězslava Nezvala*, vol. 25, edited by Milan Blahynka, 483–486. Praha: Československý spisovatel, 1974.
7. Kalandra, Záviš. "Nadskutečno v surrealismu." In *Surrealismus v diskusi*, edited by Karel Teige, and Ladislav Štoll, 84–93. Praha: Knihovna Levé fronty, 1934.
8. Teige, Karel. "Socialistický realismus a surrealismus." In *Socialistický realismus*, 120–181. Praha: Knihovna Levé fronty, 1935.
9. Štyrský, Jindřich. "Surrealistická fotografie." *České slovo* 27, no. 25 (1935): 10.
10. Chalupecký, Jindřich. "Slovo o situaci nadrealismu u nás." *Čin* 8, no. 14 (2. 7. 1936): 217–219.
11. [Novomeský, Ladislav]. "Česko-slovenský kulturní vztah." *Slovenské zvesti* 1, no. 125 (13. 11. 1936).
12. Štyrský, Jindřich et al. "Pokus o poznání iracionality fotografie." In *Surrealismus*, edited by Vítězslav Nezval, 35–40. Praha: Josef Janda, 1936.
13. Teige, Karel. *Surrealismus proti proudu: surrealistická skupina odpovídá Vítězslavu Nezvalovi, J. Fučíkovi, Kurtu Konradovi, St. K. Neumannovi, J. Rybákovi, L. Štollovi a. j.* Praha: Surrealistická skupina, 1938.

5. Alternative Modernities: New Myths, Art, and Science

1. Obrtel, Vít. "Právo na teorii." *Kvart* 1, no. 2 (léto 1930): 117–118.
2. Navrátil, Václav. "Rozbití osobnosti a poesie." *Kvart* 1, no. 2 (léto 1930): 143–146.
3. Rykr, Zdenek. "Úvodem." In *Z. Rykr: obrazy: katalog, Topičův salon 8.-27. května 1931*, 1–2. Praha: Topičův salon, 1931.
4. Obrtel, Vít. "O stavbě věží." *Rok* 1, č. 1 (říjen 1931): 1.
5. Navrátil, Václav. "Kvart." *Rok* 1, č. 1 (říjen 1931): 4.
6. Obrtel, Vít. "K pracovní metodě." *Kvart* 1, no. 4 (1931): 291–292.
7. Navrátil, Václav. "O krisi kriseologie." *Kvart* 2, no. 1 (1933): 4–11.
8. Rykr, Zdenek. "[Za dnešních okolností...]." In *Katalog výstavy Z.* Rykra *: od 30. prosince 1935 do 17. ledna 1936, Topičův salon*, 2–5. Praha: Topičův salon, 1935.
9. Bednář, Kamil. "Projev k situaci nejmladší poesie." *Kritický měsíčník* 1, no. 1 (1938): 120–121.
10. Bednář, Kamil. "Poznámka o 'dnešku', 'skutečnosti' a 'češství' v poesii." *Kritický měsíčník* 2, no. 5–6 (1939): 268–270.
11. Navrátil, Václav. "Předmluva"; "Mythy." In *O smutku, lásce a jiných věcech*, 9; 47–61. Praha: Václav Petr, 1940.
12. Bednář, Kamil. *Slovo k mladým*. Praha: Václav Petr, 1940.
13. Chalupecký, Jindřich. "Svět v němž žijeme." *Program D40*, no. 4 (1940): 88–89.
14. Chalupecký, Jindřich. "Dějiny." *Život* 17, (1941): 20–21.
15. Chalupecký, Jindřich. "Umění napodobí skutečnost." *Život* 18, (1942): 11–19.
16. Součková, Milada. "K problému současného románu." *Čteme* 4, no. 16 (11. 11. 1942): 185–186.
17. Jakobson, Roman. "O dnešním brusičství českém." In *Spisovná čeština a jazyková kultura*, edited by Bohuslav Havránek, and Miloš Weingart, 85–122. Praha: Melantrich, 1932.
18. Mukařovský, Jan. "Dialektické rozpory v moderním umění." *Listy pro umění a kritiku* 3, no. 11/12 (1935): 344–357.
19. Mukařovský, Jan. "Individuum v umění." In *Studie z estetiky*, edited by Květoslav Chvatík, 311–315. Praha: Odeon, 1966. [French original from 1937]

List of Illustrations

From Laughter to Forgetting: The Configuration of an Anthology

(afterword and editorial note)

Czech literature, an original representative of European literature, is geographically situated in the very heart of Europe; however, in its influence and significance it rather finds itself on the margins of interest. Studies and monographs are, with a only a few exceptions, published in Czech, which is not a complaint, but a fact — Czech literature is a "minor" literature and Czech is not among those languages which European researchers naturally have at their disposal. One of the ways in which to encourage the interest of researchers in the works of a minor literature leads, therefore, to translations. In this respect, the situation is relatively satisfying: modern Czech literature is systematically and well translated, especially into English. The list of translated Czech works demonstrates a clear orientation towards canonical works, while other "layers" reveal a certain chance in the selection, as for example in the presence of practically the entire works of poet Miroslav Holub in every foreign library. On the other hand, the works of a range of artists who with their innovative and formally courageous works have formed the development of Czech literature continue to remain only in Czech. Such a situation is also the case of the Czech interwar avant-garde, specifically its theorizing part. One of the most significant and original epochs of modern Czech literature is represented in English especially by the studies of Karel Teige. This fact was one of the motivations for preparing a representative anthology of the manifestos and theoretical studies of the Czech interwar avant-garde, which presents the given epoch to foreign researchers and readers in a more complex and diverse way, even with the awareness that every anthology is once again only a selection, a slice, an enumeration viewed through the individual eyes of the editor.

One work that bears a distant kinship with the current book is *The Czech Reader: History, Culture, Politics*, (eds.) Jan Bažant, Nina Bažantová and Frances Starn (Durham, NC: Duke, 2010), the aim and function of which is, however, evidently entirely different: It reaches across Czech history and each period is represented only by a handful of texts (e.g. four from the First Czechoslovak Republic). *The Weimar Republic Sourcebook*, (eds.) Anton Kaes, Martin Jay and Edward Dimendberg (Berkeley: U of California P, 1994) presents a concise description of the selected cultural period by means of a generous selection of well-known and unknown texts. The English version of *A Glossary of Catchwords of the Czech Avant-Garde: Conceptions of Aesthetics and the Changing Faces of Art 1908–1958* (Prague: FF UK, Togga, 2012) offers a whole range of sophisticated analyses, but assumes a detailed knowledge of the development of Czech literature. Derek Sayer's *Prague: A Surrealist History* (Princeton: Princeton UP, 2013) is the most recent treatment of the Czech avant-garde, which demonstrates its international significance and unjustified neglect in post-war historiography; Sayer's widely reviewed monograph prepared the ground for publications such as the current volume — that is, a sourcebook of the Czech interwar avant-garde.

In modernist studies, under which field research into the avant-garde abroad often falls, in the recent period a heightened attention has been devoted to texts and traditions that have for a long time stood in the shadow of the French, German, and British traditions, which dominate the canon of the European avant-garde. A revision of the avant-garde — with the aim of calling into question the stance that only the West offers canons, hierarchies of values, and stylistic norms — has become one of the key tasks for contemporary researchers. In the last decade the concept of an "alternative modernism" — which contends that the basic dynamics of modernism created, in the many various cultural contexts in which it established itself, an enormous range of forms — has become at least the theme of conferences and specialist monographs, and is inspiring new research paradigms. The modernist canon has been expanded to include previously neglected writers, especially female ones, of both major and minor literatures; at the center of research are themes connected with queer, gay, and lesbian literature, as well as art created by people of color; a significant space is devoted to the relationship between literature and xenophobia, racism, colonialism, and the like. Over the last decade a whole range of studies have been published, not only extending this concept to include new authors and themes, but also expanding it temporally and geographically (global modernism, transnational modernism). The situation of minor literatures is being heard more and more attentively, but nevertheless under a persisting condition — that is, that the given problem (author, work, context) is made available in the language of the major literatures, especially in English.

In many respects the Czech avant-garde is the ideal "alternative" avant-garde that can be presented in detail to an international readership: it systematically followed Central European developments, it often had an international influence (especially in architecture, the fine arts, and photography), and at the same time it was deeply anchored to a specific Czech culturally dynamic context. In the international context, a dominant role is played by the fine arts and architecture — that is, media for which no direct language barrier exists. However, if the concept of an "alternative" modernism and avant-garde is to be something more than merely a superficial or decorative gesture, then it must be based on a deeper understanding and more thorough approach to the complicated nature of these traditions. In the case of the Czech avant-garde, the irony of its current peripheral status in the research of the European avant-garde is the fact that in the 1920s and 1930s it was a lively international force which engaged with and established connections with many of the central figures and movements of European modernism, such as Bauhaus, Le Corbusier, Man Ray, Breton's Surrealists, and even with the first pioneers of Hollywood, such as Charlie Chaplin and Douglas Fairbanks — even though it is necessary to add that this engagement was often one-sided. In short, the Czech interwar avant-garde is still awaiting for a return to recognition that its place is firmly anchored in the tradition of the European avant-garde.

In addition to the basic historical context, the present anthology offers readers in particular a conceptual orientation in the development of the Czech interwar avant-garde by means of primary documents concerning the most important cultural debates of this period. The central narrative that this sourcebook presents is the development and sources of what can be called the "classic" Czech avant-garde: the movement from proletarian art in the immediate postwar years, through the dualism of Poetism and Constructivism connected with the Devětsil group in the 1920s, up to the Surrealist Group and the inclination towards the trends of European modernism in the mid-1930s, and finally the break-up of avant-garde forces face to face with the political pressures in the later years of that decade. This movement produced not only many individual works worthy of greater recognition, but also polemics and personal dynamics that, even though they emerge from the specifics of the Czechoslovak context, also often throw light on fundamental tensions within the framework of the fundamental dynamics of the European avant-garde as a whole. (For instance, the debates in the mid-1930s and at the end of that decade concerning the relationship between Surrealism and the Socialist Realist paradigm imposed with growing insistence from the USSR.)

Alongside this canonized Czech avant-garde, which was mostly politically leftist orientated, there existed personalities and movements (adopted thematic concepts) which, even in contemporary research, continue to be of rather marginal interest. This book also narrates their story: avant-gardists who followed a less radical political programme (the Brno-based Literární skupina — Literary Group), as well as the Slovak DAVists (present in the book to a lesser extent in particular because the cooperation between the Czech and Slovak avant-gardes was not as intensive as might be expected). Also included are studies of authors associated with Devětsil but reacting to a different cultural context; studies of the Pražský lingvistický kroužek (Prague Linguistic Circle), many of whose members were friends and colleagues of the main actors of Devětsil and the Surrealist Group; as well as personalities *sui generis*, such as Richard Weiner, Karel Čapek, Milada Součková, and Zdenek Rykr, representing stances *de facto* negating the initial postulates of the avant-garde. The aim of this book is to present to an international public not only the canonical form of the Czech interwar avant-garde, but to expand it by including names and themes that are only now seeking their place in contemporary research into the Czech avant-garde. In spite of this attempt to extend the avant-garde canon, the anthology represents the real form of historical development and for this reason, with only a few exceptions, women's names are absent. It is true that avant-garde female artists — that is, authors, creative artists, translators, journalists, and so on — played a significant role in shaping the form of Czech art between the wars. We can mention at least Toyen, Růžena Svátková, Milena Jesenská, Hana Wichterlová, Staša Jílovská, and Milada Součková. Nevertheless, because these authors with only a few exceptions did not engage in theoretical discussions or polemics of the avant-garde, they are outside the limits of this book.

The present volume contains a representative selection of the theoretical deliberations, manifestos, and essays of the Czech avant-garde. Most frequently we make available translations of the first magazine or journal printing of a text. In cases where this was not accessible, we translated the version that came out in book form as selections. In spite of the variety of genres, the book forms a thematic whole. However, it varies in its approach to language and linguistic norms. For this reason in the case of each text we have attempted the greatest possible comprehensibility. We have intervened in individual details of the text: for instance, we have changed lower case to upper case when referring to institutions (muzeum — Muzeum) and other similar matters. We fully respect the personality and particularity of the typography of the period, and especially when this bears significance we have left it in its original form. With some exceptions, period usage did not encourage the use of Christian names, and therefore we have not added these. In view of the tendency to make use of deviations from linguistic norms as an artistic means, we sometimes have retained even phenomena that appear symptomatic. We have also retained and translated into English as faithfully as possible the lexicon and morphology at all stylistic and historical levels. We have also corrected obvious mistakes in the texts (in typesetting, missing words, etc.). We have acknowledged previous translations of the selected texts. However, we have not systematically listed the translators' names and do not provide a comprehensive overview.

The anthology is divided into five parts which in the broadest sense map the historical development of a newly-built direction, as well as its emerging themes and trends. The division selected was aimed at providing an easier orientation for the reader. However, the Czech interwar avant-garde was an organic phenomenon, whose development cannot be enclosed into phases bordered temporally or thematically, and every such attempt demonstrates an insensitivity towards the development of literature. The first part, The Birth of the Avant-Garde: Between Avant-Garde, Expressionism, and Proletarian Art, is devoted to the birth of the Czech avant-garde — that is, the formation of the Devětsil group and the Literary Group. The discussion about the character of the Czech avant-garde, including manifestos and treatises of the purely Czech movement of Poetism, forms the second part, From the World of Acrobats: Poetism and Constructivism. The third part,

Coming of Age: Crises and New Perspectives, represents the crisis of Poetism and a general crisis of avant-garde approaches, which culminated in the falling apart of the Devětsil group. Roughly from the 1930s, the Czech interwar avant-garde took a more complex and complicated stance towards the phenomenon of modern art, both within the framework of avant-garde groups and also more and more often in individually constructed authorial poetics. The fourth part, Complicating the Real: Czech Surrealism, presents the foundation of Czech Surrealism and its possibilities for continuing with the aims of the avant-garde of the 1920s. On the contrary, the fifth part, Alternative Modernities: New Myths, Art, and Science, brings together texts demonstrating a turn on the part of authors towards approaches generally connected with Anglo-American modernism. The title of the anthology, *From Laughter to Forgetting, A Sourcebook of Czech Avant-Garde Discourses*, not only freely paraphrases the title of one of Milan Kundera's books, as an internationally known Czech writer, but also contains within it the path from the smiles of the workers and the laughter of acrobats up to the turn of the avant-garde back towards the past, to memory, to forgetting and being forgotten. The present book aims to resist that forgetting.

Zuzana Říhová

Index